DATE DUE

GAYLORD   #3522PI   Printed in USA

Hunger for the Wild

Hunger for the Wild

America's Obsession with the Untamed West

MICHAEL L. JOHNSON

UNIVERSITY PRESS OF KANSAS

© 2007 by the University Press of Kansas

All rights reserved

Published by the University Press of
Kansas (Lawrence, Kansas 66045),
which was organized by the Kansas
Board of Regents and is operated and
funded by Emporia State University,
Fort Hays State University, Kansas State
University, Pittsburg State University, the
University of Kansas, and Wichita State
University

Library of Congress Cataloging-in-Publication Data

Johnson, Michael L.

Hunger for the wild : America's obsession with the
untamed West / Michael L. Johnson.

p.   cm.

Includes bibliographical references and index.

ISBN 978-0-7006-1501-8 (cloth : alk. paper)

1. West (U.S.)—Civilization. 2. West (U.S.)—History.
3. West (U.S.)—Geography. 4. Human geography—West
(U.S.) 5. Frontier and pioneer life—West (U.S.)
6. Wilderness areas—West (U.S.)—History. 7. Wilderness
areas—West (U.S.)—Psychological aspects. 8. European
Americans—Attitudes—History. 9. Public opinion—
United States—History. I. Title.

F591.J617 2007

978—dc22   200603278

British Library Cataloguing-in-Publication Data is
available.

Printed in the United States of America

10 9 8 7 6 5 4 3 2 1

For Walter Isle,

mentor and compadre

I suspect the wild calls the loudest

when it has largely disappeared from our lives.

—Jim Harrison, The Road Home

Contents

Acknowledgments

Thanks to Kathleen Johnson, who presided as muse for this project; to Walter Isle, Lisa Slappey, Terrell Dixon, Alex Hunt, Tom Bailey, SueEllen Campbell, and Scott Slovic, who inspired me to think through issues of Western wildness afresh; to Steve Tatum, who shared his eclectic cultural insights about the West; to Robert Murray Davis, Jim Work, and Phyllis Doughman, who reminded me to keep a sense of humor about the West; to George Day, whose appreciative remarks helped me stay poetically tuned to the West; to Luci Tapahonso, from whom I learned much about the Native West; to Bud Hirsch, keen scholar of Native American literature, who has been a boss roommate at Western Literature Association meetings; to David Wrobel and Michael Steiner, whose criticism and suggestions greatly helped shape the manuscript; to Fred Woodward, who, at several stages, offered valuable advice concerning this project; to Matt Edge, Samantha Bartelloni, and Ann Meckstroth, who skillfully played their roles as my research assistants; to Robin Holladay, who helped me chase permissions; and to the staff of the College of Liberal Arts and Sciences Word Processing Center at KU, who labored tirelessly to civilize my savage scribblings.

Preface: A Conference in Reno

> Come on in. Cherish
> your wilderness.
>> Maxine Kumin,
>> "You Are in Bear Country"

"Wild? Hell, you people don't know what wild is!" That's part of a lengthy excoriation I heard from a member of an audience of about two hundred when, late from a delayed flight, I eased my way through a door in the back of the auditorium to catch the last half of a midafternoon plenary session on the first day of the Seventh North American Interdisciplinary Wilderness Conference.[1] The date was February 29, 1996, and the setting was John Ascuaga's Nugget, a casino-hotel, in Reno, Nevada. That vociferous member of the audience was a flinty-eyed Old Wester fed up with theories about wilderness and how to save it from the hoof-and-mouth depredations of cattle. His diatribe was punctuated with questions. Has anybody here ever seen a wolf? How do we decide what is and what isn't wilderness? If we can, why do we want it? I remained standing, not far from the door.

The title of the session was "Working Wilderness: Beyond the Rangeland Conflict," and the speaker was Dan Dagget, author of a 1995 book about experimental ranching, illustrated with Jay Dusard's photographs, titled *Beyond the Rangeland Conflict: Toward a West That Works*. An environmentalist honored for his grassroots activism, Dagget came off as cowboy-honest as Roy Rogers as he grappled with the issues raised by that interrogator and continued to show and comment on slides of Arizona countryside restored from overgrazing and now supporting restrained foraging by cattle that keep the land healthy by pushing seeds into the soil and fertilizing it.

Some in attendance seemed convinced by Dagget's case for working wilderness. Others wondered how grazed land could be regarded as wild. Still others offered renditions of the argument that wilderness is a culturally constructed idea with a distressing history—and explained how what Dagget proposed was just another play on it. A rugged buckskinner averred that wilderness is where nature is red in tooth and claw and you don't go in there unless you're packin' major iron. A young scholar started to set everyone straight on how Western wilderness was an icon of Rooseveltian machismo, but he was cut off by a cowgirl who was tired of so much philosophizing and wanted a hamburger. When the laughter subsided, someone ventured to remind all present that a great deal of what's now called wilderness can be kept as such only by removing weeds that aren't normally part of its biota—that the managing of wilderness is fraught with intractable ironies.

Dagget looked a bit crestfallen about the reception of his plan for ranches that could embrace both commerce and nature, prudent husbandry and laissez-faire biology. His vision, allied with that of the Malpai Borderlands Group, was of an American West where river water again ran free, biodiversity was the rule and not the precarious exception, road building and leapfrog development were held in check, and domestic livestock was kept in a balanced relation with the natural environment. What he wanted was a West that, by God, *worked* the way it once did and still should. What he got wasn't a consensus of aspiration but a smidgen of agreement and a lot of dissent, quibbling, posturing.

I lingered at the back of the auditorium as the crowd spilled out, watching a handful of doubters and well-wishers gather around Dagget at the podium. Then, frustrated but stimulated by the melee I'd witnessed and still shaky from flying fear, I headed for the lounge.

There the mixologist fixed me a double Wild Turkey on the rocks. I sat alone at the bar and pondered why I'd come to this meeting of diverse sensibilities in the Biggest Little City in the World. Well, to read an essay of mine on the hazards of spelunking in the Ozarks. To escape the wearisome winter of Lawrence, Kansas, where I teach in the Department of English at KU. To go west into the mountain-and-desert country that's my heart's desire. To see friends who had founded an organization called the Association for the Study of Literature and Environment (ASLE)—an endeavor of humanists who were, most of them, put off by the race-and-gender wars that literary studies had become and yearned to engage different matters. I'd come also to learn about the conference's sponsor, the new Center for Environmental Arts and Humanities at the University of Nevada at Reno, an undertaking crucial to the future of the kind of Western studies that intrigued me. I'd come to experience the conference itself, whose maiden voyage had been the forum for papers collected in a book I admired, *Wilderness Tapestry: An Eclectic Approach to Preservation*. And, of course, I'd come to participate in games of chance.

But there was a deeper reason why I'd come, one I couldn't yet clearly articulate. I'd just finished writing *New Westers: The West in Contemporary American Culture*, soon to be published by the University Press of Kansas, which surveyed, celebrated, and critiqued America's latest craving for things Western. I'd tried to cover what the West was all about for fashion designers, revisionist Western historians, filmmakers, line dancers, tourists. I thought I'd done a good job. Still, I couldn't throw off the feeling that I'd neglected something. I was in Reno because I believed it might involve the notion of the West as wilderness. I was toying with the idea of writing another book, and I was trying to figure out what it would be.

In the midst of those meditations, fellow conferees began turning up in the lounge. I forgot my woes and chatted with a riveting cast of characters: a mountaineer who relished climbing frozen waterfalls, a ranch woman who'd gentled a hundred horses, a Bigfoot enthusiast, several people doing research on nuclear testing in Cold War Nevada, a muzzle-loader devotee, plenty of academics who'd arrived at the alerting awareness that they were part of nature and its friskiness and fragility. Heli-skier or rendezvous freak, whatever, everyone had some sense of connection to the tough, the primitive, the unknown, the risky—wilderness of some sort. Those folks gathered in the lounge were sure interdisciplinary, and many knew more about "what wild is" than that curmudgeon in the auditorium had given them credit for.

That night a bunch of us continued to drink and talk, ate Mexican food, gambled. I went to bed full of wildness both vague and distinct, turning over my book problem as I nodded off.

During the next two days I listened to presentations on the cosmology of the casino as a simulacral wilderness, hiking in the Sierra Nevada, and much else. I sat spellbound while Ann Zwinger and Rick Bass told, respectively, of running the Colorado through the Grand Canyon and of (maybe) encountering a grizzly bear in the San Juan Mountains. I immersed myself in accounts of Western wilderness and reports on research projects devoted to it. Read my essay to an advertent group. And, at last, after good-byes to old friends and new acquaintances, departed.

As the plane rose over the Virginia Mountains east of Reno, I looked down on their snowy desolation and suddenly understood that my book would have to do not just with the wilderness of the West but with its wildness, a more general phenomenon, cultural as well as natural. Arrogantly, I thought of the people at the conference as being like the proverbial blind men examining an elephant: each knew some portion of the creature, maybe without quite concluding that the trunk is a snake or a leg is a tree, but none of them was seeking to know the whole of it. Neither, as far as I could tell, was anyone else.[2] I had a sense of what I wanted to deal with: the multifold wildness, both real and imagined, of the West that had powerfully and long—and ambiguously—fascinated its explorers, invaders, exploiters, legendizers, and dwellers. The pieces of the puzzle were all over the table.

Above the Shoshone Mountains I remembered my previous trip to Reno—in 1992, for a meeting of the Western Literature Association (WLA). I'd taken a tour up to Donner Pass in the Sierra Nevada, with the novelist Doris Betts as my companion. What she'd learned there about the fate of the Donner party had inspired her to start on a novel, partly about the dangerousness of the West, that would be published in 1997 as The Sharp Teeth of Love. Perhaps I would have a similar inspiration as a result of this trip.

I was on to something. In New Westers, I'd focused on contemporary America's hunger for the heritage of the West but hadn't fathomed the extent to which that heritage—however now attenuated, artificial, commodified—was a matter of wildness. Wildness, tangled up with tameness, was inherent in all of it: cowboys,

Indians, horses, buffalo, land—the whole caboodle. Wildness seemed to be very complex in its relation to tameness, civilization, Eastern-ness. Pairings floated through my mind: raw and cooked, strange and familiar, Indian and European, rural and urban.

By the time I was over the Rockies, my musing had become more analytical. Lots of historians had dealt with what was old about the Old West, but most of them hadn't dealt with exactly what was wild about the Wild West. They seemed to take that part for granted. Nostalgia for the Old West—and how it figured in an epidemic passion for the New West—was the subject of many studies, but what about nostalgia for the *Wild* West, surely something more basic? Isn't Western wildness the heart of Western oldness? Hasn't what is meant by wildness in the West been different for different times? How different have Native and European notions of wildness been during the past four-and-a-half centuries? Questions abounded.

The rumpled relief map beneath me leveled out into eastern Colorado, then western Kansas. The planar geometry of road-bordered sectional squares and circles drawn by center-pivot irrigators slipped past. Emblems of the drive to define, control, and profit from the West, to tame its wildness.

America's westering was on the increase. Many of the people involved were—and are—those whom Brooke Williams calls "new barbarians," people who "would rather be under stars than roofs" and long for "wild space."[3] People who have what I was beginning to formulate as "hunger for the wild." People who want to keep their own wildness alive in the only place left in this country where they can do that—the West, where the land remains more open and more wild than it is in the non-West. For such people the West is a place to which they feel themselves deeply related. They go there, even if more in fantasy than in fact, both to embrace wildness and to shun scourges like "the big Hum," Bill McKibben's term for "the constant barrage of chatter from the world," the harvest of excessive information technology.[4]

Aloof in my high-altitude aluminum cocoon, I oversimplified, of course. Westering was more complicated than that—other kinds of people were involved, other motives—but I'd made a start on putting the puzzle together.

Wildness appeared to be the enveloping theme when I got back to Lawrence. My wife, Kathleen, was reading Clarissa Pinkola Estés's book *Women Who Run with the Wolves: Myths and Stories of the Wild Woman Archetype.* My six-year-old daughter, Lauren, gave me a crayon drawing of a cowboy boot with its upper adorned by a rattlesnake, a reptile that Elizabeth Atwood Lawrence labels "the least tame and most lethal creature of the wild."[5] My son, Jarrett, showed me a seashell he'd found on a junior-high field trip to a quarry, reminding me how *really* wild the West once had been. In the pile of my mail, I found a letter from a friend informing me that her daughter and son-in-law, a Wall Streeter, had burned out on big-city life, bought a ranch in Montana, and moved there forthwith. I read a piece in the newspaper backlog about the enlarging diaspora of urban baby boomers into rural areas of the West.

In the months ahead, there turned up more signs that I was on the right track. Several colleagues were planning an anthology about "drinking in the wild." One of my students was preparing to search for wolves in Yellowstone National Park. Kathleen was scouting for rural property.

That summer the family and I visited Woolaroc, a ranch southwest of Bartlesville, Oklahoma, that once had been the retreat of Frank Phillips, founder of the Phillips Petroleum Company. We discovered there, in the wildlife refuge and museum, remnants of an earlier Western wildness: bison, longhorn cattle, Indian artifacts, antique firearms, no end of paintings and bronzes of woolly personages and scenes. I was struck by the way those artworks expressed Western wildness in a multiplicity of images: William R. Leigh's painting *Navajo Fire Dance* (torchbearing Indians in a frenzy of motion), Charles M. Russell's painting *Flying Hoofs* (horses fighting off wolves), Jo Mora's well-armed bronze *Belle Starr*, Sally Farnham's bronze *Payday, Going to Town* (four trail-begrimed cowboys barreling toward a night of fun), Frederic Remington's painting *The Last Stand* (cavalrymen holding off unseen Indians), and others.

Returning home from Woolaroc, I knew I was committed, but I had to decide how to proceed.

I finally did proceed, of course, and this book is the result. If I share it with mild trepidation, that's not so much because (to borrow a translated term from Jean-François Lyotard) it's something of a presumptuous "grand narrative," however essayistic, as because I'm not a professional historian. But I am an informed student of Western history and have tried throughout to bring to my study a poetic attentiveness to the significance of selected specifics. That method is due partly to temperament and partly to the scale of the subject; so I empathize with Frederick Turner's admission in the preface to one of his books that "the way I chose to write may be closer to that of the literary artist than to that of the historian" since "I have been forced by the formidable scope of my subject to choose my materials with an eye for the symbolic, the revealing detail." Likewise, I empathize with his humility in confronting "the mass of material that bore on the subject," but, like him, I couldn't wait for the unachievable goal of complete knowledge and so got on with the writing I had to do.[6]

Introduction:
A Wilde Wesste

*The hunger for a Wild West . . . arose well before 1900 and . . . continues to
the present.*
    Richard W. Etulain, *Re-imagining the Modern American West:*
    A Century of Fiction, History, and Art

While making notes for this book, I reflected on my own customs in regard to wildness—on how, for instance, I categorize weekends as "wilder" than weekdays or
how I had divided with a gentle curve the four acres on which I'd built a home
into cultivated and uncultivated areas (the former close to the house, planted with
brome and fescue, the latter away from the house, thick with weeds and wildflowers). Such basic research led me to see that the book I was outlining must itself
begin with basics, both conceptually and historically. Thus I acknowledged that to
say the American West once was—and in many respects still is—a wild place is to
utter an image-conjuring cliché. But I wanted to dig down to the roots of that cliché
and investigate how the West came to be known as wild, how the kinds of wildness
implicit in that generalization have manifested themselves, and why they have been
and remain fascinating—a line of inquiry that might help explain and even suggest
solutions for the social, economic, and ecological problems that currently plague
the West. That project, I saw, would require a topical approach first taking a long
view and thereafter concentrating on the postfrontier West. So the present book
is a loosely chronological study that, after briefly discussing Western wildness in
terms of its prehuman origins and pre-European Native views of nature, concerns
itself with how, during the last four hundred and fifty years or so, ideas of wildness have profoundly influenced Euro-American—and, more specifically, Anglo-
American—interpretations of, attitudes toward, and activities in the West.

By investigating those ideas and their implications, I have tried to lend a hand to
the writing of the "deeper history" of the West that Donald Worster has called for,
an "inner cultural history"—the kind that Patricia Nelson Limerick presents in her
1987 book *The Legacy of Conquest: The Unbroken Past of the American West*—which asks
questions about "how people in the West have thought and felt in distinctive ways."
Such historiography (writing of history, which is always what someone *says* happened), for me including inquiries as to how people *outside* the West have thought

1

and felt about it in distinctive ways, discloses "a mental life that has gone on apart from, or even in opposition to, the external reality" and pays heed to habits of mind "that stubbornly persist even when they are inconvenient or expensive or self-destructive."[1] Such historiography seeks to elucidate not only what happened but also why—as revealed by a range of evidence—it happened as it did.

In that regard, my argument in *Hunger for the Wild* runs as follows. Though the West has always been, in some sense, a wild place, its human inhabitants and visitors, from the earliest Native Americans and first explorers and nineteenth-century pioneers to postmodern tourists, have perceived or misperceived the wildness of the West in various ways, construing its meaning by their own culturally tailored ideas. For Euro-Americans intent on settling or otherwise exploiting the West, some of those ideas—originating in the Old World, evolving from the time of the Spanish *entradas*, and ridden with increasingly muddled and even bizarre contradictions—have defined the West in its most fundamental aspects. In doing so, they have determined how Euro-Americans have reacted to and acted upon the West. Slow to be recognized for what they are, such motivating ideas, animated by an ambiguous dialectic (of savage and civilized, chaos and order, and the like) and configured into a changing and ever more ambivalent ideology of conquest, thus have played, for several centuries, the principal role in shaping both the physical and biological environment and the mythology and iconography of the West, as well as their interconnections. While those ideas have fired much of the West's peculiar cultural colorfulness, they also have contributed mightily to creating the daunting problems—enduring political conflicts, overtaxed and polluted water supplies, degraded wilderness areas, endangered wildlife species, sprawling suburbs, ersatz heritage, and more—that have brought the West to a state of grave worry about its future. If such problems are to be tackled effectively—and there is reason to believe they can be—then the ideas that have given rise to them and still in some form perpetuate them must be better understood. This book, which traces the twisting history and mixed consequences of those ideas, is one writer's effort toward that end—and thereby, I hope, toward helping to ensure a viable Western future.

To stay with the stress on basics, let's consult *The Oxford English Dictionary* regarding the word *wild*. From a long entry we learn that the etymology of the word "is complicated by uncertainty as to its primary meaning" as either an adjective or a noun—though in the former case some of the derivatives carry meanings, such as "bewildered," "astray," "confused," that must cluster close to what that meaning might be. The usages of the word in different stages of English over the last thousand years or so, however, are clearly comprehensible. In reference to an animal, for instance, *wild* means "not domesticated," "living in a state of nature." In reference to a person, it means "uncivilized," "savage." In reference to a place, it means "desolate," "uninhabited." Other meanings include "resisting control," "unruly," "erratic."[2] All of those meanings, not always negative and sometimes strongly positive in connotation, still obtain in certain contexts when people speak of the Wild West.

Among the citations of usages, this one, concerning *wild* used in reference to a place, jumps out: "a wilde wesste."[3] The phrase occurs in the *Ormulum*, a poetic commentary on the Gospels penned in Middle English around 1200 by a monk named Orm (or Ormin). His words, translatable as "a wild waste" (and not, as you might guess, as "a wild west"), refer to Egypt, which was, from the Mosaic point of view he assumes, an area full of serpents and other abhorrences—in other words, a sort of Wild West in its negative aspects for Israelites, to the west of whose land it does in fact lie. The significance of Orm's label here is that it codifies an attitude toward uncultivated places that's recurrent in the Bible (and in writings from other ancient Middle Eastern cultures), was transplanted all over Europe, carried into Caribbean and Atlantic colonies in the New World, and later brought to bear on the American West.

In addition, that attitude has long been conflated with one that harbors the hope of a promised land on the far side of or within a wild waste. James H. Maguire may recall the Israelites at the beginning of their wandering as much as he foreshadows Euro-Americans on the verge of entering the trans-Mississippi West when he argues that "the earliest European immigrants arrived in America with preconceived, conflicting notions about the wild new lands: they had heard (1) that the wilderness was a new Garden of Eden and (2) that it was an earthly hell."[4]

Numerous historians and others have studied the origins and legacies of this double attitude. Their publications in recent decades range from Roderick Nash's *Wilderness and the American Mind* (1967, in its first edition) to Frederick Turner's *Beyond Geography: The Western Spirit against the Wilderness* (1980). Max Oelschlaeger's *The Idea of Wilderness: From Prehistory to the Age of Ecology* (1991) and other books have illuminated issues that emerged through and subsequent to the research of groundbreakers like Nash and Turner. Such works, along with those of historians as diverse in approach as Henry Nash Smith, Worster, and Richard Slotkin, have brought coherence to our understanding of wilderness, particularly that of the American West, and of the changing relations of humankind, mostly Euro-American humankind, to it. The insights provided by those works have proven valuable for me, and I draw upon them, with gratitude, in the pages ahead; but none of their authors has ventured quite what I have in *Hunger for the Wild*: a study that deals with wildness not just in conjunction with Western wilderness and closely related topics (the Noble Savage, for example) but also in conjunction with a wide variety of Western cultural phenomena, with special attention to the increasingly knotty ambivalence of the American attitude toward Western wildness during the pell-mell of technological innovations that brought the nineteenth century to a close and continued thereafter.

That wildness may be thought of as inhering in the West as a place or a natural environment, in the West as a state of mind or a cultural construct, or in the inter-relations of those two realms—the last, I contend, being the conception most pro-ductive, through research, of understanding. In the Age of Reptiles, the West was wild in ways beyond the direct ken of humankind. And it may have appeared some-how wild to Native Americans when they initially set foot in it. But Euro-Americans would perceive it as rifely wild in very distinctive terms from their first incursions and, in important respects, still do. The history of that wildness may be read as one in which a seemingly concrete fact has been more and more translated—by mythifi-cation, etherealization, virtualization—into an abstraction, a process accompanied and occasioned by another in which relatively unpeopled Western nature has been more and more turned into overly peopled Western culture.

However you describe the American West geographically (as everything between the hundredth meridian and the Pacific Ocean, as only the central West of the purist, and so on), all its early non-Native explorers found it a place, in Maguire's words, of "vastness and strangeness" about which they had to write "in a language they had learned back home, a language suited mainly to the cultivated and more familiar lands of Europe and the East."[5] Though that language often pretended to be objec-tive, it was always freighted with imported ideas. Their experience of the West may have changed its explorers from what they were back home, but through their ideas they changed the West remarkably from what it was before they came.

Moreover, the first Euro-American settlers in the West effected, as Rita Parks notes, "an uneasy truce with the land." That uneasiness had to do, again, with a quality of the land she, following Bernard DeVoto, labels "strangeness." It's a qual-ity that derives from dryness, poisonous animals, harsh terrain, thorny plants—all of which were adversaries in "Westerners' never-ending struggle to make the land less hostile and more like the world they had known." Those many Westerners baffled, discouraged, or defeated by that strangeness found themselves in a fable-making desperation that generated, "first, embellishments of history and histori-cal characters, then tall tales, and finally a full-blown body of legend." Meanwhile, Easterners, "backed by the classical [including Biblical] mythology they preserved from European philosophy, art, and letters, applied it freely to the western lands they had never seen."[6] Gradually the two kinds of narrative intermixed to form myths both anciently, Europeanly archetypal and contemporarily, locally legendary.

Given its attributes of rawness and danger, the strangeness of the West that has necessitated such interpretation and transmogrification is part and parcel of its wildness. And that encompassing quality subsumes other attributes that have fig-ured in the experience of westering. One of them, unknownness, had to do with the directionality of that adventure, as Richard C. Poulsen explains in his discus-sion of the beginnings of the European cultural transformation of the West: "The term *West* itself sounds deeply of what might be termed European sensibilities: of direction, of time, of place, of destiny. To the Native American the West was not the West, because it was not primarily a place of direction. But to European travelers moving into the maw of the unknown, . . . the West was being defined as a place of direction." There was a sense of teleology, rightness, comfort in that defining, for westward movement, aligned with the movement of the sun, was valued in European culture as expressive of order. That valuation would undergird Manifest Destiny, but before that it functioned in rationalizing a protracted encounter with what Europeans tended to scorn as "interminable chaos." For Poulsen it was that chaos, another attribute of wildness, that gave rise to "outrageous caricatures of the West and its inhabitants by discoverers, by those searching, however unconsciously, to fix an image" of the place.[7]

Thus, though much associated with outlawry and white–Indian conflicts during the thirty years or so in the late nineteenth century conventionally termed the epoch of the Wild West, chaos textured images of the West well before then. In that role it shared traits with another attribute of Western wildness: otherness. Marking what is different from us, beyond our control, otherness has figured aplenty in centuries of westering. It's incarnated in the magnitude of Western nature indifferent to human life that has never been more unforgettably portrayed than in Thomas Moran's huge (seven-by-twelve-foot) 1872 painting *The Grand Canyon of the Yellowstone*, where two men out on a ledge are shrunken and overwhelmed by encircling cliffs and slopes. It's what "compels our attention," as William Cronon notes, when, while visiting a wilderness, "we find ourselves surrounded by plants and animals and physical landscapes" that, by "forcing us to acknowledge that . . . they have little or no need of our continued existence, . . . recall for us a creation far greater than our own." For Euro-Americans today, inheritors of a romantic legacy of wilderness as "more a state of mind than a fact of nature," that acknowledgment tends to involve marveling.[8] For their ancestors in the West it involved a large measure of unromantic fear. That dissimilarity pertains, with adjustments, to the acknowledgment of the cultural otherness of Native American tribes indigenous to or driven into the West, whose people whites have habitually associated with wilderness and its natural otherness.

Strangeness, unknownness, chaos, otherness—those and related attributes of wildness have constellated changefully over time in Euro-Americans' perception of the West, serving as key elements in their rationalizing the dubious doctrine of Western exceptionalism. That "shaping perception," as Simon Schama calls it, "makes the difference between raw matter and landscape."[9] What such perception shapes are images. They're essential to making sense of a place. As Poulsen explains, "the land itself . . . is literally invisible, enigmatic, to the culture unless it is transformed into a predictable image." Through that transformation the land can express and corroborate the culture's values. If it fails, "there is no landscape— only a wasteland of cultural oblivion"—a proposition that, Poulsen argues, "seems

Thomas Moran, The Grand Canyon of the Yellowstone (1872): the magnitude of Western nature indifferent to human life. (Smithsonian American Art Museum, lent by the Department of the Interior Museum.)

particularly true in the waste places of the American West, areas that defy ideas of human (at least Anglo) utility."[10] The Anglo transformation of the West into predictable images hasn't exactly failed, but it has certainly been problematic, yielding images that, like the values expressed and corroborated by the land as they represent it, ultimately are ambiguous and tensional.

Those images, whether conscious or subconscious, tethered to reality or afloat in fantasy, are constituted by the interplay of the opposites wildness and tameness—and their thematic variations, such as savagery and civilization or nature and technology. Though ostensibly rigorous binaries, such oppositions have proven historically to be deeply complicated and implicated in the interplay of other complicated oppositions, so that, for example, preserving and exploiting Western wilderness get blurred together and Western cities that aspire to be centers of civilization wind up being centerless mazes of savagery. As we'll see, the opposing qualities of wildness and tameness, variously yoked, become, when the images they constitute are quickened in narratives, the terms for order (to borrow a phrase from Kenneth Burke) of myths that in turn validate those images.

Myth, analyzed this way, conforms to Slotkin's definition of it as "an intellectual or artistic construct that bridges the gap between the world of the mind and the world of affairs. . . . It draws on the content of individual and collective memory, structures it, and develops from it imperatives for belief and action." In that office a given myth participates in a mythology, which he defines as "a complex of narratives" that gives dramatic form to a culture's worldview and sense of history, thereby "reducing centuries of experience into a constellation of compelling metaphors."[11] Such general definitions seem to me sound, and they're congruent with David Daly and Joel Persky's definition of myth as "a means of deriving usable values from history and placing those values beyond the reach of critical thinking or demystification" whose appeal "is to ritualized emotions, established beliefs, habitual associations, nostalgia, and memory."[12] Furthermore, such definitions accord both with Roland Barthes's notion that myth "organizes a world which is without contradictions"[13]—of the kind exemplified, in the present book, by love and hatred of Western wildness—and with Claude Lévi-Strauss's characterization of mythical thought as "a whole system of reference which operates by means of a pair of contrasts" like "nature and culture."[14] Which pairing brings us back to my main theme, which concerns, among other things, the hero of myth, who grapples, in Daly and Persky's words, with some threatening situation typified by any number of "symbolic netherworlds," not the least of which is "the wilderness," Western in this case.[15]

That line of conceptualization is accurate and fruitful as far as it goes in describing what myth is and how it operates. But, as we'll see, the myths of the West will, in different times and circumstances, turn out to qualify the generalizing above as they are frozen into icons or commonplace ideology, become self-conscious or parodic or ironic, indeed come within reach of criticism and demystification. Such are the consequences for myths interwoven with a history that began with the imperative to conquer wildness and finally has arrived, after a lot of wavering en route, at the imperative to save what's left of it. And it's well to remember that that history has run from a time when only a scattering of Euro-Americans immediately dealt with a place they perceived as a vast and daunting wilderness until a time when much more culturally diverse though still dominantly Euro-American inhabitants, most with only rarefied and remote connections to any wilderness, have urbanized it to far too great an extent. Though the wildness of the West was more "reality" four hundred and fifty years ago than it is now and is now more "myth" than it was then, it's well to remember also, as Smith came to admit twenty years after making "an unduly rigid distinction between symbols and myths on the one hand, and on the other a supposed extramental historical reality" in his 1950 book *Virgin Land: The American West as Symbol and Myth*, "that there is a continuous dialectic interplay between the mind and its environment."[16] Thus any experience of the wildness of the West, near or distant, as literal as that of wrestling a grizzly bear or as symbolic as that of watching a John Wayne movie, is, as Stephen Tatum observes, "precisely what we make of it as we endure it."[17]

What we make of it tends to be mythic, to involve, in Smith's words, drastically simplified images that possess "clarity of form"—the impulse toward which can cause their associated myths to "become dangerous by inciting behavior grossly inappropriate to the given historical situation."[18] Yet that clarity can be confused by underlying ambivalence that mythmaking, in working for a consistent ideology by suppressing contradictions among images, leaves unresolved, particularly when those images instantiate categories as foundational as the wild and the tame. To some minimum degree such wild/tame ambivalence may be innate in humankind, but I doubt that it's ever been more extreme—and more dangerous—than it has been in the case of Americans possessed by the dream of establishing an essentially European civilization in territory for the most part inhospitable to that goal.

The tradition behind such extreme ambivalence toward the wild and the tame goes back a ways, as I noted earlier; but let me return for a moment to Orm's medieval world and then travel forward in a few leaps to the contemporary West in order to share a preliminary thumbnail history of the persistence of that tradition.

Winifred Gallagher, writing about the European heritage of "mixed feelings about nature," argues that they "were augmented by elements of the Judeo-Christian tradition and later by the economic imperatives of the emerging bourgeoisie: for the glory of God and the family fortune, civilized people had the right, even the duty, to subdue the unruly wilds and the 'heathen' who inhabited them." She zeroes in on the Middle Ages as illustrative of that heritage: during that time "vast stretches of the untamed European forest were regarded as living symbols of chaos and danger that teemed with demons and monsters. Just as evil lurked in raw nature, good was to be found in civilized communities and gardens"—a dichotomy that still emotionally structures fairy tales, yarns about Bigfoot, and the like.[19] Therefore medieval Europeans cut down much of that forest and built cathedrals in its place, through that substitution re-creating in their own mode what Greeks and Romans (from whose Latin word *silvaticus*, "of the forest" or "wild," the English word *savage* derives) before them had done when they chopped down the trees in sacred groves and replaced them with temple columns, making divinity less an immanent aspect of nature and more an imposed formation of culture.

Simultaneously, however, Gallagher reminds us, "more harmonious approaches to nature existed," as exemplified in the thirteenth century by the nature-loving ways of Saint Francis of Assisi. Such approaches survived to be adopted and adapted by Thomas Jefferson, not the first idealist to promote a middle landscape between wild country and civilized city, whose diaries, she notes, "reflect a desire to understand and cooperate with rather than conquer nature"—in a time, before Romanticism made wilderness fashionable and encouraged the protection of it, that would witness the United States engaged much more in conquering than in cooperating with Western nature.[20]

Prior to Jefferson's time the old medieval ambivalence was strongly evident in New England. In the late seventeenth century the Puritan theocrat Increase Mather found his people, as Slotkin explains, torn between "fear of the physical terrors of the wilderness" and idolatrous enthusiasm about "the promise of the wilderness" as a place for settlement.[21] After Jefferson's time that ambivalence, now in regard to areas further west, was reconstituted in widely read works by Henry David Thoreau and Herman Melville.

For all his praise of the "vital wildness" of the West he opposed "to the dead tameness of civilization," Thoreau, in Smith's phrasing, "conceded, grudgingly, that for the wise man civilization offered advantages superior to those of the savage state." He thereby manifested a tension discernible in his 1854 book *Walden* between the celebration of "transcendental 'higher laws'" and "an equal impulse toward a primitive rank and savage life." Less primitivistic than Thoreau, Melville was also more ambivalent in his attitude toward the West, for to him it, "like nature in general, came to seem in the highest degree ambiguous." As Smith notes, in the 1840s Melville's negative attitude toward the farming West of the Ohio Valley differed little from that of typical conservative Easterners—as may be seen in his 1849 novel *Mardi*. The West beyond that temporary frontier, however, had a contradictorily bifurcated value for him, as may be seen in Chapter 42, "The Whiteness of the Whale," in *Moby-Dick*, published two years later. There he elaborates two images, one of the White Steed of the Prairies and the other of a peaceful New England colt still possessed of wilderness instincts, both of which he uses to infix "the sinister blend of majesty and terror which Ishmael perceives in the White Whale." Yet, Smith stresses, through those same images "Melville adopts the theme of the paradisiacal innocence of the Wild West."[22] For Melville that West, in his own words, is thick with "demonism" but nonetheless "unfallen."[23]

Melville displays an ambivalence that has a less metaphysical analogue in the world of rodeo, a Western sport that was just beginning when he died in 1891, as a passage from Elizabeth Atwood Lawrence's summary of her anthropological study of it makes clear: "Through performance and contest rodeo intensifies, dramatizes, and glorifies the taming of the wild. Yet at the conclusion of each event the bronc is not 'broke,' the bull is not defeated; ordinarily the 'dogged' steer and the roped calf spring to their feet and run free out of the arena. In a sense, then, the wild have not been tamed." That's a logical outcome, because in the conquering of the West, which rodeo metaphorically reflects, "wilderness attributes exerted both attraction and repulsion." Lawrence's research affords lots of examples of the ambivalence thereby elicited, and she finds it still expressed in situations where the desire to control or kill a wild animal is mixed with respect for its defiance and empathy with its intractability. She concludes that the contradictions informing such ambivalence "are an important part of what makes possible rodeo's assurance that the wild-to-tame transformation which is its central concern will be a continuing process involving two opposing forces, not simply a human conquest that will ultimately come to an end."[24]

That that ambivalence, as Lawrence implies, pertains as much to inner as to outer wildness—a pertinence steadfast in the history of the contradictory compulsions to "end" and to preserve Western wildness—is revealed in Tatum's investigation of the American public's reactions to Western myths. Recognizing the validity of Limerick's point that "such theme parks as Disneyland, whose Frontierland essentially promotes the same mythologies as the Wild West shows of the last century, constitute difficult terrain because they . . . force us 'to stumble in the uncertain turf along the border between the imagined and the actual,'" he expands upon it. He notes that audiences' identification in response to the texts of popular culture can be so fluid that they swallow myths directly contrary to their own real-world experiences. He mentions specifically their "potential ability to identify with outlaws as well as agents of civilization" and finds the whole matter of what visitors to Disneyland are thinking to make for a complex problem.[25] An observation from Slotkin confirms his take on it: "the response of a given audience to myth tends to reflect that group's ambivalence toward its own ideology: The genteel reader may, in his dismay with modern society, identify simultaneously with the primitive Indian of an idealized past and with the elite agents of modernity; the proletarian reader may identify his own suppressed rage with that of the defeated Red Man in certain moods, while in others his aspiration to power and respectability will be paradoxically invested in the conquering white man."[26]

I'd argue that the complexity of the problem on which Tatum has fastened is, in these particular terms, a matter not just of ambiguity about the imagined and the actual but also of a deep ambivalence, itself ideological, at which Slotkin hints and to which I'll return continually, in Euro-American identification with the wild and the tame. I don't know that I've solved Tatum's problem in the pages ahead, but perhaps I've managed to discover something useful about its complexity.

F. Scott Fitzgerald, in his essay "The Crack-Up," asserted that "the test of a first-rate intelligence is the ability to hold two opposed ideas in the mind at the same time, and still retain the ability to function."[27] Since there isn't and never has been a plentitude of first-rate intelligences, Fitzgerald's aphorism can be taken to imply that most people in some wise can't function when they hold two opposed ideas at once. Maybe, then, it's no wonder that, during the history of their dealings with a West relentlessly conceived in terms of opposed ideas (as to whether it's independent or colonized by the East, rural or urban, and so on—oppositions generally subsumed by that between wild and tame), most Euro-Americans have occasioned all manner of dysfunctionalities, crack-ups galore. Though, as Elliott West argues, many late-nineteenth-century newcomers to the West as well as settlers already there could hold "the twin narratives of civilizer and seeker of the wild" in their heads at the same time, "apparently without noticing any contradictions,"[28] those ideas have never had simple—rather, have always had increasingly complicated and consequential—relations with each other in an encompassing high-stakes dialectic.

What follows is a history of that cyclical-and-yet-advancing dialectic, a history that, while intellectual in some respects, is primarily cultural. As such, it partakes of that field of history concerned, as Slotkin describes it, "with giving a historical account of the activities and processes through which human societies produce the systems of value and meaning by which they live and through which they explain and interpret the world and themselves."[29] In *Hunger for the Wild*, I'm engaged in giving that sort of account with regard to the American attitude toward the wildness of the West. Since that's a broad project, I draw integratively upon a broad range of sources. Therefore I hope that the history here, besides being the deeper kind that Worster calls for, replies as well to the need, which became apparent in the early 1980s and remains insufficiently addressed, for "broader studies and creative synthesis" in the fields of American and Western history Gerald D. Nash has pointed out. Perhaps in replying to that need it can join the small but growing company of studies that have "attempted to provide an interpretive stance for the whole sweep of Western history."[30]

The historical periods into which I've divided my account mirror—though not without some overlapping, of course—verifiable shifts of emphasis in the way Western wildness has been perceived and (in several senses) treated. To some extent they correspond to divisions now historiographically conventional, quite apart from issues of wildness, but they also relate directly to those issues, with each being a distinguishable context for characteristic stories about America's obsession with the untamed West and what it has wrought. Those stories should be of interest not only to general readers intrigued by the West but also to Western and Native American historians, ecocritics, conservationists and other kinds of environmental activists, American-studies and cultural-studies specialists, nature writers, cowboy-culture aficionados, art and cinema historians, recreationists of diverse types, maybe even rodeo fans—anybody with a hunger for (or just a curiosity about) the wild, Western-style.

PART ONE
A Brief History of Wild

Eastward I go only by force; but westward I go free. . . . The West of which
I speak is but another name for the Wild.
  Henry David Thoreau, "Walking"

The Prehuman West

Much of what we mean by the West is what we have found there in a state
of nature.
  Donald Worster, *An Unsettled Country: Changing Landscapes of*
  the American West

What sort of place was the West before any humans were there? How far back do we have to go to get to what SueEllen Campbell calls "the Age of the Pristine" in the West? Mulling such questions, she offers a few answers, along with more questions:

> We've been here a long time—fifteen, thirty, maybe even fifty thousand years.
> . . . When we first arrived, the land was very different. . . . There were saber-
> toothed tigers and giant sloths. . . . And further back, when the dinosaurs lived
> here, what did the land look like then? . . . I think about the amazing exhibits at
> the dinosaur museum in Vernal, pictures of drifting continents matched with
> charts of evolving animals and chunks of fossils. The state of Utah floats around
> the globe like a leaf turning on a slow eddy. What does it mean to say dinosaurs
> lived here?

One thing it means is that "the dream of the pristine is a sweet onion of illusions, . . . every layer peeled leaving another below."[1] Another thing it means is that the West was wild before we were there and will be when we are gone.

In the West, in the beginning was wildness. But isn't that true of every place on Earth? However, the difference in the case of the West, at least when comparing it to the rest of the United States and to Europe, isn't in how its wildness began but in how it unfolded and, most significant, in how, past a certain point, it went untempered by natural phenomena common to those other geographies. Worster vivifies that difference in his description of the environment Euro-Americans encountered in the nineteenth century: "Westward-moving pioneers . . . came into a country of raw physical nature, less mediated by the forces of life than that on the eastern side of the continent. The sheltering forests thinned out, then disappeared over most of the terrain, leaving the earth exposed like a massive brown body, every crevice, bulge, and scar from the past relentlessly revealed." Engulfed by broad sky, many of those would-be settlers felt exposed—to the eyes of God and otherwise—on land far barer than any cleared for farming east of the Missouri River. What they beheld was a space almost devoid of any sign of the possibility of human control, "an altogether new kind of wildness beyond European or Eastern American experience."[2]

Worster emphasizes also how the West's landforms confronted the future-oriented pioneers "with a time scale that was older than anyone had once supposed possible" and that can astonish even today's most seen-it-all traveler.[3] The West, patently showing its age in deep canyon strata, craggy buttes, high mountain faces, brandishes itself as temporally other and thus wild by chronological as well as immediate geophysical extremes.

Moreover, the West was and remains, as Worster stresses, "a highly unstable place" whose complexity—meteorological, hydrological, geological, what have you—we scarce grasp fully.[4] Testimony to the unpredictability and other qualities of wildness to which that mutability has given rise and which were the quintessence of the prehuman West is not hard to come by. Let me offer some.

In western Kansas, an area whose Minium Quarry reveals in its rock record that bamboo grew there seven million years ago, the Sternberg Museum of Natural History at Fort Hays State University houses a double fossil discovered by the museum's namesake, the fossil hunter Charles H. Sternberg: "the fish within a fish, the *Gillicus arcuatus*, about six feet long, inside the *Xiphactinus audax*, about 14 feet long."[5] There's little certainty as to how this configuration came about, but there's no doubt that its setting was the water that covered Kansas back in deep time. When I saw that fossil in the early 1990s, it was mounted on a wall above a display of human skeletal remains in a glass case. Stepping back to take in the size of it, I bumped into something's tibia as massive as a railroad tie—another memento mori. How odd, I thought, that such a huge creature once lived in Kansas and then ended up, all its kind, nothing more than bones, much the same insensate stuff as that lying in the case beneath Sternberg's famous oddity.

I was—and am—in no wise alone in such meditating on the wild doings and undoings of the prehuman West. Louis Jacobs, for instance, does plenty of it in his book *Lone Star Dinosaurs*, in which he tells of the giant reptiles that once flew over Texas or stomped through its mud.

But return to the central prairie. Imagine it at a later time, yet one well before human hunters, when, as William Heyen portrays it,

> sun now directly overhead, clouds gather,
> & rains come, again, to prairie,

as they had the day before, & will the next,

as buffalo graze in rain, tasting
the wet grass, rain running from their fur
in rivulets. . . .[6]

That miracle of water on grass and buffalo was then, as it is now, a critical part of what Worster terms "the intricate weave" of the prairie's ancient fabric. The sky from which it falls "brews the continent's most unstable patterns of weather." The earth beneath it, he explains, "is the product of ten thousand years of organic chemistry, though before that Holocene soil existed, there were other soils."[7]

Now let's go further west. Into the Southwest, where the air clarity is well suited for telescopically viewing cosmic wildness. There you can find any number of historians—and others—willing to follow Worster's urging "to get outdoors more often than we do and look at all that has been going on."[8] What they observe and write about is wild indeed. Douglas Preston, for example, reminds us that "one hundred million years ago, a flat seashore extended from Mosquero Creek in Harding County [New Mexico] to near Fort Collins, Colo.," which stretch of paleo-littoral is called "the Dinosaur Freeway, because great herds of dinosaurs once migrated along this route."[9] Michael Tincher describes how "the great heat engine of the Earth" volcanically created the Río Grande rift from central Colorado to Mexico and then its see-sawing brought about a topsy-turvy in which "the same rocks that form the top edge of Sandía Crest are part of the original floor of the rift . . . and lie more than 4 miles beneath the city of Albuquerque."[10] Tony Hillerman details how Ship Rock, the towering volcano core sacred to the Navajo, "probably formed during the great Neogene volcanic period which thrust Mount Taylor 11,389 feet into the sky, caused the mind-boggling Valle Grande explosion over near Los Alamos and scattered ashes from Utah to Kansas."[11] Halka Chronic informs us that 570 million years ago, when North America was included in Pangaea and "the western part of this megacontinent tilted just a little, a sea crept across it," preparing the way for the late-Paleozoic embayments along what's now the Texas–New Mexico border, where "a great barrier reef developed."[12]

Northwest of there, the Rockies developed in two stages of large-scale geomorphology. First were the Ancestral Rockies, which grew, in Campbell's words, "until they were as tall as the Himalayas, then wore away into lush, dinosaury plains." Thereafter the Rockies we know today surged through those plains until, unlike mountains in the East, they rose well above the timberline. Their patterns, like their orogenies, are wild: "lots of colors and all shapes, . . . jagged spires and knife edges, hogbacks and palisades, huge rounded mounds, crazy quilts of miscellaneous mountain parts welded together inside the earth and then shoved upward into the thin high air to be cut and honed by glaciers."[13]

Follow those mountains up into Wyoming, with John McPhee as your guide.

Learn that all that rock is the result of only the latest episode of mountain-making, that there were many earlier ones in the last two billion years, and so there have been many sets of Ancestral Rockies that have arisen and been deposed. This long story of repeated upheavals features planing of crustal sheets as wide as Vermont, erosion capable of deroofing and leveling and spreading thousands of feet of rock, lava by the cubic mile, some of it witnessed by rhinoceroses and "horses that had three toes and were . . . the size of collies."[14]

Cross those mountains. Taken back in time by McPhee, you gaze upon brick-red flats extending into Utah, "the signs of the Triassic," two hundred million years ago, "when the earth in its rutilance may have outdone Mars." Cross another line of mountains in eastern Nevada, and soon you discern more mountains in the distant west. Make your way across central Nevada. Climb to the top of them. Once there, "you look out upon (as it appears in present theory) open sea." If you climb down the cliffy slope in front of you and move on, you'll be in the realm of volcanoes once surrounded by water—and "above ocean crustal floor that reaches to the China Sea."[15] That floor is slowly being swallowed by subduction zones in depths pressed by hydraulic tonnage your lungs can't imagine.

Where you are is where California, along with the land's end of the West, later will be formed. McPhee explains—again, according to present theory—how the state was tectonically cobbled above that mobile rock beneath a crushing weight of ocean:

> An island arc here, a piece of continent there—a Japan at a time, a New Zealand, a Madagascar—came crunching in upon the continent and have thus far adhered. Baja is about to detach. A great deal more may go with it. Some parts of California arrived head on, and others came sliding in on transform faults. . . . The dynamics that have pieced together the whole of California have consisted of tens of thousands of earthquakes . . .—tens of thousands of examples of what people like to singularize as "the big one"—and many millions of earthquakes of lesser magnitude.[16]

Who knows but what there may be many millions more, big and lesser, after the human dream of the West is done.

Native Nature

We did not think of the great open plains, the beautiful rolling hills, and winding streams with tangled growth as "wild." Only to the white man was nature a "wilderness" and only to him was the land "infested" with "wild"

animals and "savage" people.
    Luther Standing Bear, *Land of the Spotted Eagle*

Now we situate ourselves hundreds of miles north of California. In the Northwest, a word that for Euro-Americans signifies, according to present but polemical theory, the direction from which the forebears of indigenous Westerners probably first entered what is now the United States.[1] We are just inside Canada. At the Museum of Anthropology at the University of British Columbia in Vancouver. In the Rotunda Gallery. There's a large, raised bowl of sand in the center, which serves as a platform for a sculpture about a cubic yard in volume titled *The Raven and the First Men.* Carved in yellow cedar by Haida artist Bill Reid, this piece was unveiled in 1980 by no less a Euro-personage than the prince of Wales, as members of the Haida Nation looked on.

The dominant figure in the piece is Raven himself, a creature of prolific significance in the cultures of the Haida and other indigenous peoples: creator, transformer, fire-bringer, shape-shifter, trickster, and more. Here he's depicted in a moment of eternally present ancestral past: the first men cower in a clamshell while he perches atop and coaxes them to venture out onto the sand—and the viewer to behold all Raven's spirit wings unfold above. And what do they unfold above? Well, a world different from that to which the forebears of people like the prince of Wales were accustomed. But there are other ways to answer that question. Each has something to do with pre-Euro-American times in the West.

Here's one way. I once asked Navajo poet Luci Tapahonso if Navajos have a word that means "wilderness." She replied, "No, we don't. You can speak of places that are far away or places where there are few people, but that's all." Her response correlates with George R. Stewart's observation that Native tribes in the past named places that were local—and then only if they were somehow important—and seldom had names for "anything as large and vaguely marked off as a region or territory."[2] That more grandiose place-naming would be the business of Euro-American conquerors, who would want all the land they could get, in the name of beings quite different from Raven—a remote Christian God, a king, a president, or some other white embodiment of august principles. When their traditional societies were still intact, before the conquerors greatly undid them, Indians in the West, like Indians elsewhere in North America, saw the land the way their maps showed it, as proximate, concrete, and ancestrally familiar; it was the non-Native outsiders who saw it as vast, abstract, and novelly wild and named big tracts with names either imported from their own cultures or borrowed from those encompassed (Nueva España, Louisiana Territory, Oklahoma)—though they were capable of more descriptive names that often betrayed their assessment of the wilderness (Death Valley, Crazy Mountains).

Here's another, related way to answer that question. It's inherent in a joke I first heard told over the PA system at a powwow. It goes as follows:

> An Indian needs to speak with God, and so, obedient to his Christian training, he travels to the Vatican, where the pope has a red phone, a hotline to God. But the Indian can't talk at length because it's a long-distance call. The next time the Indian needs to speak with God, he remembers his disappointment and decides to drop by the tribal medicine man's house. Turns out the medicine man also has a hotline to God. On that phone, however, the Indian can talk as long as he wants because it's a local call.

The joke makes Indians laugh almost as much as it makes whites squirm—for reasons that have everything to do with why Raven's wings unfold above a West that was locally suffused with familiar natural-spiritual presence for those who lived there ages before the coming of intruders for whom it was distant from a celestial Heaven and therefore wild.

Let me approach more methodically the question of what the Native West was like before those intruders arrived. Richard White makes two points on which I wish to elaborate: first, that "long before the first Europeans reached what is now the western United States, Indian peoples shaped this land"; second, that "Native Americans' beliefs about nature varied widely, but as a whole they can be distinguished from whites' attitudes by their tendency to endow nature with a spiritual dimension largely lacking in white thought." Thus there's abundant evidence that Indians set fires on forest land—in California, the Pacific Northwest, and the Rockies—in order to augment grasslands and the deer population, that they diverted streams in the Great Basin in order to irrigate wild plants, and that they farmed in the desert Southwest, along the edge of the Great Plains, and in the Missouri Valley. The impact of their shaping was such that "if by 'wilderness' we mean environments uninfluenced by human actions, then the lands that would become the West had ceased to be wilderness long before the first whites ever arrived." True enough, but, as White makes clear in amplifying his second point, the Indians' spiritualization of the environments they influenced imbued their animals and plants with meaning far beyond the commodity value whites attributed to them—so that it's also true that Indians and whites "perceived different landscapes."[3]

Still, there are some subtleties that need to be marked; though not free of controversy, they may sharpen or qualify our understanding of the pre-European Native perception of Western landscape and its enfolding nature. Roderick Nash writes of how, in his search for the deepest roots of the notion of wilderness, he became interested in "what seemed to be a central turning point in the human relationship to the natural world: the advent of herding and agriculture some 15,000 years ago." Before then, he explains, human beings were hunters and gatherers, essentially predators united with nature and starkly dependent on its cycles. When herding and agriculture began, there began also the possibility of "a civilized way of life based on controlling natural processes. . . . For the first time humans saw themselves as distinct from the rest of nature," and they originated "the concept of 'wild'" as a classification for any of it they couldn't control. In a real sense, then, they created wilderness; the notion was meaningless "until there were fenced fields and walled cities." As such provisions suggest, civilized people feared what they couldn't control. When their aspirations turned toward the American West, "the frontier was their invention"—a precarious borderland between civilization and wilderness.[4]

Nash goes on to relate his insights to the prehuman and human abandonment of forest for open land (because of the visual advantage) and to the fact that, in the westward expansion of America, "the civilizing process was thought to be an enlightening one" during which "evil retreated to the West."[5] But his discussion is most striking for its implication that, across the thousands of years during which pre-European humans inhabited the West, there was a good deal of variation, across both time and space, in how different peoples perceived the rest of nature as one with or disjunct from themselves. The general tendency must have been a slow movement toward dualism as hunting and gathering yielded to herding and agriculture—though never to the extent of allowing the sort of split between wild and civilized that prepossessed non-Natives.

Consider early phases of the Native habitation of the West, when the nature of which humans variously thought themselves a part was surely "wild" in our present popular sense of the word. Twelve thousand years ago, around the end of the Ice Age, nomadic Paleo-Indians on the Great Plains hunted mammoths with five-yard tusks.[6] Over ten thousand years ago their cousins in the Tularosa Valley witnessed volcanic eruptions in what would much later be called the Malpais, badlands north of White Sands National Monument in New Mexico.[7] About six thousand years ago, so the theory goes, the peoples living on the Great Plains experienced the peaking of the postglacial Altithermal period of heat and drought that virtually eliminated large animals from their land for the next two millennia.[8] And so on. You get the broad picture.

But let's zoom in. Here's the exacting imagination of Kiowa writer N. Scott Momaday at work:

One hundred centuries ago. There is a wide, irregular landscape in what is now northern New Mexico. The sun is a dull white disk, low in the south; it is a perfect mystery, or deity whose coming and going are inexorable. . . . A cold wind runs along the ground. . . . Beyond the wind the silence is acute. A man crouches in the ravine, in the darkness there, scarcely visible. . . . He wears skins and carries a spear. These things in particular mark his human intelligence and distinguish him as the lord of the universe.

Soon a long-horned bison appears, upwind from the man. It moves closer. An intake of breath at the end of a paragraph, and "then the scene explodes."[9] In a vertigo of motion, the man emerges from cover and hurls his spear, driving it into the flesh in flight. The beast staggers, falls, dies. And the ritual of the kill, for the moment, is finished.

For this man, as Momaday portrays him, the hunt is absolutely necessary for survival, and "his relationship to the land has not yet become a moral equation." He is a small-scale exploiter of a still-unmeasured plentitude. But this Paleo-Indian is the predecessor of a later man who, certainly by Columbus's time, possesses a panoply of skills—venatic, piscatorial, medicinal, agricultural, architectural—and with his bow and arrows "is only incidentally a hunter. . . . He has fitted himself far more precisely into the patterns of the wilderness." In the interim between the two men, there evolved "an idea of land as sacred."[10] After that evolvement Earth mothered beneath fathering Sky.

The Indian's fittedness is the indispensable factor: the way Native and nature fit together, culture conformed to environment. As arch-conservationist Aldo Leopold once noted, "the culture of primitive peoples is often based on wildlife," so that, for example, "the plains Indian not only ate buffalo, but buffalo largely determined his architecture, dress, language, arts, and religion."[11] Such thoroughgoing linkage was a matter of adaptation, something Indians across the West—Paiutes with their itinerant strategies of survival in the Great Basin, say, or Chinooks with their reliance on less mobile fishing and farming as well as hunting and gathering—generally did well long before Europeans showed up. In this respect, as Richard Rhodes argues, they differed much from the Europeans who entered the New World. Lacking "the genius that might transform them into a new kind of people," the latter chose not to accommodate themselves to the wilderness but to plunder and destroy it—and so chose also "to remain European, with European notions of land ownership and European beliefs in man's authority over the natural world." They believed the land belonged to them and were short on the Indians' ability to feel the opposite. The Europeans tried to remake the wilderness in their own image; the Indians "made the wilderness their own" in quite another way.[12] For them it was, in Carolyn Merchant's succinct phrase, "simply home."[13]

The Indians' sense of home derived in large part from what White earlier called their "beliefs about nature," beliefs that dovetailed with the exigencies of adaptation and thus varied widely from tribe to tribe—and radically from the beliefs about nature held by Europeans. But there were common features among those beliefs, according to Catherine L. Albanese. The Indians who populated the West, numbering in the millions by the sixteenth century, shared certain religious assumptions with their counterparts in other regions north of the Río Grande: that nature consisted of "a universe of persons and personal relations"; that "the numinous world of nature beings was always very close"; and that, since "the material world was a holy place . . . harmony with nature beings and natural forms was the controlling ethic, reciprocity the recognized mode of interaction."[14] Such assumptions determined how the Indians perceived nature and how it was present in their lives. However mundane, all activities had a spiritual dimension, and spiritual journeys could be undertaken on this side of death.[15]

The world of Native nature was above all an interconnected one, its time, to quote from Gary Short's poem "Shoshonean," a time when animals and humans spoke to one another and "all things echoed / like an owl's call in the black night."[16] The interconnectedness of that echoing world is elucidated by a logical schema Richard C. Poulsen constructs. In it man (humanity), earth ("temporality beyond the human"), and sky (the unseen world of deities) make up the fundamental realms of the Native American universe. For Anglos these realms are discrete, but the mythos of Native Americans sees them "as continuous, interlocking circles," interdependent in being and meaning. Poulsen illustrates this divergence with two Venn diagrams: one, representing the Anglo view, with the three circles of man, earth, and sky clustered but untouching; the other, representing the Native American view, with the three circles all mutually overlapping. In contrast to the first, the second depicts a cosmos of unities rather than disparities, of balanced interlockings rather than opposed forces, of harmony with "the enigmatic" rather than fear of it. For those who live in that cosmos, there's no perception of sharp separateness to rationalize the category of the wild—nor any demand for "the eradication of evil" associated with it, for that (as Poulsen shows through examples from the cultures of the Navajo and the Maidu of upper California) "would . . . be tantamount to needlessly eradicating part of oneself."[17]

The Indian's love of harmony embraced nature as essentially hospitable. That story of nature and humankind intertwined is told in petroglyphs scratched and pecked into dry volcanic rock a thousand years ago in New Mexico as well as in totem poles carved by long-dead artisans in the wet Northwest. A key reason for the story's continuity across the West lies in the fact that Indian religions, unlike Christianity, contained no doctrine of nature's fall, along with Adam and Eve's, into corruption. For those religions, the essence of creation, as Vine Deloria Jr. emphasizes, "was that all parts of it functioned together to sustain it." Correlatively, those religions, unlike Christianity, adhered to no doctrine that humankind is sanctioned "to downgrade the natural world and its life forms"—in contrast to a remote supernatural world—and to exploit it toward economic ends as "a mere object."[18]

On the other hand, Poulsen, like many students of the pre-European West—perhaps most notably, in recent years, Shepard Krech III—cautions that "the Indian was not romantic" and seems so in retrospect only because of images promulgated since the eighteenth century by, among others, poets like Philip Freneau and William Cullen Bryant.[19] Those images entail idealizations that rarely suggest how real Native people lived in relation to their natural environment. Such romanticization, in its postmodern strain, ecologically pedestals Indians and tends to accompany what Martin W. Lewis calls "an inverted form of Eurocentrism—one that focuses on the West [Western civilization] as the center of everything vile and destructive"—and to overlook evidence that early human occupants of places all over the world, including what's now the American West, "brought ecological devastation" on some scale. As an integral warrant for his argument, he cites Paul S. Martin's controversial thesis "that some 10,000 years ago, late-Pleistocene Paleo-Indian migrants may well have exterminated some 80 percent of all large mammal species in North and South America."[20]

During the decades since Martin first advanced his thesis in the early 1960s, dissension over its accuracy and implications, in which Deloria has played no small part, has burgeoned until now it's fair to say, with Gary Paul Nabhan, that "a debate is raging with regard to the 'nature' of the North American continent." The issues in that debate have bearing on whether or how, in light of our understanding of the past ecological practices of indigenous peoples, present wilderness areas in the United States should be managed. In Nabhan's characterization, those on one side of the debate contend that Native Americans have had little impact on their home environments and left large areas unchanged, while those on the other side contend that they have, to say the least, employed "farming, hunting, and gathering techniques . . . often ecologically ill suited for the habitats in which they were practiced." He surveys explanations for why Europeans failed to notice that North America "looked 'lived-in,'" concluding that in any case "it was easier for Europeans to assume possession of a land they considered to be virgin or at least unworked and uninhabited by people of their equal," and he suggests that a resolution to the debate may lie in his argument that pre-Columbian North America was not pristine wilderness "for the very reason that many indigenous cultures actively managed habitats and plant populations within their home ranges as a response to earlier episodes of overexploitation."[21]

Such arguments, sobering in how they deromanticize, go beyond Simon Schama's assertion that "it is difficult to think of a single . . . natural system that has not, for better or worse, been substantially modified by human culture."[22] Indeed, the modifications adduced by debunkers like Lewis, Martin, and Nabhan are startlingly substantial. Even Gundars Rudzitis, a geographer who admits that there's a spate of scholarly disagreement about the romanticization of Indians' land use and also acknowledges the special relationship they have with the earth, nonetheless points out that "there are examples where environmental and ecological desecration and damage have been inflicted by Indians themselves." Though recent examples may have occurred partly because of "imposed non-native economic incentives and value systems," those of the more remote past—his prime one being the Kalapuyas' profound alteration, by annual fires over several thousand years, of the Willamette Valley—of course did not.[23]

While we must recognize that Indians typically accepted the natural world on what they construed as its own terms and maintained a remarkable give-and-take in their interactions with it, we must recognize as well that harmonies in those interactions may have been skewed or broken for various reasons. Steven R. Simms makes a case that Indians' "simple societies may have caused as significant an environmental damage as have more complex societies." The evidence: "the waste of dozens of bison carcasses at the Olsen-Chubbuck site on the high plains more than 8,200 years ago," foraging practices in the Great Basin and elsewhere in the West that may have endangered species such as deer and elk, widespread slash-and-burn clearing, excessive deforestation undertaken by the Anasazi dwelling in the Chaco Canyon area, on and on. For Simms, these data dispute the platitudes that the Indians' ideology could "ensure harmony between behavior and nature" and that progress, as popularly conceived for two hundred years, inexorably runs "from a humanity that was ostensibly in harmony with nature to one now in a shambles of disharmony." He counters such platitudes with his argument, which I here summarize with a phrase borrowed from Henry F. Dobyns, that the so-called virgin land Euro-Americans headed west during widespread settlement beheld was already, through the devastations of Indians as well as those of white diseases and aggressions, well on the way to being "'widowed' land."[24]

Granting that Native ecological strategies were imperfect and that a succession of cultures—and probably climatic changes in addition—wreaked some havoc on pre-Columbian Western nature, the fact that a larger number of whites wreaked much worse havoc in far less time still must be acknowledged. Whites wreaked their havoc, through hunting and farming but in many other ways as well, on an astounding abundance. You can get a sense of its scope by juxtaposing estimates of wild fauna in the West before whites came in droves with estimates of that fauna in modern times. Donald Worster, drawing on the calculations of Ernest Thompson Seton, who in the late 1920s made "the first systematic effort to arrive at pre-Lewis and Clark faunal populations," offers juxtapositions of that sort. The grizzly bear, a wide-ranging carnivore found only in the West, was once a common sight, but by 1922 a mere eight hundred remained, most of them in Yellowstone National Park. Wolves, distributed throughout the West and elsewhere on the continent, once numbered at least two million, but by 1908 the population had declined to a tenth of that, the majority in Alaska and Canada. Juxtapositions for animals lower on the food chain are even more contrastive. Consider the figures for several Western herbivores: there were thirty to forty million pronghorn, as many as two million bighorn sheep, and ten million mule deer—all of whose numbers were reduced to no more than tens of thousands by the early twentieth century. The figures for bison, creatures once multitudinous also in the East, are appalling: Seton's "'primitive' population of 75 million" had been diminished to only eight hundred by 1895, most of them too in Yellowstone. Even if Seton's dismay led him to calculate, in

Worster's phrase, "too liberally," there's little reason to mistrust the orders of magnitude of his figures.[25] In each instance the early figure enhances the imagery of nature in the West as a faunal cornucopia.

From the first European encounter with that nature and the cultures interwoven with it, there began a tragedy of difference that would be manifested in a havoc dismaying not only in static retrospect but in the process of its expansion and intensification. What did the white invaders, their hearts full of greed and Christian piety, think of all the seeming boundlessness before them? What did they feel about societies that worshipped bears and bison and venerated medicine bundles packed with pieces of eagles and mountain lions or petroglyphs of a humpbacked flute player with a bestial erection? Above all, what were they going to do, given that they had severed what T. H. Watkins calls "those spiritual connections that bind us to the land" and were disposed to "pretend they had never existed"?[26]

What those whites did, according to Watkins, echoing Rhodes, was make choices, much the same ones they had made in the East and in the New World as a whole. The tragedy, as he describes it, is that "the choices they made were almost invariably those which continued the long alienation from the wilderness that had nurtured their beginnings."[27] What they thought and felt compelled them not only to exploit Native nature but to try to alter it, and that meant battle with it. Such battle (and, correlatively, battle with the Europeans' own inner terrors) entailed what Donald Johanson summarizes as "extremely detrimental consequences." Many of those consequences are tragic; not the least of them is that the battle, continuous into the present, has more and more "distanced us from nature and lessened our reverence for the natural world."[28]

Well, maybe not all of us. But the battle is quite unlike any known to pre-European Indians. They had their weapons, but those weapons were nothing compared to what the whites would bring to bear. The trickster Coyote, who the Shoshones of the Great Basin believed had engendered them, knew, as Zeese Papanikolas has it, that, "if there is going to be Culture, the first thing to do is to tame the women" and "the next thing to do is tame the men," but his sort of taming wasn't what the whites had in mind. They had bigger plans, and the dissimilarity between what the West once was for the Shoshones and what it has become at the hands of whites, as articulated by Papanikolas, is instructive. Though lamenting that the old Shoshone world is mostly lost, he acknowledges that "the Dust People—the Gosiutes—still remain," but they live in trying circumstances on their reservation land in the Nevada-Utah desert, an area of mining refuse that serves as the site for a striking collation: "The Indians replaced what they took from the earth, left a bead, a charm, a bit of tobacco. The miners and engineers have only taken. For the Indian, the desert was rich, a place full of story and sustenance. For the white man any land barren of material wealth is empty, a place to store nerve gas and detonate weapons, to bury nuclear waste." The desert where the Gosiutes dwell on the margin of extinction is, as are they in Papanikolas's characterization, "still burdened by the imposition of an alien culture."[29]

And yet you—Gosiute, white, whatever—still might look out across that desert and sense a kinship in the hemoglobin of your blood with the palette of iron oxides and hydroxides whose constituents date back to the origin of Earth and beyond, through the abysm of time, to the primal wildness of the big bang. Also, struggling with the mental impediments to discerning familiarity in such strangeness, you might be tempted to ask if what Montezuma said to Hernán Cortés in the context of another scene of difference—"None of us is native to this land"—applies here as well.[30]

PART TWO

From the 1530s to the 1840s: The West as Waste and Promised Land

Earth. Rock. Desert. I am walking barefoot on sandstone, flesh responding to
flesh. It is hot. . . . I must quicken my pace, paying attention to where I step.
    Terry Tempest Williams, "Earth"

Prelude and Overview

& I think how far we are going,
how big the world will be when we stop.
    Pamela Alexander, "We Lose St. Domingue"

From the earliest Spanish intrusions and colonizations to the explorations of Meriwether Lewis and William Clark to the establishment of trails that piped in trickles and then surges of Euro-American settlers, the siren of the West entranced many generations of outsiders, would-be conquerors of her natural beauty. That beauty was both different from and more dangerous than that of Europe or the East, whose denizens culturally constructed it in variegated fantasies. Recounting the development of the imagery of the West, Richard W. Etulain reminds us that it took centuries to crystallize. Europeans dreamed about the West long before they visited it: "Some dreams drew upon age-old visions of the West as Eden, as paradise, as the destiny of nations" while others "envisioned the West as Cíbola (the Spaniards' fabled Seven Cities of Gold), as a passage to India, as the home of larger-than-life heroes, or as the Great American Desert and Garden of the World." Some of those dreams were more like nightmares, construals, from New England Puritans, of the frontier as "a howling wilderness, infested with the Devil and his minions"—which construals nonetheless would never negate the mix of passions that drove Europeans west.[1]

Through those dreams and the successive forays they motivated and rationalized, the West was a place doomed to be turned figuratively (and then in sundry literal ways) into something else. Like immigrants into the New World, immigrants into the West were energized by "vague expectations," most of which affixed to three images, those, as Leonard Lutwack distinguishes them, of "a garden, a wilderness, and a place of treasure." Each image metaphorized the unknown into a more or less familiar—and symbolically loaded—class of experience, and complications in that triplet arose from the beginning. Each of the images encouraged migration to America and its westward settlement, but none suggested new practices for undertaking such enterprises. And each called for a different approach: "the garden wanted cultivation, the wilderness taming, the place of treasure quick consumption." Moreover, the three images were mutually opposed: "The garden encroaches on the wilderness, the wilderness in time reclaims the garden, and Eldorado ever extends its domain over the garden for its produce and over the wilderness for its timber, furs, ore, and oil." Those oppositions, Lutwack concludes, tell the story of "the relation of the American to his land."[2] That conclusion is true in spades of the American's relation to the West, where wilderness has been most vividly the element common, as his outline shows, to all of them.

Thus the West became the ultimate battleground for the conflicts among those three images and suffered the more because each was not only an idealization but one both compelling in principle and ambivalent in fact. In combination they promoted an ideal West, like the ideal New World or the ideal America, "standing high and free above the details of place" and existing as "a means rather than an end." The force of such idealizing created a situation in which the ideal has been more important than land itself, according to Lutwack, but it's also a situation in which stranger ironies are embedded, ironies born of vacillations between "abstract motivations." Thereby, though wilderness has been much cherished by Americans, it also has been ruthlessly plundered; though agrarianism provided Americans with a bond to farmland, "their feelings toward it . . . have always been ambivalent"; and the cities that many yearned to see rising in cleared wilderness have proven less than estimable. In short, Americans "have wavered between appreciation of the unspoiled wonders of a virgin land and determination to transform it for the uses of civilization they inherited from the European past"[3]—a wavering that appears tellingly encoded in the name of Wildorado, a town just west of Amarillo, Texas. Americans moved rapidly from East to West, wavering all the way, never bringing that schizophrenic wiggle to a deliberated equilibrium.

If the Spanish began the process of using New World land to reify ideals in the late fifteenth and early sixteenth centuries, then Americans began the process of similarly using the land of the West, from which they would displace the Spanish along with Indians, about three hundred years later. It was a process, however abstract and at odds its motivations, that, like its antecedent, involved concrete and straightforward assault and seizure. Though some Americans strove "to sacralize the land" they were out to take, their sacralizing was problematically Christian in flavor, with only occasional—and mostly sentimental—respect for that of the Indians. Conflicting and airy images and ideals, continuous movement across the continent, violent displacement of other cultures and theft of their territories, plundering of nature—all were fiercely under way by the middle of the nineteenth century, and all were implicated in a blend of feelings that Lutwack sees as determinative of the evolving attitude toward land: "love of the land when it represented the symbol of American aspirations for a new life, hatred of the land as an obstacle in the way of survival and material progress, and guilt over misuse of the land, or guilt inspired by recognition of the gap between love and hatred of the land."[4]

In the West, especially before the middle of the nineteenth century, that land meant wilderness, what Roderick Nash calls "the basic ingredient of American civilization," for two reasons: "From the raw materials of the physical wilderness Americans built a civilization; with the idea or symbol of wilderness they sought to give that civilization identity and meaning."[5] That those two activities weren't easily made compatible should be clear, and the contradictions entailed were alive and well from the beginning of the European presence in the New World—indeed, even in the nascent dream of that presence.

How so? Because that dream contained a jeopardous doubleness. On the one hand, it was wefted with what Watkins terms "the racial memory of paradise lost"[6]—and the expectation, partly in reaction to the deepening corruption of the Old World, of recovering in the New what had been lost. On the other hand, that dream was also shot through with, in Frederick Turner's words, "ancient fears and divisions" that summoned such an exercise of power that "within three centuries of Cortés's penetration of the mainland a world millions of years in the making vanished into the voracious, insatiable maw of an alien civilization."[7] In the New World, as in the American West that came to embody its best hope, it was necessary, by the logic of an oxymoronic dream, to undertake the destruction of wilderness in order to build the civilization for which it would serve as an identity-grounding symbol. (Today much the same logic obtains every time a suburban housing development is thrown up in a once naturally charming but now bulldozed rural locale whose name—Quail Creek, Fox Woods, and the like, all designed to help consumers feel like Jeffersonian rustics—is derived from what was destroyed to make the development possible.)

From the time the Spanish first entered the West, there has always been some program to build there an essentially European civilization for which it would provide both physical and symbolic sustenance. Such programs have been justified by ideology that in its religious dimension saw nothing immanently sacred in nature (only humans have souls—opinions about salvaging the Indians' varied) and in its economic and technological dimensions urged exploitation and mastery of a world thereby objectified.[8] But the bold thrust of that ideology wasn't adequate to what was discovered. "For the European who came from a community of congestion and confinement, the West," as N. Scott Momaday sketches it, "was beyond dreaming."

In such an environment "he was surely bewildered, wary, afraid. The landscape was . . . desolate and unforgiving, and yet it was a world of paradisal possibility." The cardinal word here is "bewildered," for bewilderment is the condition of one confused by wilderness, in this case by wilderness inhabited by inscrutable and dangerous people where he was an intruder narcissistically intent, by the politico-military tradition of his culture, on conquest and, by imperatives both religious and technological, on "sacrilege, the theft of the sacred."[9]

Since the West was a place beyond dreaming, it was also a place where dreams were discarded. As Donald A. Barclay, James H. Maguire, and Peter Wild note, explorers of the West prior to Lewis and Clark held a lot of outré beliefs—for instance, that mammoths lived beyond the Mississippi—but their findings "undid the mythical possibilities." Realities replaced those undone possibilities, realities that sometimes "have proved far more complex and unyielding than illusions projected by the mind."[10]

Still, of course, despite disillusionment and the acknowledgment of realities, dreams of new mythical possibilities would continue to arise as the spring of exploration grew into the summer of settlement, as sobered consciousness of the wilderness gave way, in the course of the nineteenth century, to conflicted romance. But in the early part of that century Americans were embarked on stretching their empire across the interior of the continent, which expansion, Henry Nash Smith reminds us, required an increase of agricultural population toward the end of "creating new states in the dreary solitudes of the West."[11] Of those who contemplated moving into such solitudes, some may have been blessed with clear-eyed expectations, but many entertained anticipations that concerned either the possibility that the wilderness would degrade them into hellish wildness or the possibility that they would refine it into an Edenic tameness.

To give a sense both of what those two possibilities meant by the early nineteenth century and of the respective ambiguities in what they meant, let me adduce images from the Norman-born American essayist and agriculturist J. Hector St. John de Crèvecoeur and the American painter Edward Hicks.

In his 1782 book *Letters from an American Farmer*, a collection of fictionalized epistles about the American character, Crèvecoeur, through his persona, writes of the degeneration that occurs among people who live on the Western (at that time barely Midwestern) frontier. Remote from the centers of civilization, such people abandon farming for hunting, eat "wild meat," become farouche like the Indians they live among, and wind up "half civilised, half savage." And yet, because he's a composite of Enlightenment rationalist *and* Rousseauistic romantic, Crèvecoeur elsewhere in *Letters* contradicts himself and finds much to admire in the world of savages and even endorses the choice of some white captives, "thoroughly naturalised to this wild course of life," to live among their Indian captors.[12] His dreadful vision of the wilderness, which after all makes its European inhabitants only *half* savage,

Edward Hicks, The Peaceable Kingdom (early 1830s): a primitivist reverie of the American wild transformed into an Eden. (Oil on canvas, 18 x 24 1/8 in. Brooklyn Museum, Dick S. Ramsay Fund.)

cannot dispel an opposed vision that exalts wilderness for the freedom, ease, stoic moral code, and natural democracy that, according to him, it affords.

Hicks, a Quaker given to flat and stylized renderings of biblical subjects, painted many versions of The Peaceable Kingdom in the first half of the nineteenth century, most successfully in the 1830s. It's a literal-minded illustration of Isaiah 11:6 ("The wolf shall dwell with the lamb"), with assorted wild and domestic animals tended by children in the foreground of a soft wilderness that extends back into rolling forested hills, frequently featuring William Penn signing a treaty with friendly Indians. The painting freezes a primitivist reverie of the American wild transformed into an Eden. But when you attend to the transfixed stares of the animals usually regarded as the most ferocious—the lion and the leopard—you see in their eyes a hint that their wildness may be only tentatively arrested.

Those two perspectives represent extremes (virtuous wildness, treacherous tameness) on a spectrum of expectations about the West in the early nineteenth century, but variants of them can be discovered well before and after that time. So can the mid-spectrum perspective that envisions a West whose "natural settings" have been only moderately made over into a middle landscape Winifred Gallagher exemplifies by "pastoral vistas that combined woods and lawns, deer and cattle."[13]

Or, to borrow from the argot of golf (while laying aside the figurative suggestions of sand traps, tees, and such), roughs and fairways.

> The total mythos of comedy . . . has regularly what in music is called a ternary form: the hero's society rebels against the society of the senex ["old man"] and triumphs, but the hero's society is a Saturnalia, a reversal of social standards which recalls a golden age in the past. . . . The green world has analogies . . . to the dream world that we create out of our own desires. This dream world collides with the stumbling and blinded follies of the world of experience.
>
> Northrop Frye, Anatomy of Criticism: Four Essays

Conquistadors and Colonizers: The Spanish Encounter with Unbridled Wilderness

> "What do you suppose the conquistadors saw when they looked into the Grand Canyon?" I ask John. "I don't know," he says. "Maybe just a barrier to conquest? A terrifying wasteland?"
>
> SueEllen Campbell, "Grandeur"

Roughs and fairways: let me begin this chapter by playing with that contrast as an enduring metaphor for the American West. It's entrenched in a European habit of mind much in evidence when the New World was discovered and that multistage event, in Roderick Nash's formulation, "rekindled the traditional European notion that an earthly paradise lay somewhere to the west." Early reports from the New World led the Old to believe that America might be that place of beauty, riches, and long life. Promoters of discovery and colonization, many of whom had never traveled to the New World, embellished those reports, representing it in fairway terms, paying no more attention to the rough than a golfer would—unless, maybe, it had to be dealt with. That representation was expectable, given that "for Europeans wild country was a single peak or heath, an island of uninhabited land surrounded by settlement. They at least knew its character and extent."[1]

For those Europeans who actually came to the New World, the fairway dream became a nightmare reality of rough that was not enisled but enveloping. For them, in Nash's words, "the seemingly boundless wilderness of the New World was something else. In the face of this vast blankness, courage failed and imagination multiplied fears."[2] Fears compounded with greed and righteousness bred violence against the rough, along with an obsession with wildness that would permeate European interpretations of the New World at large and then of the West in particular—starting with the Spanish. For them, as for their rivals and successors from Northern Europe, the glooming comedy of New World exploration would be concentrated in the West and lead on to the romance of extended conflict with wilderness, the tragedy of its despoiling, and the irony attendant upon its diminishment.

The Spanish who came to the New World and then the West—who were they? Southern European dreamers, Don Quixotes before there was a *Don Quixote*. Catholics intent on conversions. Imperialists. Questers after a quick route to Asia and its treasures. Warriors and conquerors in a tradition stretching back at least as far as Homer's *Iliad* (an Old World epic clearly recalled in Gaspar Pérez de Villagrá's 1610 New World epic *Historia de Nuevo México*, in which Troy is reborn as Ácoma and valiant but reluctant Gicombo is an avatar of Achilles). Above all, they were, initially, Cristóbal Colón, born Cristoforo Colombo, known in the United States as Christopher Columbus, a Genoese sailing under the Spanish flag.

Campbell, after a visit to Dominica, muses on 1492: "Five centuries ago, when Columbus first reached the Caribbean, he was moved by the beauty of the land, the variety of trees, the abundance of birds. . . . Columbus, amazed, wrote in his journal that parrots darkened the sky."[3] Fourteen years after that exotic and prophetic moment, Columbus died blind and forgotten. Between 1492 and 1506, during which time he made three more voyages to the New World, lies a story of difficulties with wildness.

What happened? No one knows all of the story, of course, but Frederick Turner, drawing on several sources, offers for my purposes the most pertinent version.[4] What follows in the next three paragraphs is, except for citations, a condensed adaptation of it.

On October 12, 1492, Columbus landed on a small island of the Lucayos (Bahamas), carried the royal standard ashore, and took possession of the island in the name of Ferdinand and Isabella. He judged the unclothed people there (the Arawaks) to be convertible to Christianity. He thought them passive enough to be easily made slaves. Soon, however, he was distracted from "prelapsarian visions" and such speculations by his noticing that the Natives wore gold and his subsequent fantasizing about more gold on "the yet-to-be-discovered mainland."[5] But he didn't acquire much then or ever, though he took hundreds of Arawak slaves back to Spain on his second and third voyages.

Possession for Columbus was an act of nomination that took no account of any inherent qualities of what was named: "To each bit of land he saw he brought the mental map of Europe with which he had sailed. . . . The Admiral scattered the nomenclature of Christianity over those lands, firing his familiar names like cannonballs against the unresisting New World."[6] Thus the Adamic Christ-Bearer (what

Christopher means by Greek etymology) brought light to the tropical night through his naming of parts: San Salvador, Santa Maria this and that, Los Santos. Thus would his Spanish successors colonize the West with similar names: Las Cruces, San Antonio, Los Angeles.

In the years that followed 1492 came all manner of frustrations, contorted relations, and strife between Spaniards and indigenous peoples (and within both groups)—and madness. Futile searches for instant wealth. Disgust toward those peoples. Orgiastic sex with their women. More slavery. Increasing awareness of the "devilish nature of the native beliefs." A labor-and-tribute system that would murder countless Natives. Columbus, turned dictatorial and cruel, was sent back to Spain, along with his men, in irons. When, deranged in his lust to force-bloom a paradise in the New World and now disgraced, he returned on his final voyage, he spent a year in Jamaica raging about disorder in the settlements, still wanting to reach Cathay, longing to rebuild Jerusalem in the Indies, raving to his sponsoring royals about, among other grotesqueries, "apes with human faces and hogs with tails like tentacles." He became Joseph Conrad's Kurtz in the heart of darkness, the prototype of many a European power-and-riches dreamer who would meet the West on his own stubborn terms and get lost in "greed and haste and estrangement," especially an "estrangement from place" that wouldn't let wilderness be anything but otherness at last uncontrollable.[7]

Columbus's estrangement from the Indians themselves was similar but subtler. As Tzvetan Todorov observes, though he early thought of them as human beings capable of assimilation by conversion to the Gospel, he gradually came to see them only as objects for enslavement. In that way Columbus is "associated with . . . two apparently contradictory myths, one whereby the Other is a 'noble savage' (when perceived at a distance) and one whereby he is a 'dirty dog,' a potential slave," both of which concern blindness, despite differences, to a common subjectivity. Those contradictory myths effect an ambiguity in which "human alterity is at once revealed and rejected" that, Todorov argues, marks the whole history of discovery in America. Certainly, as he concludes, Columbus "participates in this double movement," but it's repeatedly enacted, with variations, far past his time.[8]

A measure of the problem of estrangement resided also in the fact that the Spanish, as the bent of Columbus's madness suggests, were chasing an abstraction they were prevented from catching. Their eastern land access to Asia blocked by the Ottoman Empire, they had gone west and, in Carla Mulford's words, come upon "a land they were seeking to get around, not inhabit." However, like the French searching a century later for the legendary Northwest Passage through America to the Far East, the Spanish reevaluated their situation, and soon "Europeans generally acknowledged that a significant section of the world, a section about which they had known nothing, was available to them."[9] For the Spanish, then for the French, then for Jeffersonian entrepreneurs, and then for multitudes of their descendants, the West (in one sense and then the other) was at first a barrier, a nowhere between some here and a fabled somewhere further on. But the exploration of it led to the recognition of its exploitability.

Unknown, uncivilized, seemingly unlimited, and therefore wild, the New World inspired wonder. Columbus's voyaging there "initiated a century of intense wonder," in Stephen Greenblatt's phrasing, a time during which Europe "experienced something like the 'startle reflex' one can observe in infants: eyes widened, arms outstretched, breathing stilled, the whole body momentarily convulsed."[10] In this same vein, Lawrence Weschler remarks that the booty Columbus brought back from America "was so strange and so new as to seem to sanction belief in all manner of wondrous prospects and phantasms for years thereafter." As he more emphatically puts it, "for a good century and a half after the discovery of the Americas, Europe's mind was blown."[11]

What was discovered may have inspired wonder in Europeans, but it inspired also impulses to appropriate and transform. Those impulses were enacted in the decades after 1492 by what Greenblatt describes as "a complex, well-developed, and, above all, mobile technology of power." The jingoistic culture wielding that technology was confident of its importance in the universe and, accordingly, expected strangers "to abandon their own beliefs, preferably immediately, and embrace those of Europe. . . . A failure to do so provoked impatience, contempt, and even murderous rage."[12] That culture expected also that the wilderness in which those strangers lived could be made to submit to civilizing; its failure to do so provoked similar responses.

Such was the start, as dreams devolved into clashes, of the New World tragedy of difference. The essence of that difference was mutual resistance. The vast land, from islands to mainland, physically resisted subjugation by the Spaniards; its Natives resisted both physically and culturally, their conversion to the European worldview never immediate and often impossible. European resistance to New World wilderness also was physical and cultural but in the latter aspect pointedly spiritual. When the young Cortés in 1504, before he assailed Mexico and the Aztecs, glimpsed (as Turner reasonably fancies him doing) "the Admiral himself as he passed through the port [of Santo Domingo] on his last return, maddened, mocked," the conqueror-to-be must have intuited that, "whatever else this New World might be, it was a place of death and terror where Christians might be swallowed into the maw of the wilderness."[13] He must have sensed that it was a place whose wildness he should resist with his very marrow as well as a place that would, to borrow a phrase Stephen Tatum uses in discussing the Sahara Desert as metaphorized in Michael Ondaatje's novel The English Patient, "resist territorialization."[14]

Greed, wonder, weaponry, righteousness, resistance—a combustible coalition in a story of disillusionment Turner finds retold again and again in the Americas, in texts that range from William Bradford's Of Plymouth Plantation to F. Scott

Fitzgerald's *The Great Gatsby* to Carlos Fuentes's *Terra Nostra*. "There is," he says, "something brooding, somber here: the memory of bright hopes dashed by first encounters with magnificent lands and seascapes, of a paradise poisoned by dreams saved from a fantastic pettiness only by their size and tragic consequences."[15] The tragedy occurred—and recurred in literature as well as in fact—because of its heroes' hamartia, their lack of the personal resources to perceive, conceive, and inhabit the New World other than as they did. The Spanish who first entered it never were really *there*: they were in their own nowhereland, America as later spun by the language of Montaigne's essay "Of Cannibals" and Shakespeare's romance *The Tempest*, what Zeese Papanikolas characterizes as America in "its true location, which is the geography of the European mind."[16]

Be that as it may, the Spanish after Columbus advanced south, west, and north beyond their Caribbean staging area. Juan Ponce de León stepped onto a beach in present-day Florida in 1513 and inaugurated an expanding tenure of the Spanish empire in North America that would come to take in around half of the continental United States and would endure until Mexico won its independence from Spain in 1821. As their exploration and colonization spread during the sixteenth century, the Spanish created a New World heritage not just of European culture but also of life-forms they introduced (horses, cattle, sheep, and their forage grasses), diseases (transmitted efficiently by trade routes) that destroyed whole tribes of Indians, overt violence against people and places. Their presence at that time and subsequently "changed the natural world beyond recognition," according to David J. Weber, with the result that "all across the continent, tall native grasses and climax forests have vanished, swiftly flowing streams have slowed, and flora and fauna alien to precolumbian America have established themselves."[17]

Several of Weber's comments suggest the degree of the Spaniards' inability to engage the New World in non-European terms and how that inability contributed to such devastation. Those who occupied their empire's blurred frontier in North America may have "sought to include Natives" in their society, but irreconcilable cultural differences between themselves and Natives in need of Christianizing led to no shortage of bloody contentions. Moreover, to the sensibilities of the Spanish, "unbridled wilderness held little aesthetic appeal." Thus, when, in 1540, one of Francisco Vásquez de Coronado's scouting parties, led by García López de Cárdenas, was taken by Hopi guides to the edge of the Grand Canyon near what is known today as Moran Point and had no way of crossing, the Spaniards, "impressed by the immensity of the canyon, . . . saw it as a formidable obstacle, but they appear not to have regarded it as a place of beauty"—nor would members of later Spanish expeditions who witnessed (or avoided) that gorge. Finally, the Spaniards who were proudly attempting to tame North America by genocide, the thinning of forests, and the like "regarded the natural world as existing largely to serve them."[18]

And yet the implications of Weber's observations are qualified by what we know of the first Spaniard to enter the American West, Álvar Núñez Cabeza de Vaca. Noting that Cabeza de Vaca and his three companions were not so much discoverers as men who "were merely lost," Richard White summarizes the bare facts of their adventure as follows:

> These men had left Cuba [in 1528] as part of the disastrous Florida expedition of Pánfilo de Narváez in the hopes of pillaging and enslaving the Indians of the Gulf Coast. Instead they were shipwrecked and themselves temporarily enslaved on the Texas coast. [In 1534] . . . they began a journey back to Mexico that took them across Texas . . . and into southern New Mexico. From there they crossed into Arizona and traveled south to the Spanish outpost of Culiacán. Their journey wasn't simply geographical, though, for the Indians they met in villages en route believed them to be—and convinced the Spaniards themselves that they had become—supernatural agents with the power to heal.

White acknowledges that the men's experiences changed them to the extent that they were, "at least for the duration of the journey, no longer typical sixteenth-century Spaniards," but he doesn't delve into the details of their metamorphosis.[19] Those details aren't central for him; they are for me, however.

While it's true, as many historians have remarked, that Cabeza de Vaca and his companions deceived the Indians, unintentionally, as to how most village-razing and enslaving Spaniards would treat them and later misled Spanish officials, more questionably, in telling second-hand stories of golden cities to the north, the lost adventurers were indeed genuinely changed as they wandered through unmapped land where, as Patricia Nelson Limerick stresses, "the advantages of 'civilization' . . . counted for nothing."[20] While one may argue, as John Murray does, that in many of its passages Cabeza de Vaca's narrative of his experiences (La Relación, published in 1542) "destroys the myth that Rousseau and others would later try to perpetrate on Western civilization—that somehow the natural life was superior to the civilized life"[21]—it also stands, in other passages, as a record of the value of an attitude toward wilderness that was thoroughly uncharacteristic of typical sixteenth-century Spaniards. It speaks of cruelties among the Indians, but it also conveys a vision, momentary in centuries of mostly violent conquest, of rapprochement between two worlds.

Several discussions of Cabeza de Vaca bolster my interpretation of that vision.

Papanikolas reads Cabeza de Vaca as a man who survived as a healer—and bartering merchant—among the Indians "by trading on his Otherness." Distant from European history and his God, he went naked, turned mystical, and created for himself an identity uniting "the shaman of the Indian" and "the picaro of Spain," a figure who could mediate "between reality and utopia's fatally flawed schemes of hope."[22]

For Turner, La Relación is not just the first work of Western literature: it's also the first North American captivity narrative. Though such, it doesn't simply invoke God to retrieve the captives from the savages; instead it provides an alternative rescue, a "true initiation" into a sort of nativist imitatio Christi, for Cabeza de Vaca and his companions: "From bringers of death, . . . they had become enhancers of life. Forced to participate in the native beliefs, they had discovered the vast, untapped spiritual reservoir the New World had always constituted. And discovering this, what had been a fatal, sealed wilderness to them magically opened."[23]

Richard Slotkin considers Cabeza de Vaca an exemplar of what happened to a number of subsequent would-be conquerors, Spanish and otherwise, when they ran up against a wilderness that "could isolate them from their civilization, captivate and imprison them, and compel them to learn and live by its laws." Thus, like Papanikolas, he portrays Cabeza de Vaca as a cultural mestizo, but he casts his division in terms of loyalty to Spain and its church, on the one hand, and adherence to a lifeway he learned from the Indians, on the other. The process of his learning is reflected in a change Slotkin detects in his descriptions of wilderness in La Relación: "Land that he found barren and waste when he was with the blind and blundering Spaniards now appears to flower and be abundantly fruitful for the Indians, who know how to see and how to use it." Upon returning to civilization, men such as Cabeza de Vaca, who refused to accompany Coronado in his search for Eldorado, remained unable to accept wholeheartedly the romantic myths that had once charmed them—while their more orthodox cohorts continued obliviously and callously "concentrating on the idea of America."[24]

Implicit in these discussions are the basic elements of Cabeza de Vaca's vision: peaceful coexistence with the Indians, their conversion to Christianity by gentle means, the New World as a practicable paradise to be experienced harmoniously rather than plundered, and a more acceptive and less imperially abstract perception of the West as a place. Each of these elements is predicated on the possibility of a negotiated reciprocality between European civilization and American wilderness. It was a possibility seldom realized in the centuries ahead, and Cabeza de Vaca was deluded if he believed the contrary would be the case. That possibility haunts many still, but Coronado and his kind easily brushed it aside—or never thought of it.

With Coronado the entradas commenced in earnest. For three years he mulled Cabeza de Vaca's tales of the gold-laden Seven Cities of Cíbola to the north of Mexico, weaving fantasies of himself as suzerain of a domain of assets comparable to the ones Cortés had seized from the Aztecs and Pizarro from the Incas. When the northern reconnoitering of Fray Marcos de Niza in 1539 yielded rosy reports of Cíbola's existence, Coronado was ready to act. In Mexico City he organized a party in excess of a thousand young Spanish adventurers, padres, and Indian retainers and, cannons in tow, traveled horseback for six months through fifteen hundred miles of harsh country into what's now New Mexico. At last he arrived at something much less than what he'd anticipated: a mud-brick pueblo. Cíbola had been a mirage. On the sun-fired ground Zuñi warriors drew lines with sacred cornmeal, which they warned the Spaniards not to cross.

But cross the disillusioned Spaniards with their crosses did. Combat ensued. Then passed an uneasy aftermath, during which the outnumbered but victorious Spaniards demanded no end of food and other supplies as well as submission to Spanish king and Christian God. Tiring of such oppression, the Indians rebelled, with months of skirmishes as the sequel.

In early 1541 Coronado attacked and burned the pueblo, burned also the warriors who had survived the assault, and soon herded his band north and east in pursuit of Quivira, another golden kingdom, this one located, according to a Plains Indian called the Turk, in the buffalo-blanketed interior of Spain's new continent-for-the-taking. Quivira turned out to be no more than Wichita villages of grass-covered lodges in the middle of present-day Kansas. Coronado's gold turned out to be straw. The Turk, forthwith garroted, turned out to be as full of nonsense as Fray Marcos, who had long since made a hasty departure back to Mexico City. Coronado reluctantly returned to that same city in 1542, his conquering-hero rainbows in ruins.

From its oneiric outset, Coronado's expedition was a disastrous disappointment waiting to happen. The seductive song of Cíbola that Cabeza de Vaca had crooned to him was an old-hat yarn by the sixteenth century, a canard about seven nebulously illocal cities whose glories had been magnified by generations of hardworking Iberian imaginations. But when the Spanish pushed north, ever enlarging their empire's borderlands, they had to believe there would be something to be gained in the wasteland that stretched before them, something that made it more than mere uncultivated immensity. Thus they weren't prepared to comprehend the cosmos of the Zuñis—nor, as Weber observes, were the Zuñis prepared to comprehend theirs. Like most Indians, the Zuñis, "in contrast to Spaniards, . . . interacted more intimately with the natural world . . . and tended to regard the users of land as possessing greater rights than the nominal owners of land," owners whose God was outside nature and who believed they had a "divinely inspired message to subdue the earth."[25]

As the imagery of Cíbola and Quivira, hallucinatory cities auric in architecture and accoutrements, indicates, the Spaniards, as Weber synopsizes it, "had material as well as spiritual motives" for their subduing. Central to their conflict with the Indians and to their alienation from nonhuman nature was their extraordinary craving for gold (and all the other treasurable metals and minerals—silver, emeralds, and the like—that it, by metonymy, summoned to mind). They were going through what was to them hell in an attempt to get more of a metal the Indians knew about but little valued—at least until they figured out how precious it was to the Spaniards. "Cortés exaggerated only slightly," Weber notes, "when he sent a message to Montezuma saying that the Spaniards had a disease of the heart that only gold could cure."[26] Since they wore alchemical spectacles, the wild of the West held either gold or little but grief.

There's no surprise, then, in the Spaniards' not really seeing the Grand Canyon and the leagues-long herds of bison on the plains they marched across. Coronado and his retinue roamed, as Papanikolas argues, a place so different from Spain with its waning chivalry that it was almost an ideal blank to receive the impress of fantasies shaped by "an overwhelming nostalgia for a mythic past." What he says of Cortés applies to Coronado and other Spaniards as well: he was "a wide-awake man walking in a dream." The Spaniards perceived the American wilderness as an absence always soon to reveal a miraculous presence, a measureless *infierno* that somewhere concealed a specific and material *paraíso*: "Because the Spaniards desired them . . . Seven Golden Cities were there. And the name Cíbola . . . would become a kind of ghostly Signifier floating before the Spaniards from one huddled Indian village to the next like a flag," with each successive disillusionment paradoxically stirring renewed determination.[27] Undaunted by their failure to find Cíbola, they set out for Quivira—and hardships on the featureless Llano Estacado that drove many of that visionary company into hysteria and rage.

The word *visionary* is pivotal here, for it connotes exactly the kind of projection through which the Spanish imaginatively transmogrified an alien wilderness into a familiar figment. Thereby they were seeking in the West of the New World not something new but something old, and that transmogrification demanded not only that the land speak a cultural language known to them but also that it metaphorically carry a promise of great wealth, an expectation, in Richard C. Poulsen's words, "it continued to provide, sucking Spaniards further and further into the wastes of the interior"—until, as later tales of lost Spanish mines persist in teaching us, "the open secrets of the desert became hidden secrets of gold."[28] Since the gold stayed hidden for those first trove hunters, the desert became a place of disappointment. The great piñata of the West was yet to be broken.

"Lies. Lies, all of it," concludes Papanikolas on behalf of Coronado depressed by loss, but his dream didn't end with his failure, maybe hasn't yet. What got missed in his quest, the deepest loss, however, was at least one open secret of the desert: the lifeway of Indians who lived attuned to it. Indeed, Papanikolas laments, "at Zuni the Spaniards might have . . . found a version of Utopia, had they only been able to see it." Pedro de Castañeda, chronicler of the expedition, glimpses that version, but "the door Castañeda has opened to the Indian world shuts and is never opened again."[29] Still, a sense of the lost opportunity the wilderness held haunted him, as it haunted Cabeza de Vaca, as it would haunt others in the future.

What is opened—and never closed again—is the West as land to be further claimed, explored, mapped, colonized, politically cut up, crisscrossed by competing cultures. With that opening, the Spanish dream of conquest continued to anticipate, in Tatum's words, "that country hovering over there just beyond the visible distance, . . . that country where, as the Ry Cooder song 'Across the Borderline' would have it, there are streets paved in gold, beckoning endlessly."[30] But that dream came to be immingled with and gradually succeeded by projects of a more practical and even pedestrian order: conquering and (after the Pueblo Revolt) reconquering New Mexico, controlling and incorporating the Indians, caring for livestock, irrigating and farming arable land, settling California, holding together an unsteady economy with governance overstretched in territory that by the middle of the eighteenth century was of more than passing interest to other Europeans.

Those other Europeans would carry on the multiplication, beyond Etulain's earlier list, of largely preconceived, imported images of the West the Spanish had begun. In Ray Allen Billington's summarization, "a kaleidoscopic succession of images shaped Europe's attitude toward the New World during the ages of discovery and colonization," images that by the late eighteenth century had run from the Eden of Renaissance dreamers to the satanic forests of Puritan colonists to the wonderland of Noble Savages cooked up by Romantics—all, depending on the time and the transmitter, variously colored or intermixed.[31] But the images, likewise colored or intermixed, that shaped the European, increasingly Anglo-American, attitude toward the West would constitute an even more kaleidoscopic succession. Many of them are included in William H. Goetzmann's chronological inventory of the West as everything from "the great empty continent" to "a barren waste of heathen savages and Spaniards" to "a beaver kingdom" to "a land of flocks and herds" to "an agricultural Arcadia, a military and administrative problem, a bonanza of gold and silver, a safety valve, a haven for saints, a refuge for bad men, and ultimately, toward the end of the nineteenth century, an enormous laboratory."[32]

Motley enough, and yet, as Anglos impinged upon, seized, and settled Hispanic (Spanish and then Mexican) territory, probably the most significant relative changes in attitude toward the land were three: from community-oriented to individualistic, from reverential to disruptive, and from complexity-tolerant to simplifying. Though, as White notes, "the Hispanic peoples of the West tended, like Anglo Americans, to see nature as a set of commodities and resources," they differed from their successors in regarding them, by a less prodigal ethos, as communal as well as individual possessions. Furthermore, though those peoples worked the land hard, they did evolve "a deep reverence" for it; the Anglos, more agriculturally zealous than either the Spanish or the fur-trading French, would be harder on it and less reverent not only as they intentionally interfered with natural systems by deciding which resident species of plants and animals should thrive and by introducing new ones but also as they accelerated the effects of such decisions. While the Hispanic peoples perceived and coped with their *frontera* as a zone of intricate biodiversity, most Anglo immigrants wanted something tidier and more economically productive; thus, "when [Anglo] farmers viewed a native prairie in bloom or saw deer, elk, or buffalo grazing in the distance, they were likely to look through the scene before them and see beyond it a future landscape of corn fields, wheat fields, or cattle. . . . What a farmer meant by 'improved land' was simplified land."[33]

In many ways Anglo-Americans wanted a massive simplification of the West, a purging, by agricultural and then industrial means, of the piebald wild that contained Hispanics as well as Indians, unprofitable plants, dangerous animals, landforms that hampered movement, aridity, rock between greed and gold, anything between the ego and its surfeit—or maybe just anything between more and more families and their necessities. But they didn't want that piebald wild made wholly homogeneous, either. The story of simplification would turn out to be far from simple.

The Antipode of Paradise: William Bradford and the Hatred of Wilderness

Not only did this powerful experience of trying to live amid nature in the raw . . . engender dark feelings of fear and hatred, . . . but it also produced bewilderment, dislocation, disorientation, a sense of being out of place.
    Kirkpatrick Sale, *The Conquest of Paradise: Christopher Columbus and the Columbian Legacy*

If, as Roderick Nash proposes, one may conceive "of a spectrum of conditions or environments ranging from the purely wild on the one end to the purely civilized on the other—from the primeval to the paved"[1]—then what the Pilgrims encountered in 1620 upon arriving at Cape Harbor (now the harbor at Provincetown, Massachusetts) surely seemed to them near the primeval pole. William Bradford, soon to be elected theocratic governor of Plymouth Colony, on the other side of what's now Cape Cod Bay, recalled, years later, that the late-autumn prospect was bleak indeed for his fellow immigrants, half of whom would die within a few months:

> what could they see but a hideous and desolate wilderness, full of wild beasts and wild men—and what multitudes there might be of them they knew not. Neither could they, as it were, go up to the top of Pisgah to view from this wilderness a more goodly country to feed their hopes; for which way soever they turned their eyes (save upward to the heavens) they could have little solace or content in respect of any outward objects. . . . If they looked behind them, there was the mighty ocean which they had passed and was now as a main bar and gulf to separate them from all the civil parts of the world.[2]

In this locus classicus reside many of the leitmotifs that will, with variations, thematize Anglo-American experiences of Eastern settlement and westward movement to come: terrible, encircling, and indeterminate wildness; absence of any viewpoint from which to see a promised land beyond; turning upward, not toward the surrounding environment, for consolation; and demoralizing divorce from civilization. "Soon after he arrived," as Nash puts it, "the seventeenth-century frontiersman realized that the New World was the antipode of paradise."[3]

This wasn't the first English entanglement with that antipode. An ill-fated settlement, the second phase of which became the "lost colony," had been established on Roanoke Island, off North Carolina, in the mid-1580s, and Jamestown had been established in 1607, its population doomed to decline over the next two decades much faster than it grew—from starvation, disease, Indian attacks. The New World was tough on its coastal conquerors; those who managed to hang on were much indebted to the "wild men" who taught them the skills necessary to benefit from the wilderness. Nonetheless, opposition to and warfare with Indians would increase as English settlements grew in size and dispersed into the continent. The most successful of the early settlements, Bradford's at Plymouth, was unified largely by the common purpose of building what John Winthrop, governor of the Massachusetts Bay Colony, would later call, in his famous biblical borrowing, "a Citty upon a Hill."[4] That project of bringing God's light into the darkness of North America required subduing the wilderness and its denizens, redeeming it, exploiting it. The wilderness may have been the Puritans' salvation from the corrupt civilization of the Old World, but it would have to yield to their vision of a better civilization for the New World. "Paradoxically," Nash observes, "their sanctuary and their enemy were one and the same."[5] They were carrying forward what Yi-Fu Tuan, in his study of "topophilia," the affective bonding between people and place, describes as "the ascetic tradition in Christianity [that] maintained the dual and opposed meaning of wilderness" as "at once the haunt of demons and the realm of bliss."[6] Their descendants would keep up that tradition as they made their way westward.

But in the early seventeenth century the preponderant attitude toward that sanctuary/enemy was one of hatred driven by fear. The fear arose partly from awareness of the physical threat posed by wilderness. The first pioneers, like their westward-advancing successors, faced something indomitable, and yet their survival depended on somehow controlling an environment whose darkness, as Nash puts it, "hid savage men, wild beasts, and still stranger creatures of the imagination." The fear arose also—and ultimately, I'd argue, in greater part—from the same faculty that manufactured those stranger creatures. For the Pilgrims and their historical progeny, its typological productions were imbued with Calvinist (or at least Protestant) tints, but a deeper phantasm-molding force, one they shared with the Catholic Spaniards, underlay such tints: "the long Western tradition of imagining wild country as a moral vacuum, a cursed and chaotic wasteland." For them, in the erection of a city upon a hill or "in the morality play of westward expansion, wilderness was the villain, and the pioneer, as hero, relished its destruction" and rejoiced in transforming what he feared into utilitarian artifice. Nash credits Bradford with being the initiator of the Anglo-American translation of this "tradition of repugnance."[7]

While in the West that repugnance would be agoraphobic, in the East, where wilderness was more forested, it was claustrophobic. The land of the Pilgrims' pride was benighted and bedeviled, physically and spiritually sequestering. It was the milieu with which Adam and Eve had to struggle after their ejection from Eden, the abode not of God but of Pan, the pagan deification of Satan. Its rawness could be redeemed only by labor, suffering, and constant self-vigilance. That vigilance was prompted by a very specific fear that, according to Catherine L. Albanese, accounts for the Puritans' generally interpreting the "spiritual force" of the forest, however ambiguous, in a negative way: "the fear was that, in the primitive forests with the beasts, one would become confused, *bewildered*, losing a sense of self and society that was essential to civilized life and to salvation thereafter."[8]

That fear has roots in the mainstream Christianity that attempted to resolve its early heterogeneity of attitude toward nature when, according to Paul Shepard, it "took a critical turn away from the natural world in the fifth century by separating the divine from the physical in Jesus and, by implication, in all 'incarnation.'" As a result, in Western Christendom animals became mostly "either demons to be trampled or adoring faces in the manger scene." Such a stance wasn't without its ambivalences or contradictions, of course (for example, Gothic cathedrals are architecturally aswarm with animal monstrosities whose meanings remain muddy), but that turn helped rationalize the Christian domination of nature. Though there were traditions of nature love in Europe, as we've seen, for the most part animals with any trace of wildness were regarded "as envoys of the dark side of a dualistic world."[9]

Hence the Puritans' fear of natives who lived like beasts and their hatred of the beasts within themselves (for which wilderness was a metaphor). Hence Bradford's alarm at Thomas Morton, an English lawyer who sailed to Massachusetts in 1622 and in 1626 set up a trading post at Passonagessit, which he renamed Ma-re Mount (Mare Mount, or Marry Mount, Mary Mount—the sexual undertones not lost on Bradford, who preferred to call the place Merry-mount). There Morton, a religious amphibian with one foot in Christian ideology and the other in a Greco-Roman-Native medley of myths, soon presided over revels involving Indians and whites costumed as beasts and in the spring of 1627 put up a phallic maypole on which to center their cavorting. From then until his death, probably in 1647, he was twice banished back to England or otherwise punished by the Puritan authorities not only for his licentious practices but also for his impious praise of the virtues of Indians and his satirical attitude toward his Pilgrim peers, all of which he amply evidences in his heavily fictionalized 1637 book *New English Canaan*.

Morton, as his book makes clear, was the antitype of Bradford. He was a man who symbolized to the Plymouth Separatists, in Richard Slotkin's words, "everything evil and threatening in both the New World and their own culture." The contrasts between Morton and the Puritans, even those not as strict as the Separatists, are illuminating. They traded with the Indians; he too did that (and he may have illegally sold them rum and arms), but he also fornicated with them. To the Puritans the Indians were wild people; to Morton they were innocent primitives. What the Puritans saw as wilderness he saw, in Slotkin's codification, "as a new Arcadia, a land rich in the promise of spiritual and erotic fulfillment and renewal." The Puritans withheld themselves from wildness; he merged with it. The Puritans wanted "divine law and order in the wilderness."[10] Morton wanted pagan orgy there.

The sweet fancy of this Anglo Cabeza de Vaca was Bradford's horror movie. As Ma-re Mount's "Master of the Revells," Morton was dredging the unconscious and dragging up unspeakable shapes and, in Slotkin's phrase, "going native with a vengeance." In their original ambitions, Bradford's Pilgrims differed from the Spanish in that they weren't out to take over any Indian empire or recover some immemorial Golden Age; rather, they sought "a tabula rasa on which they could inscribe their dream: the outline of an idealized Puritan England, a Bible commonwealth."[11] The wilderness was to be that tabula rasa. Their dream was precisely what Morton, in inscribing on that wilderness a roisterous Canaan instead of an orderly Israel, scorned.

Still, the Puritans would have to displace the Indians, and they were interested in a recovery—though not the sort that Morton undertook. If, as Frederick Turner maintains, "with the establishment of the whites in North America the captivity narrative became the first form of popular literature, changing its emphasis as the settlers' needs changed, yet retaining always a certain recognizable core that could evoke powerful responses,"[12] then likewise the recovery narrative, the story of the *reinvention* of the Garden of Eden, became North America's first popular myth, one that both comprises and extends beyond the dream of a city upon a hill. From the Puritan viewpoint, Morton's *New English Canaan* contains rudiments of the Anglo-American captivity narrative, though it fails to end properly—since there's no salvational rescue from the wilderness. From the same viewpoint, Bradford's *Of Plymouth Plantation* contains the ur-text of the Anglo-American recovery narrative. In several respects those two narratives tell the same tale, particularly in that both conclude with victories over wilderness. Indeed, the Anglo-American recovery narrative in its general pattern is itself a sort of tabula rasa on which have been inscribed, with changing details, all manner of Anglo-American wilderness-subduing ventures, from the earliest acts of Indian genocide in the East to the most recent attempts by the federal Bureau of Reclamation to supervise nature in the West.

Let me consider those two fundamental narratives in their most typical forms in order to show how they dovetail thematically and logically in their treatment of wilderness.

As Turner indicates, the "interior" of the increasingly fictionalized captivity narrative persisted as the advancing frontier translated it westward. By the time it reached the Northwest, it had "gradually succeeded scripture as the means of understanding why things had developed here as they had." Indeed, its staple story hints strongly the ageless myth of the heroic quest with its cycle of separation, initiation, and return. Here, to follow Turner's condensation, is that story: it opens with a scene of innocent, tranquil domesticity, a frontier family about its daily routines (the father plowing or planting in the field, the mother at her spindle with a baby in one arm, the older children playing or doing chores); suddenly fiendish Indians erupt from the surrounding woods, slaughter the father, bash out the baby's brains, ransack and burn the cabin, and take the mother and children away on a long flight through brambly, dark wilderness; the group arrives at a clearing and enters the hellish hive where the Indians live; the captives are tortured, maybe adopted into the tribe, the mother or a daughter forced to marry a swarthy warrior; and then at last—by escape, ransom, or prisoner exchange—comes a redemption, the captives' joining civilization once again. Such a happy-ending narrative, repeated interminably (in American literature from the seventeenth century on, later in other media as well), was itself, Turner says, "the perfect scripture . . ., for in the redemption that rounded it out there was victory." That victory brought assurance that, despite setbacks, civilizing would go on, leading to "mastering . . . the wilderness."[13]

Notice, however, as Turner remarks, that the narrative significantly alters the mythic pattern it has adapted, a pattern more fully realized in the story of Cabeza de Vaca, in two ways: "there is only resistance" rather than true initiation at its center, and "nothing new is brought back out of that fearsome other world"—except more determination to subdue and transform it. In this tradition of the captivity narrative, the triumph at the end is preceded not by the acceptance of some opportunity for a life-change but by the rejection of it because of "fear of becoming *possessed*, possessed by the wild peoples, yes, but also, more profoundly, by the wilderness and its spirits." The fear was of becoming possessed by the wilderness while trying, through "a rigidly maintained spiritual distance," to possess it—thus of becoming a renegade lost in it forever.[14] The fear was of what happened to Morton, to Mary Jemison (a Pennsylvanian captured by the Shawnees and French in 1755 who, after being sold to the Senecas, spent the rest of her long life with them by choice), to any of the many other men and women over the centuries who went native, turned into Calibans.[15]

The fact that such apostasies occurred confirms that the attraction of the opportunity resisted in the story was real enough. Though the captivity narrative became a "gothic cliché," as David Mogen labels it, the genre, beginning with the Puritans, clearly discloses the powerful mingling of "apprehension and aspiration which have defined the characteristic tone of frontier mythology ever since." Though

American romantics might later feel otherwise, the Puritans certainly feared being changed by the wilderness they wished to change; but their fear was indeed an
alloyed thing. From its earliest examples, most notably Mary Rowlandson's 1682
narrative *The Soveraignty and Goodness of God, Together with the Faithfulness of His Promises
Displayed: Being a Narrative of the Captivity and Restauration of Mrs. Mary Rowlandson*, the
genre not only dramatizes the seductiveness of what might transform the victim
but also tends to betray, whether or not by conscious design, ambivalence toward
the prospect of that transformation. Thus Rowlandson's chronicle of her struggle
to survive the ordeal subsequent to her capture in 1676 tells of an encounter with
Indians that is permeated by an ambiguous "tone of shocked wonder" that, along
with a tone of sorrow, is "inseparable from . . . receptivity to the terrible beauty of
the other world impinging on comfortable complacency."[16] For Rowlandson, as
for other victims of Indian captivity, real or fictional, and for all the Puritans and
the future generations of their cultural legatees, that bittersweet potentiality of the
wilderness would never be completely submerged by any complacency, comfortable or not.

Carolyn Merchant elucidates the structure and meaning of the American recovery
narrative by a comparison of two origin stories, one from the Penobscots and one
from the Bible. The first concerns a beautiful maiden who gives up her life in order
to transform the natural world from a desert into a garden. The second concerns a
woman, Eve, whose actions bring about the fall from a happy paradise by way of a
plot whose movement is "from garden to desert." But—and here's the crux—"historical events reversed the plots of the European and the Indian origin stories. The
Indians' comic happy ending changed to a story of decline and conquest, while
Euramericans were largely successful in creating a New World garden." The story
of that success since the seventeenth century thus can be understood as "a grand
narrative of fall and recovery" whose plot is the process of restoring Eden, the goal
of which is to make a garden of all the earth—with the help of the principle of
Christian redemption, modern science and technology, and the ideology of capitalism, the last having as its own origin story "a movement from desert back to
garden through the transformation of undeveloped nature into a state of civility
and order."[17]

By the terms of that transformation and its reversal of the lapsarian plot, "Adam
becomes the inventor of the tools and technologies that will restore the garden,"
Merchant argues, and "Eve becomes the nature that must be tamed into submission." Through this logic, Adam appears as the redeemer of the fallen land and "the
image of God as patriarch, law, and rule, the model for the kingdom and state."[18]
In other words, someone like Bradford.

Bradford therefore may be conceptualized as the archetypal hero of the narrative that urged the European settlement and "improvement" of America. Applying Vladimir Propp's schema of the basic heroic myth to *Of Plymouth Plantation*,

Merchant explicates how Bradford performed that role in leading settlers as they began their conversion of hideous desolation into cultivated land. Here, in an abbreviation of her analysis, are the six phases of the story in which he stars: (1) the land lacks its hero and is vacant, the cornfields of diseased Indians left fallow; (2) the hero is transferred from the Old England of the Antichrist to the New Canaan of New England; (3) the hero is tested through his battle with the villain, Satan as he exists in the wilderness; (4) by God's intervention the hero gains a helper (the Indian Squanto) who shows the Pilgrims how to plant corn and the like; (5) the hero is victorious, and crops are harvested, cabins and stockades built; (6) the Pilgrims, reborn after surviving their first year, "celebrate their triumph over wilderness . . . through the miracle of the re-created garden."[19] And so the recovery narrative, like the captivity narrative, stories an encounter with wilderness, a resistive religious struggle with it, a redemptive triumph over it, and a restorative establishment of civilized order that promises to continue and enlarge.

Henceforth the two parallel narratives, variously revised, would spur the civilizing of the Atlantic coast, in the northern reaches of which Thomas Cole in the early nineteenth century would produce paintings that depict both the progress of recovery, whose desecration of the wild he deplored, and the perils of not staying the race. But Bradford's heirs, heading west, would stay the race, though the complications implicit in their narratives of wilderness hatred would rattle along behind them, as vexing as tin cans tied to a cat's tail, all the way to the Pacific.

Understanding those complications requires some clarifications regarding the Puritan attitude toward wilderness. First of all, the wilderness really wasn't just a symbolic domain of darkness for the Puritans, for it did present them with discouraging practical difficulties, from awful winters to soil that had to be made tillable by clearing forest to inhabitants who bucked displacement—difficulties as real to the colonists as they were to the Indians, who didn't always enjoy pleasant dealings with either New England weather or neighboring tribes in competition for food-gathering territory. Nonetheless, it's also true that the Puritans as a rule interpreted the wilderness and indexed their relationship to it with a binary severity alien to the Native world. As Richard C. Poulsen stresses, their notions of profane and sacred were configured by "decisive linearity: opposites of black and white." The Puritan divines kept their congregations apprised of the nuances of such linearity, but there was no doubt, officially, that, as captivity narratives admonished, *good* was living by "the Puritan way and worldview" and *bad* was Indians metaphorized "as snakes, wolves, yellow jackets, and other creatures of the wilderness reigned over by Satan."[20] The dogma inherent in that split provided a rationale, by the logic of the recovery narrative, for construing the land as depravedly feminine (bad) and in need of masculine mastering (good).[21]

Also, the land and peoples the Puritans encountered in America represented a profound challenge to them in good measure because, as Turner asks us to remember, they were immigrants with psychic roots in an Elizabethan culture that valued order and was "obsessed by the fear of chaos." One of that culture's principal images of chaos, inherited through European folk tradition, was that of the Wild Man. This shaggy, priapic creature was supposedly much given to raiding villages and abducting white maidens for unspeakable purposes, and the tradition therefore mandated "the hunting down and conquest of the Wild Man [read, in the present context, Indian] by the forces of civilization." He, like wild animals in general, was aligned with the Devil in his combat with God and God's orderly universe and had to be domesticated or destroyed. Moreover, the Wild Man's threat was doubly potent since he was both in the wilderness without and "within the jungle of the single body."[22] He was the Mr. Hyde (or Mr. Morton) hiding in even the most civilized person, ever ready to render him or her a savage bereft of Heaven.

Given such a mind-set, it's no surprise that the Puritans and their firsthand offspring could not, as Turner puts it, "seek God in nature." No surprise that, after decades of the self-repressing war against wilderness, demonism would reappear in Salem. And no surprise that in time progress would press the "malign spirits . . . westward into the sinking sun, with the skulking tribes themselves."[23]

To ferret out the complications that freighted this superficially uniform mind-set, you have to get behind the cliché of uniformity. Lawrence Buell proves helpful in doing that. He notes that, although for early settlers in New England "old world frames of reference became defenses against the heart of darkness," not all the Pilgrims saw their world as Bradford recalled it. Buell reminds us, as Leo Marx has shown, that "the equation of new world with nature . . . could yield antithetical schemas: arcadian utopia or dystopian desert." While it's easy enough to associate the stereotypes of the latter schema with New England Puritans and those of the former with Virginia planters, Buell argues that such dichotomies shortchange reality. Citing evidence that questions or qualifies them and even suggests that the Puritans' deeply negative view of wilderness arose only after they had been hard tried by frontier life, he concludes that "both arcadian and dystopian imagery might best be reckoned a stockpile of prefabricated imagery subject to development, deformation, and commingling according to need."[24] Complications indeed.

The cogency of Buell's argument is striking once you think about the complications it asks you to expose. The examples of Morton, Anne Hutchinson, Roger Williams, and others suffice to demonstrate a diversity in early New Englanders' beliefs about the wilderness, God's presence in the world, and Indians—and in efforts to correct the distortions of dystopian thinking. In fact, at some point you have to admit, with Slotkin, that the Puritans were responsible for mythologically developing and articulating several viewpoints with respect to the wilderness. He inventories them, along with the names of persons who instanced them in their writings, as follows: "the outward-looking, wilderness-loving viewpoint of [John] Underhill and [Benjamin] Church; Mrs. Rowlandson's combination of Calvinist sensibility and frontier realism; and the superheated vision of those like the Mathers, who saw the wilderness as a nightmarish dream-kingdom."[25]

These viewpoints would move westward with the moving frontier and be expressed, according to Slotkin, in four mythological structures, "each of which is a variation on the great central myth of migration into a new world and a new life." Of those four—conversion, sacred marriage, exorcism, and regeneration through violence—the last three, since the first involves only the soul's salvation by direct interaction with God, are the most relevant in revealing the conflicts in the multifaceted Puritan attitude toward wilderness. In the second, the protagonist "is united with a female who is both the embodiment of the god-spirit immanent in nature and the 'other half' of his own individual nature (anima)." In the third, the entities thought to compose the anima "are treated as if they were representations of the id, being sought out and recognized only that they might be repressed or destroyed." In the fourth, "the anima-id paradox is embodied (not resolved) in an intimate conflict between male avatars of wilderness and civilization for possession of the white female captive—a figure who embodies the Christian moral and social law that the [mythic] hunter both defends and tries to avoid and who therefore, like the Indian opponent, is at once the hero's anima and his soul's most feared enemy."[26]

Slotkin concedes that these structures don't receive equal treatment in the Puritans' writings, but he rightly insists that all of them arose from the confrontation between Puritanism and a wilderness both threatening and promising and that they and the mental states that generated them "continued to conflict and evolve" through the next century and the founding of a new nation.[27] And, as he well knows, they continued in their conflicted evolution long past that time and continue still. They turn up as subtexts in a plethora of perplexed ambivalences—in relations between self and other, male and female, destruction and preservation, and other oppositions, always hatred and love—that pertain to wilderness.

Those ambivalences pervaded Puritan reactions to the New England wild. Look at a few examples. Though many Puritans considered Indians assistants of Satan, some entertained the possibility that they were descendants of the ten lost tribes of Israel and therefore not outside Christian history. Some Indians were "good" and others "bad." The wilderness was Satan's domain, but it was also, as Albanese tells us, "the backdrop for a spiritual purification in which the corruption of old England might be permanently purged." Less biblically rigorous Puritans were awed by the vastitude around them. Whether fearful of or awed by wilderness, the Puritans "understood that the best wild country was subdued wild country."[28] For them the wilderness had no value in itself but was to be exploited—forests turned into lumber, prairies plowed, and so on—yet such "war against wildness," as Nash calls it, was indeed against their own sanctuary.[29] That made for a situation guaranteed to blossom with ironies, not the least of which inheres in how, in Richard Rodriguez's capsuling, God had given those early settlers an exhilarating and terrifying Eden in which they "dammed the waters, leveled mountains, broke their backs to build our regret."[30]

When Anglo-Americans pushed beyond the Alleghenies, they entered a part of the continent that Ralph Waldo Emerson, for one, regarded as the real America—because the country east of that range seemed essentially an extension of Europe. Those pioneers may have been getting away from Europe, but they were still Europeans by virtue of their mind-set about the wilderness. For most of them, that mind-set, however much tempered by a heterogeneity of beliefs, was negative and enwrapped two interlaced, definitive components: a sense of separateness from the wilderness and a desire to dominate it.[31] Both prevented a balanced engagement with the wilderness; both had costs.

The sense of separateness is documented not only in Bradford's history but also in, among other texts, the writings of eighteenth-century Puritans, preeminently Cotton Mather and, later, Jonathan Edwards. Even though Mather, in his 1721 book *The Christian Philosopher: A Collection of the Best Discoveries in Nature, with Religious Improvements*, "counseled readers to contemplate nature and go on to praise its creator," in Albanese's words, his thought betrays a paucity of direct experience of it. Edwards may have been more sensuously aware of the natural environment than Mather, but, as can be seen in his "Personal Narrative" (written in 1739) and other works, he tended to perceive it as an analogical shadow of the ideal order of Heaven. For Edwards, God spoke revelationally through nature, but nature in its materiality was spiritually defiling. He thus contributed to an American tradition; for, by such logic, Albanese stresses, "if nature was sensuous presence, it was also—in a paradox that hinted the later dilemmas of Emerson, Henry David Thoreau, and assorted other Americans—material absence."[32]

This tradition of spiritual separateness from nature, of denying its *mattering*, paved the way for feats of exploitation and degradation. In time the multiplication of those feats and their effects and the continuous, if sometimes subtle, strengthening of the tradition—ever restyled, progressively more secular, at least on the surface—that rationalized them increased American alienation from the wilderness. Richard Rhodes ponders that alienation and its cost. The wilderness, he says, reveals "a world that mirrors our own depths, that delights in acts we have thought depraved, have worked from the beginning of our consciousness to fence in and legislate away." Because of the success of those efforts, we have annealed an illusion that allows us to believe we're divided from the world of the wild and to forget too easily that, "if we destroy it, we destroy ourselves."[33] Thus the upshot of a heritage of beguilement handed down in its most intense form by Bradford, Mather, Edwards, and company, creatures of spirit who hankered to be cleansed of that world.

With such deceptive separateness came "an assumption of innocence," as Rodriguez terms it. Through "the Atlantic myth of wilderness," which would be translated into "a myth of the West," that assumption radicated itself in our Protestant ancestors and still thrives. Because of the self-ignorance it afforded, Americans rapaciously proceeded west with a guiltlessness queried only periodically. In the perspective of innocent separateness, their expanding domination of the wilderness was wholly defensible, predestined; its outgrowths, like the transcontinental railroad tracks that Rodriguez poeticizes as "vestigial stitches of the smoke-belching Judeo-Christian engine, Primacy o' Man," bespeak a cosmic arrogance.[34]

Robert Frost got it right in his poem "The Gift Outright": "The land was ours before we were the land's." But I doubt that many of us, our cultural umbilicals attached to Massachusetts and Virginia, really became "possessed" by that land as it was "vaguely realizing westward." Also, I disagree with Frost's notion that the land was then "still unstoried," for it was storied from the start.[35] The Europeans' story from the start was what Zeese Papanikolas classifies as "a fiction of their own devising," and it told of "the light of grace that gleamed at the end of the continent justifying the westward thrust of the Europeans, their massacres, and their appropriations." Living it out, they turned into the Indians' "savages."[36] Living it out, they brought with them from the Old World many of the plants they would come to despise as the weeds that threaten to this day our idealized gardens.[37] Ironically, the West was made wilder in some respects by the imposition of the European will bent on taming it. Just as the abstract denomination of the land led to the concrete (more or less) domination of it, so did a fictional cause lead to quite nonfictional effects—with attendant costs, not all intended or anticipated.

But, if I may ignore for a moment whatever else brought it about, the pioneers' fiction followed from the vertical orientation they carried to the West. As A. Carl Bredahl Jr. explains, that orientation was distinctly Eastern, a conceptual custom of people who grew "used to tall, enclosing pines, oaks, and maples that stretch from Maine to Florida" and for whom the only distant horizon was the watery one drawn by the Atlantic. He finds evidence in the writings of Bradford, John Smith, and others that such overwhelming arboreal geography promoted an imagination that "works within forests." When that imagination moved west beyond the forests, the transition shocked it with disjunction: "Quite suddenly, the eye begins to sweep across great distances, horizon is now all encompassing. . . . In the East, with the eye confined, the rational powers seek ways of isolating and protecting the individual. But as the western experience strips away enclosure, . . . the eye is confronted with such space that the idea of domination becomes illusory." Expectably, therefore, the first pioneers hurried across that openness, "seeking Oregon or California, a world physically more congenial to the eastern mind and cultural patterns."[38] Thus did those pioneers go in quest of Papanikolas's light at the end of the continent—an assertion supported both by demographic data (remember that states in the Far West were admitted into the Union before those on the plains) and by the rationale for the transcontinental railroad, which originally was intended to be a method for vaulting what some Easterners and Far Westerners now deride as "flyover country."

For pioneers to whom the geography of the West Coast beckoned less seductively or who couldn't get there for any number of reasons, there was an alternative: "to bring along structures that permitted the illusion of dominance." Principal among those structures, according to Bredahl, were physical and psychological forts. The first, which "embodies all the values of family, stability, and military order held dear by the European mind," was a stronghold that both imposed those values on the wilderness and fended it off. The second, which functioned even in the absence of the first, was a redoubt born of the imagination, a correspondent psychic enclosure against the wilderness. These two structures, each supportive of the other, permitted some illusion of dominance for a while; as Bredahl notes, however, they were to prove "both impossible and violently destructive. As so many later western stories demonstrate, the individual must eventually leave the structure—either return East or learn to live within the environment."[39] But most of Bradford's heirs who stayed in any part of the West would never live entirely "within" it. They would always inhabit it ambivalently, at various removes—across a spectrum of incomplete accommodations.

A spectrum, to be sure, and one on which attitudes shifted over time. The westward migrators built their forts, but they knew gladness as well as anxiety once they left the woods behind. When they "emerged to the openness of the Great Plains," as Nash envisions them, "suddenly they could see and their spirits brightened." If there was hatred of the wilderness, there was hunger for it as well, a hunger expressed in the "rhapsodic language," never found in descriptions of Eastern forests, that pioneers such as James Hall, in his 1838 book *Notes on the Western States*, elaborated to portray the beauties of that openness. The plains may have lacked civilization, but the pioneers generally seem to have preferred them; and in their accounts "the term 'wilderness' gave way to 'garden.'" Still, however, the pioneers were definitely ancestors to future Westerners in that they didn't all always experience the less and less brave new world of the West in the same way. For some, the receiving garden, as seductive virgin or enwombing mother, would come to seem inimical wilderness again. Some, in the mood of eighteenth-century rationalism, would see Western wilderness as merely a chaos on which they felt compelled to impose the ordering canons of European intelligence. Some, moved by the teachings of deism or the enthusiasms of Romanticism challenging the decreased authority of Puritanism in the nineteenth century, would continue to rhapsodize. Many, like explorer Zebulon Pike and mountain man Zenas Leonard, would look "through, rather than at, wilderness," assessing its "value as potential civilization."[40] For most, antipathy toward it might turn more secular, but the westward progress of civilization would remain largely a providential mission of regeneration that used as raw material the wilderness in its path. Only a few would truly go native.

The consequence of such diverseness, as Nash summarizes it, "is simply that the American attitude toward wilderness is far . . . more complex that we usually assume." Like the majority of his fellow historians, he concludes, nevertheless, that that complex attitude was skewed centuries ago by a bias against wilderness so strong that it would endure long after pioneering ceased and, to follow my earlier metaphor, considerable Western rough had been smoothed into fairway. Alongside that bias, he admits, "more favorable responses haltingly took shape," but they required a protracted and embroiled while to achieve their present sophistication, pitch, and breadth of sympathy.[41] Even so, the dead hand of William Bradford still grips.

Ravage through the Garden: The Wild according to Boone, Lewis and Clark, and Crockett

Leaving the snakeskin of place after place,
going on.
> William Stafford, "For the Grave of Daniel Boone"

As Euro-Americans moved west in the late eighteenth century, out of New England, away from the Southeastern coast, across the Appalachians, and then into the Mississippi Valley, the wilderness too moved west; and their ideas about the wilderness became more Western. Explorers and exploiters of the West put positive mythic spin on the old Puritan ideas, even inverted them, but never left them entirely behind. That mythologizing was well under way before the West was unmeasured plains and rock-ribbed mountains. It really took off when the West was the Kentucky frontier. Its first consummate spin doctor was a schoolmaster and land speculator named John Filson, and his bombast imparted such momentum to the eddies in the wake of Daniel Boone's trailblazing that they became mythic whirlpools drawing the nation's expansionist attention to the Western wilderness as never before. Through the mythologizing of Filson and those influenced by him, it was presented not at all as a place to be shunned but as one to be embraced. But the truth beneath, entangled with, betrayed by that presentation was, of course, more complex.

In an essay on nature and work, Richard White mulls the subject of "the first white man" in the West. He notes that we tend to tell a story of a white man who encounters an immaculate paradise and alters it by his work upon it, which amounts to "environmental original sin." He easily refutes this story: Indians had already shaped that seemingly untouched world, and "French métis trappers and traders penetrated and lived in the West long before more famous first white men came along." But myth still overpowers such refutation, so thematically inappropriate mixed-bloods are kept out of the picture, the pre-Anglo West retains its virginity, and "the most popular first white men" to enter it "remain Lewis and Clark and Daniel Boone."[1]

True enough. But who were those first white men? Who are they yet? How and to what extent did Boone, as an actual adventurer and as a mythical figure, define the Western wilderness? What was it for Meriwether Lewis and William Clark, explorers who went west in—and then beyond—Boone's wake? Since Boone's salient exploits preceded Lewis and Clark's, which I suppose makes him the "real" first white man in the West, let me address those questions as they relate to him first.

However much he wound up being an icon shrouded in myth, the basic facts of Boone's life are well known and laid out in several modern biographies, such as John Bakeless's *Daniel Boone: Master of the Wilderness* (1939) or, more recently, John Mack Faragher's *Daniel Boone: The Life and Legend of an American Pioneer* (1992), perhaps as close as we'll come to a complete portrait. For an initial sketch of his life, though, I'd like to draw, in part, on the entry for him in the *Encyclopedia of the American West*, because it typifies the rhetoric usually employed in popular depictions of him.

According to that entry, Boone, with "a lust for the wilderness and an adventurous spirit, . . . epitomizes the American frontiersman." Born into a Quaker household in 1734 in rural western Pennsylvania, he explored the woods around his home as a boy. Later, after his family moved to North Carolina and while he was a volunteer during the French and Indian War, he heard stories from a companion "of abundant game and virgin lands in Kentucky," stories on which he ruminated for years after his service, years that saw him married to Rebecca Bryan (in 1756) and then providing for a growing family. In 1769 he left his brood behind and led a small party of hunters from North Carolina through a gap in the Cumberland Mountains and into Kentucky, a place he "found to be everything he had expected." He and his fellows amassed a peck of furs and skins, but they were robbed of them—and Boone was captured—by Shawnees. After two years in Kentucky, Boone returned home, deep in debt. In 1773 he went back with a group of family and friends, which was attacked by Indians, suffered several deaths (including that of Boone's oldest son, James), and soon returned to North Carolina. In 1775 Boone acquired a large tract of land from the Cherokees, cut across it a trail running from Virginia through the Cumberland Gap and on to the Ohio River that became known as the Wilderness Road, led settlers to the Kentucky River, and on its banks established a settlement named Boonesborough, which endured numerous Indian attacks. During one, the Shawnees took female captives. Boone retrieved them but was himself later captured—and adopted—by the tribe. After some months he escaped back to Boonesborough. Meanwhile, settlers kept coming to Kentucky, and Boone sold them part of his land—ineptly, however, so there were lawsuits over titles. That kettle of fish, debt, and other problems, along with his need for elbow room, motivated him to relocate several times and then to conduct his extended family into Missouri in 1799. There he obtained land from the Spanish government, lost it as a result of the Louisiana Purchase in 1803, but had part of it returned to him by Congress in 1814 "as a reward for his effort in opening the West." Thereafter, though haunted by his boondoggles and misfortunes, he was able, until the last three years before his death in 1820, "to hunt, trap, and enjoy the wilderness, which he had been so instrumental in exploring and opening for America's westward push."[2]

In his essay "The Discovery of Kentucky," William Carlos Williams portrays this wilderness-enjoying Boone as "a great voluptuary born to the American settlements against the niggardliness of the damming puritanical tradition." In his interpretation, Boone should be seen as a man "full of a rich regenerative violence"—an attribute that, Williams seems not to notice, suggests Boone's linkage back to the Puritans. Be that as it may, Williams's Boone, in line with my sketch, differed from those who clung to the Atlantic coast in that he wanted to partake of "the forbidden wealth of the Unknown." Unlike those who wrestled with founding a better England, he "lived to enjoy ecstasy through his single devotion to the wilderness with which he was surrounded."[3]

And yet, though Williams's Boone felt that "if the land were to be possessed it must be as the Indian possessed it," the reader has to be uneasy about his desire to make a fortune from it and his un-Quakerly "killing with a great appetite." Though this Boone "never wavered for a moment in his clear conception of the Indian as a natural part of a beloved condition, the New World, in which all lived together," the land speculator in him was excluding the Indian from togetherness.[4] In such incongruities Williams's short biography of Boone dramatizes more than mine—albeit he doesn't examine it self-consciously—Boone's contradictory attitude toward the wilderness. It's even more evident in the "autobiography" of him written by Filson.

Filson's narrative about Boone, The Adventures of Col. Daniel Boon, was appendixed to his book-length 1784 promotion brochure titled (in shortened form) The Discovery, Settlement and Present State of Kentucke, a text crafted to sell farmland to Easterners and Europeans. The language of that narrative, like that of the whole brochure, is, to be sure, inflated, but it's also shrewdly employed to showcase Boone as, in Richard Slotkin's words, "the archetypal hero of the American frontier." Through the dissemination of that narrative and imitations of it, Boone became "the man who made the wilderness safe for democracy."[5] He became also the premier overblown personification of America's ambivalent hunger for the wild.

Since Slotkin shrewdly analyzes the milk-and-honey rhetoric of Filson's brochure and the mythic structure of the appendix on Boone, let me bring into play some of his insights concerning late-eighteenth-century America's changing vision of Western wilderness and how the Boone myth, itself subject to change within its developing cultural context, helped to "sanctify" that vision.[6]

Filson may not have been conscious of the contradictions threading through his *Kentucke*, but he appears to have been aware of the intellectual traditions that had shaped the American notion of the frontier. He knew the formal conventions of Puritan narrative and effectively adapted them, and he made good use of in-process frontier legends. In short, he knew how to excite the reader's interest in the wilderness and then mold it into an identification with Boone so thorough that "Boone's initiation into the wilderness becomes the reader's own experience." A romantic with a physiocrat's faith in nature as the source of public wealth, Filson foresees Kentucky as the Western seat of America's empire, and the coherence of that vision depends upon an idealized "interdependence of the people's will and the land's requirements"—a proviso iterated in the Boone narrative in the hero's conflict with the wilderness that leads progressively to "a reconciliation of man and land." Moreover, just as Filson's Boone learns to see Kentucky as a possible utopia, so Filson himself concludes his sermonizing in the brochure with a peroration in the mood of Manifest Destiny that ideates Kentucky as a new Eden. Since that Eden will have to come about through immersion in and battle with the wilderness (and its Indians), according to Filson, Slotkin associates his conceptions with Cotton Mather as well as with Thomas Jefferson. The whole enterprise, the reader of this promotional spiel is told, will make great demands on its undertakers. The role of the Boone narrative is to convince the reader that he—like Boone, "a hero produced by his intimacy with the wilderness"—is the man for the job.[7]

Filson's story filled that role to a tee, its success evidenced both by Kentucky's becoming the first state west of the Appalachians to enter the Union (in 1792) and by the amazing proliferation of Filson's version of the Boone-based myth into future American and European literature and other art forms. *The Adventures of Col. Daniel Boon* was gravid with meanings beyond its author's intent. Those meanings, appealing so broadly and long, are many and frequently discordant, as Slotkin shows. While Filson retains the Puritan idea that the wilderness Boone experiences can serve to implement God's plan for human regeneration, he treats it not as a hell but as a symbol of divinity whose beauty resides in "the extent to which it imitates cultivated nature and implies that civilization is itself the crown of natural evolution." It's a landscape in which Boone, a melancholic as Filson portrays him, can find solacing kinship. Indeed, in making the wilderness capable of liberating Boone from his melancholy, Filson anticipates many a writer who will extol the power of the West's wild country to cure virtually every malady flesh is heir to, from asthma to neurasthenia. Attuned to it, fearless, Boone turns stoical, lives as the wilderness requires him to live, "rejects both the comforts of civilization and the commercial values which characterize established urban societies."[8] He prefers the wilderness even when its pastoral brilliance gives way to dark sublimity, horridness, disorder. He may go native, but he's not Thomas Morton, not quite Williams's voluptuary; for his approach to nature is that of the rational philosophe, and he's self-reliant, to boot.

In Slotkin's interpretation of Filson's story, the ups and downs of Boone's life in the wilderness repeat an experiential pattern that is "the essence of Filson's 'myth.'" That essence has everything to do with Boone's rationality and the reader's sympathy with his rage for order. The pattern consists of several stages: Boone's immersion in the wilderness, his both terrifying and promising encounters with Indians, his reaching a deeper understanding of the wilderness and himself, and his exercise of control over the wilderness. The reader's response is "to assume that the result of this assertion of control will be to realize, through agrarian cultivation, nature's inherent power to sustain civilization."[9] Boone's *Bildungsroman* anticipates the building of Arcadia in Kentucky.

Ambiguities abound in Filson's account and in its relation to fact. Not the least of them arises through how, as Slotkin puts it, "the roles and characters of hunter and husbandman are ambiguously equated"—a confounding of boomer and sticker, to borrow Wallace Stegner's nomenclature, that still curses the West. The historical Boone was far more hunter than husbandman, and the commercial values he rejected were mainly those of lawyers whose craftiness ensnarled the ownership of land he was stealing from Indians; but Filson must have him undergo a metamorphosis through his "discovery of the husbandman and agent of civilization within the husk of his hunter's identity"—a metamorphosis that was, if ever real at all, certainly incomplete. Filson resolves some of the Puritan flip-flopping on nature's gender (as female seductress of the male renegade or male captor of the female Christian innocent and the like) by having nature play the feminine prey to Boone's masculine predator, but he does so by making both "beings of the wild"—even though Boone is also an agent of civilization—and further perplexes the whole matter by having Boone's wife act as both "a symbol of the establishment of civilization" and "a symbol of the spirit of nature."[10] Such fusions of contraries recur in remakes of Filson's story.

The Boone narrative, however read (as a Puritan tale of recovery, as a Rousseauistic fable of redemption through primitive nature, or as something else), displays what Slotkin sums up as a "welter of apparently contradictory images." But the welter does have correlations among its disparities. Thus Filson paints a landscape in which he, like Jefferson describing landscape in his *Notes on the State of Virginia*, "blends images of order and disorder," and he correlatively locates Boone characterologically in the range between Quaker and savage, presenting him as a man who seeks involvement with nature but doesn't surrender himself to outright primitiveness, one who "abstracts a code of natural laws from the wilderness and brings these laws and his own passions under the control of his own civilized reason."[11]

By the logic of such correlations, the hunter's assignment is to clear the way for the husbandman, and the goal of knowledge from the wilderness is the establishment and maintenance of civilization in opposition to it. Of course, the historical dialectic of what Slotkin sees as "antithetical values" expressed through Filson's Boone would never be locked so neatly into furthering one ideal. Because of America's generally ambivalent attitude toward the wild, as well as intellectual dispositions that differed over time and across the nation's regions, the myth of Daniel Boone would vary. But those variations nonetheless manifest two major themes, which in turn mirror tensional extremes in that attitude: "the Filsonian vision of the frontier hero as an untutored republican-gentleman-philosophe and the folk vision of Boone as the mighty hunter, child of the wilderness, and exemplar of values derived from sources outside Anglo-American civilization."[12]

The more closely you examine this double Boone, the more he seems to contain in nuce the cultural history of the Western wilderness during the last two centuries. Boone's image defined the question for a debate central to any rendering of that history that began in his time and hasn't yet abated. Henry Nash Smith discerned its original terms in *Virgin Land: The American West as Symbol and Myth*. There he keynotes his discussion of Boone with a contrast between Francis Parkman's observations in 1842 concerning Eastern farmers, recorded in one of his journals, and his portrayal, in 1849 in *The Oregon Trail*, of "men of the wilderness" he had met in his 1846 trip to the Far West. In Parkman's view, the farmers were as boorish as the animals they raised, but the Westerners, though coarse, were heroic—brave, independent, expert in the ways of the wild. Typical among his contemporaries, those opposed takes illustrate that Americans of the time saw "two quite distinct Wests: the commonplace domesticated area within the agricultural frontier, and the Wild West beyond it." The first was an insipid place, but the second was a place of rousing adventure. Smith finds implicit in Parkman's love of the West a rejection of conventional society that's understandable since he, with his Bostonian affluence, could afford to indulge "in the slightly decadent cult of wildness and savagery which the early nineteenth century took over from Byron,"[13] who had praised society-rejecting Boone in a tribute inserted into the eighth canto of his *Don Juan* as "even in age the child / Of Nature" who lived "in wilds of deepest maze."[14]

Parkman wasn't alone in his "refined hostility to progress" any more than he was alone in his favoring the Wild West over the agricultural West. Those in agreement with him hardly hampered the march of Manifest Destiny, but they did ensure the strength of one of two antithetical attitudes toward westering, both of which were conspicuous in the common conception of Boone, whose doubleness Smith capsules by reference to "the official view" of him as "empire builder and philanthropist" and the unofficial view of him as "a fugitive from civilization." He finds the official view articulated in Horatio Greenough's marble sculpture *The Rescue*, installed in the national Capitol in 1853, which allegorically "depicted the contest between civilization and barbarism as a fierce hand-to-hand struggle between Boone [as the public made out the figure] and an Indian warrior," with the white man appearing to prevail; in George Caleb Bingham's 1851–52 painting *Daniel Boone Escorting Settlers through the Cumberland Gap*, which pictures Boone leading the way into a dreamy wilderness soon to be plowed (a work, I'd note, that, with its suggestion of Boone as Joseph taking Mary into Egypt, recollects William Ranney's 1849 painting *Boone's First View of Kentucky*, which apotheosizes Boone as Moses headed into the Promised Land); in Filson's *Kentucke*; and in *The Adventures of Daniel Boone*, an 1813 epic by Daniel Bryan, Boone's nephew.[15] The unofficial view was set out in the press, tall tales, circulating anecdotes—less sanctioned media.

The two views were confused as the debate dragged on in the early nineteenth century, most notably, for Smith, in Timothy Flint's widely read 1833 book *The Life and Adventures of Daniel Boone, the First Settler of Kentucky, Interspersed with Incidents in the Early Annals of the Country*. And, as Smith remarks, James Fenimore Cooper was unable "to explore to the end the contradictions in his ideas and emotions" about social order and natural freedom personified in the Boone-like protagonist of his frontier romances—as was his readership, apparently as beclouded in its interpretation of Leatherstocking as it was in that of Boone. Muddied by such confusion, the issue of Boone's character and motivation remained unresolved. Argue for Boone as a herald of civilization or for him as a primitivist, his image, Smith concludes, "could serve either purpose."[16]

That image still can, for the issue remains fluid, much as does the related issue of whether the postmodern West should become more civilized or be left in as primitive a state as is now feasible. Though New Western Historians have tended, in the debunking mood of recent decades, more to scrutinize Boone as a businessman than to eulogize him as a child of nature, the latter impulse isn't defunct.[17] Given the equivocality of the case (and of opinions on Western wilderness), a lot of assessment winds up in between. Contrary to the simplex legend of Boone as a land-hungry Indian killer, a legend fervently disputed by his descendants, Leonard Lutwack characterizes him as a man, like John James Audubon, who, "while deeply respectful of the wilderness, could still engage in its exploitation."[18] Frederick Turner labels him "the original violator" of the West, regrets that he didn't turn out to be more Indian, but admits that he "early on . . . had become aghast at the destruction that had been unleashed."[19] Patricia Nelson Limerick sees him as the eponymous instigator and prototypical victim of "the Boone paradox," which involves those fleeing to the West there "replicating the problems they had attempted to escape."[20] Faragher argues that he symbolizes a number of discordant American sentiments, among them "a love and admiration of nature coupled with an almost desperate desire for development and material advancement," and concludes that he "was a man of contradictions."[21] David Daly and Joel Persky speak for many when, after surveying fantasy-ridden treatments of Boone from Filson's narrative

Horatio Greenough, The Rescue (1853): the contest between civilization and barbarism. (Architect of the Capitol.)

to Walt Disney's 1960s television series, they sum him up as "a curiously ambivalent figure."[22]

The same might be said of the man who conceived and authorized the Lewis and Clark Expedition, the most significant wilderness exploration undertaken in the New World. Thomas Jefferson played the seminal role in promoting the physiocratic view of land beyond the Mississippi he purchased from the French in 1803, and yet the philosophe in him was alloyed with aspects of the Puritan theocrat. As is often true of gifted utopians, he was contradictory—though more complexly so than Boone. His vision of the Western wilderness was no less conflicted.

George Caleb Bingham, Daniel Boone Escorting Settlers through the Cumberland Gap (1851–1852): a dreamy wilderness soon to be plowed. (Oil on canvas, 36 1/2 x 50 1/4 in. Mildred Lane Kemper Art Museum, Washington University in St. Louis, gift of Nathaniel Phillips, 1890.)

The West that seized Jefferson's imagination already had been explored and settled some by the Spanish, French, British, and Scottish. But on the whole, as William H. Goetzmann and William N. Goetzmann observe, outsiders knew almost nothing about it. On the basis of tales of skirmishes with Indians, deprivations in deserts, or plentitudes of wildlife, "the West was what you made it—or how you looked at it." Jefferson "made it an American mystery," in Goetzmann and Goetzmann's formulation; yet it was he also who "was determined to de-mystify it and exploit it in the name of science and the United States of America."[23] That twofold exploitation, ostensibly for the sake of disinterested knowledge and (not very) covertly for the sake of commerce, was itself conflicted, its twinned aims no more suited for one another than much Western land was for Jefferson's ideal of a national future of yeoman agriculture.

The man who sent Lewis and Clark and their Corps of Discovery to find a riverine route for trade with Asia, which unfulfilled quest would lay a symbolic roadbed for the Oregon Trail that many a farmer would follow west, "held a positive religious vision of life in tune with the land," as Catherine L. Albanese puts it.[24] But the idea of God's chosen people living virtuously in small-scale idyllic pastoralism must be examined in the context of other Jeffersonian ideas with which it wasn't entirely consonant.[25]

First of all, nature for Jefferson, as he had characterized it in the Declaration of Independence, was, in Albanese's words, "a fixed source of right and order in the world," and his ideology of it was pragmatic. Not the immaterial vapor of Edwards, spirit as he conceived it was invested in the substance of a nature that, however idealized, was politically real, and it "had no existence apart from matter—and more, if the whole truth would be told—matter on the American continent." That sense of spirit-in-matter privilege is pronounced in Jefferson's *Notes on the State of Virginia*, most of it written in the early 1780s, where, as Albanese remarks, his notions about a special American destiny included a "religion of the soil" that was in fact "a charter for expansion." Since the agriculture of a growing nation required space, it implicitly required also dealing with wilderness. That kind of hunger for the wild involved Jefferson's beholding "the national landscape as American sublime," and for him, by Albanese's compressed logic, "the sublime equaled wilderness equaled power. The equation had been shaped in Europe, but it was being reshaped in America under the aegis of forces that stressed magnitude as a way of being. . . . American sublime hinted of empire and dominion."[26] Empire and dominion demanded that wilderness be brought under control. That control would come about in a manner contrary to sublimity and, moreover, would have little to do with living "in tune with the land."[27]

Although Jefferson had an appreciation of nature, he was no lover of nature in its rawest state (Monticello was, after all, a thoroughly *cultivated* neoclassical environment) and charged Lewis and Clark not just with exploring the Louisiana Territory but, in Winifred Gallagher's polysemous phrase, "with charting the wilderness."[28] Thus a *charter* for expansion into the wilderness led to the necessity of *charting* it, mapping it (Jefferson was fond of maps), defining it with *cartographic* exactitude. All three words derive from the Latin word *charta*, "paper," and imply Enlightenment abstractions of entitlement that had scant connection with the fractal actualities of the wilderness. But a new nation competing with other nations for land, keen to preserve democratic principles as it expanded, and interested in the economic possibilities of the West needed certainty about its boundaries and who laid claim to what within them. Those concerns absorbed Jefferson immediately after the Louisiana Purchase, and Lewis and Clark's charting would lay the groundwork for the later and more formal definition of not only the Louisiana Territory, which they went beyond, but all of the West by mapping based on orthogonal townships and sections, the invention of none other than Jefferson himself some years earlier.

The impact of Jefferson's invention as it was applied to the West shouldn't be underestimated. Lawrence Buell, noting that in 1785 Congress had approved a modified version of it, describes that invention as a system by means of which "the spatial physiognomy of American egalitarianism, entrepreneurialism, and privatism was rolled into one diagram." Therefore its clearest importance, he argues, is that it figured in "a strategy for consolidating control of 'unsettled' regions." The cartography involved was, of course, quite different from that of the Indians—not to mention, as John Wesley Powell later would, that its geometry ignored watersheds and other nonrectilinear features of Western topography that any thoughtful mapping for settlement ought to take into account. But the official maps, particularly the big map Clark was making for Jefferson and the War Department, weren't intended to be records of such features: they were to be, among other things, "agents of cartographical imperialism."[29] By charting wilderness, Lewis and Clark set the stage for the mechanical gridding of the West necessitated by Jefferson's vision, but none of those men could have foreseen that by the 1860s, as John R. Stilgoe observes, "the grid objectified national, not regional, order, and no one wondered at rural space marked by urban rectilinearity."[30]

In 1804, though, neither the American West nor the Louisiana Territory that had become a substantial part of it was yet gridded. On May 14 of that year the Corps of Discovery, a group that would vary between forty-five and twenty-nine members, began boating into what Rita Parks calls "land that stretched to what might well be infinity—with the possibilities seemingly infinite as well."[31] Lewis and Clark perused old maps with broad blank areas, what John Logan Allen terms "the geographical lore characteristic of their own milieu," lore they shaped into images of what lay ahead that would be reshaped during their journey. They wouldn't be the first white men to cross the North American continent in search of something long vivid "in the geography of the mind," the Northwest Passage through a vast garden, the all-water link to the Pacific, the Passage to India.[32] That had already been done—through the western Canadian wilderness—by a small 1793 expedition led by the Scottish fur trader Alexander Mackenzie, whose 1801 book about his attempt to open new territory for Britain and the North West Company, *Voyages from Montreal* (its title in brief), Jefferson, Lewis, and Clark pored over.[33] Lewis and Clark's party would, however, be the first American white men to do so—via a very different course, in obedience to a meticulous plan with flexibly drafted (if not wholly compatible) multiple goals, and under the joint command of two admirably qualified leaders (especially Lewis, whose preparation included instruction, by the American savants of his age, in everything from chronometry and botany to mineralogy and medicine).

Still, no amount of perusing maps, poring over books, planning, training, and interrogating of experts (much of whose knowledge of the West was hearsay or hypothetical) could have prepared Lewis and Clark for what they faced. If contemporary Europeans thought "the whole continent was a 'great incognitum,'" as Goetzmann and Goetzmann put it, borrowing the name that Philadelphia painter and museologist Charles Willson Peale had given to his exhibit of a reconstructed mastodon in 1801,[34] then those two Americans headed up the Missouri surely thought the West before them was such. If they and their men negotiating that river's sandbars to enact what Jefferson's enemies condemned as a moonstruck project didn't think that when they left St. Louis, they did when they broke camp after wintering in 1804–05 with the Mandans in what's now North Dakota; for past that point loomed what was for them a guesswork world. After they there took on a young Shoshone woman named Sacagawea, she, like other Indian helpers, didn't so much guide them on westward, which is what legend tells us, as, among other contributions, keep them at times from losing their way in distances that struck them dumb.[35] Not since the Renaissance had anyone white grappled with so much geographical unknownness.

Leaving the huts of Fort Mandan, Lewis and Clark traveled the Missouri through Montana to the Three Forks, then the Jefferson River, then, after a winding path (and 340 miles of arduous portage) that included Lemhi Pass, the Clearwater, and then the Columbia out to the Pacific Ocean. Having wintered in 1805–06 at the site of the small palisaded structure they called Fort Clatsop, about seven miles southeast of the Columbia's mouth, they returned by a partly different route; the two leaders split up most of the way, to just below the junction of the Missouri and the Yellowstone, whence, reunited, they descended the former back to St. Louis. When they arrived there in late September 1806, they had been gone for over two years and had variously navigated some eight thousand miles of wilderness. They had learned a lot—and recorded it in notebooks and journals that copiously documented their trip. They had measured everything measurable. They had made astronomical observations to determine positions that could be used in creating maps, far less erroneous than the ones they carried with them, of the Western incognitum. They had studied Indian cultures, soils, plants, animals, collecting all manner of artifacts and samples. Their tidings of bountiful beaver set off a rush of trappers who shortly would kill and peel that creature's kind mercilessly. The general upshot of their labors was a fuller comprehension, more objective and more rational, of the young nation's new hinterland. "The Garden of Jefferson's theories and pastoral ideal still existed," Allen remarks summarily, but "now the dreams of an agrarian utopia in the fertile Northwest could be grounded in the detailed and specific accounts of American explorers."[36] True, but William H. Goetzmann's blunter assessment more accurately shadows the future: what Lewis and Clark brought back suggested "the immense value of the interior to all kinds of American enterprise."[37]

Most of that enterprise wouldn't get its depredations into swing quickly. Despite the significance of Lewis and Clark's trove of information, the report of their expedition wasn't published in book form—most of it a paraphrase, with extensive omissions, of their journals—until 1814. Not until then, as Goetzmann says, "was there even a satisfactory cartographic representation of the whole region south and west of the Missouri River. Instead, for a long time the West remained an immense unknown, whose limits were gradually being defined by the explorers sent out into it by the governments and fur-trading companies along its margins."[38]

As their journals show, however, Lewis and Clark defined not so much the limits of the West they experienced as the nature, in both senses, of it as a wild place. The process of that defining was characterized by a fundamental ambivalence that involved the perception of the West as a dangerous paradise. On the one hand, as hardly a page of the journals will let you forget, the men of the Corps of Discovery had, in Stephen E. Ambrose's phrase, "cut themselves off from civilization" and taken on a military mission that might well run into hostility. On the other hand, as is clear from any number of passages, those men were at times unguardedly, even deliriously, responding to a "wonderland," as Ambrose puts it, "just bursting with animal and plant life."[39] Thus throughout the expedition there was a tension, repeatedly reflected in the journals, between viewing the environment as one demanding soldierly discipline and viewing it as one inviting the utmost in sensuous, aesthetic, or scientific engrossment.

The tension arises from two opposed attitudes held, to recall F. Scott Fitzgerald, in the mind at the same time, alternating in ascendancy, one insistent on a tending to duty, the other on an attending to beauty. The difference between them is apparent in the juxtaposition of two entries in the journals, both written by Clark, one on June 29, 1804, while the expedition was at the mouth of the Kansas River, and the other on July 4, when it was headed north from there on the Missouri. The first entry relates to two men of the party who during the previous night had stolen whiskey from the expedition's supply, an act "'contrary to all order, rule or regulation'"; gotten drunk, one of them while on guard duty; and then been sentenced by a court-martial to lashes on their backs. The punishment was meted out not merely for theft but for breaking discipline and for lack of vigilance. The second entry relates to the country around an abandoned Kansa village, where the expedition had stopped for the night. Clark writes of plains on which "Groops of Shrubs covered with the most delicious froot is to be seen in every direction, and nature appears to have exerted herself to butify the senery by the variety of flours Delicately and highly flavered raised above the Grass, which Strikes & profumes the Sensation, and amuses the mind."[40]

This contrapuntal oscillation went on in the month ahead, as it did for the rest of the trip: on July 9 everyone was on the qui vive for an Indian attack that didn't occur, and on July 12 a man was sentenced to lashes for falling asleep at his sentry post; but then on July 30 Clark and Lewis gave themselves to taking delight in a grass-covered prairie with "the most butifull prospects imagionable."[41] Such oscillation is understandable: those Anglos knew that the Garden of Eden held a serpent, that lotus-eating had a price, that the warm land of plenty could be a place of privations as well as of mosquitoes, syphilis, dreadful weather, and so on.[42] Ambrose speaks volumes about that oscillation when, in less than a page of text, he waveringly indexes Lewis's situation eight days west out of Fort Mandan: "Lewis was now step-ping into the unknown. . . . He was entering a heart of darkness. . . . He stepped forward, into paradise. . . . Not quite paradise." He may speak even more volumes when he brakes the wavering by affirming that "this really was paradise," only to get it moving again, implicitly, by invoking two points of view, the ecological and then the militaristic, regarding the beneficiaries of the country about: it was para-dise not only for wildlife in all its interactions but also "for the human hunters who declared war on the predators and lived off their prey."[43]

There were yet other ambivalences toward the wilderness inherent in this ex-pedition. On the one hand, Lewis and Clark were engaged in—and more or less succeeded at—demystifying the West. Donald A. Barclay, James H. Maguire, and Peter Wild, for instance, remark that they would blemish "the West as dream-scape" by showing how "the laws of physics apply west of the Mississippi River as they do everywhere else on the planet."[44] White argues that Lewis and Clark "replaced the search for what the West did not contain with a search for accurate and detailed knowledge of what the West did contain."[45] However sensitive to the land's beauty, they were, he says succinctly, "matter-of-fact"—though the men who practiced seemingly neutral matter-of-factness would "serve both to reveal the un-touched continent and to set its destruction in motion."[46] And Richard W. Etulain stresses that they carefully avoided the "imaginative reshapings" of "the strong-armed, hairy-chested school of Wild West literature."[47] But while Lewis and Clark demystified—and, in some respects, demythologized—the West, they also cultur-alized—and, in other respects, remythologized—it. As Richard C. Poulsen's read-ing of their journals has it, they made the wilderness through which they traveled a "domesticated" space. They thereby stamped a tenacious image on the nation's psyche for two reasons, both of which have as much to do with making the un-known known in their own cultural terms as with demystifying it: "First, they were pushing the mythology of motion called manifest destiny into the waste places, which motion itself effected a transformation. And second, through their percep-tions of and dealings with the landscape and its various inhabitants, . . . they made predictable what had been only chaotic." Indeed, Poulsen argues, "the culturaliza-tion of the landscape"—the Anglicizing of the wild—"seems to have been their major mission."[48]

Predictability, a recurrent topic in Jefferson's and Lewis's planning, was the prime desideratum of culturalization, the establishment of Anglo society and com-merce in the West. Yet predictability was at odds with what the West of the early nineteenth century was all about, the freedom it meant to those who entered it from the more constricting spaces of the East and South. As Donald Worster observes, Lewis and Clark were among the first white travelers to experience that West as a place where "all physical restraint seemed to be removed." To illustrate their re-action to it as such, he cites Clark's description of prairie along the Platte River, written after he and Lewis had left their pirogues for a better look at the interior and in which he declares that "the most butifull prospect of the River up & Down and the countrey Opsd. prosented it Self which I ever beheld." Worster acknowledges that Clark "gives no indication that any deeper thoughts occupied his mind at this moment" but opines that he must have felt "a sense of utter release" and goes on to say that we who read the passage certainly believe that, had we been there, we would have felt "freedom made possible only by the dry air, the short grass, and the horizon running off to infinity." If Clark felt that freedom, then he may have had an inkling of how the West would get embrangled in "the coils of paradox," paradox still unresolved, when it tried to "achieve material success and yet maintain the landscape of freedom."[49]

Or maybe not. Certainly Clark and his cocaptain tasted what Thomas J. Lyon calls "the genuine excitement of space and wildness the West offered," and there's no difficulty in detecting an "Adamic undercurrent" in their descriptions of trans-fixing scenes of beauty.[50] Lyon's exemplary passage is in Lewis's entry for April 25, 1805, when the expedition, having left Fort Mandan behind, was nearing the Missouri's junction with the Yellowstone. Lewis writes that he and four men had disembarked and were proceeding to the Yellowstone's entrance. The passage details what Lewis saw on that march:

> Our rout lay along the foot of the river hills. when we had proceeded about four miles, I ascended the hills from whence I had a most pleasing view of the coun-try, perticularly of the wide and fertile vallies formed by the missouri and the yellowstone rivers. . . . the whol face of the country was covered with herds of Buffaloe, Elk & Antelopes; deer are also abundant, but keep themselves more concealed in the woodland. the buffaloe Elk and Antelope are so gentle that we pass near them while feeding, without apearing to excite any alarm among them, and when we attract their attention, they frequently approach us more nearly to discover what we are.

Well and good. Lots of Adamic undercurrent there—and witnessing of the space of freedom. But remark, as Lyon does not, the passages that closely precede and fol-low that one. Here's the former: "falling in with some buffaloe I killed a yearling calf. . . . ; we soon cooked and made a hearty meal of part of it" (and, presumably, pitched the rest). Here's the latter: "in our way to the place I had determined to encamp, we met with two large herds of buffaloe, of which we killed three cows and a calf. two of the former, wer but lean, we therefore took their tongues and a part of their marrow-bones only."[51] The scene of plentitude and peace is framed, both in the text and in the sequence of events it reports, by two scenes of wasteful killing—with no apparent recognition by Lewis of the incongruity of appreciating the wilderness in one breath and abusing it in the next. This white man brought to the wilderness something quite unlike the total-use predation that was the wont of Western nature and its longtime human inhabitants.

Two days later, after recounting a morning walk near the Missouri–Yellowstone junction, during which he pondered setting up a military and fur-trading post there, Lewis states that, "altho' game is very abundant and gentle, we only kill as much as is necessary for food."[52] The game was abundant indeed: elk, deer, beaver, on and on, many species new to Lewis, their numbers uncountable. The second half of that sentence, though, is untrue. Of course, the hard-working men of the expedition needed large quantities of food, mostly meat, but the killing happened far in excess of what Lewis asserts. For one thing, animals were killed for scientific purposes, and they were killed also for sport; but even those killed for the pot were often done in with prodigality. God's plenty of buffalo gave only their tongues to the party's diet. Grizzlies were shot as a matter of routine.

Some of the slaughter seems to have been arbitrary, committed out of a disregard for beauty otherwise appreciated. Such disregard is easy to spot. For example, on May 31, 1805, Lewis made an entry that contains a passage in which he describes the White Cliffs area of the Missouri Breaks. His description, a transposition of the scene into European geometric, geological, and architectural terms, part of it redolent of paintings of Roman ruins by eighteenth-century painters like Panini or Piranesi, goes apace, detailing an entrancement that, in passing, focuses on a fox Lewis saw and then, without missing a taxonomic beat, tried to kill before sliding his attention to a seam of coal in a sandstone wall:

> I saw near those bluffs the most beautifull fox that I ever beheld, the colours appeared to me to be a fine orrange yellow, white and black, I endevoured to kill this animal but it discovered me at a considerable distance, and finding that I could get no nearer, I fired on him as he ran, and missed him; he concealed himself under the rocks of the clift; it appeared to me to be about the size of the common red fox of the Atlantic states, or reather smaller than the large fox common to this country; convinced I am that it is a distinct species. The appearance of coal continu[e]s.[53]

Et in Arcadia ego. Ego, to be sure.

The disregard didn't have to do merely with beauty, however. In a discussion of animals in the West, Worster gets at the broader implications of the attitude Lewis exemplifies above. Commenting on our nescience of animals and proposing that historians read the provocative nature writing of Barry Lopez, experience animals in the wild, and "join in a move to change the relationships we have had with animals," he argues that we must radically rethink how we treat them.[54] Doing that means foremost complying with a requirement he finds voiced in one of Lopez's essays: "to rise above prejudice to a position of respectful regard toward everything that is different from ourselves and not innately evil."[55] Such regard is exactly what Lewis, Clark, and their party lacked. Since they were the first white Americans to enter the overflowing world of Western animal life, Worster offers their treatment of that life, the opposite of what Lopez deems now crucially appropriate, as Exhibit A in his revisionary "overview of western wildlife."[56]

Though the extraordinary wildlife the men of the Corps of Discovery beheld impressed them just by its presence, it often was perceived as nothing more than game—an ambiguous word that signifies its reduction to a source of either food (a must for explorers living off the land) or sport (a more disturbing must). Desensitized by that reductive perception, the explorers, in Worster's wording, "raised their muzzleloaders and shot at animals of every species they saw, killing them in large numbers on both banks, all the way from Saint Louis to Fort Clatsop," for a total, by his estimate, of between five and ten thousand.[57]

Clearly, the amusement of sport accounts for a good part of the killing, but other motives were involved in some of it, motives that had to do with more than just wildlife as game. Scientific objectification (of which Lewis's taxidermy, freezing wild creatures into tame statues, was the epitome) played a role, as did "idle curiosity"; but a measure of the slaughter was, in Worster's categorization, "an impulsive, vague gesture toward pacifying the wild." If the explorers seemed at times—in their killing of mountain lions, marmots, badgers, snakes, et cetera et cetera—like, to paraphrase Gloucester in Shakespeare's King Lear, wanton boys killing flies and thus imitating the gods killing humans, the resemblance resides not so much in the common denominator of acts committed for the sake of enjoying sport, which is what Gloucester literally says, as in that of acts committed for the sake of expressing power. Worster judges the explorers' pacifying murder "banal," but he discerns in it "no Ahab-like violence visited on the natural world for the sake of domination, no fierce implacable hatred against the wild lodged in a puritanical heart."[58] I'm not so sure, however, for the men did intend, ultimately, to dominate the natural West by the power of a culture that would become, if it wasn't already, Ahab-like; and their attitude toward wildlife does seem informed with at least vestigial Puritan hatred, certainly with the other Christian sentiment (not novel, I assume, to the majority of the party who attended mass in St. Charles on May 20, 1804) that wild animals counted for little in the hierarchy of their universe.[59]

Still and all, Worster does hit the mark when he interprets one of Clark's acts of violence from a Lopezian point of view. On the evening of May 29, 1805, Clark was walking on the bank, not far from the mouth of the Judith River in Montana, and came upon a pile of a hundred-odd bison carcasses, probably the result of a mass drowning and not, as he speculated, of Indians' stampeding them over a buffalo jump, an ancient method of hunting. "Great numbers of wolves were about this place & verry jentle," he writes; while they were dining on the carrion, "I killed one of them with my Spear."[60] Concerning this casual killing (with a short pike or spontoon), Worster comments that Clark "would never have done that to any Indian on the scene; he was not that kind of man. But the wolf was in Clark's mind not another being like himself, to be tolerated and respected."[61] Needless to say, there wasn't much respectful regard in that lethal violation.

Nor was there much such regard in the expedition's treatment of Indians—though more than was shown Western fauna. Lewis and Clark, like Jefferson, considered the Indians they were charged to study to be for the most part capable, with tutoring, of becoming American citizens. Granting them more social potential than they did African American slaves, those Virginians, as Ambrose puts it, "thought the only difference between Indians and white men was religion and the savage behavior of the Indians, which was caused by the environment in which the Indian lived"[62]—and that could be tamed.

Which is to say, Lewis and Clark were as ignorant of the Indians and their histories as they were of their habitat, especially once they had traveled beyond the Mandans. Their initial ignorance is forgivable since, as Allen shows, the French sources they consulted differed greatly in their descriptions of the inhabitants of the Northwest, a place those sources "peopled with the hosts of fantasy" that included everything from dwarf Indians to white Indians dwelling in magnificent cities. In the main, though, the duration of Lewis and Clark's journey didn't see that ignorance corrected. Lewis delivered long speeches to Natives who couldn't have understood them, referring to his listeners as red children of the Great Father back east. He told them how they must behave and threatened them with penalties for disobedience. Baubles and certificates were given to chiefs who, unfortunately, would rather have had whiskey and rifles. Some men in the party took advantage of the Indians' sexual generosity, with syphilis passed around. Much as their French sources had characterized Natives "as noble savages living in near-civilized splendor, or as rude and barbarous tribesmen little above the level of the beasts of the forest,"[63] so Lewis and Clark classified them as "good," like the Mandans, who assisted the expedition, or "bad," like the Teton Sioux—the latter standing in need of harsher taming into dependence on the will of the Great Father's nation. Indians who were too wild would have to be somehow removed—a proposition as problematic as the cruel procedures and results to which it would lead.

Behind all this intercultural mismatching lay Jefferson's as-yet mostly subjunctive Indian policy, of which Lewis was, in Ambrose's appellation, "the advance agent." His goal in that capacity was to increase the Indians' participation in trading, so that "guns and other manufactured goods would come up the Missouri; prime furs would float down to St. Louis."[64] If such an arrangement, far cheaper than war, worked, the Indians would be peaceful, have jobs, befriend the white middlemen, join in the all-around prosperity, be civilized.

This policy was, however, only the beginning of Jefferson's long-term but hazardously hypothetical expedient (in part originated during Washington's presidency) for coping with Indians. As Ambrose, among others, has pointed out, two conditions, at least, would ensure its unsustainability and the downslide of both the kind of commerce and the coexistence it was designed to promote: the overtrapping of beaver, which had already happened in the East, and the unstoppable migration of non-Natives into the West. Nonetheless, Jefferson intended to block settlement in the northern part of the Louisiana Territory, civilize Indians east of the Mississippi as extensively as possible, and ship those who couldn't be converted from barbarism "west of the river, into what would be a vast reservation."[65] By that mechanism the progression of the frontier could be regularized after the Indians had been either made members of the republican club (and allowed to intermarry with whites) or banished into the indefinite outback.[66] Land would be deeded and farmed without red–white conflicts. Taxes would be collected. Law and order would triumph. Wild nature would be culturalized into a middle landscape.

"But," as Ambrose's conjunction announces, "it was all a pipe dream." The wild that Lewis and Clark plumbed was never to be so systematically tamed and used. Their brokering of Jefferson's relatively compassionate policy would come to naught, with Jefferson himself much to blame, for he had arranged the exploration, had its leaders' journals printed and distributed, and (skeptical or not about the extent of the West's inhabitability by whites) "was thus encouraging what he said he wanted to restrain." Ambivalence thereby blurred into hypocrisy, and hypocrisy themed his treaty-greased Indian policy: "Join us or get out of the way, the Americans said to the Indians, but in fact the Indians could do neither." Finally, since those Americans soon would want most of the West for themselves, the policy devolved into a grimmer directive that would hold for some time: "get out of the way or get killed."[67] Such a policy, ironically implicit in Jefferson's hope for the Indians' future, guaranteed that the West would become the arena for cultural wildness far surpassing any occasioned by endemic intertribal squabbles.

Lewis and Clark's expedition and its aftermath thus were infested with ambivalences, hypocritical or not (since their age wasn't as conscious of them as ours has come to be), toward the Western wild. John R. Milton, in his discussion of influences on the Western novel, ranks Lewis and Clark's journals high in that regard partly because their record of experiences with a strange landscape exhibits a combination of objectivity and awe that would recur in myriad narratives, fictional as well as nonfictional, written over the next two centuries. Intrinsic to it is something else that also would recur: "the ever-present ambivalence toward a land which is both beautiful and plain, rejuvenating and deadly, desolate and free, and harsh but spiritually refreshing."[68] You feel it throughout the journals, where, in Frank Bergon's phrases, at one point the explorers "seem like new men in a new Eden" and at the next confront "monsters and dark powers." But, he argues, all along they betray by many of their actions that the real evil in the garden is their own, and from them "we get sad glimpses of the coming dark side of American imperialism." Yet, that said, Bergon, by an ambivalence of his own, swings from darkness back to light:

> In their timeless struggle through a dominating wilderness, Lewis and Clark present a counterimage to the mythical frontiersman alone in a western land-scape. . . . They are dependent on each other, on the other members of the ex-pedition, on the native peoples of the West, and especially on the natural world through which they pass. . . .
>
> When the expedition finally reaches the Pacific . . ., we see that moment when the whole community—including a black man and an Indian woman—votes on where it wishes to encamp for the winter. Rather than striving to conquer the wilderness, these people learn to make a home within it.[69]

Well, maybe so—at least for that epic moment.

That moment of acknowledged interrelation, even respectful regard, would yield to a quick succession of others of another sort. "It is remarkable," observes J. Golden Taylor, "that in a mere seven decades . . .—the period from the Lewis and Clark expedition to the explorations by John Wesley Powell of the Colorado River and its plateaus and canyons—the unknown, fabulous West should become the known—and largely exploited—West."[70] It may be equally remarkable that Jefferson, for all his anticipatory intelligence, did not foresee the devastation to come—how soon, as Annette Kolodny puts it, "the pastoral impulse found itself danger-ously confused with the myth of progress."[71] Still, his blind-spotted vision of the ·
wilderness may seem less contradictory than that of Lewis (a man whom Ambrose describes as "full of contradictions")[72] or that of present-day authenticity-seekers who trace the expedition's circuit with jetboats, high-tech RVs, and pricy bicycles.

Early on during those seven decades, even as the information journalized by Lewis and Clark was seeping into the realm of public knowledge, the opening Western wilderness was being storied anew, remythologized again by the incred-ible tales told by and about explorer-adventurers such as John Colter. But the most incredible tales began disseminating in the middle of that period, and they told of an entrepreneur who established himself as a larger-than-life folk hero—surely, to adapt White's phrasing, the most popular *second* white man to enter the West—and who endures in legend as a caricature of Daniel Boone: David (Davy) Crockett, whom Faragher dispraises, in distinction to Boone, as "a hater and killer rather than a civilizer or a philosopher."[73] Above all, this Gargantua of the sticks, so en-tertaining to Americans from the 1830s to the 1850s, vividly reveals the fate of Jef-ferson's vision of the West in the generation after his death in 1826. If Boone was ambivalent in his relation to the wilderness, Crockett, more arrogant and consum-ingly destructive, was surely less so—on the surface, anyway. Examining the chiar-oscuro of the dream that Jefferson's vision became, Albanese finds the light shades of its nature religion in the meditative romanticism of Bryant and the dark shades in the "cannibalism" of Crockett.[74]

The "exorbitant fictions," as Albanese calls them, that turned David Crockett the man into Davy Crockett the myth—mostly the former's own self-aggrandizing 1834 text *A Narrative of the Life of David Crockett of the State of Tennessee* and a series of almanacs that began appearing the following year—portray a figure who recalls Enlightenment nature religion but also appears, in his slaying of bears and other wildlife and his ability to "outsavage any savage in hunt or fight," wilder than the wilderness itself.[75] In the *Narrative*, especially, as Slotkin notes, the Crockett persona is self-contradictory—for example, "both vicious Indian killer . . . and friend of the victims of Removal," both "'frontier wastrel'" and bourgeois farmer.[76] Pre-eminently, though, those fictions disclose him as an avid partaker of "the cannibal Eucharist," Slotkin's term for the devouring of "the spirit and substance of the wilderness and the Indian" that was abhorrent to the Puritans in their campaign to exorcise the wild and replace it with New England but was adopted into the mythos of later generations (think of Lewis and Clark eating the wilderness as they plumbed it).[77] As embodied in Crockett, the racist proponent of Manifest Destiny, this fusion of self and wilderness was, Albanese argues, both "the ultimate act of conquest" and "the ultimate form of nature mysticism, an eating in which external foe and victim became internal sustenance."[78]

That Anglo-American variant of common Indian mythology manifests a hunger for the wild, indeed. The hunger was Crockett's, but it was also that of the many immigrants—into Tennessee, the Texas in which the real Crockett died (at the Alamo in 1836), and other portions of the Midwest and West—for whom he was the fictional-mythic delegate. The logic that directed it thus hosted a symbolization by which, in Albanese's formulation, "the war and hunting cannibalism of the forest became the collective political cannibalism of empire." Hence, in the heroic hunter's both celebrating and ingesting nature, she detects a dissonant echo of Jefferson's American sublime—much as I detect one of J. Hector St. John de Crèvecoeur's worry that civilized people's partaking of the wild would make them half savage. She concludes more specifically: "The twisted vision of Crockett and the contorted figures with whom he grappled reflect the twists in a popular American mentality grown arguably overlarge. . . . nature religion had become dominance over the land and, simultaneously, escape and illusion. . . . The Puritan dialectic of fear and fascination had played itself into another key; and the Enlightenment had yielded its rationalism to the powers of the irrational."[79] Like Boone and Lewis and Clark but in a more grotesque and wilderness-gormandizing way, Davy Crockett, canonized by Walt Disney as "King of the Wild Frontier" in the theme song for its 1950s television series about him, was, in several senses, as that ballad from a singularly innocent decade asserts without an inkling of irony, "leadin' the pioneer."[80]

But there are other twists to that twisted vision, and they have to do exactly with Crèvecoeur's worry and with what Crockett's leadin' meant. In a psychohistorical essay on the fictional Crockett, Carroll Smith-Rosenberg analyzes him as a charismatic young man who strongly intrigued "the male Jacksonian imagination"—an independent spirit with a crude conceit of progress, a ruffian clad in animal skins who, with his rough cohort, revolted against an increasingly governmentalized and industrialized society and fled into an ambiguous wilderness where nature was "a chaotic power that simultaneously enticed and demanded taming." Within its context Crockett and his ilk assumed the violent qualities of the animals they were pitted against and consumed. He became, as he often said, half man and half alligator. On at least one occasion he ate an Indian. He, like the frontier itself, straddled classifications: he was "the man turned beast, the white man who scalps Indians, the uncultured civilizer." Finally, of course, as Smith-Rosenberg reminds us, the myth of this oxymoronic bandersnatch is "a joke."[81] But its functional meaning was serious enough to a willing audience. Whatever else it did, Crockett's bizarre myth prompted the plans and guided the actions of many bent on going west.

Mountain Men and Other Explorers: The Vanguard of Western Exploitation

"I was on the 40th Parallel Survey with Clare King," Jefford rattled on. He sounded as though he had gotten into Buchanan's whiskey jug. "I remember our commission still! . . . We were to inform the nation of what it possessed in the way of scenery and minerals. We were opening the West! Well, what has become of the West?"
Oakley Hall, Separations

Howard R. Lamar notes that the goals of Lewis and Clark's painstakingly blueprinted trek "were to prove contradictory." The problem, which I earlier adumbrated in other terms, was that those goals—developing fur trade with the Indians, searching for new farmland, and finding an easy route for commerce with Asia—were inherently at odds. How so? Because, as Lamar articulates the cross-purposes, "developing a fur trade meant preserving the Indian tribes and the wilderness; settling the vast Louisiana Purchase with farmers meant Indian displacement or assimilation and an end to wilderness; developing commerce threatened the status of both Indians and farmers."[1] In the decades to come, many activities would further mesh that web of contradictions, few more, at first, than those of mountain men and, early and late, those of other explorers who entered the West after Lewis and Clark, most of them trailblazers with motives, like Jefferson's, mixed.

"For the American West to come into national consciousness as a concept," according to Lamar, "it had to be invented or defined, then explored, and then occupied and redefined on the basis of actual experience." If, as he argues, Benjamin Franklin, Jefferson, and James Monroe were the "progenitors" of the West's inventors,[2] then the progenitors of its explorers after Lewis and Clark were the mountain men, whose explorations, generally in the name of fur, contributed to bridging the gap between the first and third of those processes (and to blurring them with the second).

Prominent among those hundreds of survival-skilled worthies who, as legend has it, disdained the constraints of both cities and farms and plunged into the wilderness were, in no special order, these: Hugh Glass, handfuls of Bents and Sublettes and Smiths (Jedediah being the most famous), Bill Williams, Jim Baker, Joseph Meek, John McLoughlin. Such men found exhilaration in their audacious and often parlous investigations of the wild (and in the cut-loose celebrations of their annual rendezvous). They got addicted to their woolly lifeway, a point Ian Frazier emphasizes: "A trapper with a good gun and two mules and a partner to share the watch at night was liable to leave the settlements for the West and never look back. . . . Jim Bridger, sometimes called the King of the Mountain Men, first crossed the plains at eighteen, did not return to the settlements until he was thirty-five, stayed a short while, then went back."[3] Of all the white roamers of the nineteenth-century West (a host that included Indian fighters, miners, lawmen, outlaws, gamblers, cowboys, and other itinerants and vagrants), the mountain men were the first. Even after trapping went belly up and many of them, their halcyon two-decade heyday passed, retooled themselves as traders or guides, they were still the most wed to the wild. Whatever their backgrounds, those men had, as Winfred Blevins, echoing the tenor of accounts like George Frederick Ruxton's *Life in the Far West* (1849), briefs it, "gone back to nature" and were "on the way to becoming Indians, with the outlook, habits, cuisine, languages and customs of red men, with red wives and children."[4]

Well, yes and no. If the mountain men went back to nature, most of them also went, so to speak, back to culture—or never actually forsook it. Escape and adventure were reasons for their peregrinations through the wilderness; so were space, solitude, simplicity. Some of them—such as Jim Beckwourth, a mulatto who joined the Crow tribe in the 1820s, married several Crow women, and died among his adopted people in 1866—became Indians in all but racial heritage. But most mountain men always had an ulterior motive, the same one the fur companies for which they trapped had: money. Trapping, especially from the early 1820s until the end of the 1830s, was very profitable, with the fruits of one man's labor for a year bringing him a thousand dollars or more at rendezvous time (which gain usually got squandered in debauchery or wound up in the pockets of company-store suppliers charging extortionate prices). Even marriages to Indian women, however much in another way motivated by hunger for the wild, served the end of profit in the multi-cultural economic networks of trapping and trading, as Richard White and others have shown.[5]

Thus, as Richard Slotkin argues, "the Indian trappings of the Mountain Man concealed his essentially Jacksonian character," a Crockett-like character shaped by an exploitative ethic: "get what you can from the territory, then move on, rely-ing on the bounty of nature to repair the waste of timber or game and to provide those who have been defrauded with the opportunity to renew their fortunes."[6] William H. Goetzmann offers a description with more specificity (and pathos) by taking account of two prevalent stereotypes of the mountain man. In one of those stereotypes he's portrayed as a Byronic outcast in love with the hunt, in the other as merely "a member of the backwoods proletariat" used and abused by fur companies, dependent on London's taste in hats, and symbolic "of a wilderness fast disappearing before the crush of civilization." Goetzmann acknowledges the truth of those stereotypes, but he also spotlights what they neglect: the mountain man's "close resemblance to the common business-oriented people of the time all across the country."[7] What that resemblance shows is that the mountain man was indeed a laissez-faire capitalist—albeit one with more than ordinary mettle, since his profession had a 25 percent mortality rate. Ray Allen Billington, rectifying Eu-ropean novelistic depictions of mountain men as nature's wealth-spurning nobles, employs more judgmental language: their real-world counterparts were "half-civilized illiterates" who "risked their scalps and their lives daily simply because such risks were necessary if they were to amass the fortune of their dreams."[8]

Still, Goetzmann stresses, the mountain man differed from the Spanish ex-plorer, who saw the West as a place to be conquered, and the British explorer, who saw it as a place to be exploited from afar, in that "he looked with imagination and flexibility upon the West." Though a fur trafficker, he was open to other business possibilities—farming, mining, freighting, real estate, and such. Since he likely knew, by personal experience or otherwise, the fate of previous frontiers east of the Mississippi, he tended to see the wilderness "as simply a stage in the civilizing pro-cess—a place to be settled and developed in the future."[9] Though romanticized or self-dramatized as a hero of the wild, he wanted eventually to have Western land of his own to live on and rode point for a domesticating migration—with the Boone-paradox blues not far behind.

Given the often conflicting roles of mountain men—as agents of Manifest Des-tiny, individualistic entrepreneurs, employees of fur companies, storytellers, hus-bands of Indians, on and on—it's no surprise that their loyalties, not just to the people associated with them but to the wilderness itself, were, in White's word, "ambiguous." So in 1807 John Colter was persuaded by a scoundrel named Manuel Lisa to apply the knowledge he'd acquired on Lewis and Clark's expedition to the advantage of Lisa's fur company, soon to be headed by Clark himself (who was also the federal Indian agent for tribes in the West) and succeeded in the early 1820s by what would become the Rocky Mountain Fur Company, which was organized by William Ashley and Andrew Henry, famous for their advertisements, in St. Louis newspapers, for enterprising youths ready to ransack the wilderness—to which invitations many of the mountain men of the time responded. So Jedediah Smith, who worked for—and then for a while was a partner with—Ashley, pursued a career that White offers as illustrative of "the peculiar blend of adventure and business that gave the western fur trade an appeal far greater than its limited economic importance."[10] So Thomas Fitzpatrick, another Ashley man, stumbled on a notch in the Rocky Mountains, later to be called South Pass, that opened up new beaver country and became a floodgate for immigrants on the Oregon Trail.[11] So Jim Bridger, after trapping and exploring for Ashley, guided wagon trains into the West and outlined a trail for the Corps of Topographical Engineers to follow in its survey of the West (part of which trail was later incorporated into the routes of the Overland Stage and the Union Pacific Railroad) and founded a profitable supply post on Blacks Fork of the Green River. So Joe Walker divined the locales not only of beaver for trappers but also of wagon routes for immigrants (including the first one all the way to California) and of gold for prospectors. And so Osborne Russell, though he did his bit to push the beaver toward extinction, was profoundly moved by what he records in his journal as "the wild romantic scenery" of the Lamar River valley.[12]

Despite loyalties that now seem obviously ambiguous, "it is possible," J. Golden Taylor surmises, "that many of the mountain men who became guides did not realize that, ironically, they were aiding in the destruction of the wild, free West they had left civilization to enjoy."[13] It's possible, of course, even probable; but, whatever the degree of their self-awareness, they all, in Elliott West's convincing brief, "helped destroy the way of life that, according to tradition, was the only home for their anarchic souls." First, they trapped beavers as if there were no tomorrow. Then around 1840, when the beaver business collapsed along with the prices that supported it, they became middlemen in the trade between white outposts and Indian camps, the primary product being bison robes Indian women made from the skins of animals Indian men killed—an arrangement that favored intermarriage. And then when, more than once in the West, gold was discovered, "every trader who had the chance jumped into the flow of development." The evidence for such sequential exploitations gives the lie to the distorted remembrance of mountain men "as running away from cities, not building them."[14] All those activities, all that building, depended upon pillaging the wilderness they supposedly esteemed.

The mountain men's building in the wilderness thus involved an ambivalence of attitude, and that ambivalence relates directly to the ambiguousness of their role as middlemen—not just between Indians and whites or fur and money but, more fundamentally, between wild and tame, unknown and known, nature and culture. That ambiguousness goes deeper than—and underlies—the ambiguous loyalties I discussed earlier. Mountain men reveled in the wild, but they also had what Richard C. Poulsen diagnoses as an "obsession with naming the puzzles of geography and terrain—and other anomalies—in a landscape of extremes"; by that practice they were "baptizing mountain, tree, buffalo, beaver, and plain in the image of their own culture"—controlling by denomination, once again. A cognate process of making the hostile friendly and the strange familiar was entailed when the mountain man fashioned himself as half-Indian—another aspect of middlemanship—and by such appropriation in effect fashioned the Indian as half-white. Mountain men acclimated themselves to the anomalies and severities of the West, but through their notorious tale-telling they also made it, by a paradox, "more extreme"—in order to render the enigma of it "usable and believable."[15]

Poulsen finds in ambiguities and paradoxes of this type the manifestation of a loyalty seemingly free of both that explains their ubiquitousness: the mountain man, he argues, was "*always* an emissary for his own culture." He may have been a half-Indian roamer of the Indians' world, but he assessed that world by the indices of its marketability. His occupation as a trapper was never just trapping. It was as well the larger business of searching for land and the opportunities it could afford. Through that search mountain men were able to accomplish something still larger, the affirmation of the culture that commanded their basic loyalty, with signal consequences for the wilderness. They surely did borrow from and adapt to the cultures of Indians and cohabit with them, but, Poulsen stresses, "they returned . . . to a culture they never really left, a culture that dictated how and what they saw in the vastness of western spaces." Because of that mind-set, which prevented their full acculturation as Indians and compelled their return to the white world, they left behind a place transformed into an extension of that space-hungry world. The trappings of mountain men—clothing, powder horn, knife, possible sack, rifle—"have become artifactual (are hollow icons of a past gone forever)," Poulsen perorates, because the men returned.[16] But before they returned, before silk succeeded beaver in the fancies of top-hatted dandies, there must have been many men like the man in William Ranney's 1850 painting The Trapper's Last Shot (and in other, similar oil portrayals), men, in William H. Truettner's exegesis, who were "looking over their shoulder, as if their anxiety echoed that of a nation overextending itself—rushing westward to conquer and exploit land rather than nurture its productive capacity."[17] Men who already knew they would return from nature already being remade in the image of their culture.

At the end of "the era of William H. Ashley and Jedediah Smith," as Goetzmann labels it, "most of the important features of Western geography had been revealed and the Rocky Mountain heartland had been opened up to American exploitation." At the start of the 1830s, a decade framed by the deaths of Smith (by Comanches) in 1831 and Ashley (by pneumonia) in 1838, "a second set of fur-trader explorers appeared"—a set overlapping with the first that included not only Joe Walker and Osborne Russell but also men like Kit Carson, Benjamin Louis Eulalie Bonneville, and Zenas Leonard—and harbingered "the era of Manifest Destiny" (that phrase coined by New York journalist John L. O'Sullivan in 1845).[18] In some ways more adventurers than mountain men, they were succeeded by government surveyors, John Charles Frémont and others, "officials on a mission," as Lyon characterizes them, who before the end of the century would have "corrected and completed the mapping of the West, made it known to all through their reports, and served thus to edge the 'country in the mind' out of the unknown and mythic, toward the account books."[19] Along with such later explorers (literally so, in many instances, and under their auspices), an assortment of scientists, artists, and less official travelers undertook other forms of exploration in the West. Among them all, ambivalent attitudes aligned with mixed motives with respect to the wilderness were the rule.

Carson is a salient case in point. Even a cursory survey of the fiction, biography, and portraiture in other genres and media readily reveals diverse Carsons. The man who was first blessed with fame through Frémont's reports of his exploits as a Hawkeye-like guide—or, as Henry Nash Smith puts it, through "Jessie Benton Frémont's skillful editing of her husband's reports of his exploring expeditions in the early 1840s"—was, according to DeWitt C. Peters's 1858 biography The Life and Adventures of Kit Carson, the Nestor of the Rocky Mountains, from Facts Narrated by Himself, a "pure and noble" person who acquired the wilderness virtues of the mountain men but avoided the savage vices that made them creatures of moral incongruity. This Carson, with amplifications, carries through subsequent biographies by Charles Burdett (in 1862) and John S. C. Abbott (in 1873). But another, less genteel Carson, "the rip-roaring Kit Carson" who fought Indians, slew grizzlies, and the like, turned up in two 1849 novels that inaugurated a different tradition, Emerson Bennett's The Prairie Flower; or, Adventures in the Far West and Charles E. Averill's Kit Carson, the Prince of the Gold Hunters; or, The Adventures of the Sacramento. In Averill's story, Carson is a "gigantic figure" bereft of humility and the purer Carson's "power to commune with nature," an isolated hero in a dreary wasteland.[20] Yet another Carson, if you accept Alex Nemerov's reading of the painting, may be descried in Charles Russell's 1913 oil Carson's Men, which "represent[s] the early western explorer as messianic victim," a Christlike trailblazer, his usefulness past, sacrificed to progress.[21] And, of course, other Carsons—or variations on earlier Carsons—star as protagonists in a number of films produced in the twentieth century. There's also the veridical Carson whom more scrupulous biographers such as Harvey L. Carter, in his "Dear Old Kit": The Historical Christopher Carson (1968), have tried, not without difficulty, to catch.

The fact is that Carson the man was as contradictory in his transactions with the wilderness as would be the frontier Frankenstein you might assemble from characterizations like those above. In the understatement of David Daly and Joel Persky,

Charles M. Russell, Carson's Men (1913): the early Western explorer as a Christlike trailblazer sacrificed to progress. (Gilcrease Museum, Tulsa, Oklahoma.)

his "relationship with the Indians was somewhat inconsistent" since he had at least two Indian wives early in his life and later led ironfisted military operations against the Kiowas and Mescalero Apaches.[22] He may have been a valuable white–Indian go-between and an Indian sympathizer, but he also annihilated a Klamath village. Nature's Nestor, a legend-in-his-own-time hero who would have a national forest named after him, he slaughtered sheep and burned land to deracinate thousands of Navajos (as well as hundreds of Mescalero Apaches)—before forcing them to walk three hundred miles from their homeland of Dinetah to the deprivations of Bosque Redondo in a relocation that resulted in many deaths from exposure, disease, starvation, and other causes.

A failure as a fur trader, an obscure Army officer in whom Andrew Jackson mysteriously took special interest, Bonneville spent five years in the 1830s leading trappers through the Rockies for reasons on which, as Goetzmann notes, "historical opinion . . . has been sharply divided." There's little doubt, however, that, through the information he collected, he promoted national expansion. Certainly that's true also in regard to his sending Walker and a big party of trappers further west, beyond the Great Salt Lake, with the hope that they could discover a trail to California. When they finally descended from the Sierra Nevada—after a ferocious and apparently unwarranted attack on a band of so-called Digger Indians, tough trail breaking, and near-mutiny—they found themselves in the Merced River valley, the first white witnesses of the magnificent falls in what would become Yosemite National Park. Traveling on to the coast, "they were continually dazzled" by everything from towering redwoods to the pounding Pacific itself. Dazzled they may have been, but Walker and his party also saw California as "potentially the province of the American settler."[23] Leonard, Walker's clerk during this 1833 expedition, nicely exemplifies that double reaction: in his account of California, first published in book form in 1839, he tells both of his wonderment—so convincingly that Richard Dankleff, in his poem "California," writes that Leonard "rose up in his stirrups marveling"[24]—and of "this vast waste of territory" and "what a theme [it is] to contemplate its settlement and civilization."[25]

Few scientists and artists ventured into the West in the very early nineteenth century—there were none, for example, in Lewis and Clark's party. However, when they began to go there, most notably as members of Major Stephen H. Long's 1820 expedition up the Platte River to the Rockies (which included artists Samuel Seymour and Titian Peale and geologist Augustus E. Jessup and zoologist Thomas Say, among others), their work instanced and encouraged what Goetzmann terms "a new kind of contrapuntal image of the West," one certain to engender ambiguities: "To the artist and the scientist, European and American alike, the West was important not as a place for settlers and civilization; it was important as a source of new experiences, new data, new sensations, and new questions. . . . For many who had no need to hack home and farm out of the sod, it represented the very symbol of the good life." The effect of that image was the casting of "serious doubt, at least for a time, upon the validity of the slogans of Manifest Destiny."[26]

That doubt would flourish indeed only for a time and tentatively—though it would never quite fade away and later would return in other forms—because there soon came another wave of explorers, most of them, in Goetzmann's words, "soldier-engineers trained at West Point." Supplementing the knowledge of mountain men with new maps and topographic surveys, they sought solutions to "the problems of settlement on the widest possible scale"—very much matters of expansionist politics.[27] In concert with them and behind them advanced the hackers, Americans, as Lamar sums them up, who "came to know and want the mysterious and different western lands described by these explorers."[28] But, abristle with ambivalent feelings about the wilderness, they too were implicated in ambiguities, ones related to those Goetzmann adumbrated above.

Apart from Lewis and Clark, the precursor of Long and the scientists, artists, soldier-engineers, and other explorers who followed him was Zebulon M. Pike. Subsequent to his leading an expedition from St. Louis to the Rockies and then down the upper Río Grande in 1806, he made the assertion, later confirmed by Long, that the Western plains were too arid to be farmed and thus weren't suitable for white habitation. Thereby originating the myth of the Great American Desert (a myth both truthful, given the agricultural technology of his day, and stocked with sobering intimations that soon enough were ignored), he also set in motion afresh the dialectic of the West-as-desert myth and the more assuring West-as-garden myth. It was a dialectic that prefigured variations, none ever resolved, in his successors' attitudes toward the wilderness.

Long's confirmation, in his 1823 report, of the limits to the dream of the West as Eden may have discouraged some of those Anglo-Americans whom Frederick Turner typifies as "citizens who meant to grab lands and then clear them of all vestiges of nature," but it also renewed thinking about the plains as a dump for uncivilizable Indians east of the Mississippi and helped rationalize the forced migrations sanctioned by the Removal Act of 1830.[29]

Long's position was anathema to expansion-minded Frémont, who promoted settlement in the West almost as much as he promoted himself. While Long believed that the inhospitable plains would moderate America's westward sweep, Frémont, reporting (with the assistance of his wife's romanticizations) on his expeditions to the Rockies in 1842 and to Oregon and California during the next two years, discounted the drawbacks of the West and overstated its advantages. Indeed, as Goetzmann and Goetzmann note, his boosting of California—which could be reached either by boat (and, if you wanted to short-cut the loop around Cape Horn, a less-than-first-class crossing of the Isthmus of Panama) or by overland trails like those he had mapped—made it "seem a pastoral paradise ripe for the taking."[30]

Such rhetoricating helped pump up the lust that drove hundreds of thousands of settlers (along with miners, land speculators, and others) into California and Oregon over the next quarter-century—though it had less effect on immigration into other areas of the West. Granted that Frémont, unlike Long, usually wasn't sensible about—or sensitive to—the desert environment of the West, he still did occasionally have, in Lyon's phrase, "an enjoyment of mountain wilderness." When he forgot for a moment his membership in the Army Corps of Topographical Engineers or let his booster mask slip, he could be as disarmed by admiration as Lewis and Clark sometimes had been. The Wind River Range in Wyoming, for instance, "seemed to speak to him in terms quite other than the march-tempo tunes of manifest destiny, future railroads, and future mines which he heard nearly everywhere else" during his 1840s expeditions.[31] His response is illustrated (if we may trust the wife-mediated text) by his extolling the Wind Rivers for how they "impress the mind" with their "savage sublimity of naked rock."[32] As Lyon dryly observes, however, though he "saw a lot of wilderness, and was impressed by it," he wasn't "detained."[33]

Not the most eccentric scientist to visit the West (that honor probably should go to botanist Thomas Nuttall, an unworldly Brit as unsuited to the early-nineteenth-century West as you could imagine), John James Audubon nevertheless was paradigmatically contradictory in his views of the wilderness. As an artist, he saw it as a biotic Shangri-La; as a naturalist, he saw it as a source of specimens to be killed, stuffed, and carried away for scrutiny in more civilized surroundings. In 1843, at Fort Union, he seems to have lost his sense of balance between the two views, for he briefly became an ardent buffalo hunter—but then later expressed sorrow over the unrestrained slaughter of buffalo well under way before he died in 1851.

When William Hemsley Emory, then a lieutenant in the Topographical Engineers, completed his 1846 investigation of the Southwest, which he had conducted between Fort Leavenworth, on the Missouri, and San Diego, he compiled notes he would submit to Congress at the end of the Mexican War. While those notes, which contained the first reliable scientific information about the area, made clear his commitment to Manifest Destiny, they also made clear a problem that would vex Powell thirty years later: the ordained settlement pattern based on a gridwork of 160-acre tesserae was at odds with the character of land so dry that farming could be done only near its infrequent and nonrectilinear water resources. As Goetzmann points out, Emory recognized (though Powell, Goetzmann claims, didn't) that the problem involved issues of politics as well as of practicability, for any approach to the planned use of water in the West would clash with "the basic Jeffersonian agrarian philosophy of the independent entrepreneur"[34]—a recognition hard lessons would bring home to Bureau of Reclamation functionaries in the twentieth century.

Translations of the garden-desert dialectic may be discerned in the attitudes and values associated with other nineteenth-century surveyors of the West. Howard Stansbury, who surveyed the Great Salt Lake and the desert around it in 1849, though dedicated to his mission as a captain in the Topographical Engineers, was keenly aware of the wild beauty that settlement could wreck. When Clarence King was surveying California in the mid-1860s, he dreamt of railroad tracks from the Great Plains to the Pacific; but he also portrays the geology of the arid West, especially in his 1872 book *Mountaineering in the Sierra Nevada*, with a literary responsiveness to its peculiarities rivaling that of John McPhee.[35] Scientifically minded Powell may have fancied himself a romantic conqueror of the Colorado after he explored that waterway to the end of the Grand Canyon (the Great Unknown to most Americans of the time) in 1869 and went on to help bureaucratize the surveying of the West, but he also recognized both that the place's aridity required (though it would never see put into effect) land policies far more environmentally attuned than those applied in the East and that the most beautiful parts needed to be protected from ranchers and railroaders.[36] However much his wide-ranging surveys of the Great Plains in the late 1860s informed him of their implacable dryness, Ferdinand V. Hayden endorsed (to his later embarrassment) the theory, imported from Europe and propounded by Cyrus Thomas, a botanist and entomologist in his 1869 party (by then titled the U.S. Geological Survey of the Territories), that "rain follows the plow"—that, as more and more settlers tilled Western land, rainfall, by an obscure causality, would increase.[37]

Among all the nineteenth-century surveyors, Clarence E. Dutton may have been the most alert to the treacheries of that dialectic. In his critical assessment of Dutton's *Tertiary History of the Grand Cañon District* (1882), Lyon remarks that he "raises an epistemological and aesthetic point which, in the works of subsequent writers about western wilderness, has become an important theme: that which is totally wild cannot be easily assimilated into the prepared categories of civilized perception. In fact, it will be distorted by them." Heedful of that distortion, Dutton endeavored to nurture in himself an apprehension of "terrain-as-it-is" that would enable him to write of it without recourse to a long tradition of conventions such as giving Christian names to natural features. As a result, his accounts of geological phenomena in the Grand Canyon startle with their freshness. He failed to perfect such apprehension, but by his cognitive swerve he at least "avoided any explicit comments in the area of the dialectic which has, from the beginnings of American literature, been suggested by the opposition of civilization and wilderness."[38] If his commendable, albeit psychologically exacting, example had been commonly followed, the subsequent history of the West might have been quite different.

While the purpose of surveyors' explorations of the West was to render its crooked concreteness into abstract and neat linear representations, the purpose of artists' explorations was to create vividly concrete and particularized representations of a world unfamiliar, except as an abstraction, to most people living outside it. The latter purpose, like the former, however, tended to gradate into other purposes, so that the resultant artworks betray contradictory or ambivalent attitudes toward the wilderness and its inhabitants. Indeed, Seymour and Peale were so overwhelmed by it that their dedication to precise depiction quickly lost ground to fired-up imagination—a slipping of emphasis illustrated by Seymour's *Distant View of the Rocky Mountains* (1823), a painting at once pragmatically pictorial and infused with awe that served, in the form of an aquatint, as a frontispiece for the report on Long's expedition. "None of the topographical artists," Goetzmann and Goetzmann argue, "was really able to be objective." That generalization holds true for most of their successors in the nineteenth century. American science and art of the time were idealized as having "a symbiotic relationship"; but it wasn't an entirely concordant one because, in a point Goetzmann and Goetzmann make repeatedly, though artists went west with the intention of accurate documentation, "so stunned were they by what they saw—ranging from rock formations to immense herds of buffalo—that they inevitably produced romanticized interpretations of the unknown territory."[39]

In the early nineteenth century those interpretations, as Barbara Novak makes clear, were shaped by ideas projected onto nature that were increasingly variegated and complex, replete with unresolved contradictions. At least four such ideas were in vogue: "nature as Primordial Wilderness, as the Garden of the World, as the original Paradise," and as "the regained Paradise" America was awaiting. It was a labile brew whose intermixed mutability gave rise to a situation in which each artist could interpret nature "according to his needs." That situation and the evolution of the art—for Novak, landscape painting—it influenced occurred at the same time that much wilderness was being unremittingly destroyed. Responding to that destruction, artists of the time, painting along the Hudson or beyond the Missouri, helped preserve "the last evidences of the golden age of wilderness";[40] yet many of their interpretations, most notably those of the West, because of the individual needs and contradictory ideas governing them, consciously or unconsciously fostered ideology that was anything but favorable to preservation.

Although not as venal and obvious in that fostering as the works of some later artists—Albert Bierstadt, for instance—those of George Catlin suffice to demonstrate the way it operates. During the 1830s he traveled all over the northern and southern plains, creating hundreds of paintings of Indians, their villages, ceremonies, games, natural environs. As an ethnologist and collector of artifacts, he was interested in recording Indian lifeways, but his painterly imagination, coupled with his moral sympathies, transported him outside science. Attracted by the exotica of societies foreign to his own, Catlin, in Goetzmann's characterization, "became a primitive limner of the redman's world, not only documenting in concrete detail everything he saw, but managing to capture the romanticism and nobility of an Indian culture as yet unspoiled by the white man." His passion for the panoply of a world soon to be minified impelled his efforts as a defender of it and a critic of the forces civilizing it. He was "a naturalist who loved nature."[41] He loved especially the people his pigments saved for posterity, and yet in subtle and unintentional ways he colluded in their exploitation and demise.

How did that happen? It happened because Catlin in one crucial respect differed little from most white Americans, including artists, who, in Julie Schimmel's predication, "perceived Indians through the assumptions of their own culture." As his portraits reveal, he perceived Indians in terms of "a portrait process that cherishes individuality, material status, and vanity—all notions less highly regarded in Indian culture." But additional preconceptions distinguished his relationship to his subjects, and they have bearing on the then-prevalent idea that Indians, like those amiable Noble Savages posed agaze in various directions in Charles Bird King's 1822 studio oil *Young Omahaw, War Eagle, Little Missouri, and Pawnees*, "could perhaps be persuaded by rational argument as well as the formidable presence of the United States government to abandon tribal tradition for a more civilized lifestyle."[42]

Catlin's portraits sometimes almost unnoticeably harbor the telltales of such preconceptions, but you can easily find them, with Schimmel's assistance, in a pair of portraits of Osages, Romantic in style, he did in 1834, *Cler-mónt, First Chief of the Tribe* and *Wáh-chee-te, Wife of Cler-mónt, and Child*:

The two adults assume conventional poses. . . . But Catlin's subjects are placed outdoors; their home is not in the city but in nature. The attire and hairstyles of husband and wife suggest their "natural" state. . . . Yet neither is the couple uncivilized. Clermont may wear leggings and hold a war club fringed with scalp locks, but his war trophies, brass armlet, and wampum earrings are as decorative as they are menacing. . . . His threat as warrior is further diminished by his passive seated pose and by the peace medal hung around his neck. . . . Wáh-chee-te has been similarly, if more highly, touched by civilization. Although still "primitive," her demeanor is gentle.[43]

Catlin's Indians are somewhat literary, Rousseauian, in a measure tamed, co-opted, prepared for citizenship and abandonment of the world he deemed worth saving. Such summary may oversimplify a mite, and Catlin did paint some less pretty and more authentic pictures (of buffalo hunts, scalpings, ceremonial mutilations, and so on); but in none of his visual pieces did this artist who was ever a commercial showman—ultimately one in favor of Christianizing Indians—really show the cost, through disease and other destructive agencies, of bringing Anglo civilization to people whose welfare he sincerely had at heart.[44] (An arguable exception is his late–1830s cartoonlike painting titled, with some variations, Pigeon's Egg Head (The Light), Going to and Returning from Washington, which depicts, by before-and-after images, the corruption of the Assiniboine chief Wi-jún-jon by civilization.)

A more talented painter, Karl Bodmer, who with his sponsor, Prince Maximilian of Wied-Neuwied, traveled further up the Missouri in the 1830s than Catlin did, may have committed a similar sin by overemphasizing the exotic beauties of at-risk Plains Indians while neglecting the coarsenesses of frontier life among the traders. Alfred Jacob Miller, an escapist painter, is perhaps equally culpable because of his dreamy pastoralizing of Indians and their environment and his making the mountain man (despite knowledge of behavior at rendezvous) into a figure that would captivate latter-day imitators, what Goetzmann and Goetzmann term "the Anglo 'noble savage.'"[45] Certainly the celebration of idealized Western nature in Thomas Moran's late-nineteenth-century paintings of the Grand Canyon was compromised by their placement, through an advertising agreement that granted him free travel and lodging, in the parlor cars and other properties of the Atchison, Topeka and Santa Fe Railroad, which wasn't in the business of leaving wilderness untouched.[46] ("One's soul is shaken by contradictory thoughts and feelings," Alexis de Tocqueville wrote, perhaps apropos of such gestures, while traveling through Michigan in 1831 and meditating on its timbered wild: "Thoughts of the savage, natural grandeur that is going to come to an end become mingled with splendid anticipations of the triumphant march of civilization.")[47]

George Catlin, Cler-mónt, First Chief of the Tribe (1834): an Indian who is "natural" but not uncivilized. (Smithsonian American Art Museum, gift of Mrs. Joseph Harrison Jr.)

Indictable here also, of course, is Bierstadt, whose highly commercialized career of painting big canvases of a picturesque West is epitomized by his six-by-ten-foot 1873 oil *Donner Lake from the Summit*, a promotional painting commissioned by Collis P. Huntington, one of the four partners who launched the Central Pacific Railroad, that proffers the splendor of a Sierra Nevada unchanged, except for unobtrusive snowsheds in the middle distance, by the digging and blasting required

George Catlin, Wáh-chee-te, Wife of Cler-mónt, and Child (1834): an Indian who is "primitive" but gentle in demeanor. (Smithsonian American Art Museum, gift of Mrs. Joseph Harrison Jr.)

to make a rail path through spiring rock. Some artifice of subject might be expected from a painter who did his grand-manner works in the studio, contrived what Hans Huth calls "composite scenes," and titled them with the names of nonexistent places.[48] There's also an artifice of technique, however, and it's ideologically more foreboding for the wilderness and its denizens. In his critique of Bierstadt, Lee Clark Mitchell finds the mythic landscapes in his popular paintings of the 1860s

Albert Bierstadt, Emigrants Crossing the Plains *(1867): the effect of aesthetic taming. (Oil on canvas, 60 x 96 in. 1972.19. Museum Permanent Collection, National Cowboy and Western Heritage Museum, Oklahoma City, Oklahoma.)*

and 1870s marked by an "overaestheticization [that] suggests a theatricalizing of experience, transforming the West into a safe stage set, thereby assuaging the viewer's potential uneasiness about the unknown"—a technique appropriate for an artist enthusiastic about the West as a spectacle to be consumed by railroad travelers. The effect of such aesthetic taming, in paintings from *The Rocky Mountains, Lander's Peak* (1863) to *Mount Whitney* (1875), is the creation of "a cosmic drama always on the verge of becoming moral and social"[49]—which is to say, civilized. In its implications for Indians, that effect is perhaps most remarkable in a painting Mitchell doesn't consider, Bierstadt's *Emigrants Crossing the Plains* (1867), at the center of which an Indian village is smothered by all the golden Western light toward which the settlers and livestock in the foreground are advancing. Scarcely dangerous, it's as good as gone.

Like other ironies I have discussed, those through which the artistic representation of the Western wilderness forwarded its spoliation are, by the retrospective character of ironies, far more evident to us, even as we perpetuate them, than they were to their original perpetrators—a concession that sanctions some forgiveness. Still, the posthumous prize for such ironies has to go to the team of photographer William H. Jackson and Moran, both of whom produced depictions of the Mountain of the Holy Cross in the Colorado Rockies, a mountain with snow-filled fissures on its peak that form a white cross. In 1873 Jackson, accompanying Hayden's

156. MOUNTAIN OF THE HOLY CROSS.

William H. Jackson, Mountain of the Holy Cross (Colorado) (1873): God and nature wed in an image signifying God's blessing on the westward course of empire.

surveyors, took a photograph of it, a picture that, in Goetzmann and Goetzmann's explication, "wedded God and Nature in a single frame." Upon seeing the photograph, Moran decided to paint the same scene, made an arduous climb to get the right view (a longer one than Jackson's), did a sketch, and in 1875 finished a Bierstadt-size oil. When the two famous works were displayed together to adoring crowds at the Centennial Exposition in Philadelphia the following year, the romantically sublime peak "became an archetypal image of a Christian nation, an outward sign that God himself had blessed the westward course of empire."[50] Whether that image—the consummation of the idea, as Novak puts it, "of the West as a 'natural church,'" a prosaic trope by then, as characteristic of Clarence King's writing as of Bierstadt's painting[51]—was a sign that He had blessed also the empire's westward curse was a question for future artists to engage.

Similar ironies arise in nineteenth-century travel narratives. You can find a plethora of them in the texts of visitors to the West like Washington Irving, Thomas H. Gladstone, and Robert Louis Stevenson. Exemplary—but maybe not altogether typical—is The Oregon Trail, Francis Parkman's 1849 chronicle of his 1846 trip from St. Louis into wilderness far beyond the frontier towns along the Missouri. He witnessed in those towns what Taylor calls "a surprising and ironic array of the contradictions between civilization and the wild brought together,"[52] but his narrator views them, in A. Carl Bredahl Jr.'s phrase, "through romantic lenses"—as he will later view the disconcertingly wilder world of Indians. Because of those lenses, "the imagination shaping *The Oregon Trail* linguistically encloses itself from involvement with the physical experience" of what's encountered and idealizes in more comfortable Eastern terms. The upshot is that, though the book is attentive to experiential details, "permeating both construction and thought is the enclosed stance of an individual who came West in order to reinforce eastern superiority."[53]

As the nineteenth century churned on and bold exploration of the West gave way to safer, more rapid movement through it and epidemic tourism succeeded supposedly mind-broadening travel, the old perceptual limitation held and redoubled. American tourism, an industry beginning in the East and spreading west during the early part of the century, was, as Hal K. Rothman argues, from its inception a self-fulfilling activity: "It worked to confirm the understanding that people already had about the world around them." By dint of that confirmation, travelers heading west after reading Cooper or Charles Brockden Brown or guidebooks and other sources of information saw what their culture told them they would see. After the Civil War, when trans-Mississippi tourism started to boom, the West thus became "a place less real than a representation of qualities missing in mainstream society." In quest of those qualities—all of them aspects of wildness—tourists there at that time traveled quite differently than Lisa, Catlin, Prince Maximilian, and others did earlier, but they had in common with their predecessors—"prototourists," as Rothman dubs them—the fact that they went to the West to apply the elite interpretive conventions of another world. As a result of that contradictory intention, the West seemed to them "knowable yet incomprehensible."[54]

And so what befell the Wild West because of all the exploration—commercial, scientific, artistic, and otherwise—that began in the early nineteenth century and both climaxed and began anew with the completion of the surveys?

One answer to that question may be discovered in *Separations*, Oakley Hall's novel, set in the 1880s, about, among other things, the exploration of the Grand Canyon by the rapacious railroader Charles P. Daggett, a man, given to singing Verdi's *Rigoletto* while steering his boat through the Colorado's white water, who is emblematic of "the whole daring of western exploration, of violent men taming the West and big men civilizing it." Such flatulence aside, however, it's apparent from the grumblings of some members of his party that the West "'has gone rich man/poor man like the East'" and that the opening of it, which "'was like the dawn of the world,'" has quickly led to chewed-up mountains, desolated valleys, and the like—with more to come.[55]

Another answer may be discovered in *The Abstract Wild*, Jack Turner's cri de coeur about the loss of wilderness in the West and elsewhere. The surveys, he laments, "redescribed" the land in a manner that created the template for rectangular farms, parks, reservations, counties, states, as well as towns and cities that, seen from the air, look like computer-chip matrices—geography rationalized, ordered, controlled by pioneer values that made it possible "to sell the grid for cash," with the result that "the places long sacred to the indigenous population simply vanished behind the grid, behind lines arrogantly drawn on paper. With the places gone, the sense of place vanished too—just disappeared."[56] Powell's ill portents come true—and more direly so those of the indigenous population, which, watching the surveyors' instruments cut up their living places, felt, in Angie Debo's words, "the horror of dismemberment."[57]

Another answer to the question of what befell the Wild West is that it became "the Wild West," places—or ghosts, vestiges, or reconstitutions of places behind the grid—touristically exploited for their natural beauties and historical redolences, turned into iconic playgrounds for equivocal impulses, pre-Disneyland theme parks.

Howbeit, there was (and may still be), to reformulate Wallace Stegner's oft-repeated phrase, hope for saving as places part of all that geography not just gridded by greed and sold but inventoried almost down to the last swale, arroyo, and boulder within the lifetime of Bridger, that tough-as-nails mountain man who died, blind and long absent from mountains, on a Missouri farm, the kind of tame milieu of drudgery he'd once shunned, in 1881. The hope resided in the fact that, as White assures us, early explorers and scientists in the West did experience "enchantment, and it sometimes carried them away from the utilitarian ends for which their investigations were intended." It resided in the fact that some of those men were able to apprehend the wilderness as more than a warehouse to be robbed and even "began to speak the language of ecological interdependence."[58] It resided in the fact that neither that enchantment nor that language was dead in 1881. And it resided in the fact that both together signaled the possibility, however faint, of what Frank Waters, in his 1946 book The Colorado, calls "the deepening relationship of a people to their earth." The truth of that relationship was still available in 1881, as it was also in the 1940s, when Waters could "read [it] here in this vast heart of America, the upland basin of the Colorado. In the conquerors, whom it defeated. In the padres, whom it rejected. In the trappers, who overcame the land physically and were caught by it psychically." Moreover, he continues, with a relevance that ought to have set the spirits of those with ears to hear humming like tuning forks in resonance, "the secret of its hold upon us is the treasure the prospectors sought. Until we find it—the profound and haunting secret of the reciprocal relationship that must exist between man and land—we will still remain outcasts."[59]

Perhaps, if we today decide, as T. S. Eliot writes in "Little Gidding," that "we shall not cease from exploration" of the West—by which I mean deeper, more comprehensive exploration—we yet will find that reconciling secret. If we do, we'll no longer be outcasts; then, as goes the poem's prophecy, ironic but positively so,

the end of all our exploring
Will be to arrive where we started
And know the place for the first time.[60]

Inventing the Indian:
The Noble Savage

*There's horror in the act of invasion and, for conquerors, a need to compensate
through willed ignorance and sentimental distortion.*
    C. L. Rawlins, review of "Why I Can't Read Wallace Stegner" and Other
    Essays: A Tribal Voice, by Elizabeth Cook-Lynn

In 1621, after suffering the deprivations and deaths of their first winter in the New
World, the Pilgrims were visited by an Indian named Samoset, the last member of
a tribe wiped out by sickness earlier imported across the Atlantic. They cloaked his
naked back. He spoke to them in broken English of his lost folk and their home east
of Plymouth, along the coast. Then he departed, promising to return with a powerful sachem and a more fluent speaker of English. In several days he did return, with
Massasoit, the Wampanoag sachem, and Squanto, soul survivor of his tribe, whose
English was sufficient to expedite, through Massasoit, a treaty between the Indians
and the whites. The latter, after months of Indian help, gathered their first harvest
and held a feast attended by Massasoit and many of his people.

So runs the grade-school legend of the beginning of that white holiday on which
God is offered gratitude for his providence and the land's provender, but that legend embeds another, what Frederick Turner calls "the utilitarian legend of the
Good Indian: faithful, a little doglike in his patience and kindness, teaching the
whites how to plant their corn and where to take fish, serving as their interpreter as
they penetrated 'unknown places for their profit.' A very prerapine Caliban."[1] And
also, apparently, an avatar of a ripening concept arisen from the customarily mixed
European perceptions of Indians: the Noble Savage.

That concept, which wouldn't come to full fruition until the eighteenth century,
wasn't, of course, one Bradford and company normally favored, however useful
they found friendly Indians, by a lopsided treaty, to be; any of the Pilgrims who
flirted with it later in the seventeenth century probably were disabused by King Philip's War in 1675–76 (especially since Philip was, like Massasoit, a Wampanoag).
But the concept would otherwise hang on, through varying accentuations and regardless of anthropological degaussing, all the way to the present, and the sundry
images that embody it thus constitute a heritage of ambivalence, part and parcel of
that toward the civilized and the wild, regarding exactly the two terms of the oxy-

moronic phrase that names it, the *noble* and the *savage*. First in the East, then in the West, it would be one of the concepts employed, more and more problematically, in an attempt to define the "authentic" Indian as a timeless being living in what Elliott West calls the "historical limbo"[2] of a wilderness that seemed static to both the Spanish, who (like the French) by and large were intent on the religious conversion of people they thought culturally deficient and on the joint Euro-Indian occupation of land, and the English, who tended to want the Indians, by turns, banished, assimilated into invisibility, or at least safely peripheralized. It was a concept associated with the proposition that, to paraphrase Thoreau, wildness is another kind of civilization—and with its flip side, that civilization is another kind of wildness.

In seventeenth-century Europe, however, that concept was pretty much a nonstarter. Evidence was mounting that the natives of the New World might not be "civilizable." Diversity reigned among opinions about their subhumanity, morality, manageability. Many expansionists believed that, as Ray Allen Billington has it, "a holy crusade of extermination was justified." Though quandaries abounded, the dominant view of the learned was rationalist: the civilized was superior to the primitive; nature needed to be tamed by intelligence. Persistent into the eighteenth century and beyond was the idea, propounded by George Louis Leclerc, comte de Buffon, and others, that Europeans were better qualified to occupy the Americas than Indians too dependent on nature. That idea was a component of a fashionable "revolt against the glorification of Nature" visible even in the design of seventeenth- and early-eighteenth-century gardens, and it "doomed the Indians to a Hobbesian state of perpetual chaos."[3] It didn't weaken in its persuasiveness until its excesses were countered by the nature-worshipping Romanticism that emerged during the late eighteenth century and was in full swing by its end, at which time praise of the Indian's natural nobility was on many a European poet's tongue.

The invention and popularization of the Noble Savage stereotype usually are attributed to Jean Jacques Rousseau.[4] As Geoffrey Symcox has shown, however, that creature, whose tradition Columbus and the New World chronicler Bartolomé de las Casas augmented centuries before, had been around awhile when Rousseau adopted him. Rousseau re-emotionalized a Wild Man figure that by the eighteenth century already had been rendered "refined and rational" and conducted a "study of primitive man [that] was not an idealization of his subject, but . . . was nonetheless an indictment of the overelaborate society in which he lived."[5]

Indeed, the Noble Savage was a concept that had been kicked around since at least the time of the ancient Greeks and expressed a perennial nostalgia for an earlier state of human innocence. By the late eighteenth century it was polished enough that a French philosophe (Rousseau, Diderot, Voltaire) could use it as a touchstone for criticizing his own corrupt society or for recommending its reformation (though not its reversion to savagery). Or that an Anglo-American could use it for picturing Indians not as the ignoble and mostly intractable beasts that affrighted the colonials of a previous age but as beings of sensibility amenable to management and exploitation.

Despite that seeming clarity, the significance of the concept at its apogee was a muddle that made for debate. To what extent was the syncretized Noble Savage no more than, as Montaigne and others in the sixteenth century posited him, a Wild Man antitype of depraved courtly or urban life? To what extent did he still abide within the civilized breast? How rational or wise or sentimental was he? Was he merely a wish-fulfilling hypostasis of contradictions implicit in the Baroque and then the Rococo imagination of Europe? Such interrogatory currents and cross-currents were characteristic not only of the late Enlightenment but of the whole stretch of "the transitional period between the medieval and the modern ages," as Hayden White designates it, during which "many thinkers took a more ambivalent position, on both the desirability of idealizing the Wild Man and the possibility of escaping civilization."[6]

Much of that debate centered on the Indian of the New World, and its main issue, in James K. Folsom's condensation, was a fundamental question: "Was this classic 'man in a state of nature' a 'noble savage,' as good primitivist theory would have it, or was he, as actual contact in the field suggested, merely a savage whose nobility was presumed rather than demonstrated?"[7] Though the reports of seventeenth-century French Jesuit missionaries in Canada about the Indian as the prototypical Noble Savage had artfully and optimistically discounted what Symcox calls "his more obviously disturbing features" and inspired some European thinkers to take an affirmative view of "his progress from ambivalent primitiveness to nobility,"[8] others, more Puritan in mind-set, were less sanguine about nature, in Richard Slot-kin's simile, "as the vehicle of civilized European values." So Americans reading the literature of late-eighteenth-century Europe found two dominant stereotypes of themselves and the Indians: the image of "the good Quaker and the good savage" and that of "degeneracy, whose chief signs were intermarriage and amalgamation." Clearly the images differed, but Slotkin argues that they shared, among other features, an association of the Indian with the unconscious. Correlate with the stereotypes thus were two theoretical schools. Proponents of the good-savage theory considered the unconscious innately good and trustworthy when curbed by the intellect. Proponents of the degeneracy theory believed the intellect too weak to control the unconscious, which they deemed the dark wellspring of human bestiality. The schools diverged correspondingly in their teleological forecasts: "For the proponents of the degeneracy theory, the marriage myth-metaphor . . . presaged the biological and moral decline of the [white] race in America. Those who took the pastoral view . . . saw the outcome as a natural movement of all Americans toward a republican-arcadian polity."[9]

Whether or not miscegenation was taken into account, during the eighteenth century Americans grappled more and more with what Roy Harvey Pearce states as "the problem of the relation of savage to civilized life." It occasioned plenty of ambivalence-laced questions, especially as its pertinence, like American society, moved west: "How hold to a God-ordained moral absolute and to an assurance of common humanity, and still understand whatever good there might be in savage societies? How relate that good to the obviously greater good of civilized societies? How believe in two ideas of order?" The enigmas of what came to be known as savagism led Benjamin Franklin "to make primitivism into a game" and compelled J. Hector St. John de Crèvecoeur in his *Letters from an American Farmer* to concoct a sanitized Indian, among other oddities. Such responses were attempts to defend the soft fantasy of the Noble Savage against the hard fact of unnobly westering civilization. Around the end of the eighteenth century, American poetasters like Josias Lyndon Arnold, William Prichard, and Sarah Wentworth Morton took sides pro and con primitivism and presented Indians accordingly stereotyped in poems that instantiated two contradictory themes: "the Indian as nature's nobleman, perhaps superior to his civilized conquerors; and the Indian as subhuman, waiting fiercely to be wiped out."[10] As time would show, these two themes could, with some philosophical tinkering, be melded into a makeshift solution to an overarching problem.

Whatever the complexities that sprang from their interrelationship, each of those themes, along with its respective image, was at base, to borrow nomenclature from Lawrence Buell, a way of "simplifying"—as well as "exoticizing"—Indians that "abetted the 'otherization' of the 'native.'"[11] Paradoxically, of course, Anglo-American otherization of the Indian, by either ennoblement or damnation, was but a method of trying to categorize conveniently people who constituted, in Richard C. Poulsen's words, "perhaps the most unnerving puzzle of all on the western landscape."[12] The two images generated by otherization determined not just who Indians were for Anglos but how they might be handled. Those images, though, had been in conflict with one another, each, as Gary B. Nash notes, "wrestling for ascendance," since the first colonies were established. The image of the backward yet friendly Indian the English sometimes entertained derived from both utopian hope and desire for trade, but, Nash stresses, that creation "could never blot from the English mind the image of the hostile savage." Of course, imagining the Indian in the latter mode availed "a way of predicting the future and preparing for it and of justifying what one would do."[13]

As such ominousness suggests, the matter most relevant to these images, first in the East and then in the West as well, wasn't trade or treachery but ownership of land. In that respect, to follow Nash's analysis, there were two ways to deal with the Indians. One way was to acknowledge their humanity, share land with them, and extend to them the benefits, particularly Christianity, of Euro-American culture. The other was to take their land by the argument that savages weren't equipped to possess it. By the late eighteenth century, when Euro-Americans populated the verge of the full West, "the colonial intelligentsia" may have been sympathetic to the first way, but "the ordinary farmer and frontiersman found less and less to admire in Indian life" and were growing more committed to the second.[14] Though the Noble Savage thrived in art at that time, there were maturing doubts about his actuality.

In the early nineteenth century, as the expansionist zeitgeist intensified, the conflict of those two images was getting partly resolved. In the first quarter of the century, to follow Pearce's time line, the Indian's noncivilized life was taken as an example for measuring how far American civilization had evolved from such a condition. In the second quarter, however, the mood of that exemplification shifted from indicative to imperative, for by then Americans pushing beyond the Mississippi, like their ancestors pushing beyond the Atlantic coast, were acutely aware of the dangers waiting, "should they venture west toward noncivilization." They had come to affirm strongly the importance of their own culture; by the rationale of that affirmation, Indians constituted not so much an image as a counterimage—of "what Americans should not be." Thus Americans convinced themselves they were morally right in their advance, a necessity since "only with such conviction—cruel, illogical, and self-indulgent as it was—could they move on."[15]

There was, of course, ambivalence in this state of affairs, but frontier pragmatism muted it. The pioneers' response to the West was, as Roderick Nash tells us, a complicated mixture of "appreciation and repulsion," but they, like many fur traders, were far from literal-minded about the Noble Savage. "Contact with the red man," in his summation, "served to undermine their Romantic hopes."[16] That assessment is echoed by West's conclusion that, for most new migrants to the mid-century West, Indians "might be allowed some fuzzy, abstract nobility, but face-to-face, as potential neighbors, they were considered somewhere between marginally tolerable and barely human."[17] Even in her less peremptory analysis of attitudes toward the Indian in the mid-1850s, Julie Schimmel urges us "to remember that one person's Noble Savage was hopelessly indolent to another, and that white audiences probably viewed paintings such as [Catlin's] *Mandan Village* with mixed reactions. Indians might not suffer from the ills of progress and civilization, but neither did they exhibit the virtues admired by white society."[18]

All of which is to say that the conflict of those two images and their dueling dualities was fully resolved, in a fashion, by the middle of the nineteenth century. The resolution was effected as part of a catchall solution to America's savagism-civilization problem that involved not a critique of progress in terms of its ills but an embrace of it as an inevitability whose smug logic, enwrapping a heartless sophistry, Pearce details as follows:

> Cultures are good, it was held, as they allow for full realization of man's essential and absolute moral nature; and man realizes this nature as he progresses

historically from a lesser to a greater good, from the simple to the complex, from savagism to civilization. Westward American progress would, in fact, be understood to be reproducing this historical progression; and the savage would be understood as one who had not and somehow could not progress into the civilized, who would inevitably be destroyed by the civilized.[19]

Savagery may still have been associated to some extent with nobility in the late-nineteenth-century West, but, whatever its primitivist attractions, its differences from mainstream civilization were stringently determinative: it meant, in Patricia Nelson Limerick's synopsis, "hunting and gathering, not agriculture; common ownership, not individual property owning; pagan superstition, not Christianity; spoken language, not literacy; emotion, not reason."[20] Savagery would have to yield.

Nonetheless, Noble Savages—however attenuated or vestigial—endured. In Cooper's fiction as Indians like Chingachgook and Uncas (opposed to bad Indians like Magua). In dramatic productions in New York or Boston, as Peter L. Thorslev Jr. points out, "at the same time as their less domesticated and real-life brethren were scalping settlers in the western territories" (thus demonstrating that whether the Wild Man is good or bad "depends not upon facts but upon the symbolic purposes he is to serve when he appears").[21] In a photograph from the 1870s by John K. Hillers, a member of Powell's team surveying the Colorado Plateau, of an Indian woman posed among boulders as a sentimentalized odalisque.[22] In those Indians who were, in Momaday's epigrammatizing of the unkindest irony of all, "given in defeat that compensation we call savage nobility."[23] In the wise old chiefs, most of them homogenized into Plains Indians, in Western novels and films. In the 1960s countercultural nostalgia for Indian lifeways. In collector-plate prints of Diana-like White Doves and Herculean Running Bears. In the daydreams of New Agers convinced of their having a fraction of Indian blood because of a distant grandfather's coupling with a dusky "princess." In PC documentaries demonizing white people (with their premeditated vices) while angelizing Native Americans (with their spontaneous virtues). In the cliché-ridden conscience of a West uncertain about its connection to both the noble and the savage, the civilized and the wild.

In fine, though he had mythic antecedents, the Noble Savage of eighteenth- and early-nineteenth-century America was essentially a construct of happy-ending Romanticism, the comedic Indian, a white invention contrapuntal to Puritan and rationalist concepts of the Native American. As later chapters will show, the Noble Savage did indeed endure—in versions defined, directly or indirectly, by Euro-Americans' changing yet ever ambivalent views of the Western wilderness—into the succeeding and overlapping eras of the romantic (or Victorian satanic) Indian, the tragic (or dispossessed modern) Indian, and the ironic (or revisionist postmodern) Indian, during which last era he still endures.[24]

Trails and Trials: The Inroads of Commerce

A typical landschaft . . . objectified order not only in its intricate arrangement of dwellings and fields and mills and pastures but in its juxtaposition with chaos. . . . The roads that passed from landschaft into wilderness promised excitement and fortune.
John R. Stilgoe, *Common Landscape of America, 1580 to 1845*

Commerce: the buying and selling that have propelled the development of the West. The controversies surrounding the revisionary 1991 exhibition "The West as America" at the National Museum of Art and its simultaneous semblable "Albert Bierstadt: Art and Enterprise" at the Brooklyn Museum had to do with how, in Bryan J. Wolf's phrasing, both worked not only to demythologize "the popular claims made by art" about the West but also to uncurtain "the West as a form of enterprise"—and to expose artists like Bierstadt as themselves enterprisers shrewdly aware of how to cash in on Western ideology.[1] The spirit of commerce sent Lewis and Clark into the wilderness. What has made the West grow as a society, according to Gundars Rudzitis, is the double economy of "the export industries and the 'residentiary' industries (those that produce for the local market)," the second dependent on the income the first gain from the sale of their lumber, cattle, silver, and so on.[2]

The recent proliferation of service industries throughout the West now qualifies Rudzitis's explanation, but the capitalism it implicates has had what William G. Robbins terms "revolutionary consequences" for a place non-Indians early on saw as property waiting for proprietors. All too quickly occurred a substantial altering of the landscape, dramatic shrinking of the Indian population, and extensive settlement by whites, among other effects. From such consequences it's evident that capitalism, in reaching across the West, "destroyed as it created." Part of what it created, contrary to the bromide that business thrives best in the midst of stability, was "institutionalized economic instability," a market environment that waxed far wilder, even as capitalism tried to rein it, than that east of the Mississippi.[3] In any case, the open sesame for money's westward expansion was trails—and then railroads, highways, flight paths, as well as the more gossamer trade routes of copper wires, electromagnetic waves, fiber-optic cables. But first came the trails. And the trials entailed in cutting them through recalcitrant country.

Many of the trails began as wildlife paths, such as the ones buffalo trod between water holes, and then became Indian migration routes. The Spanish etched the Southwest with trails: El Camino Real, the Old Spanish Trail, the Chihuahua Road, several routes that bore the carts of *comancheros* (traders with Indians). In time such trails and others lost their woolliness, slowly and then, as Anglo-Americans took them over, more rapidly. For those invaders trails were more than circuits for seasonal movement, missionary work, or local barter. They constituted an empire's courses into a virgin land "awaiting its white American groom," and, in Richard White's sexual transcription of the classic Old Western dream logic into the historical present, "the people on those trails have to be virile, strong, and brave. They carry the seeds of a new society into the West."[4] (In nineteenth-century usage the word *commerce* referred almost as readily to sexual *intercourse* as it did to the buying and selling of goods.)[5]

Metaphorical overtones in tow, the trade David Dary endows with the epithet "the civilizer of the West" penetrated the West initially by waterways. Apart from roundabout ocean travel to the West Coast, that meant proceeding by rivers. The first to be utilized by entrepreneurs was the Ohio. Flatboats and barges floated goods down that river, then down the Mississippi to New Orleans. Later came keelboats, which could go upstream, up the Missouri (as Lewis and Clark's did to Fort Mandan), carrying goods. Likewise, in 1819, the first steamboat that headed west out of St. Louis. But in that same year Major Stephen H. Long, en route to explore the upper Missouri in a steamboat christened the *Western Engineer* and decked out like a smoke-spouting dragon to impress and perplex the Indians, learned what precursory explorers already knew: although a large craft might travel a portion of the Missouri into the northern West, its usefulness in that respect really ended around what's now Kansas City, rivers like the Kansas and the Platte being "too shallow for reliable riverboat navigation."[6] The Great American Desert presented yet another deterrent. But unnavigable rivers wouldn't, any more than would the unamenable land itself, make U.S. citizens do what Pike in 1810 said they would do: "leave the prairies incapable of cultivation to the wandering and uncivilized aborigines of the country."[7] Those citizens would find a way into and a way to do business in Pike's desert. Those ways would be overland trails.

That desert was already crisscrossed with trails worn by trade among Indian tribes. Long before the Spanish *entradas*, the Plains Indians and the Pueblos had a system of trade involving the exchange of buffalo hides for blankets and the like, as well as traffic in slaves. In his discussion of that system, Dary explains that the Spanish pushing north not only tapped it but also introduced new items of barter, the most significant for the Indians being the horse, which animal "changed their way of life forever by making them vastly more mobile."[8] That way of life was irreversibly changed again when, later, the French headed west across the plains, for they, like other Euro-Americans to come, further enlarged the Indian system by attracting more tribes into it and supplying products undreamt of in the old days of swapping tobacco for pemmican or pumpkins for moccasins, products, such as axes, knives, mirrors, and guns, forged by European technology.

In such change originated the most egregious calamity of nineteenth-century trade between Indians and whites. Frederick Turner's description of its unfolding highlights how it culminated in destruction barely suggested by the word *change*. In the West, as previously in the East, with the entrance of the whites trading became different from what Indians traditionally had engaged in: it "took on a new and sinister velocity, for the new party to the bargaining had no relationship whatever to the lands other than what could be realized economically from them." The white traders set up their posts in the hope of making a killing, moving on, and quickly going back to civilization. To ensure the fast turnover and high-profit volume that would hasten their exit, the Indians "had to be made to want" the items offered. They had to be made to want them a lot—and, soon, dependently—by a relentless seduction that spelled spiritual doom for many of the whites' customers. Indians wanting their lives made easier were drawn onto "the hidden and devious byways that lead inevitably from the consumption of the new luxuries to the destruction of the myths that give life its meaning."[9]

The Indians of the West were caught in exactly the trap Turner describes. When alcohol was introduced into trade to lubricate dealings, an old ruse by the nineteenth century, it aggravated Indians' exploitation and dependency. Each trader, having secured his profit in a hunted-out area, would pull up stakes and proceed further west, leaving ruined land and people behind. For most Indians, only after decades of this repeating process and their anger at and bafflement by it, "only when it was all over," as Turner puts it, "would they know that the whites had not only wanted beaver, buffalo, rights-of-way, parcels of land for expanding settlements, and military posts to protect the settlers. They had wanted all of it. Everything."[10] Each act of trade had chipped at the Indian will and made an inroad into the Indian world. Each, like each treaty (another kind of shell-game trade), had exchanged home and meaning for very little—Manhattan for twenty-four dollars' worth of trinkets, ancestral nature for alien culture, again and again.

As we'll see, trade with Mexicans, those other ambiguous "children of nature" in Anglo eyes, though it took place in territory Mexico would lose to the United States, didn't lead to the disaster that befell the Indians. But there were trials aplenty for whites on the main artery of that trade, an Indian track that came to be known as the Santa Fe Trail. To get a sense of the desolateness, to nineteenth-century Anglos, it passed through, imagine yourself on a mesa in Mora County, New Mexico, looking south and down on ruts of the trail's mountain branch still so deep they're visible for miles as they converge toward their distant joining with the ruts of its Cimarron Cutoff at Watrous, whence the two trails descend as one before fishhooking around the end of the Sangre de Cristo Mountains and up to Santa Fe. The land is dry, limitless, seemingly empty. Not unlike the land in West Texas in the early 1840s encountered by Woodrow Call—soon to join an abortive military excursion, with Gus McCrae and other Texas Rangers, to conquer Santa Fe—in Larry McMurtry's novel *Dead Man's Walk*. Identify with Call: "The land before him, which looked so empty, wasn't. A people were there who knew the emptiness better than he did."

Those people were Comanches, and they "were wild men."[11] And there were other wild men between civilization and Santa Fe—Apaches, Kiowas, Cheyennes, Arapahos, as well as Comanches attacked whites on the trail until late in the nineteenth century—and wild creatures of other kinds, wild circumstances possible at any moment, in the early 1840s and before and after. That wildness wouldn't easily allow the uneventful passage of men with a yen for jack.

But the Mexicans themselves weren't quite so wild. They wanted to be dealt in. Prior to 1821, when Mexico declared its independence from Spain, outsiders enjoyed only politically troubled and irregular trade with Santa Fe, a prime target for business, given the needs and wants of its several thousand people, its distance from Mexico City, and the dearness of goods sent from there over the Camino Real. But in 1821, the year also of Missouri's statehood, that situation started to change. In the late summer a plainsman named William Becknell gathered a trade expedition in Franklin, Missouri, and set out with a modest pack train for the Southwest. He intended to trade with Indians, but he wound up in Santa Fe, where his party was warmly received and grossed a handsome profit from the sale of merchandise. According to Dary's version of the occasion's lore, when Becknell returned to Franklin, having left most of his Santa Fe–enchanted fellow traders behind, "rawhide packages of silver dollars were dumped on the sidewalk" of the main street.[12] Whatever the tales of argent glory, regular trade had begun. Becknell would undertake future trips—and, by the advantage of the Cimarron Cutoff, with wagons. So would many other traders, caravan after caravan—along with settlers, storekeepers, gold seekers, and all the rest—for decades ahead, as east–west commerce thickened.

One of the traders in Becknell's wake was a Missourian named Josiah Gregg. A young man of frail constitution, he decided in 1831, following his doctors' advice after a long bout with dyspepsia and consumption, to make a curative journey to the High Plains. At Independence he joined a caravan bound for Santa Fe. In the course of the six-week trip, he recovered enough to give up his carriage for a horse, taught himself Spanish, was hired by one of the merchants as a bookkeeper, and developed a passion for trading. Over the next nine years he indulged that passion with more trips to Santa Fe, including one that took him on down to the interior cities of Mexico and another that proved the feasibility of wagon-training into New Mexico along the Canadian River, a route that would later be followed by forty-niners. During those trips Gregg kept notebooks on matters ranging from merchandise inventories to natural history. In 1843 he turned them into a manuscript that was published the following year as *Commerce of the Prairies; or, The Journal of a Santa Fé Trader*.

The two-volume work was Gregg's encyclopedic masterpiece. Reprinted over and over, it shaped several generations' impressions of the Southwest as a place of both highflying adventure and down-to-earth finance. "Here for the first time," Howard R. Lamar observes, "Americans began to learn about the exotic, unknown

American Southwest." Gregg described Mexican and Indian life at length. He offered Americans the exotic, to be sure; but the land he documented was exotic in another sense as well, for it "represented a totally different West from what they had known previously. Here was a frontier already with a sizable population . . . [that] gave the lie to the assertion that American pioneers were advancing into uninhabited virgin land."[13]

Gregg's portrayal may have given the lie to that assertion, but, like his translations of trail hardships into romance and of fractious territory into visions of profitable Anglo settlements, it didn't do so without vacillations of attitude. His account of Becknell's second expedition, for instance, is inconsistent in its narration of "the terrible trials which awaited him across the pathless desert," which trials Gregg also calls "thrilling incidents"; and, though he speaks of a later Santa Fe expedition as a journey involving "many . . . exciting incidents," he concludes that its route "appears to have presented fewer obstacles than any ordinary road of equal length in the United States." As an adventurer, he foregrounds the unusual; as a trader, he reassures his readers of predictability and makes light of difficulties—apparently without discerning any contradictions. Consider, for example, his description of the rendezvous of Council Grove (now a town and the seat of Morris County, Kansas) as he experienced it on his first trip, a description rendered just a few pages after his referring to "the prairie wilderness" the Santa Fe Trail passes through:

> This point is nearly a hundred and fifty miles from Independence, and consists of a continuous stripe of timber nearly half a mile in width, comprising the richest varieties of trees . . . and extending all along the valleys of a small stream known as "Council Grove creek," the principal branch of the Neosho river. This stream is bordered by the most fertile bottoms and beautiful upland prairies, well adapted to cultivation: such indeed is the general character of the country from thence to Independence. All who have traversed these delightful regions, look forward with anxiety to the day when the Indian title to the land shall be extinguished, and flourishing "white" settlements dispel the gloom which at present prevails over this uninhabited region. Much of this prolific country now belongs to the Shawnees and other Indians of the border, though some portion of it has never been allotted to any tribe.[14]

The details are revealing in their contradictoriness: this wilderness is "delightful" and wonderfully arable; whites who have seen it "look forward with anxiety" (uneasy anticipation) to its being seized and settled; and "gloom . . . prevails over" this "beautiful" place, which is "uninhabited" except for "the Shawnees and other Indians" to whom much of it "belongs."

Also remarkable in that regard is Gregg's zeal for settlement, which, Donald Worster rightly says, "may seem a strange sentiment for a man whose life in the white settlement had been so sickly." Yet, as Gregg healed in the thin open air, he became an enthusiast for Manifest Destiny—a turn Worster explains by the fact that he found the town of Santa Fe a shabby excuse for whatever Cíbola he expected it to be. What he came to envision in place of such a disappointment was "the prospect of a bigger and broader America . . ., of a nation extending the blessings of its free institutions to the benighted Mexican and Indian peoples that it would conquer and subdue."[15]

Through his envisioning, Gregg foresaw also, in a passage toward the end of *Commerce of the Prairies* that revises the West-as-desert myth with rain-follows-the-plow folklore, the flowering of the most arid land the trail traversed because of the influence of more cultivation. The New Mexican people, he says, "assure us that the rains have much increased of latter years, a phenomenon which the vulgar superstitiously attribute to the arrival of the Missouri traders. Then may we not hope that these sterile regions might yet be thus revived and fertilized, and their surface covered one day by flourishing settlements to the Rocky Mountains?"[16] Here Gregg is no less superstitious than his sources, and his hope derives not from fact but from what he expected. That had to do with the psychocultural baggage this businessman brought to the wilderness. Specifically, it had to do with the belief that the West could be, as Richard C. Poulsen puts it, "transformed into a land of gold, of out-flowing rivers, of the blessings of God (running with milk and honey), simply by being graced by whites, by those intent on wresting a living from the land through the plow." By that wishful transmutation sterility would be "abolished—and in this case, sterility is not a simple lack of productive soil; it is a chaos destined to be transformed by a world of order imported from Europe."[17] Gregg's hope for civilization's reviving "these sterile regions" (a phrase implying the immanence of evil) may be traced back to Bradford and beyond.

But there's another twist in Gregg's personal road. Despite his rage for civilized order—and despite a fear of Indians—he was unable to remain long in the world to which he returned following his last trip to Santa Fe. After receiving a degree in medicine from the University of Louisville in 1846, he headed west again for a series of adventures that would terminate with his death, in 1850, on a trail-seeking expedition north of San Francisco. His explanation in *Commerce of the Prairies* for why he felt he must soon recur to the wild rewards examination:

> I have striven in vain to reconcile myself to the even tenor of civilized life in the United States. . . . Yet I am almost ashamed to confess that scarcely a day passes without my experiencing a pang of regret that I am not now roving at large upon those western plains. Nor do I find my taste peculiar; for I have hardly known a man, who has ever become familiar with the kind of life which I have led for so many years, that has not relinquished it with regret.

He goes on to extol the life of the prairie trader for its excitement—and for its freedom, which lures even men of high station. He brushes aside the physical dangers of such a life, but he dwells on a subtler danger of it: the obliteration of civilized manners and practices that leaves the adventurer vulnerable to so much criticism and ridicule that he may light out for the territory once more. Still, Gregg adds, in conclusion, "It will hardly be a matter of surprise then, . . . that this passion for Prairie life, how paradoxical soever it may seem, will be very apt to lead me upon the plains again . . .—there to seek to maintain undisturbed my confidence in men, by fraternizing with the little prairie dogs and wild colts, and the still wilder Indians—the unconquered Sabaeans of the Great American Deserts."[18] Thus does he romantically hyperbolize life in the unsettled Wild West that his profession was striving to settle and tame. If ever the West had a white-American wanting-it-both-ways Every(business)man, surely Josiah Gregg was he.

Meanwhile in the 1840s, up on the Oregon Trail, Americans by the thousands, many of them traders, were wending their way to the agricultural paradise of the Willamette Valley and vicinity. The white commonwealth multiplying there was subduing the land not just through farming but also through killing or displacing of Indians that would continue so implacably over the next decades that Oregon (a territory until 1859) can be seen, in Lamar's retrospect, as starkly exemplary of "the darker side of American expansion."[19] Equally stark in such exemplification, storying ecocide rather than genocide, was the fate of the trail itself. Drawing upon the reports of travelers, White offers a catalogue of trash along the dust-clouded, manure-strewn trail, much of it items jettisoned to lighten loads, that includes iron bars, grindstones, stoves, barrels, harnesses, clothing, bacon, a diving bell, scads of abandoned wagons.[20] Debris of that kind is of special interest here because it speaks not only of trials (in coping with which the countless liquor bottles on the trail had been drained) and unrealistic planning but as well of the presence of merchandise in the pioneers' West. All those discarded items tell and foretell a wilderness littered with the artifacts of metastasizing and profligate commerce.

Just before the proliferation of railroads in the West, a major impetus in that metastasization was commercial hauling, of both people and freight, particularly during the migrational frenzies of the gold rushes to California, beginning in 1849, and to Colorado, beginning a decade later. In the mid-1860s West, Elizabeth Johns declares, "no other artifact was so clear a symbol of progress as the stagecoach, at least for a while."[21] By then there were thousands of miles of stagecoach routes in California, the Pacific Northwest, the central West, and the Southwest. What they boded for the wilderness may be inferred from Elliott West's discussion of the spread of overland stage service between Missouri and the Front Range in the early 1860s. He re-creates a sweep of map on which the stage lines, with their road ranches and nodes of appurtenant businesses from grog shops to groceries, elaborated "a nearly continuous thread of posts throughout the valley of the Platte and both its branches." About every ten miles a station stood ready to tend the swelling numbers of travelers and immigrants bound for Denver. The swift and profound changes all that mercantilism brought weren't merely the obvious physical and financial ones, however; there was also a psychological change, and it augured an even more changeful future: "Stage service was . . . a vital step in reimagining the region. It seemed suddenly more natural to picture the river towns, plains, and mountains not as distinct and widely separated entities but as parts of a geographical and economic whole." In that perspective, soon habitual,

> the plains and their edges were literally re-vised. Further change took on an inevitable air. The string of tent stations, an orator announced at the twelve-hour celebration [after the first stage trip to Denver], was introducing "civilization, cultivation, and refinement" into what had been thought a desert. And next? The routes "could not but become the . . . iron arteries of inland commerce . . . over which the iron horse would yet snort on his road to the Pacific."

The stage drivers drove toward a West of interlinked cities their passengers would populate. Much the same might be said of the drivers of the huge cross-plains freight wagons and their goods on board, for a freight train, in West's words, "was a cultural invasion. . . . In its particulars, its sheer bulk, and its consequences, a freight train summed up the vision of a seamless region. . . . In that, it was a rolling undeniability."[22]

Another undeniability rolling on its own trails through the West of that time was the commercial freight known as cattle. In the early years of wild-longhorn ranching in the Southwest, as Dee Brown recounts, gathering cattle and taking them to market was more like a hunt than a roundup; and when the trails north to railheads were worn some later on, there was no shortage of hell-raising after the herds had been delivered to the pens at Kansas City, Abilene, Dodge City, or similar termini across the Great Plains. As trail driving increased and the cattle industry spread into the northern West, though, the drivers' work—albeit never quite losing its wild aspects—"gradually became routinized."[23] The routinization was in no small measure due to what the cattle trails—the Shawnee, the Chisolm, the Goodnight-Loving, the Chisum, the Bozeman, and others—meant to the cowboys who used them.

Poulsen approaches a specification of that meaning through a contrast between the significance of Chimney Rock, a formation in western Nebraska, for the mountain man and then, later, for the cowboy. For the former, it marked a transition from civilization to wilderness and all its stimulations; for the latter, it signified "that the trail was being accurately and predictably followed, which passage would lead to an inevitable occupational expectation." The trail on which the cowboy drove his herd thus "was the prime image in the transformed landscape," since it was the channel by which the drive to market was accomplished. It existed for the sake of the herd, just as the cowboy did. In Poulsen's strongest language, the herd (and everything occupationally associated with it) "was defined against the western landscape" (the controlled against the wild) to such an extent that, "to the cowboy, the trail was the West."[24] By that equation America's premier icon of white wildness furthered the taming of the West through commerce.

All the trails I've discussed were, as West maintains concerning those crossing the plains between the Missouri valley and the Rockies, "more than part of the landscape; they became actors themselves" in the drama of Western expansion, binding together settlements, towns, and cities "by safe and sure arteries of commerce" and diminishing the wilderness that once appeared so daunting.[25] True to the genre in which those trails played their roles, the diminishment was dramatic; that brought about by nomadic Indians and their horses was supplemented exponentially by whites and their constant freight trains, stagecoaches, cattle herds, and immigrant wagons, not to mention military troops and vehicles. Pasturage along the trails was overgrazed. Grassbeds were trampled and abraded by hooves, wheels, and soles until gullied with ruts. Wildlife was slaughtered remorselessly. River valleys were stripped of trees. Such ruinous activity direly affected the lives of Indians. It occurred in the course of America's engineering what White calls "a more complex West in which the traffic out of the West—whether gold, silver, wheat, cattle, lumber, or people—mattered as much as the traffic into it," a West in which the trails "seem more a maze than a simple line from one point to another."[26]

In the wink of an eye, railroads would succeed rutted trails. One of them, the Atchison, Topeka and Santa Fe, would enter into a partnership with a restaurateur named Fred Harvey, who would build and operate restaurants and hotels along its routes. Once the Indians were beat down and the depression of the 1890s was past and tourism in the West had begun to boom, Harvey would contract with Indian artisans and artists in the Southwest to sell their pots, blankets, baskets, jewelry, and whatnot to the tourists hankering for things "Indian" who ate in his restaurants and slept in his hotels. Through such bargaining he would add another chapter to the co-optation of the Native world of spiritualized nature by the white world of cash-nexus commerce. As David Binkley, the curator in charge of the exhibition "Inventing the Southwest: The Fred Harvey Company and Native American Art" during its late–1997 stay at the Nelson-Atkins Museum of Art in Kansas City, Missouri, puts it, the items those Indians produced "'moved from ritual to retail context.'"[27] Just so.

When Becknell first packed into Santa Fe, he couldn't have forefelt all that would follow from his unassuming enterprise. All the caravans of men with visions of sweet cakes, tequila, gambling, and whores dancing in their heads. All the Punic treaties. All the battles. All the business that would be created. All the wilderness that would be destroyed. But, were he alive today, he might understand what the speaker in Richard Dankleff's poem "Route 56" notices while driving on blacktop that approximates (except for paralleling the Cimarron Cutoff) Becknell's original route:

Along this trail bulldozed
through the ancient brush, the scalped
Kansas landscape leads back. On the hill to make
their stand by the orange billboard, ghosts.[28]

Like most of us today, though, Becknell might not understand what it could mean to stop the car, get out, then saunter off the trail, back into the world of those ghosts. "'Off the trail,'" teaches Gary Snyder, "is another name for the Way, and sauntering off the trail is the practice of the wild"—something done "not for the sake of newness, but for the sense of coming home to our whole terrain."[29]

PART THREE
From the 1840s to the 1890s:
The West as Frontier

The fire ignites. My longing returns. When we want everything to change we call on fire.
   Terry Tempest Williams, "Fire"

Prelude and Overview

To the laborer in the sweat of his labor, the raw stuff on his anvil is an adversary to be conquered. So was wilderness an adversary to the pioneer.
   Aldo Leopold, "Wilderness"

The West as *frontier*. That term, long evocative of innocent imperialism, was the subject of hot debate among Western historians in the 1980s and early 1990s. The debate has now cooled or, for many of those historians, ended. In fact, the term seems to be having a new vogue, mostly because protracted debate instigated re-thinking that has enriched our understanding of what a frontier is and how particular frontiers came about. Originating in old mental habits, the concept of the frontier, like that of the wilderness, was one imposed by Euro-Americans on what they perceived as "the West." That's what the zone where their world *fronted* a world other than itself came to be called. But at no time was it only a line where, in Frederick Jackson Turner's frontier-thesis terminology, civilization met and then overcame savagery: it was also a changing area of complex interactions, contestations, and adaptations both cultural and natural. And it was, of course, thoroughly mythologized by its inventors.

Such emphases need to be amplified. The traditional European notion of a frontier may have referred to an immobile and maybe fortified geographical boundary (forest or mountain range, say), but from the beginning of Atlantic colonization the American notion denoted a *moving* demarcation of where (white) settlement bordered on (Indian) wilderness. The idea that American society was shaped by the extension of the frontier—most intensely in the latter half of the nineteenth century—across a "vacant" West seemed new to some when Turner stated it in his 1893 essay "The Significance of the Frontier in American History," but it had been adumbrated well before that by Franklin, Emerson, Lincoln, Whitman, and others;

it was a delayed regional corollary of the idea that American society was shaped by the frontier's extension across a whole vacant continent.

Because that frontier changed, it was really multiple frontiers. By Richard Slotkin's reckoning, there were about half a dozen major ones, each shorter in duration than the last: first, the "transoceanic" frontier; then that between the seaboard and the Alleghenies; then the trans-Allegheny, the trans-Mississippi, and the Mexican frontiers; then that of California and Oregon; then, finally, that of the Great Plains. Because the frontier was a sequence of frontiers over several centuries, the mythology of it changed as settlers moving from Plymouth to the Pacific dealt with different realities—and as their culture changed. The image of the wilderness as a Zion was succeeded by that of the wilderness as a place of inexhaustible economic opportunity and inexpensive property for those prepared to work it, which was succeeded by that of the wilderness as a safety valve for America's growing and disaffected lower classes. Though these successive ideological phases differed in their ideas of what the land offered, they all carried "a common implication that transformation would be part of the experience."[1]

Certainly that implication held for the frontier West; but since it was very different territory from the frontier East or South and was settled by people whose worldview was molded by a relatively late stage of white American culture and was settled moreover with a vengeance, even if sparsely by Eastern standards, from the 1840s to the 1890s, the ideas about the kind of transformation it offered differed from those associated with earlier frontiers. They were more secular and overtly politico-economic in tone. Whatever vestiges of previous ideas they carried, they had been cast, at least in rough form, in the die of the American Revolution, a watershed whose importance shouldn't be underestimated. As David Mogen makes clear, after that revolution the colonial drama of wilderness confrontation was rebuilt into a myth of national character invested with "the ambiguous and often contradictory values projected into visions of Manifest Destiny." That myth was new, but its values were indebted to the older notion of confrontation. As a result, the dominant frontier mythology, even when Manifest Destiny was at its fever pitch in the technologized late nineteenth century far removed from the Puritans' world, still was based on "the fusion of the traditional gothic theme of psychic disintegration with the larger theme of metamorphosis, of regeneration in the wilderness." That mythology, its "heightened atmosphere of ambivalence" retained in much frontier literature, evoked "both horror and a primal sense of union."[2] Small wonder that the real-life romance of climactic Western settlement would be bleakly gothic as well as brightly optimistic.[3]

That settlement definitely involved a transformation of white people by their contact with an unaccustomed environment and its inhabitants—as popular history has it, they grew rugged, self-reliant, individualistic, and so on—but the converse transformation was at least as powerful; it now seems, in some registers, indefensibly terrible. The post-1840s West wasn't the first frontier where, as Christopher A. Conte summarizes its narrative, "white settlers, bent on the conquest of indigenous peoples and their environment, reorganized ecological relations to suit their own economic and political imperatives."[4] But it was one where the reorganization of ecological relations (in the most compendious sense) occurred—in great part because of advances in white agricultural, industrial, and military technology—with unprecedented violence as well as rapidity.

By the 1840s violence had become ingrained in the experience of westward expansion. To borrow from Leo Marx, any idyll that experience included had been long since interrupted. White Americans already had a heritage of violence against the British, the French, Indians, African Americans, one another, and the natural environment when they headed west out of Missouri. By then, as Slotkin notes, violence was central not only to the history of the frontier but also to its representation in myth. One of the principal representations born of the "Myth of the Frontier" concerned progress. The particulars of that representation varied from Puritan to Jeffersonian to Jacksonian to later times, but always, in Slotkin's formulation, "the Myth represented the redemption of American spirit or fortune as something to be achieved by playing through a scenario of separation, temporary regression to a more primitive or 'natural' state, and *regeneration through violence*." In this perspective, he stresses, what's distinctive may not be so much the violence itself as the use made of it symbolically and politically. In the Myth of the Frontier, that use entails positing a moral landscape that serves as an arena for the conflicts of settlement and delineating those conflicts in terms of the settlers' paradoxical relationship to the wild. That landscape, as Slotkin explains it, is divided by a border between civilization and Indian country the settler has to cross in order to experience regression—"so that the false values of the 'metropolis' can be purged and a new, purified social contract enacted." Wilderness and Indians are his enemies, but they "also provide him with the new consciousness through which he will transform the world." The situation is rendered knottier by the requirement that the heroes of this quest "must therefore be 'men (or women) who know Indians'—characters whose experiences, sympathies, and even allegiances fall on both sides of the Frontier"—and who emerge victorious from conflicts that are for them "spiritual or psychological . . . by learning to discipline or suppress the savage or 'dark' side of their own human nature."[5] Thus was William Bradford's shade welcomed in the West.

Well, yes and no, and the unsureness derives directly from the question of how that dark side figured in the gradually fading romance of the West's historical summertime. On the one hand, celebration of the dark side—or aspects of it—was what the Western quest was all about, a fundament Richard White emphasizes: "When Henry Thoreau wrote, 'Eastward I go only by force; but westward I go free,' or when Mark Twain's Huckleberry Finn 'lights out' for the territory to escape the constraints of 'civilization,' both spoke to an audience for whom westering, and thus the trans-Missouri West, had already taken on an identification with freedom and independence in a country that regarded freedom and independence as its peculiar hallmark." Americans associated those qualities preeminently with single males in borderland conditions. As heroes defined by their liminal wildness, those males, in Crockett-like fashion, "became violently and dangerously natural." Though their assaulting could be mutual and general, their targets were mostly the wild animals they consumed and Indians. Thus, despite their incivilities, such men were needed, for they helped clear the wilderness for white settlement. On the other hand, however, as they exultantly warred against others with guns or against nature with mining gear, their dark side posed a threat to the settlers' image of the West as peaceful, pleasant, cultivated. Which is to say, at a certain point "domesticating . . . natural male violence became a part of the mythic agenda."[6]

Implementing that part of an agenda was mainly the job of westering women, often stereotyped as prairie madonnas and the like, who successfully soothed the savage breasts of many violent men. More self-sufficient than their Eastern sisters, facing perils unknown to them, they rode in ox-drawn wagons or walked through the duple male-female romance of the West—desert and garden, hell and hearth—till settlement would make the ever-onward days they stoically recorded in their diaries and letters little more than memories. On the weary miles of trails, rehearsing in their heads their husbands' booster tales, they birthed and lugged children, packed and unpacked wagons, tended to the cooking, endured bad weather and broken axles, stared out across desiccated flats, ate their oxen, climbed mountains barefoot, and finally got to the San Joaquin or some such tramontane destination. Each year there were more women—especially after the Kansas-Nebraska Act of 1854 and the Colorado Gold Rush and the Homestead Act of 1862—who stopped on the plains and learned to suffer the loneliness and wind there.

As penetration of the wilderness for exploration and quick plunder yielded to penetration for settlement and longer-term earning, conflicts with obstacles—Indians, scofflaws and outlaws, the land itself—multiplied. The obligation to participate in those conflicts and to try to end them heightened both the single-male romance of adventure and the married-female romance of domesticity. With the second slowly achieving a measure of ascendance, the century passed and then closed with a sense of consummation that included the glad consciousness of a new society gained as well as the crescent recognition of a wilderness lost. But meanwhile there were constant conflicts, the stuff of romance not only for distant Easterners and Europeans but even for those (from Karl Bodmer to Bret Harte to Custer to Bill Cody) who knew something of the unromantic West.

Most of the settlers engaged in those conflicts were motivated by a desire to win, to vanquish their adversaries and adversities at nearly any cost to their new environment and turn a family-supporting profit or more. That desire is exemplified by a passage in a letter written in 1853 by a Washington Territory settler named

Walter Crockett, who asserts that his foremost goal is "to get the land subdued and the wilde nature out of it" and that "when that is accomplished we can increase our crops to a very large amount and the high prices of every thing that is raised heare will make the cultivation of the soil a very profitable business."[7] But such subduing, though certifying American progress and often proving profitable, was accomplished through what Gerald F. Kreyche calls "a series of contradictory drives" tangled together in the desire to win the West, drives "toward subjugation and freedom, exploitation and exploration, destruction, conservation, and liberation." Analyzed in terms of these drives, the development of the West in the nineteenth century can be viewed as "a dialectical struggle attempting to produce a new synthesis," a struggle of the opposing forces of different religions, races, tribes, business interests—and, he stresses, "above all, man and nature."[8] All those oppositions, he rightly argues, helped determine the character of the cultural West, but the last left the deepest imprint; for it was complicated by a cross-grained dialectic between the *quest for* nature and the *conquest of* nature that would reach no more than a partial and shaky synthesis.

Technological innovations intensified many of the conflicts between opposing forces, escalating the violence inflicted on human beings, wildlife, and the environment at large. As, in Kreyche's clause, "brawn gave way to brain," what the double-action revolver and magazine repeater did to conflict between man and man, improvements in mining techniques, for example, did to that between man and nature: "First there were placer methods (panning), then pick and shovel work, sluice boxes, hydraulic means of washing down banks, and, last, dredging streams"[9]—not to mention coyoting (shallow-shaft mining) with blasting powder, river damming, and other destructive refinements. Increasingly during the late nineteenth century, the white occupation and exploitation of the West was a matter of firepower, the power of fire, technology, which originates in fire (both literally and according to the Prometheus myth) and enables, through its material mediation, fire's agency of transmutation.

Study John Gast's 1872 painting *American Progress*—also titled, tellingly, *Westward Ho*—which was distributed in thousands of chromolithographs by George A. Crofutt to promote his Western travel guide, and you'll see the whole story of technology's role in Manifest Destiny condensed onto just over a square foot of canvas. An angelic woman, the spirit of civilization, forehead adorned with the Star of Empire, floats westward through the sky, carrying a schoolbook and paying out telegraph wire. While some of the pioneers beneath her proceed west on foot or horseback, Indians and buffalo and a bear fleeing before them, most are transported by vehicles symbolic of successively upgraded technology: a covered wagon, then a stagecoach, then three locomotive-pulled trains abreast. On the left side, telescoped to a few inches' breadth, lies the still-benighted land extending to the Pacific the pioneers long for; on the right, beneath a miniaturized East (urban

John Gast, American Progress (1872): the whole story of technology's role in Manifest Destiny. (Museum of the American West Collection, Autry National Center, Los Angeles.)

buildings, suspension bridge, sailboats and steamboats), is foregrounded a scene they must be dreaming of turning the wilderness into: cozy cabin, field being tilled by a farmer with a plow behind oxen, tidy split-rail fence.

The post–Civil War impulse toward national unity, like most of the nation's internal migration, was directed west, and its engine was ever-more variegated, sophisticated, pervasive technology. That technology evolved at such a pace that arresting juxtapositions of wild Old Western events and the appearances of technological novelties that would shape the tamer New West can easily be arrayed: cattle drives up from Texas and the development of the automobile (and hence the pickup of later cowboys) both began in 1866; Custer died at the Little Bighorn and Alexander Graham Bell made his first telephone call in 1876; when the initial land rush into Oklahoma occurred in 1889, the motion-picture camera had already been devised; Butch Cassidy and the Wild Bunch had their holdup heyday just a few years before Orville Wright's first airplane flight in 1903.[10] Indeed, the impact of such novelties was so sudden and detrimental that the blessing of their civilizing influence—like philistine cheerfulness at the news that, according to the 1890 census, the frontier was closed—was soon doubted by those able to see lucidly what was happening to the West. Whether or not what was happening corroborated French statesman Georges Clemenceau's snotty dictum that America had gone directly from barbarism to degeneracy without the usual interval of civilization in between, there loomed abroad in the nation by the end of the century a malaise, its treble mood ranging from apocalyptic to regretful to nostalgic but its swelling bass mood tragic, relating to the technologically accelerated white spoliation of the wilderness.

> The complete form of the romance is clearly the successful quest. . . . A quest involving conflict assumes two main characters, a protagonist or hero, and an antagonist or enemy. . . . The enemy may be an ordinary human being, but the nearer the romance is to myth, the more the attributes of divinity will cling to the hero and the more the enemy will take on demonic mythical qualities. The central form of romance is dialectical: everything is focused on a conflict between the hero and his enemy. . . . Translated into ritual terms, the quest-romance is the victory of fertility over the waste land.
>
> Northrop Frye, Anatomy of Criticism: Four Essays

Settlement and Its Discontents

A tale half told and hardly understood;
...
     a tale it was of lands of gold
That lay toward the sun. Wild-wing'd and fleet
It spread among the swift Missouri's bold
Unbridled men, and reach'd to where Ohio roll'd.
     Joaquin Miller, "Pilgrims of the Plains"

In 1832, Massachusetts-born William Cullen Bryant visited his brothers in Illinois. Romantic author of "Thanatopsis," a poem about nature's claim on everything, he was stirred by the oceanic grasslands there and commemorated them in "The Prairies":

    These are the gardens of the Desert, these
The unshorn fields, boundless and beautiful,
For which the speech of England has no name—
The Prairies.

Viewing those gardens (inaptly named by the French word for "meadow"), the speaker muses on the Indians, beaver, and bison that recently were there and now dwell only far to the west. Nonetheless, he rejoices that "Still this great solitude is quick with life"—insects, flowers, birds, reptiles, deer. But near the end of the poem, as he listens to the "domestic hum" of bees, imported creatures, an aural hallucination takes hold of him. He thinks he hears

The sound of that advancing multitude
Which soon shall fill these deserts. From the ground
Comes up the laugh of children, the soft voice
Of maidens, and the sweet and solemn hymn
Of Sabbath worshippers. The low of herds
Blends with the rustling of the heavy grain
Over the dark brown furrows.

Then suddenly, at the poem's close, the wind rises "and breaks my dream, / And I am in the wilderness alone."[1]

Soon a restitution of that sort of solitude in Illinois—and points further west—won't be possible. More Indians, beaver, and bison will disappear on across the continent. The multitude will advance, in fact, to fill the land with what Bryant foresees. Some members of the multitude won't be so docile; the prairies may become rural, but they will become urban as well. After a few decades hardly anybody, in Illinois or in Utah, will really be in the wilderness alone. The westering that began in Massachusetts and Virginia two centuries before and that in 1832 was bringing more and more families into the valleys of the Ohio and the Mississippi and into the states and states-to-be whose eastern borders were defined by that latter river would surge beyond the Missouri in the 1840s and thereafter as hundreds of thousands and then millions of settlers moved, generation by generation, into a place ever less Indian country.

But in the midst of that settlement seethed an unappeasable restlessness. Continuing and extending westward "the unsettling of mid-America" from 1700 to 1850 that Elliott West attributes to "tumultuous events" given momentum by the advents, from different directions, of consecutive Spanish (southwest to northeast), French and British (east and northeast to southwest), and American (east and south to west) frontiers,[2] that restlessness was a presumable characteristic of people whose ancestors had risked all in a gamble on the New World. However, the extremity of it in later westering suggests that in the makeup of many pioneers, champions of civilization or not, it was, as expressed in and reinforced by vast openness, something of a wild-card trait of another order. Rita Parks's research reveals that among those who migrated into the West "almost everyone pulled up roots at least once and moved still farther west" and that nineteenth-century Westerners were so restless that Easterners tended to regard them as mavericks who were "exuberant, exasperating, explosive," even "dangerous"[3]—in other words, as Westerners themselves referred to Indians, untamed or uncivilized. Frederick Turner speaks of the unsettledness of Western settling in terms of a broadening and intensification of the impulse that had caused earlier pioneers to depopulate parts of Connecticut, Massachusetts, and New York. The further west that impulse thrust, the more it inspirited a pace of settlement that astonished visiting foreigners, who marveled at "the frenzied ways of the settlers" in their consuming, selling out, and moving on.[4] Settlement involved settling down; but it involved also saddling up as Americans went nomadic in an increasingly spoiled and nominal wilderness.

In the 1840s, though, the West wasn't a wilderness in name only. Nor would it be for a while; nor is it, wholly, even now. In 1843, when settlers in force began departing from Independence, Missouri, on the Oregon Trail (a mazy passage only explorers, merchants, missionaries, and go-it-aloners had used during the preceding several decades), they believed in the work ethic, progress, and the future. The world into which they wagoned would test those beliefs and others, many of them no more than fantasies about what lay in wait for them. The rule was that the cowardly never started on the trip and the weak died on the way. On average, for some time after 1843, one in ten, weak or not, did die on the way—mostly from cholera, but drownings and other accidents, a few from guns seldom used to fend off usually friendly Indians, also took lives. What became the largest human migration ever was tough on women and children, but the women and children who saw it through got toughened up to the challenge of what was essentially a family event (except for gold seekers who, beginning in 1848, struck off at some point for California). As the years passed, along the road and its branches lay buckled wheels, a discarded this or that, crudely marked graves, scattered skeletons of horses and cattle. When the settlers stopped, to stay or not quite stay, after months of difficulties and delays, relations with Indians strained into craziness and genocide; the land demanded never-ending labor; time moderated high hopes with orphans and despondence.

In August 1844, at his graduation from Harvard, Francis Parkman delivered a commencement oration titled "Romance in America" in which he both ecstatically eulogized America as he imagined it had been in Columbus's time—"the sublimest object in the world"—and bemoaned what civilization had done to it. In the latter vein, he concluded that "the charm is broken now. The stern and solemn poetry that breathed from her endless wilderness is gone; and the dullest plainest prose has fixed its home in America."[5] He concluded that, of course, before he made his journey on the Oregon Trail during the summer of 1846, a journey that crippled his health but also, as Roderick Nash notes, "readied him intellectually to give wilderness the Romantic interpretation in history that Bryant had given it in poetry, Cooper in fiction, and Cole in art."[6] What Parkman subsequently discovered, contrary to his oration, was that even in 1846—a year so fraught with a sense of the changes wrought by American expansion that Bernard DeVoto dubbed it, by the title of his 1943 book, *The Year of Decision*—the poetry of the wilderness wasn't gone. That poetry—stern, if not solemn—still contended strongly in its duel with American culture's prose, each imposing its characteristic threats and destructions on the other.

What did that poetry impose? A Pandora's box of troubles that eroded settlers' European veneer. Plains whose level spaces yawned like horizontal abysses.

Daunting mountains. Desert topography beyond the Rockies that disoriented, at times mortally. Droughts and the losses they caused (according to Matilda Armstrong Steele, whose family came to eastern Kansas from Illinois in 1860, that year's drought "swept the calendar," leaving "no spear of grass . . . no shade, no fruit, no flowers").[7] Lightning that was hard to hide from in open country and especially frequent along the Front Range. Tornadoes that could demolish a soddy in a heartbeat. Sun, kilning sheltered and unsheltered settlers alike, that, in Walter McDonald's words, "burned the truth of what they were, / one crop away from being meat for buzzards."[8] Floods, when the shallow riverbeds the settlers camped and lived along overloaded with rainwater or snowmelt. Crop-crushing hailstorms, their stones of ice maybe Texas-size. Tallgrass fires that raged like rolling infernos across acres as far as flame-fighting or skedaddling settlers could see. Days-long blizzards as late as mid-spring that caught careless or tardy travelers and lulled them into refrigerant sleep, buried the housed in hibernal boredom, and resculpted the earth with impassable drifts. Wind, with or without a cargo of sleet or heat or something else out of Revelation, that in some areas unceasingly scoured land and mind (there are enough peevish mentions of high wind in Howard Ruede's 1937 book *Sod-House Days: Letters from a Kansas Homesteader, 1877–78* to qualify it as a leitmotif). Mosquitoes. Snakes, poisonous and otherwise, that wanted to share tents and less-than-tight domiciles. Grasshoppers, once in a while (as in 1874) cubic miles of them, crowding the sun out of the sky, then alighting to eat up corn or wheat by the fieldful. Bears, wolves, mountain lions, and other fanged mammals that far more unnerved than hurt or killed settlers or their livestock. And Indians, helpful to settlers in untold instances, about whom horror stories—many of them mule-skinner balderdash and many not—freely circulated, stimulating as much irrational fear as justifiable watchfulness.

What did American culture's prose impose? Millions of domestic hooved animals. Epidemics that decimated Indian tribes. Religion that sanctioned the subduing and undoing of the natural environment and its inhabitants. European social habits transplanted from the East and Midwest (snatches of classical music fiddled around the campfire, awkward enactments of the current rituals of family life, and the like). An artistic custom of pastoralizing raw land into culturally cooked landscape, thereby, in Buell's synopsis, "translating what had traditionally been a sophisticated intellectual game into an ideological program for an actual society."[9] Folklore that testified to the settler's ownership of territory he took, iconized him as a hardy naïf who wandered into the Western wasteland to battle nature and eventually find peace, and concealed his role as an interloper, in Richard C. Poulsen's exposure, committed to "homogenizing, as far as possible, all of his surroundings into an image of himself," eliminating whatever didn't "fit the image."[10] Military power, mostly to control Indians. New technologies of transportation, communication, and metal and mineral extraction. Agricultural technology (axes, hoes, shovels, mattocks, tempered-steel plows, windmills, barbed wire, reapers, threshing machines) and science (experimental planting of barley, oats, sorghum, potatoes, new varieties of wheat).[11] Distinctly nonindigenous and dominating architecture (frame houses, forts, towns, cities).[12]

Of all the implements, mental or material, the early Western settlers brought to the nature–culture duel, the plow is perhaps the most emblematic. As Poulsen explains, it "is a prophetic tool—one wholly concerned with the order of the row, of the reduction of the landscape to a homogeneity: to an agricultural presence speaking clearly and exclusively of the destiny of those who are God's supreme creation."[13] Ousting whatever doesn't conform to that order, the plow acts not only as a symbolic phallus that breaks and fertilizes the earth but also as an actual tool that dispels its sterility. The plow therefore had a role in both making and remaking the West. The latter was, however, the more important, for the settlers' goal, as Richard White stresses, "was ultimately the restoration of the familiar world that they had left behind." That goal would prove elusive, but the pursuit of it would nevertheless lead to remaking the West into a place of agricultural bounteousness (in some areas) as well as "the most urbanized region of the United States."[14]

The function of agriculture in the settlers' pursuit of that goal is of special interest to Frieda Knobloch, who has investigated two related "historiographical tropes" in the story of Western settlement: "the present emerging, as if inevitably, from the past, just as culture emerges inevitably over time from nature." That story begins and unfolds by a rationale of naturalization: "It cannot not happen that something primitive, simple, and primordial (associated with the past) gives way to something complex and sophisticated, just as it cannot not happen that an organism grows and develops or a child matures." From this analogizing ensue both the notion of the Indian as childlike and the understanding that untouched land awaits the plow. And thus does the fateful inference of the manifestness of destiny follow from the premise of a nature whose sole purpose is to yield to culture. Or from the fact of a world where, as Knobloch puts it with a more aggressive verb, the instrumentalities, physical and otherwise, of agriculture could "turn nature into culture," a transformation especially legible in the West because of its incompletion there—that is, "because of the West's continuing identification with wilderness."[15]

That agricultural transformation required a *colonization* of the West etymologically synonymous with its *cultivation*. Both words derive from the Latin *colere*, the meanings of which include "to till" and "to foster" as well as "to dwell in" (all of which are linked to another derivative, *culture*), and, as Knobloch explains, "the two words work together: colonization is about enforcing landownership through a new, agricultural occupation of lands once used differently."[16] What issues from the disruptive dialogue of colonization/cultivation with nature is a consummation that justified all manner of initiatives, from the Homestead Act to the filigreed branching of railways to the establishment of the U. S. Department of Agriculture, apposite to settling the late-nineteenth-century West.

In her critique Knobloch is careful to take into account Annette Kolodny's argument that the records of western settlement show white men and white women to have had quite different views of the West: the former, ideologically preponderant, saw it as virgin land to be mastered by the individualistic "imposition of fantasies of exploitation and large-scale transformation," while the latter, qualified by uncertain feelings about the damage caused by settlement, saw it "as a garden to be tended" (and thus a place of possible domesticity and cooperative community).[17] To borrow Stegner's distinction, the men were boomers, and the women were stickers. That's a drastically simplified contrast, of course, though it has some cogency. But it ignores the extent to which women were implicated—directly or indirectly, willy-nilly—in the enterprise urged by the male view (the gardens, homes, and communities they wanted necessitated, after all, exploitation and transformation on some scale). That view was co-optive, and the settlement it sanctioned occurred under the aegis of a European Enlightenment concept of progress renovated as unmistakably American—and Western—in both rhetoric and results.

The rhetoric was the work of men like John Charles Frémont, Congressional speechmaker Thomas Hart Benton, expansionist visionary William Gilpin, railroad president James DeBow, Whig newspaper editor Jessup Scott, and nationalist painter Emanuel Leutze. Collectively they recontextualized and literalized George Berkeley's declaration in his 1752 "Verses on the Prospect of Planting Arts and Learning in America" that "Westward the course of empire takes its way" beyond the decay of Europe and toward some vague culmination in the drama of history.[18] They trafficked in the imagery of white people inexorably vectored west for fresh starts, inexhaustible as-yet-untapped wealth, upward social mobility, new markets, a renewal of civilization, the end of political tyranny, on and on.

This "rhetoric of destiny," as West terms it, was intertangled with "a living myth—of a superior people finding their true home in a rising nation's exuberant heartland." All those who had lived there before them, from Clovis hunters and Mound Builders on, doubtless had perceived that land as meant for themselves and their lifeways, but the changes occasioned by white settlement "were so astonishingly quick, their results so seemingly sure, that they deluded people more than ever. The illusion of inevitability and control was nearly irresistible."[19] As frontier succeeded frontier, the plot of the myth became more inflated; but in all its versions it included some rewrite of the recovery narrative.

That narrative had long been artfully invoked by others—by William Bradford, of course, in his history of Plymouth, by Thomas Cole in paintings he did in the late 1820s and 1830s, by Ralph Waldo Emerson in his essay "The Young American" in 1844, for instance—but, Carolyn Merchant argues, "Euramericans acted [it] out

. . . in transforming the western deserts during the second half of the nineteenth century." Epitomized by Frederick Jackson Turner's 1893 essay on the closing of the frontier, that narrative, as translated into the terms of trans-Mississippi expansion, tells of men subjugating fallen land and making it into a garden safe for women and capitalism (except for the Rooseveltian remnants that "must be preserved as test zones for men . . . to hone male strength and skills"). The climax, never quite—or at least not yet—reached in the West, is dictated by an apocalyptic logic: "Civilization is the final end, the telos, toward which 'wild' nature is destined. . . . Civilization is thus nature natured, *Natura naturata*. . . . The unruly energy of wild female nature is suppressed and pacified. The final, happy state of nature natured is female and civilized." Such an "ascensionist narrative," Merchant observes, is exactly what's depicted in Leutze's 1862 mural in the U.S. Capitol, *Westward the Course of Empire Takes Its Way* (with armed men axing and uprooting the wilderness, preparing the way for women in wagons to their rear), or in Gast's *American Progress*.[20]

If the rhetoric of progress, with its selective and idealized myth of Western settlement, was (seemingly) unmixed in its message of subjugation and transformation, the results of progress were not, as we know. Nature and its denizens did not simply submit to the dream of recovery. Some settlers held on and lived more or less happily ever after, but some got along less well with the wilderness. The Homestead Act, though intended to provide opportunities for property ownership, made problems for many settlers, mainly because, as John Wesley Powell knew would be the case, most of the 160-acre homesteads lacked access to water and were located far from railroads. Homes on lots of those plots were no more than small boxes in nonarable backland. Women and preachers were formidable civilizers, but some towns, particularly those at the ends of cattle trails or in mining districts, held more hazardous wildness than the plains and mountains around them. The second big boom in settlement, which commenced as the West bounced back from the Panic of 1873, was attenuated by merciless cold and dryness in the 1880s.

Western wilderness was hard on settlers, but they were hard on it, too. Farming, mining, ranching, logging—all took a heavy toll. So heavy that, as the end of the century approached, any number of people, Westerners as well as Eastern onlookers, would have agreed with a character in Oakley Hall's *Separations*, William Jefford, when he says, "'The stump is the American symbol of progress and destruction. . . . From the beginning, settlers have sought to transform the wilderness into a garden, but their success is destroying the natural paradise that was the gift.'"[21] Probably those mourners would have agreed also with Patricia Nelson Limerick when she observed some years ago in regard to the West of the 1990s that "one thinks that one has seen all the possible variations on the injuries, costs, and disadvantages of uncontrolled human settlement, and reliably, one turns out to be wrong. . . . Human nature has met and matched nature in wildness and novelty."[22]

So goes the continuing dialectical tilt of restless settlers and resistive environment. The stakes are higher now than they were a hundred or a hundred and fifty years ago. The scale is larger. The outcome, as promised by rhetoric or predicted by science, is less guaranteed. And the engagement, by virtue of the mediation of postmodern technology, is more distant, less concrete, generally (in the short run at least) safer. Progress has blunted its sharpness, and therethrough something has been lost. Whatever their shortcomings, the nineteenth-century settlers of the West met the wilderness they hated and loved more fully than present-day Westerners meet it. John Ise, author of the 1936 classic Sod and Stubble, an account of his family's pioneering in western Kansas, vivifies that sentiment with existential details:

> These pioneers were in contact with reality. They felt the tingle of the cold, the kindly warmth of the fireside; they knew hunger, as we never know it, and the keen relish of needed food; they knew what it was to be dead-tired, and to sleep dreamlessly; they experienced the thrill of danger, the joy of solid achievement. . . . Theirs was the robust youth of a civilization; and, as the bent and gnarled old men and women so often said to me, "It was a good life," in some respects, perhaps, "a better life than folks have now."[23]

Ise wrote those words in the middle of the Great Depression. Think how much more tenuous our "contact with reality" has become since then, how much more we have distanced ourselves from the once far-less-mediated basal reality of natural wildness. Whatever their shortcomings, Ise's Old Westers understood better than their more recent—and maybe envious—New Western counterparts what Helen Vendler means when she remarks that "the best moments of all are the ones when the wild and the settled parts of being do not forget each other."[24]

To California Go: The Thar in Them Thar Hills

With knives they dug the metal out of stone;
Turned rivers back, for gold through ages piled,
Drove knives to hearts, and faced the gold alone;
Valley and river ruined and reviled.
    Yvor Winters, "John Sutter"

"Those of you on the left side of the aircraft might want to glance out your windows. That big hole down there is what used to be the largest truck-operated open-pit copper mine in the United States."

Obeying the pilot, I peered through the plastic. Not long airborne after departing Missoula, where I'd been attending the 1997 ASLE conference, and en route to Kansas City, the plane had just flown over the Deer Lodge Mountains and was now flying south of Butte, the hole known as the Berkeley Pit visible behind the port wing. It looked like the pit of Dante's Hell, complete with circles. The pilot said it was a mile and a half long, a mile wide, a quarter of a mile deep, the millions of gallons of contaminated water in the bottom of it making it the deepest lake in Montana. Lake? I saw no sign of life anywhere near it (in fact, as I found out later, recordings of eerie sounds have been used to ward off any migrating birds that might be tempted to land on that lethal soup).

The pilot went on: there were plans to clean up the mess with money from the hastily-established Superfund, to convert Butte, the city copper built, and its waste site into some sort of minescape park, a reproving remembrancer of the environmental cost of unchecked corporate greed. Would Westerners learn much from it? I noticed that a new pit was being dug to the east of the old one. Somebody across the aisle joked that locals called the place Butt, Montana. I could see why. It seemed less "The Last Best Place," Montana's slogan for the state's more naturally splendid parts, than just "The Last Place," a nether no-man's-land full of eschatological (as well as scatological) warning about the excesses of the West's extractive economy.

Operation of the Berkeley Pit began in 1955, marking a colossal continuation of the Butte copper-mining boom that had cranked up in 1880, when America's swelling demand for electrical wire was in its infancy. But Butte had experienced metal madness before that: a small boom in hard-rock silver mining in the late 1870s and, with the discovery of substantial placer deposits in Montana Territory in the early 1860s, a half-baked gold rush that eventually turned hydraulic and fouled creeks and reduced pine-covered hills to rubble—and made robber barons rich.[1] Given the fat profitability of those two metals in late-nineteenth-century Montana, it's no surprise that the official motto of the state, which entered the Union in 1889, is "Oro y Plata." Nor is it a surprise that the first word in that phrase capsuling so much deplorable history is "gold"; for if there ever was a first cause in the taking of the West, from the Spanish *entradas* on, it was gold.

J. E. Cirlot defines gold emblematically as the image of sun "in the earth" and "the essential element in the symbolism of the hidden or elusive treasure which is an illustration of the fruits of the spirit and of supreme illumination."[2] In concordance with those definitions, John Wilmerding, in his reflections on the luminist movement in America during the third quarter of the nineteenth century (in which movement he includes painters and photographers of Western landscapes such as Bierstadt, Carleton E. Watkins, and Timothy H. O'Sullivan), writes of "the pull of American 'light,' that palpable, spiritual beauty of the American wilderness," felt by early explorers of the New World: "Almost from the beginning were fused the real vastness of space . . . , the sun's golden radiance setting in the west, and the sense of spiritual as well as physical riches in this new continent. Looking to the glowing western horizon, therefore, promised the gold of this world and of the next"—a confluence of the interests of Catholic missionaries, Puritans, and then transcendentalists with those of the bedazzled searchers who participated in the 1849 Gold Rush and "its initiation of a truly gilded age of acquisitiveness."[3]

Elliott West discusses the Buddhistic and Christian associations of gold with "heavenly light" and the alchemists' confidence that making it from lead would teach them how to transform human baseness into holiness. Its appeal he attributes to three facts: "It is rare. It is remarkably inert and will combine with almost nothing around it—the source of its 'incorruptible' image. And it is shiny." To the Incas "it was the solar essence fallen in fragments" and thus "promised fertility, resurrection, and renewal." Loaded with such associations, qualities, meanings, it "clearly had the power to reshape places." The heart of that power, as West explains, was its allure, which altered perception, in this instance perception of land already viewed optimistically: "The American West had long been called the 'golden land.' The term expressed a general promise and a powerful, unfocused attraction. When gold was found in a particular place, that appeal took on a terrific, specific intensity, like light through a lens." The auriferous West toward which ideologues of Manifest Destiny like William Gilpin directed America's ambitions in the decade after 1849 thereby multiplied in its attractiveness to people wanting "to redream their existence."[4] No wonder Karl Marx, around that time "scribbling away through the winter of the British Museum," as Richard Rodriguez visualizes him, "believed the California Gold Rush was a more significant event than the discovery of the Americas by Columbus."[5] No wonder Americans lost sight of the Western wilderness, the base earth itself, in their quest for what it could yield of a metal invested with cultural magic. No wonder they confused the gold of this world and of the next.

Though miners in the Old West had as little esteem for geologists as they had for dowsers, such scientists have gleaned how gold wound up where it did. The process, chthonic and wild indeed, began, in Snyder's poetic résumé, a long long time ago:

First a sea: soft sands, muds, and marls
    —loading, compressing, heating, crumpling,
        crushing, recrystallizing, infiltrating,
several times lifted and submerged.
intruding molten granite magma
        deep-cooled and speckling,
            gold quartz fills the cracks. . . .[6]

After eons of rising and folding strata and surface erosion, some of the prize turned up within reach of pan, shovel, and more invasive tools in California, Colorado, New Mexico, South Dakota, and other places located, in America, mostly in the

West. Minor deliriums over gold occurred before the forty-niners were caught up in their major one—on Cherokee land in 1820s Georgia (a motive for Indian removal there), for example, and on land now in Los Angeles County in 1842—but the true lunacy centered first in the foothills of the Sierra Nevada east of Sacramento in 1848.

Those foothills slope into the Central Valley of California, which on February 2, 1848, when the Treaty of Guadalupe Hidalgo was signed (mere days after the discovery of gold on the American River) and the United States assumed ownership of the present Southwest and more, was populated by dozens of Indian tribes. Michael Kowalewski describes it as then being "a rich palimpsest of tribal customs, technologies, beliefs, and local ecologies," all interfused with biological diversity now almost unimaginable—an "American Serengeti" of antelope, elk, deer, grizzlies, pigeons, quail, trout, salmon.[7] Even in the summer and fall of 1848 that scene wasn't yet seriously disturbed. Most of the early birds were *Californios*, California-born Mexicans, not that many of them, and those seasons, in the words of Malcolm J. Rohrbough, "presented an idyllic, almost pastoral view of individuals and families camped alongside streams harvesting gold through the most rudimentary techniques, a vision of Arcadian harmony set off against the occasional examples of exploitation in which large numbers of Indian peoples worked the streams for little or nothing, a promise of harsher things to come."[8] Then (Snyder again) "came the white man," who was intent on "going after that old gravel and the gold."[9] For him the treasure is mostly all that matters; through what Leonard Lutwack calls his "Eldoradan use of land"—celestial connotations be damned—"both land and the people engaged in its exploitation are wasted or reduced to some infernal condition."[10]

The transmutation that made California what the Chinese of the 1850s referred to as Gold Mountain began midmorning on January 24, 1848, when James Marshall, constructing a sawmill in Coloma for self-invented grandee John Sutter, glanced idly into the millrace his Yalesumni workers were digging. He saw some fleeting glistening beneath a foot of sluicing water. He reached in and picked up what he was certain was a nugget of gold. Then he saw another and another, the size of BBs. Then he grew less certain; the color didn't seem right. But some amateur assaying proved his original guess correct. He and Sutter tried to keep the cat in the bag, but the cat was too big. Soon Sutter's mini-kingdom of Nueva Helvetia was overrun by squatters and he and Marshall left ruined—along with tens of thousands of others, cupidity-crazed castle-builders who scampered west only to end up as scavengers lost in booze and wandering excavated land they never really saw. After the Gold Rush, the West, environment and people, would never be the same again.

The rush to California, like later rushes to other fields of dreams, was, headmost and hindmost, a wild event. A largely male happening, it designates the start, in the popular mind, of the get-in-and-get-out West. Reverend Randall Hobart, a member of the Wolverine Rangers, a gold-mining company that left Marshall, Michigan, for California in the spring of 1849, wrote a letter to his hometown newspaper on May 24, 1850, in which he described the country around the Feather River as a place where "gambling is carried on to the highest extent" and "everything . . . is, so to speak, out of joint." On August 20, Elmon S. Camp, another member of the company, wrote likewise from Bidwell's Bar, in the same area, of "the moral degradation of California," where "vice of every description strides . . . with bold front, in open day," and "nineteen twentieths [of the population] are in the habit of drinking." Moreover, as Camp wrote from Smith's Bar on the Feather River on February 16, 1851, the miner, as if his wearying toil and coarse meals didn't make life sufficiently dismal, "is in continual danger from wild animals, savages, and difficult places in traversing the mountains through which it is necessary to pass."[11] Add to that list frostbite, heatstroke, blue devils, infectious illnesses, lynchings, and, as miners became more daring, rockfalls, cave-ins, tunnel fires, and other accidents.

The avaricious wildness of the Gold Rush, like the nitroglycerine in dynamite later used in mining, was a dangerous compound—of excitement, anarchy, dislocation, unfamiliar nature, ideological ambiguity, genocide, moral darkness. As a whole nation conjured up visions of auric wealth and a fair portion of its citizens headed west to trample and gut much of the land John Charles Frémont had depicted as a bucolic paradise, social critics of the rush argued that those sucked into its topsy-turvy bacchanal might prove indefinitely ungovernable or be destined for the nuthouse.[12] Laissez-faire Pollyannas may have felt the thrill of progress at play in such turmoil, but others were less sanguine. Even Bayard Taylor, a well-traveled editor for Horace Greeley's *New York Tribune* and a man usually composed when confronted by outlandishness, found 1849 San Francisco consternatingly astir in its "excess and dissipation of business" and warned that "he who but ventures into the outer circle of the whirlpool is spinning, ere he has time for thought, in its dizzy vortex." He complained that "never have I had so much difficulty in establishing, satisfactorily to my own senses, the reality of what I saw and heard."[13] For Taylor, who recently had reveled in the vicissitudes of the Isthmus of Panama, that city epicentral to the rush was, in David Goodman's description, "an altogether bewildering place, a place in which previous habits of perception were of no use at all."[14] Like the rest of California's gold-gaga localities, it was a cultural wilderness in the midst of a natural one.

Civilization disordered by greed was an old story in the Old World, and it would be repeated in the New—in Nevada, Colorado, Idaho, Montana, Arizona (Tombstone, its miner-funded business district once two-thirds saloons, gambling halls, and brothels, still advertises itself as "too tough to die"), South Dakota, and then the last-gasp fin-de-siècle frontier of the northern West, Alaska—but it was writ largest in California. Rohrbough reminds us that those who first joined the Gold Rush, primed with enthusiasm by sensationalistic journalism, entered a state just relinquished by Mexico (a nation ignorant of how much gold was there) that actually "was still part of a war zone." On the eve of their arrival, the rush internal to California already "was out of control." In that situation, "access to the rivers, streams, and valleys was, for all practical purposes, without limits." The miners, most of them clumsy novices, initially worked in and along only a few waterways, their sites jumbles of tents and shanties and picks and piles of dirt. They labored in a frenzy that "reflected the random and quixotic character of the mining experience."[15]

In time, as the frenzy spread and miners from everywhere descended into the belt of the Mother Lode, entropy climbed like a bull-market graph. Some miners lived like wolves in their earthen holes. Amenities were few and far between and astronomically expensive. Swindles were commonplace. Weeks wore long, their travail likely little rewarded, and R and R could be grotesque: "On Sundays," as John McPhee sums it up, "while you drink your tanglefoot whiskey, you can watch a dog kill a dog, a chicken kill a chicken, a man kill a man, a bull kill a bear. You can watch Shakespeare. You can visit a 'public woman.'"[16] In his 1994 account of a tour through California, Bill Barich writes of washing dishes at his campsite on the South Fork of the American River while trying to imagine how phantasmagorical that reign of entropy must have been, "how the foothills must have looked in 1849, throbbing with the energy of all the wistful souls pursuing the Vast Unknown, men as avid for experience as they were for gold." Such cogitation leads him to conclude that "the Gold Rush, as in adrenaline rush, was something not to be missed. In the mining camps and in the sudden, new cities that exploded into being like flares, the world's biggest party was going on, and the boldest, baddest, wildest, most free-spirited people around couldn't resist the invitation."[17]

Indisputably, that party was, in Goodman's understatement, "a disturbance to the normal order of things," and it raised no-nonsense ideological questions. Because of its chaos, the rush was rife with contradictions. It brought prosperity—but by a troubling means. Whatever progress it promised, for many it also was producing social decline. In its tumult Goodman discerns the cause for differences of opinion: "It was difficult even for this pre-Darwinian generation, habituated as it already was to modes of hierarchical or evolutionary explanation of human history, not to think of the activity of gold seeking as regressive."[18] On the basis of his reading of literary texts concerned with the rush, Kowalewski makes a similar point: the event "was assessed in radically divergent and contradictory terms from the start, both by the argonauts themselves and by outside observers.... Either a triumph of American enterprise and determination, or the final proof of an American insanity of greed and restlessness . . .—the gold rush was open to either interpretation."[19]

Interpretive teetering about the California Gold Rush, like that about other rushes, remains alive and well today, but the sorry results of its wildness were and are vividly apparent. Its deleterious impact, on both land and inhabitants, occurred because to those new to the place, as Kowalewski has it, "there was no 'there' in California to understand in a cultural sense, only a physical landscape to possess and reshape." The consequence of such blindness was pervasive "environmental havoc"—on all levels.[20]

That havoc has been thoroughly recorded. In *Roughing It* (1872), Mark Twain wrote of how miners in the 1850s had disfigured California land and of how mining towns had boomed and then fallen into shambles. Bret Harte melodramatized the degradations of mining in *The Story of a Mine* (1878). Helen Hunt Jackson and others wrote poems that elegized topographical and botanical beauties, wildlife, and human life trashed by it. Late in the nineteenth century, naturalist and environmentalist John Muir lamented that the foothills around the Stanislaus River "have been cut and scalped, and every gorge and gulch and valley torn to pieces and disemboweled." He wrote of the area's leftover miners that they "linger languidly in the washed-out gulches or sleepy village [Murphy's Camp] like harried bees around the ruins of their hive"; however intriguing he found those characters to be, he also judged them "perhaps more exhausted than the mines, and about as dead as the dead rivers."[21]

The more gold seeking became technologized and industrialized, the more it violated and destroyed places and people in California and elsewhere. Underground mining did its share, but no environmental damage related to mining in the nineteenth-century West exceeded that inflicted by the water cannons used in hydraulic mining to get at gold-bearing deposits. "In effect," as Richard White summarizes it, the technique "took mountains and washed them into rivers. In places the accumulated debris filled mountain canyons to a depth of 100 feet and more."[22] Though hydraulic mining would later be regulated by law, such mammoth messes had severely clogged rivers by the late 1860s—with gritty Noachian aftermaths for farms and population centers downstream.

McPhee offers an illuminating description of the action of the water cannon, along with a quotation that reveals the attitude toward nature of those who wielded it:

> At a hundred and twenty-five pounds of pressure per square inch, the column of shooting water seems to subdivide into braided pulses hypnotic to the eye, and where it crashes at the end of its parabola it sounds like a storm sea hammering a beach. . . . Benjamin Silliman, Jr., a founding professor of the Sheffield Scientific School, at Yale, writes in 1865, "Man has, in the hydraulic process, taken command of nature's agencies, employing them for his own benefit, compelling her to surrender the treasure locked up in the auriferous gravel by the use of the same forces which she employed in distributing it!"[23]

The diction—both McPhee's and, less subtly, Silliman's—betrays the technocratic arrogance that informed the emprise of disintegrating mountains in the chase of buttery metal. Equally revealing, with more disturbing undertones, is Silliman's couching his proclamation about the power of giant nozzles in the language of sexual conquest.

The Anglo-male attitude toward wilderness displayed here is old stuff, of course, but its symbolic specificity is striking. Much that same specificity—though articulated less overtly and from a female point of view—may be teased out of an oil done by Margaretta (Mrs. Jonas W.) Brown sometime in the 1870s titled *Mining in the Boise Basin in the Early Seventies*. Studying her painting, you can discern a hierarchically organized man-against-nature battle scene, one, even if prideful about progress, overflowing with visual double-entendres. Below, down in the canyon, men in identical pale slickers are shooting water onto the eroding slope, flushing tons of gold-laden dirt into gullies. Up above, on the ridge, before a backdrop of soft, rounded peaks half peeled of timber, men in suits look on, the well-dressed women with them perhaps, like the artist, finding something telltale in such rapine that makes the landscape, to borrow language from Katharina at the end of Shakespeare's *The Taming of the Shrew*, "like a fountain troubled, / Muddy, ill-seeming, thick, bereft of beauty."[24]

Indeed, the effects all the mastering practices of mining had on the Western wild might well be described in like terms. They ravaged it directly, of course, by making sludge and rubble of geological splendors, but also indirectly by propelling urban growth and the overnight blooming of boomtowns that often subsided into ghost towns. Cities like San Francisco and Denver that profited from mining in the nineteenth century should be understood not as isolated imperial nodes but as hubs—economic, industrial, cultural (and, increasingly, multicultural)—on the periphery of a meridian-leaping metropolitan society bent on rebuilding the wilderness in its own image.[25] The boomtowns, with names like California Gulch and Gold Hill and Silver City, to which mining gave rise were—despite the zealotry of reformers, the moral authority of betterment-minded women, and the civic pride of sanctimonious magnates—mostly incoherent communities dithering with the chicaneries of business and mired in vice and violence. When a boomtown went belly up and the interests (typically Eastern) that created it pulled out, what remained was keenly illustrative of Bernard DeVoto's description of the West as a "plundered province."[26] In her examination of the history of extractive industry in the Rockies, Anne F. Hyde synopsizes the ecological upshot of this flip-flop: "When industry boomed, people were too busy making money to worry about industrial waste, and when it busted, no one had the money or the desire to clean up, leaving the region as combination charnel house and toxic junkyard."[27] If the town in the midst of that botchery got abandoned, its ruins soon resembled, in Muir's image that summons up the bad days of another sort of extractive industry, "the bones of cattle that have died of thirst."[28] A town in that condition, as Lutwack puts it, "is the symbolical end-product of American Eldorado."[29] All the trash left for nature to deal with,

Margaretta (Mrs. Jonas W.) Brown, Mining in the Boise Basin in the Early Seventies (1870s): a hierarchically organized man-against-nature battle scene. (Oil on canvas, 26 1/2 x 20 3/4 in. 349. Idaho State Historical Society.)

from graying lumber to tailings by the acre-foot, amounts to not just a ghost town but a ghost wilderness as well.

To be sure, many people were dubious about the future of any society based on mining that trumpeted America's triumphal march across the continent. Goodman documents Californians who early on set the tone for such pessimism by proposing alternatives: either "the agricultural society" or "the natural world in its un-cultivated state." The press persistently offered agrarianism, in prose and poetry, "which deprecated gold mining and praised the agricultural life." Nor was it hard to find advocacy of pastoralism as an alternative. Taylor exulted in the spirituality of the California wilderness, as did the pantheistic Unitarian minister Thomas Starr King and others with a transcendentalist penchant; and, Goodman notes, "often within a religious framework . . . the natural world was harnessed to the criticism of the values of gold-rush society."[30]

Predictably, however, ambivalence permeated Euro-American attitudes toward the wilderness mining was unmaking. Goodman detects it in the 1850s writings of Franklin Langworthy, a Universalist minister, and Alonzo Delano, a merchant-banker turned humorist (and then successful Yuba River miner). The former, re-counting his arrival in California, "wrote repeatedly *both* of the danger he faced from the Indians *and* of the beauty of the scenery he encountered" in what he saw as vacant land waiting to be taken. The latter was able to give himself to both "ad-miration of the sublimity of the natural scene" and "celebration of the intruders who are 'tearing up the soil' in the cause of civilisation."[31] For Hyde, such am-bivalence is plentifully turned up by her investigation of the "deeply conflicting values" inscribed in the extractive-industrial history of the Rockies. While she ad-mits there have been Westerners who incarnate a sort of Sagebrush Rebel's mythic redaction of those conflicting values, individuals who were "deeply devoted to the land, but also intent on extracting wealth," she deduces from historical evidence that "most people went to the Rocky Mountains to make a quick killing and leave." Yet that's not quite the end of the matter; for, albeit Rocky Mountain communities have held to a mobile-home architectural aesthetic and encouraged plundering, still "the beauty of the landscape is continually celebrated." Thus she concludes that the people of the Rockies, if they wish "to have an impact on the future, . . . have to see the shape of their history more clearly and recognize the conflict at its core," a conflict that "explains much of how we use, imagine, and fear the Rocky Mountains themselves."[32]

For Euro-Americans, recognition of that conflict in the history of the Rockies—and the rest of the mined West—and resolution of the ambivalence that empowers it have come about and, as Hyde implies, will come about, to the extent that they have and will, predominantly through a *transvaluing* retrospect. By that I mean a retrospect that evaluates the past in terms of a new, more sobersided, fuller un-derstanding of it—specifically, of what, apart from artificially valorized metal, was discovered by those who hurried west. They discovered the kick of risk all gamblers crave, of course, but many of them later realized that the lasting significance of their mining experiences had to do with something about the "there" that Kow-alewski says they failed to grasp while enslaved by greed and that, moreover, they yearned to return to.

Call that something, as Wilmerding might, the spiritual riches of Western nature or, as Aldo Leopold might, its "cultural harvest."[33] It involved an urgent sense of connection to the wilderness. Rohrbough hints at it in his account of elderly New England argonauts who in 1890 organized and undertook a train trip back to the mining camps of 1849. Like the members of other such groups around the country, they shared a "strange and shimmering past"; their trip was motivated by "the prospect of recapturing the sense of the place and the time of the Gold Rush in a direct way." When they reached the sites of what were once their claims, they found them radically changed, some of the hills they'd worked obliterated by water cannons. Whatever their responses to such alteration and erasure, they were there not because of "the luxury accommodations that they enjoyed on the train and in California" (the fruits of the tame present) but because of "the memories of the greatest adventure of their lives" (the fruits of the wild past).[34]

Jack London gets at that something in his story "All Gold Canyon," written in 1905, seven years after he departed from the Northland, a wilderness he had decided, according to Earle Labor, "was a hostile place to be escaped *from*, not *to*." The story tells of the "newly awakened ecological conscience" of a writer who, having settled in the Sonoma Valley and gotten past his fascination with Klondike bonanza kings (who, "like their Puritan forebears," behold "in wildness not the preservation of the world, but profit"), portrays a more pastoral wilderness in which "the roles between Man and Nature are reversed from what they were in the Northland: it is Man who now becomes the savage destructive force, Nature the helpless victim."[35]

William W. Bevis deals with that something in his 1999 novel *Shorty Harris; or, The Price of Gold*, the fictionalized account of a real-life Death Valley prospector whose search for gold gives way to a quest for a deeper relationship with the desert he has exploited. It's a novel that recalls Robert Service's 1907 chestnut "The Spell of the Yukon," whose speaker, another Klondiker, has learned that "somehow the gold isn't all," that what's really valuable is the beauty and stillness of "the great, big, broad land 'way up yonder."[36]

Would that the legacy of the Gold Rush were so simple. It isn't. An innocuous national nostalgia about the event persists unflaggingly—witness the two sesquicentennial exhibits concerning it at the National Museum of American Art in late 1998 and early 1999 that later traveled to California venues—but so do the harmful delusions that energized it—witness the A&E documentary miniseries *California and the Dream Seekers* broadcast in January 1998. (As Zeese Papanikolas remarks of the so-called Dream Mine of Utahans, which "exists in a tantalizing mental area between fiction and reality," it is—no matter its promise before, during, or after the automotive gold rushes of the Great Depression—"the dark side of America.")[37] Gold greed still thrives in the West, where mining companies now extract the metal from cheaply purchased federal land on a zillion-dollar basis, leaving rearward more and more Buttes, land turned into trash by strip mining with loaders and haulers the size of mansions and contaminated by the cyanide that leaches gold from low-grade ore. And the conversation of conflicting values drags on, its polarities codified in the title of a public conference held at the University of California at Santa Cruz in the summer of 1998 called, maybe with a note of transvaluational hope, "Green and Gold: California Environments—Memories and Visions."[38]

Barich offers, in a sentence, what may have been the principal lesson of his tour of the Golden State (whose motto is "Eureka"): "Every true California story, I would learn, begins in yearning and ends in transformation."[39] That may apply to every true Western story in general. If it does, then what each one's transformation yields, green or gold or some balanced marriage of the two, depends on what's yearned for.

Reinventing the Indian: The Red Devil

The only good Indians I ever saw were dead.
General Philip H. Sheridan

For several hours on June 26, 1867, near Fort Wallace in western Kansas, Company G of the Seventh Cavalry fought a superior force of Cheyenne and Sioux warriors. Sometime after the Indians had withdrawn, Dr. William A. Bell came upon the mutilated body of Sergeant Frederick Wyllyams, one of six cavalrymen killed in the battle. Outwardly, he may have conducted his autopsy with clinical objectivity, but Bell doubtless felt twinges of the fear Josiah Gregg had known back in the 1830s (the whiz of an arrow in the rebounding of a branch, the snap of a gunlock in the clacking of pebbles). An amateur photographer, he took a picture of the corpse. It's an unforgettable image: a head battered and crusted with blood, torso pierced with arrows like St. Sebastian's in Mantegna's painting of that martyr, eviscerated abdomen gaping open, thorax emptied of its heart, arms mangled, thighs slashed lengthwise to the bone. No man like the Eton-educated Wyllyams could have done such a thing, Bell, though not ignorant of white enormities against Indians (or Native ways and beliefs about the afterlife), may have thought; only incorrigibly evil savages were capable of it. Certainly conclusions of that kind would occur to others, not only those who had seen such things with their own eyes but also the less venturesome who encountered pictures of Indian atrocities as horrid as Bell's in *Harper's Weekly* and elsewhere. If you needed ocular proof that the Indian was a devil, it was available.

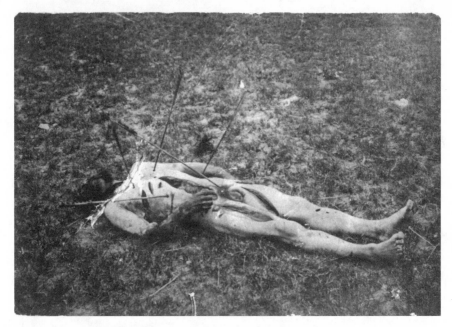

Dr. William A. Bell, The Remains of Sergeant Frederick Wyllyams (1867): *ocular proof that the Indian was a devil. (Fort Sill National Historic Landmark and Museum.)*

That idea wasn't new, of course. All along there had been equivocality in the Puritan-colonial tradition as to whether the wilderness to the west was spiritually renewing or degenerative, but the demonization of Indians (as Satan-worshipping, trapped in sin, and the like) had never let up, Noble Savage sentiments to the contrary notwithstanding. Longfellow's Indian-heroizing epic *The Song of Hiawatha* didn't speak for all Americans when it was published in 1855. Even if the demonizing of Indians in the West lacked Matherian fanaticism, it was nonetheless common and often vehement—especially after the Civil War, when settlement crowded more and more Indians off their land, hemmed them in, and provoked the violent defensiveness that made them seem like devils. Such seeming was, of course, expedient.

When the British explorer Richard F. Burton boarded a Concord coach on August 7, 1860, in St. Joseph, Missouri, to visit the Far West, he already knew something of—and would come to know more of—that defensiveness and the desperation prompting it. On his way to Salt Lake City and then California, he kept copious notes about Indian cultures, but, for all his humane sympathy and anthropological sophistication, his study of their peoples often led him to observations trimmed with the terminology of demonization. "The Prairie tribes," he proclaims, "are untamed and untamable savages. . . . the Shoshonees and the Yutas (Utahs) are as cruel as their limited intellects allow them to be." The pupil of the Indian's eye, which some travelers describe as "'snaky and venomous,'" reminds him of "the Evil Eye." He detects "a peculiar animality to the countenance" of the Indian. Indian religion "is a low form of fetichism." The Indian "never tells the truth." While Indian women "in their teens have often that *beauté du diable*, which may be found even among the African negresses," it's "evanescent"—so that the aging Indian woman, who has no belief ("not even in the rude fetichism of her husband"), "rapidly descends in *physique* and *morale*: there is nothing on earth more fiendlike than the vengeance of a cretin-like old squaw."[1]

The contemporary white perception of Indians as ugly signaled another reversal of axiological poles, one that's indexed not only by Burton-like views of Indian customs and countenances but also by the typical take on Indian languages. As Jill Lepore demonstrates, it involved both a change from and a recurrence of earlier European and American assumptions about Indians. Although Columbus held the opinion that the Indians he encountered really had no language, the whites of Jamestown and Plymouth tended to believe that Indians "did have languages—barbaric, guttural, grating, ridiculous, impossible to learn, and possibly satanic." During the Enlightenment, in turn, their speech was regarded as eloquent, exemplary of the Noble Savage. That perception, however, "changed in the late nineteenth century. After years of Plains Indian warfare, Native American speech was again seen as ugly, unredeemable, unevolved. 'Ugh' emerged as the ubiquitous Indian exclamation"—and its like would later turn up in reams of movie scripts.[2]

A hard-to-shake habit of projection obtained in this bad-Indian fixation. The projection, as Robert F. Berkhofer Jr. analyzes it, entailed Euro-Americans' "using counterimages of themselves to describe Indians and the counterimages of Indians to describe themselves." By that expedient, if Euro-Americans "could project their own sins upon people they called savages, then the extermination of the Indian became a cleansing of those sins from their own midst as well as the destruction of a feared enemy." Though such counterimages can function ambivalently, depending on how you feel about Indians' lack of white civilization, and in the process give rise to "two fundamental but contradictory conceptions of Indian culture," the conception dominant in the late nineteenth century clearly was the one that deemed that culture cankered by sin and not the one that valorized it.[3]

As the Talmudic maxim goes, we see things not as they are but as we are. Or, as Richard C. Poulsen puts it, "we see what we have been taught to see—or rather, we see what our transforming images allow us to see."[4] Since Indians in the way of God-decreed settlement were prone not, in Donald Worster's words, "to disappear peacefully, nonviolently, abstractly, cleanly" but to act quite otherwise, many pioneers judged them less than human "and had no qualms about shooting as many as they could."[5] For a good number of those pioneers, as for Burton, the Indian's subhuman nature was not only physical but correlatively moral and spiritual as well. In more than one sense they "made an enemy" of the Indian.

The Western enemy that white America made was wild, therefore antagonistic to Christianity and progress, therefore evil. Therefore a devil. As Indian antagonism increased in response to increasing settlement, the mythology of the Noble Savage steadily fell out of favor—a declension, as Peter L. Thorslev Jr. notes, attendant upon "the diminution of Romantic faith in nature" and "the rise of a Victorian faith in evolution, in progress, and in the benefits of a mercantile and industrial civilization"—and the Indian was reinvented as the lowercased ignoble savage, a figure I earlier termed, here echoing Thorslev's eponymous modifier, the Victorian satanic Indian.[6]

Coincident with accelerating industrialization and urbanization, a more and more utilitarian attitude toward the natural environment, and a concomitant lowercasing of Romantic celebration of wild nature into a romantic conflict with it, that reinvention carried a change in cultural imagery whose beginning William H. Truettner dates back to the 1840s and that occurred because Indians threatened migration into the West: "Either they had to be cast in the role [Asher B.] Durand chose for them in his [1853] painting *Progress*—as thoughtful witnesses to the passing of an age—or they had to be portrayed as belligerents . . . whose chief delight was attacking trappers, wagon trains, or defenseless women and children." The latter portrayal required hatred of Indians, which rose as lust for their land rose. Thus, as settlement enlarged, "contact between whites and Indians was generally shown as conflict, and violence became condoned as the triumph of good over evil."[7] In Berkhofer's tarter terms, in a West where federal troops and local law were seldom effective in protecting Indians from whites, many citizens "saw little reason not to violate Indian country or to kill Native Americans at will, justifying their actions by summoning up the image of the Indian as a horrible savage."[8]

Late-nineteenth-century images of Indians as evil belligerents (and whites as victims) survive in various media, but none is more blatant than Theodor Kaufmann's 1867 oil *Westward the Star of Empire*. In that painting Indians are portrayed crawling on their bellies in the moonlit darkness beside a railroad from which they have pried free sections of track and on which a distant train, headlight bright, chugs toward the viewer. Those Indians, like the real Sioux and Cheyennes assailing railroad-construction crews on the northern plains in the late 1860s, thereby, in Julie Schimmel's interpretation, "attack one of the preeminent symbols of American progress and westward expansion. As the light of civilization approaches, the forces of evil skulk in the dark, carrying out their devilish plans to derail the approaching train and, by extension, the progress of white civilization."[9] Indeed, Kaufmann's Indians have the air of reptiles so "unincorporated" by that civilization, as to be, in Poulsen's designation, "unimaginably dangerous, untouched by the transforming image: an autonomous evil."[10]

While some whites still fancied Indians to be noble spectators of their own dying out, exposed the U.S. government's despicable treatment of them (most fa-

Theodor Kaufmann, Westward the Star of Empire (1867): Indians as reptilian forces of evil working to derail the progress of white civilization. (St. Louis Globe-Democrat Archives of the St. Louis Mercantile Library at the University of Missouri–St. Louis.)

mously, but not unambiguously, Helen Hunt Jackson in her 1881 book A Century of Dishonor), or even attempted to expiate injustices against them, others busied themselves with exterminating the brutes. Like General William Tecumseh Sherman, they believed, in Frederick Turner's words, "that the Plains, as the last stronghold of the savages, would have to be cleared before settlers could feel safe and before the nation could achieve its special destiny."[11] Many among them considered Indians merely obstructing varmints and the slaying of them an honor or a divine right, an opinion maintained by Colonel John M. Chivington, who in November 1864 set up cannons on high ground near a peaceful Cheyenne camp on Sand Creek in eastern Colorado Territory and oversaw a binge of shooting, gutting, scalping, and dismemberment.[12] In the same spirit, leading the Seventh Cavalry, Lieutenant Colonel George Armstrong Custer stormed a Cheyenne village on the Washita River in Indian Territory in November 1868, killed more than a hundred men (including the peace-minded chief Black Kettle) and uncounted women and children, shot hundreds of horses, and burned everything else. After Lakota and Cheyenne warriors wiped out Custer and his regiment at the Battle of the Little Bighorn in June 1876, national fear of savagery's overwhelming civilization in the West deepened, justifying more severe military suppression or destruction of Indians.[13]

As many historians have argued, military success in crushing Indians in the 1870s and 1880s came about more through doggedness and attrition than anything else. The Great Sioux War, which was actually about gold in the Black Hills, ended that way in the winter of 1876–77. Other wars—with the Cheyennes, Comanches, Kiowas, and Apaches, tribes relentlessly pursued, afflicted with disease, and denied shelter and food—likewise ended with weary Indians ignominiously surrendering. That was true as well in the case of the Nez Percés, an obliging people who had been bullied into war by eviction from their land in northeastern Oregon.[14] It was their Chief Joseph who in 1877, his flight to Canada cut short, at his last war council declared, "I am tired. . . . I will fight no more forever." He thus represented many Natives who had lost out against white depredations in the West, but the efficient end of protracted warfare between whites and the peoples they sought to control or eliminate didn't come to pass until Sioux factions brought together in reaction to the Wounded Knee Massacre on December 28, 1890, surrendered to General Nelson A. Miles on January 15, 1891, on the Pine Ridge Reservation in southwestern South Dakota. That massacre had to do with the Ghost Dance movement, and that movement had to do with differences between white and Indian attitudes toward the Western wilderness.

On July 6, 1876, ten days after the wipeout of Custer and his troops, the *Bismarck Tribune*, a newspaper in what was then Dakota Territory, published an extra concerning that disaster. Following several front-page subheadings (one of which announced that some of the Indians' victims had been "Tortured in Fiendish Manner" while another beseeched, "Shall This Be the Beginning of the End?"), the account opened by recalling that the paper had sent a special correspondent, Mark Kellogg, to accompany General Alfred Terry as he led one of three advances against the Sioux in the basin of the Yellowstone River. When Custer's regiment detached and proceeded along Rosebud Creek toward the Little Bighorn, Kellogg, readers found out, had gone along for the ride. His last words sent to the editor of the *Tribune* were, as quoted in the account, these: "'We leave the Rosebud tomorrow and by the time this reaches you we will have MET AND FOUGHT the red devils, with what result remains to be seen.'"[15]

In 1876 "red devils" was a matter-of-course white epithet for Indians, particularly for those who were troublemakers, "hostiles," and its currency, like the rekindled Puritan zealotry ensuring that currency, lasted awhile. With ignorant ease the military and the public attached it—or similar nomenclature of the demonic— to Indians whose activities were bruited about the most, the leaders of the hostiles: Satanta, Crazy Horse, Dull Knife, Lone Wolf, and others. In 1890, four years after the menace the Mexicans called Geronimo had surrendered and he and his Chiricahua Apaches had been made prisoners of war, the red devils still weren't under control, especially in the northern West, where for many whites the main bugbear was a Hunkpapa Sioux medicine man who for thirty-three years had been a tribal war chief and who was strongly identified with the demonic: Sitting Bull. To them he remained, even after an 1885 tour with Buffalo Bill's Wild West, what he had been when he held the Sioux confederation together in the 1870s, the Indian whom Robert M. Utley summons up as "the man to get, the archdemon of the Sioux hold-outs, the architect of Custer's defeat and death, the supreme monarch of all the savage legions arrayed against the forces of civilization"—the leader who "had indeed come to mean, for Indians and whites alike, the hostile Indians."[16]

In 1890 that meaning was reinforced by Sitting Bull's influential (though maybe skeptical) espousal of the Ghost Dance. He spent the year, until he was killed on December 15, living in a cabin by the Grand River on the Standing Rock Reservation in northern South Dakota, where the U.S. Army had sent him in 1883. Ian Frazier describes him as a magnet for "the wildest and most unreconstructed Indians on the reservation" and the camp around his cabin as the place where, once the Ghost Dance religion had made its way to reservations across the West, the local Ghost Dancers gathered. That religion was, in Frazier's sketch, the handiwork of a Paiute named Wovoka who was acquainted with Christianity and at times claimed he was "the Messiah returned." His inspiration was a vision he'd experienced during a solar eclipse: "He said that he went to heaven and saw God, who told him that if the Indians did a dance which He would teach him, and danced long enough and hard enough, all white people would be submerged under a layer of new earth five times the height of a man, and the buffalo would return, and all the Indians who had ever lived would come back to life, and the land would become a paradise."[17] The Ghost Dance, with its promise of restoration, obviously was attractive to Indians—but scarcely to white people, especially those on or near reservations. To them Wovoka seemed more Antichrist than Christ, for they had little interest in being "submerged" and wanted the West not restored to a less manageable wildness but further tamed and civilized. In practical terms, they wanted what Indian agents sought to—and gradually did—accomplish: the arrest of leaders of the Ghost Dance movement and the quelling of their followers.

The arrest that went most wrong was that of Sitting Bull, which escalated from a tense situation into a riot during which he was killed. The quelling that went most wrong was that of the Lakota Ghost Dancers of the Miniconjou tribe at Wounded Knee on the Pine Ridge Reservation, which ended—after less than an hour of fire from Colonel James W. Forsyth's soldiers' rifles, pistols, and Hotchkiss guns—with a snowy killing field littered with the bodies of several hundred Indians. Questions sprang up about Sitting Bull's death, and the public soon suspected that the incident at Wounded Knee had been not a battle but a butchery; but what had precipitated both disasters was fear of the return of the demonically wild. A decisive determinant of the extremity of response instigated by that fear was, as Turner makes clear, historical context, for such atavism "seemed so safely buried beneath the towns, cities, and railroads," with Indians relegated to the hazy realm of nostalgia; yet the wilderness began "to howl again with the chants of these dancers." Moreover, the dancers belonged to tribes on both sides of the Rockies. The thing was spreading—"so once again commenced the Hunt for the Wild Man, the sha-man, the ultimate doer of this evil." The main suspects were the Sioux war chief Red Cloud and Sitting Bull. Since the former was old and no more than ceremoni-ally connected to the movement, Sitting Bull had to be cast in the role of ultimate evildoer. When talk couldn't persuade him to forswear his adherence to the Ghost Dance, "plans were laid." Indian police, acting on "ominously vague orders," car-ried out those plans.[18]

The removal of Sitting Bull didn't, however, remove the image of the red devil. It stayed. In the portraits for which Sitting Bull had sat after his surrender in 1881—and in portraits of other chiefs of other tribes, like the Cheyenne and Comanche and Apache, whose members whites regarded as extremely cruel and inscrutable. In dime novels about the West and in visual stereotypes of Indians derived from the canvases of Remington and other painters and displayed on movie and televi-sion screens. Cinematic representations, with few exceptions before demythologiz-ing (and somewhat more culturally informed) films like *Cheyenne Autumn* (1964) and *Little Big Man* (1970) and *Ulzana's Raid* (1972), were of Indians far from "friendly" (or even human): they appeared instead as icons of savage villainy ever on the warpath, whose indelibility in the American mind served as a justification for genocide and as a reminder of the dangerous wilderness Western expansion supposedly overcame.

While the red devil was the dominant image of the Indian in the West during the latter half of the nineteenth century, it's important to remember, again, that the Noble Savage didn't evaporate during that time. The basic images of good and bad Indians that had persisted for centuries continued to persist. After the 1840s that double persistence guaranteed an ongoing contest of images correspondent with opposed desires among white Americans: for expansion to be incremental or for it to happen rapidly, for assimilating Indians or for exterminating them, for allotting land to them on an individual basis and habilitating them as farmers and ranchers (finally by the provisions of the Dawes Severalty Act) or for simply restricting them to reservations without consideration of their wherewithal, and so forth. Despite their divergences, such paired desires had in common an implication to which I'll return in a later chapter: the extinction, in one sense or another, of tribal Indians.

That implication, however, folded within itself a subtler one, a certainty that gives Woodrow Call, in Larry McMurtry's novel *Comanche Moon*, pause as he pon-ders, in the mid-1850s, the coming plight of the Comanches he has fought for years but for whom he feels a "contradictory itch of admiration":

> They were deadly, merciless killers, but they were also the last free Indians on the southern plains. When the last of them had been killed, or their freedom taken from them, their power broken, the plains around him would be a dif-ferent place. It would be a safer place, of course, but a flavor would have been

taken out of it—the flavor of wildness. Of course, it would be a blessing for the settlers, but the settlers weren't the whole story—not quite.[19]

An Animal Holocaust: Wildlife Management in the Old West

> *Lying still,*
> *I felt an earthquake rumble, a herd*
> *stampeded by rifles, miles of humpbacks*
> *galloping, about to disappear.*
>   Walter McDonald, "In Fields of Buffalo"

One day in August 1930 the Nebraska writer John G. Neihardt, working on his narrative poem *The Song of the Messiah*, went to the Pine Ridge Reservation in search of "some old medicine man who had been active in the Messiah [Ghost Dance] Movement and who might somehow be induced to talk to me about the deeper spiritual significance of the matter."[1] With the help of the Indian agent at the Pine Ridge Agency, he met a Sioux holy man named Nicholas Black Elk, who was old and nearly blind. They spoke together from noon till after sunset, then planned for Neihardt to return during the following spring. Beginning in early May 1931, Neihardt and Black Elk had many lengthy conversations, from which Neihardt acquired not only information about the Ghost Dance and events related to it but also Black Elk's biography and the vision of creation winding through it—all of which he would soon fashion into *Black Elk Speaks: Being the Life Story of a Holy Man of the Oglala Sioux*.

In that book Black Elk, telling of his boyhood, recalls the Lakotas' fear of the white men invading their land in the mid-1870s and how by and by he learned "what the fighting was about." His explanation of the cause of war interweaves the concerns of several of my previous chapters:

> Up on the Madison Fork the Wasichus [whites] had found much of the yellow metal that they worship and that makes them crazy, and they wanted to have a road up through our country to the place where the yellow metal was; but my people did not want the road. It would scare the bison and make them go away, and also it would let the other Wasichus come in like a river. They told us that they wanted only to use a little land, as much as a wagon would take between the wheels; but our people knew better. And when you look about you now, you can see what it was they wanted.

That bitter recounting prefaces a moment of both wistful remembrance of the La-kota world before the Wasichus arrived and regret for what they did to it:

> Once we were happy in our own country and we were seldom hungry, for then the two-leggeds and the four-leggeds lived together like relatives, and there was plenty for them and for us. But the Wasichus came, and they have made little islands for us and other little islands for the four-leggeds, and always these is-lands are becoming smaller, for around them surges the growing flood of the Wasichus; and it is dirty with lies and greed.[2]

Commenting on this passage, Donald Worster points up the natural companion-ship in the country Black Elk evokes and what happened to those who shared in it: "They were linked together in an ecological league of nations, and they went down together in defeat—dying out, retreating into the earth, or confined to res-ervations."[3]

Whatever belated efforts intervened on behalf of those companions, from com-passion or conservationist anxiety or some other motive, and prevented their extir-pation to the last germ cell, the wildlife of the West, like the Indians of the West, didn't just wane into death, retreat, or confinement: the invaders inflicted such lessenings upon it. They had no real idea of what Worster calls "the peoplehood of animals and plants"; if they anthropomorphized at all, they usually attributed vice, not virtue, to life-forms. Thus to them beavers "appear as 'fur'" and wolves as creatures of crafty evil.[4] While Indians' active participation in fur trade must be acknowledged, that perception of wildlife as merely commercially valuable or mor-ally negative had consequences of a very Euro-American stripe.

Consequences—along with other consequences stemming from other, related perceptions. Though some of the first whites in the West, Zebulon Pike among them, refrained by conscience from freely killing animals that still make the place distinctive and though opposition to such killing crescendoed in the last half of the century, the death toll snowballed. For decades, most intensely in the 1870s, herds of bison miles long were reduced to millions of putrid hide-stripped car-casses. Once the Indians were out of the way, partly because of the depletion of bison, bluebloods and lowlifes alike, unrestrained by game laws, blasted through the West, bagging or leaving to rot untold myriads of turkeys, elks, ducks, herons, badgers, hawks, antelopes, owls, doves, raccoons, cranes, on and on. "No won-der then," Worster concludes, "that . . . the wildlife numbers of the West plum-meted" and that in time "blank uniformity was often all there was, the abundance had become rarity, and much of the grandeur had gone out of the landscape"—a conclusion soon true not only of the plains and mountains of the West but of its rivers and bordering ocean water as well. No wonder that domesticated animals would multiply to take up the vacated space and that economics would necessitate the killing of any predators (wolves, bears, coyotes, mountain lions, and the like) threatening (or seemingly threatening) to those animals. No wonder then that for a long time, well into the twentieth century, conservation was compromised by "its categorization of nature as either useful commodities or useless encumbrances." No wonder then that after the 1920s, when some Western wildlife began to make a comeback, it did so in the only way it could—"from the edge of extinction" (and partly by dint of conservation measures). No wonder then that our growing awareness of mixed consequences brings us, with Worster, face to face, again, with an inveterate ambivalence: "Since Lewis and Clark shot their first grizzly in 1804, the West has been a place where Americans have come to kill animals as well as to raise and preserve them."[5]

Mixed consequences thus derive from a mix of perceptions, of evaluations. In the case of the settlers migrating into the West in the second half of the nineteenth century, the mix was inordinate, polarized, variable—to a great extent because many of them encountered kinds and numbers of wildlife beyond their tenderfoot ken. The bison was as "startlingly unfamiliar" to the inexperienced as it had been to the Spanish, whose fancies had molded it, in Richard C. Poulsen's phrasing, "into a shaggy monster of immense proportions, an image of cultural expectation, not a biological verity."[6] Those overlanders, says Elliott West, "were not surprised to see new species of beasts. . . . But the actuality of these creatures jarred them." Bison in the thousands amazed them. Antelope, with their speed and agility, left them "slightly giddy." Wolves (or coyotes), wicked in symbolism, "swarmed along the roads."[7] Oftentimes unfamiliarity bred awe as readily as contempt—or a blend of the two.

Eugene D. Fleharty has documented the variety of responses that native animals elicited from new-arrived immigrants to the Great Plains between 1865 and 1879. The extremes of those responses, "ranging from terror to the sublime," he exemplifies by a pair of newspaper accounts from 1870s Kansas. One relates a teenage girl's death from a snakebite, "one of the most shocking and heart-rending sights the imagination is capable of picturing," for the poison from "the fangs of a hateful rattlesnake" had "driven her to frenzy" before she died. The other account tells, in first person, of a man on "a grand buffalo hunt" who, after some shooting, found himself enisled between two streams of a stampede: "I had such a view of buffaloes as I never could have expected. . . . As far as the western horizon the whole earth was black with them. The desire to shoot, kill, and capture utterly passed away. I only wished to look, and look till I could realize or find some speech for the greatness of nature that silenced me." Through such experiences the Great Plains came to seem both "a dangerous place" in want of housecleaning and "an awesome spectacle" that could still murderousness into veneration.[8]

Awe, however, little impeded the juggernaut of wildlife destruction. Of course, there were Westerners—and Easterners—apprehensive about the holocaust, a few determined to head it off, but, as Fleharty's chronicle makes clear, "there were strong factors working against them."[9] Many settlers believed the wild creatures of the West existed in such numbers that no species could ever be much diminished, let alone extinguished. Even so, farmers and ranchers dedicated themselves to trying to eliminate wild herbivores and carnivores that ate their crops, pasturage, and livestock. Their killing of prairie dogs, jackrabbits, coyotes, and the like upset the interrelations of many species, as did the alteration or cancellation of habitat by all the comings and goings of settlement, causing some faunal populations to shrink, maybe to extinction, and others to increase. Hunters, especially those out for high-body-count recreation or profit, profoundly imperiled or deleted some species. In some respects, the white hunter, whether Little Red Riding Hood's righteous hero or just a slovenly slaughterer, was the most destructive of Fleharty's factors—and the most revealing of the Western invaders' tangled-up attitude toward wildlife.

Consider the following reminiscence, first published in 1886 and written by Scott Cummins, a man of several occupations but best known for his poetry, who was at the time he recalls a buffalo hunter lately come to Barber County in south-central Kansas, then still untamed enough to harbor a handful of grizzlies. One January day in 1871, afoot and alone, he left his camp near the junction of Elm Creek and the Medicine Lodge River and headed west. He walked "over hills and through canyons that now appear to be but barren gulches, but at the time I write of, the sides as well as the bottoms were covered with trees so dense as almost to exclude the light of the noonday sun." His wandering took him to a spot where he "came full in sight of the 'Flower Pot' mountain," and its presence so impressed him that he decided to climb it:

> When I had reached a point from which I could look through the foliage out on the plateau, I was somewhat surprised at seeing a huge buffalo grazing complacently on the rich sward of buffalo grass that covered the entire summit, excepting that portion occupied by the fringe-like trees. My first impulse was to let him go, as I had little use for so much meat, yet I could not resist the temptation of killing a buffalo in such a romantic place, so with one shot from my Spencer I laid him prone on the earth.[10]

The movement of this reminiscence, from wide-eyed wonder at wild nature to the gimlet-eyed killing of one of its splendid creatures, is the reverse of that structuring the buffalo-hunt account Fleharty quotes, but in both the hunter-narrator betrays appreciation cheek by jowl with destructiveness. Cummins is poignantly aware that in only fifteen years the thick-timbered canyons of Barber County's Red Hills had been turned into barren gulches, and yet he tells without a hint of regret of succumbing to the temptation to violate the very scene that moved him, to contribute to the death ad nauseam of life once ad infinitum. Wanton hunting in the Wild West involved a compulsion so ingrained that even a man with Parnassian sensibilities could yield to it after only an instant's hesitation.

Richard Slotkin argues convincingly that, while pre–Civil War Western settlers and their earlier Puritan counterparts in the East shared similar hopes and fears, the former differed from the latter not only in having a fund of their predecessors' knowledge of how to cope with wilderness but also in believing that their superior skills, coupled with more efficacious technology, made them equal to its obstacles. As such confidence grew and emboldened them, their motivation changed from that of their ancestors: "Where the Puritan cleared the country in the name of converting heathendom to an exemplary Christian commonwealth, the heirs of Daniel Boone did the same in the name of 'getting ahead' (or merely 'getting on') and of self-realization through the prideful display of individual prowess and independence of social or other external restraints." Hunters, like Western entrepreneurs, "relied on material success on a massive scale to prove the power of their manhood in a threatening world."[11] The hunter's success was measured by the quantity of his kill.

This ethos of hunting stayed in effect for a good while after 1860, and it dovetailed with any number of the mythical and more or less unconscious rationales, discussed by Slotkin and others, by which whites engaged in hunting as a means of gathering the power of wilderness into themselves, as a marriage of man and nature, as an initiation ritual, as an exorcism, as a lethal expression of the human dominance of the wild otherwise expressed in amusements like bearbaiting (see, for example, James Walker's 1877 painting Roping a Wild Grizzly, a view of that diversion as he imagined it in an earlier California), and so on. Whatever the matrix of incentives for an activity that was getting rid of what it thrived on, the quantity of kill, the scale of it across so many kinds of animals, was what at last drastically curtailed the wildlife of the West. Market hunting to provide meat for railroad crews, loggers, and miners, and meat and hides and feathers for Easterners, was responsible for much of the carnage, but it doesn't account for all the profligacy through which mammals were harvested with repeating rifles, birds with giant nets, and fish with dynamite.

You can get a sense of that profligacy from research on the destruction of animal species in nineteenth-century America conducted by Conger Beasley Jr. He reminds us that the millions of people who inhabited North America (excluding Mexico) five hundred years ago lived in "a cornucopia of wildlife" and that, according to his findings, "despite certain excesses perpetuated against select species, their overall impact on the landscape was minimal." The wholesale disappearance of species within that time frame did not begin until white civilization advanced across the continent. The passenger pigeon, his primary example, a bird once numbering in the billions east of the hundredth meridian but extinct by 1914, was for years the object of community holidays during which the wing-overlaid sky was emptied by means of muskets, rifles, pistols, cannons loaded with nails and glass, any weapon at hand—an avian annihilation to which the leveling of forests in the Ohio Valley after the Civil War contributed. The real abattoir after 1865, however, was further west; there, as the white population ballooned, "a willful and systematic slaughter of native species" accelerated into unprecedented immoderation.[12]

Documents detailing that outrage are easy to come by, but two examples Beasley discusses are notably appalling. One is a report about a professional hunter in northwestern Kansas who steadied his Sharps rifle on a tripod in the middle of a buffalo herd and by rotating his fire from that position "described a complete circle in less than 20 minutes, knocking off 85 buffalo." The other is the menu that Chicago railroad proprietor John B. Drake presented to his guests on Thanksgiving Day in 1886. That list of culinary goodies—sixty-nine by my count, only one of them, celery salad, not a meat dish—amounts to a catalogue of hard-hunted and furiously fished Western animals and testifies damningly to the American upper class's "hunger" for the wild. A sampling: Baked Black Bass with Claret Sauce, Leg of Mountain Sheep, Ham of Bear, Venison Tongue, Partridge, Wild Turkey, Leg of Elk, Sandhill Crane, Fillet of Grouse with Truffles, Pyramid of Wild Goose Liver in Jelly—on and on until reading that necrology gives you a feeling of Neronian surfeit. No wonder Beasley imagines Drake's cronies as he does: "Corpulent people, puffing fat stogies, bellying up to linen-draped tables groaning with dead game, feasting smackingly. . . . America as a devouring, greasy-lipped monster."[13]

Beasley traces this monster's psychology back to Davy Crockett, to something in his tangled character "emblematic of the prevailing frontier mentality—a messianic urge to extirpate from the landscape those figures, animal and human, that might be regarded as obstructive and evil." Yet Beasley also offers the heartening tidings that simultaneous with that extirpation "the seeds for a profound shift of consciousness were . . . being sown." Their sowers were champions of preservation, Easterners like Thoreau and Emerson and then Westerners like Muir, Mary Austin, and John C. Van Dyke, who articulated "a different attitude toward wildlife."[14] Before that attitude really caught on, however, great damage had been done. As is often the case when the zeitgeist changes, violence foreran the shift of consciousness.

The buffalo's fate is always invoked as the paradigm for what happened to the wildlife of the West. Rightly so. For Plains Indians, once upon a time, the buffalo was a spiritual and material general store. Venerated and worshipped, it was also, when killed for either tribal needs or trade, typically thoroughly used: skin for clothing, bedding, shelter, shields; flesh for roast meat, jerky, pemmican; hair for rope and pillow stuffing; bones for tools or toys. The intimacy of the Indian's relationship to the buffalo can be intuited even through images of the hunt composed by white men like George Catlin, as exemplified by his 1844 painting Buffalo Hunt (A Surround), and Charles Russell (a man who knew that the end of the buffalo, its skull his trademark, symbolized the death of the Old West), as exemplified by his

1899 painting *The Buffalo Hunt, Wild Meat for Wild Men*.[15] For Euro-Americans short on foresight, who had shot the last buffalo east of the Mississippi in 1825, the animal was nothing but an Indian support system that had to go, a natural resource to be mined for salable ore (hides, many of which were made into conveyor belts, and tongues, mostly) and abandoned for bone peddlers, or game to be killed for railroad-crew food or for sport. Photographs of the result of this mind-set may still be dug out of trunks in grandparents' attics: a snow-dusted prairie littered with inert dark mounds; a hunting camp in Texas where dozens of hides are stretched on the grass to dry and dozens of tongues hang from a rack; hides in Dodge City awaiting transport, stacked in a pile as high as a boxcar. By the end of the century, tens of millions of buffalo had been whittled down—by mounted Indians, imported diseases like anthrax and brucellosis, drought, decreased grazing, as well as whites' holocaustic gunning—to a few hundred.[16]

But there's a strange twist, itself paradigmatic, to the buffalo's story. Jane Tompkins, recounting her 1988 visit to the Buffalo Bill Museum at the Buffalo Bill Historical Center in Cody, Wyoming, uncovers it through her discovery that Buffalo Bill, who achieved his first fame as a buffalo hunter for the Kansas Pacific Railroad, had been a conservationist and may have saved the species from extinction by keeping a small herd for his Wild West extravaganzas. She sees him as typical of his time, for, oddly enough, "the men who did the most to preserve America's natural wilderness and its wildlife were big-game hunters." She reminds us that the sport-hunting Boone and Crockett Club, which was founded by Theodore Roosevelt and conservationist George Bird Grinnell in 1887, was among the first environmental-protection organizations in the United States. Then she sees a twist within the twist, and it directs her to the heart of the matter. The suggestion that big-game hunters were interested in conservation only to maintain prey for the pleasure of sport is, she thinks, too simple, since "the desire to kill the animals was in some way related to a desire to see them live. It is not an accident . . . that Roosevelt, Wister, and Remington all went west originally for their health. Their devotion to the West, their connection to it, their love for it are rooted in their need to reanimate their own lives." This insight has to it the familiar ring of contradiction-ridden truth about the white-male relationship to the Western wild, as does Tompkins's speculation that Remington's paintings of wild animals and taxidermists' stuffed memorabilia symbolize and thereby preserve "the life of the observer."[17] However you analyze that paradoxical theme, some variation on it helped ensure that, as Patricia Nelson Limerick puts it, "intervention came in time" to save the buffalo, as well as the grizzly, "before the real West was entirely lost."[18]

Because of that intervention—and subsequent preservation efforts—there are now tens of thousands of buffalo (far fewer grizzlies, though) in the West. But most of them are no longer really wild. If you peer into the onyx eye of a bison bull on a ranch in Nebraska, you may discern a disposition Richard Dankleff calls "unforgiving";[19] but you won't see all of what the Ghost Dancers wanted to dance back. Fenced-in buffalo provide their white promoters with scenery and lean meat, but little of their progenitors' spirit lives in them.

Lots of Indians want to remedy that situation. Talking with Osages on their reservation in northeastern Oklahoma in 1995, Frederick Turner learned that the tribe had participated in the release, in 1993, of three hundred buffalo onto the five thousand acres of the Nature Conservancy's Tallgrass Prairie Preserve near Pawhuska but that "participation had hardly been completely enthusiastic because many tribal members were uneasy about white attitudes toward the buffalo." From their standpoint the animals, each with a microchip implanted in one ear, were not treated with proper respect. The objection had a religious basis, of course, but it had to do also—and correlatively—with an issue of wildness that comes up when you compare Indian and white treatments of buffalo. As Fred DuBray, a Lakota from the Cheyenne River Reservation and founder of the InterTribal Bison Cooperative, explained it to Turner, Indians allow the animals to be themselves; white ranchers, though, "'don't appear to understand that these are wild creatures—big, dangerous ones that should be kept that way. They want . . . to totally control their buffalo herds to maximize the profit. But they're not looking at the long-range aspects. If you domesticate the buffalo, then you haven't got a buffalo anymore.'" Intensive management of buffalo, with its inclination "'to eliminate the ones that are the hardest to handle, . . . eventually shrinks the gene pool, whereas,'" DuBray argued, "'we should be working to expand it.'"[20] If we don't, we'll wind up with nothing more than well-behaved herds of shaggy cattle.

That bovine eventuality boils down analogically what's happened to Western wildlife since the nineteenth-century holocaust. Like the human-occupied places in the West, the preserves and parks set aside for the remnants of a glorious biological past are, in the parlance and mode of postmodern bureaucracy, managed habitats. A wolf or bear that wanders away from where it's supposed to stay may anger or alarm locals, but, for the most part, the only truly dangerous animals in the West now, as before, are white humans, especially those who are male and have gone rogue. The type is illustrated by a young construction worker from Reno, Nevada, who, along with two Marine buddies, was arrested in January 1999 for killing thirty-four wild horses with high-powered rifles. In an Associated Press story, his neighbors, denouncing him (a hopeful sign!), mentioned that he had a habit of shotgunning birds in the yard outside his apartment. One spoke of his bragging about all the animals he had killed and described him as "'dumber than a bag of hammers.'"[21] Doubtless, but in the Old West the sickening act of which he was accused probably would have brought only a sprinkling of condemnation and no prosecution at all; he might even have been, as other killers of wild animals were, as coyote hunters in some venues still are today, applauded.

In without Knocking: The Cowboy as Wild Man

Cowboys are romantics, extreme romantics. . . . They are oriented toward the past. . . . Nature is the only deity they really recognize and nature's order the only order they hold truly sacred.
   Larry McMurtry, "Take My Saddle from the Wall: A Valediction"

Brutal work tends to bring out the brutality in all of us. And that's probably why most cattlemen, as a class (I emphasize this, as a class), tend to hate nature. Hate wildlife. Especially anything they dream might compete with their cattle.
   Edward Abbey, "Something about Mac, Cows, Poker, Ranchers, Cowboys, Sex, and Power . . . and Almost Nothing about American Lit"

Having his say about the three aforementioned young men arrested in Reno for horse killing, one neighbor described them as "'cowboy-style punks' who liked to start fights."[1] I'm sure the cowboys I know would be quick to take exception to that epithet. But they would be quick also to recognize (and take in stride) one of many stereotypes of the cowboy, a figure that has been multifariously interpreted—by everyone from Hollywood directors to cowboys themselves. Sifting through that mélange of interpretations, you'll get befuddled fast unless you see that most, maybe all, images of the cowboy characterize him somehow in conjunction with wildness. That's as true of the mythical cowboy as a natural Western aristocrat as it is of the historical cowboy as a low-wage laborer exploited by Eastern capitalists, as true of the cowboy as a knight in shining leather as it is of the cowboy as a liquored-up cow-town reveler. Indeed, the more closely you examine the cowboy, fictional or real, in all his psychocultural shape-shifting, the more you understand how thoroughly he embodies, now as in the past, the paradoxes of America's obsession with the untamed West.

Let's begin with Charles Russell's 1909 painting *In without Knocking*, which portrays the cowboy in terms of one of his archetypes, the Wild Man, in apotheosis. Here men tired of the herd are out for a bender in town. Montana sun low, the street bursts with a swirl of horseflesh, gunsmoke, hats, lariats, dust, poker cards scattered about. One horse has pushed its hoof through the plank walk in front of a saloon these men intend to enter without dismounting. They are men of the kind Remington had in mind when he spoke of men with bark on whose breed would never die out. This painting of Russell's, simultaneously raucous and sentimental, was, Goetzmann and Goetzmann apprise us, "inspired by a story his wrangler companions once told him about one particularly wild night on the town. . . . the event occurred in the early 1880s."[2] Despite the immediacy of the action represented, the work is based on Russell's memory of a story, heard many years before, about an event he hadn't witnessed. By 1909 the breed with which he peopled his over-stated scene, which had by then nearly died out, was already well romanticized.[3] A twentieth-century glorification, *In without Knocking* expresses a wistfulness about a wildness, of beast-straddling men almost centaurs, largely passed.

Other paintings—and bronzes—by Russell, Remington, and their contempo-raries and successors in Western artistry express a similar wistfulness. You can feel it even in late-nineteenth-century photographs of cowboys decked out in studio paraphernalia so that they might seem—and be remembered as—wilder than they were: gun-totin' roughriders in woollies, denizens of raw distances. The cowboy showcased in such images suggests a range of qualities—recklessness, persever-ance, what have you—but he is associated, even when indoors, with the outdoors, where he does his job. Like other Western writers of the time, Emerson Hough, in his 1897 book *The Story of the Cowboy* and in his novels, idealized the cowboy as a man perfectly suited in temper and appearance to the natural milieu through which he rides. In his 1939 book *We Pointed Them North: Recollections of a Cowpuncher*, E. C. "Teddy Blue" Abbott presents the cowboys he worked with in the 1880s as men full of alfresco vim who shunned, except for "saloons and brothels," what Stephen Tatum describes as "the interior, somewhat feminized space of culture, not nature, where entanglements with the social order erupt in ways that threaten masculine mobility and, hence, independence."[4] And what Barre Toelken calls "the stereotype of the cowboy as 'macho'" usually depicts him in close—and dominating—rela-tion to wild animals, often with a Paul Bunyan–like savor to the description, as in these lines from a cowboy song Toelken quotes:

> As I was a-roundin' Scorpion Butte on a routine cattle inspection,
> Who should I meet but Hairtrigger Pete, ridin' hell-bent for election.
> The lion he was ridin' at full speed was kickin' up plenty of dirt,
> He used a Bowie knife for a bit and a rattlesnake for a quirt.
> The wildcat he carried under his arm chewed the loose end of the reins,
> A gila monster for a charm was drug by a barb-wire chain.[5]

Such imagery suggests a longing for connection with natural wildness that's not only mythical but contradictory (since the wildlife featured has been brought into utility or at least restrained).

Attenuated avatars and abstracted vestiges of this mythical-natural cowboy turned up throughout the twentieth century. In six-gun-armed singing cowboys gathered around campfires, yodeling in the cactus-thronged cinematic darkness after a day of heart-pounding action. In Roy Rogers atop Trigger rampant. In the iconography of John Wayne as a mounted man tougher than any of the evil he dispatches. In cowboy humor, which, as Lawrence Clayton and Kenneth W. Da-

Charles M. Russell, In without Knocking (1909): the cowboy wistfully portrayed as the Wild Man in apotheosis. (Oil on canvas, 20 1/8 x 29 7/8 in. 1961.201. Amon Carter Museum, Fort Worth, Texas.)

vis analyze it, "still mirrors a way of life involving . . . close contact with a some-times beneficent, sometimes uncaring nature; exposure to the beauty as well as the stubbornness of different animals; and personal isolation."[6] In the lifestyles of quasi-cowboy truckers and clinic-trained steer wrestlers. In the sentiment of a highway-billboard advertisement for Copenhagen chewing tobacco that declares some men (that is, cowboys with the right stuff) "don't compromise"; instead, "they cope." In the *narco-corridos* that lyricize the exploits of "cocaine cowboys," the pseudo-*charros* who keep drugs moving across the Mexican-American border and sport ostrich-skin boots and thousand-dollar Stetsons.[7] In the ambience of retail establishments with names like Le Cowboy, Cowboy Snowmobiles, Cowboy Heaven, ad absurdum. Even in such rock-music magnificos as Little Richard and Prince, according to Perry Meisel's 1998 study *The Cowboy and the Dandy: Crossing Over from Romanticism to Rock and Roll.*

The historical cowboy differs significantly from such translations. If he was a romantic, he was one with a pragmatic sense of nature's ups and downs. In some cases he was modestly educated, not just a non-Indian child of nature. His mobil-ity and solitude (and bachelorhood) were facts of his existence—though seldom glamorous ones. He tended to be young, with a tad of the craziness of youth but also with a solid measure of self-discipline. On average, his career, like his heyday that ended in the late 1880s, following the cattle-felling winter of 1886–87, was brief. He partied a lot more with his coworkers than with soiled doves. He was given far more to card playing (unless his boss forbade games of chance) than to gun play. His profession may have had to do with chaos barely under control, but the emphasis was always on the latter.

After Columbus brought cattle and horses to Hispaniola in 1493, both ranching and the animals that were its raison d'être proliferated. "By the late seventeenth century," Richard W. Slatta informs us, "the foundations for Western Hemisphere equestrian cultures had been laid. . . . Throughout Latin America, plains horsemen hunted and slaughtered wild cattle for their hides, tallow, and by-products." Early in that century the British colonies had imported cattle, and Anglo cowboys were hunting their less-domestic descendants in Texas two hundred years later and then learning from Mexican vaqueros the wonts of the Spanish-English crossbred longhorns they would drive north after the Civil War. By the late nineteenth century, cattle and the practice of tending them had spread across the Great Plains, up through California, to Canada, even to Hawaii, but in the West—what with increased settlement, railroads, fenced range, docile breeds—cowboying was far less breakneck than it once had been (though to some people, as it had been to Spanish gentlemen of the sixteenth century, it was still "undignified," labor for "Indians and other nonwhite charges" whose identification with it has contributed to its being thought of as a wild calling).[8]

The cowboy's world of work and recreation sometimes compassed exciting moments, but mostly that world, to draw on Richard C. Poulsen's reading of We Pointed Them North, "is stark and bland compared with the popular image decorated by the media." The cowboy, after all, was a member of a team dedicated to the herd—not a carefree wanderer. His world was one of dull utility centered by "his reverence for the steer" (an animal tamed by castration). The cowboy, in this demystifying perspective, was a man whose life was directed by a commercial trail—the thrust of Andy Adams's 1903 book The Log of a Cowboy, in Poulsen's construal—and was therefore "a more visible tool for the needs and advances of civilization than was the mountain man."[9]

The strict-interpretation cowboy of the period from 1865 to 1888, by which year overgrazing as well as foul weather had terminated America's first big experiment in ranching, was thus an instrument of civilizing forces rather than a Tarzan of the equines. That period saw his end. The result of his years of what Donald Worster calls "cowboy ecology" was "an unmitigated disaster," a huge environment degraded "through turning pastoralism into a capitalistic enterprise."[10]

But that cowboy is still around, sort of. Today's cowboy, if he's the real thing at all, has a regimented job, and he spends a lot more time doing routinized work or dealing with "wrecks" than making chivalric gestures or communing with nature. However courteous he may be, he's not a natural nobleman. There was a time when, as Paul Shepard imagines it, "the splendid beauty of the great aurochs, or wild cattle, was beheld in ecstasy by hunters/gatherers," the contemporary cowboy's prehistoric predecessors, but that time is gone, along with much natural beauty besides the aurochs'. Though he may at leisure behold the wild in ecstasy, he's heir to a tradition of herding that has much effaced it. "More than axe or fire," says Shepard, "cattle-keeping is the means by which people have broken natural climaxes, converted forest into coarse herbage, denuded the slopes, and turned grasslands into sand." Among other outcomes of this perverse ecology are the unhealthily excessive consumption of beef and cattle-hosted infectious diseases that affect humans. "If the auroch was the most magnificent animal in the lives of our Pleistocene ancestors," he concludes, "in captivity it became the most destructive creature of all."[11]

A jump-cut search of characterization of and commentary on the cowboy over the last century or so discloses numerous instances in which his mythical and historical aspects are brought into curious relation to each other or even somehow reconciled. For example, in the preamble, titled "The Cow Boy," to his poem "The Maid of Barber," written sometime before 1903, Scott Cummins is at pains to persuade the greenhorn reader that the cowboy, who "in the East / Is oft compared to savage beast," ought to be counted among "gentlemen."[12] In 1902 in The Virginian: A Horseman of the Plains, Owen Wister, who was ambivalent about Indians as well as cowboys, also makes that case—but in more complicated terms. If it's true, as Jane Tompkins argues, that "historically . . . the Western is a reaction against a female-dominated tradition of popular culture" and that "it buries its origins by excluding everything domestic from its worldview,"[13] then Wister's story at its conclusion unearths those origins and affirms the domestic by summarily finishing the evolution of its cowboy protagonist from a rollicking buckaroo (whom we never espy actually tending cattle) to "an important man, with a strong grip on many various enterprises."[14]

The dialectics of this progression, though it occurs in the context of what Wister classifies as "a colonial romance" with few documentary elements, reveal much about the historical as well as the mythical American cowboy—that is, about the mythical-historical amalgamation he turned into. In his paragraphs prefatory to the narrative, Wister counsels the reader to remember that "Wyoming between 1874 and 1890," the setting of his story, "is a vanished world" and that "the horseman with his pasturing thousands . . . will never come again." Yet when Wister inquires as to what has happened to that "last romantic figure upon our soil," he answers that "he will be here among us always, invisible, waiting his chance to live and play as he would like. His wild kind has been among us always." Early in the narrative we learn that "the sons of the sagebrush . . . live nearer nature" than city people, and yet we learn also that the Virginian, though an "ungrammatical son of the soil" and a canny prankster, is capable of "cold and perfect civility." The body of that Southerner displays a "tiger undulation" in its movement, but its heart chambers "the creature we call a *gentleman*," one to be gradually externalized into more refined demeanor and more civilized accessories and surroundings. Once the main action of the story is over and the Virginian has disposed of his old foe Trampas and married Molly Wood, he and his bride spend their honeymoon on an island in the mountain wilderness. In that isolation he tells her, "'Often when I have camped here, it has made me want to become the ground, become the water, become the trees, mix with the whole thing. Not know myself from it. Never unmix again.'" But, he explains to her, he can't, for "'the trouble is, I am responsible.'"[15]

The trouble is also that the wildness the Virginian has desired has, by the end of the story and its historical moment, indeed largely "vanished"—for him as for an increasingly industrialized America. It's true, as Thomas McGuane contends, that we revere the Virginian because of his "cleaving" to nature; still, we have to acknowledge that his own nature as "a 'knight' of the open range" ensnares him in a love that "is heading him toward the domesticity he abhors"[16]—and in a gentlemanly ambition that will cleave him (in the opposite sense of that word) from nature to the extent that he can exploit it as a mining magnate. Like the West, he, by turning from pastoralism to capitalistic enterprises, became what he abhorred. But what he became was also, paradoxically, what he strove to be.

Such contradictoriness isn't just a product of Wister's puppetry, and it can be unriddled some, both within the context of *The Virginian* and within the context of Western history. *The Virginian* is, as Robert Murray Davis terms it, "a portrait of the 'natural man,'" but it's a portrait in which he shifts "from wildness to responsibility." Moreover, in the process of that shift, he functions "to reconcile a number of oppositions in late nineteenth-century America: North and South; East and West; democracy and aristocracy; past and present."[17] The most capacious opposition he reconciles, however, is one that Davis doesn't include in his list (though it's implied by two pairs there): wild and tame.

Zeese Papanikolas's analysis of our double vision of the Virginian elucidates how that opposition is reconciled in him and suggests a way to understand how he emblematizes the fate of his kind. In the vision in which we prefer to see him, he's "standing alone in the long sundown of our collective imagination," heroically ready for the good fight; then suddenly "it is all over. Trampas lies dead at the other end of Main Street and the Virginian . . . rides off to the tall timber: a Western myth has crystallized into its final form." In the other vision, which foregrounds the ideology disguised by the imagery of that myth, the Virginian is no "splendid, free-spirited pagan" but a racist, a social Darwinist, a Christian, "a frugal saver," and a natty capitalist who "even—so much for the myth—ends up married." Through the accretion of this second vision, Papanikolas argues, Wister "calms his eastern audience by assuring them that in spite of the six guns and chaps the Virginian is no threat to either their morals or their ideology, but rather is their defender. In fact, the Virginian is only another version of themselves."[18] So he's a true-blue colonial after all, reconciling the wild-tame opposition by repressing—with some reluctance, the honeymoon scene indicates—the first term in favor of the second. In that respect he resembles the cowboy of history and the modern West itself. Still, if you were to write a "ghost chapter"[19] to continue the story of the Virginian beyond Wister's text, I think it would have to depict him—like many cowboys, like many earlier and later Westerners—regretting the decisions that led to such a repression. The regret would have to do with why, though "the horseman . . . will never come again," nostalgia keeps "his wild kind . . . among us always," at least in mythic consciousness—there not invisible at all. The repressed, the Wild Man in his wilderness, always returns—somehow.

Wister's story, already nostalgic a century ago, isn't the whole story, however. The wild/tame cowboy, both mythically simplified and historically bristling with ideology, has remained iconically vivid and ubiquitous in the interim, the ratio of his contradictory aspects (and the evaluation of them as positive or negative) changing with the times, as William W. Savage Jr. and others have shown.[20] In 1950 Henry Nash Smith traced those aspects back to the 1870s, during which decade the cowboy came to be seen alternately as "a semibarbarous laborer who lived a dull, monotonous life of hard fare and poor shelter" and was prone to violence and depression and as a herdsman with "a touch of the picturesque" who lived by a civilized code of honor that committed him to generosity, bravery, and honesty.[21] In the mid-1980s Gretel Ehrlich attempted to redress American culture's "hellbent earnestness to romanticize the cowboy" by offering humdrum explanations for his only apparently uncivilized character: he's the strong, silent type because he doesn't have many opportunities for conversation; he rides into the sunset because his long day of work is over; given his lot, it isn't "toughness but 'toughing it out' that counts."[22] And the cowboy's toughness was further recast by David Daly and Joel Persky in 1990 in their noting that in Westerns his masculinity "is identified as the only source of stability in a frontier world where the clash of savagery and civilization threatens cultural and social order," that its defining quality is "the ability to be tough," and that it is cowboy heroes with their toughness—the sort "restrained by internal checks," not that of the freewheeling Wild Man—"who are able to make that important leap from savagery to civilization."[23]

The image of the cowboy as possessor of an unrefined quality that, with internal checks, ensures the progress of Western refinement has long been present in the concept of cowboys as, in Robert G. Athearn's phrase, "knights, mounted and ready to serve their lords."[24] It's present even in Marilynne Robinson's idea that the cowboy, his ambiguities equilibrated by myth, "is the image of the worker in glory" (a glory through which he's "associated with violence").[25] Chivalric valiance, glorious violence, toughness, stick-to-itiveness—whatever you call that wild essence ironically in the service of a taming civilization, it's part and parcel of the imaginational West that McMurtry says "no Westerner has wanted to think . . . was lost.

For if that West is lost, then it's all just jobs."[26] That's the West Montana rancher Joel Bernstein talked to Dayton Duncan about in the early 1980s, when Duncan was retracing Lewis and Clark's route and writing his book *Out West: An American Journey*: "If the West has become a symbol of America's identity, Bernstein says, then the cowboy is the human symbol of the West and imbued with as many romantic myths. . . . 'His life wasn't romantic. . . . Sure it's been romanticized, but there's nothing wrong with that. I don't know why people are ashamed or afraid of that.'" Duncan assures us that Bernstein "certainly isn't," but he adds that Bernstein has given himself not only to "explaining" but also to "exploding" such myths.[27]

Well, is there anything wrong with a myth that makes a national-heroic natural man out of a ranch laborer? That question has been answered in lots of different ways. I'd like to avoid it because fussing with it makes a sticky issue of an appealing ideal of open-air existence in a stifling world. Nonetheless, I must admit there is something wrong with the myth, though the wrongness inheres not so much in the myth itself as in its functioning to conceal, with an affirmative imagery of Western wildness, precisely what imperils that wildness. If you explode the myth, you can see how it hides a taming process that seems bound to destroy the very West it commemorates.

Sharman Apt Russell explodes the myth by looking at the "dark side" of the cowboy. She knows that, "as our last frontier urbanizes, we need the psychic ballast of people who make their livelihood directly from soil, grass, and water," the people the cowboy myth iconizes; but she concludes that, "although he or she would not admit it, the cowboy's job is to transform the wild West into something that resembles, prosaically, a feedlot."[28] An apt condemnatory image, for the feedlot, nothing more than fenced rectangles of fecal mud, an agribusiness phenomenon born of traditionally quarreling farmers and cattlemen finally in total cahoots, illustrates well how far we've come from the open range of the nineteenth century: in such immobilizing confinement cattle are merely machines for making beef and leather.

Sara L. Spurgeon, in an analysis of Cormac McCarthy's *All the Pretty Horses*, puts this dark-side process into a longer, more subtly unmasking historical perspective. In that 1992 novel, she says, "we see the modern embodiment of the ancient myth of the sacred hunter—that of the sacred cowboy. The figure of the hunter engaged in holy communion with nature has . . . been replaced with that of the cowboy digging postholes, preparing to string barbed wire across the tamed body of the wilderness in order to populate with cattle what he so mercilessly emptied of buffalo." The latter figure, she contends, is, like its predecessor, "hollow at its core" and thus vulnerable to being deconstructed in the course of McCarthy's story, which bares the disjunction between austere reality and a myth promising that "a worthy young man should end up with a ranch of his own, a lovely young wife, and 'all the pretty horses' simply by virtue of being Anglo, male, a cowboy, and the descendant of colonizers."[29]

Spurgeon accounts for the hollowness of this figure and its impracticable myth through a discussion of the horse, the animal that "defines the cowboy's status as sacred, special, uniquely American" (and she's as aware as McCarthy that *caballero*, the Spanish word for "gentleman," literally means "horseman"). Pointing out the popular attractiveness of that definition and its usefulness in advertising (for Marlboro cigarettes and several of Ford Motor Company's cars), she explodes as she explains the myth by drawing out the implications of "an uneasy juxtaposition" of two images. The first is that of the mounted cowboy, who signifies the conquering of the Western wilderness, in which image the horse symbolizes his connection to it. The second is that of a herd of wild horses, a primary signifier of untamed nature. The uneasiness in their juxtaposition Spurgeon attributes to the tension between them, which originates from a force field manifold in its own imagery,

> lurking off-screen, so to speak, behind the wild herd and just out of our sight: the cowboy with his lasso, the empty corral, the waiting saddle, bridle, bit, and spur. The process of breaking the wild horse, branding it, claiming and utilizing it in the further subduing of nature through fences, cattle, roads, for instance, follows unseen, behind the image of the wild herd. It is a complex and powerful metaphor of desire and domination, of colonialist nostalgia and Manifest Destiny.

That process involves a deep-seated paradox Annette Kolodny has discerned in the American pastoral: the "destruction of the dream in the act of achieving it." For us as for McCarthy, the two images deceptively silence that paradox, and the myth of the sacred cowboy has the effect of "disguising not only its own violent and disordered nature, but the true nature of the world and its effect on it as well."[30]

Perhaps, though, all this gets too astringent. Surely, in his fullest realization, the cowboy, past and present, is somewhere in the middle ground—or middle landscape—between knight and laborer, myth and history, especially nature and culture. Hasn't he always, to follow J. E. Cirlot's expounding of the image of the Wild Man in heraldry, expressed "base forces, while sustaining certain spiritual and sublimating elements"?[31] As a sort of Anglo Noble Savage (a figure often conflated with that of the Western gunfighter who, however much uncontrolled by white society, battles on its side), hasn't he been—like the iconographic Wild Man during the High Middle Ages, according to Hayden White—"both good and evil, both envied and feared, both admired and calumniated"?[32] Like Thoreau, in some ways the prototype of Anglo-American natural men, when he confronted what he called the "Chaos and Old Night" of the wilderness ("savage and awful, though beautiful") in the Maine woods around Mount Ktaadn in 1846,[33] hasn't the cowboy been, in Simon Schama's words, "deeply ambivalent about the primitive instinct within humanity"?[34] Surely so.

A humorous tidbit from Savage may say as much in its compressed scope about the cowboy's middle-ground relation to the wild and the domestic as my disquisition above. In his 1979 study of the cowboy's image, he comments on an interview with two Colorado ranchers he witnessed on the PBS program *Bill Moyers' Journal* in February 1976. Both men, Monte Sheridan and Menford Beard, "believed that history had passed them by," and they praised "the virtues of rural living." In the lives of such men, Savage opines, "myth and reality coalesce . . . because they like it that way," and everything of which they spoke, "all those things—the relationships, the work, the way of life—merged in Menford Beard's joyous monologue on the disposition of his corpse: when he died, he hoped to be skinned in order that his hide might be made into a woman's saddle. Then he would 'always be between the two things I love the most.'"[35]

Or scrutinize the images in recent advertisements for Nocona cowboy boots: a boot-pinned rattlesnake that's about to be decapitated by a redoubtable knife, a Gila monster with a boot toe in its jaws whose clasp is about to be broken by wire cutters, others in the same vein. In every instance the wild is *about to be* defeated or annulled by the wearer of boots made from the skin of some animal killed and thus rendered useful. Each image resembles the "Cold Pastoral" scene of which John Keats writes in his "Ode on a Grecian Urn": there's a suspension of action just before a consummation both wished and not wished.[36] In each image nature is subject to an imminent instrumentality of culture (rope, whip, fire, and others, as well as those mentioned previously) but not (yet? ever?) undone. Each image tells the same allegorical story: the American cowboy, that mythical-real Westerner, has always wanted to have his land and eat it (or let his cattle eat it) too.

Romancing the Gun: Outlaws and Man-Killers in Helldorado

> *Lewis had the frontiersman's faith in his rifle. As long as a man had his rifle, ammunition, and powder, he would take on anything the wilderness could throw at him.*
> Stephen E. Ambrose, *Undaunted Courage: Meriwether Lewis, Thomas Jefferson, and the Opening of the American West*

In 1882 the New Mexican Printing and Publishing Company in Santa Fe published *The Authentic Life of Billy, the Kid, the Noted Desperado of the Southwest*. The book was written, with the help of a ghostwriter, by Pat Garrett, sheriff of Lincoln County, New Mexico, a place still territorial and therefore in transition from wild outback to civilized statehood. He was the man who had shot and killed Billy the Kid in Fort

Sumner on July 14 of the previous year. Garrett and his ghost had stuffed the biography of their subject, a young man born Henry McCarty in New York City's Irish ghetto, with fictitious concoctions that painted him as a worthy opponent to Garrett, who nursed political aspirations—and that served as seed crystals for the Kid's future eminence in American folklore. Of special interest, in the present context, is the conclusion of the addenda attached to this yarn.

As Stephen Tatum explains, that conclusion "draws on conventional romance images of a restored world to illustrate, however flamboyantly, the regeneration of the human and natural worlds after a perilous conflict with the Kid's demonic vision of experience."[1] Though Garrett's political successes would be small and questionable, those images imply that he has played the role of a gunfighting Parsifal in such regeneration. "Whatever may be the cause of the effect," the narrator humbly declares, "Lincoln County now enjoys a season of peace and prosperity to which she has ever, heretofore, been a stranger." Indians and desperadoes no longer frighten the county's citizens, and "stock wanders over the ranges in security." The wasteland is redeemed: "vast fields of waving grain greet the eye."[2] The Kid is gone. Good has triumphed over evil, civilization over savagery. It's quiet at last.

But, as the pioneers girdled by wagons at night in the old Westerns used to say, it's too quiet. The tale is too ironed out, not finished. We have heard it told that way again and again and want—most of us, most of the time—to believe it, but we know that Billy the Kid and Jesse James and Clay Allison are still around and that Garrett and Wyatt Earp and Elfego Baca, cops less perfect than Parsifal, still contend with them. We're still romancing the gun. By and large, for Americans, that romance, even in the inner city (where, after all, Billy the Kid started out), is a Western one, and it's knotty in the extreme. The vagaries of America's ambivalent attitude toward wildness have significantly shaped the history of that knottiness and are graven in it.

The romance began around the middle of the nineteenth century. In his *Arming America: The Origins of a National Gun Culture*, Michael A. Bellesiles disputes the truism that the United States was always a country in love with guns. His study has been vilified as fraudulent by the National Rifle Association (NRA) and some of its documentary data, primarily those derived from eighteenth-century probate records, questioned by scholarly peers, but on the whole it appears to offer a well-supported argument concerning the changing presence and meaning of guns in American society. Bellesiles's most crucial premise, that the first transatlantic migrants came from a world where "handheld firearms developed slowly and in the face of great suspicion and even hostility," seems justified by his citations. And I see no reason not to accept his thesis that ownership of guns in America "was exceptional in the seventeenth, eighteenth, and early nineteenth centuries, even on the frontier, and that guns became a common commodity only with the industrialization of the mid-nineteenth century"—quite apart from issues such as whether or not statistics uniformly indicate that the gun wasn't "the weapon of choice" for murder prior to the Civil War.[3]

Whatever the criticisms of Bellesiles's Early American sources and his methodology, that war, whose contagion of violence was in no wise cured by Robert E. Lee's surrender at Appomattox, *was* the watershed. With it, as his later evidence shows, commenced a reconstruction of national history "to promote the necessity of a heavily armed American public." This made-up tradition was institutionalized within a generation after the Civil War. Those who had experienced that ordeal believed guns were central to America's selfhood and "essential to its survival." There was no scarcity of guns by then, either, for the war had marked "an exact historical coincidence of increased productivity of and demand for guns," a moment of innovations in arms manufacturing from which "emerged a distinctive American gun culture"—a widespread idolization of and fascination with guns unique to the United States. Within a decade of the end of the war that saved the Union, the word *gunfighter* was coming into currency, and males in this country "had a fixation with firearms that any modern enthusiast would recognize and salute."[4]

Hence by the mid-1870s, thanks to Samuel Colt and others, guns were everywhere, in the West, short on gunsmiths before the 1850s, as much as in the South and East. "By that time," Bellesiles notes, "a gun seemed to most men a requisite for their very identity"—not just national but personal—and guns were becoming strongly associated with the cowboy. At midcentury, rifle production may have lagged behind that of pistols, but both now were at full steam. Still, though, the pistol was the preferred personal-identity weapon. Colt had died in 1862, but his company and others sold "the perfect weapon for a gun culture" like hotcakes, mostly to people who didn't need it, because they continued to do what he'd done so well: link the revolver, through advertising, with the heroic imagery of the romantic West. Women in the families heading west "not only disapproved of aggressive behavior, but also usually put a quick stop to it," says Bellesiles; thus many of their men had been persuaded to bear what was functionally little more than "a tourist accoutrement."[5]

Well and good. Such history, even if polemical, helps to clear the air of some unexamined notions about the gun in America and the West. But its presence and meaning as a distinctly Western object invite more investigation into how the fixation with it has deepened until, by an oxymoronic irony, it has become, in Bellesiles's ill-boding catch phrase, "the icon of a savage civilization."[6]

In Stephen Crane's 1898 short story "The Bride Comes to Yellow Sky," the anticipated gunfight between Marshal Jack Potter and the besotted Scratchy Wilson doesn't happen because Potter has gotten married to a woman who symbolizes all the influence of the East that's insinuating itself into the Texas town of Yellow Sky. When Potter and his bride, just off the train from San Antonio, run into Wilson on the street, he menaces the marshal with one of his two pistols (he's dropped the other in surprise) but then notices that the man isn't wearing a gun. Nonplussed, staring at the woman "like a creature allowed a glimpse of another world," he acknowledges that the fight is off, holsters both pistols, and walks away.[7] Without a gun you can't have a gunfight. Without a gunfight you can't have a Western with any traditional feel to it (so you get something else, maybe the first anti-Western, in the case of Crane's narrative). When civilization comes to the West, guns are put away, age into antiques. Well, not entirely. Guns, after all, were instrumental in bringing civilization to the West; they were—and are—part of the culture of the West, essential to its continuing romantic mythology of the conflict between the wild and the tame. That's where the knottiness sneaks in.

If you've ever held in your hands one of the firearms used in the Old West (where *gun* usually meant "handgun")—a Springfield carbine once carried by a cavalryman, say, or a pepperbox once owned by a gold seeker or a Model '73 Winchester (sometimes dubbed the "Gun That Won the West") once racked above a rancher's mantel—you've sensed that it's a tool. If you've fired such a weapon and seen what it can do, you've grasped that it's a tool of a special kind. Elliott West discerns its specialness in the fact that it is "more than a stretch of old killing tools." Unlike the energy of a stone ax or lance, which was simply that of the user, the energy of the gun "was recruited elsewhere—from natural materials that were found far away, processed into a powerful combustible, then stored and carried long distances. A loaded gun or rifle was an addition to the basic source of a person's power." Obviously, such an instrument required trade, but whoever was in the loop had "a potential edge."[8] In the West, Euro-Americans, from the start, had that edge on the inhabitants, human and otherwise, of the wilderness.[9] Firearms—along with railroads, windmills, and other mechanisms—were one of the deciding technologies in the later settling of the West.

Intriguingly, however, the gun, most notably the Winchester rifle and the Colt revolver, became representative of all those technologies. Like the "jar in Tennessee" in Wallace Stevens's poem "Anecdote of the Jar," it seems to have almost magically made "The wilderness [that] rose up to it, / And sprawled around, no longer wild."[10] It's because of such synecdochic inclusiveness and transformative power that, as Jane Tompkins remarks in reporting on her visit to the Winchester Arms Museum at the Buffalo Bill Historical Center, firearms are reckoned as "inseparable from the march of American history" and "venerated."[11]

In great measure, though, the status of the gun as an icon of westering has to do with its being inseparable not only from history but also from its owner. The gun, particularly the handgun, was indeed personal. Lots of guns in museums have a label that states, among other things, the person (the more famous, the better) to whom it once belonged; if it were possible, I think, all of them would be so annotated. Few people care about who owned which locomotive in nineteenth-century Utah, but Bat Masterson's pistol is a horse of another color. That's history with a human face just up the arm.

But there's more to this matter. A gun isn't merely a technology that belongs to someone. As Robert Bringhurst describes it, a gun is "a dark beauty with a steel sheen, / caught in the cocked / mind's eye and brought / down with an extension of the hand."[12] That is, a gun is a continuation of its user, as intimate as a prosthesis. Much of its beauty derives from how well it conforms to its user. James C. Work says of the 1873 Colt .45 single-action revolver that "the plow-handle shape of the grip fits the hand as if molded to it."[13] Robert Starrett, the boy who narrates Jack Schaefer's 1949 novel Shane, perceives its gunfighter hero's gun as "part of the man, of the full sum of the integrate force that was Shane."[14] And David Daly and Joel Persky comment that through early descriptions of the cowboy the handgun "strapped to his body . . . became thought of as another part of his nature."[15] There's nothing figuratively malapropos, therefore, in referring to those who wear guns simply as "guns."

"For an American boy," Jonathan Holden writes, "the feel of a firearm in his hands extends way beyond all rational considerations. It touches upon his identity." Thus the legacy of this male romance. But that feel doesn't just touch upon identity: it changes it. Holden notes that a six-gun makes "my right hand vital like a wand."[16] Work speaks of "some undefinable power the pistol has to change a man's image of himself."[17] Though you might define that power in terms of phallic enhancement (shooting as puissant, if ersatz, ejaculation), such definition would be insufficient. Something else is involved. West gets at it as well as anyone has when he observes that in the nineteenth century a firearm was close to "a Promethean force, an elemental source of power that raised whoever held it to what seemed another human category." Taking a longer view, he asserts that it was "no wonder the earliest European emissaries bestowed guns on favored indigenous leaders. A flintlock was as much talisman as weapon, an outward sign of the mystery offered when two creative universes suddenly touch."[18]

No wonder, either, then, that the gun was not only a means of protection from the inhabitants of the Western wilderness but also a means of connection to them. It made its user bigger and more powerful, equal to that daunting wilderness; its ubiquitous mediation led to a condition in which, as Holden says, "weaponry is woven into the American landscape itself."[19] The gun became a naturalized nexus in the relationship between self and any other interpreted as threatening—human and bear, white man and Indian, good guy and bad guy.

And therein lies another subtlety. With the diminishment of Indians and wildlife, to a good extent by guns, and the intensification of white immigration, the wildness of the West increasingly was symbolized by guns and their wielders, most opprobriously outlaws, who thereby became the new enemies of civilization. The outlaw wielded his weapon in a wild way; his hand, though it was an appendage of a creature of culture (in a poem about John Wesley Hardin, Raymond Carver describes his right hand as "slender, delicate-looking"),[20] held his equalizer like a viper he could aim at anyone he pleased. Law-abiding people metaphorized him as a skunk or other undesirable fauna (something N. Scott Momaday does to Billy the Kid, though with but slight negative judgment, when he imagines how "He wanders in the high desert / Like a coyote").[21] The wildly wielded gun took the place of what it destroyed.

Whether or not the gun-bearer was really an outlaw or just some fool full of testosterone and alcohol, wild wielding meant violence—just as the controlled wielding of the lawman did. Historians differ in their views of violence in the West, with debate about its kinds and their extent, its causes, and its impact on postfrontier American society still lively. Depending on whom you read, you get the impression that the frontier was constantly violent or only infrequently so, that everybody was always shooting everybody else or hardly ever was, that the most widespread violence was that of domestic abuse or labor–management disputes, that vigilantism either perpetrated violence or prevented it, that the inheritance of Old Western habits of violence has made America the Grand Guignol we watch on the nightly news or is only vaguely implicated in it. I agree with Roger D. McGrath's opinion, largely as valid now as it was when voiced in 1984, that Western historiography presents "a less than complete—in some cases a highly selective and perhaps unrepresentative—picture of frontier violence and lawlessness." On the other hand, there's no reason not to agree also with his conclusion—derived from the research of Kent Ladd Steckmesser, Joseph G. Rosa, and others—that "gunslingers were involved in a considerable amount of violence."[22] It's a conclusion that requires qualifications, however.

In his discussion of the work of those he calls "frontier-was-violent authors," McGrath finds a focus on the classic factors (of the sort rank in HBO's recent series *Deadwood*) that allegedly promoted violence: "an exaggerated sense of individualism encouraged by the lack of legal, religious, and educational institutions"; "the presence of few woman and the absence of the stabilizing influences of family life [that] fostered the establishment of brothels, gambling houses, and saloons"; "the consumption of great quantities of alcohol, a sense of honor that allowed no insult to go unchallenged, the vast sums of money afloat in the West because of insufficient banking facilities, and the often tenuous difference between outlaw and lawman"; the frontier's attractiveness to "the bold and strong" as well as "the rootless and . . . desperate"; and the like. Yet he notes, regarding gun violence, that "none of these authors really demonstrates whether this violence was typical of the frontier as a whole or was only typical of the gunfighters themselves." It seems clear, however, from McGrath's discussion of the work of authors who argue that the frontier wasn't especially violent, that the first typicality is the more mythical of the two—

and that the violence of gunfighters has been grossly exaggerated and overempha-sized by dime novels, movies, all the apparatus of romance. Moreover, he cites per-suasive arguments that the frontier was a safer place than present-day America is, that its conditions and personality types didn't engender inordinate violence, and that in some respects the Old West was not so much a wild place that underwent taming as a relatively tame place that was subject to imaginative "wilding."[23]

Corroborating such arguments are observations like Ian Frazier's that, "in all the years of the cattle boom, fewer people were shot or stabbed in Dodge City than die violently in New York City in three days; what gave Dodge its fame, partly, was the fact that the town had several weekly newspapers chronicling each gunfight and its aftermath in detail."[24] Even when you take the population difference into account, such data dissipate your gunslinger reveries a bit. So you're likely to ac-cept the argument, as McGrath condenses it, that "violence in America has been a problem more related to postfrontier urban development than to the Old West."[25] And you need to keep in mind, as Frazier implies, that celebrity followed public acts of violence, gunplay perhaps predominantly, and not private ones in the Old West and that such celebrity was promulgated journalistically not only through detail but often through rhetorical augmentation that would give pause to the most ghoulish of today's talking heads on the ten-o'clock news.

To refine further McGrath's conclusion that gunfighters were involved in a con-siderable amount of violence in the Old West, let me bring to bear on it a few quali-fications from Richard White's "It's Your Misfortune and None of My Own": A New His-tory of the American West, a 1991 study that's about the West as a dynamic pastiche of conflicts, many of which escalated into gun dramas. Ringing down the curtain on his discussion of social conflicts—vigilantism, social banditry, range wars, strife grounded in differences of race and class, and the like—he concludes that their violence "was an intrinsic part of western society." That's orthodox New Western History by now, but, White argues early in his discussion, most Americans still don't understand conflict in the West in terms of clashes between social groups; rather, they think of it through the image of a confrontation between lone gunmen on a deserted street. Myth, with its built-in resolution by violence, thereby "has preempted history in explaining conflict," and its explanation allowed nineteenth-century Americans to hold the comfortable belief that violence was merely personal and generally eliminated by the civilizing process. That explanation thus evades the fact that "the social order itself sometimes encouraged violence."[26] By this reason-ing, myth persists because of the reassurance it affords: the West was once wild with gun crazies practicing interpersonal homicide, but they're as rare as dinosaurs in these times of peace and harmony.

White admits, of course, that there was personal violence in the Old West, much of it involving guns, but he also stresses that, even if it overlapped some with social violence, it was far from universal, occurring within limited domains such as mining camps and cow towns. But even those places weren't exactly what myth makes them out to have been. Law officers didn't like showdowns, and gun control, always a ticklish topic, was usually effective. For the majority of people, excepting unmarried young men given to drinking, "life remained secure," and they were content to let Western myth "obscure a far more pervasive social violence."[27]

White's argument seems wholly defensible as far as it goes, but he may not emphasize enough the ambiguousness of the role of the gunfighter in the myth of Western violence. It arises from the reality that in the legal donnybrook of the Old West there were gunfighters on both sides of the law and that frequently a given gunfighter was at different times (sometimes at the same time) on both sides.[28] It arises as well from the corresponding fantasy that gunfighters were both the basic cause of much Western violence (as homicidal scofflaws or anything-goes hirelings in the service of corrupt institutions) and the capital solution to it (as Robin Hood–style outlaws opposed to corrupt institutions or morally solid lawmen in the service of civilized values). A close look at the ideological muddle of such ambiguousness deeply implicates an old acquaintance: America's ambivalent attitude toward Western wildness.

In Cormac McCarthy's novel *Cities of the Plain*, which begins in 1952 in New Mexico, occurs the following exchange between the main protagonist, John Grady Cole, and an old cowboy named Johnson on the ranch where he works. Johnson has just told his young listener, with a realism "the movies don't ever get . . . right," about a shooting he witnessed in a bar in Juárez in 1929:

> He looked out across the country to the west where the sky was darkening. Tales of the old west, he said.
>
> Yessir.
>
> Lot of people shot and killed.
>
> Why were they?
>
> Mr Johnson passed the tips of his fingers across his jaw. Well, he said. I think these people mostly come from Tennessee and Kentucky. Edgefield district in South Carolina. Southern Missouri. They were mountain people. . . . They always would shoot you. It wasn't just here. They kept coming west and about the time they got here was about the time Sam Colt invented the sixshooter and it was the first time these people could afford a gun you could carry around in your belt. That's all there ever was to it. It had nothin to do with the country at all. The west.[29]

However you might quibble with Johnson's geographical prejudice (it's not all amiss), his account (of a shot in the back of an unsuspecting victim's head) and unadorned history say or intimate much that's relevant here: few killings in the West came about through the sort of walk-down gunfight whose tradition began with a duel between James Butler Hickok and a luckless gambler named Davis K. Tutt in

Springfield, Missouri, in 1865 and later became a mandatory ritual in Hollywood Westerns; gun violence had its roots east of the Mississippi (where plenty of shooting had happened and, especially in the South, manly duels in the Old World style were prevalent); and, as Belleisles noted earlier, breakthroughs in gun technology and marketing coincided opportunely with heavy westward migration.[30]

But Johnson is mistaken in saying that "it," his pronoun referring to chronic aggressive gun-toting, had nothing to do with the West. The West differed from the East (and South), as it still does, in being what Eastern gun manufacturers were happy to have it be: a laboratory for testing new weaponry. That and other factors made it a wilder place than the East, but it was also a place engaged in establishing itself as a projection of Eastern civilization. That double character created an ideal cultural climate for the flourishing of the romance of the gun, those "tales of the old west" that, like the contradictions they both foster and attempt to resolve, have held Americans like a spell.

From the dramatis personae in this romance, pick out the Western outlaw. Always a gun-bearer, he (ordinarily a he) was a sociopath who brought bullet death to fellow humans and otherwise fretted the advance of civil society. There were few lawmen to pursue him for his crimes. If they—or vigilance committees—did, he, as McGrath notes, "had the advantage. His chance of capture and punishment was remote, since he could simply disappear into the wilderness for a time."[31] So, for all who opposed him, he was one with the wilderness and its dangers. Simultaneously, though, some of those and others romanticized him. For them, their pastoral idealism shaped by "stories about Romantic Outlawry" and populist individualism, the outlaw, according to Steckmesser, "served as surrogate for all those other westerners who disliked industry, corporations, and progress."[32] Such romanticization functioned to obscure whatever caused the outlaw's sociopathy, and by its inverting transvaluation, in McGrath's synopsis, his "violent characteristics . . . were often turned into virtues"—so that he became a hero legendized for his independent derring-do. Because such a hero mirrors Americans (males, even the most law-abiding, anyway) as they like to see themselves, he has hung on and furthered "an overemphasis on the violent side of the frontier and an underemphasis on the peaceful and orderly side."[33] A composite of fact and fiction, he abides as bittersweet as the land shadowed by Sierra Blanca Peak in southern New Mexico that Billy the Kid once roamed, land, in Momaday's phrase, "anomalously wild and luxurious."[34]

Think too, then, about the Western lawman. Like that of the outlaw, his image is a double exposure, his toggle-switch disposition appositely hinted by Andy Warhol's 1963 serigraph *Double Elvis*, in which two identical and imbricated stills of Elvis Presley in his half-breed (half-savage, half-civilized) *Flaming Star* mode, six-gun drawn, face the viewer head-on. The legendary gunfighter (or, to use an older word, man-killer) lawman stands between the wild and the tame, attached to both worlds. He gets rid of the outlaws. Maybe by killing or maybe by the force of his reputation for killing, as Wyatt Earp, who "cleaned up bad Ellsworth . . . and tamed Wichita," does in Dodge City in Richard Dankleff's poem "The Legend," just through "the way he strides to meet Clay Allison / killer of sheriffs."[35] Or so goes the story of the town-tamer whose gun made the West safe for women and children that Rosa and others assure us isn't true—though such men did on occasion serve as stays against anarchy. Nonetheless, we want to see our pistol-slick hero that way: a mythically magnified intervener between savagery and civilization, a liminal presence like Tom Doniphon in John Ford's 1962 film *The Man Who Shot Liberty Valance* who ends violence with violence for the best of reasons and then passes on. We continue to believe that only the half-wild could have repulsed the wild, only the gun could have been the adequate tool.

A remarkable ideological fluctuation runs through this fable. It provides for the gunfighter lawman's having undergone what Christine Bold, speaking of the late–1880s heroization of the cowboy, calls a "decisive gentrification" that changed him "from hell-raiser to half-wild, half-cultured frontier hero and democratic individualist."[36] That's a provision that persuades us to remember James Butler Hickok as Wild Bill Hickok because of what Eugene Weber praises as "his *admirably impetuous* actions and reactions" (my italics).[37] Yet, even if gentrified, such a gunfighter is more outlaw than lawman at heart, therefore a perpetually expendable—indeed, self-expending—function of what he defends. Marilynne Robinson, discussing the myth of the showdown and its role in legitimizing social order, annotates this paradox in terms of the hero's mediation between "the ungovernable souls beyond the frontier" and the civilization, whatever its faults, flowing toward them. "The hero identified with it for his own reasons," she says, "but for deep and obvious reasons, having to do with personal style, he belonged with the outlaws. In the myth, every concession is made to the way of life being suppressed. . . . Westerns are always elegiac." Referring specifically to post–World War II American culture in relation to its post–Civil War analogue and speculating that "perhaps the myth of the pacification of the frontier rehearsed the emotional and psychological readjustment of the population to the norms of peace," Robinson suggests that it "transacted a good deal of important business in its obsessive return to this imagined moment." And then, she says, "the moment vanished."[38]

Or did it? Imagined moments that impel obsessive returns in which important cultural business gets transacted tend to last, especially if they seem to freeze a fluctuation, dehorn a dilemma, resolve an ambiguity or ambivalence. Maybe the durability of Robinson's moment is more understandable if it's redefined as the moment at which "the Western story is set," according to John Cawelti: "that point when savagery and lawlessness are in decline before the advancing wave of law and order, but are still strong enough to pose a local and momentarily significant challenge." Though relatively brief, it has been culturally constructed as "a timeless epic past" with a prototypical hero who possesses abilities and a lifeway that connect him to the wilderness as a savage landscape but whose moral character connects him to it as "the setting for a regenerated social order."[39] Thus, however wild he may be (or however much he belongs with the outlaws), he is, as intermediary, pledged to the townspeople, who constitute the third major role in the romance. And, Cawelti contends, in this recurrent moment we recognize his doubleness (if in no other way) by his trappings, and we experience its mythical resolution in favor of civilization by how he uses his gun.

From Cooper's Leatherstocking on, the Western hero has worn clothing that, as Cawelti analyzes it, combines "naturalness and artifice" and echoes "the nineteenth century's fascination with the mixture of savagery and elegance." He may be a little drabber now than he was in Hopalong Cassidy's day, but he's still inclined to dress both white/Anglo and Indian/Mexican. Doing so, he expresses his position between two lifeways. Symbolic of his transcendence of both, his costume embodies the same principle that thematized the end of my last chapter: that "of having your cake and eating it too."[40]

If, though, the hero is complex enough, heir to the tradition of Leatherstocking rather than that of movie mannequins, his doubleness isn't so simple. Then his costume may be an outward sign of an internal tension between savagery and civilization, an axiological tug-of-war between his bond to the wilderness and his loyalty to the townspeople. Because of his self-division, the outcomes of Westerns featuring him "are invariably more ambiguous and tragic"—attributes that prompt Cawelti to find his archetype in Achilles, the heroic warrior split between personal honor and allegiance to the Achaeans. Like Achilles, he's doomed to an end he resignedly accepts, but there's an ambivalence in our response to it: "In the destruction of the gunfighter or the sad departure of Shane, we lament the hero's fate, and we feel nostalgic about the passing of a time when men were men, but at the same time we see their sacrifice as a necessary contribution to progress."[41]

The gunfighter's contribution isn't, of course, just that sacrifice: it's also his killing of those who hinder progress. And it's his approach to killing them, an approach that affirms values consonant with progress—hence Cawelti's argument that the gunfighter's most distinctive characteristic isn't what he accomplishes with a gun but how he uses it. In that characteristic he differs from the knight, to whom he's often likened. Whereas the knight took on his opponent in hand-to-hand combat, the gunfighter takes on his at a distance of some yards and dispatches him through the mandatory and exacting ritual of the draw. The difference is fundamental, for this procedure associates him with qualities that constitute the sine qua non of his heroic status: "Killing is an act forced upon him and he carries it out with the precision and skill of a surgeon and the careful proportions of an artist"—and without the bloodlust of his opponent, whom he allows to draw first. Since he kills in such a clean, restrained, detached manner, he continues to appeal to the citizens of a nakedly violent but peace-preaching nation for whom "he resolves this ambiguity by giving a sense of moral significance and order to violence."[42] He's civilization's hero because he, never a back-shooter, is a civilized killer.

Still, despite how adamantly we may believe that the gunfighter's gun will save us from wildness that yet inhabits him (and us), we're uneasy about him. Meeting him in the dreamscape of the West, say in Mesilla, New Mexico, where the speaker in Edward Dorn's long poem *Slinger* meets the "Cautious Gunslinger," we are impressed by his "impeccable personal smoothness," but the swiftness of his signature move induces an edginess deference can't conceal:

> You make the air dark
> with the beauty of your speed,
> Gunslinger, the air
> separates and reunites as if lightning
> had cut past.[43]

Which brings us back to Billy the Kid country—and the Kid himself. Denying such smoothness as he possessed (intelligence, literacy, charm, according to some reports), the famous photograph of him standing homely and slope-shouldered, pistol at one side, rifle at the other, presents him as a cretinous juvenile delinquent with a short fuse. Otherwise, notwithstanding many treatments of his life, we know little about who he really was, this best known of Western desperadoes. On the other hand, *what* he has become since his death is amply evident: a kind of human Moby-Dick of the desert, the figure most burdened with the shifting symbolic load of America's ambivalence toward the wildness of the West.

To understand the construction of this posthumous Billy the Kid, we must consider briefly the way visions of his career have oscillated, in Tatum's interpretation, "between self-consciously ironic and romantic treatments." His study of how the Kid as "a wild man in wild times" has been seen at certain historical moments says much about America's relation to the West's wild places.[44]

When he wasn't gambling, pulling off practical jokes, or participating in gunplay, the Kid may have been the romantic fool that Pinkerton detective Charles Siringo once said he was—by virtue of his having "a señorita in every cantina from Fort Sumner to Fort Stanton"—but after his death he was what America (and the civilized world) needed him to be: another type of romantic figure, one cast in a romance darker than that acted out in cantinas. As Tatum's inspection of his obituaries shows, images of him were typically satanic. Later images would be different, but in 1881 he was portrayed as incorrigibly allied with the forces of lawlessness. By the logic of that portrayal, Garrett is indeed the redeemer who, in achieving the goal toward which he quested, the killing of the Kid, ensures "the emergence of order and control over the competing human and natural forces of chaos."[45]

This obituary romance takes place smack-dab at Cawelti's epic moment when, in Tatum's formulation, the dialectic of civilization and wilderness was poised to legitimize the violence of a man who resided in both of those worlds and to found "a Southwestern Eden that synthesized civilized values and a close contact with Nature's beneficent influence." Like Roosevelt's Rough Riders seventeen years later, Garrett undertook his mission because cumbering others—Cubans and desperadoes among them—"were unable or unwilling to transform the wilderness into a pastoral garden."[46] If a utopia that combined the best of Eastern and Western life was to happen, some taming was necessary—on all levels.

Given that objective, it's not surprising that by the end of the century Garrett came to be seen as "the representative of an ideal agrarian West" and the Kid soon thereafter as "an anachronism in a society devoted to confirming that railroads and the wilderness could coexist." But there would be another shift in the popular conception of the Kid when the genteel world of the Roosevelt era began to feel oppressively conservative; for then, in a time of heightened nostalgia for the wild, his defiance of order seemed heroic to some. And Tatum tracks yet other shifts, in the literature and films of the 1920s, 1930s, and 1940s, as the Kid was reconstituted as a romantic or tragic figure, with his death (in Walter Noble Burns's 1926 book The Saga of Billy the Kid) symbolic of a loss of the spirit of adventure. By the early 1950s, reinventions of him had turned ambivalent. In the late 1950s he "resembles a Southwestern rebel without a cause," exemplified by Paul Newman's version of him in Arthur Penn's 1958 film The Left-handed Gun. By 1973, with the release of Sam Peckinpah's Pat Garrett and Billy the Kid on the heels of Stan Dragoti's Dirty Little Billy, the Kid had been converted from a romantic or tragic figure into an ironic one who moves through a "broken world." Things haven't gotten any better for him since that belated, wintry "shattering of the basic Western formula," what might be deemed a second closing of the frontier.[47]

No matter the conversions or inversions of the Kid's mythic role, some of the aura of romance still clings to him. It's what guarantees that, as the jailed Kid tells an interviewer in Michael Ondaatje's The Collected Works of Billy the Kid, "I'll be with the world till she dies."[48] His endurance, according to Tatum, has much to do with an aspect of his story's appeal that dime-novel authors thoroughly exploited: his story allowed those who entered it to "cross over into the forbidden world of the barbarous Kid for a brief moment before returning to the ordered daylight world of restraint and responsibility Garrett validated by shooting the Kid." It still allows that transgression. The Kid's story not only plays effectively with "the public's love-hate relationship with its outlaw heroes" (as well as with its more general love-hate relationship with Western wildness) but also addresses two deep human needs that underlie that relationship.[49] Harry Berger Jr., in a passage Tatum cites, describes them as follows: "First is a need for order, peace, and security, for protection against the terror or confusion of life, for a familiar and predictable world. . . . But the second . . . is contrary to the first: man positively needs anxiety and uncertainty, thrives on confusion and risk, wants trouble, tension, jeopardy, novelty, mystery."[50] The contrariety of the two needs causes a psychic conflict, and it's that conflict, Tatum suggests, the Kid "synthesizes."[51] But let me, building on that suggestion, offer a further one: Billy the Kid is the Wild West that America has tried, with dogged perseverance, to defeat and yet through which it has avidly sought escape, adventure, deliverance; has abhorred and hungered for; has wanted both dead and alive.

In 1999, as tens of thousands of people gathered in Littleton, Colorado, to mourn the shooting victims at Columbine High School and call for more gun control, other people were growing interested in plans for the gated community of Front Sight, to be located in Nevada roughly halfway between Death Valley and Las Vegas, because it was to include thirteen shooting ranges.

The NRA was founded in the East in the wake of the Civil War, but it, like its controversies, has for some time been commonly identified, in spite of nationwide membership, with the West. That's another way of saying that, by and large, when Americans think of the gun, they think of the West—with mixed feelings.

(En)closing the Frontier

In 1890 the Census Bureau reported the disappearance of that line between white civilization and wilderness that from the beginning had really defined what America was.
    Frederick Turner, "Wounded Knee III"

The 1890s in the West weren't entirely gay. The romantic summer there was waning, and the autumn of tragic anagnorises was waxing. Early in the decade, the West, like the rest of the nation, slid into an economic slump and a crisis of identity. Much of the open land had been closed in one way or another, and imperialist America's post–Civil War haste for a new beginning in the West had led rapidly, through greed and violence on personal and social and industrial scales, to an ending—not the first of many reversals that in time would concatenate and cross-link to make the story of the West, eventually almost as exhausted of tragedy as that of Billy the Kid, postmodernly ironic.

Indeed, a century later the irony of that beginning at an end had been compounded to a daunting extent, as Thomas J. Lyon makes clear in his description of the "two Wests," one mythic and one all too real, that, by the windup of the millennium, had grown jarringly divergent. The first West, he says, "is mostly a mental place, a projection. Wild and open, this West is everything the over-civilized East, or Europe, is not. . . . In the big new space, you create a new life, a liberation from the past. The very soil is untapped, so even being a farmer is a kind of adventure. Plant seed and jump back." This is an Anglo rendition of the West that inspired dreaminess in sixteenth-century Spaniards. It has given Americans their national iconic imagery of the frontier. Over a century ago "it became 'stock.' The Wild West." The second West Lyon exemplifies by what can be seen from the air between Denver and San Francisco. Much of that is beautiful—mountain forests and peaks, canyons, stretches of sagebrush, more mountains—but there are also feedlots, gas and oil wells, open-pit mines, cities and their freeways, reservoirs, highways, much that isn't. You'll notice as well other airplanes that additionally interlace "this well-developed region," but what you won't see, "except for the tell-tale bristle of repeater towers on mountaintops, is the network of electronic communications that smoothly integrates the American West into the global lifeway." This is the West in which "people actually live and have effects on the landscape," and it, Lyon stresses, "isn't the stock one."[1]

Americans wanted the first West—and still do—but they wanted it subdued—and still do. They have been like a man who wants a woman who'll be both his tempestuous mistress and his submissive wife. They have wanted the West to be always somewhere yonder, unlimited, spiritually other but also here, containable, materially theirs. They couldn't accept it on its own terms, so they imposed theirs upon it—till it now looks like the creation of Thomas Jefferson's gridding gone berserk and as near gridlock as you can get in country with much asperous terrain. Puritans at heart, they opted more for the West as wife than for the West as mistress they still dream of. They went too far.

In 1890 many people knew they had done so, people as unalike as Helen Hunt Jackson, Theodore Roosevelt, Bill Cody, and John Muir, the last having fought for the establishment of Yosemite National Park in that year and soon to be founding the Sierra Club. They knew, as Harold P. Simonson has it, that the generic American facing west had faced an epic choice: "to conquer nature or, in a mystical sense, to fuse with it; to appropriate it for the progress of civilization or, instead, to conform to its ineffable laws for the sake of realizing selfhood; to emulate an Andrew Carnegie or to follow a Henry David Thoreau."[2] They knew that the westering American had chosen—if not uniformly, then still overwhelmingly—to emulate a Carnegie rather than to follow a Thoreau; to dwell more in the grid fed by Henry Adams's dynamo than in the West's indigenous ecology; to accent the pride and not the shame of conquest, the pride at a trammeling of the wild that would deprive that pride of its informing myth's basis in reality.

That American was the hero of Frederick Jackson Turner's recovery narrative, but soon enough he would be haunted by what had been lost and, like Turner, anxious about the future of a frontierless people. He was beginning to think like Jody Tiflin's ex-pioneer grandfather in John Steinbeck's short story "The Leader of the People":

> The man old smiled. "There's no place to go. There's the ocean to stop you. There's a line of old men along the shore hating the ocean because it stopped them."

"In boats I might, sir."

"No place to go, Jody. Every place is taken. But that's not the worst—no, not the worst. Westering has died out of the people. Westering isn't a hunger any more. It's all done. . . . It is finished."[3]

Never say never. Census figures in 1890 and thereafter certainly indicated that the West might be on its way to filling up with people and that a lot of them were clumping along the coast. But Jody's grandfather is in error, as some of his real-life peers were, about the hunger for the West: it was still alive in his time (the early twentieth century), and it's still alive today. However, it *has* changed from what it was, become (as Turner foresaw) increasingly frustrated, more tenuous than what the pioneers felt, sometimes parodic in comparison to that. It's not what it once was—in that sense the old man's *consummatum est* is vindicated. To borrow a phrase that Robert Frost, in his poem "The Oven Bird," applies to nature in seasonal decline, the hunger for the West is now—on the surface, anyhow—"a diminished thing."[4] But it's still there within the multitudinous grid that strangles it and that it, ironically, made Americans build. Moreover, though 1890 is a defensible year for marking (by average population density) the onset of that hunger's diminishment, the grid's loom was affecting it long before.

"During the nineteenth century," Donald Worster reminds us, "a growing number of Americans discovered the beauty and value of wild nature, qualities that brought them excitedly into landscapes that had been for earlier generations dark, dangerous, forbidding places that should be avoided or cleared away." Under the sway of Romanticism, their aesthetics promoted a conservation of forested land, the wilderness thus saved being "a standard by which to judge civilization, rather than the other way around." The enthusiasm was for "the vertical" rather than "the horizontal," however; so places without forests or mountains "tended to become unimportant, unvalued, uninteresting." Much of the West and Midwest was places like that, and none of the grasslands therein would be federally preserved until 1996. What did happen to it, as a consequence of the Ordinance of 1785, was what didn't happen, except on paper, to the most vertical land: the U.S. Rectangular Land Survey, which laid out a grid westward from where the Ohio River leaves Pennsylvania that "was arbitrary, abstract, and imperial" but appropriate to "a new market orientation in the perception and use of land."[5]

Worster is right that the most devastating result of that grid was the rectangular plowing of millions of acres of prairie, which practice not only widely obliterated native ecology but led to dramatic erosional losses of topsoil, and that it had the ironic sequel of permitting "the counter-ideal of wilderness to flourish elsewhere"—in New England, where forest made a comeback in the late nineteenth century, for instance, and in several areas of the West beyond the prairies. But the damage didn't stop with farming. Jefferson's ur-grid dictated how cities were raised in meshes of streets extrinsic to any natural formation of the land, and its lines were supplemented by others: lines of railroads, dirt roads, barbed-wire fences, and so on. Some of those, for various reasons, "diverged from the grid," but their asymmetries didn't so much supersede the original grid as complexify it and finally incorporate it into "an ever-changing network of power, with lines aggressively crossing, competing, and converging"—a super-grid rationalized by the naïve dream "of civilization replacing nature."[6]

The construction of that network was well under way in 1890. The frontier, that movable ecotone between wild and tame, had hazed into geographical oblivion as the web of human technology had overrun that of natural community, a process sponsored by what Stephen Tatum calls "the map and icon worldview invested . . . in boundaries that edge and divide and in space as a homogeneous void ripe for exploitation."[7] The projection of grids onto landscape, a custom in a number of ancient Old World cultures, had already gone to excess in the West. A great deal of that projection was materialized in steel. In James C. Work's construal, "steel in the Great Plains marked its closure, bound it with rails and wire." In the late 1870s barbed wire not only bound land but also tamed men: it "made ranch hands out of trail drivers, made sedentary farmers out of westering pioneers, and made section-line surveyors out of explorers." Soon the Atchison, Topeka and Santa Fe Railroad fingered across the southern plains to interconnect with the Southern Pacific ("the 'octopus' of Frank Norris"), and in the north, by 1893, the Great Northern reached all the way to Seattle and the Pacific coast—those systems thus containing the West "within a box of steel, webbed with barbed wire."[8] In 1890 the wildness left in the West, human and otherwise, was in almost the same situation as the caged panther in Rainer Maria Rilke's poem "Der Panther" that at last sees nothing beyond the bars that prison him but only the bars themselves.[9]

Let's examine the bars—railroads, fences, and more—that were enclosing and occluding the Wild West.

Telegraph lines. The first transcontinental telegraph line was completed in 1861, a feat that put an end to the eighteen-month-old pony express and installed the spine to which spreading Morse-code reticula in California, Missouri, Texas, and elsewhere would quickly be linked. The lines, spreading over trans-Mississippi land like crazing on a glaze, usually paralleled rail lines, which became transcontinental in 1869. The name of the game was instant communication, and instant communication—resisted by, among others, Indians (whose downfall through telegraphy may be suggested by Henry F. Farny's 1904 painting *The Song of the Talking Wire*) and Mormons—was the key to decreasing the West's cultural and political isolation and, in conjunction with railroad shipping, to more closely directing business operations dispersed through its vastness. As Richard White explains, such operations accomplished a transformation that had its "proper economic symbols" in the telegraph and the railroad: "They tied the larger world and the West in a tight embrace. Across the telegraph wires came the instructions and information that coordinated eastern financial markets and western production sites. Along the railroads traveled the raw materials of the West and the finished manufactures of the East."[10] Those wires aligned with rails were merely the precursors of many others that would crisscross the West in the century to come.

Railroads. First iron, then steel, their trunks, branches, and branchlets traversed the West on several latitudes by 1890. Their owners boosted the West and provided trains equipped with palatial cars for financiers that huffed through "Hell on Wheels" towns toward plusher accommodations on down the line.[11] As that epithet implies, the vascularization of the West by rails, though many people profited by it (especially those who received federal grants of land along the routes), meant high costs not just to natural but to cultural environments. In the second half of the nineteenth century, Western railroads, which, to use Frederick Turner's simile, "began to spur out across the stretches like cactus" during the 1850s, bred "the thorns of bribery, political corruption, manipulation of public opinion through the newspapers, land speculation, discriminatory rates, hatred." They bred also towns "full of what Robert Louis Stevenson saw as 'gold and lust and death,' towns that shriveled into dead husks when the rail routes changed." Wrapping up his somber meditation on the machinations of railroad magnates, Turner concludes, "Here again was that hunger beyond consumption."[12]

Late-nineteenth-century visual portrayals of the rail-based ravening of that hunger reveal much about America's changing wishes concerning the railroad in the West. Borrowing concepts from Richard Slotkin, William H. Truettner discusses the depiction of the encounter of progress and wilderness in American painting around the middle of the century in terms of a distinction between West and East: the first was popularly fantasized as a place "in which personal greed and the national good became magically associated"; the second was a densely urbanized place in which the problems attendant upon progress were all too actual. Consequently, Eastern scenes treating progress "rang a warning bell," and artists were advised to be sure such treatments "tactfully diluted the more obvious manifestations of progress"; whereas a Western scene treating them less dilutedly "was tolerable because in that fictional space the implications of progress hurt no one (except Indians, foreign powers, and others who were expendable in the eyes of an expansionist society)."[13]

To illustrate the difference in treatment, Truettner asks us to compare two paintings, Andrew Melrose's *Westward the Star of Empire Takes Its Way—Near Council Bluffs, Iowa* (1867) and Jasper F. Cropsey's *Starrucca Viaduct, Pennsylvania* (1865), the two celebrating, respectively, a new roadbed between Chicago and Council Bluffs and an engineering feat of some renown. In the first, which features an immigrant family's log cabin surrounded by stumps on the left, "a locomotive steams through a raw cut in the wilderness, its headlamp silhouetting deer fleeing before a literal engine of

Andrew Melrose, Westward the Star of Empire Takes Its Way—Near Council Bluffs, Iowa (1867): announcing the railroad's presence with unhesitating approval. (Museum of the American West Collection, Autry National Center, Los Angeles.)

progress" bearing down on the viewer. In the second, a gentler train "moves away from the viewer, its size is small compared to the breadth of the landscape, and many picturesque touches 'naturalize' its presence." Thus, in Truettner's summarization of these two treatments of the machine in the garden, "Cropsey downplays the disruptive quality of the railroad and what it portends for the future, Melrose announces its presence with unhesitating approval."[14]

As the century wore on into that future and the wilderness wore more and more rails, though, treatments of Western scenes in the vein of Melrose's fell out of favor; patrons (many of them railroad magnates) and viewers alike were partial to treatments more in the vein of Cropsey's that put a happy spin on progress.[15]

Bierstadt applied that spin, of course, and so did other painters—Joseph H. Becker, for instance—and photographers such as Carleton E. Watkins; but nobody did it like William H. Jackson. Subsequent to his stint as official photographer for Ferdinand V. Hayden's survey during the 1870s, he put himself at the magnates' service as a publicist. White observes that his pictures, even from his early days as a freelancer, "did not so much capture" the transformation of the West by settlement "as mythologize it"—in restatements over a long career. Moreover, those pictures composed by his landscapist's eye made that mythologized West look factual: "Precisely because photographs do not seem so much created as found, . . . they became the ideal means for giving the imagined West a simple actuality." In his early pictures the actuality is that of "a potential garden." In his survey pictures it's that of a pristine laboratory in which scientists can research nature's mysteries. In his

Jasper Francis Cropsey, Starrucca Viaduct, Pennsylvania (1865): downplaying the railroad's disruption and what it portends. (Oil on canvas, 22 3/8 x 36 3/8 in. 1947.58. Toledo Museum of Art, purchased with funds from the Florence Scott Libbey Bequest in Memory of her Father, Maurice A. Scott.)

railroad pictures the actuality still appears simple, but, White's analysis shows, it disguises a remarkable ideological juggling act that presents nature as vanquished by rails and yet unaltered: "These pictures often show tourists disembarking from the trains to stop in meadows, pause at streams, or view spectacular mountains and canyons. Nature no longer threatens; it heals the alienated and overcivilized. It exists easily beside the technology that makes modern civilization possible." Such pictures were artistic wish fulfillments that avoided realities railroad companies didn't like displayed to people who didn't care to see them. They were intended to persuade Americans to go west. Hiding the panther's bars, they dispelled any anxiety about the erasure of the wild and "appealed to a middle-class audience that wanted to both conquer the West and retreat into it."[16] Most of that audience did its conquering and retreating through pictorial illusions that, like Jackson's photograph *Double-headed Work Train in Rio de las Animas Cañon* (circa 1880), which invites the viewer to discover a train integrated into the mid-height of a rock face that dwarfs it, supported convenient beliefs, with no sign (except, perhaps, for the talus below) of what such engineering required. Jackson's railroad pictures show nothing of digging, blasting, and forests denuded to make ties and, in the case of many canyons, intricate trestles (grids again), some of them over a hundred feet tall.

Barbara Novak finds Jackson's *Double-headed Work Train* especially striking in how "the train, snaking through the rock, suggests . . . fusion of the natural and the

William H. Jackson, Double-headed Work Train in Rio de Las Animas Cañon (circa 1880):
the fusion of the natural and the man-made. (William H. Jackson Collection, 124, Colorado Historical
Society, all rights reserved.)

man-made." It's a fusion illustrative of a time, as iron-horse-enthusiastic America continued its equivocation between nature and civilization "in a kind of perplexed vibration," when "the rhetoric of the technological sublime developed concurrently with the nature rhetoric." That fusion can be detected in lots of paintings and photographs from the latter half of the nineteenth century that include railroads within expansive landscapes. Many carry the message "that nature and the machine would both be harnessed to the same purpose—to fulfill the American concept of a future clearly blessed by an understanding God"—but the tensions of their component oppositions, between country and city or silence and noise, aren't always resolved. So it's not surprising that many artists, like Jackson, were inclined to show trains at a distance and minimize their "linear imperialism."[17] Viewers of such works were somewhat like the people who traveled by rail in the West of the 1880s as Hal K. Rothman describes them: since the speeding train insulated them from the world they comfortably watched pass by through framing windows, it "made tourists out of travelers," passengers, of the kind White mentioned earlier, "divorced from the realities of any visited place" who were free "to re-create its essence in the context of the cultural baggage . . . brought along."[18] Railroad art, like railroad technology, contributed greatly to making the (en)closed West at least as unreal to Euro-Americans as the open one had been.

Fences. They kept stray livestock (and some wildlife) out of cultivated crops; they also served to contain livestock and to indicate property lines. They distinguished and separated me from you, mine from yours, order from chaos, civilized from savage, and they often didn't make good neighbors. In most of the West, materials at hand suitable for building fences (wood or stones) were far less available than they were in the South, parts of the Midwest, and East; moreover, expedients like embankments and hedge rows were impractical or imperfect alternatives, especially for large acreages. An industrial solution was needed, and it wasn't the single-strand smooth wire tried out for a while but a kind that was barbed, an invention ascribed to several people, among them an Illinois farmer named Joseph Glidden (with the help of his second wife, Lucinda), who patented his twisted double-strand "armoured" wire, inspired by the thorns on an Osage-orange fence he saw on a trip west, in 1874.[19] Worster remarks, following Walter Prescott Webb, that barbed wire offers an example of how "the westward movement of agriculture was at once a process of conquest *and* adaptation." Which concession appears to bode well—until you realize, as Worster qualifies his remark, that barbed wire is more accurately taken as an example of how the technology of conquest "had to be adjusted to meet environmental exigencies."[20]

Barbed wire may therefore have participated in what Worster calls "a story of reciprocity and interaction rather than of culture replacing nature," but it, like the irrigation dam and the stock saddle, has done so as "an instrument of domination."[21] If its teleology isn't the imitative replacement of nature by culture, that it also little maintains any balance of the two can be inferred from the names of a few of the types patented in the late nineteenth century, some of which are classified as "vicious" by Henry D. McCallum and Frances T. McCallum in their book *The Wire That Fenced the West*: "Thorny Fence," "Hold-Fast," "Burnell's Four-Point," "Neck-tie," "Buckthorn," "Spur-Rowel."[22] Fences of such wire weren't so much interfaces as barricades. Built by farmers, ranchers, or railroaders (to bound rights-of-way), those pales were a means of control. As Richard C. Poulsen puts it, they "choked the open spaces of the plains," and many of their owners still engage in hanging "slain predatory wildlife" on them.[23] David Daly and Joel Persky observe that, "in Westerns, barbed wire is usually a symbol for the relentless encroachment of technology" and that in films like King Vidor's *Man without a Star* (1955) and David Miller's *Lonely Are the Brave* (1962), elegies that mourn such encroachment, it "becomes the symbol of the passing of the West."[24] It's that symbology, stretched, after the devil's hatband came to be stretched around the West and more, that prompted William Stafford, visiting the grave of Daniel Boone nearly a century after Glidden secured his patent, to write, "Children, we live in a barbwire time."[25]

Reservations, Wild West shows, and other encirclements. In the late nineteenth century, reservations both fenced Indians in and kept them out of the white world. Some Indians, though, became entertainers of the citizens of that world, most notably as actors in Buffalo Bill's Wild West. Confined within that circus (etymologically, a "circle"), they executed safely scripted reenactments of their savage deeds. They thereby were critical to Cody's success, the secret of which, for Frederick Turner, was his fame as a terminator of Indians and buffalo:

> He was symbolic of that process of taming the wilderness that had seemed so imperative to whites even while the wilderness had been so perilously seductive. In his figure this ambivalence was delightfully resolved, the heroic killer displaying to his audiences the trophies of his triumphs. Inside the ropes and canvases of hundreds of arenas the wilderness lived on in the only way whites could accept it: tamed, scaled down, and under the direction of the white hero/ magician.

Cody as Prospero vividly symbolized what civilizing was about, but the resolution he effected didn't stay delightful, either for him or for anyone else sensitive to the results of Western conquest. Late in his career in showbiz, "as the real Wild West steadily receded into memory, there came a change in the mind of the hero. He began to be haunted by the suspicion that he and his kind had killed the thing he had most loved." Like many of his fellow Americans touring the West, he grew confused as to what should be leveled in the name of civilization and what should be saved of what was left of its wildness. While he got into Western real estate and more in his cups and "came to feel himself less hero than romantic mortician,"[26] those fin-de-siècle and then twentieth-century tourists vacillated in what they thought about a wilderness sundered, abridged, exploited, and piecemeal preserved in national parks, rodeos, Indian curio shops, zoos, museums.

Years before the deliria of his last days, Cody enjoyed having a whirl in an automobile, the very machine that soon would supplant the train as the Western tourist's conveyance of choice—though he wouldn't drive one into the arena and violate the illusional kingdom of his more and more preposterous circus.[27] When he died in 1917, after making a film about the massacre at Wounded Knee, there was a tussle over where his tourist-drawing corpse should be buried; the site finally decided upon was the crest of Lookout Mountain, above Denver. From there, according to Turner's paraphrase of a passage in a contemporary article in the *Denver Post*, Cody "could look eastward toward the ever-rising dawn that each morning would reveal anew the concrete realization of his dream: a great city humming where once there had been nothing but a wild New World."[28]

Cities and towns. White offers the datum—eye-opening to most people, I suspect—that the West "very quickly became an urban region whose cities held sway over vast hinterlands. By 1880 the West had become the most urbanized region of the country." Already, by that time, "the western universe began to take the shape of a collection of discrete solar systems, and the suns of these systems were cities"—San Francisco, Denver, Salt Lake City, Omaha, and a dozen more.[29] In terms of that conceit, the planets of the systems were towns, and the systems in the aggregate, which had a formidable ecological footprint by the end of the century, were tentacled together with railroads. Before the Civil War, railroads intertied frontier and city subregionally; thereafter their transcontinental extension and knitting, in Carl Abbott's words, "allowed townsite speculators to fill in the gaps between the earlier cities with communities like Cheyenne, Tacoma, Colorado Springs, Bismarck, and Fresno."[30] Such towns followed the inorganic evolutionary patterns of the cities preceding them and became gridded, webbed, networked in manifold ways.

That process can be seen in the development of Junction City, Kansas, during the late nineteenth and early twentieth centuries. As I learned back in the 1970s while working as a consultant on a documentary film about the town, located in the east-central part of the state, it was from its beginning a place of junctions: of rivers (the Kansas, Republican, and Smoky Hill), immigrant trails, and railroad lines (one of the east–west trunks of the Union Pacific and a branch of it that ran northwest to Concordia and Belleville). The director, Robert Richards, and scriptwriter, Roy Gridley, of the film, titled *Junction City, 1890–1915*, sought suggestions for their use of the photographs, most of them done by Joseph J. Pennell, that were the building blocks of the project. The idea was to sequence them so as to relate the story of the town's rapid growth from a railway station to a full-blown, if relatively small, urban community. By the time I came on board, that idea had been pretty much translated into documentary art; it was, with all due respect for the filmmakers' talents, a cinch. Once the pictures with the most illustrative images were arranged in a dated series, they immediately said almost everything about how a strict geometry got stamped on that spot on the plains: grassy open land, a railroad track, a telegraph line, tidy houses that rustic visitors found stiff and squeezed too close together, dirt streets laid out in squares, a mesh of electric lines emanating from the power plant that started operating in 1886, telephone lines, cars (the first in 1905, a Ford) and then trucks as well chuffing in straight rows back and forth on yet more streets laid out in squares and bordered with houses or stores or other businesses and all strung with wires high and low—until you couldn't decide exactly when the outer grid must have become an inner one as firm, for the majority of the citizens in that bureaucratized junction box of a town, as a panther's cage.[31]

Photographs like Pennell's aren't exceptional. The archives of any town or city in the West contain similar ones that tell similar stories of end-of-the-frontier transformations. Each story is about settling, settling down, settling for an anthill existence of more abstract frontiers that wasn't quite what the romance of immigration promised those who wanted something, well, maybe the same as it was back East but also not the same. Such transformative settling always originated in the desire, again, for control, especially when land speculation was involved. For instance, Elliott West comments, concerning town-promoting immigrants along the South Platte during the gold rush in Colorado, that, "as easterners competed among themselves, they reached out to bring this country into their common grasp, and the central ritual in this act of faith was the survey. Notice was given: Society from the Missouri valley, with its grids of streets lined with mercantiles and saloons, would control the area."[32] Control was indispensable to what Jon Roush calls the Western town's "most important historical mission," which was "imposing man-made order on the wilderness."[33]

But that mission, to the extent it was fulfilled by 1890 or shortly afterward, had a cost, one rousing remorse that still—and perhaps more deeply, if diffusely, after another century of imposing man-made order—gnaws at the innards of all Westerners not hopelessly alienated from nature by urbanization. During exploration and settlement the psychological urgency of gridding surely was palpable for Euro-Americans responsive to the principle that, as Roush expresses it, "the more wild the reality, the more important the reassurance of straight lines." Such lines mean nothing to a bison that wanders beyond the rectilinear bounds of Yellowstone, but they were the means of creating a "cookie-cutter space [that] conformed to the mind of nineteenth-century America" and allowed a West of interchangeable geographic parts to be governed from points east. The strategic medium for the ramification of rails and their spawning of towns, the gridded arrangement of that space "was as efficient as the corporate blueprints are to McDonald's." And irrelevant to, opposed to, the need for something other than bureaucratic efficiency. Which is why, as 1890 approached and the West was less dotted with the forts of a half-century before and more checkered with towns and cities that, like the straight-

Joseph J. Pennell, Firemen's Parade, *photograph of Washington Street in Junction City, Kansas* (1905): *the strict geometry of the urban grid imposed on the plains. (Pennell Collection, Kansas Collection, Spencer Research Library, University of Kansas Libraries.)*

fenced, straight-furrowed fields surrounding them, "walled out the wild" even as they sprawled out into it, some Westerners got serious about preservation. They wanted "to wall the wild in, to protect it from the incursions of civilization," but, ever entrepreneurial, they didn't want it to "interfere with business"—so they kept it in square parks and its people on square reservations. Quite apart from Indian issues, belated measures like those were inadequate and remain so. Millions of townspeople and urbanites in the West still want more wilderness. Sympathizing with them, Roush concludes that "we feel something missing from the compartmentalized spaces in which we have caged ourselves. . . . The rigid fragmentation of western space has walled us away from essential parts of our own being."[34]

When, in 1901, Pattillo Higgins and other Texas wildcatters struck big oil at Spindletop and touched off a boom in the black gold that would be distilled into the gasoline to fuel unprecedented human circulation through the West, he gave no thought to the primordial plants and animals that had been compressed to make the buried soup that shot skyward for nine days before the well was capped. Nor would he care that the derricks soon springing up all over Texas, Oklahoma, and

California like forests of trees made from giant Erector Sets were, just as were the buildings rising in Western cities, unstoppably verticalizing Jefferson's grid. Nor, in his actualized dream of wealth from a liquid quickly to become the West's most profitable extraction, would he ever have a glimmer of the kind of balanced vision of the wild and the civilized that a sane future for the West required—and requires yet. He was imprisoned in the panther's cage, hypnotized by its bars. And he wasn't alone. But what those bars repressed, outwardly and inwardly, wasn't really gone, not by a long shot.

PART FOUR

From the 1890s to the 1960s: The West as Region

We are water. We are swept away. Desire begins in wetness.
Terry Tempest Williams, "Water"

Prelude and Overview

Turner's frontier narrative moves away from the Old World where elite romance and subaltern tragedy fought for control of human consciousness and into American democracy where conflict resolves into the balanced harmony of high comedy. . . . Its concluding democratic synthesis evades the dangerous antinomies of romance and tragedy.
Kerwin Lee Klein, *Frontiers of Historical Imagination: Narrating the European Conquest of Native America, 1890–1990*

During an interview a few years ago, Frank Bergon was asked if the violence in his 1987 novel *Shoshone Mike*, based on events in 1911 in Nevada that involved a posse's massacre of a Shoshone family accused of killing some white men, was "inevitable" or "just the result of a series of fatal misunderstandings." Bergon answered that "the violence grew out of misunderstanding—a conflict between two cultures that couldn't talk to each other. It was tragic." He explained that "history, in hindsight, only seems inevitable" and that "the massacre was the result of attitudes, perceptions, and values that might have been different. . . . Tragedy is the consequence of choices." While Bergon granted that revenge was a significant motive for the posse's actions, he stressed that the attitudes and values of the posse's culture weren't about that but about "the belief that 'savagery' and 'primitiveness' needed to be eliminated for 'civilization' and 'progress' to thrive." Hence, he said, he intended for the novel, set in a time of many new technologies, to dramatize the tension between the Old West and the New West, a durable one since "technological progress couldn't expunge the values of the Old West, which . . . still survive in the contemporary West." Such survival is possible, he concluded, because "the way we think changes much slower than the material surfaces of our lives."[1]

Much of what Bergon says about that massacre and its circumstances might be said about the closing of the frontier, an event whose effects and aftereffects remained powerful in 1911. It wasn't simply inevitable that it had happened as it had. Plenty of misunderstandings came into play in the conquest that brought it to pass. In sundry ways that closing was tragic, the fruit of attitudes, perceptions, and values that might have been different and urged other choices. The arrogant belief that savagery and primitiveness needed to be eliminated for the sake of civilization and progress rationalized it. Tensions between the Old West and the first of a succession of New Wests figured in it, as did disjunctions between slow-changing habits of mind and fast-changing material surfaces of lives.

Misunderstandings, tensions, disjunctions. Guilt over the past of the West and exuberance about its future. A mélange of moods. All of which, in the 1890s and early twentieth century, gave rise to a more complex ambivalence about the Western wild than ever before, ambivalence informed, for many, with a sense of tragedy. Like all tragedies, that of the West wasn't generally recognized in medias res but only in the hindsight that made it seem inevitable—and then made clearer what had happened, why, what it meant, how bungles might have been avoided. After the spring morning of exploration and the summer afternoon of conflict, autumn evening, as occupation kept thickening, brought a recognition of disaster—and lamentation and nostalgia. Romantic excesses led to tragic exegeses.

"There was little inclination among nineteenth-century Americans to think about tragedy," Harold P. Simonson remarks, as long as the frontier was open; once it was closed, though, there formed "the necessary climate for tragedy—specifically, for American tragedy." That tragedy had much to do with the dourest implication of the closing: "the end of the Edenic myth and the illusions it fostered."[2] The unfolding (uncovering, apocalypse) of that tragedy in the twentieth century would expose the human limitations and flaws that had caused it and still perpetuated it—though such exposure would do little to prevent the Edenic myth and its illusions from returning in new guises.

Prior to the 1890s many Americans may have thought the West was surrounded by a cordon sanitaire that would protect it from the bad habits of the rest of the world, but, as David M. Wrobel has shown, there was "a widespread frontier anxiety" that "emerged in embryonic form in the 1870s and became more pronounced in the succeeding decades." Initially more an intellectual than a popular anxiety, it originated in a stark, if mythy, fact: the Eden of the Edenic myth "was in peril." The tide of immigrants into the United States and the West was rising. Cities were getting crowded. Expanding commerce and industry threatened America's "agrarian heritage."[3] What was once wild, open, and free was becoming mild, closed, and fettered. Pressured by progress, a lifeway was passing away, more swiftly and less intellectually all the time. The rural West was becoming less lawless, more respectable, even as Western cities were becoming culturally wilder. Frontier anxiety was a mixed bag.

But in the early years of the twentieth century, as that anxiety, its constituent misgivings now nationally epizootic, increased, the cause, however diffuse, had a unitary feel. During that time of excitement about the future, in Robert G. Athearn's words, "it was as if America was cutting itself loose from the past, surrendering a treasured family possession as one of the conditions for embarking upon some uncertain but necessary new course. Somehow, old values were to be traded for new ones. . . . there lingered a sense of impending loss. Philosophers and forecasters who pondered these things thought they could identify the missing item: it was the West." Though singular in name, what was missing—or at least fading—wasn't only the geographical West but also "the West of the mind, of the spirit," a "mystical West" that had long been the fantasy of America's future.[4] That West was the baby being thrown out with the bath water of the past; in its place were coming tramways, gaslit streets, automobiles, urban sprawl. A nervous-making prospect.

The unevadable truth was that the West was turning into a region (from the Latin *regio*, "a space enclosed by lines"). A congeries of disparate territories was melding into a quilt of states possessed of characteristics, as Patricia Nelson Limerick describes them, "that do not appear in every part of the West but that overlap in enough Western places to give the whole some conceptual unity"—characteristics such as "a scarcity of water; the presence of Indian peoples; Mexican influences; a focus on the Pacific Ocean; vast amounts of federal land; a distinctive regional relation to the federal government; long-term involvement with boom-or-bust economies; myths of romantic escape and danger; a history as the nation's dumping ground; and, finally, a continuing legacy of conquest."[5] What her list, in most of its specifics and in toto, suggests is that the overarching common characteristic of places in a West being "ruled" into relative tameness as a region was a continuing legacy of wildness. That wildness requiring continuing conquest was direly at risk during what Richard W. Etulain terms the West's "postfrontier or regional stage," a stage defined by the "ambivalent marriage of celebration and lament," which would lead, after World War I, to the reinvention of the West as a place "beyond a frontier of cowboys and Indians."[6]

That reinvention involved changes, some already under way but now accelerated, transitions tautened by issues ultimately of wildness. It meant the extensive conversion, to borrow terms used by William Cronon, of "first nature" into "second nature."[7] By that techno-economic alchemy, as Hal K. Rothman explains, nature "organized to feed and clothe the self and the family" was transmuted into nature "designed to market the world," the prototype of which was, by Cronon's argument, Chicago, "a place apart from first nature but intrinsically tied to it." The conversion was essential to how "Americans saw themselves as 'nature's nation,' with an updated appreciation for their own technological prowess," and how they fathomed in the West "a firm bond between this visually exceptional region and the people who believed they had mastered it." The industrialization that enabled such mastery, however, was also destructive. Technologically proud Americans thus also "felt ambivalence" about machines and cities in the West and "wanted its physical nature to defy the efforts of civilization."[8]

After recounting the arrival of the first railroad line at the South Rim of the Grand Canyon, late in 1901, and then of the first automobile, early in 1902, at that location above a gorge where John Wesley Powell and his men had gambled their lives only thirty years before, Donald Worster observes that the explorer had witnessed in his lifetime, from 1834 to 1902, "a revolution in the direction of the nation's development—from agrarianism to industrialism, a change that brought a deep shift of power and a profound redefinition of values." The reinvention of the West through later decades carried on that redefinition, a signal benefit of which was the articulation of "a more thoughtful, scientifically informed ethic of conservation" in opposition to "a careless, unplanned exploitation of nature."[9]

But the redefinition of values brought by that change had aspects that were problematic. Industrialism, more radically than agrarianism, undertook the commodification of nature and in the twentieth-century West furthered what Carol Steinhagen calls "the re-creation of land into landscape"[10]—most of the latter (etymologically, "shaped" land) not the sort idealized by the pastoral tradition. At the same time, however, Americans were loath to let go of their frontier mythology, tragic ambivalence and all. The result was a tailoring both logical and irrational, here capsuled by Richard Slotkin: "Faced with the choice of 'liquidating' the concept of the Frontier or 'renaturalizing' it, Americans chose the latter. By a systematic and highly selective reinterpretation of the language of the myth, they adapted it to suit the ideological purposes and needs of the new industrial society."[11] That adaptation started in the nineteenth century, and it would go on, with tweakings and improvisations as new "frontiers" (with their wildernesses, opportunities, and so on) dawned thereafter, into the twenty-first.

Ambiguously concomitant with such redefinition were changes, during the late nineteenth and early twentieth centuries, in how the West was, in a broad sense of the word, *seen*. John D. Dorst points out the most determinative of those changes in his *Looking West*. The visual categories once typically applied to the West, European categories even today not quite defunct, the *picturesque* and the *sublime* (opposites bookending a range from the genteelly pretty to the terrifyingly transcendent), were, according to him, largely replaced by the end of the nineteenth century by those of another language. The more Americans read survey reports and came to know the West firsthand, the more obvious was the inadequacy of the traditional aesthetic vocabulary to much of the physical West—Southwestern deserts, endless plains, alkali flats, and such that that vocabulary could picture only negatively. The new language, in contrast, was empirical and empowered "a new, more self-confident, and more distinctively American discourse of looking, through which the West could be seen in much greater variety and complexity." Seen that way, the strange West became the familiar region that epitomized America for the rest of the world; but such change also entailed a shallowing of wildness, so that "the West of adventurers, explorers, and scientists, a West of 'views,' is supplanted by a packaged and marketed West of touristic experiences."[12] That supplantation registered the resurgence, in a modern form, of the utilitarian conception of Western nature.

And there were other, related changes in how the West was seen. Aligned with the movement toward conservation was a change in the idea of wilderness that began in the nineteenth century—through the efforts of Thoreau, Muir, and others—and gathered momentum in the twentieth. Max Oelschlaeger describes it as "a shift . . . from viewing wild nature as merely a valuable resource (as a means to economic ends) and obstacle (wilderness must be conquered for civilization to advance) toward a conception of wilderness as an end in its own right and an endangered species in need of preservation."[13] That shift generally accorded with a reordering of priorities with respect to the West that Gene M. Gressley says occurred at the advent of the twentieth century: "From a presumption that the domain was inexhaustible and for private reward arose the commandment that the domain was a national treasure, some of it inviolate and to be guarded, some to be used, and all of it to be strictly supervised for generations to come."[14]

There were, of course, changes counter to such reasoned ones as well. As Gressley argues, most of them had to do with the exploitation of wild nature through which "Americans' speculative ardor unleashed chaos on the West." If the heating-up of the ardor of conservationists as the twentieth century unrolled was arithmetic, that of developers of various kinds was geometric—and topsy-turviness reigned. Indeed, Gressley proposes, "if one searches for a scenario setting in which to examine, define, and analyze the twentieth-century West, the development of the West's natural resources—land, minerals, water—provides the theater (often of the absurd)." Pursuing his metaphor, he stresses that "the dramatization would encompass a long litany of western and national visions and despair," featuring clashes on end, many over issues of wildness, from "urban sprawl versus rural shrinkage" to "conservationists versus all."[15]

The first decade of the twentieth century witnessed the sprouting of regionalist literary and artistic colonies in the Southwest and the completion of the last transcontinental railroad; the second, the burgeoning of the Western-movie industry and the founding of the National Park Service; the third, the proliferation of dude ranches in the West and the first one-day, coast-to-coast airplane flight; the fourth, the Dust Bowl, the passage of the Indian Reorganization Act, and the dedication of Boulder Dam; the fifth, the beginning of smog in Los Angeles and the explosion, in New Mexico, of the first atomic bomb; the sixth, the expansion of Cold War defense industries across the West; and the seventh, the establishment of California as the most populous state in the nation and the passage of the Wilderness Act.[16] Such watersheds made those decades of Western regionalization a time of tremendous changes, many of them at odds with the Old West and its mind-set or with one another, all of them within the historical context of an increasingly complicated dialectic of the wild and the civilized to which they contributed.

> In full tragedy the main characters are emancipated from dream, an emancipation which is at the same time a restriction, because the order of nature is present. . . . Tragedy is a paradoxical combination of a fearful sense of rightness (the hero must fall) and a pitying sense of wrongness (it is too bad that he falls). . . . If we are right in our suggestion that romance, tragedy, irony and comedy are all episodes in a total quest-myth, we can see how it is that comedy can contain a potential tragedy within itself.
>
> Northrop Frye, Anatomy of Criticism: Four Essays

Ending the Indian: Civilization (f)or Extinction

> A long time ago my father told me what his father told him, that there was once a Lakota holy man, called Drinks Water, who dreamed what was to be. . . . He dreamed that the four-leggeds were going back into the earth and that a strange race had woven a spider's web all around the Lakotas. And he said: "When this happens, you shall live in square gray houses, in a barren land, and beside those square gray houses you shall starve."
>
> John G. Neihardt, Black Elk Speaks: Being the Life Story of a Holy Man of the Oglala Sioux

The last word Thoreau said before he died in 1862 was "Indians," supposedly. If that's true, what did he mean? What was the rest of the sentence in his head that went unvoiced? I like to believe that it was about the predicament of the Indians, that at his end America's premier naturalist, troubled during his short life over the end of wilderness, was acutely aware of the possible end of its longtime human inhabitants, most of those left by then in the West. If that was the case, he had plenty of reason to be worried. In 1862 the end of the Indians, one way or another, really was possible. That issue, like the related issue of the end of the wilderness, most of what was left of it by then also in the West, had been growing more worrisome—and more complex.

To be sure, in the late nineteenth century there was no shortage of white Americans more interested in the extermination of Indians than worried about their termination. Whatever his sympathies for their situation, General Sherman wasn't unique in wanting to do to them what he had done to Atlanta during the Civil War—

a desire that swelled after the Custer debacle and was allied with the assumptions that Indians were hindrances to the progress of civilization and on the whole either weren't civilizable or shouldn't be granted the benefits of civilized life. But that attitude was only one extreme on a spectrum that became more variegated as the nineteenth century closed and gave way to the twentieth. There were still whites who engaged in what Richard Slotkin, discussing Longfellow's The Song of Hiawatha, describes as "the Romantic association of the Indians with those characteristic virtues acquired by the Americans in their transit from the Old World to the new."[1] After Custer's Last Stand in 1876, for many people the myth of that cavalier, as Richard White puts it, "became a way to talk about race and class, a way to demonstrate the necessity of subordinating savages of all kinds"; thus Indians "had to be reformed and taught the meaning of work and order."[2] There were also inclinations to blame Indians for their own demise, to attribute their undoing to God's will, to see them as too fallen to resist the vices of civilization that had corrupted them, or to explain their dying out (a fact for most ethnographers) as a result of natural (Darwinian) winnowing. There were people who believed that cultural assimilation could save the remaining Indians, and there were people who believed that such assimilation was inconceivable—just as there were those who condoned white-Indian intermarriage and those who detested it.[3]

The European image-makers of the late nineteenth century whom Ray Allen Billington surveys occupied just as dizzying a spectrum. They generally agreed "that the Indian was doomed, but they differed sharply on whether his fate was justifiable." Some believed that Indians couldn't be assimilated and must yield to progress as hunting was surpassed by farming and manufacturing, the teepee by the house. Some believed in "the true mission of the Anglo-Saxon: to transmute lesser people into civilized citizens useful to mankind." Many saw Indians in another light: "as tragic victims of frontier greed, and hence deserving of sympathy and aid"—Noble Savages done wrong.[4] And so on.

Stateside, the upshot of such a spectrum of disparate—and shifting, intermixing—attitudes was rampant ambivalence about the place of Indians in American society. Were they to be included or excluded? Were they mythically central or marginal to the nation's identity?[5] Reactions to the deepening dilemma those questions indicated, by both whites and Indians, were themselves dilemmatic. The mission of the U.S. Army in dealing with Indians during the closing decades of the nineteenth century was much the same as Elliott West says it was in the 1860s: "typically ambivalent. Soldiers were told to help the starving Creeks [removed to Indian Territory in the late 1830s]; they were to police the starving Cheyennes." Plains Indians were torn between "two dreadful choices. They could try to accommodate, surrendering their vision [of their way of life], or they could try to resist the irresistible," which "awful alternatives coincided with two trends already dividing the tribes, a fracture arising from their own choices and actions."[6] Largely irrelevant to the choices and actions of those overrunning the land on which they were trying to live, Indians grappling with this damned-if-you-do-damned-if-you-don't double bind got little assistance from Congress. Traditionally duplicitous in its policies toward Indians, that body, like other governmental agencies, was divided by what Robert F. Berkhofer Jr. labels "the traditional East-West conflict over Indian policy." That conflict concerned the possibility, desirability, and pace of civilizing Indians and produced a "dual vision" that guaranteed ambivalence—as well as contradictions, "consistent inconsistencies," and "paradoxical assumptions"—in Indian policy through the late nineteenth century, for most of which time white America was at war with many of the peoples it debated assimilating.[7]

Armed strife would stop, but the ambivalence would go on. It was nurtured by and nurtured in turn a mishmash of images of the Indian, all variations on hackneyed themes, together sending jumbled messages. Writing about the first photographs of Plains Indians to reach Easterners, Larry McMurtry reasons that they "must have awakened at least a little ambivalence in the viewers, for the pictures themselves contradicted some of the most wildly propagandistic aspects of the rhetoric of conquest. Here indeed were the people Rousseau had been thinking about, and yet the military men and journalists were describing these handsome specimens as murdering, scalping devils."[8] Ambivalence must have been awakened by subtler mixed messages within individual images as well. For instance, in her research on the ideology of geological-survey photographs of landscapes and Indians by William H. Jackson, John K. Hillers, and others, Susan Hegeman has discovered that those photographs, which were included in reports but also made available to the press and sold to individuals, reflect "competing desires and interests." However much readable as scientific records or artworks, those photographs served "as a way of producing stereotypes of the West's indigenous people, which could be used to both justify and create the conditions of their colonization." Thus if, as was typical of Jackson's practice, photographic depiction downplayed the Indian, the photographed Indian still dwells in the West (and is part of its charm, perhaps) but only as "a relic of a receding presence"—so that "empty vistas" are open for settlement. Portraits of individual Indians, sometimes in faked settings, may have a romantically savage air, but they also make the subject an object of control by "turning the 'place' of the personal image into the organizable and impersonal data of bureaucratic 'space.'" Such photographs present Indians as captured, photographically and otherwise, and sequestered under bureaucratic control, but they also, to stretch the application of one of Hegeman's phrases, hold what's unknown about them "at arm's length, by *keeping* it strange."[9] For contemporary viewers the Indians were there but not there, familiarized and yet remote and exotic.

That's how a stereotype works. It offers a game of cultural hide-and-seek. The image is of an Indian, but it annuls the real Indian; the image may seem authentic, but it expunges the truth of history.[10] It functions to simplify what it portrays and make it comfortable. It's therefore highly marketable. But the simplification is always tentative. The expunction is always incomplete. Ambivalence is prepatent in the image; it may be veiled, but it can be teased out to tell the story of America's unfinished business with the Indian. It's in the wooden Indian (the savage congealed into stoic harmlessness), the war dance on a bubble-gum wrapper, the horsed Indian chief in a Santa Fe System Lines advertisement who salutes with his spear the Super Chief streaking through sage-bedecked land toward a Fred Harvey meal, the Indians played by white actors in most of the Westerns ever filmed.[11] Look closely.

In the 1890s and the first decades of the twentieth century, the photographer of Indians was Edward S. Curtis. He was also their principal photographic stereotyper. In her biography of him, Barbara A. Davis discusses an anonymous poem titled "The Passing of the Red Man" published in *The Western Trail* in May 1901—a time when "public interest in the subject of Indians was on the rise." Printed around an 1899 Curtis portrait of a Nez Percé man, the poem is crammed with stereotypes of Indians being militarily shellacked by whites but refusing to be pacified, disdaining reform, and so on. The poet, says Davis, "echoes the still-developing idea that the Indian was unable to live in civilization: a 'domesticated' Indian could only be one whose spirit had been broken. As the notion took hold that there could be no future for the 'true,' 'wild' Indian, notes of admiration and poignancy intensified in popular depictions of Indians. America's romance with its Western past was about to burst into full bloom."[12] So was Curtis's career. Many photographers had recorded Indians in transit from traditional lifeways and the adversities of reservation Indians, but for the next thirty years Curtis would exercise what William H. Goetzmann and William N. Goetzmann term "a special talent . . . that inevitably made the corpus of his work a new sentimental myth of 'the vanishing American.'"[13]

The sentimentality as Curtis—and others—elaborated it is unmistakable, and there's a good deal of emotional contrivance to lots of his photographs. As Berkhofer observes, he "reconstructed the past when he could no longer find the disappearing Indian ways of life," using wigs, culturally inappropriate clothing, and other props to make his subjects appear as he wished.[14] His often theatricalized images are filled with inaccuracies most viewers failed to notice and for whom he succeeded in creating, as Goetzmann and Goetzmann describe it, "an aboriginal West that never was."[15] Yet, for all the artifice and hyperbolized sentiment that made Indians into postcard romantic figures and even celebrities and suppressed the severe realities of their lives, Curtis's images betray—and betrayed to his knowing contemporaries—the regretful truth suggested by words like "poignancy" and "vanishing": the Indian, in N. Scott Momaday's synoptic phrase, "has been compelled to make his way under an imposed identity of defeat."[16] Beneath the romance—or perhaps behind it, like the backgrounds Curtis blurred with wide apertures to conceal any fixtures of modernity—there was a loudening undertone of tragedy about the real aboriginal West that had been lost.

From this stew of emotions, moods, and attitudes would emerge the preponderant Indian stereotype in the early part of a century characterized, in Kerwin Lee Klein's metahistorical perspective, by historians' "growing willingness to imagine America's past as tragic conflict" and its "democracy founded on a Native American holocaust": the doomed Indian.[17] Dispossessed of his land, the buffalo gone, the hoops of his world snapped, he was the victim of a civilization holding the beliefs, in Roy Harvey Pearce's phrasing, that "he must die, since noncivilization is not life," and that "the good society could sustain and prove itself only by destroying the remnant of a savage past." The notion that he was thus predestined fit perfectly with the "pattern of pity and censure" that had long determined his treatment by whites.[18] But the elevation of pity renewed emphasis on the Indian as a Noble Savage, a reversal of the process that had made him a red devil.

Some American artists, as we've seen, had been furthering that emphasis since the beginning of the prevalence of red-devil imagery in the 1840s. In addition, study Tompkins H. Matteson's 1847 oil *The Last of the Race*, a painting of an Indian family, contemplative elder standing tall, halted before an ocean, whose distributed prints, in Julie Schimmel's interpretation, addressed "sentiment in the East for pictures that constructed a romantic fade-out of Indian life." Or think of Ferdinand Pettrich's 1856 marble sculpture *The Dying Tecumseh*, a representation of the final moments of the Shawnee chief killed in 1813 who had come to symbolize quintessentially the Indians' antagonism to westward expansion; though by such memorialization "whites recognized his greatness," his death, "tragic as they made it out to be, signaled the inevitability of white advance." But the perennial exemplar of artworks influential in the reversal is James Earle Fraser's *The End of the Trail*. First modeled in 1894 and then repeatedly revised (by the artist) and myriadly reproduced in various media to the present, the sculpture was displayed in monumental form at the 1915 Panama-Pacific Exposition in San Francisco, a fair that proclaimed the triumphal march of Euro-American progress across a cosmopolitan nation. It became the emblematic centerpiece of that festival, a distinctly Western distillation of the mighty mounted and armed Indian now exhausted and defeated, the whole structure defined by "downward arcs," declivities that unify it in "a bow to the modern world." Fraser sympathized with the Indians in that world, but, Schimmel concludes, "this particular formulation of the ill-fated Indian has projected a powerful stereotype through the twentieth century," one that even today turns up on everything from belt buckles to "signs designating retirement communities."[19]

Fraser's ubiquitous beaten Indian might be featured on the cover of any of the books, from Helen Hunt Jackson's *Century of Dishonor* on, that Patricia Nelson Limerick accuses of peddling "the standard, sympathetic version of Indian-white history," which "casts Indians as victims, passive people who stood frozen in place as a great wave of white expansion crashed down on them and left them broken

Tompkins Harrison Matteson, The Last of the Race (1847): a romantic fade-out of Indian life. (Oil on canvas, 39 ¾ x 50 in. 1931.1. Collection of the New-York Historical Society.)

and shattered." She notes that most American historians now reject such bathos, and she argues that it disserved the people it might have meant to help. "But," she admits, "one ends up shaken in one's orthodoxy. Consider the condition of Indian people at the end of the wars, and the term 'victim' keeps coming back to mind."[20]

The more you consider that condition, the more shaken your orthodoxy becomes. If Indians hadn't been merely the victims of violent expansion, they were indeed the victims of the civilization it had brought and into which many whites hoped they could assimilate. Roderick Nash reminds us that around the turn of the century "too much civilization, not too little, seemed at the root of the nation's difficulties" and that, "in regard to primitive man, American opinion was also tending to reverse the flow of two and a half centuries. Increasing numbers joined Helen Hunt Jackson in sympathizing with the Indian and identifying the disease, whiskey, and deception of civilization, not his savageness, as the crux of his problem."[21] They weren't just weepy softheads. If they embraced the "morality of pity" that was the trend in the early twentieth century, they had, Momaday argues, good reason:

The contact with the white man's civilization—it was all too clear at the turn of the century—had failed to enrich the Indian. To the contrary, that civilization had debased him. Surely the white man was hard put to retain his image of the noble savage. For what he saw in actuality—if he dared to look—was not the creature of his imagination but a poor, syphilitic, lice-infested wastrel whose only weapon against despair was alcohol. The death rate among Indians had begun to exceed the birth rate. The reservations had at last become contagious colonies and concentration camps.[22]

Reservations: an ambiguous idea that became a double-dealing institution that produced contradictory results that aroused ambivalent feelings (disgust and others as well as pity) that motivated, gradually, confused redress.

If it's true that in 1856 Lame Bull, head chief of the Piegan subtribe of the Blackfoot (a tribe, in Angie Debo's words, "not enthusiastic about 'civilization'"), told a Presbyterian missionary named Elkanah Mackey that he wanted the whites to tame his people, he undoubtedly had something friendlier than the reservation system in mind.[23] The idea of that system had been hatched in a white mind. Responding to requests from settlers on the trails to Oregon, California, and Santa Fe that Indians be gotten out of the way and their populations concentrated, the commissioner of the Bureau of Indian Affairs (BIA) proposed in 1849 that the obstructors be confined in limited areas with strict boundaries where, to borrow bureaucratese from Berkhofer, "they would undergo civilizational transformation." Implementation, through the usual specious treaties, of this "second phase of removal" was, of course, advantageous for railroaders and other entrepreneurs as well as for settlers.[24]

But civilizational transformation on gridded tracts assigned tribe by tribe didn't work smoothly. Not all the Indians hoodwinked into accepting treaties complied with them. Some raided settlements. And some settlers raided reservations—places that were supposed to be, in Pearce's words, "savage islands in the midst of civilized seas"[25]—killing buffalo and stealing timber and horses or the land itself. Later, white ranchers grazed their cattle on them. By 1871, the year Congress halted the negotiation of treaties with Indians and the establishment of reservations became a matter of less-respected titles authorized by executive order, reservations had the look of ill-maintained wildlife refuges.[26] They didn't function well even as zoos, since they failed both at protecting savages and at eliminating them from the outside world.[27] Life on them was dull and frustrating and worse. Warrants for Momaday's appraisal of them aren't hard to come by. Travelers in the West who visited the reservations found what Billington describes as "maladjusted discontent," and their accounts projected the image of a bestial race "doomed to extermination."[28] There's little exaggeration in Frederick Turner's contention that even in the early 1880s, by which time the reservation system was well implanted, "the whites could not rest easy with the least whisper or rag of the old 'wild' ways.

Within the eroded little enclosures of the reservations the rage for white order . . . continued unabated."[29]

In 1887 Congress formalized that rage and worsened the reservation mess by passing the General Allotment Act (Dawes Act). Its basic provision was for a mechanical procedure, variations of which had been tried since the 1830s, whereby a given tribe's reservation land was diced into quarter sections (for heads of families) and eighth sections (for single persons over eighteen years old and orphans) and allotted to enrolled members of that tribe, with any "left-over" land—more than half, by one device or another, it turned out—to be secured for white settlement. Though Southwestern Indians largely avoided this procedure and such completion as it came to required forty-seven years, it ground on, keeping Indians, inconversant with its numerical abstractions, in what Debo describes as "constant fear of dispossession."[30] Since their communities were being torn apart by geographical individualization, their relations to the natural environment abbreviated, and their preallotment lands, some 138 million acres, taken in chunks by subterfuge, that fear was justified.

Whatever humanitarian hopes the Dawes Act raised thus were dashed by the damage it caused. But those hopes had been naïve and ambivalent from the start. They were affixed to what Debo calls "the centuries-old aim of changing Indians into white people" and inflated by the conviction "that smaller holdings would advance the Indians' 'civilization'" (because "too much land encouraged their roaming tendencies") and that "they would learn the superior ways of the white people settled among them" on confiscated land.[31] If big, open spaces made Indians wild, then small, closed spaces would make them tame; and tameness meant detribalization (the abolishment of communal ownership of land and other such practices) and the simultaneous supplantation, through education, of tribal values by those of the Protestant ethic and the spirit of capitalism, an acculturation by which Indians would wind up being, in White's summation, "Christian farmers living in nuclear families on their own land."[32] Cultural extinction (deculturation) and cultural rebirth—so went the theory, which at first said they would happen fast—would prevent physical extinction and enable assimilation. The role of education was, to quote the infamous dictum of Richard Henry Pratt, the foremost educator of Indians in the late nineteenth and early twentieth centuries and their steadfast if dubious champion, to "kill the Indian and save the man."

George Washington believed assimilation was the best answer to the Indian question. So did George Catlin, in whom, in Limerick's trope, "admiration and concern came mixed with plans for remodeling."[33] So did John Muir, who thought that Indians' wildness, unlike that of Yosemite, could not be preserved. So, though his knowledge of Indians should have prompted him otherwise, did John Wesley Powell.[34] Even as Indians, denied self-government and their traditional cultures, were more and more turning into dependents of reservation agencies, there was a general concurrence in favor of assimilation—though intermarriage and the racially heterogeneous society it implied were still fiery themes. Indians as Indians wouldn't do in the white world. Their vestigial wildness had a certain charm, but it finally had to go. It indicated deficiencies that had to be remedied by whitening. Indians, like the Western wilderness in which they lived, needed to be improved, developed. The Indians' old cultural circuitry would have to be rewired so that they could assimilate new self-images. Something like that.

What would those images be like? For many whites they were exemplified by two oil portraits, John Mix Stanley's *Eleanora C. Ross* (1844) and Charles Nahl's *Sacramento Indian with Dogs* (1867), both of which Schimmel interprets as stereotypes of Indians remodeled "for white consumption." In the first, a Cherokee girl sits stiffly within a vaguely natural setting, wearing a pink dress, hair combed and braided, a pencil in her right hand, a book in her lap open to a page showing a sketch of an idealized landscape—she is "constructed to convince whites of her capacity to absorb the gentle arts of reading, writing, and drawing." In the second, Wahla, once chief of the Yubu but now a coachman for Milton S. Latham, governor of California, who had adopted him and seen to his education, sits with the mien of a gentleman—nice suit, closely clipped hair—in a parklike setting, seemingly relaxed. The whole, says Schimmel, "suggests that Wahla has overcome his 'Indianness' and made his way in white society as a responsible citizen." She observes, however, that there's an unease about the painting (just as there is, I think, about Stanley's—and for the same reason): "He is too neat, too fixed, too conspicuously part of a contrived environment." The portrait, probably commissioned by Latham and never identified by the subject's name, feels hollow to her: "Wahla is still just a servant—one among many domestic animals owned by Latham. Surely this is a portrait of a 'white' Indian painted to naturalize a ritual similar to the one enacted the first day pupils arrived at Indian boarding schools."[35] All the ambient tameness—serene landscape, flightless fowls, fawning coach dogs—that protests too much may betray a cultural unease about the rehabilitation of the portrait's once-wild subject with his straight-out gaze (compare his eyes to those of the lion and the leopard in Hicks's *The Peaceable Kingdom*). Nahl's painting, like Stanley's, presents a stereotype that must have been convincing to many, but the unease the discerning viewer could have sensed in both paintings, clear enough in retrospect now, may be much the same unease that would inform later whites' ambivalence about the efficacy—and humaneness—of boarding schools designed to forge children of night into Eleanoras and Wahlas.

The prototype for federal boarding schools was founded by Pratt in Carlisle, Pennsylvania, in 1879. Like its imitations, soon all over the Midwest and West, it was an off-reservation school, intended to remove Indian children from the tribal influences that apparently had guaranteed the failure of experiments with acculturation through on-reservation schools. Boarding schools were in effect prisons

John Mix Stanley, *Eleanora C. Ross* (1844): *an Indian remodeled to absorb the gentle arts.* (*Gilcrease Museum, Tulsa, Oklahoma.*)

whose charge was to strip their wards of Indian heritage and replace it with white values, minimal white literacies, white domestic and vocational skills. Children were taken from their families and then shorn of long hair, dressed in uniforms, subjected to military-style discipline, compelled to speak only English. When they graduated, they were supposed to be able to merge quickly into the mainstream of American society.

Charles Christian Nahl, Sacramento Indian with Dogs (1867): an Indian who has become a responsible citizen. (Oil on canvas, 42 1/16 x 49 ¼ in. 41988. Fine Arts Museums of San Francisco, gift of Mrs. Milton S. Latham.)

Such schools dominated Indian education until the 1920s; some were still in operation a half-century later. While they could claim individual successes—for instance, many of their graduates became tribal leaders—the program as a whole wasn't a success. Far from it. "In the final analysis," as David Wallace Adams argues, "the boarding school story constitutes yet another deplorable episode in the long and tragic history of Indian-white relations."[36]

The slow finale of boarding schools started in the 1920s because that decade was when more-clear-eyed reformers such as John Collier and Lewis Meriam dedicated themselves to exposing the schools' problems. The schools were expensive, inefficient, and often unsanitary. Few Indians were effectively assimilated into the white workforce through the schools, which in their Euro-American ethnocentrism both imposed white culture that didn't fully take and blotted out Indian culture, with the result that lots of graduates returned to their reservations, as Debo puts it, "suspended in vacancy, separate from both cultures"[37]—and spiritually disconnected from the natural world of their tribes. The schools failed at what Adams terms "cultural metamorphosis" for a reason obvious to critics like Collier and Meriam:

their educational philosophy was based on "the presupposition that the acculturation process was a relatively simple matter of exchanging one cultural skin for another."[38]

Adams considers that process as carried out in boarding schools to have been
"the last great Indian war," one "waged against children" but children who didn't
passively receive "the curriculum of civilization." They resisted it, fled it, variously
strove to undermine it, and "even the response of accommodation was frequently
little more than a conscious and strategic adaptation to the hard rock of historical
circumstance, a pragmatic recognition that one's Indianness would increasingly
have to be defended and negotiated in the face of relentless hegemonic forces."
Those forces weren't without effect, though: Indians were changed by the schools,
and they changed in white ways the reservations to which they returned. And yet
there was an unexpected consequence, most significant, as well: off-reservation
students from wholly different tribes gained "an enlarged sense of identity as 'Indians.'" By an irony that would usher in the era of the ironic Indian to come, "the
very institution designed to extinguish Indian identity altogether may have in fact
contributed to its very persistence in the form of twentieth-century pan-Indian consciousness."[39]

It was that identity as pan-Indian consciousness, for whites a new complica-
tion to the image at which they directed their efforts both to control Indians and
to help them, that sustained Indian cultures through the political ups and downs
of the middle decades of the twentieth century: the bestowal of citizenship upon
all U.S.-born Indians in 1924; the passage of the Indian Reorganization Act, which
ended allotment and in other ways enhanced the status of Indians, in 1934; the
predominance of what Momaday calls the white "attitude of impatience" toward
assimilation during the 1940s;[40] the setbacks to tribalism of the federal policy of
termination and relocation, which expedited the urbanization of Indians, in the
1950s;[41] and the sanguine ameliorations—a growing national respect for Indian
heritage, bicultural education, increased self-determination, and the like—of the
1960s. Those ups and downs reflect the old white ambivalence as to what to do
about Western wildness, and it was that very wildness in white eyes, that otherness
of other human beings, that both eluded convenient stereotypes and hid Indian
personhood from bureaucratic rationales and rationalizations. For the Indian the
core of that ostensible wildness was—and is—the desire, as Debo puts it, "to be
with his own people, to preserve his inner values, his cultural integrity." To it, she
says, "he owes his remarkable record of survival . . . ; but it has been baffling to
well-meaning 'civilizers' determined to throw him into the melting pot."[42]

The attempted extinction of Indians through detribalization and assimilation,
though it caused grief, at last came to grief because many Indians, even as they
"changed and accommodated" like the twentieth-century Arapahos whose resil-
ience White finds admirable, "did so in order to try to maintain a basic fabric of

life and not to become like whites."[43] To the extent they maintained that fabric, modern Indians stayed Native and became, as we'll see later, postmodern Indians who would continue to change and accommodate but by revised—resistive but also radically self-affirmative—means.[44]

Thou Art Lost and Gone Forever: Postfrontier Anxiety and the Recall of the Wild

> We in America have from the beginning been cleaving and baring the earth, attacking, reforming the immensity of nature we were given. We have explored, on behalf of all mankind, this paradox: the more matter is outwardly mastered, the more it overwhelms us in our hearts.
>> John Updike, "Packed Dirt, Churchgoing, a Dying Cat, a Traded Car"

With the closing of the frontier came an opening of attention, a nervous alertness as to what that event portended. The turn of the century betokened a turn of attitude William Cronon summarizes in a single sentence: "The wastelands that had once seemed worthless had for some people come to seem almost beyond price."[1] Thoreau, with his declaration that the preservation of the world lay in wildness, had foreseen the turn; so had Muir. So had Americans in general, for most of whom the turn signaled an etherealization by which *frontier*, the customary metonym for wilderness, became, in Richard Slotkin's formulation, "primarily a term of ideological rather than geographical reference."[2] As frontier anxiety, which David M. Wrobel finds to have been at its height in the 1890s,[3] consequently in the twentieth century took the more subtle and clinging form of what I would call postfrontier anxiety, the emotions entangled with that ideological reference grew in depth and complexity. Such anxiety, an "inward uneasiness" Roderick Nash detects beneath America's "outward confidence" early in the century, manifested itself in the nation's "middle-aged mood," its realization that "frontier conditions were on the wane," and its citizens' growing increasingly "critical of the urban environment, nostalgic for a return to nature."[4] A manifold phenomenon, it involved as well remorse, envy of forefathers, doubts about the nation's democratic spirit and masculinity, misgivings about the future of industrial civilization—but most strongly that nostalgia for a return to nature. And nature meant, eminently, the West, a place now conquered, much of its wildness lost and gone forever.

The white men who conquered the Western wilderness learned too late, to borrow from Dylan Thomas, that they had grieved it on its way. Even those most callous about the inexorability of its taming, themselves aging during America's middle age, must have felt a conqueror's regret, the melancholy of Leatherstocking and his Indian companions through which Cooper, in Leonard Lutwack's elucidation of the end of *The Prairie* (1827), "helps to create and keep alive both the sense of wonder over the original forest and the sense of guilt over its destruction."[5] Unlike the Indians, Euro-Americans inhabited a nation that had no cultural antiquity, only a natural one; many were appalled that they had taken a jackhammer to their Acropolis.

Or, in the case of many Euro-American men, that they had also, in a sense, castrated themselves. As Cronon notes, "nostalgia for a passing frontier way of life inevitably implied ambivalence, if not downright hostility, toward modernity and all that it represented. If one saw the wild lands of the frontier as freer, truer, and more natural than other, more modern places, then one was also inclined to see the cities and factories of urban-industrial civilization as confining, false, and artificial." And feminizing—since many men of the generation of Owen Wister, Frederic Remington, and Theodore Roosevelt, born around the time of the Civil War, believed "the comforts and seductions of civilized life were especially insidious for men, who all too easily became emasculated by the feminizing tendencies of civilization." Such men advocated preserving what was left of the frontier so that, if they had the pocket, "they might enjoy the regeneration and renewal that came from sleeping under the stars, participating in blood sports, and living off the land."[6] From Carolyn Merchant's feminist point of view, American men of the late nineteenth century began "to lament the loss of wild nature" because of "an apparent need to retain wilderness as a place for men to test maleness, strength, and virility and an apparent association of men with nature" (and of women with manliness-suppressing civilization).[7] Just as the closing of the frontier cued, in Frederick Jackson Turner and others, a solicitude about whether American democracy could survive without open land, so, in Michael S. Kimmel's words, the twenty years before the United States entered World War I "witnessed a striking resurgence of concern about masculinity," a quality that requires wild nature but whose "stability and sense of well-being" paradoxically also depends on "a frantic drive to control its environment." That concern, which Kimmel relates directly to the closing of the frontier, had to do with an uncertainty that within a few decades, in an overly artificial world on the razor edge of nuclear madness, ballooned into a "pathological insecurity" still with us today.[8]

Concern about masculinity was augmented and complexified by an old menace made new in the late nineteenth and early twentieth centuries by the theories of Sigmund Freud: the beast within. Even a person as committed to preserving outer wilderness as Muir brooded about preserving the inner one. Studying his writings during a time colored by "the fear that modern man . . . was beginning to degenerate as the result of overcivilization," Ann Lundberg shows how in *The Mountains* of *California* (1894)—particularly in that book's climactic essay "A Near View of the High Sierra"—Muir "constructs a model of wilderness experience by which modern man can recover the original, or 'wild,' strength he has lost in the process of becoming 'civilized.'" As she notes, however, he was preoccupied with the question of "how to distinguish the realm of human and natural violence, or 'the savage,' from the harmonious world he so devoutly sought in 'the wild.'" Constrained by his Calvinist heritage, he answered that question with his concept of a cleansing through which "all that is lawless and uncontrollable within the self, including savage instinct and fear, is . . . absorbed into the greater harmony that exists on the grand scale of geologic time." Thus did he, as Lundberg says of a passage in his essay "Shasta Game," "ambivalently affirm the survival of the wild self beneath the trappings of our 'mean, lean,' civilized lives."[9]

So it's understandable that in the early years of the twentieth century what Nash terms "the compulsive urge to prove the national vitality and to heed the multifaceted call of the wild" expressed itself in postfrontier sublimations: Wild West shows, rodeos, dude ranches, Roosevelt's "strenuous life" of "sheer gusto," Boy Scouts and Girl Scouts, organized sports (the rise of which "coincided almost precisely with the disappearance of the frontier and the advent of industrialization" and entailed competition between teams with names like Indians and Bears and Cowboys), rebellious experiments in literature and dance, the art of the Armory Show ("newer, 'wilder' forms"), jazz ("uncontrolled music"), faster cars. The civilized primitivism of many such sublimations received the imprimatur of Robert Underwood Johnson, the "self-styled upholder of America's 'standards,'" when he popularized the paradoxical notion that "appreciation of the primitive was a mark of superior cultivation." That was the notion he brought into the controversy, which raged through congressional hearings from 1908 to 1913, over plans to dam the Tuolumne River and make a reservoir of the Hetch Hetchy Valley in the northern part of Yosemite National Park. When Congress approved the O'Shaughnessy Dam—and thereby voted in favor of supplying San Francisco with more water and electricity and against preserving wilderness—it spotlighted the incertitude of America's reply to the call of the wild that elicited the sublimations Johnson's notion endorsed: "The claims of civilization and the claims of wilderness [had] both pulled strongly"—to such a degree that the dam bill was passed by a Senate vote about which nearly a third of the members "could not make up their minds."[10]

The doubleness of mind that brought about such indecision and, as Nash stresses, made "many proponents of the dam in Congress . . . ambivalent" is symptomatic of postfrontier anxiety.[11] It was defined partly, of course, by conflicting political interests—populist versus progressivist, conservationist versus corporatist, and the like—but more fundamentally it was defined by the "contradictory images" of the West that Richard White sees as central to the "cultural crisis" of the day: a place of freedom or one of "freeholding," a wilderness or a garden, open land or overcivilized cities.[12] In this instance the main pair seems to have been that of the "bifurcated geography" Slotkin argues the frontier traditionally demarcates: "the 'Metropolis,' the civilizational center; and the 'Wilderness,' into which the heroic energies of the Metropolis are projected."[13] As David Teague observes in a discussion of John C. Van Dyke's 1901 book *The Desert: Further Studies in Natural Appearances*, that geography mirrored a bifurcation in the nation's thinking about nature—so that Van Dyke's Southwest "existed as a sort of holding pen for beautiful nature" while the East was where "the U.S. Steel plants of his friend Carnegie converted nature into rails and dollars."[14] By the time of the Hetch Hetchy controversy, however, the boundaries of such places had become blurred. Without a frontier, how was anyone to discriminate between Wilderness and Metropolis, Southwest and East, beautiful nature and nature converted into technology and money? How to choose, during a national identity crisis, between the two realms that comprised America's greatness? No wonder Congress agonized so long and its deliberations left so many members flummoxed.

A different, though related, confusion of categories entered into nostalgia for the premodern West, an affliction to which legislators weren't immune. According to Susan Stewart's psychocultural analysis of nostalgia, it is a paradoxical emotion, "a sadness which creates a longing that of necessity is inauthentic because it does not take part in lived experience." Yearning for an absent past, nostalgia "turns toward a future-past," an imaginative reunion of nature and culture in a utopia of authenticity. Distant from the here and now, that utopia is a place whose antiquity tends to be "linked to . . . the pastoral" and often promotes an "aestheticization of rural life." Nostalgia thus involves "reconstruction," and the aim of that narrative process, its "false promise," is restoration, which "can be seen as a response to an unsatisfactory set of present conditions" that produces "a conservative idealization of the past and the distanced for the purposes of a present ideology."[15] Stewart's general description of nostalgia matches up illuminatingly with the variety that arose in reaction to the closing of the frontier and that affects, if not afflicts, us yet, but some further particularization is in order.

First of all, nostalgia for the lost West was in large part "imperialist nostalgia," which, as Renato Rosaldo explains, is the nostalgia of colonists who "mourn the passing of what they themselves have transformed," and it entwines a paradox illustrated in his example, most relevant here, of "people [who] destroy their environment, and then . . . worship nature." In all its versions, he argues, such nostalgia "uses a pose of 'innocent yearning' both to capture people's imaginations and to conceal its complicity with often brutal domination."[16] Americans' Western nostalgia, in accord with this pattern, harbored an inauthentic longing to restore what they had destroyed (Western nature as it was) and to incorporate it into their vision of a guiltless future (American culture as they hoped it would become). Since Easterners as well as Westerners had such nostalgia, it didn't always have to do with distorted memories of the previous West; but in its "celebration of an unindustrial West" it was, as Lee Clark Mitchell tells us, "a barely disguised effort at restoring cultural hegemony" during a period of national instability.[17]

Is that what the old-timers who could remember—those, as McMurtry invokes them, "who began to wish that they could have it again, bring the great wild place back"—were up to? All those antimodern cowboys who changed the open range into a fenced checkerboard of ranches that "left them with a confused, unhappy, bittersweet feeling, unable to forget the paradise they helped destroy"—is that what they were up to?[18] Well, maybe so. If so, the reason was not only dissatisfaction with the present but also worry about a rapidly arriving future—because of which more and more historians, in Gerald D. Nash's reading of them, "began to question the positive impact of the West, and instead focused on its assumed negative influences."[19] Still, whatever of the Western past they wished for—cultural hegemony, open range, virgin land, the whole idealized show—all that those old-timers, like other Americans, restored amounted to little more than what McMurtry classifies as "an Edenic fantasy."[20] That fantasy, however, would prove to be ideologically enveloping and durable, fostering not just an aestheticization of rural life but a thoroughgoing etherealization of the great wild place America wanted back.

Euro-American narratives that nostalgically captured the apparent authenticity of the Western past, imaginatively restoring a wild to whose increasing etherealization they contributed, are plentifully represented in dime novels, pulp Westerns, and films of the postfrontier period. Perhaps the most prominent examples of them, in condensations, are to be found among the paintings and sculptures of Remington and Charles M. Russell, artists who had their homesick say with minimal competition since regionalists would not fully reinvent the West as a more realistic place until well after World War I. Like Wister and the aging Francis Parkman, both were men who in the 1890s dreaded the modern world and lamented the passing of the Old West. Both replayed their renditions of that West into the early years of the twentieth century. Both were mythmakers.

Because of the impression of authenticity his paintings and sculptures (as well as his fictional and nonfictional writings) give, Remington was long thought of as a realist. Even as late as 1960 Harold McCracken, then director of the Gertrude Vanderbilt Whitney Gallery of Western Art in Cody, Wyoming, declared that "he was strictly a documentarian."[21] He was such, however, only in the details (mostly taken from sketches made during trips from New York to the West) and not in the overall composition of his best-known works, which have, on inspection, the look of studio constructions (what they largely are) that, as Richard W. Etulain notes, "became increasingly nostalgic, romantic, and mythic."[22] Do some inspection. *Rounded Up* (1901) is as organizationally contrived as the West Remington wanted immutable. *Fight for the Water Hole* (1903) has a stronger feeling of authenticity, seems less self-consciously assembled; yet that very fact, as Alex Nemerov points out, allows it "to

Frederic Remington, Fight for the Water Hole (1903): the classic experience of Western nostalgia. (Hogg Brothers Collection, Museum of Fine Arts, Houston, gift of Miss Ima Hogg.)

deny its own making" and by virtue of the illusion of naturalness offer the viewer the classic experience of Western nostalgia, an etherealization through which "the image of the West becomes the West."²³ In *The Rattlesnake*, an undated bronze, a mounted cowboy's encounter with underived wildness is suspended inconclusively in an eternal moment, horse and rider twisted contrapposto-style with the invigoration of danger, the whole piece as tensely posed as a Nocona boots ad. And *The Outlier* (1909), with its Van Gogh–like brushwork, stages a solitary Indian at once authentic in trappings and unreal in epic stature within a dreamy setting of moonlit pastel hills.

Whether showing white men testing their manhood against the wild or Indians as embodiments of the savage essence etiolated in the Anglo-Saxon race, these and other works by Remington refer, as Nemerov argues, "not so much to a common reality, to a real object existing or once existing in the world, as to the rest of the collection of which they are a part"—so that "it is through other images that each picture comes to define the real." Indeed, he argues further, "before they ever went west, . . . Remington and other artists had virtually completed their frontier iconographies." The result is that in many of their works, as in N. C. Wyeth's *Wild Bill Hickok at Cards* (1916)—a painting, like lots of Western-themed paintings of the time, indebted to Baroque models—"the action takes place in its own separate world, shut off from the real."²⁴

N. C. Wyeth, *Wild Bill Hickok at Cards* (1916): *a world shut off from the real. (Oil on canvas, 32 x 40 in. L.3.89.4. Buffalo Bill Historical Center, Cody, Wyoming, loan from Mr. and Mrs. W. D. Weiss.)*

That's certainly true of Russell's works. His *In without Knocking*, which I discussed earlier, presents the sort of world shut off from the real he usually produced. It's one of what William H. Truettner calls his "re-creations of the Old West," lighter on the surface than Remington's but with similar tragic undertones, as romantic as the myth Russell made of himself, a self-invention "that eastern patrons suffering from post-frontier blues at the turn of the century appear to have swallowed whole."[25] The unreality of those re-creations isn't hard to descry, though, if you critically refrain from such swallowing. (It may be helpful to keep in mind that in the 1890s Russell did a series of paintings of Indian buffalo hunts that he likely never witnessed.)[26] In *The Tenderfoot* (1900), a drunken cowboy employs his pistol to teach a dude to dance, the scene as cutely (un)real as a Norman Rockwell (in terms of which quality the painting might be compared to W. Herbert Dunton's 1908 oil *Rodeo Rider*, a depiction of sanitized wildness in which the rider of a bucking bronc, as described by Kate F. Jennings, "is a sort of Gibson girl in Western dress—serene, pretty, feminine and wearing a clean, neat shirt and starched white blouse, despite the rigors of her task").[27] *Bronc to Breakfast* (1908), like *In without Knocking*, illustrates a "fascination with horsemen frozen in vignettes of violent activity" that Etulain finds characteristic of Russell, for whom "this scene of campfire confusion seemed to epitomize the untamed West, full of surprises and pleasing disorder"—an apt idealization from a man trapped in the predictable and displeasing order of modern society who had "participated in the cultural *ubi sunt* of the 1890s that mourned the passing of the West Out There."[28] Another painting I mentioned earlier, *Carson's Men*, pictures a Southwestern wilderness some Easterners of the day may have rightly thought as fantasticated as a landscape by Maxfield Parrish.[29] *Buffalo Bill's Duel with Yellow Hand* (1917), though less surreal in atmosphere, is as theatrical in the action it bodies forth as one of Buffalo Bill Cody's shows. And *The Fireboat* (1918), painted from the Indian point of view Russell favored in his portrayal of white-Indian encounters, idealizes, through linked coloration, the oneness of foregrounded Indians on horses with their rocky land, which is being invaded by a small paddle-wheel steamer (a painting thematically reminiscent of several earlier bronzes by Russell, especially his *Piegan Maiden* [1910], in which Indians are blended with the rock on which they are seated).

The ontological paradox of the etherealized Wild West of Remington and Russell can be summed up by juxtaposing two observations from Joni L. Kinsey. On the one hand, they, like other artists of their time, "were inventing their notions of the region's glory or pathos nearly wholesale" (even Montana cowboy Russell "relied more on his imagination in his paintings than actual experience"). On the other hand, their art and that of Charles Schreyvogel and others is now "the archetypal representation of the 'Wild West'"—an observation "borne out by the continuing adherence to these artists' formulas by countless 'western realists' today."[30] The poignancy of the paradox lies in the lasting pertinence of Russell's obsession with "the tag end of a dream" that William H. Goetzmann and William N. Goetzmann suggest when they remark that "the Old West and its pioneer people who lived mainly through nostalgia were as real to him as they were to his many admirers in his own time and even more so today."[31] The poignancy results from the quandary of a culture that wanted (and still wants) the West back—but not the warts-and-all West. Instead, it wanted a simulacrum, a pretend reality only spectrally connected to what was plowed under, responsive to ideals that must be ever reasserted even in contexts remote from the one that nurtured them.[32] So there came the ideological necessity of nostalgia narratives—selective images, expurgated stories, tall tales of the once-and-future perfect wild.

Tall tales. Of big wild men who were, of course, ironically, tamers: postfrontier hallucinations whose birthplace was, as Etulain has it, "the fertile twilight zone between fact and imagination" and who comprise "a pantheon of manufactured, gargantuan western heroes whose mien and deeds vivified the fearless, mighty people needed to save and settle the West."[33] Paul Bunyan, the giant lumberjack who dug Puget Sound with a glacier. Pecos Bill, the supercowboy who rode a mountain lion across the Southwest. Febold Feboldson, the titanic Nebraska farmer who tied knots in the tails of tornados vacuuming the plains. And others. All of them populated, Barre Toelken stresses, "a factitious folk tradition" established by "authors who wanted to satisfy a demand of a . . . political variety: the hero chock full of brag and fight and patriotism."[34] Exactly the sort of hero postfrontier America believed had to be somehow, like his wild world, restored to life—in spirit if not in flesh. Richard C. Poulsen accurately pigeonholes Pecos Bill as "an image of the popular press, not of the folk mind," but that colossus holding barbed-wire reins did, interpretational haggling aside, satisfy the demand of Western geography—America's projected desire—"that men match its mountains." He's equally correct that Paul Bunyan "is a figment of fakelore, a product of American advertising"; but he's mistaken in arguing that that redoubtable logger "is not, and was not, meant to be a hero at all but an expectation of geographical boundlessness,"[35] for he, like his similars, was—and is—meant to be both. America, impossibly, wanted back its taming Western heroes as well as what they matched.

Thus recalling the wild, America called back in fancy what it had loved and killed—in a voice never more clear, whatever the contradictions antiphonal to it, than that of Jack London's 1903 novella The Call of the Wild, which was an immediate best-seller and is still one of the most widely read books by an American author. It's the story of Buck, an outsize dog, half Scotch shepherd (collie) and half Saint Bernard, that's stolen from his master's California ranch and sold to pull sleds in the Klondike. In the harsh conditions there, Buck, in Roderick Nash's summary, "gradually sheds his domesticated habits and becomes a superdog." By the end of the book, Buck has "reverted to the wolf,"[36] a state in which both narrator and reader rejoice: "When the long winter nights come on and the wolves follow their meat into the lower valleys, he may be seen running at the head of the pack through the pale moonlight or glimmering borealis, leaping gigantic above his fellows, his great throat a-bellow as he sings a song of the younger world."[37] Commenting on this story, Nash notes that it never was rivaled in popularity by London's White Fang (1906), about a wolf's becoming a family dog; and he highlights its importance as an allegory to postfrontier America, for the author implies that his contemporaries, like Buck, "suffered from overcivilization, and in the early 1900's the idea struck a sympathetic chord." Absent a brave new America, "the millennium once expected," many were those who, whatever their fretting about the beast within, identified with Buck and pined to run in a West as wild as the North still was.[38]

But in more pragmatic moments, in sensibilities less captivated by the retrospective imagination, the draw toward Western wild nature quickened not so much the wish to restore what had been as the wish to preserve what, like Buck's hunting ground, still was. The narratives of that wish were the writings of Muir, Aldo

Leopold, and others. Some of them concerned conservation—"which became a household word in the Progressive era," according to Nash—a matter more of husbanding resources than of leaving places that contain them alone.[39] Other narratives, more products of back-to-nature cultism, were genuinely preservationist in purport—but with nostalgic tones—and insisted, as Ray Allen Billington puts it, on setting wild areas aside "not only to protect natural vacation lands from urban sprawl and corporate greed, but to assure future generations the spiritual, physical, and emotional rejuvenation that contacts with unspoiled Nature made possible," contacts that "had endowed the Founding Fathers with the wisdom and spirituality needed to establish the Republic" and now were crucial to its survival.[40] Yet other narratives, Thoreauvian rather than nationalistic in advocacy, urged a deeper rapprochement with a nature that, as Frederick Turner argues, "must have made a thousand . . . revelations to the Indians that it had never made to the conquering white man."[41]

Preservationism, strict or otherwise, wasn't, however, an uncomplicated movement. It was cursed by the irony that wilderness, in Cronon's words, "came to reflect the very civilization its devotees sought to escape," because those devotees were mainly "elite urban tourists and wealthy sportsmen [who] projected their leisure-time frontier fantasies onto the American landscape and so created wilderness in their own image."[42] As Catherine L. Albanese points out, the national park system, the strenuous life, and such were the dreams not only of people disaffected by modern civilization but also of "those who felt the need for greater control and mastery."[43] So, Nash stresses, the cult of wilderness, though encouraging "a favorable opinion" of it, wasn't ideologically dominant in the early twentieth century and was limited in its efficacy by those, even among its adherents, possessed of "pride in the accomplishments of American civilization and a belief in the virtues of further development of natural resources"—both of which traits pushed preservation in the direction of conservation.[44]

Preservationism, conservationism, and nostalgia may have been distinct currents of thought with different ideological moods about the West, but they got intertwisted. In his discussion of the back-to-untamed-nature impulse in the early twentieth century, Wrobel concludes that there was no shortage of Americans who embraced some combination of "these seemingly contradictory tendencies." He takes the Janus-mindedness of the combination Roosevelt typifies, future-oriented "reordering of priorities" cum past-oriented longing for a prior order, as an index of how difficult was the nation's "coming to terms with the perceived loss of the frontier." Rightly so. And the way that loss was perceived made certain that the frontier's "influence—or at least, the influence of the myths that had sprung up around it—remained a central presence in the cultural climate of the early decades of the century."[45] Remained and remained. Remains yet, an unlaid revenant.

Long Live the Weeds and the
Wilderness Yet: Preserving the West

What we tend to do is surround ourselves with ourselves, and then we prize the wilderness, where we aren't surrounded. Pretty soon we create little areas called "the wilderness." Like zoos.
> William H. Gass in H. L. Hix, "An Interview with
> William H. Gass"

It's June 19, 2001, and I'm standing on the South Rim of the Grand Canyon at Mather Point, about fifteen miles west of Moran Point, the approximate spot to which Hopi guides had taken García López de Cárdenas in 1540. Ten miles across the gorge in front of me lies the Kaibab Plateau. To get there in one of the SUVs or RVs parked in long rows in the lot behind me would require a trip of over two hundred miles. A mile down, in a lower weather system, the Colorado River, just the tiniest segment seeable from here, courses toward Lake Mead. Between here and there: strata of limestone, sandstone, shale, metamorphic rock carved open, *wide* open, by water's erosive flow; ravens, black dots in the gulfing distance, afloat on thermals; cubic miles of haze (much of it smog that has ridden the wind from urban and industrial areas). Tourists cluster and mill around the overlook like flies on the lip of a gaping wound. Gazing out at all that geological space and time and stretching play of light, they ooh and aah. Glancing down, they feel their heads go empty; they step back. They have come to see the natural West in its most stunning manifestation. Like millions of others every year, they haven't been disappointed.

"No place spoke to fin de siècle America like the Grand Canyon," writes Hal K. Rothman in his study of Western tourism. Just over a century before my visit, its vertiginous vistas, rich palette, and, more hubristically, "Americans' ability to master it" furnished a confirmation desperately needed: "Here was the entire package, a place the people of the time regarded as God's handiwork that reflected what Americans wanted themselves and their nation to be. It offered assurance and wonder, power and humility intertwined; it became the icon of the moment that explained Americans' complicated relationship with the land they possessed."[1] For many it still serves as some such icon, though it may explain less satisfactorily the more complicated relationship Americans now have with their land: it's a set-aside place only more or less preserved in a wild state, more or less safe from Americans' compulsion to despoil and develop.

The man who officially set the Grand Canyon aside was Theodore Roosevelt, who in 1908 designated it a national monument (which Congress made a national park in 1919). Roosevelt himself incarnated his contemporaries' relationship with Western land. If the West was the handiwork of Brahma, he was its Vishnu and

Shiva together, both preserver and destroyer. While it may be true, as Rothman argues, that ambivalence wasn't in Roosevelt's makeup, contradictoriness was another matter. The same man who, acting on the advice of Gifford Pinchot, his chief forester—and in opposition to Congress—created so many national monuments and parks, bird refuges, forest reserves, and wildlife preserves in the West during his two terms in office also denatured the West by bringing "the resources of civilization and his will to bear on what he sympathetically regarded as an uncivilized place," its wildness "romanticized by the very people who sought to tame and restructure the West along their own lines of thinking." Roosevelt knew the West was tougher than the East. Like the tourists above the chasm at Mather Point, he recognized that it "provided both serenity and terror, that it was to be simultaneously loved and feared." Acting on that recognition, he "impressed the hegemony of eastern values on the West, choosing the aspects of western culture he found laudable and presenting them to the world as virtues and castigating others,"[2] but at least, heeding John Muir, he chose to save some of Western nature, used his bully pulpit to enforce his choices, and set a standard for future presidential efforts at keeping pieces of the Wild West wild.

Muir was very much the catalyst for that keeping. No provincial Johnny Appleseed, he was well traveled, not only in the West but in many of the world's wild places. Botanist, glaciologist, and more, he fought for the establishment of Yosemite National Park in 1890, subsequently served as the founding president of the Sierra Club (a post he held until he died), and helped create the National Park Service, which began in 1916. Like Roosevelt, he was influenced by Pinchot but was less a timber-supply utilitarian than the efficiency-minded forester, more rapturous, not given to food-chain realism. He advocated the isolation of wild nature, particularly if it was mountainous (vertically purified), from human use, but he went in quest of it for his own religious purposes. Though, as Michael P. Branch argues, in his differences with Ralph Waldo Emerson he pinpointed "a significant ideological conflict between East and West, between Boston and Yosemite," he "finally understood culture to be subsumed by and subordinate to nature."[3] Through his life's work, whatever its philosophical perplexities, Muir certainly may be seen as a man who was, to borrow the title of Frederick Turner's biography, "rediscovering America" on new terms.[4]

Nevertheless, those perplexities can't be dismissed. They all have to do with how Muir profoundly culturalized the nature to which culture was supposed to be subordinate. Because of that contradiction he may have confused as much as he clarified the status of Western wilderness as something to be preserved. For instance, Simon Schama finds problematic Muir's adherence to the presumption that that wilderness "would be the antidote for the poisons of industrial society"— since wilderness conceived that way "was as much the product of culture's craving and culture's framing as any other imagined garden." It still is, more so than ever before, maybe most so in the case of Yosemite, where, Schama points out, "we still imagine Yosemite the way Albert Bierstadt painted it or Carleton Watkins and Ansel Adams photographed it: with no trace of human presence. But of course the very act of identifying (not to mention photographing) the place presupposes our presence, and along with us all the heavy cultural backpacks that we lug with us on the trail." Such wilderness, he emphasizes, does not represent itself, in the mode of its painters and photographers and of lyrical writers like Muir, "as the holy park of the West; the site of a new birth; a redemption for the national agony; an American re-creation." Its votaries metaphorized sequoias as the columns of "America's own natural temple" and reversed the custom of separating "the beastly" from the garden "by keeping the animals in and the humans out." Like some earlier American painters and writers (the painter Frederick Edwin Church is Schama's exemplar), they shunned negative classical and Puritan attitudes toward the wild, but there was a paradoxical cost to eliding people, including Indians and mining companies; it's clear enough in Schama's clinching quotation from Adams, who revered Muir and followed in his footsteps: "To protect Yosemite's 'spiritual potential,' he believed, meant keeping the wilderness pure; 'unfortunately, in order to keep it pure we have to occupy it.'"[5]

The paradoxicalness was resolved after a fashion by that occupation's being itself, in large part, spiritual—though not in a sense comprehensible to either Indians or mining companies. The preservationism of Muir and his disciples resolved it by culturalizing the wilderness more through an occupation at a distance than through an immediate one. That process began with what Catherine L. Albanese terms "Muir's complex response to wilderness," which was shaped by his home-made theology concocted from Calvinism (which his father fanatically professed), transcendentalism, idealism, pantheism, and vitalism; and it intensified as he "joined a personal religion of nature to a rhetoric inspiring his readers to direct action to preserve the wilderness."[6] All to the good, it would seem, except that such culturalization etherealized what it sought to preserve, making the remnants of a tangible Western wild into a discarnate iconic simulacrum that would become as exploitable as the original.

You can observe the effect of that etherealization by flipping through Adams's photographs taken in Yosemite, elsewhere in the Sierra Nevada, or elsewhere in the West, most of which are images that include no humans or human artifacts. In *Paradise Valley, Kings Canyon National Park* (circa 1925); *Thundercloud, North Palisade, Kings Canyon National Park* (1933); *Pinnacles, Mount Whitney, Sierra Nevada* (circa 1940); *Cathedral Spires and Moon, Yosemite Valley* (circa 1949); on and on—such images, in Adams's glossing of them, "must stand or fall, as objects of beauty and communication, on the silent evidence of their equivalence" to what he experienced.[7] But the equivalence consists in planar patterns of light that engage directly only sight, the most abstract of the senses, and the slippage between fact and film has significant consequences. Therese Lichtenstein, in her praise of the beauty Adams's photographs communicate, betrays how they accomplish an etherealization that Adams, as dedicated to preservation through images in celluloid as Muir was through those in words on paper, surely didn't intend. She speaks of how the beauty of what has been photographed "radiates beyond the surface—into a metaphysical realm of essences"—and of how "the images, like the actual landscapes that inspired them, become . . . metaphors for physical, emotional, and spiritual desire." Some of the forms in his photographs seem palpable, but the viewer is nonetheless "psychologically distanced" from them. It's expectable, since his images evoke "nostalgia for a lost paradise," that "many people who have visited the same areas that Adams photographed are often disappointed by the actual views."[8] Many people in Adams's time, as in Muir's time, desired the lost paradise of the West, but what they experienced and increasingly accepted as desirable was increasingly mediated—photographically and in other ways—and thus more and more estranged from what the least artistic forty-niner had known of the natural West.

People now visiting the Grand Canyon may not be disappointed, but the majority spend a lot of time not hiking its trails or rafting its river but framing its vistas in the removing viewfinder (telling word) of a camera. What they preserve isn't the Grand Canyon but what they need to take (another telling word) from it, a souvenir of an encounter that occurred for the most part in only one sensory dimension. That is, after all, what the quotation from Roosevelt on a plaque at the Canyon View Information Plaza advocates in advising that visitors (literally, by etymology, "seers") should keep the canyon unmarred for future generations "as the one great sight which every American should see."

As the twentieth century rushed on, that necessity to see the set-aside West heightened. Timothy Egan is correct when he asserts that President Grant's establishing Yellowstone National Park in 1872 "started something. Instead of the government giving away the West, or trying to remake it, or disparaging it, the land was cherished for simply what it was—America in the raw."[9] But the cherishing wasn't that simple, seldom would be. It would become more complexly mediated, and in the process the land as Americans experienced it would become less raw and more etherealized. As park after park was instituted across the West—Glacier, Rocky Mountain, Grand Canyon, Grand Teton, Olympic—and more railroads and highways brought centipede-like lines of tourists to those parks, they soon weren't so much places set aside as stage sets of "scenic nationalism," a result quite other than what Muir had wanted, which was, in Richard White's words, not nature reduced in scale "to fulfill human needs" but "nature preserved in all its diversity . . . so that humans might momentarily escape their human condition by mystical communion with forces greater than themselves."[10]

This last, of course, also involves a human need—though one deeper than that for scenic nationalism—and it has been described in various ways relevant to

Ansel Adams, Cathedral Spires and Moon, Yosemite Valley (circa 1949): an etherealization in the slippage between fact and film. (Center for Creative Photography, University of Arizona. © Trustees of the Ansel Adams Publishing Rights Trust.)

Muir's ideas about how and why nature should be preserved, especially for people, however much kept outside it, who would *see* it, however much etherealized, more than scenically. While it's true, as William Cronon reminds us, that "the movement to set aside national parks and wilderness areas began to gain real momentum at precisely the time that laments about the passing frontier reached their peak"[11] and that, as Dennis Cosgrove argues, the movement occurred in a context that "locates the discourse of wild nature . . . within a historically deep-rooted cultural tradition that embraced ideas of order, civilization, empire, and both personal and national self-consciousness,"[12] it's also true that for many people such a concerted effort at preservation addressed that deeper need. That need was for what British travel writer Isabella Bird intuited during her 1873 ascent of Longs Peak (which she later narrated in her book *A Lady's Life in the Rocky Mountains*): a sense of interconnection with the entire world of life, a world that contains, in Richard Rhodes's words, "the complexities that lie dormant within us, the possibilities we have not yet understood."[13] The need was to respect nature as a holistic ecosystem and not, as conservationism envisages it, as a warehouse to be prudently looted. The need was to do what the Wilderness Act of 1964 did more comprehensively than any previous act of Congress: keep a small portion of American land (just over nine million acres) and its communities of life as unviolated by humans as practicable—in response to the wisdom that, as Samuel I. Zeveloff, L. Mikel Vause, and William H. McVaugh express it, wilderness is "simply an inextricable part of being human."[14]

That's where the snake bites its own tail: the injunction of preservationism is to disconnect ourselves from wilderness in order to save it, and the reason we must save it is the depth of our connection to it. Its features "seem indelibly etched in our psyches" for Zeveloff, Vause, and McVaugh, who submit that without it "we might not reach our potential or maintain our identity."[15] We crave what we want to save from ourselves. For our preservation-minded forebears a century ago, that approach/avoid predicament was becoming tragically ironic, and its irony involved other ironies and like conundrums, all of which came into play in a story of increasing etherealization.

Conventional in American preservationist literature is the distinction between preservation and use, but, of course, as Muir and company knew, preservation also means use of a kind.[16] Even the most puristic of that company—"hypersensitive persons," as Keith Thomas terms them—would have admitted that, in part at least, "it was not for the sake of the creatures themselves, but for the sake of men, that birds and animals would be protected in sanctuaries and wild-life parks."[17] Nonetheless, naïve notions of nonuse contributed muddlement to already heated conflicts over the possible uses of land set aside, conflicts whose battle lines had been drawn around the turn of the century by differences between Muir's spiritual naturalism and Pinchot's pragmatic Benthamism and that were fierce with respect to the West, the region being most dramatically developed.[18] Such notions tended to forget Indians who happened to dwell in national parks, and they generally failed to recognize the extent to which what they hallowed was a cultural product.[19]

Naïve preservationism, in other words, was blind to the fact that, to cite a particular instance, the Grand Canyon—"the first western national tourist destination," as Rothman styles it—"had been invented, mirroring the nation's structures and blending the values of the Progressive Era with the benefits of industrialization."[20] According to Alison Byerly, that blindness came about largely because of an "aestheticization of landscape" through which the American wilderness was transformed, step by step, into "picturesque scenes," an appropriation that "removed it from the realm of nature and designated it a legitimate object of artistic consumption." She explains that that process, which may require a "tasteful 'improvement'" of landscape, "permits the viewer to define and control the scene, yet fosters the illusion that the scene is part of self-regulating nature." During the first half of the twentieth century, that aestheticization, which left a legacy of unreality, happened roundly to the West, a region where "nature's text" would have to wait awhile before many would learn to read it "as something other than fiction."[21]

The areas that were invented and aestheticized in that way became what Barbara Novak calls "artificial enclaves," places where, sometimes, "nature's prolixity had, apparently, to be edited."[22] They became terraria, selective Noah's arks, even corrals—a situation consonant with Kenneth R. Olwig's reminder that "the etymologically primary meaning of the word 'park,' found in many early European languages, is an enclosed preserve for beasts of the chase." Though the semantic ambit of the word was later extended, that underlying meaning doesn't comfortably accommodate, any more than did early Western tourists afraid of bears, the conception of wilderness as "the place where the beasts . . . ran wild." So there's a profound contradiction in the conceit of a wilderness park, and it can be overcome only by controlling not just how such a place is experienced but what of it is experienced; thus national-park guidebooks "are full of references to vantage points from which one might view natural 'scenery'" (a term derived "from the realm of theatrical illusion"). Once you have followed Olwig through the implications associated with that contradiction (that, for example, the word *paradise*, Iranian and then Greek in origin, carries the primary meaning of "'enclosed park,' and the first paradises were indeed hunting grounds"), you're little fazed by the fact that Muir, who thought of the Garden of Eden as a prototype reserve for Yosemite, operated his sawmill there to manufacture "lumber for tourist development." There was "a dark side" to the artifice of idolized wilderness—after all, "Muir's temple was bloodied from the start by the violent eviction of the native Indians"—and always the eventuality that wilderness would turn out to be "not 'wholly other' but 'wholly us.'"[23]

Hence, from the start, the maintenance of wilderness required management, especially in the West. Such management was what one of Sharman Apt Russell's aphorisms says it still is: "an oxymoron we all have to live with."[24] Its paradoxes, as Patricia Nelson Limerick traces them, "had already, in 1842, taken root on the Great Plains"—as evidenced by John Charles Frémont's saving buffalo calves by reducing wolves so that those calves could become the full-grown game he and his men loved to kill. By the early twentieth century more enlightened management hoped "to study how a particular place would work naturally, maneuver things around until natural balances return, and then get out of the way," but that procedure had weaknesses, obvious enough in practice, because of ecosystems' complexity and politically determined boundaries that ensured that "no national park makes ecological sense."[25]

Such difficulties gave rise to questions of the sort that engage Stephen J. Pyne in his study of fire management in wild and rural areas, for years a matter of dispute in the tinder-rich West where summers see millions of acres eaten by flame. He stresses that the paradoxes of fire in wild areas are "ideological" as well as "operational" and have been so for some time because "'wilderness' is not a state of nature or a state of mind but the interaction between a continually changing state of nature and a perpetually evolving state of mind."[26] Understandably, there have been disagreements about what constitutes "natural" fire and when to prescribe "controlled" fire in such areas, all of which have come to the fore in a forum where Gundars Rudzitis finds "much debate about how 'wild' wilderness and other public lands should be." That debate, though vexed by paradoxes, comes down to "a choice between protecting either humans or the wildlands." But implicit in that choice is a paradox far older than the history of American preservationism that still baffles the West, its elements apparent in Rudzitis's observation about Western ecosystem management that, "while professing that humans and nature are interconnected, programs and policies continue to assume they are separate or that one is dominant over the other."[27]

The reason for the perdurance of that nettlesome paradox can be deduced from Limerick's retelling of the story of Americans' relationships with nature in the past, which reinforces—and enlarges the relevance of—points I've previously made. The version of that story customary until the early 1970s consists of three phases: in phase one Euro-Americans reacted to wilderness with a shudder of fear; in phase two they struggled in a vengeful mood to master it; in phase three, jolting in its onset, they began to appreciate the wilderness and steward it through "congenial management." The problem with that version, as we've since learned, is in the strict narrative ordering of the phases, for they "probably do more in the way of coexisting and coinciding than they do in the way of preceding and following each other." Indeed, in the new version Limerick tells, "the attitudes they represent are more braided and intertwined than they are separate and distinct."[28] Some specifics in that version may invite quibbles, but it helps explain the paradox expressed in Rudzitis's observation in terms of the conflicting attitudes, long bound together, toward preserving Western wilderness: of appreciation and congenial management (because humans and nature are interconnected), of fear (because nature is separate from humans and dominant over them), and of mastery (because humans are separate from nature and dominant over it).

Ambivalence breeds ironies, and the ambivalence occasioned by such conflicting attitudes, combined with congenial mismanagement and the American appetite for unregulated individualism, bred the most tragic irony yet for Western wilderness: the possibility that, in Roderick Nash's words, it "could well be loved to death."[29] Fueled by nationalism and a sightseeing itch as well as a passion to preserve, the enthusiasm essential to producing that irony was high even in the 1870s, during which decade the watershed in that respect may have been 1873, the year in which Thomas Moran accompanied John Wesley Powell on his second survey of the Grand Canyon and painted *The Chasm of the Colorado*, a work that started what Egan calls "an esthetic stampede to the Southwest."[30] Splendors like Hetch Hetchy Valley and Glen Canyon that were on the margins of the stampede garnered less public support for their preservation and so were lost to development, but those favored got plenty of attention, more and more as the decades passed. By the 1920s, at visually lush sites in the West, people arrived by the thousands upon thousands, debouching from automobiles and trains and then, as in Rothman's *tableau vivant* of spectators at the Grand Canyon, standing awed "before an enormous and living canvas of nature, separate from the world from which they disembarked."[31] By the 1950s, the thousands upon thousands had become millions upon millions.

By the 1960s, the monster had both grown more and mutated; there had been "a change in the nature of the beast," which Robert G. Athearn explains as follows:

> Earlier travelers had found charm and excitement in the country's isolation, its unpredictability, and its contrariness. By contrast, the new breed demanded two things above all else: the wonders of the West must be accessible, and the action must unfold on schedule. . . . Planners of national parks built ever-more roads and facilities for the Bermuda-shorts crowd. . . . A western tour was becoming less and less an adventure and more and more an entertainment. And a big, big business. Edward Abbey coined the best term for it—"industrial tourism"— mass produced, streamlined, and with a high yield of pollutants.

It all added up to a "delicious irony." People like Muir and Stephen T. Mather, the first director of the National Park Service, "had set out to save the western wilderness from the philistines by promoting its romantic image and by begging Americans to come and see just what a treasure they might lose." Americans did—and did and did. Too many of them, too many times. "The contradiction had always been there," Athearn says in closing, "but it took the westward rush to bring it fully into the open. By the seventies the movement that had been set in motion at the turn of the century was bearing down on the wilderness with all the subtlety of a road grader."[32]

The physical impact on Western wilderness, with the clotted traffic now called greenlock just around the historical corner, wasn't subtle, but for most people the changes in America's experience of that wilderness over the preceding century had been. Insidiously the "wholly other" had become a planned adventure and then a living canvas and then an entertainment complete with soft-drink machines, restrooms, and shops where the Bermuda-shorts crowd could buy film to record what they hadn't really seen and souvenirs to remind them of what they hadn't really done—a mass entertainment only thinly akin to the natural West of the past and so colonizing of the present one as to be on the brink of making it "wholly us."

In his famous "Wilderness Letter," written in 1960 to David E. Pesonen of the Wildland Research Center at the University of California, who was working on a report for the Outdoor Recreation Resources Review Commission, Wallace Stegner pleaded for "not so much the wilderness uses [fishing, hiking, and the like], valuable as these are, but the wilderness *idea*, which is a resource in itself." Speaking mostly of the West, he argued that wilderness had been foundational to the American character, that its destruction would lessen the nation's people, that Americans had renewed themselves through the wild, that for the sake of future generations it should be kept "as a reserve and a promise—a sort of wilderness bank." He concluded, "We simply need that wild country available to us, even if we never do more than drive to its edge and look in. For it can be a means of reassuring ourselves of our sanity as creatures, a part of the geography of hope."[33] While the letter would be read and reread as a classical text in the canon of the postmodern environmentalism that began in the 1960s, it is, for all that, symptomatic of the ironic circumstances of postwar Western preservationism.

First of all, that Stegner pleaded on behalf of the idea (another word whose etymology has to do with seeing) of wilderness rather than the fact of it is an index of its tragic diminishment—of how, in an important sense, by Irene Klaver's caveat, "as soon as one stakes out the wild, it is gone."[34] Moreover, that idea was one about which Americans had changed their minds and would again—so that soon, while the commodifiers of Western wilderness were transforming it from entertainment into the "prepackaged vacation moments" William Fox says it is today,[35] most environmentalists would come to understand that what they mean by the wild exemplifies, in Yi-Fu Tuan's phrasing, "the orderly processes of nature" and that "true wilderness exists only in the great sprawling cities."[36] Also, Stegner's invocation of nationalistic sentiments ignored the extent to which they had confused nature and culture and convinced many Americans "that an empire could be built that did not destroy nature"—a belief Truettner finds reflected in the way "Moran could paint the wonders of Yellowstone and factories pouring smoke across the Rockies without apparent conflict."[37] Finally, even in 1960 there were too many visitors to Western wilderness, most of them doing about what they do today (when they get their noses out of the picture books), Stegner's minimum: driving to the edge, that safe minifrontier, and looking in.

In the decades ahead, arrangements for that looking, quite apart from other uses (such as citizens' going to Western national parks to repair their identities as Americans after 9/11) and however much it may have reassured visitors of their sanity, became more costly to the geography of hope being preserved. Later generations would have to face a bleak redaction of Nash's love-it-to-death irony: the possibility, in our age bewitched by the virtual and neglectful of the real, that, to paraphrase an infamous justification from the Vietnam War, Western wilderness could be saved only by its being destroyed—and resurrected as something else.

Wild West Shows, Rodeos, and Dude Ranches: Wildness as Specious Spectacle, Ritual Reenactment, and Tenderfoot Travesty

Rodeo . . . is no less than a folk ritual that reenacts and sanctifies the Myth of the West before an audience of modern North Americans who no longer have firsthand experience with the initial civilizing of the West.
Michael Allen, *Rodeo Cowboys in the North American Imagination*

In October 1940, driving alone in his Cord between Tucson and Phoenix on Highway 89, cowboy movie star Tom Mix swerved to avoid some construction, sped into a dry wash, flipped over, and died quick, his neck broken by a hurtling metal suitcase that, as the lore has it, was filled with twenty-dollar gold coins. Born into poverty in 1880 in Pennsylvania, the man dead in that wreck had left school after the fourth grade. He'd twice enlisted in the U.S. Army—though later accounts of his participation in well-known military campaigns were falsehoods for publicity—and then gone AWOL. He'd tended bar. He'd been an apprentice entertainer in the Miller Brothers' 101 Ranch Wild West Show. He'd first gotten into the movie business in 1910. During the ensuing decades he'd come to love fast cars, bought several ranches and a mansion in Hollywood, dabbled in another Wild West–show enterprise, kept himself dressed in glitzy Western duds, been married five times, made a fortune and lost most of it, and become America's favorite hard-ridin' and straight-shootin' hero in more than two hundred films. In 1934 he'd returned to the arena and then started his own show. After just over a century of changing exhibitions in all manner of venues, that arena, from which Mix had borrowed for his brand of cinema, closed around the same time he did. What had transpired there had been ambiguous in meaning, at once as physically real and as mythically unreal as Mix's glamorous life, one step away from the cinematic—and soon televisional—West he'd helped to create.

Paul Reddin argues that Wild West showmen attracted public interest "by tantalizing people with the proposition that they had missed something special because a particular phase of Plains history was nearing its end or had already passed." They satisfied the curiosity stirred up by employing "authentic props and real western-ers—even if they did not always follow through—to reproduce for audiences the most significant sights, sounds, and experiences of the Plains." To ensure broad appeal, they had their reproductions always somehow involve "scenes featuring he-roic figures performing adventurous deeds in wilderness settings." By that charac-terization, George Catlin, who in 1830 started his career of exhibiting the West—in his painting, writing, and otherwise—was the first of many entrepreneurs of Wild West spectacles. Just as he in his shows "glorified Plains Indians and eulogized them as 'vanishing Americans,'" so Buffalo Bill Cody in his "celebrated the Anglo-Saxon settlement of the frontier" and the Millers in theirs "tried to rally enthusi-asm for cattle kings" and Mix, in his, "adulated the romanticized cowboy."[1] But never, in either those shows or less famous ones, without equivocal results—surely clear to some among their leads, supporting actors, and audiences—for, though the West reproduced may have been commemorated, it was also selectively repre-sented, misrepresented, parodied, shrunk to a place no wilder than a movie set.

Catlin undertook his rudimentary Wild West show with the belief, as L. G. Mo-ses summarizes it, "that just as Indians should be educated over time in the ways of civilization, so also should American citizens be instructed in the ways of nature and nature's noblemen"—and thereby initiated the tradition of claims by Wild West showmen that their spectacles were educational. But turning that belief into action was complicated by Catlin's combining "the seemingly incompatible motives of artist, scientist, and showman."[2] Albeit his paintings were intriguing, the neces-sity of displaying them indoors restricted the kind of performances that could ac-company them to lectures, tableaux, Indian dances, and the like; his showmanship may have been constrained in some ways, but his commitment to it—and to artistic interpretation—raised questions about his integrity as a scientist. Still, Reddin ar-gues, he did "try to foster enthusiasm for the material, spiritual, and mythological aspects of Indian cultures" not only by treating them in paintings and lecturing (sometimes histrionically in Indian costumes) and writing about them but also by tirelessly assembling and presenting, first in the United States and then in England and Europe, "a museum-like aggregation he called his 'Gallery unique,'" a collection "so grand that an admirer designated it the 'raw material of America.'"[3]

From the time Catlin's career went into full swing—with exhibitions of his In-dian Gallery in Pittsburgh, Cincinnati, and Louisville in 1833—he experienced, in Reddin's euphemistic phrase, "credibility problems." Like later Wild West show-men, he had a taste for authenticity, but it was mostly in carefully chosen details and came, as it always would, in an ideological package—one, in Catlin's praxis, constructed of his advocacy of the Indian as a Noble Savage and his condemnation of the cankering influences of civilization. What Reddin terms "another contrari-ety" is evident in his both denouncing the unchecked slaughter of buffalo and of-fering exhilarating tales of hunting them, and another is patent in his stories, told with illustrative "grisly trophies," of atrocities perpetrated by the people he commended as virtuous.[4] Similar contrarieties, along with the credibility problems they bred, would permeate the Wild West show put together by Cody, who in 1872, the year of Catlin's death, was just beginning his career as an actor.

Cody was a born performer, and he inaugurated the Wild West show as a whole-hog ripsnortorama (though, to safeguard the illusion of it, he never said the word *show* when referring to his enterprise). His show had predecessors in productions undertaken by P. T. Barnum, Joseph G. McCoy, and others, but nothing matched what he, in short-term partnership with William Frank Carver, first mounted in 1883 in Omaha. Following on the Fourth of July "Old Glory Blowout" outside North Platte, Nebraska, in the previous year, in which Cody had participated, and now highlighting the handsome buckskin-clad man famed as "Buffalo Bill" in dime novels, stage melodramas, and regional anecdotes, it was clearly a happening of another order. When the show opened on May 17 to an audience estimated at eight thousand, the program commenced with a parade consisting of a twenty-piece band, assorted Indians in full regalia, buffalo, more Indians, Buffalo Bill and Carver (self-legendized as the world's finest rifle shot), cowboys, a Concord stagecoach, and yet another band. The acts that ensued, though more would be added in later years, previewed the fare for many a Wild West show to come: a demonstration of the pony express (for which Cody, irrespective of his claim to the contrary, never rode), an attack on the Deadwood Stage (with Cody, Carver, and scouts at last thundering to the rescue), an exhibition of marksmanship, a buffalo chase, a grandiloquent closing speech by Cody.[5]

That show, Cody's subsequent shows, and dozens of shows undertaken by imitators were exactly what Reddin says they were: "self-consciously American institutions devoted to defining their nation's values and history through the lens of the frontier experience." Ever-evolving spectacles of spellbinding sensuousness—brassy music, acrid blasts from firearms, earthy animal smells, pounding hooves, war-dancing Indians—they gave the public what it wanted: adventure, battles, heroic bloodshed in the name of progress. Showmen explored something of the West's cultural diversity, but they neglected mundane facets of Western life that had no box office, leaned toward portraying white Americans as innocents, and—like Mix's movies—helped elaborate "the glorious mythology that infixed a positive view of the frontier in the psyches of Americans." It was a mythology of victory that glossed over any gnawing awareness of tragedy that spooked those psyches, and through it, eventually, "the white cowboy emerged as the most memorable icon of the West."[6]

Wild West shows were opportunities for a nationalistic public to escape momentarily from its urban-industrial world, return to a simpler time, and experience vicariously the regenerative wildness it had missed. They were also occasions when, as Ian Frazier puts it, "old-time plainsmen who would never have 'real' fun

Joseph E. Stimson, photograph of Cody's Wild West in Omaha, Nebraska (1908 or 1909): a whole-hog ripsnortorama of spellbinding sensuousness and glorious mythology. (Wyoming State Archives, Department of State Parks and Cultural Resources.)

again were paid to have imitation fun."[7] But because plainsmen, along with others in the shows, were frequently the genuine article—Cody, in his quest for déjà-vu authenticity, enlisted Indians who'd actually fought Custer to reenact his final battle—and because all the trappings and animals provided a context to stimulate a willing suspension of disbelief, what was witnessed through that ersatz fun had an appreciable verisimilitude for nostalgic Americans. For them, as for Europeans captivated by the shows, that verisimilitude—which would continue past 1940 only partially in rodeo and only in rarefied form in media such as radio, film, and television—was sanctioned by both superficial and deep-seated desires.

In her discussion of the significance of Buffalo Bill and his show, Jane Tompkins, inspired by a French placard for a performance that carries beneath a picture of Cody the announcement "JE VIENS" ("I am coming"), singles out those desires. Though she considers them in relation to the lure specifically of Cody and his show, much of what she says pertains to Wild West shows in general. He comes, in her construal, as a redeemer "who will lift us above our lives, out of the daily grind, into something larger than we are." He appeals to "childish desires," but he appeals also, now as he did a hundred years ago, to "something more profound in us." Since he, as Tompkins emphasizes, "was" the West, his mission was to show people that, whatever their imaginings about the place, it really existed. Therein lies the key to "the deeper legacy" to which Cody and his show appealed: "He and his cowboys played to an inward territory; a Wild West of the psyche that hungered for exercise sprang into activity when the show appeared. *Je viens* was a promise to redeem that territory, momentarily at least, from exile and oblivion. The lost parts of the self symbolized by buffalo and horses and wild men would live again for an hour."[8] And live again they did, those lost parts of the hungry inward Wild West, over and over, for many years.

But not without ambiguities that would require those years and more to be anything like fully perceived and understood. The most disturbing concern the "wild men" who were Indians. Some of those Indians, like the sharpshooter Princess Wenona, were not Indians. Most of those who were got uniformized into the stereotypes that would be passed on to other media (and white actors). On the other hand, Indian gatherings and performances for Wild West shows, especially Cody's, did educate the public some about the lifeways of people often disdained as Stone Age curiosities, and they helped found an institution of great importance to twentieth-century pan-Indianism, the powwow. Whatever images of the Indians' nobility were available, however, intertwined with images brought to the fore by the Indian attacks that, Moses tells us, "became set pieces in all Wild West shows." Doubtless Indians in the shows were exploited, even denigrated, but they made a better living than most Indians on reservations did. They may not have upheld reformers' ideals, but Cody, for one, Moses argues, "saw the employment of Indians in the shows as a method to ease the transition of a proud and capable people to the cultural demands of the majority."[9]

The most famous Indian Cody employed was Sitting Bull, who toured with the Wild West in 1885. Since he was one of the architects of Custer's demise, he himself was a figure of surpassing wild-tame ambiguity to the show's audiences. In a promotional photo made while the show was in Canada, which features him standing beside Buffalo Bill, each man with his left hand on the barrel of an upright lever-action rifle and both looking off to their left, his ambiguity may be seen as exemplary of the general play of ambiguities that characterized Indian participation in not only Cody's show but others as well. The photo, as John D. Dorst scans it, is an icon on the theme of reconciliation between the white and red races, "the apparent concord" of a "now-automatic pairing enshrined in our common parlance—cowboys and Indians." But, of course, he notes, those terms connote conflict, and indeed the tone of concord is undercut by crafty details. The index finger of Cody's right hand points to something outside the frame he's looking at, a gesture that "puts him implicitly in charge of the scene," but Sitting Bull seems to be looking elsewhere—a divergence that might be interpreted "as a small moment of resistance, or at least an indication of an alternative to Buffalo Bill's imperious gaze." Cody's face is higher and brighter than Sitting Bull's, his body less shadowed, so

W. Notman, photograph of Buffalo Bill and Sitting Bull taken in Montreal (1885): a general play of ambiguities. (P.69.2125. Buffalo Bill Historical Center, Cody, Wyoming, gift of D. F. Barry.)

that "the conventional contrast between the 'light and dark' races is deeply coded in the lighting arrangements." Also, in the placement of hands on the rifle, there's "at least a hint of the idea that the Indian, though visually obscured and compositionally subordinated, really has a firmer grip on a symbolically important artifact."[10] You get the picture.

Still, though, the heroic notable who was both the man William F. Cody and the persona Buffalo Bill enwound, not just in photos but in himself and the show that was an extension of himself, the most revealing ambiguities involved in reproducing the West that was. That Western jack-of-all-trades (buffalo hunter, army scout, Indian fighter, guide, and more) was once the real thing, but as a showman he lived and died "in ambivalence and ambiguity" in N. Scott Momaday's assessment of him: "Buffalo Bill was a plainsman, but the place he might have held on the picture plane of the West was severely compromised and ultimately lost to the theatrical pretensions of the Wild West Show. Neither did he see the Indians. What he saw at last was a self-fabricated reflection of himself and of the landscape in which he had lived a former life."[11] Long before revisionist Western history was picking up speed, Henry Nash Smith argued that Cody was so enamored of costumery—for instance, he was sporting a vaquero-like outfit from his stage wardrobe when he fought his actual but soon-legendized and much-reenacted 1876 duel with the Cheyenne chief Yellow Hand and took a scalp to avenge Custer (whose affected mien of the scout Cody copied)—that his get-ups alone "illustrate the blending of Cody with his theatrical role to the point where no one—least of all the man himself—could say where the actual left off and where dime novel fiction began."[12]

The more Cody has been studied, the more evident has become the extent of his blurring of authenticity and fakery. Discussing Buffalo Bill as the antitype of Frederick Jackson Turner (both made brilliant use of Western iconography but to tell, respectively, two different sanitized stories—one about the conquest of Indians, the other about the conquest of nature), Richard White sums Cody as a genius who "re-created himself as a walking icon, at once real and make-believe." His show, with its inversions (conquerors as victims and so forth), included a related ambiguity about "where representation stopped and lived experience began." Through that beguiling vagueness, Cody "created what now seems a postmodern West in which performance and history were hopelessly intertwined" and imitated one another. Thus, to pick White's most striking example, "actual Indians . . . inhabited their own representations" and "were imitating imitations of themselves."[13] The show, like Buffalo Bill and like Robert Altman's 1976 film *Buffalo Bill and the Indians; or, Sitting Bull's History Lesson* (itself an imitation of Arthur Kopit's play *Indians*, first performed in 1968), finally wasn't about the West so much as about representations of the West.

In her analysis of the mythopoesis through which the Western hero is created (or self-created), Rita Parks attends to how "the historical person is transformed into a media persona." She notes that early heroes underwent only a limited transformation in that respect and remained aware of the discrepancies between person and persona—Boone, she says, "was resentful of his portrayal by popular biographers as an 'anarchic fugitive from civilization,'" and Carson "slyly admitted to the exaggeration of his exploits"—but that Cody, a later hero, underwent a nearly total transformation.[14] Just as Cody's obsessive showmanship made him inseparable from his persona, so his show, in Joy S. Kasson's words, "made frontier life inseparable from its embodiment as a spectacle." But, she argues, that inseparability, in keeping with the involutions of the postfrontier spirit, possessed a peculiarly modern complexity. It resides in the fact that "the Wild West's blend of theatricality and historical pretension had a certain self-consciousness." All of which, like Altman's stagy film, makes Buffalo Bill, as Kasson accurately interprets E. E. Cummings's portrait of him in his poem "Buffalo Bill's," a figure "radiating complexity."[15] Hardly reconciling the contradictory values of individualism and civilization, wilderness and progress, he left them in a more confusing tension than ever before.

Cummings's Buffalo Bill, Kasson says, "is indeed an apt hero for the modern era, an age when images have become indistinguishable from what they purport to represent and the content of national identity seems identical to its performance." True enough, and when she speaks of the "air of hyper-reality, assumed to be authentic but more 'splendid' than ordinary experience," of the performed images of Cody's Wild West, the conspicuous word is "air";[16] for, whatever the seemingly concrete immediacy of its wildness, his West was airy. Also apt, therefore, was the presence of his show (unofficially) at the World's Columbian Exposition (also called the Chicago World's Fair) of 1893, which hosted not only the meeting of the American Historical Association at which Turner presented his famous essay on the closing of the frontier but as well an erection of airy idealism known as the White City. Richard Slotkin describes it as "an architectural extravaganza in ersatz marble representing the pinnacle of Euro-American civilization" and "the antipode" of Buffalo Bill's Wild West: "Moving up the Midway to the White City, the visitor passed from the Wild West to the metropolis of the future, and from . . . displays of primitive savagery and exotic squalor to a utopia of dynamos and pillared façades." Two representations, equally ethereal: one that offered a prophetic vision of alabaster perfection and one that offered "something like a poetic truth" about the frontier.[17]

The more you contemplate that conjunction, the richer in implications it grows. Delving the meaning of the White City, Reid Badger suggests that the basic teleological story it told, particularly as a fairyland in Chicago, is wholly analogous to Cody's Wild West narrative of victory over savagery, for "the construction of the White City at the site of what had formerly been a swamp was seen as nothing less than the reenactment of the purpose of American civilization, to bring order out of chaos." Likewise, though it offered a tame "pretense of harmony" in the future rather than a wild pretense of conflict in the past, the White City resembled Cody's show in endeavoring "to create a dreamlike scene under the spell of which the problems and complexities of modern life seemed to vanish."[18] Moreover, both had double effects: while many who saw the White City marveled at it and found hope in it, many criticized its irrelevance to the dreary actualities of urban life; while

what Slotkin calls the "historical ritual" of Cody's Wild West signaled "the integration of the Indian into 'American' life as 'Former Foe—Present Friend,'" it also re-
aroused "the 'savagery' or warrior spirit that is latent in the civil sons and daughters
of the heroes who won the West"—and, since the show incorporated more-global
struggles (casting "cowboys and Indians as Rough Riders and Cubans," for instance), incited them to further imperialist actions against "'regressive' races."[19]

Perhaps the most significant similarity between the White City and Cody's Wild
West lies in the way each in its insubstantiality would go on to excite a secondary
nostalgia. In the case of the White City with its eclectic and antique European architecture, that nostalgia wasn't for a past ideal civilization but for a futurized myth
of some such civilization long dreamt and in time to outplace the Western wild. In
the case of Cody's Wild West, that nostalgia, which originated during the show's
final tours before it closed in 1916, wasn't, as Slotkin puts it, "for the reality, but for
the myth—not for the frontier itself, but for the lost glamour of Buffalo Bill's Wild
West."[20] The extent to which early-twentieth-century American cityscapes and civic
architecture commemorated the White City more than they did premodern Europe
may be debatable, but it's inarguably true, as Moses asserts, that attempts late in
the century "to re-create the Wild West show . . . commemorated the show itself"
and "represented a nostalgia for the show more than for the history presumably
re-created in the show."[21]

Whatever problems of modern life Wild West shows, Cody's and others, seemed
to make vanish, there was one problem they not only couldn't poof away but indeed
typified and heightened: Americans' schizophrenic hunger for both the wild and
the tame, the savage past and the civilized future, opposites that would beget ever-
stranger combinations on ever-more factitious frontiers. Much the same is true of
rodeo, which developed simultaneously alongside and through Wild West shows.

In 1884, when Cody hired an amiable and talented young man named William
Levi ("Buck") Taylor and made him his star cowboy, he invented the cowboy as a
hero of the arena; but he didn't invent rodeo. Like the Wild West show, rodeo in
one form or another had already been in existence awhile. Though *professional* rodeo may have begun with the equestrian contests featured in Cody's 1882 blowout,
competitive work-skills tournaments among cowboys and between ranches had
been held on holidays since the 1860s. There are disagreements about the origin
of rodeo as a formal affair; what is certain is that rodeo, formal or informal, was
an elaboration of the spring roundup. That was a time not only for work (branding
calves and so on) but for festive get-togethers, which means it was also a time, Michael Allen reminds us, "for 'cowboy fun'—horse racing, roping, and bronc-riding
contests." Rodeo, he explains in brief, evolved as "a direct descendant of the work
festivals of early North American cowboys and vaqueros," and the word itself "is
derived from the Spanish verb *rodear*, meaning 'to encircle' or 'to round up'" (another enclosing of the wild).[22]

Allen carefully distinguishes early rodeos from Wild West shows. He grants that the two shared "event motifs and the larger symbolism and nostalgia of cowboys taming wild animals in an open-air performance," but he stresses that Wild West shows were more purely entertainment than rodeos, less closely tied to real folk traditions, more commercial (with contracted performers and not competitors who paid entry fees), and more oriented toward city audiences. He argues, however, that in the course of the twentieth century, rodeo, as it became more professionalized and profitable, "moved away from folklore toward fakelore."[23] In that respect it wound up being much like the Wild West shows it outlasted: it too turned into an etherealized reproduction/representation of its original, one replete with similar ambiguities and ambivalences.

Elizabeth Atwood Lawrence observes that, though we're prone to visualize him otherwise, in fact, "over time, the figure of the cowboy seems to have traversed a path further and further from cattle, even to the point of becoming an 'urban cowboy' today."[24] There are several ways to characterize that path. You might think of it as leading from the open range to the fenced ranch to the rural and then the urban arena. Or from spontaneous cowboy fun to more programmed and organized imitation cowboy fun to nothing less than a professional spectator sport. Or, as Beverly J. Stoeltje's folkloristic analysis shows, from "operational customs" to "ritualized customs" in a planned performance that assumed "the quality of display as the size of the audience and the difference and distance between performer and audience increased."[25] Or, in Allen's construal, from a folk festival of "*real cowboys*" (his italics) to rodeo of "the 'golden age' of rodeo" in the 1950s that still "exuded real western flavor" to rodeo of the 1960s and thereafter that was "a folk-based popular-entertainment spectacle" with too many competitors who were trained not on ranches but in arenas (often at rodeo schools or clinics), each "an actor who has fully embraced his persona" of the *real cowboy* and whose kind would acclimatize to indoor stadiums. When Allen concludes that such athletes and their rodeos nonetheless were—and are—"symbols of our frontier heritage," he's dead right: they are, precisely, symbols—ritualized, performative, their obligatory displays only emblematic reenactments of encounters with the West's real wildness.[26]

Yet, of course, to take the word *symbol* more in the sense Allen intends, rodeo has always been symbolic, closely and then remotely, of "our" frontier heritage and, especially in its hairiest events, of that real wildness that was intrinsic to such heritage. Its symbolism is rife with the tensions of opposites that mirror American—a fortiori postfrontier American—ambivalence about the West that was. Rodeo, in Lawrence's minimal anthropological description, "picks up the main themes from the pastoral life of the cowboy, . . . identifies and exaggerates them, and makes them explicit through patterned performances," but her explication of those themes discloses the underlying meaning of rodeo, what it's really about:

The sport of rodeo, like the duties of the working cowboys from which it was derived, deals with the relationships between man and animals . . . and on a deeper level with the human relation to the land—the wilderness and the wild. . . . As an outgrowth of ranching, rodeo embodies the frontier spirit as manifested through the aggressive and exploitative conquest of the West, and deals with nature and the reordering of nature according to the dictates of this ethos. It supports the value of subjugating nature, and reenacts the "taming" process whereby the wild is brought under control.

But, she goes on to say, this symbolic drama of human domination betrays an anxiety about the way "the sphere of the tame inexorably expands at the expense of the wild," and so rodeo, "at its deepest level," much as she noted earlier, gives "assurance that there are still wild elements to tame while at the same time expressing ambivalence concerning the nature-to-culture transformation which is symbolized in the various events." Thus, from its beginning, rodeo not only has served "to revitalize the sense of exhilaration arising from the past conquering of a formidable wilderness": it also has proclaimed that that exhilarative conquering paradoxically isn't past, hasn't and won't come to an end.[27]

Amplifying Lawrence's explication, Allen focuses on the rodeo cowboy as representative of the taming muscle of civilization in a ritual that "sanctifies the Myth of the West" for a culture profoundly marked by "ambivalence over the loss of a real or imagined agrarian Eden," and he finds that figure instructively contradictory and ambiguous. First of all, he notes, there's trenchant irony in the fact that, since "the rodeo cowboy is himself wild, or at least aspires to that distinction," when he's engaged "in civilizing the forces of the frontier he is in many ways taming that which he loves best." He thereby embodies a wild-tame tension, and to the degree that he succeeds in taming the wild he's a tragic character who, in classical Western-heroic fashion, "must die or . . . must move on"—to the next rodeo. Also, he's both a man of his age who sleeps in motels, drives a truck, and carries credit cards and "*a cowboy*—representing facets of North America's past that evoke powerful rural and preindustrial images." Finally, rodeo cowboys, like real cowboys, have long been influenced by representations of themselves in popular culture, so much so that not too far into the evolution of rodeo "what we get is pop-culture artists making art about art based on lives that were and are influenced by art"—a situation in which "cowboy and rodeo-cowboy life and art have gotten all mixed up" and the original Wild West, whatever it was, is offstage from that tangle.[28]

The mix-up, both aesthetic and ideological, that defines the rodeo cowboy is nowhere more pronounced than in bull riding. Replacing safer steer riding as a regular event in 1929, it was intended to electrify audiences and not to demonstrate any ranching skill—no real cowboy ever rode a bull because his job required him to; more than one rodeo historian has wondered if the event owes its origin to after-hours boredom or drunkenness. It was—and is—a crazy exploit in which, to follow Lawrence's interpretation, "the stark simplicity of equipment is symbolic of the very low degree of control which culture is seen as exerting over the nature of the bull." Contestants don't try to subdue the animal the way calf ropers or steer wrestlers do: all they attempt is eight seconds of their niftiest riding, by the standards of the event, on a bucking and lunging and spinning bull. They "do not want to destroy the bull's male force; they want to first enhance it and then equal it by opposing it with their own. . . . they pay homage to it, and come to identify with it."[29] A logic of chiasmatic suspension obtains here, and it has historical resonance: they want to be wild tamers of an untameable wild.

Although a quick ride never compels the bull to, as Lawrence puts it, "enter the human sphere, it seems that in a strange and illusory way man enters the bull's sphere." Entering it, bull riders become, in her description of their self-image, the kind of frontiersmen that made J. Hector St. John de Crèvecoeur nervous: "strong, dumb, crude, and wild, tough and brutish as the animals they ride—a breed apart."[30] Maybe what boredom or drunkenness once upon a time inflamed was the desire not just to bronc-ride horses that could be broken but to straddle something unbreakable and affirm, against historical momentum, the survival of that breed of man and his invigorating interlock with the dangerous wild. Rodeo cowboys of that breed thus may be less tragic than contestants in other events; indeed, they more resemble the bullfighter clowns who protect them on the ground in that they, to borrow phrases from Stoeltje, both enact "the role of hero" and provide "burlesque of the role of the cowboy."[31] In their duality they seem to have anticipated, during the middle decades of the twentieth century, the more ironic rodeo (suburbanized, gay, and so forth) of the postregional West—to which I'll turn later.

Concurrent, though slower in proliferation, with Wild West shows and rodeos were dude ranches, places where visitors, for a long time almost exclusively wealthy Eastern urbanites, could participate through regulated experiences in the wildness of the big-sky outdoors. Dude ranches (whether guest ranches, which pamper their charges, or working ranches, which put them to work, or maybe combinations of the two) offer what Hal K. Rothman calls "recreational tourism."[32] There's dissension about which ranch first took paying guests, but it probably was the Custer Trail Ranch in Dakota Territory in the early 1880s. As transportation routes increased, especially in the northern West, so did the number of dude ranches, their high tide coming in the 1920s and 1930s (Robert G. Athearn notes that in 1937 "Wyoming alone had 102 such establishments").[33] They began thriving when, to apply Patricia Nelson Limerick's terms, "the violent history of conquest" was past and "a new, tame history of buying souvenirs and taking photographs" was accelerating. That was a time in which "one could sometimes make more money by herding tourists down a trail than by herding cattle," just as "skills once used for work" on the range could be more profitably "used for show" in rodeos.[34]

Successful tourist herding depended preeminently on "the accenting of western distinctiveness," a highly selective process, as Limerick limns it, of "disconnecting cattle-working techniques from their real-life context, and locating them instead in a timeless moment when real westerners were cowboys." At guest ranches that process required Western scenery, leathery ambience, and riding on bridle paths; at working ranches it required authenticity sold as "the experience of simulated work."[35] In either case, dude-ranching recreation had to deliver one thing on which, according to Athearn, American travelers in the West insisted: "the expected." They wanted the West to be how their mythologized fantasies told them it was. That's what they got; for "dude ranchers were the first to face this peculiar American attitude, and they learned to play it beautifully."[36] Peculiar indeed, but familiar: the dudes wanted wildness free of anything disconcerting—that is, they wanted it tame.[37]

What the dudes sought may have been a travesty of real Western wildness, but their motivation, as Athearn explains, is understandable: "It was indicative of a change in outlook on the part of those who were tired of summering at the eastern spas and whose interest in the West was not unlike that of other Americans who feared that the Old West was gone, or at least was slipping, and wanted to taste the flavor of that much romanticized place while time allowed." Also, many were conservation-minded and glad to discover that "primitive beauty was a main stock in trade of the new herdsmen."[38] They were motivated as well by a yearning for what Rothman describes as "more than a temporary release from the feeling of overcivilization that seemed omnipresent in American society." Like the many people hot to visit archaeological sites in the West, a diversion, thanks to Charles Lummis and others, in vogue prior to the 1930s, dudes may have been "roughing it in style," but they nonetheless went to ranches for recreation that was "truly distant from mainstream life."[39] They went west, as others had before them, both to find something and to escape something.

As the tame wildness of "roughing it in style" implies, however, the dudes couldn't escape a modern version of the Boone paradox. They may have gone west with the faith that a rural respite could repair the harm done by cities, but in doing so they only proved out the old irony that, as Fred Erisman puts it, "the act of escaping to the land brings civilization to the land."[40] (Think of the episode in Ron Underwood's 1991 film *City Slickers* in which a battery-powered coffee grinder triggers a cattle stampede.) In Rothman's terms, when "the civilized of the twentieth century . . . experienced what they regarded as the primitive, as they conquered it with their actions and ideas, they reinforced the hierarchical modes of fin de siècle America," with the result that dude ranching "simultaneously mirrored the patterns of industrial America while holding out the image of a different life, chock full of the meaning that an industrial economy . . . seemed predestined to destroy."[41]

"IT'S NEVER TOO LATE TO BE A COWBOY!" shouts a recent magazine ad for the Lost Valley Ranch, an outfit located between Denver and Colorado Springs that's puffed as an "authentic 112 year old AAA 4-diamond working cattle/horse ranch." It offers, among other amusements, horseback riding and roundups, of course, but also a couple of tenderfoot extras (in Tom Mix's time) now become musts in the postindustrial economy of services for mobile Americans: "Pool. Spa."[42] And if mountain scenery and rustic authenticity get to be overwhelming, you could, I suspect, easily hook into the Internet.

Dust Bowl: The Great American Desert with a Vengeance

The place was a mess, and it became a young nation's job to fix it with geometry, democracy, seeds, steam, steel, and water.
    Richard Manning, *Grassland: The History, Biology, Politics, and Promise of the American Prairie*

When the roaring of the twenties ended, the Great Depression had already begun; then, to make things worse, came the Dust Bowl, the name for that area of the southern plains of the West that was the parched center of a catastrophe that extended, in space, across many millions of acres and, in time, across a decade of little roaring except for that of scouring wind. The agricultural boom that had brought so much civilization to the West turned into a bust as farmland from Canada to Texas devolved toward desert. In 1936, after traveling through sandstorms and dust storms in Colorado and Kansas and seared, grasshopper-eaten, maybe even God-curst cornfields in the Dakotas, Scripps Howard reporter Ernie Pyle told his readers what such withering misery was like: "Day upon day of driving through this ruined country gradually becomes a sameness that ceases to admit a perspective. You come to accept it as a vast land that is dry and bare, and was that way yesterday and will be tomorrow, and was that way a hundred miles back and will be a hundred miles ahead."[1]

In the long view, a severe Western drought is nothing unusual. In June 1895, William Allen White, editor of the *Emporia (Kansas) Gazette*, wrote of abject eastbound fugitives from rain-starved western Kansas who "have tossed through hot nights, wild with worry, and have arisen only to find their worst nightmares grazing in reality on the brown stubble in front of their sun-warped doors. They had such high hopes when they went out there; they are so desolate now. . . . They have come out of the wilderness."[2] In fact, many previous severe Western droughts—in the 1750s, the 1820s, the 1860s, the 1870s, the 1880s, for instance—are a matter of record, and after the 1930s another would occur in the 1950s. Nor was that of the 1930s the worst of them, but its particular tragedy had to do with how much white Americans contributed to the calamity it wrought. They, as Elliott West says, "were hardly the first to imagine their way into trouble," for "in countless variations of trial, success, and failure, dozens of cultures had dreamed their way into this landscape of desire"; but no other people, he stresses, "ever pressed the land so far. None inflicted deeper wounds by failing truly to look at the place and to listen to its past."[3] If they had looked and listened, they would have realized that some years in the West are wetter than others, that the contradictory information from explorers and settlers about farming the place depended not only on where they were but when they were there.

Such information doubtless raised the red flag of grave ambiguity in the minds of some—ambiguity of the kind reflected in the titles of two books partly about the vulnerability of the West to drought, Bruce Bair's Good Land: My Life as a Farm Boy (1997) and Jonathan Raban's Bad Land: An American Romance (1996)—but they usually resolved it on the side of hope, not despair. Likewise for any ambiguity about the ability of technology to take charge of nature. Just as others in the West didn't accept the absence of, as the phrase in Harry McClintock's song goes, "the Big Rock Candy Mountains," so the farmers there didn't accept the typical paucity of rain, the truth of one of Wallace Stegner's wise aphorisms: "Aridity, more than anything else, gives the western landscape its character."[4] They had to face a question he sets forth as follows: "what do you do about aridity if you are a nation accustomed to plenty and impatient of restrictions and led westward by pillars of fire and cloud?" The answer: "You may deny it for a while. Then you must either try to engineer it out of existence or adapt to it."[5] In great part the tragedy of the Dust Bowl occurred because those farmers decided to engineer rather than to adapt. Why did they do so? To answer that question, as the framing of Stegner's implies, you have to analyze the complex of causes behind the Dust Bowl, all of which, except for the vicissitudes of Western weather and locust swarms, were finally attitudinal.

Donald Worster, whose 1979 book Dust Bowl: The Southern Plains in the 1930s is perhaps the definitive environmental history of its subject, acknowledges the role of nature in what he calls "as dramatic an example of maladaptation as any in human ecological experience," but his aim is to explain the role of culture in what happened. The linchpin for the data that warrant his explanation is high-altitude photographs of the dust storm that stunned Oklahoma in 1977, the worst since the 1950s. They show that "the source of the dust was west Texas farms, plowed and planted to seed, while neighboring New Mexico lands left in grass remained stable." The documentation afforded by aerial perspective handed down a clarifying indictment: "it was not the ragged, pervasive specter of drought but the human mind and its ill-considered land practices—a mind marking its presence by straight fence lines—that was the main culprit in the 1970s; and the cameras show persuasively that the same was probably true in the 1930s." He concludes that "there can hardly be any doubt now that the destruction by plow of the grass cover on vulnerable lands—semiarid lands where the soil is loose and the horizon flat and open to winds—has been the leading reason for the devastating scale of dust storms in the twentieth century."[6]

That scale owed much to the implements of power farming, but the use of machinery that accomplished what's sometimes called the Great Plow-up had to have motivation. What motivated plowing up an immense carpet of native grass was, in Worster's summative phrase, "agricultural capitalism," an ideology that urged the transformation of "unproductive" land into "little more than a form of capital that must be made to pay as much as possible." Ensorcelled by its worldview and imbued with its values, agri-entrepreneurs ignored scientific research, commonplace cautionary advice, and criticism and commodified Western soil as never before. Economic individualists, they savored risk, played dice with nature in the name of expansionist greed, and created the conditions for what became "that other great tragedy of the decade."[7] Wrecking nature to make money, they also wrecked their culture—at least for the duration of the "dirty thirties."

Related causes aren't difficult to inventory. An extractive mentality that viewed the land as disposable was one. So was the zeal to take advantage of a booming wheat market during World War I or to increase production when wheat prices fell afterwards. So was the habit of forgetting the agricultural disasters of the late nineteenth century. So was adherence to the misconception—"the most persistent and harmful vagary in the West," according to Walter Prescott Webb—"that 'the country is becoming more seasonable'"—somehow wetter, tamer.[8] So was the belief that dry-farming techniques in the West would prevail over aridity, that Americans, as Blake Allmendinger puts it, "could conquer the Great Plains eventually."[9] That belief is a variant of "the notion that 'man conquers Nature,'" which Worster notes was listed first among the "attitudes needing reform" enumerated in the 1936 federal report The Future of the Great Plains as "the root causes of the Dust Bowl disaster."[10]

That notion rationalized what Frieda Knobloch sees as "a thoroughly colonial operation" in effect from 1862 to 1945 that involved domination connoting "a progressive history from the wild to the domesticated, the natural to the cultural," with agriculture "the means by which an object became valuable (as a crop) and was released from its past into the history of improvement."[11] It was an operation encouraged by propagandists for irrigation like William Ellsworth Smythe, whose historical study The Conquest of Arid America (1900), Stephanie Sarver argues, was instrumental in "facilitating a shift in public perceptions that made possible the development of reclamation projects throughout the West in the twentieth century." Like others who disregarded or explained away facts that contradicted their visions of the West as the place where an agrarian utopia could be founded, Smythe "perceptually transforms the very real land into a set on which events are played out." By means of this theatricalization, Sarver observes, "the land becomes abstract as its distinguishing features, and its previous human and nonhuman inhabitants, are erased from the scene." All the mechanisms of land modification are kept out of sight. It was a trope of simplification repeated in Western boosterism during the early decades of the twentieth century; its rhetoric of mastery would survive the test of the Dust Bowl until finally its fuller etherealization of the West would ensure, Sarver concludes, that Smythe's vision of massive Western reclamation has come true "through a collective public agreement to overcome the natural conditions of the land regardless of cost, either economic or environmental."[12] The improvement achieved through a consensual fantasy of conquest is at the minimum as dubious now as it was in the 1930s.

To return to that earlier time, what were the effects of such causes? Retrospectively prophesied, if you will, in Thomas Hart Benton's painting *After Many Springs* (completed sometime between 1940 and 1945), which portrays, in William H. Goetzmann and William N. Goetzmann's interpretation, fecund and neatly tilled land sepulchrally haunted by a past of violent conquering (symbolized by a human skull and a rusted pistol) "awaiting a time for revenge,"[13] those effects were undeniable evidence of Americans' mis-taking the wildness of the West. You see exemplifications of them in the black blizzard of Dorothea Lange's photograph *The Great Blow of 1934* and the shriveled landscape of Arthur Rothstein's 1936 photograph *Stock Watering Hole Almost Covered Over by Erosion, Cimarron County, Oklahoma*. In Alexandre Hogue's farmer-villainizing paintings, especially *Dust Bowl* (1933), with its atmosphere of a nighttime battlefield, and *Mother Earth Laid Bare* (1938), with its criminalization of the plow (which appears as ugly and broken as the land it has raped). In Jackson Pollock's painting *Going West* (circa 1934–35), which updates the Western pioneers' optimistic migration, envisaging it as a bleak trek through a minatory nightmare of wasteland turmoil. In John Steinbeck's 1939 novel *The Grapes of Wrath* and John Ford's 1940 film of it. In Ian Frazier's evocation of the grievous phenomena of "the first of the great modern eco-catastrophes": days plunged into throat-clogging darkness, dust in drifts six feet deep in Kansas and inches of it all over Chicago, "'snirt' storms" in winter, asphyxiated wildlife and livestock—ad nauseam.[14]

Frazier's evocation prefaces an account of what farmers learned from the Dust Bowl—"to hold on to their topsoil by contour plowing, leaving crop stubble standing in their fields after harvest, strip farming, and planting windbreaks"—and of how, with government help (crop support and the like) and the resumption of rain and then higher grain prices during World War II, many who survived the 1930s made respectable rolls. But he also suggests that those who were parties to that decade's ecological wreckage and their heirs may otherwise have learned little more

Alexandre Hogue, Dust Bowl (1933): the atmosphere of a nighttime battlefield. (Smithsonian American Art Museum, gift of International Business Machines Corporation.)

from it about the natural West than the gullible Southwestern nesters in Conrad Richter's 1937 Dust Bowl novel *The Sea of Grass* knew when they started plowing under native herbage—and that ultimately in Smythe's Eden reborn through increased irrigation by high-efficiency pumps drawing down the Ogallala Aquifer there'll be the devil to pay again. If that reservoir runs dry—and it will, at the present rate of takeout, within the next half-century—"the desert which came in the 1930s," Frazier safely prophesies, "will return."[15]

Patently, some lessons that should have been learned weren't, for after the 1930s the dream of unlimited Western agriculture resurged in the 1940s and, despite dampening during the lesser dust bowl of the 1950s, looked like it would stay resurgent indefinitely. Farming became more mechanized. Environmentally damaging but production-boosting pesticides, herbicides, and fertilizers were more intensively and widely employed. Much of California was agronomically geometrized into one huge farm. Large tracts of scrubby grassland in eastern Colorado were plowed and sown with wheat. Dread of drought ebbed from the late 1940s through the 1960s, the period Richard White terms "the golden age of the Bureau of Reclamation," as "river systems became elaborate plumbing" for farms.[16]

Some of the lessons of what Gene M. Gressley views as "the collision between man and nature" symbolized by the Dust Bowl were apparently—given the Western agricultural boom after the 1960s—learned only "temporarily."[17] Among them was what Curt Meine labels a "moral lesson" about the need "to strike some balance in a world so increasingly blind to beauty and hungry for bread that the environmental conditions necessary for balance were threatened."[18] Another lesson was, Hans Huth argues, "that nature could not be relied upon to produce . . . crops as an assembly line produced automobiles."[19]

Whether the lessons stuck or not, the 1930s were the time, in Worster's phrase, "of reappraisal of conventional thinking about the West." In the decades that followed and as the realities of the region were better understood, that reappraisal continued. By the end of the century, a deeper comprehension of the physics of weather had shown the Western sky to be far wilder than any rain-follows-the-plow fanatic or old-time meteorologist could ever have conceived. "Climate, we are now beginning to acknowledge," Worster warns, "is so complicated a series of events that we may never be able to make predictions that a farmer can rely on." Its patterns are stochastic, nonlinear, exceedingly multivariate. The recognition of such complexity at play in the climatic history of the Great Plains helps you grasp why all the "technological fixes" tried there—planting drought-tolerant varieties of crops, constructing bench terraces, and so on—"have limits and drawbacks."[20]

Which means that postmodern agriculture now proceeds in a contingent, if not precarious, way in a West that has proven to be neither an infinitely fertile Eden nor an obstinately infertile Great American Desert. But, as Worster stresses, no foreseeable innovation in technology, pioneer-spirit determination, or federal assistance to farmers will be of much avail "as long-term desiccation sets in." Even that gloomy forecast may not be entirely certain, however, for, he reminds us, the environmental history of the West reveals "a pattern of erratic cycles that go back as far as we can look." On the other hand, such a pattern itself may imply even gloomier possibilities. "Nowhere in the West," he admonishes, "have we any reason to think we have escaped that pattern of nature, or even escaped the cycles of boom and bust created by our own deeds and mistakes. We have not mastered the place nor built a secure civilization with its raw materials."[21] What is entirely certain is that we must stop thinking of the West either as a place to which we can escape or, in this case, as a place from which we can escape while we're there. The final lesson of the Dust Bowl, all in all, is surely this: if we want to steer clear of the truly apocalyptic dust bowl of the future, we'll have to adjust our farming to the realities of the West and not to those of some tamer elsewhere we'd like it to be.

With regard to that possibility, there are signs of hope. You can see them in the activities of the Nature Conservancy and in the accomplishments of the many individuals and organizations advocating and practicing sustainable agriculture in the West.[22] You can see them specifically in the projects of the Land Institute, a nonprofit research center located on the banks of the Smoky Hill River in central Kansas. The best introduction to the institute's agricultural philosophy might be found in Richard Manning's discussion of the Buffalo Commons, an idea—for large areas with a natural grassland economy—with which media mogul Ted Turner and others have experimented: "The West that John Wesley Powell described has always been that West, despite our attempts to remake it. It took the old cowboy of the Turner ranch, Bud Griffith, long enough to realize that the way to herd buffalo was to figure out where they were going and go with them. It has taken us much longer to figure out the way to inhabit the West is just the same." But it didn't take geneticist Wes Jackson, who, with his wife, Dana, founded the institute in 1976, very long to figure out the way to farm the West also is just the same. And that got him into a passion Manning nutshells as "the business of reinventing agriculture."[23]

Jackson's way started with his insight that conventional agriculture with all its problems and destructive shortcomings (nitrate pollution, soil salinization, and so forth) is, in Manning's formulation, "nothing but a determined effort to keep nature from taking its course." Granting that the cultivation of grain is absolutely essential, Jackson is committed to discovering how to go about it without high-energy fossil-fuel technology, aquifer-depleting irrigation, herbicides, and the like, as well as the plowing that promotes erosion. His proposal is for "farm fields that copy the design of the mature communities of the prairie," systems of perennial crops that don't need annual plowing and reseeding, polycultures that include insect-repelling plants and legumes that fix nitrogen from the air for fertilizer—fields with a viable yield that flourish on whatever rain the empyrean drops. Research at the institute on domesticating exotic and native perennials, breeding perennial varieties of annuals now cultivated, and such "has established and successfully assembled the key pieces" to the puzzle of how to reach Jackson's sustainable agriculture, but implementing it on a West-wide scale calls for a lot more work; "the task," avers Manning, "is sufficiently ambitious to require generations."[24] Whether or not we have them is anyone's guess. For some years now much of the West has been edging into record dryness. An extended drought cycle may lie ahead.

In the meantime, at any rate, the institute is trying to help Westerners be "homecomers," Jackson's name for people who face blunders like the Dust Bowl, admit that Jeffersonian agronomy is a dog that won't hunt on arid land, stop growing sweet corn in Arizona, and "get native" by participating in "a second settling of the West" that will do it right this time by husbanding the economy of indigenous nature rather than imposing that of industrial culture—the theme of his 1994 book *Becoming Native to This Place*.[25] Learning to be at home in the West, to go with its way, may not be easy for many people, no easier than Jackson's mimicking wilderness and redoing what's been undone by inventing a Western agriculture for the future based on nature's own agriculture of the past, but continuing to go against that way will end, after who knows how many springs on a warming globe, in something to which no degree of the adjective *easy* could be applied.

Re-imagining the Wildness:
Modern Mediations

She shrilled the great scenes out defiantly, as if it were her place to defend them,
as if they belonged to her, and were better, even at second hand, than anything
that any of the townspeople had ever experienced.
    H. L. Davis, "Old Man Isbell's Wife"

Larry McMurtry contends that revisionist historians like Patricia Nelson Limerick and Donald Worster, though they rightly emphasize the terrible cost of Western settlement, can't quite understand what he, as a novelist, may better make out: "that the lies about the West are more powerful than the truth about the West—so much more powerful that, in a sense, lies about the West are the truths about the West—the West, at least, of the imagination." He says that in his own novels about the West he's tried to deromanticize the cowboy but that "people won't have it." He thought, he recalls, that his 1985 novel *Lonesome Dove* "was antimythic," and yet the book's fans heroized its antiheroes. "Readers," he sighs, "suck so hard at the old myths that they turn stones into grapes."[1]

A century ago there were readers, as there are now, who favored historical realism over mythical romanticism in their view of the West of the past, but they weren't in the majority—nor are they now. A lot of stones have been turned into grapes, though the grapes may be only wax or glass or plastic. The illusionary artifices of narratives of restoration have proven hard to resist. Taking the West as sure-enough stones or turning it into grapes—either is a postfrontier response to its tragedy. Modern Americans preferred the second way. As the twentieth century ripened, that preference, like the increasingly etherealized West imagined in literature and other media, involved an ever-more intricate mix of values and attitudes.

Helpful in explaining that preference is Anne F. Hyde's investigation of how "cultural filters" shaped Americans' perception of the West during the nineteenth century. Those filters were constructed by explorers like Lewis and Clark, by painters like Albert Bierstadt and Thomas Moran, and especially, since their medium seems to secure literal truth, by photographers like Carleton E. Watkins and Timothy H. O'Sullivan. Watkins, for instance, "used a combination of painterly aesthetics and photographic truth to make the western landscape appealing to American audiences," and O'Sullivan magnified the drama of it by angling his camera oddly or by masking or playing up certain features. They filtered what they saw through their own idealizations; their work thereby bolstered a "perceptual tradition" ideological to the pith.[2] By means of such filtering, they, like others in other media, composed the West that Americans craved.

That tradition lasted into the twentieth century, and its perceptions, as Hyde says, still affect ideas and behaviors whose "tension between wanting to expand

and develop agriculture and industry and wanting to enjoy splendid scenery has not been resolved." Despite actualities that might have discouraged those perceptions, the West of the twentieth century thus was in large part their offspring. Nevertheless, even as most of their filters remained in place, many Americans were reinterpreting the West, generating both new misperceptions and a new sense of what the region might mean for their culture. In either case, the imagery of the West grew more complex. Always entangled in that complexity was an irony that continues in force: "much of the West that seems so important to our self-perception either never existed or has disappeared, but we have re-created it as we imagine it must have been."[3]

Re-created indeed, in far more images in various media and genres than I can compass in the present book. But in this and the next chapter I can offer a survey and examples essential to understanding the modern operation of the wild-tame dialectic in the more and more profoundly mediated West.

David Mogen, Scott P. Sanders, and Joanne B. Karpinski describe the heart of the frontier story as an encounter with a gothic wilderness that was "violent, consuming, intrinsically metaphysical, and charged with paradox and emotional ambivalence."[4] That story is about people who identified themselves with the land they assailed and, as Barbara Allen puts it, "measure[d] themselves in terms of their ability to meet its challenges."[5] That story, like the encounter of which it tells, is likewise charged, so that in its narration of people's meeting those challenges there turn up "ironic contradictions" of the kind Forrest G. Robinson finds throughout Cooper's *The Last of the Mohicans* (1826)—for example, in Cora Munro's being a character who is both "the embodiment and advocate of civilization" and "the witness to and bearer of its shame"[6]—contradictions so pervasive in all the Leatherstocking novels that, as Roderick Nash says, they "gave Cooper's countrymen reason to feel both proud and ashamed at conquering wilderness."[7] Such contradictions were unabated, as we've seen, in *The Virginian*, which book exemplifies what Robert G. Athearn terms "the pull between changes implied by progressivism, on the one hand, and the comforting warmth of the nostalgic past on the other."[8] And they persisted in the story of the West as region, another story charged with paradox and ambivalence, one that evolved, most dramatically in the twentieth century, alongside the story of the West as frontier.

The two stories have their two literatures, and those literatures concern the two Wests in Thomas J. Lyon's description I mentioned earlier: a frontier West that's mostly a mental construction and a regional West that's a uniquely actual place. Literature about the former tends to be romantic and, as he argues, "uses the 'frontier' set of myths and values unconsciously"; that about the latter tends to be realistic and, especially as it matured in the postfrontier decades (and, during and after the 1920s, paralleled the slow development of literary criticism focused on Western literature), takes a "stance toward the frontier and the frontier ethos [that] is conscious, reflective, and analytic."[9] That opposition correlates with the differences between two well-known nineteenth-century travelogues: Francis Parkman's *The Oregon Trail* (1849), with its romantic, idealized, and narrow view of the West, and Lewis Garrard's *Wah-To-Yah and the Taos Trail* (1850), with its more realistic view that represents what A. Carl Bredahl Jr. types as "attitudes of openness and receptivity to the physical environment" and that "conveys the experience of a strikingly new world."[10] That opposition correlates also with John R. Milton's distinction between "the lowercase *w* western" (exemplified by the writings of Max Brand, Luke Short, and company) and "the capital *W* Western novel" (exemplified by the writings of Willa Cather, John Steinbeck, and company), both of which he distinguishes from Eastern fiction—mainly because their characters engage the natural world more fully.[11] Arguably as old as the literary West itself, that opposition is a simplification—it refers less to an absolute polarity than to the ends of a spectrum well supplied with blends—but, with a little tinkering, it will prove useful.

Frontier-oriented literature draws on and ratifies the master-narrative of the triumphal West, of white men conquering wilderness.[12] Though it may seem as straightforward in its mythic resolutions as a fable, it invariably smooths over thematic snarls, preeminently, in the early twentieth century, those in the mismatch of the popular Western's celebration of the progress of industrialized urban civilization with its valorization of the very sentiments that guaranteed the genre a jumbo readership—nostalgia for the preindustrial West, lust for the strenuous outdoor life, and the like. That genre is the exemplary modern form of such literature, and it began in the 1860s with the mass-market dime novel, a paperback phenomenon that Lyon characterizes as soon showing "certain consistent, indeed programmatic, elements: a hero who represented a synthesis of civilization and wildness; an affirmative finding with regard to progress; an emphasis on action; and a setting of epical import—usually vast, wild, open spaces." The hero was self-reliant and naturally noble, and he typically acted in support of civilization. The hundreds of titles, written by hacks like Edward Judson ("Ned Buntline") and Prentiss Ingraham, in which he starred, along with Wild West shows, "helped to solidify the West as a pageant-like realm of adventure . . . and the Western itself as a formulaic or 'automatized' text serving as the key to that never-never land."[13]

Thus, by the time Owen Wister succeeded in gathering the mythic elements of the frontier romance into *The Virginian*, millions of Americans were devoted to the nation's westering as what Athearn calls a "spectator sport."[14] The West of those vicarious adventurers was a miscellany of images. It was also resistant to revision, for many didn't want that sport to end. What the dominantly male readership of Westerns wanted to escape through them was what readers of Westerns, in Jane Tompkins's formulation, still try to escape: "triviality, secondariness, meaningless activity." She speculates that "the hunger Westerns satisfy is a hunger not for adventure but for meaning," but I'd suggest that it's for both, for something that might as well be called meaningful adventure—maybe even adventurous meaning. Though I agree with her that the Western is (partly anyway) "about men's fear of losing their mastery, and hence their identity, both of which the Western tirelessly reinvents," I obviously disagree with her dismissal of its having to do with "a reenactment of the American dialectic between civilization and nature."[15] Almost everything in the Western, now or a century and a half ago, has to do with that.

Accordingly, the rise of the Western must be understood as exactly what William Bloodworth says it, to a great extent, was: "a popular literary response by both authors and readers to the closing of the frontier and opening of a new, urban environment." The rise occurred because Americans deprived of a real frontier avidly turned to an imaginary one, its experiences so prescribed and perpetuated by mythical recipes that by the middle of the twentieth century Westerns centrally featured not "the West itself—the unmediated West, so to speak—but the power of prior perceptions of the West." And since that time, as Bloodworth succinctly puts it, Westerns "have been about the Western as often as they have been about the West." That self-referentiality has allowed all manner of ironic twists on the genre, as we'll see later; the cardinal point here is that the Western, in re-creating an imaginary rather than historical time and place, furnishes an archive of attitudinal conflicts since it "promoted the advance of civilization while celebrating a primitive past"—a paradox that, even if simplistically resolved, "meshed easily with the complex anxieties of a traditionally rural society that rapidly became urbanized and industrialized." Bloodworth concludes that the mythic character of this literary vessel lies not so much in its hero, setting, or plot as in "its deep and often contradictory appeals to American readers."[16]

Yet we must remember that one of those appeals in the postfrontier period of tragic acknowledgments and exuberant hopes was something Lyon deems a precious offering: "The opportunity to revel in the spacious freedom of the wild frontier and to identify with a hero who can somehow live beautifully in both the wild world and the civilized one to come."[17] And remember too, of course, as Lee Clark Mitchell advises, that this peerless contradictory hero "*was* invented"—and revised —by cultural necessities.[18]

Region-oriented literature is, however, a horse opera of another color. It's a literature written more by insiders, natives of the West or at least people who've lived there awhile, than is frontier-oriented literature, much of which has been written by outsiders more acquainted with its conventions than with the West. In some respects region-oriented literature is not only a literature in its own right (the West writing about itself) but also a counterliterature out to demythologize the West of the popular imagination (myth writing about itself). As Russell Martin observes, during the decades after Buffalo Bill Cody launched his show, the West "was, to most minds, simply the mythic locale of the nation's enduring morality plays." But for lots of Westerners that West was only a barroom daydream. Some of those

Westerners wanted to break out of the formulaic box. So writers like Frank Norris, Cather, and Steinbeck and then Bernard DeVoto, Dorothy M. Johnson, and Wallace Stegner gave their talents to "re-creating a historical West that was a palpable, believable place, . . . as if the contemporary region couldn't be addressed until the historical West had been *correctly* divined and defined."[19] That subsequent task wouldn't be taken up broadly until the postregional era of the 1960s and thereafter.

Correctly divining and defining the historical West required questioning traditional assumptions about the place, its wildlife, its people, and the interactions among them. It required debunking romance and seeing the West's perpetual issues as, in Lyon's phrase, "intensely problematic."[20] It required, he says more specifically, a "tragic vision of history," a determination "to get underneath the dominant imagery and portray life in the West in its human conflict, paradox, and sometimes sheer perversity."[21] The region-oriented literature that met such requirements, mainly that written after the shocks of World War I, grappled, in James C. Work's simile, with "ambiguities [that] began springing up like weeds in an overworked field."[22] Most of them involved increasingly complicated relationships between various aspects of the wild and the tame.

No small part of that complicatedness had to do with the fact that postfrontier Westerners, as Athearn reminds us, were two-minded about telling their story: they "reveled in their collective role as the Sagebrush Siegfried" conceived by Easterners, but they also were learning "to look within and to think more about the significance of their own region."[23] Many of them knew that history can't be wholly liberated from myth and that myth exists only through some correspondence, however oblique, with history. Although, as Fred Erisman notes, facts consistently repudiate the mythic vision of the West, it still endures, its durability evidenced by "the ambivalent and contradictory ways in which Americans look upon the western landscape in the present."[24] At least a trace of it, if only an exorcized incubus in the background, lurks in even the most modernist region-oriented literature. The opposition of frontier-oriented and region-oriented literature does indeed refer to the ends of a spectrum. Fluctuant though it was, the overall shift in tone of that spectrum during the century or so leading into the 1960s, as some annotated examples will illustrate, was from that of heroic romance to that of realistic tragedy to that of antiheroic irony, with the wild-tame dialectic wobbling all the way.

Begin with John Rollin Ridge's *The Life and Adventures of Joaquín Murieta, the Celebrated California Bandit* (1854), the first novel written by a mixed-blood Native American (Cherokee). In it Ridge created a Mexican-immigrant mestizo whom he both censures and heroizes, in Blake Allmendinger's interpretation, with the result that the book "presents two competing versions of the Mexican-as-Indian. In one of these versions, Murieta is the savage of Indian captivity narratives, who holds the entire state hostage during the course of his murder spree. In the other version, which alternates, the Mexican is an ennobled and romanticized Indian, who appears both sublime and benign due to his presumed imminent extinction." The product of an assimilationist author who believed in Manifest Destiny and yet sympathized with rebellion against the oppressions of frontier society, this text is crosshatched with "internal divisions" reflective of California's social chaos; thus the very qualities that have checked its popularity by making it "inaccessible—its vacillations, its ambivalence, and its sheer inconsistencies—are the same traits that make Ridge's 'borderland' work representative."[25]

Bret Harte, one of the originators of the local-color movement in American literature, wrote stories, such as "The Luck of Roaring Camp" (1868) and "The Outcasts of Poker Flat" (1869), that are superficially realistic, particularly in their settings. As Mitchell observes, however, middle-class romanticism presides in his narratives, through whose plots rough-and-tumble characters are revealed to be good persons. Harte's stories thereby envelop a paradox: "Beneath the wild and woolly veneer of frontier life in the Sierra foothills, he suggests, civilized values are firmly in place"—and the untamed landscape itself "usually seems already tamed."[26]

In *Roughing It* (1872), his only book about the West, Mark Twain penned a work that humorously examines the discrepancies between dream and reality and deromanticizes the territory (for instance, by portraying Gosiutes not as Cooperian Noble Savages but as filthy wretches). He was too clever, though, to do that straightforwardly. In consequence, for all its realism, *Roughing It* is a novelized autobiography in which, as Patrick D. Morrow argues, "the tall tale *is* reality"; moreover, through the book Twain sought "to create a serious, often irreverent world, paradoxically out of comedy." In creating that contradictory world, he exposed the crassness of plundering the West for riches, and he "learned a fundamental and paradoxical truth that he would carry to his grave: ironic comedy can be the most effective tragedy."[27] Interesting, given his clutching such truth, is the fact that he was never able to complete his Western sequel to *The Adventures of Huckleberry Finn*.[28]

Lew Wallace's *Ben-Hur: A Tale of the Christ* (1880), written while its author was governor of New Mexico Territory, may seem an odd member of this literary club, but, as Allmendinger persuasively argues, the novel "is a western in toga, in drag." A biblical romance about a Jew who escapes Roman bondage and finds Christian salvation, it's based on local history. At the same time he was "placing Indians on reservations and arbitrating range wars between bandits and cattlemen, Wallace was . . . narrating 'civilization's' rise over 'savagery'"—that is, Ben-Hur's triumph over decadent and pagan Rome. The narrator, however, shows signs of the same "decided ambivalence—an identification first with agents of 'civilization' then with the forces of 'savagery'—[that] plagued Wallace throughout his life and careers." It's an ambivalence that blurs the differences between civilized Jews and savage Romans, most notably through Wallace's characterizing the former as "unrefined natives" doomed to subdual and whose hero, like the standard white Western hero, is a man who moves "back and forth between (moral) civilization and (spiritual) wilderness" and, "paradoxically, . . . defends civilization by resorting to uncivilized means, as Ben-Hur does when he wreaks havoc on Rome" (the very empire that bequeathed so much to Wallace's own society).[29]

Like Crane's short story "The Bride Comes to Yellow Sky" (which, as we saw earlier, shows what Lyon describes as its author's "mixed, ambiguous response to the West," with his realism using the imagery of romance for irony both comic and tragic),[30] Frank Norris's *McTeague* (1899) concerns dispossession in a time of wrenching change in the relations of the wild and the tame. Roughhewn and hot-blooded, the novel's protagonist has a run at living a lower-middle-class life in San Francisco, the author's home at the time, but he proves to be a bull in the china shop of a civilization unsuited to his temperament. McTeague exemplifies, for Richard W. Etulain, Norris's "archetypal westerner," a crude man out of place who "eventually retreats to the open frontier when under stress"—though at last, ironically, he's lost in Death Valley, a victim of the whirling limbo of a world in transit "between a vanishing frontier and an emerging urban West."[31]

Zane Grey's *Riders of the Purple Sage* (1912), often paired with *The Virginian* as a classic Western, is a tad more realistic than Wister's book but still very much a romance—and as perplexing in its configuration of the wild-tame dialectic. Lyon is right in his assertion that in *Riders*, as in his many other Westerns, Grey (who, like Wister, grew up in the East) has the wilderness act as a redemptive force, specifically, in *Riders*, one "that somehow encourages the finest qualities in heroic people."[32] Yet such casting carries complications, for it predicates "an escapist return to nature" that, as Stephen Tatum demonstrates, is the means by which the story "affirms an eroticized myth of progress." That myth, though, is countered by the way it also critiques modernization. The upshot is that *Riders* may be read "as a force field of conflict where images and plotting motifs . . . embody the contradictory pressures of and ambivalent responses to a compelling story of transformation and conquest which haltingly ushers in the modern world."[33]

Before the 1960s, there was only a handful of gifted American poets whose works had a distinctly Western flavor, among them John G. Neihardt—heir to the romantic laureateship of lesser poets such as Joaquin Miller—and Robinson Jeffers, Thomas Hornsby Ferril, Yvor Winters, and William Stafford, all more realistic in bent. Of them Jeffers is perhaps most strikingly the poet of the critique Tatum attributes to Grey—but with a difference. From the beginning of his mature work in the early 1920s until his death in 1962, Jeffers wrote poetry associated usually with the Pacific coastline. As Robert Brophy avers, however, he was not a conventional regionalist. In poems such as "The Purse-Sein" (1937) he represented with precision the landscape he knew (and criticized progress), but that "final frontier," Brophy says, "is an ontological statement, not a geographic or cultural one. It is final as the coast is final. . . . America's violence, its rape of the land, its betrayal of

the Indians, its pillaging of resources—all of these must ultimately be faced here."
Jeffers did face them, in poems that condemn cities and urge peaceful immersion in cosmic nature. Still, despite his explicit dithyrambic rejections and embracements, his poetry houses "a deep-seated ambivalence"; because of it the shore his oeuvre delineates "was full of life, yet inhospitable, ancient and yet young, violent yet serene, a platform above the Pacific set for tragedy."[34]

Harvey Fergusson, author of *Wolf Song* (1927) and other fictional and nonfictional books about the West, was a man born and reared in New Mexico who was intrigued by the East, loved back country but was comfortable in both Eastern and Western cities where he spent most of his adult life, and was drawn to the West of the past but also skeptical about its mythology. In many ways *Wolf Song*, a thoroughly researched and lyrical novel whose protagonist is a mountain man named Sam Lash, amounts to a narrative exploration of the tensions between such contraries. Throughout the story Lash is torn between trapping and hunting in the wilderness and settling into married life with Lola Salazar, the pampered daughter of a Taos *rico*; his finally acceding to the latter resolves little, and he winds up feeling caged. "What this ambiguous, realistic ending reveals," according to Lyon, is Fergusson's "postfrontier habit of mind. The frontier mind is forthrightly dualistic: here is wilderness, there is civilization. . . . But Fergusson . . . shows the utter attractiveness of both sides of our national polarity." In his later novels, which concern a more modern and urban West, he continued to tell of what Lyon calls "the wavering at the core of the American personality," honoring "the past, which is always wilder, freer," but affirming that "just *here* is where we are now."[35] That new regional "here" became, for this revisionist, more important—and more dilemmatic—than the old frontier.

In Nathanael West's *The Day of the Locust* (1939), as in some of native Oklahoman Lynn Riggs's darker dramas, the region is portrayed even more dilemmatically, to say the least. Leslie Fiedler sums up that novel as an anti-Western in which the author, a New Yorker transplanted to Hollywood (where he was a screenwriter), "plays the parody-game, . . . not only with the movie images of the Westerner, but with those ex-real cowboys who come to play their own mythicized selves on the screen—or flock to Hollywood in the vain hope of doing so."[36] The novel is a parody, but it's a tragic one; it exemplifies a strain of Western literature that postregional writers later will either further ironize or attempt to transcend. Its tragedy is that of the closed frontier as manifested in what Harold P. Simonson terms "something surrealistic and nightmarish," the outcome when "the westward trek of Americans, growing pathological in their optimism, finally ends in Southern California, a region inhabited by the totally deluded"—and a Dantesque place of desperate artifice where migrants from Iowa, cheated out of the American dream, divorced from the natural world, suffer an "existential panic" that ends in mass violence.[37] The postfrontier West à la Goya.

The son of a white Southern woman and a man with Indian ancestry, Coloradan Frank Waters wrote about a West not as tenebrously oddball as West's but just as troubled by tensions as Fergusson's. His vision is more upbeat than West's chiefly because of his interest in a rapprochement of contraries analogous to the kind that engaged Fergusson. Charles L. Adams's conjecture that it derived from "the early necessity of reconciling the opposing forces inherent in his own heritage" probably is correct. In his attention to historical and cultural details, Waters was a realist—and certainly a revisionist in his treatment of the world of Southwestern Indians (whom he was careful not to ennoble unduly)—but his overarching emphasis, in fiction and in nonfiction such as The Colorado (1946), was on a possibility that would appeal to many a postregional Westerner: "a synthesis of the apparently opposing points of view into a wholeness in both individual and mankind."[38] Stranded between the egoistic and technical world of whites and the communal and organic world of Indians, Martiniano, the Pueblo protagonist of The Man Who Killed the Deer (1942), at last is able to reach that wholeness, which bestows a sense of deep connection to the life of the land. So is Helen Chalmers, the Anglo protagonist of The Woman at Otowi Crossing (1966), who finds herself at what Lyon discerns as a distinctly modern crossroads where two "realms of the human spirit," nuclear-scientific Los Alamos and ceremonial San Ildefonso Pueblo, intersect and, through a series of epiphanies, "undergoes an emergence into a unified, enlightened outlook" that joyfully comprehends both realms.[39]

From the end of World War II to the mid-1960s, plenty of lowercase literature was published, but the trend in work that had the aesthetic feel of uppercase literature was increasingly away from frontier romance and toward regional realism and away from modern tragedy and toward postmodern irony, with little of Waters's mystical sanguineness in tow. In his novel The Big Sky (1947), Montanan A. B. Guthrie disputed the blessings of progress and through his protagonist, Boone Caudill, rewrote the romantic legendry of the mountain men (and, by implication, hairy-chested Western history) as the realistic tragedy of white savages ironically complicit in destroying the wilderness they loved.[40] In Shane (1949), Jack Schaefer, who lived east of the Mississippi until 1955, wrote a novel that Lyon dubs the epitome of the Western as the genre that "sanctifies the outcome of American history by a ritual drama in which 'civilization and savagery' are fruitfully blended (in the person of the hero and the issue of the plot),"[41] and it may be read, like a lot of Westerns in this period, as a Cold War allegory of the victory of American family-based civilization over the Communist savagery of the Soviet Union; but, as Robinson indicates, there's enough ideological fuzziness in that blending to call into question any definite reading—not the least of which attaches to the fact that the novel's emotionally split protagonist exposes the "utopian domesticity" he defends as "shallow and constraining and vulnerable."[42] Even North Dakota–reared Louis L'Amour's Hondo (1953), another Cold War Western, although reliant on formulaic fantasy for plot and characterization, is grounded in accurate history, a well-versed awareness of place, and what Lyon calls the author's "ecological valuation of nature" in a way that partly qualifies it as a work of region-oriented realism.[43]

Realism fused with romance defines some Western literature of the 1960s—such as Idaho native Vardis Fisher's Mountain Man (1965), with its polarized depictions of experiences in the beautiful and terrifying Rocky Mountain West of the 1840s— but by then the tone of much of it had shifted noticeably. Irony edges out tragedy in more-or-less realistic works by more-or-less Westerners such as Ken Kesey's 1962 novel One Flew over the Cuckoo's Nest (a schizophrenic Indian narrates the tale of an institutionalized quasi-hero's defiant but losing battle with civilization—in the shape of a castrating nurse—that ends with his lobotomy and the Indian's "escape" back to what's left of his people and their lifeway on the Columbia River); Thomas Berger's 1964 novel Little Big Man (a fabulating white man in a nursing home who claims to have been reared by Cheyennes shares rib-nudging revisionist frontier history that features demythologized heroes, civilized Indians, and savage whites who overrun them); Sam Shepard's 1964 play Cowboys (displaced waddies struggle with the disjunctions between mythical, if laudable, Old Western ways and a fragmented postmodern world); and Truman Capote's 1966 "nonfiction novel" In Cold Blood (two male convicts on the loose on the "queer frontier" as masculine cowboy and feminine Indian murder a farm family in southwestern Kansas and hang for it).[44]

In the postfrontier period women hastened the evolution of region-oriented literature that by the 1960s would wind up being as variegated in its handling of the wild-tame dialectic as the West, with the admission of Alaska and Hawaii as "Western" states in 1959, was geographically. Writing about a land long interpreted in changing feminine terms (as virgin, loving or terrible mother, mistress, even whore), as Annette Kolodny and others have shown,[45] women changefully reinterpreted the West in turn, challenging the traditional male mythology. Mary Hallock Foote, a New York Quaker transplanted to a West that both charmed and repelled her, and B. M. Bower, a Montanan most of her life, wrote novels and short stories during the first two decades of the twentieth century that reevaluated the differences between the civilized life of the East and the uncivilized life of the West, finding gentler means for reconciling them than that mythology afforded and in effect inventing an oxymoronic genre, the domestic Western. In O Pioneers! (1913), My Ántonia (1918), Death Comes for the Archbishop (1927), and other novels, Nebraskan Willa Cather created a West of regional textures, a place of tragedy as well as possibility, pressing what Lyon praises as "her poetic sense of the redemptive, creative contact with nature that may give an individual, and perhaps even a culture, a basis for right living."[46] In Old Jules (1935), a biography of her tyrannical father, and Slogum House (1937), a value-inverting novel about a land-grabbing and heinous woman, and later in sympathetic biographies of Indians, Crazy Horse (1942) and Cheyenne Autumn

(1953), Nebraskan Mari Sandoz deglamorized pioneering and Manifest Destiny through fiercely realistic descriptions of frontier life.[47] In *The Mountain Lion* (1947), Jean Stafford, who grew up in California and Colorado, wrote a novel in which, as Susan J. Rosowski construes it, "familiar ingredients of the formula western are laid bare" (so that, for example, "the hunt represents undisguised aggression against women") and the symbolism of settings that echo traditional contrasts (civilization versus nature and the like) "is self-reflexively critical of the very formulas that they evoke."[48] In her short stories about the West, most famously "The Man Who Shot Liberty Valance" (1949), Montanan Dorothy M. Johnson wrote of what Work calls "the reconciliations that have to take place when an ideal pastoral world is in conflict with the necessities of reality."[49]

Lyon cautions that "ethnic writers are not necessarily interested in . . . the Euro-American dialectic of civilization and wilderness."[50] Nonetheless, some of the literature by such writers, which was gradually coming into its own during the early twentieth century, presented modern perspectives on that dialectic. Most of the works in that category were written by Native Americans less well known than Waters and are about white–Indian conflicts with tragic undertones. *From the Deep Woods to Civilization: Chapters in the Autobiography of an Indian* (1916), one of two autobiographical books by Charles A. Eastman (mixed-blood Santee Sioux), belongs in it, as does *Cogewea, the Half-Blood* (1927), an oral-tradition Western by Mourning Dove (Okanogan) in collaboration with Lucullus McWhorter. So does *The Surrounded* (1936), a novel by D'Arcy McNickle (mixed-blood Cree), with its ironic and pessimistic treatment of the discontinuities of reservation life. *Laughing Boy* (1929), a novel by Oliver La Farge, a non-Indian authority on Southwestern Native culture, might be read illuminatingly in relation to such works because, like much of his fiction, its dominant theme, in Everett A. Gillis's capsuling, is "the decline and ultimate disintegration of the ancient tribal structure of the Navajo nation beneath the eroding force of a materialistic Anglo-American civilization."[51]

In his assessment of Western literature published during the first decades of the twentieth century, Athearn argues that "the only genuine westerns usually were portrayals of the land itself."[52] You could argue further that the most genuine Western literature of the first half or so of the century was nature writing, a kind, largely essayistic, concerned with exactly such portrayals. Ancient in its pedigree, nature writing in America was birthed by Thoreau and others in the East and given its Western booster shots by Muir. He, along with Mary Austin and John C. Van Dyke, represents, in Lyon's judgment, "the flowering of the post-frontier vision." It was a basically ecological vision that began with "the opening of perception to a specific environment" and led to "a critique of civilization."[53] Muir contributed to it through books like *The Mountains of California* (1894) and *Our National Parks* (1901), Austin through *The Land of Little Rain* (1903), and Van Dyke through *Nature for Its Own Sake* (1898) and *The Desert: Further Studies in Natural Appearances* (1901). But others also had a hand in that flowering. Coloradan Enos Mills did, with books like *Wild Life on the Rockies* (1909). Aldo Leopold, a writer, like Muir and Austin, with a Midwestern background, certainly did, with *A Sand County Almanac* (1949). So did the Texas writers whom McMurtry refers to as "the Big Three"—Roy Bedichek, Walter Prescott Webb, and J. Frank Dobie—who "revered Nature, studied Nature, hued to Nature" in books like Bedichek's *Adventures with a Texas Naturalist* (1947), Webb's *The Great Plains* (1931), and Dobie's *The Voice of the Coyote* (1949).[54] So did Joseph Wood Krutch, a New Yorker and then a New Englander who in his later years moved to Arizona to pursue a love affair with the Sonoran Desert and wrote *The Desert Year* (1952), *The Voice of the Desert* (1954), and other books that professed his view—which echoed the views of his precursors above—of humankind and other animals as, in Lyon's ascription, "an aspect of a great, overall, interpenetrating system."[55] So did Texan John Graves in *Goodbye to a River* (1960), his elegy for a section of the Brazos slated for damming.

Lyon detects a repeating theme in the work of such writers: "the apparent need for civilized man, when confronting the wild, to develop clearer ways of seeing and a clearer consciousness in general."[56] To articulate that need was, in Glen A. Love's words, "to risk the contemptuous epithet, nature-lover." For most of those writers, however, as for later ones, nature-loving meant not just protective appreciation but responding fully to "the tug of eco-consciousness as a corrective to ego-consciousness."[57] That required their striving to do—and to help readers do—what Lyon sees as Muir's bold stroke: "to transcend the frontier mentality and its dualistic frame of reference" that separated the human self from nature. They thereby wrote "within the world of discourse he legitimatized."[58] It was a regionalist world in which they tried to mend that breach by the cultural act of writing about the natural.[59] To the extent that they succeeded, they laid the groundwork for their postmodern progeny, who would practice that paradoxical art in more sophisticated, more importunate, and more politicized ways.

Meanwhile, less back at the ranch than in urban universities—some Western, some not—historians, even disciples of Frederick Jackson Turner (himself more a regionalist than he was once thought to be) such as Herbert Eugene Bolton, Frederic Logan Paxson, Robert E. Riegel, and, later, Ray Allen Billington, were writing more-region-oriented narratives, ever pulling away from the frontier-oriented romanticism exemplified by Theodore Roosevelt's four-volume epic *The Winning of the West* (1889–96). Historians firmly and experientially regionalist in approach, such as Webb and James C. Malin (as exemplified by *The Grassland of North America: Prolegomena to Its History* [1947]), wrote more in the grain of predecessors such as Josiah Royce and Hubert Howe Bancroft, both of whom had written Pacific-centered histories in the late nineteenth century. Those historians were expounding history that concerns foremost, in Donald Worster's words, "an evolving human ecology" and were motivated by a desire to know "how a people or peoples acquired a place and, then, how they perceived and tried to make use of it."[60] They were assembling a regional image of the West, and through it they too were trying to mend breaches—between myth and reality, natural past and technological present. While not always as gloomy as disillusioning Royce had been in narrating the aftermath of conquest in his *California, from the Conquest in 1846 to the Second Vigilance Committee in San Francisco: A Study of American Character* (1886), they weren't as Darwinistically confident about Manifest Destiny as Bancroft had been. Their image of the West, especially when you include ex-Utahan DeVoto in their troupe, was more tragic than comic, more realistic than romantic, more wised up than ebullient; their West was rife with dilemmas.

By the late 1950s and 1960s, historiography of the evolving human ecology of the West was telling an increasingly more complicated story of how the region had been acquired, perceived, and used. Historians such as Earl Pomeroy and Howard R. Lamar were casting a cold analytical eye on exceptionalist notions of the West as a region, setting the stage for studies of the West as an urban, global postregion.[61] In addition, a new generation of literary historians was investigating how Americans had laminated a mythic and symbolic West onto a geographical and political one. It was a topic of central importance in Texas-born Henry Nash Smith's *Virgin Land* but also of no small moment in other studies revamping ideas put in motion by Turner and by Vernon L. Parrington in his three-volume opus, *Main Currents in American Thought: An Interpretation of American Literature from the Beginnings to 1920* (1927–30)—studies like R. W. B. Lewis's *The American Adam* (1955) and Leo Marx's *The Machine in the Garden: Technology and the Pastoral Ideal in America* (1964). Such studies illustrate the persistence of frontier-oriented approaches to Western historiography even as the regional era was closing. Although they had moved beyond what Kerwin Lee Klein terms the "Dantean comedy" by which Turner had "emplotted the European occupation of Native America as the building of a modern democracy from wild nature," they owed much to that precursory tale of the opposition of wilderness and civilization "as the dominant conflict, contradiction, or dialectic of American culture." The democracy they examined may have "looked more shadowy and tragic," but their conception of the frontier that figured in its building was at bottom Euro-American.[62] In the late 1960s and early 1970s, that conception, as we'll see later, would begin to undergo, to use one of Klein's favorite words, peripety.

While frontier-oriented visual artists pretended to representational realism but tended not to honor the actual West, their region-oriented counterparts, realists or otherwise, generally imaged a West derived from empirical experience. They eschewed the aesthetic of illustrations on the covers of dime novels and Western adventure magazines that, in William H. Goetzmann and William N. Goetzmann's phrasing, kept the myth of the West "in ascendance" while the Wild West was "on the wane"—an aesthetic that's debunked, in their example, by a Norman Rockwell cover for a 1930 issue of the *Saturday Evening Post* that shows Gary Cooper having his lips colored by a makeup man on the set of Daniel Nathan Rufin's *The Texan*, a vignette, a parable of etherealization, in which "the tough cowboy has been reduced to a meek actor."[63] Those artists also rejected the artifice of studio paintings that offered postfrontier Americans what Nancy K. Anderson construes as "assurance that the West could endure as both iconic symbol and economic resource . . . by suggesting that the natural sublimity of the land and the technological achievements of man could harmoniously coexist."[64] Unlike Frederic Remington, as Nemerov speaks of him, region-oriented artists didn't see "the very process of painting—the act of applying pigments to a flat surface—as perhaps the most fundamental obstacle to a realistic retrieval of the past,"[65] for they were interested more in veracity of expression than in the illusionary authenticity of frontier-oriented painting.

What Patricia Janis Broder says of the constitutive twentieth-century paintings that "give a new dimension to the art of the American West" may well be said of region-oriented artworks of the first half of the century: they "have two basic sets of roots—the realist vision and the modernist vision." The distinction is helpful in differentiating those artworks from romantic frontier-oriented ones, but it's not conclusive—Charles M. Russell's oil *The Roundup #2* (circa 1913), a fairly literal, if somewhat impressionistic, study of the daily chores of cowpunchers, certainly exemplifies the former vision (as do some of his bronzes), but so do many of the modernist Western paintings by Georgia O'Keeffe, whom Broder defensibly classifies as "a visionary realist." Fussing aside, however, regionalists of either persuasion interpreted the West with fresh eyes. The modernists typically came from the East, with Eastern or European ideas, and artistically discovered the West. For them it provided "a faraway nearby" that evoked an assortment of unwonted responses. Artists such as O'Keeffe and Marsden Hartley, for instance, didn't paint warmaking Indians and rowdy cowboys but "the specifics" of New Mexico, through their expression of which "'the West' is elevated to a metaphor for universal concerns: Life, Death, and Natural Force." Those artists and others—such as Robert Henri, John Sloan, John Marin, and Edward Hopper—gave their attention to a particular place, mostly the Taos–Santa Fe area, and "strove to express in their work the multidimensional world that is the twentieth-century West." Usually from the West or Midwest, the realists—artists such as Thomas Hart Benton, John Steuart Curry, and Peter Hurd—"tried to depict the world they experienced as individuals," a less intellectual project.[66] It mirrored their belief, as Etulain summarizes it, "that their paintings must emerge from the physical and cultural environment they knew best rather than from European or eastern American trends."[67]

The paintings of the realists may not have *emerged* from those trends—impressionism, fauvism, surrealism, and so forth—but many of them show the influence of such trends. Consider, for instance, Benton's 1928 painting *Boomtown*, a wry presentation of the West Texas oil town of Borger as a business beehive where automotive modernity meets and pollutes a big sky punctuated by derricks and power-line poles, what Etulain terms "a cultural oxymoron, a regionalizing Wild West"—done in an El Greco-like expressionistic style.[68] Or look at Californian Maynard Dixon's *Desert Southwest* (1944), a painting in which the land's beauty is rendered into geometric planes and cubist abstraction. Moreover, the modernists didn't completely renounce realism, as already noted in the case of O'Keeffe—and as can be seen in paintings such as Hopper's *Western Motel* (1957) and *People in the Sun* (1960), studio works but ones much indebted to the artist's trips to the West, both antiromantic snapshots in which urban figures seem as detached from blank landscapes and skyscapes as they are from the austerely linear civilized surroundings in which they sit.

Nor was the frontier as a historical subject flatly taboo among region-oriented artists. Walter Ufer, a Kentuckian who happened upon the glories of the Taos area in 1914, painted a lone covered wagon moving through a spacious, picturesque, but vaguely ominous demesne of sagebrush, crevices, and shadowing thunderclouds in his *Where the Desert Meets the Mountain* (circa 1922). And Benton did a number of El Greco–like paintings of frontier scenes featuring Indians, buffalo, forts, even Custer's Last Stand, as well as *Lewis and Clark at Eagle Creek* (1967), which reduces the men coming ashore to tiny dabs within an expanse of weirdly calm fauve and quasi-surreal wilderness.

Such artists may tax art-historical distinctions, but all of them were committed to re-imagining the natural and cultural West in perspectives afforded by an era both acceleratingly transitional and radically indeterminate, quite unlike the one any of their grandparents had known.

Tripping the Light Dialectic: More Modern Mediations

The celluloid West . . . offers equestrian dash and characters of ruthless and exuberant individualism to a population bedraggled by mechanical routine and befuddled by complex economic and domestic changes. . . . That is why the celluloid image becomes more and more vivid as the historical actuality gets dimmer.
    Marshall McLuhan, *The Mechanical Bride: Folklore of Industrial Man*

Highbrow art in the decades after 1900 dealt with the West as a region, but lowbrow art, in the form of radio, film, and television Westerns, generally did not. Its setting, its bread-and-butter theme, was the frontier, a never-ending place nevertheless always about to end, and it kept the corollary myth of the West, tweaked from time to time, emphatically in ascendance—at least until the 1960s.

During the 1930s, 1940s, and 1950s, radio Westerns supported that ascendance. Early programs, such as *The Lone Ranger*, written primarily for children, offered frontier romance unmodified by any acknowledgment of a changing West—even in the case of *Tom Mix*, which was set on an updated twentieth-century frontier. Throughout their programs Gene Autry and Roy Rogers sang songs that celebrated an unreal aural West that was dangerous but also clean and safe. Later radio Westerns, written to capture an adult audience, flirted with realism and grappled some with the knotty issues of the wild-tame dialectic. On *Gunsmoke*, for instance, as Michael T. Marsden and Jack Nachbar recall, "Matt Dillon worried about killing, about whether the fragile civilization represented by Dodge City would hold up against all the attacks, and about whether he could continue to serve as the man who stood between civilization and the savage wilderness day after lonesome day." Still, I agree with them that radio was never more than "a proving ground for variations in the Western formula which were to be more completely developed on television and film."[1] It was predominantly through those media, especially film and film adapted to television, with their smooth simulation, that the modern redaction of the mythic West, an ethereal territory of denatured wilderness, became deeply installed in the American psyche and ubiquitously institutionalized in American culture.

Motion was the key to such simulation. That point is made nicely in Guy Vanderhaeghe's 1996 novel *The Englishman's Boy*, a postmodern narrative about 1920s Hollywood's translation of the Western past into its own idealized (and profitable) present terms, during a conversation between a young screenwriter named Harry Vincent, one of the story's principals, and Damon Ira Chance, the reclusive mogul who owns Best Chance Pictures and has just spoken of the "spiritual Americanism" that he believes had its genesis with D. W. Griffith's 1915 film *The Birth of a Nation*:

> "And what is this spiritual Americanism, Mr. Chance?"
>
> "Perhaps it can't be defined in words, Harry. Pictures come closest to capturing its meaning. . . . for years I was troubled by the question, Why have the American people produced no great art? . . . We recognize the soul of a people in their art. But where is the American soul? I asked myself. Then it dawned on me. . . . The American spirit is a frontier spirit, restless, impatient of constraint. . . . What the American spirit required was an art form of forward momentum. . . . A *westering* art form! It had to wait for motion pictures. The art form of *motion*!"
>
> "I see," I say.[2]

At least the gist of Chance's insight must be true, for millions of people in the decades to come did hungrily *see* thousands of examples of an art form that seemed quintessentially American, a high percentage of them Westerns. Indeed, starting with the first Western shoot-'em-up, Edwin S. Porter's *The Great Train Robbery* (1903), the marriage of moving film and mythic West was made in cinema heaven.

It was thoroughly coded with the ambiguities of the wild-tame dialectic, and until the 1960s it was based well-nigh entirely on nostalgic romance, formulaic or quasi-historical, that ignored regional tragedy. The latter assertion is congruous with certain of Robert G. Athearn's arguments concerning a genre perfected in its fundamental imagery long before that watershed: that it was consummate escapism, that its protagonist's riding on west at the end "provided an important safety valve for his vicarious companions in the audience" and "helped to preserve the old belief that the wilderness was still offering a superior way of life," and that those companions avidly took in the diet on the screen, as multitudes still do, "because they need[ed] it."[3]

Students of mass media justly stress their extraordinary power as technologies that forge and purvey myths. Rita Parks observes, with respect to twentieth-century makers of Western myth, that they had "tools at their disposal for fabricating legends that reach beyond the wildest dreams of the early chroniclers, story-tellers, and dime novelists."[4] For several decades, the most powerful tool those mythmakers had was film, and with it they fabricated legends in terms of a variety of plots. The number of those plots depends on the classificatory method invoked, but every plot pigeonhole, whether defined by theme (justice or revenge, say) or by motivation (the need to put down Indians or clean up a corrupt town, say) or by some other factor, implicates the wild-tame dialectic.[5]

The plot taxonomy most relevant to my purpose here is Will Wright's. He constructs what he calls "a cognitive theory of myth structure" and then employs that theory to study the top-grossing Western films from four historical periods, stretching from 1930 to 1970, with attention to the social meanings preponderant in each period. The first period, which lasts until around 1955, is dominated by "the classical plot," which "revolves around a lone gunfighter hero who saves the town, or the farmers, from the gamblers, or the ranchers." The second, which overlaps some with the first and lasts, for the most part, until around 1960, is distinguished by "the vengeance variation," a plot that "concerns an ill-used hero who can find no justice in society and therefore becomes a gunfighter seeking vengeance." The third, which, Wright explains, "is more logical than temporal," is characterized by "the transition theme," a plot, anticipatory of fourth-period films, that "centers on a hero and a heroine who, while defending justice, are rejected by society." And the fourth, which lasts from 1958 until 1970, is marked by "the professional plot," which "involves a group of heroes who are professional fighters taking jobs for money." Wright evinces through examples the symbolic structures of these plots, extends his theory to analyze "how the narrative structure of a myth provides a social and conceptual *explanation* to ordinary events," and then relates "the structural meanings of each Western plot to the concepts and attitudes implicit in the structure of American institutions."[6]

That's a tall order, and the extent to which Wright fills it may be questionable; but his detailed analyses of and conclusions about the play of oppositions in films that exemplify each type of plot cogently illustrate the changing function of the wild-tame dialectic in narratives that mediate—and thus both reflect and constitute—much of the modern American experience of the West, a region many still imagined as a frontier. Let me flesh out that argument.

The classical plot sets the foundation of the genre. Wright's examples include Michael Curtiz's Dodge City (1939), Jacques Tourneur's Canyon Passage (1946), and George Stevens's Shane (1953). The characters usually seem unambiguous, as do three of what Wright distinguishes as the four basic structurally important oppositions that determine them: those inside society and those outside, the good and the bad, and the strong and the weak. The fourth opposition, which contrasts the hero with the rest of the characters, "is perhaps the typically American aspect of the Western—the opposition between wilderness and civilization." And it admits an unconcealed ambiguity: "The villains may be outside of society but are always seen as part of civilization." It's the opposition Wright singles out, and in discussing it he offers a clarification: "The difference between this opposition and the inside society/outside society distinction will become clear if by society we mean having roots, an occupation, and responsibilities, while by civilization we mean a concern with the money, tools, and products of American culture. The Indians become an easy test, for, as in [Delmer Daves's] Broken Arrow [1950], they would typically be inside society (their own) but outside of civilization."[7] For some reason, though, he doesn't pursue the implications of that second statement, and the pursuit might have led him to uncover more of the complexities accruing to the wild-tame dialectic during the regional era that historians of human ecology were investigating and postmodern Western films would find hard to avoid—indeed, would take on.

Such pursuit also might have caused Wright to rethink his contention that "the wilderness/civilization contrast is not as central as the other oppositions, and it is sometimes, though rarely, only vaguely present or missing altogether."[8] That is to say, he might have granted more exegetic efficacy to Jim Kitses's schematization of binary oppositions in Westerns, which he dismisses since he believes it can't account for the popularity of the genre's myth. If he had granted it such efficacy, he might have discerned that that opposition, interpreted broadly, may sometimes be only vaguely present but is never missing altogether in the Western, classical or otherwise, and figures foremost in the appeal of the genre. That's because it subsumes not only Wright's other oppositions but also, as Kitses argues, whole rosters of them under the subheadings of individual and community, nature and culture, and West and East. How conscious the audience of the Western was—and is—of that multifaceted appeal is a moot question, but it has been there all along, textured by a tension arising from what Kitses terms "an ambiguous cluster of meanings and attitudes that provide the traditional thematic structure of the genre" and whose "shifting ideological play can be described through a series of antinomies" linked to his master antinomy of wilderness and civilization. The factors paired in those antinomies instrumented the ostinato dialectic of the American psyche, and what imbues the genre with "a particular thrust and centrality is . . . its being placed at exactly that moment when options are still open, the dream of a primitivistic individualism, the ambivalence of at once beneficent and threatening horizons, still tenable."[9]

Nonetheless, Wright's taxonomy does avail a useful framework here, in part because he finally doesn't play down the wilderness–civilization opposition as much as he suggests he will. In fact, he speaks to the potent audience appeal of the dream of a primitivistic individualism in the classical Western when he stresses that the significance of that opposition resides in how it functions to separate the hero, the only character endowed with both strength and rectitude, from everyone else—because "he is associated with the wilderness, while all other characters . . . are associated with civilization." That logic is accurate as far as it goes and may well justify Wright's speculation that some impressive Westerns, such as William Wyler's The Big Country (1958), have failed financially because they committed the mythological sin of having the hero be "an eastern dude."[10] But it neglects the paradox that the classical hero ultimately advances civilization, and it ignores subtleties (such as Shane's psychological self-division, preserved in transferring Jack Schaefer's novel to film) that render ambiguous the hero's association with wilderness.

The vengeance variation derives from the classical plot but rearranges the characters' coding in terms of Wright's basic oppositions: "Unlike the classical hero who *joins* the society because of his strength and their weakness, the vengeance hero *leaves* the society because of his strength and their weakness." This plot thereby indicates a downhill change in the hero's relationship to society and its values that will continue through the subsequent plots' periods. Wright's main examples are John Ford's *Stagecoach* (1939), Anthony Mann's *The Man from Laramie* (1955), Marlon Brando's *One-eyed Jacks* (1961), and Henry Hathaway's *Nevada Smith* (1966). The wilderness–civilization opposition, he notes, is as prominent here as it is in the classical plot, with the optical presence of Monument Valley and the Monterey coast identifying, respectively, the Ringo Kid in Ford's film and Rio in Brando's with the wilderness. Such heroes, intent on revenge, may not succeed in avoiding society, but its image is different: "No longer is it primarily concerned with churches, schools, and progress; now the image stresses the ideas of forgiveness, marriage, and a peaceful, respectable future."[11]

The transition theme pushes the rearrangement of the characters' coding until the classical plot is reversed: "The hero is inside society at the start and outside society at the end." Wright finds only three solid examples: *Broken Arrow*, Fred Zinnemann's *High Noon* (1952), and Nicholas Ray's *Johnny Guitar* (1954). The wilderness–civilization opposition appears most remarkably in the third, a psychologically tortuous film in which the townspeople are the villains with whom not a lone hero but a heroic duo, a gunfighter named Johnny Guitar and a woman named Vienna who runs a saloon, must struggle. That opposition, intermittent through most of the story, is written all over the scenes that conclude it, the most striking being the one that occurs after the climactic fight to save a beautiful hidden valley the townspeople want to destroy by silver mining: "Johnny and Vienna, all alone, emerge from under the waterfall [the secret entrance to the valley], . . . having been purified by the water and forests of nature and baptized into a new life and strength apart from the viciousness of society." Noteworthy here, on the eve of the (markedly feminist) postmodern period in American culture and the postregional era in the West, is the way the female lead, like those in *Broken Arrow* and *High Noon*, "joins and supports the hero's separation from civilization," becoming a genuine heroine and not merely, as in the classical plot, a symbol of social goodness.[12]

Ironic variations on the transition theme turned up later in the century (in Kevin Costner's *Dances with Wolves* [1990], for instance, or Ridley Scott's *Thelma & Louise* [1991]), but it faded for a while, succeeded by the professional plot, which then ruled the genre until 1970 or so (and also turned up later, its most ironic variation being Clint Eastwood's *Unforgiven* [1992]). In this plot, society is relevant only as "an excuse for fighting," for, as Wright says, "the fight itself generates the values that replace the values of society in the myth." Conspicuous examples are Howard Hawks's *Rio Bravo* (1959), Richard Brooks's *The Professionals* (1966), Sam Peckinpah's *The Wild Bunch* (1969), and George Roy Hill's *Butch Cassidy and the Sundance Kid* (1969). The wilderness–civilization opposition recedes in structural salience in some of the professional-plot Westerns—*Rio Bravo*, for instance—but in others, such as *The Professionals* and *The Wild Bunch*, it's vivid in characters' coding. In Hill's film, Western wilderness, Wright notes, seems to have a special cultural status: "Butch and Sundance are exquisitely filmed against broad expanses of western scenery, in contrast to the townspeople, the Bolivians, and even Etta [Place]. Significantly, when they all go to Bolivia, though it is mostly jungles and forests, there is no visual sense of wilderness—of wide open land and freedom—as if, while other places may be wild, only the American West has meaningful wilderness."[13] That at a time when many Americans felt distanced from their nation's values and yet tried to redefine themselves by the most traditional American gesture: heading into the natural West to seek a new, bootstrapped lifestyle.

Looking back on the modern period, Wright shares germane reflections on the myth embodied in Western films, but they ask qualification and amplification. First of all, he emphasizes that, though history can use the past to explain the present, myths use it "to tell us how to act in the present." A signal consequence of America's decades-long engagement with Western films was the encouragement of a longing, on which many Americans acted, to visit, literally (through travel) and symbolically (through clothing, for instance), the Wild West (or what remained of it naturally and culturally) in order to confirm values being subverted by modern civilization. Such literal and symbolic pilgrimages involved the idea that Western land was an American tradition; that tradition, however, was founded less on the actual West than on the myth of the West, and its meanings are contained in the Western—specifically, in its hero, "the man who accepts the wilderness, believes in it, and communes with it" and thus "is stronger than civilization and capable of making it into something worthwhile." The puissance of that myth is that, through images structured by binary oppositions, it "can reconcile, or at least make understandable, the conceptual contradictions" in the culture that clings to it, but there's a tricky turnout to its operation, an etherealization, maybe explanatory or reconciliatory but also illusional and trammeling, to which Wright gives insufficient attention: "To the extent that the myth succeeds in making the past like the present, it also makes the present like the myth of the past."[14] To be like the myth of the past is to be dematerialized to some similar extent, and by the 1960s the myth of the Western past had succeeded in making the present West into something too much like that myth itself: a nearly seamless phantasm that was, as long as it would hold together, precariously disconnected from the reality of the place.

Moreover, as Kitses implied earlier, problems, ones not addressed adequately by Wright, reside in the myth itself. It wasn't brought down from some cinematic Mount Sinai, of course: it's America's own creature, full of as many questions as explanations, as many irreconcilables as reconciliations—though it took a while for that to become clear. "There always had been a fuzziness in the western fictional formula," Athearn observes—largely because of the hero's alienation not only from the middle landscape of the ranch but from the very civilization, in the form of new towns and their institutions, that Westerns before the 1960s tended to celebrate.[15] Parks sees that hero as near-tragic by virtue of his alienation from both rocky openness and infant town; he is, she says, "almost always a man with one foot in the wilderness and the other in civilization, . . . belonging to neither world."[16] Thomas Schatz grants that, if the Western is seen as serving to help the public cope with its transition from a rural-agrarian to an urban-industrial age, "the diverging depictions of the hero and the community seem altogether logical"; but he sees uncertainty in that divergence as it's narratively animated by "the governing civilization-savagery opposition" (typified not only in the conflict of hero and community but also in that of schoolmarm and dance-hall girl and so on). The actions of other characters (such as "the philosophical inebriate") often reveal in them some of the hero's ambivalence. Even when the crises in which they're ensnarled are resolved, there remains, he says, a "fundamental and not altogether obvious sense of ambiguity." In the epilogue to Stagecoach, for instance, as the Ringo Kid and the whore Dallas ride off to Mexico, Doc Boone, "ever the cultural commentator, muses to the sheriff: 'Well they're saved from the blessings of civilization'"—the defective social order the exiled hero has salvaged by violence. Schatz is correct in claiming that "many (perhaps most) classical westerns did not play out this ambivalence in terms of plot resolution,"[17] but some late-modern and many (perhaps most) postmodern Westerns would—full tilt. In them the formulaic seams that superficially darned deep conflicts would be pulled open, the dubious artifices of the myth exposed and ironized, so that, as John G. Cawelti avers, "the ritualistic affirmation of progress and success becomes more and more ambiguous and strained."[18] The time would come when no amount of ideological tuning could convincingly adapt an inconsistent myth ill suited to history; by then, even if we still entreated Shane to come back, we'd find it a stretch to imagine why he would want to.

By then we recognized in earlier Western films one of the issues in whose dramatization there's a legacy Joy S. Kasson attributes to Buffalo Bill Cody: "Americans' love-hate relationship with unspoiled nature and native peoples."[19] We knew, as Robert F. Berkhofer Jr. recalls for us, that "no matter how important the Indian might be to the Western plot and genre, he usually served in the end as the backdrop rather than the center of attention, for to do otherwise would have discarded simplicity for complexity."[20]

By then we could see that those dated movies betray curious gender ambiguities about the characters' relation to wildness. Blake Allmendinger points out, for instance, that, "although they exhibit some 'macho' tendencies," heroes in the Western "are actually more dandified and effeminate than most other characters"—whereas the villain "has an unregenerate status that codes him as 'masculine.'"[21] We understood why Roy Rogers had to get shut of his real name, Leonard Slye. And we noticed that women in the Western have a contradictory role, which David Daly and Joel Persky parse as follows: they are both peripheral (by acting only as spurs to the hero) and central (by being associated with his goal), aspects complicated by the fact that they "are symbols of the cultural values men must defend but, at the same time, . . . symbolic of societal encroachments on the natural male world."[22] Moreover, we finally picked up on a quirk that Jon Tuska states baldly: the Western's sweet civilizers, "if they are heroines, must endorse violence and even be willing to become violent themselves."[23]

By then we knew in a more knowing way what we'd really known long before: that the Western, as Czeslaw Milosz assays the genre, had "passed entirely into fable, formalizing its own motifs, arranging them in nearly algebraic equations"; that its soothing myths of dexterous killing show us nothing of the foul wildness of the West—"the wound which might fester for weeks on end, the fever, the stink of the sweat-drenched body, the bed of filthy rags, the urine, the excrement."[24] We wondered if Americans who had lived through the Dust Bowl (and the Depression and World War II) didn't want to bear too much reality and needed such cleaned-up idealization even more than those who had lived through the end of the frontier and died well before the Wild West shows did. Still, we sympathized with debunking

Westerners like New Mexico rancher Cleofes Vigil who, as Stan Steiner quotes him, told an assemblage of Hollywood types at the 1981 Western Film Festival in Santa Fe that "'Western movies are a bunch of lies.'" But we postmoderns, accustomed to the etherealized West, weren't surprised that as reactionary a celebrity as Charlton Heston, in Steiner's account, was quoted as saying, "Since there is no 'truth' about the West, what is the responsibility of the filmmaker to tell the 'truth'?"[25]

By then we had assented to Christian Metz's aperçu that "the classic Western was already self-parodying."[26] Lightly, in general, as in Ford's *My Darling Clementine* (1946), Metz's example, but heavy-handedly at times, as in a Tom Mix film made in 1915 that William H. Goetzmann and William N. Goetzmann describe:

> It was called *Bill Haywood, Producer.* It was the story of a cowboy who assembles his "pardners" and their lady friends and attempts to make a movie. In pure slapstick fashion the scenery collapses all around them, horses charge right through false-front buildings, riders tumble in a heap and get into a fight, the camera blows up, and finally the "cowboys" decide moviemaking is too dangerous, so they will all go back to cowboying.[27]

Thus the fate of actors whom Vanderhaeghe labels "refugees from a vanishing West":[28] in a controlled illusion of a controlled illusion crumbling into chaotic reality, they depart the parody of an illusion for what is already one of a reality.

By then we could read the cinematic land "cowboys" always ride back to when they leave the town (or set). For them, as for their audience, it isn't what Mexicans once bewailed as *el territorio perdido*, land lost to Manifest Destiny, but what Spanish-dubbed Westerns have taught that it is: *el viejo oeste*, which Jesús Martínez-Saldaña adumbrates as "a site inhabited by fictitious blond-haired, blue-eyed cowboys."[29] It doesn't belong to Mexicans or Indians or outlaws. Those cowboys might be creating a progressive society, but they ride away from it into land that also doesn't belong to women (as Lee Clark Mitchell reminds us, the Western "defines its landscape *as* 'Western' by the absence of those familiar signs encoded as somehow female").[30] They leave the town (and "a tense accommodation to society") for open range (and "a relaxed association with nature"), which is the undomesticated space of their usual filmic origin, since, as Philip French remarks of Westerns, "there are relatively few movies which do not begin with the single man or group of men riding through the countryside."[31] Even if the story supposedly is set in Kansas, that countryside is apt to look craggier than Kansas; typically it's desert, "the landscape of death" ridden by a hero whose hardness Jane Tompkins sees as continuous with its own and for whom it's the be-all and end-all: "He courts it, struggles with it, defies it, conquers it, and lies down with it at night." The horse between him and the earth on which he rides may "express a need for connection to nature, to the wild," for repairing some rupture with life, but it also "reinforces the image of mastery that a man on horseback represents," the vertical separateness of domination.[32]

Ambivalences: those of the hero but also those of the filmmaker and the audience. Yet it's just a make-believe land—or is it?

By then we were well acquainted with that hero, that icon apparently engendered by an iconic land in which he sought death, life, mastery. He was several—and one, maybe Gary Cooper, whose Western persona Stephen Tatum describes as "ultimately defining a paradoxical combination of opposing traits" in movies with "focus on the triumph of civilization over savagery."[33] But, when the dust cleared, really the one was John Wayne, a dream man invented by Ford (as the Ringo Kid in *Stagecoach*) from the raw material of a young actor named Marion Morrison. In film after film, treading his own dark wild within, he choreographically trod the dark wild without, becoming, in films like Ford's *Rio Grande* (1950), the bold-striding personification of both Manifest Destiny and Cold War American imperialism. Even today, decades after his death, he's the most popular Western hero of all time.

Why? Perhaps because "John Wayne" was and is also the peerless personification of the modern wild-tame dialectic, with all its instabilities, of the increasingly self-conscious etherealized West. Garry Wills, one of his biographers, surely unveils him as such. The man on the screen was, Wills says, "nothing but image." He was "a man from nowhere . . . riding into Never-Never Land." In Raoul Walsh's *The Big Trail* (1930), before he became a Ford star, he played a scout who articulates both "a nature mysticism" and "an imperial justification for the westward expansion." The Monument Valley that Ford gave him as the stage for his stardom "is as much an idea as an actuality." In Howard Hawks's *Red River* (1948) he acquired the "ability to convey control and menace." In Ford's *The Searchers* (1956), a warped captivity narrative, his Ethan Edwards ends up a tragic hero who symbolizes "the West that is no longer ours." In *The Alamo* (1960), which he directed, he played Davy Crockett as both starry-eyed congressman and rough but sensitive frontiersman—a double figure that mirrored his self-imaging, "the way he 'put on' his cowboy persona," so that his Crockett turns into "Wayne philosophizing about his own Wayneness." Two years later, in Ford's *The Man Who Shot Liberty Valance*, he played Tom Doniphon, a gunfighter who helps clear the way for the modern West and then is buried in a pauper's coffin as a symbol of a violent past—though in George Sherman's *Big Jake* (1971) he returned and in his final movies, Stuart Millar's *Rooster Cogburn* (1975) and Don Siegel's *The Shootist* (1976), reprised the oxymoronic role he had long since perfected, the "kindly killer." Concluding his study of Wayne, Wills asks whether he is "the most dangerous man in America" or "the American Adam." He replies with the answer he has pieced together: "He is both. He is the former *because* he is the latter. He reflects our society back upon itself, which is the source of his appeal, and of his danger. It is a mixed and terrifying image, full of the unresolved contradictions in our own ideal country."[34] All the more so in our own ideal West.

By then we understood that Ford, the supreme etherealizer of the region, the directorial tripper of the light dialectic, also was full of unresolved contradictions.

When he looked through the camera's finder to check a shot, what that Maine-born "Irishman" saw was a West he had made, in Wills's phrase, "his mythical homeland."[35] That sounds like a simple enough vision; but, because of who Ford was culturally and where he was and when he was there, it was complicated, and, since all of that changed during dramatically changeful decades, it got more complicated.

In *Stagecoach*, James K. Folsom notes, the landscape initially appears to be empty and safe; but then the camera reveals Indians, and they bespeak "the profound duality of nature itself."[36] Moreover, the perilous wilderness in the film is less accented than enclosed social space, especially that of the stagecoach, a result A. Carl Bredahl Jr. attributes to Ford's symbolistic responsiveness to the international political situation in 1939, his readiness to perceive "the West as a place to test and hone the values of civilization"—about which, ironically, as the film's epilogue attests, Ford was skeptical.[37]

Peter Wollen may be right, up to a point, that the structural play of oppositions (European versus Indian, book versus gun, and the like) that recur in Ford's films are relatively obvious in *My Darling Clementine*, with the hero, Wyatt Earp (Henry Fonda), making "an uncomplicated passage . . . from the wilderness left in the past to the garden anticipated in the future";[38] but when Earp rides on at the end, though he may have rescued Tombstone from savage forces, there remain "conflicts and contradictions . . . within American civilization" and "within Ford himself," the strain of which, as Ronald L. Davis shows, the film mirrors.[39]

In *Fort Apache* (1948), *She Wore a Yellow Ribbon* (1949), and *Rio Grande*, which comprise Ford's cavalry trilogy, white society's problems, Bredahl observes, "are ultimately greater threats than the external savages," and in the second film wilderness is present "more for its beauty than for its danger."[40] Davis notices, in addition, that the Indians in *Fort Apache* "are seen through sympathetic eyes"—more evidence that "Ford's best work is rife with tension, paradox, and contradiction."[41]

Such evidence mounts in *The Searchers*. Ethan Edwards is a deeply ambiguous figure, tangled inside with antinomies: a nomadic white loner who, as Bredahl describes him, is a relic of the past, "an intense and bitter man who becomes like the savages he hunts" as a defender of the homesteaders (and their values of marriage, family, home)—in a film in which "we are presented simultaneously with extremes of the land's beauty and with the central figure's hatred of the people who inhabit that land."[42] There's something very late-modern about this film; it has to do precisely with Edwards and the beautiful Monument Valley through which he searches for a white girl (his niece, whom he appears equally capable of rescuing or killing) captured by Comanches—and with American culture at the time. In a study of its landscape, Richard Hutson explains that "what makes *The Searchers* a film of the 1950s is Ford's insistence . . . that his narrative is the legend of the West, not the experience of the West." Americans of that decade surely sensed that the frontier had been mythicized all along, but they, like Ford, believed in the importance of myths for coherently purposing the nation's future in relation to its past. "Such self-conscious intentions," Hutson argues, "carried with them the strong possibility of disavowal," and, indeed, the film's plot, "with its disturbed and unattractive hero and its theatricalized landscape, carries an immediate disavowal: This narrative . . . could never have taken place, but even so."[43] There we have a preview of the postmodern Western to come, a more and more self-consciously mythic and mythopoeic genre, with more ingenious (even demythologizing) disavowals, through which to tell ever-more ironic stories of America's etherealized wild.

Ford's *The Man Who Shot Liberty Valance* is interlaced with irony to a still greater degree. "According to the film," in Donald Worster's terse construal, "the story of the West is one of turning nature into artifact. As the leading female character says near the end, looking from a railroad car window onto the improved scene,'It was once a wilderness, now it's a garden.'"[44] He's right, of course, and the many interior and somewhat claustrophobic scenes, along with the absence of the director's signature panoramas of Monument Valley, harbinger that transformation; but such summary doesn't do justice to the intricacy of Ford's treatment of it. Mitchell suggests the ubiquity of that intricacy by noticing how "the film's ironic tone works at every level to complicate the relation between history and myth that lies at the heart of the Western—at once confirming yet subverting the assertion by the newspaper editor, Maxwell Scott: 'When the legend becomes fact, print the legend.'" Through this double perspective Ford "insists upon both the 'fact' *and* the 'legend,' viewing them as mutually sustaining interpretive gestures rather than one as a misreading of the other."[45] Because of that perspective we puzzle out the conclusion, with Bredahl, that the film, a late-modern Western shot in black and white, is "about the death of the western, as Ford imagined that story." Because of it we feel the ambiguity in Hallie Stoddard's line Worster quoted, for what she says can digest comic myth or tragic history—or the tragicomic romance that bridges the two. And because of it we understand that Ford's Euro-American imagination has an ambivalent take on the Western wild: while it's attracted to all the superlative qualities there, it's also "committed to enclosing and reshaping wilderness in order to make it safe for young women, families, and Shakespeare."[46]

In Ford's final Western, *Cheyenne Autumn*, released in 1964, such ambivalence is further complicated—though perhaps facilely resolved—by a pattern of reversals. Whereas in his earlier films the quest for a Western home involved white settlers moving into the future, in this film Indians journey in search of the home they had in the past. In the depiction of their trek, Kitses argues, there's a transposition resonant with the rise of radical politics during the 1960s: "The Indians of *Drums along the Mohawk* [1939] and *Stagecoach*, devilish marauders that threaten the hardy pioneers, suffer a sea-change as Ford's hopes [for America's promised land, the garden of the West, his own homeland of myths] wane, until with *Cheyenne Autumn* they are a civilized, tragic people at the mercy of a savage community." With this film, the Ford of formulaic revisions has become a kind of guilt-ridden regionalist, as Kitses may suggest in his epitaphic summing-up: "As Ford grows older the American dream sours, and we are left with nostalgia for the Desert."[47]

By then we had experienced, in 1975, what Marsden and Nachbar dub "the first Westernless television season," closing twenty-five years of the video audience's satisfying, finally to satiety, its appetite for Western series. Initially the networks had aired shows, like *Have Gun Will Travel*, in which the heroes were loners, but the most successful were those, beginning in the mid-1950s, with families or family-like groups as "a collective hero"—a new formulaic approach that lent the shows a certain realism, even regionalism, and fit the cultural disposition of the time. *Gunsmoke*, the prototype, and other such ensemble shows—*Wagon Train, Bonanza, The Big Valley*, and so on—"created tiny communities of love and cooperation that were able to withstand the ravages of frontier savagery." But that small-screen, family-evening edition of the wild-tame dialectic would stop selling in the wake of the Vietnam War, Watergate, and other events that brought a stint of national self-doubt, the wrong mood for a story that "was traditionally a narrative confirming America's worthiness to venture onward."[48] Such doubt, however, wouldn't really slow us down.

By then we had been told by media-mancer Marshall McLuhan that, to paraphrase one of his famous dicta, postindustrial America was venturing onward, faster and faster, while looking in the rearview mirror. And what was in the mirror? The past, mostly, despite any televisional dips, the Western past. Well, not so much the historical Western past as simulacra that, as Richard Misrach explains Jean Baudrillard's use of the word, "so thoroughly mediated" our perception of the West "that we no longer have a genuine primary experience" of it. What we saw in the mirror was pictures "of white, rugged cowboys roaming vast open places or the uninhabited landscape spectacles of Monument Valley, Death Valley, or the Grand Canyon." Fixated on that etherealized, hyperreal wild, we little heeded what we were pell-mell venturing into, the West "of irrigation projects gone amuck, plutonium-contaminated landscapes, chemical-weapons storage dumps, forty acres of grapefruit trees on fire, tens of thousands of swimming pools, and millions of people."[49]

Derricks, Dams, Bombs, and Such: A Walk on the Dark Side of the West

They swooped low over spectacular canyons, wild and untouched. Caught up in the mission of the bureaucrats who remade the West, Josephy shouted above the

At the end of this phase we reach a point of demonic epiphany, where we see or glimpse the undisplaced demonic vision, the vision of the Inferno.
Northrop Frye, *Anatomy of Criticism: Four Essays*

Peggy Simson Curry ends her poem "Old Cowboy" with a quatrain in which her subject speaks his mind on the modern technology of extraction in the West:

They come for coal, he says,
put oilwells in the pastures—
I ain't ready yet to see
the sandhill cranes move camp.[1]

Not all of his feather felt the same way in the first decades of the twentieth century, when coal and oil production west of the Mississippi went into a frenzy. Some cowboys, old or young, and a lot of other Westerners joined in the frenzy. Many felt ambivalent, of course: they hated to see pastures hollowed out or defiled into crude-soaked, mechanized barrens. But the profits were persuasive. Besides, Westerners had for some time been intoxicated by the power of technical wizardry, from wind wagons to repeating weapons. In any case, though railroad monopolies would limit coal production in the West to about a fourth of that in the nation, oil production there skyrocketed, soon accounting for over three-fourths of that in the nation. By the late 1920s, Richard White tells us, "a motorist could drive through 150 miles of West Texas without losing sight of oil derricks, and the biggest discoveries were yet to come."[2]

The vehicle that motorist drove had everything to do with all the drilling witnessed then, with the oil boom that would follow World War II, and with the glooming of urban air in the West. Also, in retrospect you can make out a curious homology, both structural and functional, about those derricks: each looks fairly like the tower of a windmill; like a buttress on one of the reinforced-concrete multiple-arch dams engineer John S. Eastwood built all over California and other Western states in the early decades of the century; like a lattice-work electrical tower; like the shot tower at Trinity Site north-northwest of Alamogordo, New Mexico, that supported a plutonium bomb detonated on July 16, 1945; maybe, to come further forward in time, even like the gantry (later, silo) for a rocket loaded with the offspring of that bomb. All those strutted structures astride Western land once promised much through technological regnancy over nature—abundant energy, water, military might, money—but what got delivered was thoroughly alloyed with tragedy and irony, the wages of hubris.

Just after the turn of the century, there was nothing new about the idea of dams in the West, most of which was water-poor, rendered so, to begin with, by the saw-toothed Sierra Nevada raking eastbound maritime clouds out of the sky. After all, as Donald Worster reminds us, John Wesley Powell, whatever his ambivalence about it, had "sketched a future in which . . . every kind of dam would allow control over nature—a new hydraulic civilization."[3] What was new was the crazy pace at which, the scale on which, America, thoughtless of any comprehensive hydrology, was endeavoring to actualize Powell's Western future. It's true that in 1913, the year legislation to stopper the Hetch Hetchy Valley with a dam was passed, "many Americans were no longer so sure" about what Roderick Nash calls their "conquering posture" toward Western nature and its wild rivers,[4] but that didn't brake the indefatigable Eastwood, who was well along with designs for over sixty dams, their functions ranging from hydroelectric power to flood control, between 1906 and 1924—most of them constructed in adherence to his fiat that, as Donald C. Jackson puts it, "all flow in California's rivers be impounded in reservoirs" (thus formalizing "a critical aspect of the West's 'second nature,'" in Cronon's phrase).[5] In 1936 the pharaonic Boulder Dam (renamed for Herbert Hoover in 1947) on the Colorado River was completed, its example as a provider of urban water, hydroelectric power, flood control, and rural irrigation inspiring a pandemic madness of damming that was most dramatic from the late 1940s through the 1960s. Over that time the Bureau of Reclamation (BR), which was established as the Reclamation Service in 1902, then renamed in 1923, engaged, with Cold War fervor, in what Richard White calls "the race to dam the West," girding the Rockies with dams and adding "more than a dam a year to the Columbia and its tributaries," among other such feats; indeed, for that influential nationalistic bureau, "building dams was all that mattered."[6] Between 1930 and 1980 the federal government was responsible for building over a thousand dams in the United States, most of them—including monsters like the Shasta, Bonneville, Grand Coulee, Glen Canyon, and Hungry Horse—in the West.[7]

During the New Deal, explains Bruce Babbitt, secretary of the interior in the Clinton administration, the Tennessee Valley Authority "became the model for Western lands," and the BR then and subsequently played the role of "the Western TVA." In that role, acting with oblivious urgency, the bureau "geared up development programs that would eventually run amok."[8] In need of a scarce and vital resource, the West engineered an unprecedented "hydraulic empire"—but one created, as Worster informs us, by "a policy of technological domination instead of accommodation toward nature"—with ecological hell to pay.[9] For all the good it did, the damming of the West was in many ways, as Edward Abbey used to say, the damning of the West. A little instancing will validate his judgment.

Some years ago I flew to Las Vegas for a conference. As the plane approached McCarran International Airport, it soared over Lake Mead (what Abbey called Lake Merde), that city's main source of water. I peered south at Hoover Dam. The old man seated next to me, who'd been silent since our departure from Kansas City, suddenly talked—at length. The height of the dam was almost two-thirds that of the Empire State Building. Its concrete was still curing. He'd helped construct it. So many human lives depended on the water it controlled and the electricity it generated. He loved the blue-green jewel of the lake behind it. But fellow workers had been killed in accidents. And he missed the beauty of the canyon that had once been where the lake now stretched. He despised what Las Vegas had turned into. He guessed that every blessing had its drawbacks. On that note, we landed.

Hoover Dam, the supreme symbol of the Western New Deal, was five years in the making. Joseph E. Stevens dubs it "the great pyramid of the American West, fount for a twentieth-century oasis civilization." He's a positivist who recalls a 1980 tour of the facility during which he was filled with amazement at its turbines and transformers, at how such a massive yet high-precision device could have been erected in such an inaccessible place. He lauds it as the product of a time "when taming a wild river was a heroic endeavor"—an icon that "offered powerful reassurance, tangible affirmation that the American dream of limitless possibility still lived." It changed Westerners' image of the region and heralded economic independence of the East—independence to be achieved by means of water-guzzling agriculture like that in California's Imperial Valley and electricity-powered defense and aerospace industries that helped win World War II and emboldened American strategies on the Cold War chessboard. At the flip of a switch: thousands of acre-feet of water, millions of kilowatt-hours of current—all a tribute to "man's skill in bending the forces of nature to his purpose." The flooding of the Colorado in 1983 damaged, through cavitation, the diversion tunnels of the Glen Canyon Dam, completed in 1963, but those of the Hoover Dam held up well—a felicity that moves Stevens to declare that "with proper maintenance the dam's life should be indefinite."[10] At long last, so believed many in 1936 and for decades thereafter, the West was becoming a technologized garden . . . indefinitely.

While Hoover Dam wasn't as literally an anthropomorphic reshaping of the Western wild as the presidential heads sculptor Gutzon Borglum was carving on the face of Mount Rushmore in the 1930s, it nonetheless was a gesture that represented the same thing that, according to Simon Schama, those heads, when finished in 1941, would symbolize: "the ultimate colonization of nature by culture, the alteration of landscape to manscape."[11] Even without dwelling on the irony of "ultimate," however, it's clear that that alteration has, in Worster's words, "the makings for an unrivaled study in the modern domination of nature and its consequences." The inundation of the Black Canyon behind the dam spelled doom for a lot of wildlife, and it submersed Anasazi ruins. It underwrote the overpopulation of the Southern California coast and started Las Vegas down the road to being a bursting-at-the-joints boomtown. It set the stage for a necklace of other dams on the Colorado that would mute the grandeur that was once its flow and keep it from reaching the sea. Worster criticizes Stevens's swooning about Hoover Dam because it leaves significant questions unasked, particularly those regarding the buildup of salinity that's making the contained water unfit for use. And, of course, Stevens ignores a long-term threat present from the time of the ceremony of dedication: the river, with the pressure of water and accumulating silt, is "gathering force to remove this new obstruction just as it has removed everything else ever put in its way." Finishing his lesson about Western hubris, Worster warns, "Do what we will, the Colorado will one day find an unimpeded way to the sea."[12]

Similar Stevensian eulogy or Worsterian augury has been written about other dams in the West. Some may praise the technological sublimity of, say, the 710-foot Glen Canyon Dam, upriver from the Hoover, that impounds the water of Lake Powell, but those who look with a discriminating eye see something darker than its bright monumentality. Katie Lee condemns it as "the most hated blob of cement and steel ever constructed." Why? Because, among other reasons, Lake Powell, which fills a once-splendid valley, is overused for recreational boating and has stagnated into an engine-polluted sump where human waste occasions bacterial alerts. "Small wonder," she says, "that the place has acquired some unflattering names: Utah's Urinal. The Rotting Rez. Loch Latrine." Lake Foul in Abbeyspeak. Moreover, in the years since the completion of the dam, the river corridor of the Grand Canyon also has come to a sad state—sandy beaches and their flora have been washed away, and the cold water released through the dam from the lake's depths has killed a lot of fish. Like Worster, Lee laments such effects but prophesies, both bleakly and jubilantly, "the return of a free-flowing Colorado River."[13] Recent attempts to restore the Grand Canyon's aquatic and riparian ecosystems by calculated sediment-rich deluges may be of modest help in reversing damage to the natural environment; nothing on the horizon, though, will prevent the disaster, sooner or later, of a naturally dismantled human contrivance.[14]

Such contrivances, once raised by tragic hubris in a mood of lingering romanticism but now being slowly razed, constitute a deeply mixed legacy. Jackson counsels that "there is good reason to be concerned about the long-term environmental consequences of the West's dam-based hydraulic infrastructure."[15] Often I read in the newspapers that American Rivers, the Sierra Club, or some other organization wanting dams breached or removed registers dismay at what they have done and are doing to Western rivers and their biota, but it's no news. The word has been out awhile.

In 1982 Roderick Nash reckoned that, for the present, America "appears at ease with the balance between wilderness and civilization struck on the Colorado River. Parts of it 'work'; parts flow wild and free." The values associated with the two modes may have seemed to be in a placid equilibrium, but he observed, all the same, that "the legitimate ambivalence American culture feels between wilderness and civilization is quite accurately expressed in the present pattern of resource use on the Colorado."[16]

In 1985 Worster told us of dam-born expedients such as California's Friant-Kern Canal that irrigates, at the rate of several thousand cubic feet per second, the dry land around Bakersfield and indirectly induces the disorder of a social wilderness. He told us of big dams that had collapsed—the St. Francis, north of Los Angeles, in 1928; the Teton, in southeastern Idaho, in 1976; others in the interim. Concerning our prodigal expenditure of impounded Western water, he cited ancient wisdom: "The old Incas used to say, 'The frog does not drink up the pond in which he lives.'"[17]

Two years later, Wallace Stegner wrote of Westerners' failure to adapt to their place: "Instead of listening to the silence, we have shouted into the void. We have tried to make the arid West into what it was never meant to be and cannot remain, the Garden of the World and the home of multiple millions." He excoriated the BR for having as its aim, since it was first established, "not the preservation but the re-making—in effect the mining—of the West." He reminded us of the consequences of trying to master rivers with dams—of how both natural lives and human standards are destroyed therewith, of how reservoir water alkalizes an irrigated field, and the like. He mused upon the decline of the West's hydraulic empire, and he confessed his yearning for a past of free-running rivers when "the West provided for its thin population a hard living but a wonderful life."[18]

Although in the 1980s Bruce Berger had written of the ironies of so-called reclamation, of the ambiguous half-century history of the Coolidge Dam (on the Gila River in southeastern Arizona), and of how "it is unlikely we will see heroic new wedges of concrete,"[19] in the 1990s Timothy Egan discovered that politicos in the Sacramento Valley were planning to resume construction on a dam on the American River that had earlier been halted by fear of earthquakes—because the people there wanted "one last time to hold nature at bay, one last time to let new houses rise in a valley prone to epic floods, one last chance for California to start anew."[20]

An awakening Rx for such politicos might be a parable from William Kittredge that concerns an epiphany he had at the Fort Peck Dam in northeastern Montana. In the museum there he encountered the skull of a triceratops, and then he noticed that "just beyond through soundproof windows, in a metallic powerhouse control room, a man sat watching banks of motionless dials." For all who have imposed so many metaphors of alienated command on Western nature (and their literalizations in the form of dams and other regulating structures), that juxtaposition delivers exactly what he says it does: "the perfect metaphor, our interwoven biological past sealed off from the shadowless future."[21]

Be that as it may, dams enabled the modern militarization of the West that began after the Japanese attack on Pearl Harbor and foretold a regional future of shadowless technology portending deep shadows indeed. Western liabilities were reevaluated during World War II, White declares: "Vast distances, low population density, and arid climate had seemed detriments to economic development. Now remoteness, isolation, and a climate that allowed people to work outdoors much of the time became major assets as military planners scrambled to locate new military bases"—a scrambling that brought ten bases to Utah alone by 1942, shifted the center of martial gravity definitively westward, and created new dependencies on the federal government, among other effects.[22]

Other effects. Meditating on the meaning of Trinity Site, located in the northern part of the desert the conquistadors named the Jornada del Muerto (Dead Man's Trail), just west of the Sierra Oscura, Stan Steiner describes some of those effects and gets at yet others. The scene of the first atomic blast, where more jets than birds now fly overhead, seems "like a landscape of the moon after a nuclear interplanetary war." The gadget that made that lunar barren had been assembled a hundred and fifty miles north of Trinity, at Los Alamos, in laboratories built on land holy to the Jemez. Those laboratories situated in the vulcanian geology of the Jemez Mountains now are consolidated as the Los Alamos National Laboratory and devoted to a number of projects, but their focus remains what it was during World War II: the technology of nuclear weapons. Thus Los Alamos retains vestiges of what it was then: a community that in its combination of rugged individualism (of a scientific sort) in a semiwilderness and federal fosterage "was indeed a modern re-creation of the paradox of the frontier." Robert Oppenheimer, who directed the effort to build the weapon that would bring the Japanese to their knees, had long been a frequent visitor to the area, but most of the scientists there, Easterners and continental Europeans, "shared a sense of unreality about the West." The power they played with implied, in Steiner's retrospect that's also prospect, a taming not just of Asian otherness: "The nature of the West was both a temptation and an obstacle that challenged human society. At times, it seemed fit only for wild animals. And so the raw, elemental life in the West required the might of military arms to conquer it, whether by bow and arrow or the atom bomb."[23]

The bomb proved to be an economic boon. With it, as Steiner largely bemoans, "the Sunbelt was born and the Rocky Mountain boom began."[24] More people, technical personnel and others, moved west, southwest, coastward. After the war, atomic-bomb production slowed for a year or so, then picked up. Tests were few—until the Russians set off their first nuclear explosion in 1949. Until then the United States' postwar site of choice for testing had been the South Seas, but that arrangement, as David Thomson explains, "was expensive and problematic," what with shipping equipment, building bases, relocating natives. Also, American development of the hydrogen bomb was well along. A viable test site was an immediate necessity. Those whom Thomson calls the "decision makers," more or less acknowledging the dangers involved, "looked at the odds: They sought isolation for a test site, which was advantageous on grounds of security as much as safety. But didn't they also dip into that traditional and still-active American mythology that the American West is relatively 'empty,' that it matters less?" Besides, Nevada was already cursed by the sordidness of gambling, and the downwinders would be mostly Mormons, marginal religionists "famous for their obedience to, and acceptance of, authority." In 1950 President Harry S. Truman signed the papers: "Nevada was chosen. And it is still America's favorite dead ground."[25] A sunbaked province that again and again would host the bursts of man-made suns.

In the 1950s and 1960s the West was a militarized zone extraordinaire, the frequent experiments with seismic-level firecrackers justified by Cold War tension, paranoia, dread of a nationwide mushroom-cloud conflagration, courtesy of the Russians or maybe, after 1964, the Chinese. Fallout fell everywhere finally, its effects unknown, uncertain, or known and denied. Low-budget science-fiction films, lots of them plotted like Westerns, featured freakish mutant creatures, the fruits of atomic goings-on gone wrong, emerging from some Sonoran or Mojave nowhere. Las Vegas held a Miss Atom beauty pageant. Communists, allegorized as extraterrestrials in other science-fiction films, were the new Indians, intent on taking over a nation best represented by the West that Americans were busy blowing up and irradiating. Laguna land was mined for ore to make yellowcake. In 1957 a hydrogen bomb was accidentally dropped from a B-36 into Albuquerque; fortunately, only the chemical trigger charge went off.[26] And the clinching image of bonkers 1960s Wild Western militarism turned up near the end of Stanley Kubrick's 1964 film Dr. Strangelove; or, How I Learned to Stop Worrying and Love the Bomb: Slim Pickens broncrides an H-bomb dropped from the bay of an incommunicado B-52 over Russia, waving his cowboy hat and yeeeeehaaahing all the way down.

Richard Rhodes offers a terse wrap-up on the decision in 1942 that Los Alamos would be the site for the Manhattan Project: "'My two great loves are physics and desert country,' Robert Oppenheimer had written a friend once; 'it's a pity they can't be combined.' Now they would be."[27] But the combination, with either nuclear or nonnuclear physics, wouldn't be an entirely happy one for that country, its wildlife, its people. Many areas in the West, as Richard Misrach says of the U.S. Navy bombing range in Nevada named Bravo 20, whose damage he has photographically recorded, would be "transformed from pure desert wilderness to the post-apocalyptic landscape of a Mad Max scenario."[28] Such places, usually playas, would become the contested settings of frightening terminal dramas, in William Stafford's words, "for little selves / at the flute end of consequences."[29] They would be the mise-en-scènes of the military sorcerer's apprentices' covered-up screw-ups, toxic perditions, pits brimful with the pustulated carcasses of cattle and sheep. All manner of ordnance would degrade them, expediently even if by understandably desperate motives, into a generic cratered Golgotha where, as Gary Short's poem on Bravo 20 has it, "The skeleton of a mustang, dreaming its run, / rises slowly back out of the dust."[30]

But the cost of nuclear physics would be the highest. Especially to people. To get an idea, read Terry Tempest Williams's *Refuge: An Unnatural History of Family and Place*, Carole Gallagher's *American Ground Zero: The Secret Nuclear War*, or Teri Hein's *Atomic Farmgirl: The Betrayal of Chief Qualchan, the Appaloosa, and Me*. Or study the nuclear map of a West multiply nuked—by explosions, groundwater contaminated with radioactive mill tailings, ash from fallout, on and on—in the *Atlas of the New West*.[31] Or have a look for yourself at the test sites (not only in New Mexico and Nevada but Colorado as well), uranium mines all over the Rockies, the Idaho National Engineering and Environmental Laboratory, the Hanford Nuclear Reservation in Washington, the China Lake Naval Air Weapons Station in California—and know we've all been downwinders ever since that detonation in 1945 at which the witnesses were, in Reg Saner's phrasing, "taken by surprise, stunned witless through long, elliptical seconds of animal fear."[32]

After 1945 the West as oil field, dammed reservoir, military and industrial laboratory, graveyard for technological mistakes, dump for the wastes from progress, all that ugliness, was the price exacted by the devil's bargain of Western "growth." Americans paid it in the most plentiful coin of the realm: environment as open and unspoiled as they had left. But those seconds of fear at Trinity marked the start of a countermovement as well. The fireball illuminated more with its candlepower than the faces of mountains, lizards, and scientists: "For the first time," in Berger's assessment of the bomb's significance, "nature as final arbiter" was seen as "nature as fragility—fragility summed up by a single image" from a decade yet to come, one made possible by defense technology associated with the West and announcing the postmodern globalization of the region, of all regions: "the photograph of our planet from space."[33] By the end of the 1960s, many hoped that ecological stewardship, inspired by that Fabergé-like image of the round resplendence and vulnerability of all known life, would take the lead in its Western pas de deux with dangerous development.

Alas, that hope was specious. The fear of annihilation by Russia's H-bomb arsenal subsided with the waning of the Cold War, but it was succeeded in the 1990s and early 2000s by the fear of terrorist attacks that could be biological, nuclear, God knows what; must be defended against; might necessitate an all-out military response. So what you still find along Interstate 25 between Las Cruces, New Mexico, and Buffalo, Wyoming, "the Nuclear Highway" that passes about a degree of longitude west of Trinity Site, is the cordilleran armature of an ambiguous West that Tad Bartimus and Scott McCartney describe as "built up by the machines of war yet touched by an aura of serenity. Here, Star Wars . . . is taking shape in secret laboratories. Here, nuclear warheads are designed and deployed. Here, surrounded by one of the most beautiful and yet unforgiving landscapes on earth, beats the heart of the work that could save the world . . . or destroy it." War and serenity, a dream of implausible control in the dimming brain of a movie-star president, a beautiful but unforgiving landscape, salvation and destruction—it all sounds familiar. It puts us on notice that, as Bartimus and McCartney conclude, "we are all Trinity's Children now."[34] And it suggests that nature, from subatomic infinitesimals to airless space, will be the final arbiter after all.

Perhaps the most important research under Oppenheimer's direction at Los Alamos during the charette to make an atomic bomb was that done by the Critical Assemblies group in a laboratory at a removed canyon site named Omega. There scientists led by the German physicist Otto Frisch repeatedly performed an experiment to determine the critical mass of fissionable material (uranium 235 and, later, plutonium) needed for an explosive chain reaction. It involved the terribly risky procedure of bringing together, for only a fraction of a second, varying quantities of such material and measuring the energy output of what amounted to an incipient nuclear blast. Everything depended on timing, ensuring that the reaction wouldn't be sustained. There were close calls, nasty exposures to radiation. In 1946, after the race against time was over, one colleague, cavalierly making a game of that procedure, showered himself with neutrons and took nine torturous days to die. Others endured more amortized agonies. The experiment was known as "tickling the dragon's tail."[35] In the West, in our many risky dealings with nature—nuking the landscape, of course, but also pumping oil deposits and aquifers dry, harvesting forests wholesale, poisoning the wind, holding polluted rivers behind deteriorating dams, constructing high-rises near fault lines—we're still tickling the dragon's tail.

Sprawling into Western Emptiness:
The Metropolitan Frontier,
Suburban Borderlands, Misbegotten
Middle Landscapes

The civilization that erects barriers between man and nature can lead only to alienation and unhappiness.
    David Brooks, *Bobos in Paradise: The New Upper Class and How They Got There*

Let's start with figures and facts. First, some historical perspective from Roderick Nash: "In 1830 only one out of every fifteen Americans lived in a city of over 8,000 inhabitants. In 1900 it was one in every three. Ten years later approximately half the population was urban." Americans, he notes, "responded ambivalently to this basic environmental change. On the one hand, cities were the seats of intellect and refinement. They also seemed to many a new frontier—replete with opportunities. But on the debit side, cities were thought to spawn social disorder, immorality, and an indifference to the virtues of nature."[1] That ambivalence was intense in the West; so was the opening across the region of that urban frontier.

Growth in urban population in the West was dramatic in the late nineteenth century, and California exceeded Nash's average for 1910. It would decelerate during the 1930s, except for Southern California and oil-rich subregions, but it was rapid from the 1940s until the 1970s, let off some in the 1980s, then speeded up again in the 1990s. Indeed, the post-1940 surge of Western urban population, which more than doubled between 1940 and 1960 and again between 1960 and 1990, has come to be perceived, most notably by Carl Abbott, as an event defining, occurring on, and expanding not an urban but a *metropolitan* frontier. "One out of every four Americans now lives in a Western metropolitan area, up from one out of eleven in 1940," with more than 80 percent of Westerners now living in those areas, the rest about evenly divided between lesser burgs and what Abbott calls "the 'real West' of farms, ranches, lonely desert gas stations, and railroad hamlets clustered around the gray columns of grain elevators." Since a smaller percentage of people in other regions of the United States live in metropolitan areas, the West's "most important contradiction" is quite apparent: "the nation's most open and empty region is also its most heavily urbanized."[2]

That remarkable citification, largely an economic phenomenon spurred by dam building, World War II industrialization, and subsequent development, created a regional and then a postregional West whose inhabitants, as a rule, were and are out of touch with anything like the natural wild. The extent to which the regional West converted its emptiness into metropolitan areas, its outdoors into indoors, was recorded in nighttime satellite photos decades ago; recent such photos show those dozens of areas glowing noticeably broader and brighter. They may well be what they were from the beginning, "islands in the big empty," as Charles Wilkinson describes them; but they were islands that grew, spreading into and colonizing the hinterlands until they deepened the "urban-rural conflict" and became "painful places even to think about, much less go to, what with all the noise and rush and pollution."[3]

A century before World War II, Western cities served as enclaves of Eastern civilization bordered by less civilized surroundings. People from elsewhere came to dwell in them. But in the 1900s, following a migration pattern repeated in other countries worldwide, more and more Westerners too moved into them, leaving their farms and ranches for jobs in confining circumstances. The results were mixed: wealth for some, middle-class financial security for some, poverty for some, congestion and stretched infrastructure for all—painful places with trade-off advantages, if you lived in the right part of town.

Why were there ever cities in the first place? At the most basic level they have to do with the millennia-old drive William L. Fox finds symbolized in an earthwork by Nevada sculptor Mike Heizer titled City: "to signify human order impressed upon chaos, consciousness over the void."[4] At a higher level, they have to do with protecting human order as civilization from its opposite. Thus, according to Frederick Turner, the evolution, from encampments through villages and then through towns, of ancient Near Eastern cities "nurtured the belief that 'civilization' meant the walled, blocked, and grain-stocked city." The city of peoples such as the Sumerians therefore was "a kind of barricaded, fortified oasis. . . . What was within the walls, within the reaches of the irrigation ditches, was nature subdued, controlled, put to proper use; what was beyond, whether land, people, or spirits, was savage, unpredictable, malevolent."[5] In Hayden White's summary, the Greek, like the Judaic, translation of that dichotomy, which we have inherited, "set . . . the order (cosmos) of the city over against the turbulence (chaos) of the countryside."[6] To set that order was to construct a cityscape, which comes about, by John R. Stilgoe's definition (which distinguishes it from landscape, a combination of "natural and man-made form"), when people "wholly dominate the land, when they shroud it almost completely with structure and chiseled space."[7] From Sumerian stronghold to American megalopolis, the double object of the cityscape has been to exclude or minimize raw nature and to provide an extended haven for culture—and its transactions, economic and otherwise.

Yet that has always been an idealization, the emanation of a mind-set adherent to what Gretel Ehrlich terms "our rigid conception of interior versus exterior," a conception she finds questionable:

> Isn't there a commingling everywhere? We breathe air into our bodies and exhale again. . . . And aren't there wild birds in big American cities? Still we equate "inside" with a static sort of security, a maintenance dose of control, a solid defense against the commotions of nature, against the plurality of ourselves. Outside has come to signify everything that is not "us"—everything inimical.
>
> But space is not a stable entity.[8]

That last apothegm would turn out to be unusually true of the Western city, a place where the connections between inside and outside would be shot through with elasticity.

As historians of the West as a region came to acknowledge, its history since the middle of the nineteenth century has been, in many ways, paramountly that of its cities. Cities were foci of progress. They meant schools, churches, banks, material goods, comforts, conveniences. They meant safety and profits from commercial (typically more than manufacturing) enterprises. They meant, much through the efforts of increasing numbers of women, the formation of communities out of concentrated populations, men for the most part, dwelling in boomtown squalor.[9] As Metropolis, the conventional name of American cities as a collectivity, moved west, it made Western life less primitive, more complex, just as Frederick Jackson Turner said. It gendered much of the cultural West feminine (metro- derives from the Greek mētēr, "mother") and subjected it to Euro-American law (police derives from the Greek polis). It gradually assimilated ethnic otherness (Asians in San Francisco, Indians in Albuquerque, Hispanics in Denver). For a while Western cities tended to imitate their Eastern counterparts,[10] but that changed, especially after 1940, in the main because, as Abbott explains, those cities, which came to initiate trends rather than follow tradition, have had "a special relationship with wide open spaces." Such spaces have encouraged the flourishing of industries such as aerospace and tourism and, except for the California coast, have averted the densely compressed urbanization of cities in the East. "Western city people," Abbott observes, "prefer to construct widely spread and open cityscapes. They presume that direct and immediate contact with the outdoors is their due."[11] Such preference and presumption shouldn't be surprising in a populace steeped in an ideology according to which, as Richard Slotkin formulates it, "the direction of expansion is always progressive, and proceeds from the Metropolis outward," so that each successive new frontier, once it's conquered, "becomes a Metropolis, and as such the base for a new and deeper foray into the Wilderness"—an ideology through which, by mythological adaptation, "industrialization and the growth of cities constituted an internal equivalent to the Frontier of expansion at the borders."[12] That story, revised standard version.

The actual history isn't, of course, that smooth and positive. Roger W. Lotchin advises that making the urban past of the West intelligible requires "a complex vista, one sensitive to the contradictory, paradoxical, and ironic," one that takes into account, in his primary example, the fact that Western cities—the largest founded by the 1890s—"have been both conservative and revolutionary, settling and unsettling."[13] In Western eyes they have always been ambiguous blessings. Many people moved into them in the regional era and ballyhooed their benefits, but many, rural Westerners as well as new urbanites, hated and feared them; many did all those things at once.

Whatever the advantages of cities, modern Westerners tended to think of them as anthills where people, crowded together, descended, like rats jammed in a cage, into the behavioral sink. Indians resisted being hustled into them. Luther Standing Bear knew they hardened hearts. Frank Waters despised them as cancers. Little wonder that the appreciation of wild nature took root among their inhabitants or that, as Richard White reminds us, in the early twentieth century, in the West as in the East, "back-to-the-land movements and utopian colonies both operated on the assumption that cities and industrialization did harm and that the countryside and agriculture healed."[14] Western cities may have been envisioned as nerve centers of progress triumphing over rural backwardness, but that envisioning was at odds with frontier mythology vitally surviving beyond its time that, in Slotkin's well-hammered theme, "implied the existence of two geographical poles: the Metropolis, with a predominantly negative character (else why should we leave it?); and the wilderness Frontier, necessarily with a rich endowment of good things to appeal so strongly to us."[15]

The myth-tangled history of the Western city may be read as a late stage in the devolution of the city as an affirmative idea. Drawing on various sources, Garry Wills ponders the implications of a determinative datum: "Other cultures begin with a fixed and social hearth, a temple, a holy city. American life begins when that enclosure is escaped." We never really built Winthrop's City upon a Hill, let alone our Paris or Rome. We were headed elsewhere. We wanted to depart, not arrive. Thus with the national identity crisis precipitated by the closing of the frontier came an anxiousness about anomic imprisonment: "We would become all City, after being all Frontier." It was a traditional American anxiousness rising to a fever. As Wills remarks, an "anti-city note sounds throughout our history," and it was now sounding loudly.[16] But never before more loudly than it did throughout the regional history of the modern West. And the volume hasn't decreased since. As Daniel Kemmis wrote in the early 1990s, when he was mayor of Missoula, a town worried about suburbanization, "no one has been as good as Westerners at making cities feel unwelcome on the land."[17]

Such observations lead to the conclusion that many modern Westerners viewed their burgeoning cities as artificial wildernesses, places, especially in their dilapidated recesses, of savagery—more of a cultural than of a natural kind. To some extent that attitude is understandable just because, as White notes, "at the turn of the century the urban West, like the urban areas of the nation as a whole, had consisted of unruly, unplanned, and chaotic cities."[18] Several factors had contributed to that situation, among them, for example, the post-1873 business contraction that threw multiplying city-dwellers out of employment and led to what Slotkin describes as "an explosive and unplanned urbanization that produced appalling conditions of housing and public health."[19] Westerners were making mean streets as readily as overtilled fields, overgrazed ranges, overrun parks. As the twentieth century wore on, the tragedy of cities became received irony; by contrast, the countryside, if not the further wild, looked more civilized.[20] While the natural environment seemingly became more managed, the cultural environment undeniably became less manageable. By the century's end, most Western cities of any size, their development fecklessly administered from the get-go, would be sumps of pollution inured to crumbling architecture, drive-by gun violence, and gang rape referred to as "wilding."

To be sure, that view of the city had a signal psychological (and, implicitly, ideological) dimension that must be taken into account. Andrew Light traces it to an intriguing durability: "as the romantic idea of wilderness gradually came to replace the classical idea and Euro-Americans found that nature was no longer an evil place, the classical idea still persisted in some rather unusual areas"—urban ones. That happened by a transference: since culture had expanded in its control of nature, the "cognitive wilderness" was projected onto the less civilized aspects of the city.[21] Corroboratively, Nash observes that in 1890s America "many of the repugnant connotations of wilderness were transferred to the new urban environment"—a process that continued until in time it resulted in an evaluative reversal through which cities "acquired some of the old terror once reserved for the wild" and the wild was seen as "a peaceful sanctuary."[22] That reversal created a moral setting for film-noir gumshoe movies about the urban frontier, as well as for more literal urban Westerns such as John Schlesinger's Midnight Cowboy (1969) and Don Siegel's Dirty Harry (1971) and the 1970s television series McCloud, and figured significantly in the heightening of ecological awareness of the wild that began in the 1960s.

The savage city imaged by that reversal wasn't, of course, peculiar to the cultural West, but it was ideologically more sharply defined in that context, just as its physical counterpart stood out more distinctly in all that more recently colonized openness than it did in long-since-urbanized parts of the nation. The sharpness had to do with urban–rural conflict.

Such conflict wasn't new. Keith Thomas notes that by the eighteenth century England was well acquainted with "a genuine tension between the relentless progress of urbanization and the rural longing to which an increasing number of people were subject."[23] Nor were the American East and South strangers to that tension. But it was extreme in the West, where the wild-tame dialectic was everywhere writ large. Many a denizen of Western hinterlands in the early twentieth century would have sympathized with the antipathy to cities expressed by Rick Bass, who lives in Montana's Yaak Valley: "I understand they are necessary and serve good and all that stuff. I also understand I can't live in one."[24] Contrariwise, many a city-dweller of that time, however nostalgic about what Zeese Papanikolas terms the "strange and often threatening hinterlands" of Kansas that L. Frank Baum wrote about in The Wonderful Wizard of Oz (1900), would have endorsed the Emerald City of the West as a "benign metropolis" offering "regeneration" of a sort.[25] By the time World War II began, there were obviously two demographic Wests, at odds—very complexly so.

During the war and afterwards, corporate and federal dollars "brought stability and prosperity to a region whose economy had previously soared and swooped like a badly handled kite," as White puts it; but there was a tab to pay, for all the attendant bureaucratization and cityward migration more than ever intertwined the two Wests in an unbalanced relationship, with "one mostly rural and largely powerless, and the other largely metropolitan and increasingly powerful."[26] It was a relationship in which collisions of interests would intensify through and after the 1960s and become ensnarled with oppositions—between developers and environmentalists, Eastern bureaucrats and Western individualists, capital-propelled growth and neglected local needs, on and on.[27] It was a relationship by which cities, evolved from railroad and river towns and coastal ports, profoundly and even tragically, in William G. Robbins's phrasing, "conditioned life in the countryside." But it was also a relationship that was "symbiotic," a fact evidenced in the extent to which, even though metropolitan areas called the shots in everyday matters, throughout those areas "a powerful rural mythology" dating back to the beginnings of American history held sway in molding "public consciousness."[28]

These two Wests therefore were—and remain—intertwined not only on the geographical, economic, and political levels but on the personal level as well. Abbott finds the Americans Tocqueville thought of as being pulled by two opposed impulses, one toward the wildness of intense individualism and the other toward the tameness of "enthusiastic association in the pursuit of common interests," still alive and well in the West. "Like Tocqueville's Cincinnatians of 1831," he says, "the Denverites and San Franciscans of the 1990s are caught in the permanent tension about how best to be American."[29] So are the rustics. Though the rural West feels some rancor toward the urban West and beer-guzzling outbackers with rifle racks in their pickups often don't cotton to latte-sipping city slickers on mountain bikes or skis, Gundars Rudzitis argues that the polarization has been "carried to extremes" in the media, that urban and rural people share conflicted views of wildlands management and related issues.[30] This mutual internalization of the two Wests clarifies why what Lotchin calls the "rural-urban relationship of love, hate, tension, cooperation and interdependence" has been reciprocal, all the more now, in the postregional era, when cities "have comprehensively interpenetrated nature to the extent of breaking down the dichotomy of the two," with the result that, "instead of living in city or country, most people now live in metropolitan areas tied together in myriad ways."[31]

Those Westerners live in city-country syntheses, a third West where the twain have met. Borderlands of a kind, decentralized, of uncertain "nature," clustered with houses both ticky tacky and quasi-palatial and often surrounded by too-green grass. Yardscapes where the etherealized wild is so commodified that it's possible to hear on the radio, as I did recently in Kansas, that "spring is on sale at the Suburban Lawn and Garden Center." In other words, those Westerners live in, precisely, suburbia—or whatever it's turning into.

Like the urban–rural conflict, suburbia isn't new. As Stilgoe explains, the word *suburb* once "denoted inhabited land immediately below hilltop walled towns," a literally inferior place whose ancient and medieval residents longed for annexation into the protective enclosure above them. Now, however, that situation has changed; suburbs have come to mean "the good life, the life of the dream" that inspires urban dwellers "to get out of cities they perceive as chaotic, inimical to childhood joy, unnaturally paced, incredibly polluted, and just too crowded." Whatever their present variegations, their direct ancestor is "the postwar automobile suburb," the place referred to in the title of Kenneth Jackson's 1985 book *The Crabgrass Frontier: The Suburbanization of the United States*.[32]

Stilgoe traces the idea of suburbia as a superior place back to the eighteenth-century ideological progeny of the Puritans who saw westward movement as "a grand course of empire" and endorsed "fleeing the city for wilderness purity or rural virtue." Thus he argues that "the issue of commuting urban trouble" grew out of "the great immigration and westering enterprises." However grand or great the motions of its provenance, though, it's an issue that, he remarks ominously, "continues to haunt public discourse about urban problems."[33] That goes twofold for the West. All across America postwar suburban growth outran the growth of the cities from which it extended, but, White stresses, "the newer, more malleable western cities proved particularly responsive to the changes suburbanization brought." It jibed with Westerners' "cultivation of environmental amenities and an informal pace of life," and promoters supplied the overtaxed infrastructure.[34]

Changes, problems. The modern hope in the West was that suburbia would be a middle landscape combining the best of city and country and fulfilling in trans-Mississippi style the Olmstedian fantasy of renaturing places fallen from the paradise of an earlier America, but such hope for a man-made wild tameness (or tame wildness) got tragically qualified and then ironized all too soon.[35] What that oxymoron referred to wound up being as disastrous as Firestone's Wilderness AT tire, which was advertised, before all the lawsuits commenced, as having both "city style" and "frontier spirit." Like the tire, suburbia lacked stability. Not only did the suburbs allow the cities they fled to deteriorate: they, in their fashion of automotive forsaking, almost invariably turned into cities, of another kind, themselves. As Yi-Fu Tuan informs us, middle landscapes, including suburbs, are acclaimed as attempts at avoiding "the extremes of nature and city, both of which can seem unreal for contradictory reasons of thinness and inchoateness" (nature "reduced to pretty image," city "reduced to geometric streets and high-rises," either "become a jungle"), but historically the middle landscape in its conventional forms "reverts to nature, or, more often, it moves step by step toward the artifices of the city even as it strives to maintain its position in the middle."[36] Though the modern Westerner designated, in Simon Schama's words, "the suburban yard as a cure for the afflictions of city life,"[37] by the 1960s, in Jennifer Price's exemplification, "nothing symbolized the un-Real suburbs better or more visibly than the regulation lawn."[38] Nor would it be long before the suburban version of the Virgilian ideal of *urbs in horto*, the city in the garden, would find at its center a novel urban artifice, "the twentieth-century Garden of Eden," in Carolyn Merchant's construal: "the enclosed shopping mall decorated with trees, flowers, and fountains in which people can shop for nature at the Nature Company, purchase 'natural' clothing at Esprit, sample organic foods and Rainforest Crunch in kitchen gardens, buy twenty-first-century products at Sharper Image, and play virtual reality games in which SimEve is reinvented in Cyberspace."[39]

In suburbia nature became thin, inchoate, unreal, even as suburbia itself turned into thin, inchoate, unreal city—most remarkably in the West. Mid-twentieth-century suburbia was yet another avatar of the old American dream of an ideal mean between the negative, if necessary, city and wilderness that also was necessary and, in its own ways, negative. "Attempts to create and hold an imagined middle landscape, neither savage wilderness nor bloated city, run," in Denis Cosgrove's short telling of long history, "like a yearning refrain—'back to the garden'—through the centuries of American conquest and incorporation into the European *imperium*, all the way from its settlement by Europeans and its coming to self-consciousness as a nation, through Jefferson's Land Ordinance Act, and on to the contemporary suburb."[40] But that dream was and is, as Tuan says, "compounded of profoundly ambivalent and even contradictory elements"—antitheses evident enough in the nineteenth-century wish to make America both an empire of cities and a nation of farms. Laboring to realize that dream in more intellectual terms, Emerson tried tirelessly "to reconcile the idea of high civilization with the idea of untouched nature." The master metaphor for that reconciliation was "the City of the West," a place, unlike the Puritans' City upon a Hill, of "divine spaciousness." Through such images, Tuan explains, the suburb—even more the Western suburb, the twentieth-century City of the West—acquires, in contrast to the urban core, a romantic aura, but it "seems utopian (in the ambivalent sense of 'desired place' and 'no place')" and, no matter the nostalgic associations of its name with the natural or the rural, is "undergoing change, at the end of which is urban culture."[41]

In the 1950s, however, before that irony stood out starkly clear, suburbia in the West and Midwest, much influenced by West Coast imagery with frontier resonances (the horizontal ranch-style house and its accoutrements), was already a place of nature abstractly patterned and technologized by power mowers, sprayers, spreaders, and sprinklers to the point of being, in Alexander Wilson's phrase, "in suspension." It would become the plat for more and more malls, spaces within which "nature is so lavishly replicated . . . and yet so repudiated without."[42] Misbegotten, dispersed, crepuscular, autumnal, caricatural, it would become also, through that comparative with a distinctly Western flavor, Greater Kansas City, Greater Denver, Greater Salt Lake City, Greater Los Angeles—starting big in the 1960s, a decade Abbott generalizes in his history of the modern American West as "pivotal years in one area after another."[43]

PART FIVE

From the 1960s to the Present:
The West as Postregion

I hear it coming up through the rocks. It is a geyser of air that draws me farther
up the red stone staircase. I look down over my shoulder to the river valley below
and almost lose my nerve, but something pulls me higher.
    Terry Tempest Williams, "Air"

Prelude and Overview

The Old Western Historians usually write comedy, in the sense that they provide
a happy resolution (even though many of them came to distrust it). . . . New
Western Historians may lean toward tragedy, but . . . most end up with the far
less satisfying mode of irony.
    Richard White, "Trashing the Trails"

At the beginning of his 1852 work *The Eighteenth Brumaire of Louis Bonaparte*, Karl
Marx trumped the Hegelian gnome that all great events in world history happen
twice by adding a kicker: the first time they happen as tragedy, the second time as
farce.[1] He goes on to offer examples to support his qualification. If he were alive
today, he might well adduce the westering that occurred before 1940 and that which
occurred afterwards, most illustratively during the postregional era. The example
would be cogent in many ways. The follies of ballooning Western suburbanization
alone might make it so; but, as we'll see, other doings—some, though farcical, not
free of tragedy—also could be warrants for that cogency.

   First of all, suburbanite wannabes weren't the only people headed west after
1940. So were their antitypes in the 1950s, the Beats. Larry McMurtry remembers
that, when he was a graduate student late in that decade, "the Beats were like mountain men, or like Huck Finn, striking out for new territory."[2] He speaks of them as
literary explorers, but his simile rings true for literal as well as psychic geography.
What Jack Kerouac biographer Dennis McNally says of his subject and his writings,
such as the novel *On the Road* (1957), holds for many of the Beats in their rebellion
against middle-class America: "The journeys on the road that defined Kerouac to
himself and established his art were westward bound." In the 1950s he, like his
sometime companion Gary Snyder and a flock of other Beats, was drawn to a San
Francisco not yet metropolitanized. Regardless of their philosophical differences,

Kerouac and Snyder were among the leading representatives of a generation that sought "to re-create the natural state of the wilderness in the mind."[3] It was a quest that now seems to have involved nostalgia for Wild Western nostalgia as much as the high from Zen, jazz, and drugs. To put it another way, in Hal K. Rothman's words, *On the Road* is the classic Beat story about "the wild and spontaneous abandonment of New York and the East" and "reinvention in the West." The migration it narrates "presaged the obsession with individual freedom that engulfed the nation in the second half of the twentieth century" and soon would inspire, among other things, the overdevelopment of chichi Western destinations like Aspen, Colorado, "replete with Kerouac-like restlessness, transience, growing hedonism, and mobility."[4]

Also among the things that obsession inspired was the westward roving of hippies during the 1960s and, to a lesser extent, subsequent decades. They flooded into northern New Mexico.[5] Into San Francisco. Into Bisbee, Arizona. Into Oregon. They held be-ins and love-ins. They even invaded Disneyland.[6] They brought a new brand of politics to the West. Their countercultural banner might well have borne the frontier-crosser's motto blazoned on the front of the bus the Merry Pranksters took on their psychedelic odyssey across the United States in 1964: "FURTHER." They rejected false experiences and artificiality and, as Jennifer Price puts it, "pounced on one target with unanimous and utmost scorn: PLASTIC." Fleeing plastic suburbs emblematic of the aging Beats' winter of discontent, they followed Snyder's trace to "a simpler and more natural life" or at least camped out and backpacked and "used Reality and Nature interchangeably."[7] Wild things, to pluralize a line from the Troggs' anthem of the time, made their hearts sing. By 1970, Roderick Nash recalls, "'wild' had become an approbative adjective in American popular speech. The counterculture identified it with freedom, authenticity, and spontaneity or, in the common parlance, with 'letting it all hang out.'"[8] A lot of "it" was wilderness in the mind, and it hung out a lot in the West. What its bearers—like many of their forebears for centuries before, though with important differences—wanted there was contradictory. So was what they found.

Responding to the clarion call of books like Aldo Leopold's *A Sand County Almanac* (1949) and Rachel Carson's *Silent Spring* (1962), the counterculture of the 1960s embraced a mélange of biological, romantic, and mystical notions about the ecological web of life. The Woodstock generation wanted to "get back to the garden." Threading through its syncretism was what Fred Erisman describes as "an idealistic sense that the land—*any land*—is somehow magical."[9] For many members of that generation the really magical land was in the West, and what they wanted to do on it was live communally, despite the fact that writers they had read—a group as diverse as Nathanael West, Aldous Huxley, Kerouac, and Allen Ginsberg—were certain, as Richard W. Etulain points out, "that the West, especially California, was no longer the Eden, the El Dorado, and the Big Rock Candy Mountain that earlier frontier and regional writers claimed."[10]

So hippies fired up communes all over the West. Many of them believed that they, like the Ecotopians in Ernest Callenbach's popular 1975 novel *Ecotopia: The Notebooks and Reports of William Weston*, "had at last found an unending frontier" for what Patricia Nelson Limerick nutshells as "sensuality and personal development." Like their fictional counterparts in Callenbach's Pacific Northwest, they adhered to the idea that they "could make the West what it was supposed to be in centuries of imaginings: a place where nature would restore Euro-Americans to their senses." Ironically, however, most of those experimenters were like members of a New Mexico commune Limerick visited in 1971: "secure participants in Western tradition: living in a rugged environment, putting on magnificent verbal displays on the subject of fresh starts and autonomy, and still solidly connected to the system they had supposedly left behind."[11] On the other hand, they were not secure participants in "a 'traditional' West" that "had never existed," as Richard White dubs it, but that nonetheless was being vamped by the New Right, preeminently by the governor of California in the late 1960s and early 1970s, Ronald Reagan.[12]

A salient reason for the insecurity was that the hippies wanted to be not cowboys but Indians, a preference Leslie Fiedler pointed out in 1968 in his analysis of the Euro-American who is transformed by his encounter with the West in such a way that he "ceases to be White at all and turns back to the Indian, his boots becoming moccasins, his hair bound in an Indian headband, and a string of beads around his neck—to declare that he has fallen not merely out of Europe, but out of the Euro-peanized West, into an original and archaic America."[13] Proclaiming that fortunate fall, flower children adorned their walls (often those of tipis) with posters featuring Edward S. Curtis's photos of Indians. They painted their faces. They tried to build communities based on the ideal of the Noble Savage, with whose victimization by plastic progress they strove to identify. And they did all that largely with intentions (to live cooperatively, with a sense of organic relation to the land, and so on) the West would now do well to heed. No matter the naïveté of their quasi-Indian gestures and the misadventures that occurred when they, to paraphrase William Blake, damned braces and blessed relaxes too much (Charles Manson and his band of homicidal zanies come to mind), they were part of a cultural rescription that presented, in Robert F. Berkhofer Jr.'s words, "a supposedly Indian way of life . . . as a serious alternative to general American values."[14]

But the hippies were not Indians. "Heirs of the white middle class of the 1950s," as Philip J. Deloria labels them, "the communalists worked hard to counteract their parents' America, perceived in terms of consumptive excess, alienated individualism, immoral authority, and capitalism red in tooth and claw." Still, however putatively based on harmonious Indianness, most of the communes broke up. Deloria argues persuasively that their members were having a crisis of identity and that, just as some of their ancestors had done in such crises, they were "playing Indian" as a way to find assurance in a time of social bedlam. But their motives were contradictory: they may have opposed and critiqued their parents' world and taken the Indian alternative seriously, but they also wanted to be "both civilized and indigenous."[15] That Western story, postmodern version.

There were other contradictions, and they had to do with the West itself. Some arose from the fact that the West of the 1960s was, as Fiedler says, "a place of recreation as well as of risk," not so much a wild as, by then, "a park."[16] It was far more Europeanized than original and archaic. The West the hippies entered wasn't a frontier either—or even a region—anymore; it was a postregion, a megalopolitan place strikingly unlike the wilderness in their minds. The West they wanted was one on the order of the redwood world in Ken Kesey's 1964 novel *Sometimes a Great Notion* in which, to borrow from Carl Abbott's sketch of it, "the urban West appears only by implication"; the West they found was one turning into the frenetic 1984 West of Thomas Pynchon's 1990 novel *Vineland*, "a world that stretches easily and instantly to San Francisco, Los Angeles, Las Vegas, Tokyo, and Washington."[17] A world for a different generation of wild seekers.

The postregional West, in whose era we continue to live, is a place, in all its dimensions, of unparalleled multiplicity. It's a place where you mark that, as Michael C. Steiner and David M. Wrobel apprise us, "folk singer Malvina Reynolds's rows of 'little boxes made of ticky tacky' are now an endless nowhere of silicon valleys and edge cities—a World Wide Web of circuit-board landscapes." It's a place where restless urbanites bulldoze and pave more and more of the very nature they claim to cherish, where the desire for mobility is countered by "a desire for regional identity"—even as "the postmodern twilight" yields to a darkness in which the sense of place among many contending Wests "is in a constant state of flux."[18] It's a place of both deepening ecological pessimism and ever-resurgent technological optimism. It's a place, Etulain argues, that "has experienced *more* persisting cultural change than any other American region during the twentieth century."[19] It's a place not only of first nature and second nature but also, to a greater extent than in other parts of the nation, of "third nature," an essentially touristic medium, what Rothman sees as "a natural world organized to acquire intangibles, experience, and cachet" and is itself "intangible, ethereal."[20] (Old Nick may not inhabit third nature as he did the Puritans' first nature, but in the postregional West he's a seductive bargainer in selling it.)

The postregional West is *more* lots of things than the regional West was: globally interdependent, culturally decentered, illocal, hybridized, palimpsestic, abstract, artificial, virtualized, militarized, polluted, Indianized, computerized, Ralphlaurenized, feminized, Disneyfied, improvisational, conflicted, confused. Such augmented peculiarities have to do, as we'll see, with postmodern changes in the tensions that spring-load the wild-tame dialectic.

The most obvious of those changes are related to the accelerative spilling of cities into shrinking open space, agricultural land as well as biodiverse habitat. Westerners' predilection for the private automobile over public transportation contributes to that process—though remote wildlands are still off-limits to the four-wheel vehicles (if not always to ATVs and snowmobiles) that increasingly clog all but the West's outback roads. The construction of technoburbs and bedroom communities contributes mightily, as does their tendency to fuse together over time—which causes residents to move outward once again for elbowroom, creating yet more pseudo-centers for each multicentered metropolis, particularly in Texas and California. But there are more fundamental reasons for runaway urban sprawl in the postregional West. The most fundamental is that too many people live there. Also, the majority of those people congregate in cities simply because cities are where the postindustrial economy provides jobs. And, though all cities sprawl, Western cities generally have more space in which to do so, space that Euro-Americans are disposed to regard as useless unless sufficiently developed. That reason, however, should be seen as linked to a cognitive turnaround that, as John M. Findlay points out, was specifically Western: "By the mid-twentieth century, if not sooner, virgin cities had begun to replace virgin land in the minds of many Westerners as the key image in defining the region."[21]

The idea of virgin cities came about, Findlay explains, through Westerners' perception that, when compared to the rest of the nation, "the region seemed less troubled by urban problems and more open to improvements in metropolitan design, social relations, and styles of living." It was an idea reified by Disneyland, which opened in 1955 and thereafter powerfully influenced such improvements. That theme park demonstrated the possibility of an "absolute control" over urban environs and served to some degree as a model for virgin cities such as Sun City, a retirement community on the outskirts of Phoenix that opened in 1960, and the Century 21 Exposition at the Seattle World's Fair in 1962. Idealized cities of that sort seemed "magical" in the way they worked to transform the chaos and contradictions of surrounding areas through designs that "gave them greater spatial coherence and invested them with distinctly western meanings." But such proto-New Urbanism and its derivative concepts would be of little avail in managing the detriments of an immigration into virgin cities that was as out of control as that into so-called virgin land had been a century before: "Planned districts that had seemed almost utopian in the years 1953–62 offered much less room for optimism after the mid-1960s."[22]

In that key, I offer, as a transition to the chapters that follow, a Western rogues' gallery of postregional cities. Though doubtless omitting cities the reader might include (Boise, say, or Albuquerque), it should suffice. Las Vegas has a later chapter all its own.

Seattle. Gold strikes in the Klondike in the late 1890s first made it grow. Then cars made it grow—and lumber and shipping. Then, during and after World War II, the Boeing Company made it grow and contracted the world connected to it. Soon its suburbs encircled Lake Washington and stretched the length of Puget Sound. By the 1970s it was a thoroughgoing "networked city" (one economically interlinked as much with other cities as with subregional hinterlands—the kind, Abbott states, that "was becoming the rule rather than the exception among Western cities").[23] Home of the first Starbucks and (in Redmond) of Microsoft Corporation, it has become synonymous with the caffeinated technoburban lifestyle of the Virtual West, the placeless place promised by the Space Needle at the fair in 1962.

Portland. As a commercial hub in the Northwest, it has played second fiddle to Seattle. Growth in the nineteenth century was promoted by agriculture, timber, and gold (during the rush to California and then Idaho). A world's fair there in 1905 spurred population and prosperity, as did shipyards during World War II. In more recent decades the city has shifted its economy to high-tech industry, deemphasized the harvesting of Cascade forests, worked to revitalize its downtown, and tried systematically to limit sprawl.[24] Maybe it can save itself.

San Francisco. Growth here is a story of gold and then mercantile ups and downs, banking, international seaport commerce, railroads, agriculture, timber, and more. Regional dominance in shipbuilding during World War II furthered expansion, but measures occasioned by environmental conscience and tightening space have slowed growth on the tip of a peninsula being transmogrified almost entirely into (the perfect name for a dale so postmodernly morphed) Silicon Valley.

Los Angeles. A place as much of devils as of angels, it covers hundreds of square miles of coastal plain south of the San Gabriel Mountains. Lotusland of little usable water nearby, it has grown through many booms: gold, oranges, real estate, oil, movies, aircraft, tourism, computers, sex, glamour, kookiness. Railroads helped, as did a man-made harbor, water filched from other places, vertiginous freeways, a clement climate.[25] Its sprawl has fed and been fed by a car-culture lifestyle that has incurred stifling air pollution, Sisyphean commuting, and rush-hour gridlock. As Greg Hise and William Deverell have shown, the city Kerouac called a jungle might be a saner locale today if a 1930 proposal for less-dense development had been endorsed by the greedy boosters then in charge.[26] But it wasn't, and what we have instead are endless subdivisions watered by artificial rivers and surrounding desert that developers regard as, in the words of Mike Davis, "simply another abstraction of dirt and dollar signs" they can strip, pave, and belt with security walls. The growth of the city's pseudo-communities is maintained by "malice toward the landscape." The irony is, of course, that this malevolent ecology is turning suburbia into what it's trying to escape: "wreckage" spilling out "in ever-widening circles over a denuded countryside."[27] It's enlarging what William Fox calls "that ultimate urban apocalypse standing at the terminus of western expansion."[28] Los Angeles is not just a dystopian city west of the West but an image of what bigger Western cities, all of them its imitators to one extent or another, are headed for—unless something heads them off. Whatever else it may purport, that image blazons

Orange County as the most ambiguous product of an ambivalent conception. Robert D. Kaplan, writing of that county, says it's the nation's "most fully evolved urban pod, in which classic definitions of city and suburb no longer apply"—a "neither-nor landscape."[29] It's the epitome of "the mythical power of California" for Jean Baudrillard: "a stunning fusion . . . of the wonder of nature and the absolute simulacrum."[30] Los Angeles is, Maxine Scates understatedly avers, "a place where the unnatural imposes itself on the natural with sometimes disastrous results."[31] Is it already Los(t) Angeles?

Salt Lake City. Just northeast of it, at the mouth of Emigration Canyon, there's a state park commemorating the spot at which, in 1847, Brigham Young announced to his Mormon entourage that they had arrived where they would build their Zion. And build they did, raising a city with gardenlike openness that became a polestar for mining, smelting, and agriculture. Air pollution got bad, then got cleared up some; the city got beautified, became a military navel during World War II, and in the last decades of the twentieth century entrusted itself to tidier enterprises like finance and high tech. However, it still doesn't exist in any happy equilibrium with its natural surroundings. "In fact," says Baudrillard, "the whole city has the transparency and supernatural, otherworldly cleanness of a thing from outer space."[32]

Phoenix. Founded on the Salt River in 1870, it didn't really start growing until the Theodore Roosevelt Dam was completed in 1911. Thereafter it prospered from hinterland businesses (cattle, cotton, and copper) and from winter tourism. During and after World War II it grew and grew—horizontally, like most Western cities, much more than vertically. By the end of the century its multiple hubs (established or emergent), in strained relation to the downtown area, were spreading it in all directions, and it was the second-fastest-growing metropolis (behind Las Vegas) in the nation, developing square miles as rapidly as its original settlers had developed acres. But at a terrible environmental cost. "In a letter published by *Arizona Highways* in May, 1940, Frank Lloyd Wright offered southern Arizona some advice," Bruce Berger tells us: "A true civilization could grow around Phoenix, but only if it . . . fused with what the desert already possessed." After decades of realty Midases' bulldozing cactus to build air-conditioned faux haciendas and bringing in native and nonnative plants to decorate subdevelopments, Berger judges that Wright's injunction has been "honored in the eeriest sort of way. . . . It is as if the desert weren't being obliterated so much as geometrized into a Borgesian facsimile, complete with labyrinth. The desert lives—not in the flesh, but as mythology."[33] Or as nature etherealized into an edge-city chimera.

Tucson. Though not prone to Phoenix's neoplastic mania, it nonetheless now swells with computer commuters on its proliferating outskirts to such an extreme that Kaplan reads it as "a century-old speculative bubble that has yet to burst." There are water problems, dozens of gangs, drugs and their pathologies permeant. And the old wild-tame ambivalence can be seen everywhere—the city "still evinces a Wild West quaintness" and yet also appears "truly futuristic: a deliberate pod."[34]

Denver. Gold and railroads made its first spurt of growth happen in the late nineteenth century. Then it became a center for Eastern investment in the West, then got addicted to the defense industry and federal dollars. As María E. Montoya notes, the city's expansion in recent decades is much indebted to highways, especially those inaugurated by the Interstate Highway Act of 1956, which mandated a national plexus of multilanes that could be used by the military in the event of an invasion by Russians. Those highways streamlined the flow of rural people into suburbs and were the arteries for trucking goods through the hinterlands. At the intersection of I–25 and I–70, Denver embraces a "crossroads of the nation," and its residents keenly instance a habit of mind by which "Americans have come to think about their place in the American West based on their access to highways, freeways, roads, and streets instead of thinking about their place in relation to natural geography such as rivers, mountains, or lakes."[35] Driving on I–25 through suburban Denver today, with one eye on the highballing vehicles around you and one on the mountains to the west, you might conclude that the city is still what Elliott West says it was in 1861, "a blend of the refined and the rough,"[36] but you might also be hard pressed to decide which is which.

Dallas–Fort Worth. Metroplex this combo dominated by Dallas and born of cattle and oil surely is. By now well yuppied-up and technologized, it, in concert with Houston, has exerted, according to Abbott, a good part of "the supermetropolitan influence . . . [that] may have slowly reoriented the West's regional grain" into a north-south pattern "that cuts across the old [east-west] grain and draws the West away from the old national core."[37] The growth that's brought that about is indebted to the fact that "the Texan," as Larry McMurtry described him in the late 1960s, "likes . . . his cities as raw as possible, so as to allow free play to what's left of the frontier spirit." That spirit abides in Dallas, and it has a hand in making the place "one of the uneasiest cities in the country"; but it survives mostly only in "wheelerdealerism," which "is an extension of the frontier ethos, refined and transplanted to an urban context"—and now has become considerably airier than it was in the late 1960s.[38]

Omaha. Kansas City. St. Louis. All three have long been points of entrance into the West. "In the 1950s, at the peak of the Industrial Age, when the mortgage interest tax deduction and the G.I. Bill allowed for rapid suburbanization," Kaplan tells us, these cities "all expanded westward." They now have a feeling of repetitious extension, fragmented sameness. In St. Louis, particularly, where outer migration has "followed the highways that had once been Indian trails," the dispersing suburbs "suggest that . . . the frontier may, at last, be closed."[39] If that's true—and, in reference to Frederick Jackson Turner's frontier, if not to others, it certainly is—there's a profound irony entailed. As William Cronon's cultural geography shows, "for much of the nineteenth century the West began in Chicago," a city that raised large questions about "the city-country story" and "our most basic connections to the natural world,"[40] but for all of the nineteenth century and more, Chicago's favorable location notwithstanding, St. Louis, raising similar large questions, was—indeed, you could wryly argue, still is—what Eero Saarinen's Arch announces: the Gateway to the West. The meaning of that 630-foot catenary, in Yi-Fu Tuan's elucidation, "derives from ancient tradition: like the dome it symbolizes heaven, the limbs leading the eye upward to the round curve of the apex; and in analogy to the monumental portal that opens into the city or palace it regally beckons the traveler to enter the promised land. Historically, travel to the new frontiers began at St. Louis."[41] The irony is that, however regally that symbol of heaven may beckon, the West is not the promised land it once was. It has changed. So have its new frontiers.

> As structure, the central principle of ironic myth is best approached as a parody of romance: the application of romantic mythical forms to a more realistic content which fits them in unexpected ways. . . . The figure of the low-norm eiron is irony's substitute for the hero. . . . Tragedy and tragic irony take us into a hell of narrowing circles . . . . Tragedy can take us no farther; but if we persevere with the mythos of irony and satire, we shall pass a dead center, and finally see the gentlemanly Prince of Darkness bottom side up.
> Northrop Frye, Anatomy of Criticism: Four Essays

A Sewer Runs through It

> Horse and man passed other signs and stigmata of life: the petroglyph of a wild turkey chiseled in the stone, a pair of tin cans riddled with bullet holes of various caliber, brass cartridge shells, an empty sardine can dissolving in rust. They were nearing civilization.
> Edward Abbey, The Brave Cowboy: An Old Tale in a New Time

An hour's drive west of Albuquerque, enisled on a flat sandstone mesa that rises over three hundred feet above the ambient desert, lies Ácoma Pueblo. The few Indians who live there say it's the oldest continuously inhabited city in the United States. Given the evidence for something like nine hundred years of occupancy, they may be right. More spiritually expansive than the Puritans' City upon a Hill, Ácoma Pueblo is what Timothy Egan calls "a city in the sky, looking out to the world as before."[1] Euro-American cities in New Mexico or elsewhere in the West don't seem that permanent, not as permanent as Eastern cities looked to the Indians in Buffalo Bill Cody's touring Wild West, according to Philip Kimball in his novel Liar's Moon: "eternal as the woods and prairies, the buildings embedded in time, the narrow streets durable as the canyons disgorging mountain rivers out onto the plains, as the trails through the passes of the Dakota Black Hills."[2] Most Western cities have an air of transitoriness, as if each were foredoomed to boom out and become Ozymandian rubble in the lone sands, a colossal repeat of Rhyolite, Nevada, Patricia Nelson Limerick's exemplar of a twentieth-century gold-rush town gone bust.[3]

If those cities come to that sometime in the too-soon future and make the West a ghost postregion—and Donald Worster, among others, cautions that all hydraulic empires of the past have collapsed from ecological backlash—overpopulation, profligate evulsion of water, chancy exploitative investments, and the like won't be the only causes. A correlate one will be pollution, the mephitic result of arrogant indifference, if not hatred or anger, toward the natural environment that lets us imagine it as a space somehow outside ourselves where we may dispose of everything we reject or fear. Pollution is a global problem, but in the United States much of the West, because of its vastness and seeming emptiness and intractable desolateness, has long been singled out as a limitless midden for tailings and other hazardous chemicals, nuclear waste, obsolescent ordnance, unexploded bombs, toxic blunders of every sort, and the megalopolitan miasma that all that huge air presumably can carry away to *somewhere else*—to the point now that much of that much, that geographical unconscious where America stashes its bad stuff, ought to be qualified for Superfund status.[4]

As the *High Country News* (published in Paonia, Colorado) and other informative sources have declaimed for decades, the West is perniciously polluted—or, to tap into the word's Latin etymology through synonyms, befouled, defiled. The human actions that have made it so began a long time ago, but their legacy of soiling became lethal on a mammoth scale during the Cold War. Then the military-industrial complex, not to mention the suburbanization that accompanied it, altered a lot of land, María E. Montoya recalls, partly from her experience of growing up in Colorado near what's now known as the Rocky Flats Environmental Technological Site, where plutonium triggers for H-bombs were assembled: "It made deserts into proving ranges and testing grounds. It tucked secret military hideouts into mountains, and it created places so poisonous that it will be thousands of years before humans can ever inhabit those landscapes again." Those places include not only Rocky Flats and nuclear test sites but also areas degraded by spinoffs from nuclear-weapons technology such as Project Plowshares (which was intended to employ nuclear explosions for peaceful ends) and by the refining of uranium ore. Such places and others otherwise poisoned have come about through insensate distinctions between the wild and the tame, through what Montoya characterizes as a "division between what Americans deem inhabited and uninhabited, rural and urban, empty and full, [that] denies the interconnectedness of the world around us."[5]

Poisoned places. The Nevada Test Site, the zone of sacrifice for the national interest (to echo Pentagon terminology), where nuclear experiments caused "secret holocausts" (to follow Mike Davis's terminology) that affirm its interconnectedness to downwind lives, human and nonhuman, and its role in making the Great Basin the nation's memorial to the Cold War as "the Earth's worst eco-disaster in the last ten thousand years."[6] The Hanford Nuclear Reservation, which, though no longer making weapons, may never be "cleaned up," what with its retired reactors, dozens of square miles of contaminated groundwater, radioactive drains that used to eject coolant water into the Columbia River, backfilled burial grounds (some leaking) that hold tons of solid and liquid waste, disposal pools full of hellish soup—in the aggregate a time bomb for the Columbia.[7] The Rocky Mountain Arsenal, near Denver, which from 1942 until the late 1960s manufactured chemical weapons (from mustard gas to nerve agents) and then, until 1982, pesticides and herbicides (atrazine and such) and in the process deposited millions of gallons of noxious glop in basins and landfills that now constitute what William Cronon calls "one of the West's most remarkable wildlife refuges," a Superfund site so teeming with jeopardized plants and animals (and so blurring of "the boundaries between 'natural' and 'unnatural'") that it has been dubbed "The Nation's Most Ironic Nature Park."[8]

Poisoned places. Smaller ones, like those photographically recorded by Richard Misrach within Bravo 20 (a bomb crater with fetid red liquid at the bottom, a sandscape strewn with dead fish, and the like)—or the dead-animal pits documented in his sequence The Pit (the sixth canto of his ongoing series Desert Cantos) that was shot from 1985 to 1987, as Davis recounts, "at various dead-animal disposal sites located near reputed plutonium 'hot spots' and military toxic dumps in Nevada." The photos in the sequence confront the viewer with a "'Boschlike' landscape" of decaying carcasses (of horses, cattle, you name it) that amounts to "a nightmare reconfiguration of traditional cowboy clichés." In it, Davis speculates, Misrach "may have produced the single most disturbing image of the American West since ethnologist James Mooney countered Frederic Remington's popular paintings of heroic cavalry charges with stark photographs of the frozen corpses of Indian women and children slaughtered by the Seventh Cavalry's Hotchkiss guns at Wounded Knee in 1890." The sequence "builds drama around a 'found metaphor' that dissolves the boundary between documentary and allegory"—suggesting yet more interconnectedness, of a kind that has intrigued photographers such as Peter Goin and Carole Gallagher, among others, who, with Misrach, belong to a "movement of politicized western landscape photography that has made the destruction of nature its dominant theme." Confuting the "myth of a virginal, if imperilled nature" artistically favored by Adams and his Sierra Club progeny, they have elaborated an iconography that displays rawly "the fate of the rural West as the national dumping ground."[9]

Davis's reference to Wounded Knee is apt here in another respect also—because of the extent to which the West's poisoned places, especially nuclear sites, are located near reservations and in areas Native Americans look upon as sacred homelands but Euro-Americans see, as Valerie L. Kuletz puts it, "as wastelands of little

Richard Misrach, Dead Animals #1 (1987): an iconography of the rural West as the national dumping ground. (Original in color. Reproduced by permission of Richard Misrach.)

economic and productive value, suitable primarily for environmental experimentation and ultimately sacrifice." The latter is the view countenanced by an objectification whose consequence is "deterritoriality," a writing-off of certain land. These two culturally glossed landscapes, one sacred and the other expendable, "meet at nearly every point of the nuclear cycle, from uranium mining to weapons testing to the disposal of nuclear waste." Now they meet—or collide—most jarringly at the point and on the issue of disposal, for "the proposed premiere site for the nation's high-level nuclear waste repository is Yucca Mountain—'holy land' to the Western Shoshone, Southern Paiute, and Owens Valley Paiute." The faith that that controversial but congressionally approved (though not yet fully operational) repository, filled with thousands of tons of spent fuel rods, will be safe from nature's dynamics (aquiferous, seismic, volcanic, whatever) relates to a Euro-American belief grounded in a wild-tame binary foreign to Indians: that "humans live outside the world they attempt to manipulate and control"—that the savage realm (rural emptiness, Indians, and the trash they're forced to live with) there is somehow separate from the civilized realm (urban plentitude, whites, and their immaculate surroundings) here.[10] Inducing readiness to make the West a worse wasteyard than it already is, it's a belief ignorant of or oblivious to what Neil Campbell calls "the complex interactions of the New West" evidenced by "overlapping sites and perspectives: sacred native lands, nuclear dumps, airforce bases, wildlife refuges."[11]

Complex interactions. Ay, there's the rub: the rubbing of realms or overlapping of sites that belies the separation of savage and civilized, pollution and purity, and in the magnitude of its complexity distinguishes the postregional from the regional West. The social, ecological, and eschatological significance of such interactions in the postregion was recognized—and overlapping perspectives at least temporarily reconciled—by the Westerners, politicians and environmentalists and ranchers and Indians alike, who joined in 1981 to oppose and kill a plan for the mobile basing of MX missiles in the Great Basin.[12] (That rebuff, like the destruction of Minuteman II missile silos with the winding down of the Cold War, heralded a time when America's enemy would no longer be a clearly targetable nation-state but a nationless terrorism whose practitioners, postmodern avatars of diabolical Indians, would be as hard to locate as Geronimo once was.) In general, however, since the 1960s, Westerners haven't been sufficiently aware of those interactions and their often ironic implications or have been reluctant and slow, by virtue of economic arguments rationalized by a blinkered mind-set, to act on what they know.

And so the West is pocked with "ponds" containing carcinogenic mill tailings. Little towns here and there, such as Naturita, Colorado, sit in the midst of hot spots, derelicts from uranium-mining booms still monitored by the Department of Energy. National parks in the West, from Yellowstone to Big Bend in Texas, suffer from air pollution. Lots of days you can't see the Sierra Nevada from California's increasingly subdivided Central Valley, the once-crystalline air is so darkened. Navajos in and west of the Four Corners area breathe the smeech emitted from coal-fired power plants—a sad situation, profoundly ironic in country with such open sky, that moves Montoya to lament that "Westerners, mostly Native Americans, shoulder the cost of living in one of the most polluted areas in terms of air quality."[13]

But surely the most ironic and calamitous pollution in a postregion remarkable for its aridity is that of its waterways, major and minor rivers with far-flung environmental interactions, fluid sites of many quarrels over rights that have coded them, à la Thomas Jefferson, more as economic resources, when they appeared serviceable as such, than as media of life with their own implacable laws.[14] That codification has ignored other codifications—that typical of Native Americans, which takes the health of rivers as an index of the health of the cultures dependent on them, for example, or even that of "fluvial myths" of the Old World, which, as Simon Schama explains, relate rivers symbolically to "the female body as the *fons et origo* of verdant life."[15] Notwithstanding, most Euro-Americans in the postregional West, while acknowledging the hydraulic bottom line ("*Sin agua no hay vida,*" as the *dicho* goes),[16] have perceived its rivers in terms dictated by the developmental demands of an updated Manifest Destiny. Their attitude derives from—and, despite any yearning for wildness and despite what ecological science has taught in the interim, is grounded in much the same wild-tame dialectic as—that of their mid-nineteenth-century forerunners who judged the Platte, Arkansas, and Kansas, in Elliott West's words, "valueless except as a source of water" and otherwise worthy only of "dismissal."[17] As for a river, they seem to say, exploit it, or forget it; either way, you can use it as a toilet.[18]

With abominable and unpropitious results. Today the Arkansas, like a lot of rivers on the southern plains, is dry along much of its length. The Kansas is badly polluted from agricultural runoff—fertilizers, herbicides, and pesticides. Many Western rivers have been biologically degraded by siltation from sewage-treatment plants or manure washed from feedlots. The Missouri is a multiply dammed mud puddle.[19] The Rio Grande has become seriously depleted by excessive diversion—and seriously polluted, to boot. The distended portion of the Colorado known as Lake Mead is home to malformed fish; beyond the lake, where it flows southward, its tamed water is channeled into aqueducts and canals so greedily that the only outlet it reaches is the surreal sump of the inland Salton Sea. "The meandering stream in Yosemite has been preserved, but," Kenneth R. Olwig mourns, "in much of California the rivers have become linear open sewers made of concrete."[20] The Columbia, in Richard White's summation of its combined natural and cultural histories, "has become an organic machine which human beings manage without fully understanding what they have created," a freakish hybrid that "has, in turn, spawned a virtual river whose life influences the actual Columbia" very problematically.[21]

There are, though, signs of hope. More and more Westerners are, as Worster advises, "learning to think like a river"—to foster "a 'water ethic'" that inculcates "a sense of belonging to the larger community of nature."[22] Washingtonians are starting to understand that in their relationship with the Columbia they must, as White urges, "come to terms with it as a whole," as a site of "production and nature, . . . beauty as well as efficiency."[23] Angelenos are working to renew at least a portion of their urban river—in this case the Los Angeles, which the Army Corps of Engineers spent many years and dollars destroying and re-creating as the fifty-mile-long mother of all concrete sewers.[24] And, as San Antonio's less-cloudy downtown river attests, even some Texans, like Duane Moore, the protagonist of Larry McMurtry's 1999 novel *Duane's Depressed*, have grown melancholy about the baneful habit by which people "went about their lives creating waste materials and then just threw them off the handiest bridge."[25]

Without such awakenings and the responses they catalyze, we will make the West into a wilderness not of the kind we conceive as "original chaos" but of the kind Denis Cosgrove defines as "the final act of the cycle of civilization."[26] If we respect and protect and, as best we can, restore Western rivers, we may never experience the Bitterroot and its flora and fauna as Lewis and Clark did in the summer of

1805; but we still might do what Sandra Alcosser speaks of doing: "canoe the river in the amethyst / hour before dark," paddling past "the banks of aster, the flood plains / dense with white tail and beaver."[27]

Where the Wild Things Aren't:
The Last of the Breed

"Whoopie-ti-yi-o, it's your misfortune and none of my own": the old cowboy song sums up our detachment from the crash of other animal life.
    Edward Hoagland, "Vermont 1997"

Regardless of the extent to which the West has been developed in the postregional era, it remains America's wild kingdom. It is now, however, a more complex such kingdom than ever before, one in which intensifying concern for the future of wildlife, especially megafauna, has provoked bitter conflicts between protectors of animals—some revered as quintessentially Western, like wolves, grizzlies, wild horses, and spotted owls—and enterprises like mining, lumbering, and ranching that profit from the exploitation of the natural environment. Those conflicts, though rooted in centuries-old Euro-American ambivalences about the relation between the wild and the civilized, in recent years have assumed peculiarly postmodern textures—and for the most part have come only to the ineffectual pseudo-resolutions of an ideological stalemate.

In 1949 Aldo Leopold laid down a maxim that had the semblance of simple truth but that was long since debatable in its reference to most Americans: "There are some who can live without wild things, and some who cannot."[1] Inveterate urbanites and Idaho backpackers may have been unhesitating about the matter, but Westerners generally hadn't—and still haven't—made up their minds so neatly. They were—and would become more so—hyperbolic exemplars of typical Americans as Donald Worster characterizes them: both "an avid group of nature lovers" and "consummate nature destroyers."[2] Westerners can't live with wild things and can't live without them. We kill as quickly as we save the charismatic mammals few of us know firsthand. We're detached from wild things, and yet we need them. We confuse them with what they symbolize. In their unbarred presence we feel fear, hatred. In the words of Ronald Wallace,

We'll put a rattle on the tail
of nearly anything we fear,
and poison in whatever we can't master.[3]

In their barred presence we feel pity, contempt. In their absence we have substitutes—pets, taxidermic reconstructions, statues, pictures. We want them to be like us. We want to be like them, and we don't. We don't care a fig for biodiversity and academic disquisitions about how the more we simplify it by the diminishment or extinction of species, the more intractable its problems grow, the more ambiguous its implications for our own lives become. And we do care. We worry—and forget—that a good portion of Western wilderness is utterly gone.[4]

However much postregional Westerners love wild things, they have destroyed and continue to destroy them; and their destruction hasn't, to echo Macbeth, trammeled up the consequence. Quite the contrary.

As an entrance into this thicket of consequence, consider wild horses. See them through the two lenses of Western eyeglasses. One eye sees horses running, herds of them as unroped and unsaddled as Western wind, what Larry McMurtry labels "perhaps the most potent image to come out of the American West."[5] The other eye sees horses tamed, with riders on their backs, an image, says Jane Tompkins, that "celebrates the possibility of mastery, of self, of others, of the land, of circumstance."[6] The two images analogize Western wilderness itself as it has long been seen by Euro-American eyes: something glorious in its unfettered beauty that must, all the same, be dominated. Or, if it's useless or in the way, then gotten rid of. Like that wilderness, a lot of wild horses have been tamed ("broken") and put to use, but also a lot have been put to death—and still are, in spite of the protection of the Wild Free-Roaming Horse and Burro Act of 1971.

"As has often been observed," Frederick Turner reminds us, "without the horse it would be impossible to imagine the American West, and the wild horse of today is presumed to be the lineal descendant of the mustang that was so significant in the 'making' of the West." The ancestor of the mustang was the horse the Spanish rode against the Natives of the New World. Once the Spanish occupied the Southwest, the enslaved Native Americans there learned how to tend and ride horses, how to steal them (and, sometimes, eat them), how to breed them, and how to trade in them—which last explains how "the horse figured in the dream of freedom" for tribes far removed from the Southwest. But many escaped from the Spaniards' herds and foaled wild horses that foaled wild horses—until by the middle of the nineteenth century there were millions all over the West. Indians captured and trained them for riding. So did whites. Though there was no shortage of admiration for the staunch animals, most were doomed. Liquidating them was yet one more military strategy, liberally exercised, for subduing Indians, but another reason for doing so, invoked to this day, was to curtail competition for cattle and sheep forage. Because of the growing nation's need for beef, ranchers' greed, "and the prevalence of firearms that has always tempted men to randomly kill wild creatures," wild horses were viewed as "an anachronism and a nuisance" and myriadly shot outright—or caught, hobbled by any of several cruel methods, and shipped to slaughterhouses.[7]

To be sure, hundreds of thousands of captured horses were sold to the U.S. Army or exported elsewhere for military service or, before stock contractors got the hang of breeding bucking horses, supplied to rodeos, but after World War I there was little call for mounted troops and much for the pet food wild horses could be rendered into. By the 1960s so many had been so rendered, their hide sewn onto baseballs and used in other ways, that their population had been reduced to around 1 percent of what it was a century before. The wild horse was on its way to becoming, in Turner's words, "an all-but-extinct icon of the Old West."[8]

In the wake of the 1971 act, the Bureau of Land Management (BLM) established an expensive adoption program to save the horses; but its inadequate guidelines have been abused, since scores of the adopted animals have wound up in the hands of meat processors rather than in sunlit pastures—and the bureau (known as Bullshit Land Management to more than one benefactor of the Fund for Animals and the Animal Rights Defense Fund) has a deplorable law-enforcement record. Today, out in spaces remote from the roads punctuated with flattened wildlife that lace the postregional West, some thirty thousand wild horses (about half of them in Nevada) remain. But maybe not for long. Probably the only place you and I could ever see them is California's Wild Horse Sanctuary.

The wild horse is an animal that went wild after domestication, whereas the true wild animals of the West have been wild from the outset. Many of them, like the buffalo, ranged widely in the nation until restricted to and therefore strongly associated with, even if islanded in small areas of, the West. There are some survival success stories (coyotes and mountain lions, for instance), but many have been and continue to be threatened with extinction. Exemplary of them are the grizzly bear and the gray wolf.

Taxonomically, the grizzly is *Ursus arctos horribilis*, a name that conjures up the chill of terror early westering Euro-Americans felt in any encounter with the beast. Not without cause. As Dan Flores notes, there are plenty of frontier and even postfrontier stories of mortal adventures with the continent's largest predator, the first detailed one being trader Jacob Fowler's gruesome account of a hapless member of his camp near the Purgatoire who was killed by a grizzly in 1821.[9] On April 22, 1998, Earth Day, when Doug Peacock, an expert on grizzlies, showed a film of several at play to a ballroom filled with rapt viewers at the University of Kansas, they all understood the significance of his exhortation at the film's end: "Put that on your computer screen!" They had witnessed something far beyond digitized imagery: the frolics of a massive mammal that can crush a human skull with a bite of its jaw or a swipe of its paw, the prime-matter emblem of the West at its bestially wildest . . . still. They'd seen themselves as well in a creature, foul-smelling in the flesh, that, according to J. E. Cirlot, "is related . . . to the instincts" and has been deemed "a symbol of the perilous aspect of the unconscious" and "an attribute of the man who is cruel and crude."[10] Certainly the audience was impressed, distressed that the grizzly might perish; some may have sensed that "the bear within," in Louis Owens's phrase, has—as it does, for instance, in Kiowa mythology—"overwhelming spiritual power,"[11] but many must have experienced disquiet at glimpsing, to cite the topic of Delmore Schwartz's famous poem "The Heavy Bear Who Goes with Me," his or her own bundle of stifled appetites.

Indeed, fear and hatred of the bear within has had everything to do with making the grizzly without, officially since 1975, an endangered species—and one poachers kill merely to reap a gallbladder Asians prize as an aphrodisiac. Those feelings motivated a religious fanatic named Ben Lilly to leave his native Louisiana in 1906, after he'd depleted the black-bear population there, and go west, as Flores recounts, for "a career with the government's Predator and Rodent Control in New Mexico and Arizona, where in the name of Jesus and Civilization (that's exactly the way he thought of it) he waged a kind of John Brown campaign against all bears and lions." Lilly expedited the extinction of the grizzly in most (maybe all) of the Southwest, a fate whose history prompts Flores to suggest that the animal be seen as one "we should incorporate into an understanding of how we've thought about the West, and of how we're coming to think of it." His approach to that incorporation, which judges Lilly an extremist in a long tradition of "jihad against predators," interprets that jihad as an extension of the Puritan battle against the wild within ourselves, an exercise that got us into "a Freudian feedback loop" whose repetition has led to a downbeat postregional repercussion:

> For much of American history, that exercise, when we've indulged in it, has not pleased us, producing a self-hatred that we've deflected outward. And now, since the grizzly and the wolf were animals our grandfathers so labored to eradicate, many Westerners find it repugnant to confront the possibility that their own ancestors were wrong. As Paul Shepard put it in one of his last books, "By disdaining the beast in us, we grow away from the world instead of into it." That line stands as an evocative summary of much of the history of the American West.

Flores surveys Euro-American accounts that help him reconstruct how we've "created the bears in our heads," and he discusses the portrayals of grizzlies in Indian stories where "humans and grizzlies play interchangeable roles." He concludes that the bears have rights, that in killing them we've made yet another effort at self-destructively separating ourselves from the natural world, and that, therefore, "hanging on to the great bear may be nothing less than an act of self-preservation."[12] Which means that hanging on to all the natural wildness of the West that's left, lest we animals at odds with our animal natures humanize it into some suburban Disney Wild, is paramountly such an act.

So far we've hung on to neither very well. Only a few hundred grizzlies now exist in the lower forty-eight states, most of them in the Northern Rockies—in Yellowstone, especially, and in the Bob Marshall Wilderness and Glacier National Park in Montana, square mileage inadequate for their ranging needs. As SueEllen Campbell remarks, "they remind us of facts we prefer to forget, that we don't control the whole creation, that death is inevitable, that the food chain doesn't stop with us."[13] But they also can be the healing force they were for Peacock when he quested for them while recovering from his traumas in Vietnam: "the living embodiment of wild nature, the original landscape that was once our home," the grizzlies of Yellowstone, he says, "saved my life."[14] Regarding our hanging on to the grizzly and its world in the age of etherealization, Patricia Nelson Limerick may have the most cogent question. Noting that, "from the nineteenth century on, bears symbolized the power, strangeness, extravagance, and wildness of the West" and that the grizzlies in Yellowstone may be disappearing, she asks how long will it be "until bears are purely symbolic—represented in the contiguous forty-eight states only by the Forest Service's Smoky, who has never threatened humans by direct attack, but only by warning them of the consequences of their own actions?"[15]

The gray wolf, Canis lupus, has fared no better. All but a few of the last wolves native to the West were wiped out by government hunters, trappers, and poisoners by the 1930s—at the behest of ranchers. The remnant descendants, their numbers refreshed by migrants from Canada, are now scattered across a handful of states, their destiny largely under the sway of the National Park Service and the politically fickle U.S. Fish and Wildlife Service, successor to the Bureau of Biological Survey that oversaw that extermination program. Their status as an endangered species is scrutinized by both friends, such as members of Defenders of Wildlife, and foes, such as cattlemen in Montana. The thirty-one Canadian gray wolves released into Yellowstone in the mid-1990s, over strenuous objections from the cow world, have had a hard go of it, what with deaths from rifle bullets, accidents, fights with neighboring packs—though they have multiplied to several hundred. As Timothy Egan tells us, "ambivalence about Yellowstone still exists in Wyoming." Transplanting those wolves cost a lot of tax dollars and spurred a spate of animosity and litigation, and for sure the wolves have pulled down elk and bison and otherwise altered the ecology of the Lamar Valley; but "the cattle and sheep industries have not been hurt, no private land owners have suffered an egregious breach of property rights, no children have been snatched by fairy tale predators" (arguments to the contrary were, he says, unpersuasive, particularly since "the big issue—what the West should be like and who would control it—was never brought out into the open").[16] The release of eleven Mexican wolves (Canis lupus baileyi, a subspecies of the gray wolf) into the Apache-Sitgreaves National Forest on the Arizona–New Mexico border in 1998 also involved difficulties, what with ranchers' suing to stop the reintroduction, wolves shot, polemics about possible livestock losses. And so forth—matters of control. Given the enmity toward wolves, you can sympathize with the speaker in William Trowbridge's poem "The Wolf's Advice to His Nephew":

Brains and fair play went out with the dewclaw;
now it's all PR and who's got the real estate.
Try to pass for a collie, is all I can say.[17]

In *The Ninemile Wolves*, his book-length essay on wolves in northwestern Montana, where the population has been on the rise, Rick Bass relates what he learned from interviewing around a hundred people both pro and con wolves: "The ones who are 'for' wolves, they have an agenda: wilderness, and freedom for predators, for prey, for everything. The ones who are 'against' wolves have an agenda: they've got vested financial interests." But, while he admits that sometimes wolves do kill and eat cows, he knows that more than economics motivated the quick and zealous killing of wolves in the West—and that such killing allowed our prejudices against them to stay inviolate, for "we never had time to learn about them, and about their place on the land. And about our place on it."[18]

So there's a lot we don't know about wolves. Barry Lopez finds reason for cheer in the fact that "biologists have given us a new wolf, one separated from folklore." However, he goes on to say, "they have not found the whole truth. For example, wolves do not kill just the old, the weak, and the injured. They also kill animals in the prime of health. And they don't always kill just what they need; they sometimes kill in excess. And wolves kill each other. The reasons for these acts are not clear." Nonetheless, wolves aren't, he argues, *pace* wolf-haters, born killers; on the other hand, contrary to the warm-and-fuzzy fancies of wolf-lovers, in North America they have on occasion killed humans. Because of what we don't know, the wolf still powerfully affects the imagination: "It takes your stare and turns it back on you," exciting not only hatred and fear but respect and curiosity as well.[19] Through that returned stare, says Jim Brandenburg, who has photographed many a wolf, Ojibwa hunters and other Native Americans "saw in the wolf a high degree of skill, intelligence, endurance, and strength. . . . They saw a teacher. They saw a brother. They saw themselves." In a different cultural space-time, though, Westerners attributed "aspects of evil to the wolf: maliciousness, thievery, murderousness. What they saw wasn't the wolf. But they, too, were seeing themselves."[20]

Like that stare, the wolf itself comes back to remind us who we are. It's a memento of all the Western wild we killed quickly and zealously. As Irene Klaver has it, "the wolf keeps coming back to us, because we keep coming back to the wolf, the hungry shadow of our imagination, smoldering in our soul." The wolf is part of what wilderness is symbolically about, and wilderness, by her trope and to a marked degree for postmodern Euro-Americans, is "a story sliding and stumbling over a range of meanings as wide as the mountains of Montana." Ultimately, she says, echoing Bass, "it deals with the place of the other, and thus with the place of ourselves." And the place of the badly treated wolf is testimony to a plangent indictment: "The myth of the Wild West speaks with a forked tongue. The ideal of wilderness arose when we no longer knew how to live with the wild. From its beginning wilderness has been its own abstraction, sacrificing wildness on its altar."[21]

The irony here is that we oppose the wolf as nature to culture by imposing an abstraction on it when we should be trying to relate to the animal, like the West, on its own terms. Bill McKibben may be right that "it is the middle ground that we have lost sight of completely, that we misunderstand even more than we misunderstand wilderness." Our insufficiently informed opposition of nature and culture, wild and tame, has prevented us from realizing how we can and must have both. He interprets the wolf as an indicator species whose return "is an indication of human beings learning to accept real limits, to pull back."[22] Maybe, I'd argue, an indication that we're learning about the place of the wolf as the other and letting it have that place—and wolves need a Western-size place. Maybe even an indication that we are learning about the place of ourselves in a truer story of the Western wilderness than the one we've made up.

But the story we've made up keeps on being told, and it's not a tale, to borrow from the subtitle of McKibben's book from which I've been quoting, of "living lightly on the earth." We've been living heavily in the West, shooting rather than shooing wolves, and we don't know fully what the impact on wildlife amounts to. Sharman Apt Russell asks the relevant question: "How . . . is wildlife really faring in the West?" And she offers an expectable answer: "The General Accounting Office concludes, with some chagrin, that the federal government doesn't know. The high numbers of animals killed every year could mean that we have a lot of animals out there to kill. Or it could mean that we are not going to have many animals in the future." It's also expectable, in a country so ambivalent about the importance of wildlife, that different people, New Westers or Old, experts or not, "have very different visions," depending on their points of view.[23] For the moment, at any rate, elk are on the increase. Coyotes, though often hunted by gun cranks for sport, have adapted to suburbs and are holding their own (and visions of them differ—in James Galvin's part-fictional natural history *The Meadow*, Wyoming rancher Ray Worster says, "'You can admire a coyote—he's an outlaw, but it's damned hard to admire a sheep'").[24] Peregrine falcons are back in some strength, as are pronghorn and sandhill cranes; but bald eagles are poisoned to a species-menacing extent. The lynx was reintroduced into Colorado in 1999, a year after activists with the Earth Liberation Front burned ski-resort buildings on Vail Mountain to discourage further exploitation of the animal's habitat. Mountain lions enjoy an impressive range in the West; but their numbers (some tens of thousands) are uncertain, sentiments about their habitual killing of livestock and well-recorded attacks on humans vary, and more than a hundred (by a conflicted management strategy) are "harvested" each year in New Mexico to protect the endangered desert bighorn sheep.[25] Even jaguars have been spotted in southern Arizona.[26] What such ups and downs and pros and cons bode for the near-term future isn't obvious; what is obvious, for the sake of the not-very-long-term future, is the need for Westerners to liberate themselves once and for all from the wildlife-holocaust mentality and to conceive and enact a more carefully balanced coexistence with their wild (br)others.[27]

If that doesn't happen, what will we have? Probably only more of the substitutes for the Western wild we have now. We'll have the sort of "nature tourism" that, according to Alexander Wilson, has evolved since the 1960s to become the principal American way of utilizing wildlife to human ends: a safariing in which "*photographing* animals has become the preferred trophy-taking activity, especially if the beasts can be 'captured' on film in a wild setting"—and vanishing species thus "temporarily 'preserved'" in that way.[28] We'll have zoos where dispirited bears slowly pace their small spaces and wolves are safely locked up and patrons feel secure that, as Gary Snyder lines it,

> the Coyote singing
> is shut away
> for they fear
> the call
> of the wild.[29]

We'll have pets, animals Shepard terms "compensations for something desperately missing."[30] We'll have plastic deer in our yards. We'll have kitschy Bradford Exchange sculptures of an eagle ("Silent Strike") and a wolf ("Mystic Spirit")—what we heirs of Bradford get in exchange for the wilderness we failed to steward. Or, if we are possessed of more eclectic taste, a postmodern sense of humor, and an appetite for the visceral, we'll have the work of an artist such as Luis Jiménez, whose representations of wild animals (*Howl* [1986], *Bighorn Sheep* [1990], *Chula* [1987], and the like) vision the West, in Dave Hickey's words, as "a richer, stronger and sweeter place" than "a Puritan's Eden" of dangerous beauty.[31]

In the November 2000 issue of *Scientific American*, at the beginning of what so far seems a millennium of unmatched foolishness, appeared an article that, with dismissive bows to objections, proposed frozen-tissue storage as a way of retaining endangered species. Referring to that article in his introduction to the issue, John Rennie, the magazine's editor, expressed Western-flavored misgivings about the proposal. "I can," he wrote, "imagine a future time in which a land-use developer argues that there is no reason to worry about the disappearance of a given species in the wild because we can always resurrect it later through cryogenics and cloning—whereas we need that ranch land now." While he acknowledged hypothetically the usefulness of cloning as a tool of conservation, he also recommended that we "not forget that real conservation involves preserving the life and lands we might least think to save."[32]

In the United States that life and those lands are mostly in the West. About them, as well as others we might least think to save, William Kittredge, writing eight years earlier on a theme much the same as Rennie's, was more jussive. If we're deprived of the life around us, he said, "we begin to die of pointlessness . . ., even if some of us can hang on for a long while connected to nothing beyond our imaginations"; so we need a new story of that teeming realm with which we're interpenetrant. "We must," he bade, "define a story which encourages us to make use of the place where we live without killing it, and we must understand that the living world cannot be replicated. . . . Ruin it and we will have lost ourselves, and that is craziness."[33] Even if we could approximate that world by some clonal ersatz, we still would lose, in a decisive sense, ourselves; for the replacement would bear no more resemblance to the original than Frontierland does to the real West.

McWilderness: Disneyfying the Frontier

When place is silent, do we substitute, Disney-style, our own versions of its voice?
 Reuben Ellis, "A Thousand Frontiers: An Introduction to
 Dialogue and the American West"

Richard Stayton recalls that, when he went there as a boy in 1961, Disneyland was a haven of magical nostalgia he associated, via Frontierland, with "the Davy Crockett craze, when every kid longed to be 'King of the Wild Frontier.'" In 1974, when he returned there in search of a job and his lost childhood after "a decade of drugs, Haight-Ashbury communes, bisexuality, political craziness in ultra-hip San Francisco," the interviewer offered him a position, which he reluctantly took, as a popcorn seller in Fantasyland but advised him that his hair was too long: "'The Disneyland look,' she lets me know gently, 'is a neat and natural look with no extremes.'"[1]

I too visited Disneyland in 1961 and took a special interest in Frontierland, which indeed had, like the rest of that trim little utopia, such a look. I'd grown up with Disney's films and television series and once, at a rodeo, shaken the manicured hand of Fess Parker, the actor who played Disney's Crockett, so the neat and unextreme nature of Disney's sham West seemed natural enough to me. By 1974, however, a few years after my own countercultural wanderings and eight years after the death of Disneyland's eponymous founder, I, like Stayton, was well along toward comprehending that Walt's fiefdom—and all the more so Frontierland, because of its historical pretensions—was, in its hyperreality, foremost among what Umberto

Eco means by "instances where the American imagination demands the real thing and, to attain it, must fabricate the absolute fake," a creation born of "the unhappy awareness of a present without depth."[2]

Before he made (and then repeatedly modified) Disneyland, Walt Disney produced many of the films that made his name a household word. Lots of them, such as *Bambi* (1942) and *Nature's Half Acre* (1951), were "nature movies" of one kind or another, the best-known ones about nature in the West being *The Living Desert* (1953) and *The Vanishing Prairie* (1954). In February 1997 Richard White presented a lecture at the University of Kansas during which he confessed that his childhood fascination—coonskin cap and all—with Disney's version of Crockett had contributed to his becoming a Western historian and that Disney's films, most of them about nature in some way, had been the main influence on his becoming also an environmental historian. He ventured to claim—correctly, I'd say—that Walt Disney had been the strongest influence on American popular ideas about nature in the second half of the twentieth century. While he admitted that Disney's films invite diverse interpretations, he strove for some interpretive unity by discussing the nature they portray in the context of the thought of Thomas Jefferson, John Muir, and Aldo Leopold in order to demonstrate that they had in common streaks of two opposed themes inherent in the notion of America as Nature's Nation: humans as integrated with nature and husbanding it and humans as separated from nature and disrupting it. Disney, he said, created a sort of synthesis of the two by both anthropomorphizing nature and naturalizing the conservative social values with which he wanted to see it invested—with the result that the films, including those made after the opening of Disneyland in 1955, simultaneously advocate both those values and a simplistically moralized (and contradictory) environmentalism preaching that nature should be protected from society. Thus, White concluded, do the films, with all of what he called Walt Disney's "reactionary innocence," fit in the tradition of assuming that the order of nature parallels and supplies a legitimating rationale for the order of American society—and of championing the preservation of that prior order.[3] Thus do the films, I concluded, inspired by White's insights, embody a compulsively metaphorized or allegorized and ambivalent idealization of nature and of Americans' relation to it that was foundational in the design of Disneyland, most notably in that of Frontierland. White had been right as far as he went, but there was more to Disney's story of Nature's Nation—or, specifically, Nature's West—he hadn't told.

In 1968 Richard Schickel lambasted movies like *The Living Desert* and *The Vanishing Prairie* for the way they "prettified" violence, cast a snake or tarantula as a heavy, reduced a mating ritual "to a joke." He argued that the films' anthropomorphic individuating of animals cheapens our experience of them. The films succeed at "shutting down the subject instead of opening it up"; they're the products of a man who, "confronted with things that were inexplicable to him, . . . either turned away in disgust or willfully falsified them by reshaping them in terms that he understood and approved."[4]

More recently, in a more sophisticated critique, Alexander Wilson has taken Schickel's line of argument further. He admits that the early Disney wildlife movies "spoke to us of a living and intelligible world beyond the fence of civilization," but he observes that they "also came with their own constricting logic. The animal stories they trafficked in were among other things transparent allegories of progress, paeans to the official cult of exploration, industrial development, and an ever rising standard of living." Still, during the postwar years, Wilson recalls, those stories were compelling myths of utopian nature that many Americans embraced while the West that was their setting changed under the impact of stepped-up militarization, urbanization, and resource extraction. They may parade a contradiction—"this is nature as she really is even though we've staged it all—[that] only works if the culture draws a sharp distinction between the human and the non-human," but they appealed to the many Americans of the time who felt ambivalent about the natural world, finding it both a domain to be watched and managed at a distance and one "they persisted in inventing a kinship with." Through those movies—as earlier through Buffalo Bill Cody's show and later through television shows such as *Mutual of Omaha's Wild Kingdom* (which began in 1963)—"the tamed American wilderness," that peculiar oxymoron, lived on, complete with contradictory frontier ideology. (In most of the later conservation-oriented television shows, Wilson points out, humans are both "destroyers of nature" and "saviours of nature.")[5]

These critiques are shot through with words and phrases that, when strung ("prettified," "joke," "shutting down," "turned away," "willfully falsified," "reshaping," "constricting logic," "staged," "tamed American wilderness"), diffusely suggest Nature's Nation as most Americans now experience it: a place where, to cite recent examples in the media, videos of wild animals' "follies" can be obtained by dialing an 800 number and a woman decorates the pierced ears of a pet fawn with cruciform zircon-crusted earrings because it looks "cute" that way. Such words and phrases certainly suggest Disneyland itself. Christian Dior once said that his dream was to save women from nature through his fashions. Disney's may have been to save Americans from nature not only through his refashioning of it in his films but also through his additional refashioning of that filmic nature in Disneyland, a space defined by exactingly controlled removes from the tooth-and-claw original.

In the years after Disneyland opened, its guests (always "guests," a word that veils consumerism) found it to be a nostalgic home-for-a-day where, whatever the technocratic extrapolations of Tomorrowland, they could retreat from the present into the more rural and natural past. They reported to their neighbors back in suburbia that in some respects it was better than "the real thing," though few of them could have known much of what Adventureland, Frontierland, even Main Street, let alone Fantasyland and Tomorrowland, imitated. In exile from whatever it was, they were willing victims of a chicanery through which any sense of relation to it that modernism had shattered was being supplanted by a postmodern sense of enmeshment in packaged virtuality (costumery, simulacra, pop imagery, highly selective heritage—nature and history à la Disney).[6] What Louis Owens terms "the crucible of Disneyland" was California, a state he sketches as "a lovely, haunted, bitter garden where stark contradictions reign."[7] It was the perfect location for a man who wanted to construct, as Carl Abbott puts it, "a walk-through fantasy that would outdo Cinerama and Cinemascope as a 'real' experience."[8]

So, in John M. Findlay's words, "the road to Disneyland began in Hollywood," and the plan was for "a three-dimensional extension of Walt Disney's films." Though it was erected in a garden ruled by contradictions, its planners meant it to be as free of them as it would be of ambiguity and confusion (qualities Disney himself toiled neurotically to suppress). Its planners believed that Disneyland "offered an enriched version of the real world, but not an escapist or an unreal version." Continuous replanting lent to it "an artificial changing of the seasons." Horticultural technology smoothed out "the capriciousness of nature," just as technology in the form of advertisements for the park on Disney's television programs ensured a steady flow of new and returning guests who would appreciate and be influenced by its "tremendous cleanliness."[9]

With its spic-and-span replicas of a jungle, desert, coral reef, and so on, Disneyland is for William Cronon the definitive model of "the replacement of nature by self-conscious artifice" and (tongue in cheek) "a triumph of artifice over nature."[10] The self-consciousness may have reached a temporary apogee in 2001 when the latest adjunct to the park, California Adventure, opened—featuring a giant sculpture of a grizzly, emblem of the California Republic. The triumph entails moneymaking irony that Eco, starting with the premise that enjoyment of "the 'total fake'" requires that it "seem totally real," spells out as follows: "Disneyland not only produces illusion, but—in confessing it—stimulates the desire for it: A real crocodile can be found in the zoo, and as rule it is dozing or hiding, but Disneyland tells us that faked nature corresponds much more to our daydream demands." Just as nature is replaced by artifice, so hunger for the real wild is replaced by a more profitable and manipulable desire for the virtual wild—a milieu where guests who pony up "can have not only 'the real thing' but the abundance of the reconstructed truth."[11]

Nowhere is that characterization more accurate than in the case of Frontierland, its opening in July 1955 emceed by no less a virtual Western personage than Ronald Reagan. What he opened, according to Michael Steiner, was a "refabricated frontier," the product of Walt Disney's mission of "remodeling what was often a dirty, brutal, chaotic experience into the cleanest, happiest, most predictable place on earth." Frontierland was built by a perfectionist who distrusted raw nature and made sure his Wild West show narrated not a tragedy but an epic. He thus sentimentally revised the memories of his less-than-paradisal boyhood on a farm near

Marceline, Missouri (something he did also in his bucolic 1948 film *So Dear to My Heart*), though he'd had to bulldoze and burn farmhouses and thousands of trees in Anaheim in order to do so. Frontierland, the largest segment of the park, was "carefully choreographed so that guests could feel they were actors in a movie" and savor "a regenerative journey into the wilderness and back to civilization again."[12]

However, even though Frontierland theoretically was contradiction-proofed through endless alteration, it would soon enough be infected. The most significant infection, in Steiner's view, was the one that struck "the Main Street dialectic between frontier and region, nature and civilization," and that echoes both in "the tension between nature and civilization within Frontierland" and in the relationship of "Frontierland in the west balancing Tomorrowland in the east," a past vis-à-vis a future frontier. Such opposites reinforced each other until the 1970s; since then their relationships have weakened as "people have become increasingly skeptical of the urban future and wary of space-age wonders." That is, the infection was manifested as an ironic reversal through which Tomorrowland has been relegated to the past and "the western frontier may be a model for the future." Hence recent company policy for future-oriented projects, as first devised by Disney CEO Michael Eisner, has been directed by "images of 'The Montana Future' with a computer in the cabin," images of urban refugees living on the fringe of the Western wild with at least some of those space-age wonders at hand. The attraction of the frontier not just in Frontierland but abroad now in its French and Japanese counterparts, Steiner says, "indicates a deeper hunger for the open West among urban, mostly upscale Americans that Disney's Imagineers have learned to capture and perpetuate"—in the 1995 film *Toy Story*, for example, and in California Adventure.[13]

But, of course, here be dragons. The Disneyfied sunny-side story in film and scaled-down architecture and landscape of, in Steiner's phrase, "how the West was fun" has airbrushed ambiguities and helped us forget terrible truth. More specifically, he argues, working toward a disenchanting quotation from Sal Paradise, the narrator of Kerouac's *On the Road*, "Disney's Frontierlands . . . muffle memories of plundering the land and killing its inhabitants, and they postpone the realization that the frontier is dead, that the real trip is over and there's 'nowhere to go but back.'" They gloss over the very historical paradox they body forth: that of "obliterating nature in order to celebrate it."[14] Built by garden-destroying machines, they're machines disguised as gardens.

Those places are illusions of a kind carried to their highest absurdity yet in the performances of a rejuvenated Buffalo Bill's Wild West at what Steiner calls the Euro Disney "rendition of the West."[15] Based on the show Cody presented during his European tour from 1889 to 1892, it features buffalo, cowboys, real Indians, chili in period crockery—the whole schmear. As Joy S. Kasson points out, however, its participants "re-enact a re-enactment of American history."[16] It's at least a copy of a copy—with lots of airbrushing along the way—within the context of a copy of the "original" Frontierland, which is, when you think about it, also at least a copy of a copy.

But why is all this draconic? If, as Yi-Fu Tuan contends, "a human being is an animal who is congenitally indisposed to accept reality as it is," why not, without further ado, just take Disney's meticulously remade world as merely an instance of how "culture is, in a fundamental sense, a mechanism of escape" from reality? Because, to apply his qualification, humans' efforts to escape "may fail—may end in disaster for themselves, for other people, for nature."[17] Some such efforts surely are necessary for our rock-bottom sanity. But Frontierland, in all its versions with their extreme escapist mediations, seems bound to end in disaster, and it's symptomatic of an estrangement general in America today.

Sven Birkerts offers thoughts on that estrangement that both spell out its character and implicate the Walt Disney Company in its furtherance. "Our technologies," he says, "have created a secondary world that we inhabit in lieu of the first world that our immediate ancestors, and all of their ancestors before them, inhabited." We once knew that first, essentially natural world through our senses, whereas we now know the secondary, essentially virtual one more "as a field of data." We're still connected to the first, of course—you can't eat software—but we feel increasingly cut off from it even as we consume it. And we "go with the ersatz" because we trust it's better than nothing. Since most of us have few direct and full experiences of unpolluted nature, with images of which our advertising teases us, we turn to "surrogate living to take the edge off our clamorous needs." *Surrogate living.* Those words are only half digested before Birkerts asks the question waiting in the wings: "Can we really doubt that the global explosion of Disney—the corporation and the concept—is not in deep ways linked to what is befalling us in the postmodern epoch?" He answers, "Small surprise that we should so overwhelmingly look for solace where it is most conspicuously offered to us—in the wonderfully designed entertainments and simulations of a safer, more natural reality. We inject ourselves with sanitized doses of what, in rougher form, is lost to us, and we imagine we are happy." For most Americans what is lost is the natural West, and Frontierland, however configured, is what we accept as a replacement for "the older things [that] had more thingness, and places [that had] more thereness."[18]

The dangers of that acceptance are multiple and interrelated. It's true that, as Birkerts asserts, "in the substitution of commodified images for formerly organic realities we are travestying those realities," but we're travestying also our history, ourselves. The more we yield to the ersatz, the more we baffle a longing, grounded in a sense of "what constitutes a right balance between nature and domesticity," that, he suggests ominously, we will, somehow or other, relieve. In addition, since we're so isolated from immediate nature, "it becomes harder to swerve off what is at every moment sold to us as the bright unscrolling road of progress."[19] It becomes harder also to see what damage we're doing to the first world, both out there and in ourselves, as we plunder it to elaborate the more and more intricate patchwork of our less and less satisfying secondary world.[20] Perhaps the greatest danger lies in our coming to believe an equation not even decades of Gary Larson's distinctly non-Disney cartoons about wildlife have laughed out of the popular mind, a delusion Jim Brandenburg sums up in one short clause: "Nature is a theme park." We can believe that only if we've forgotten that "in wilderness is truth, and," he continues, "the truth of nature is full of passion, is all about chase and evasion, capture and death, blood and birth. If we fear these things, then it is no wonder we have long feared the wolf. It is nature's truth. It is our truth."[21]

The theme-park nature in Frontierland exemplifies what Jack Turner calls "the abstract wild," which he defines as "wildness objectified and filtered through concepts, theories, institutions, and technology," and he finds it as characteristic of national parks and "designer wilderness" as of Disneyland.[22] Given such pervasiveness, he warns of how fake "'normal' wilderness" is displacing the real wild and leaving us starved for an "exotic Other which might afford a perspective on our lives."[23] That's a centrally important point; for people who lack that perspective are doubly cursed because they're prevented from gaining what Hayden White argues Montaigne bestows in his essay "Of Cannibals": "critical distance on their artificiality, which both prohibits the attainment of true civilization and frustrates the expression of their legitimate natural impulses."[24] Without that critical distance, some people, including urban refugees moving into a Western environment with which they're able to have only a tenuous connection, may wind up in the cul-de-sac of twice-alienated John the Savage in Aldous Huxley's *Brave New World*, who, after going berserk, hangs himself on the Savage Reservation in New Mexico.

Much has been written about the complex tensions between and blurrings of nature and culture in the postmodern world. Boria Sax remarks that "the boundary between human beings and animals has become ever more elusive. We now understand that we are at once human beings and animals, yet these two aspects of identity have not merged. . . . The mermaid, half woman and half fish, is a fitting symbol for our divided selves."[25] Molly Wallace argues that "'nature,' as an autonomous object for exploitation or, alternatively, preservation, has been 'denatured'" whereas "'culture' seems to have expanded to enormous proportions"—so that the two have mixed into a hyphenated hybrid even as we've become more aware of the limits to our control of nature.[26] The present state of the nature-culture dialectic is much the result of the tireless exercise of an old ambition of Western civilization, according to Worster: "to make every part of the earth over into a thoroughly cultural landscape." But it's also the result of nature's canny contesting against that misguided ambition, which makes sure that we can't fulfill it. Such contesting is fortunate: "If nature were ever truly at an end, then we would be finished. It is not, however, and we are not."[27] Nor, despite our efforts to turn it all into Frontierland or worse, is the natural West.

The Computer in the Cabin:
Unsettling the Nouveau West

"Goddamn pirates're subdividin, stockin 'the common land' with tame elk.
Half the people buyin into it are telecommuters. That's your New West. Christ,
they're not even suitcase ranchers."
    Hulse Birch in Annie Proulx, "The Governors of Wyoming"

Here are several true stories from the postregional West.

A rancher rides his horse through the sparse grass on the Plains of San Agustin, five-hundred-odd square miles of prehistoric lake basin west of Magdalena, New Mexico. Just behind, dwarfing the rider and his mount, rises one of the radio telescopes in the Very Large Array, its dish over eighty feet in diameter collecting data from deep space.[1]

An ex–New Yorker dressed in a flannel shirt, jeans, and cowboy boots stands on the deck of his house in Jackson Hole, Wyoming, a cellular phone pressed to his right ear. Snow-capped mountains spread across the background. Next to him, on a small table, sits an open laptop.[2]

After eating a breakfast prepared by a gourmet chef, several "epicurean cowboys" leave their camp at the bottom of Mancos Canyon in southwestern Colorado and, led by a Ute guide, set out to find some Anasazi ruins. They ride switchbacks up through weather-sculpted sandstone for almost an hour, finally reaching the top of a mesa. "Here," says Tom Huth, the travel writer in the party, "we stop to take a needed rest. One of the men . . ., rattled by the height, pulls out his cellular phone and calls his office in Manhattan."[3]

A showroom-clean Lincoln Navigator sits masterfully atop a lone boulder-studded hillock. The backdrop consists of craggy mountain crests rising through mist. In the sky above them appear these words: "DITCH THE JONESES." Beneath the vehicle are these: "ALTHOUGH THERE'S SOMETHING TO BE SAID FOR GETTING AHEAD, THE NEW NAVIGATOR HAS MORE TO DO WITH GETTING AWAY. AND TAKING LIFE'S LUXURIES WITH YOU." Then, beneath the mist, these: "WITH UP TO 8,000 POUNDS OF TOWING CAPACITY AND A 5.4L V-8 TO ESCAPE CIVILIZATION, JONESES AND ALL."[4]

Each of those stories is about the postmodern technologization of the West. Each has some irony to it. Each repeats, in an updated and Western variation, Leo Marx's hallmark image of the machine in the garden. Each, in his phraseology, suggests "the yearning for a simpler, more harmonious style of life, an existence 'closer to nature,' that is the root of all pastoralism—genuine and spurious." Yet each contains machinery that startles and triggers a sense of incongruity between the setting and the technology "that provides the counterforce in the American archetype of the pastoral design," a counterforce that in the nineteenth century was emblematized by the locomotive, which comes, as "the trope of the interrupted idyll" has it, "shattering the harmony of the green hollow."[5] Such intrusion of the urban-technological world into the rural-pastoral one complicated both the ideal and the reality of the middle landscape in Nathaniel Hawthorne's time and place. All the more does it do so in the present and the West, where the middle landscape has become the place to ride a horse and do advanced science, to gaze at mountains and talk on a cellular phone, to sleep in a canyon and eat gourmet food, and to escape civilization while taking its luxuries with you—above all, as the laptop in the second story suggests, to have (to recall that consummate Disney trope) a computer in the cabin.

If the emblematic invasive machine of the frontier West was the locomotive and that of the regional West was the automobile, then that of the postregional West is surely the computer, along with its allied communications gadgetry (fax machines, cellular phones, and such), that telecommuters and modem cowboys, most of them aging baby boomers in ever larger numbers, bring with them in their search for a home that can satisfy their retrofitted longings for the wild. Plenty of SUVs sluice into and out of contemporary Western exurbia, but the computer is the real symbol and facilitator of the exurban lifestyle, of New Westers' crack at the paradoxical goal that, as Donald Worster observed earlier, has long obsessed the West: to achieve material success and yet maintain the landscape of freedom. Jordan Bonfante notes, in that vein, that the "new ethos" in the Rockies "manages to combine the yearning for a simpler, rooted, front-porch way of life with the urban-bred, high-tech worldliness of computers and modems."[6]

In an age when the World Wide Web is referred to as the Wild Wild West because of its lawlessness, there are many reasons why the nonurban West is such a popular place to live, and Patricia Nelson Limerick offers some. "When reality appears in a state so unmistakably simulated, designed, and virtual, the Old West," she argues, "gains heightened appeal as the place where people who have had enough of falsity go to find authenticity—even if that Old Western authenticity is itself a theme-park creation." Also, the nonurban West obliges the desire to live "in the presence of nature," white flight from city problems, and boomer memories of halcyon childhoods spent with Hopalong Cassidy, Roy Rogers, and Gene Autry. But she zeros in on still another reason: "the emergence of the FAX machines and computers and Internet ties that make it possible to detach the workers from the office, and let the workers choose their place of residence by its amenities and attractions, especially its scenic appeal."[7]

Historically speaking, the computer in the cabin is a wholly apt figuration for the ambivalence of New Westers in quest of, to paraphrase Gertrude Stein, space where there's more of nobody and less of somebody. "By the 1890s," as Richard White retrieves an earlier time for us, "the log cabin had long been the chief icon of the nineteenth-century frontier, if not of American culture itself. It marked both regression, as the wilderness mastered the settler, and the beginning of the reca-pitulation of civilized progress"—but progress whose message, White's analysis of an etching of an isolated log cabin by Georges Henri Victor Collot shows, could be ambiguous.[8] Add a computer, and it becomes more so, the combination the-matically consonant with having both a Southwestern climate and air conditioning; with looking at a mountain through the window of a kitchen equipped with state-of-the-art cooking tech; with wanting to be Californians in Montana (New Okies committing "Californication"); with wanting a small town nearby but not one of those dwindling Midwestern-type small towns; with wanting the remedial effects of sage and piñon as well as convenient transportation to a rodeo arena in Chey-enne, a ski resort in Durango or Vail (ideally, with a global communications center and heated sidewalks), one of the golf courses on every patch of municipal land that can pirate enough water to maintain such a simulacrum of outdoor life.

Computer-in-the-cabineers exemplify to a tee the complicated national charac-ter that Elliott West finds dominant in "the Western as myth" and indebted to the fact that "our beliefs and identity are as contradictory, confused, and ambiguous as the myth." In that regard he mentions a conflict Alexis de Tocqueville wasn't the last to remark: "Americans seem both fascinated with progress and infatuated with a glorified past, always reaching toward the new while heroizing the folk and life-ways of a vanished age."[9] In the cyberspatial middle landscape of the postregional West, this conflict is contemporized in Westerners whose lifestyle, in the diction of the Atlas of the New West, knits "the standard urban frenzy" with "laid-back ru-rality."[10] Living their laid-back frenzy and urban rurality, they constitute, in many respects, a subset of those Americans David Brooks classifies as "the new informa-tion age elite," people whom he calls "bourgeois bohemians"—or "Bobos"—and who "define our age."[11] However you describe them, they want the West's wild nature, but they want it technologized and urbanized.

That double attitude certainly has been what West terms "the Western's prob-lem," but it's now more and more the West's problem as well.[12] Like the tourism that has jammed up Arizona's Oak Creek Canyon with swimmers and hikers, set-tling undertaken with that attitude has proven unsettling, destructive of the very qualities that were alluring in the first place. It entails the conversion of rough land into false-front playgrounds, overdevelopment that brings in chains and franchises to squeeze out local businesses and turns the rural into the ruderal, homogeniza-tion that attempts to make the West as predictable an environment as the operating systems on cabined computers. It entails the injurious unrealities of what has come to be called Aspenization.

In his discussion of the changes urbanization has brought to the central West, Carl Abbott zooms in on the transformation of Aspen, Colorado, as the epitome of them. The town was just another busted mining burg until the Aspen Institute for Humanistic Studies was established in 1949 and set the stage for an influx of musicians, skiers, summer tourists. In the 1960s a boom in the construction of ski resorts and condominiums made the place "a prime example of efforts to create a modern version of the 'middle landscape' sought by nineteenth-century Americans." Aspenization occurred in subsequent decades as other high-country towns followed suit, with artists, jet-setters, consultants—"dealers in national information markets"—sharing roads with loggers, ranchers, and retirees.[13]

For Abbott, this "resettling of the frontier in urban guise is more positive than not."[14] Others aren't so sure. Neil Campbell thinks it's an ironic perversion of what Wallace Stegner once meant when he recommended the smaller towns of the West, those "balancing mobility and stability," as the best places to visit or live in. Its brand of postmodernism, Campbell observes, is disruptive of traditional customs, and the information superhighway that facilitates it is but "a new extension of the old Route 66 dream of migration and a new start." The makeover of small towns by Aspenization involves, he argues, a remodelled utopianism whose New West is the creation of "a schizoid culture," a place both natural and televisional, "real and surreal, known and unknown, imagined and factual simultaneously."[15] A growing number of its visitors seem to be "post-tourists," rubbernecks with an "ironic consciousness," as Chris Rojek diagnoses them, who are "aware of the commodification of tourist experience" but take it in a playful spirit for the trifle it is.[16] We have been there before, but never like this. And there is now, for Hal K. Rothman, like the place depicted in Stephen Morath's 1990 painting Where the Wild West Went: a jumbled landscape of kitschy, technologically garish icons threatening to eclipse the desert sunset, "a West stripped of identity and history, packaged to outside taste, and repeated ad nauseum."[17]

Also disturbing is a social eclipse—of the old-timers, the locals, the havenots and desdichados for whom El Nuevo Oeste is just more of the same old grunt work, those whose West, in Wally Gordon's words, isn't where "it is always morning" but where "it is always evening."[18] Invading amenity-minded newcomers can be damned indifferent to the fate of people they may view as reprobate riffraff cluttering up their otherwise picturesque wilderness. Gary Holthaus encapsulates the status quo this way: "Now laptop entrepreneurs who can afford it are moving in, and those who can't afford to stay, even after having lived in the region for generations, are moving out."[19] Many of the ousted feel like they're the newcomers' Indians.

The environmental and social problems of Aspenization are thus knotted together as computer-in-the-cabineers build rustic Silicon Valleys and turn landscapes into e-scapes in a West that, William Kittredge reminds us, "has always been a double-hearted dreamland: a home in paradise, and a wide-open situation where you could maybe make a killing"—but now with the two locked in an unprecedentedly complex dialectic of preservation and exploitation.[20] In large measure those problems arise from a distorted and inadequate sense of place—whatever its postmodern cast, an old Euro-American limitation. "There has grown to be a real sense of place among immigrants to the West, but," White notes, "the place has, as often as not, been an imagined place—what they intend the West to be—and not the actual place."[21] From her Laguna Pueblo–Sioux point of view, Paula Gunn Allen speaks more acrimoniously of that limitation in denouncing "the 'new' Southwesterners, those transplants who move to God's country and pave it, develop it, merchandise it, commodify it," and, in a judgment that might appertain to many recent immigrants all across the West, "seem bereft of that profoundly human capacity to be created in relationship to place—to the smells, the sounds, the tastes, the language, the rhythm that makes one region clearly different from another."[22]

Intriguing, in light of Allen's lamentation, is the issue of whether or not that computer in the cabin can help its user reach and be guided by an amended and deeper sense of place. It's an issue David Rothenberg addresses in a question with reference to "the machine in the forest": "Will we live lightly on the earth in the future, each able to find a personal place in the wilderness of our choice, or will a virtual life leave us so out of touch with nature that we will no longer know what is real, what is mediated, and what is wild and free?"[23] On the one hand, there's the possibility implied by Sam Shepard's play *Operation Sidewinder*, first staged in 1970, in which, to follow Mark Busby's interpretation, a computer in the shape of a giant rattlesnake "becomes the element of spiritual metamorphosis on the Western frontier," a sea change represented at the play's end "by merging Native American and European images in a ceremonial apocalypse that suggests the beginning of a new chance for the American dream to be achieved through a new consciousness."[24] On the other hand, there's the possibility that the computer will merely entrench the user's existence as a Disneyoid in a Cyberwest.

The best hope is for something closer to the first than to the second possibility, of course, but realizing it will take more than computers. Edwin H. Marston, for years publisher of *High Country News*, predicted some time ago that small Western communities would change in order to preserve their traditional values and that such preservation "will require almost the opposite of what was required in the past"—an emphasis not on provincialism and isolation but on education and more contact with the rest of the planet. Growing aware of undeniable economic opportunities, "rural Westerners will recognize that telecommunications, facsimile machines, satellite dishes, Federal Express, and computers have opened rural areas to the kinds of work that formerly could be done only in metropolitan areas." Decent forecasting, so far. But Marston also said that, "if the West is to survive as a rural region with a rural culture, there must be more than subdivisions of electronic cottages, tourist resorts, and retirement villages"; and he voiced the expectant prayer that, though extraction (perhaps by less damaging methods) will continue, "the new rural economy will be based on reclamation and restoration."[25]

That more wishful prophecy has yet to come true. Such an eventuality will require some adaptation of traditional values, to be sure. Above all, it will require an opposite that's more than "almost": "European settlement in the rural West," by Marston's assessment, "has transformed the scenery to match a society that had its strengths, but that was also weak and destructive in many ways"; now it's high time for that society to transform itself to match the scenery.[26] That transformation won't occur just by conservation agents' holding seminars on the enigmas of country living for Johnny-come-latelies; if it's effected, though, our grandchildren will wonder, to borrow an example from Adrian Herminio Bustamante, why we ever "created an artificial Santa Fe to maintain what some people thought Santa Fe should be."[27] And we in our cabins, more connected to both the global village and the world immediately around us than we thought possible before our graceful aging into ecological wisdom, will have an answer for Holthaus, Limerick, and Charles F. Wilkinson, who asked in 1991 if we could ever come to be "genuine *settlers*, and not unsettlers," of the West.[28]

Wild(e) Style: Ralphlaurenizing the Range

I wanted those boots, I got them, and that's all I care about. Wearing my dyed alligator boots I feel the same way that Dorothy did while wearing her ruby red slippers. I seem transported from Kansas to Oz—to the West of my fantasy.
> Blake Allmendinger, Introduction, *Over the Edge: Remapping the American West*

In spring 1882, as part of his American lecture tour, Oscar Wilde traveled through the West, making a month-long loop that took him from Omaha out to San Francisco and back to Lincoln, Nebraska. He met with both flattery and mockery from the men he encountered, and the flamboyant writer's advice on interior decor stirred many a woman far from the East to redo her parlor in accordance with his non-Western aesthetics; the curiosity is the extent to which he cottoned to the look of Western clothing. He adored the ground-length cloaks and floppy broad-brimmed hats worn by miners in Leadville, Colorado, and added them to his wardrobe. Likewise corduroys and cowboy neckerchiefs. He liked the appearance of pants tucked into boots and wore his that way.[1] He was the first fashionmonger to both take to and tout the West as style, but he wasn't in the least last. Relating to the place that way would get more complex and more fictive between then and now.

"The enthusiasm for the American West—real or legendary—generated by a century of image-making found its most revealing expression in the frontier worshipers who appeared in Europe during the 1960s and 1970s," according to Ray Allen Billington. As evidence he cites the revival of Karl May's Westerns and the affixing of that author's name to all sorts of consumer items, Yugoslavian and East German children playing cowboys and Indians, Parisians' eating son-of-a-bitch stew, the opening of the Longhorn Steakhouse in Copenhagen, an international ring in Switzerland that made a fortune selling fake cowboy-cut Levis, on and on.[2] Americans' Western enthusiasm had the Asian flu during part of that time, but it would soon swell again and become as normalized as ever. Reflecting a twice-distanced nostalgia for nostalgia, the nation's renewed fascination with things Western in recent decades has incited and been incited by an expanding commercialization of the West that has sublimated and etherealized the actual place and its inhabitants into what is for most Americans no more than mannerism. Such mannerism revealingly involves what might be called Ralphlaurenization.

Why Ralphlaurenization? Because the 14,000-acre spread outside Telluride, Colorado, that fashion designer Ralph Lauren bought in the 1980s and did over to his own standards, with hands dressed in outfits he designed, and named the Double RL Ranch perfectly instantiates the "imaginings, profound and silly," that Richard White deems characteristic of the "well-kept West" of the postregional era.[3] Because that trophy ranch demonstrates what Neil Campbell terms the New West's "almost surreal ability to juggle the commercial realities of the age and the longed-for retention of older values."[4] Because that ranch—whose "mise en scène," as Richard Rodriguez puts it, "is the American West"—richly embodies the kind of ironies with which the postregional West is shot, these among them: that Lauren goes there when he "wants to escape the mythology business," that he has erected a teepee equipped with anomalies like club chairs, that for all his professions of ecological humility he has wrapped the place in miles of white fence, and that for all his rhetoric of preservation he "has built roads on his ranch, sunk ponds, cleared pastures."[5] Maybe also because the man himself personifies so well the tenor of the wild-tame dialectic in the contemporary West, as a timely Carole Cable cartoon suggests: two women are having coffee in a ferny restaurant, one of them saying to the other, "It's all over. He turned out to be a little too much Cormac McCarthy and not enough Ralph Lauren."[6]

What, beyond the man and his ranch, are the symptoms of Ralphlaurenization? Lots of people wearing clothing in Indian or cowboy style, apparel that once was sturdy and practical but now is overly prettified and often dear. Rodeo competitors trying to look like the male models in a Corral West ranchwear catalogue. Actual cowboys who, as David Thomson interprets their identity crisis, are like the Nevada town of Rawhide ("so fake a name now, so camp, it might be set in neon above a gay bar on the outskirts of some military base") in that "they hardly know whether they're wearing their own clothes or are dressed in costume."[7] Women who slip on Western suede because, as René E. Riley commends it, that pelt induces savage fantasy: "Your mind conjures images of the wildest West. Tribal days and mystic nights. Living by spear and cunning. A Ghost Dance on a canyon rim."[8] Western second homes—log cabins, faux adobes, A-frames—furnished with Navajo blankets, lodgepole beds, wildlife-print curtains, fringed leather chairs, mining gear on the front porch, corrugated metal and chain-link touches in the kitchen. Upscale restaurants decorated with copies of Old Western photographs that serve chile dishes, elk medallions, buffalo burgers. Spas that let the clientele play cowgirl and cowboy while eating macrobiotic delicacies, taking mudbaths, and relaxing to Indian flute music. Breweries in gentrified Western towns operated by locals who've coached themselves in how to speak ranch slang. Country-Western music that— however rowdy and rural in its mixed or self-subverting messages about the West— is, as Larry McMurtry nails it, "music for the suburbs and the freeways, songs to be listened to in the cabs of the newer, more expensive pickups."[9]

None of that's all bad, but much of it tells not only of the harm of excessively selling the West but also of that of selling diverse products through advertising that exploits the mythology of the West as a wild place, both of which contribute to the confused etherealization of a postregion in need of substantive understanding and realistic amelioration. Americans like "to play at being western," in Robert G. Athearn's compact phrase, more than they like to learn what veritably being so might amount to.[10] As a result, they respond agreeably to ads for Estée Lauder makeup that lends to the face the earth tones of the desert, Stetson Country (Monument Valley, according to the promos) or Untamed cologne, StreamLine hot tubs with names such as Bronco, Maverick, and Mustang. Men who sip their morning coffee from a copper mug while imagining themselves leaning against a bunkhouse doorjamb find appealing Taos Country's pitch for reasonably priced Western duds: "RATTLERS, SCORPIONS, GRIZZLIES. WE FIGURE THERE ARE ALREADY ENOUGH THINGS THAT CAN COST A MAN AN ARM AND A LEG."[11] And women "who like to be stirred by nature, not shaken," receive assurance from Subaru's sales pitch for its Outback (seen against a two-page stretch of snow-dusted sierra): "EQUIPPED WITH THE RUGGED TRACTION AND CONTROL OF SUBARU ALL-WHEEL DRIVE, THE OUTBACK CAN GET YOU OVER ROUGH TERRAIN AND DEEP INTO NATURE. BUT THANKS TO ITS NEW SMOOTHER-RIDING SUSPENSION SYSTEM, THE GOING NEVER GETS ROUGH. SO YOU CAN GO OUT AND EXPERIENCE NATURE'S BEAUTY, WITHOUT THE TRIP GETTING UGLY."[12] Such ads evince solid market sense, but they also disclose—as Elliott West says ads for Western railroad tourism did in the first half of the twentieth century—"an ambivalent, even schizophrenic attitude toward the West as a physical environment" and thus show that Americans' penchant for playing at being Western is embedded in "complex, garbled feelings of surrender and mastery toward a mythic landscape."[13]

Western-themed ads suppress the problems with that attitude, of course, and are contrived to foreground the simplistically affirmative; but those problems are implicit in them and can be teased out if, West counsels, "we know what to look for."[14] He does. By his categorization, there are three types of such ads: those that focus on the West as a place, those that focus on it as a story, and those that focus on it as a style.

The first type entices the public with a land of "geographical grandeur, exotic humanity, and nature's balms," in West's phrasing. Ads for rail travel anticipated Subaru's emphases in promising that "the vacationer's West was savage and safe, rugged and comfortable, grandly remote and easy to reach and leave." Ads for automotive travel may be selling the West, but they have always been preeminently using the West to sell automobiles. In the postregional era, that's Windex clear, given the number of cars with names that smack of Western wildness—Mustang, Bronco, Maverick, Navajo, Ranger, and so on. The attraction is the possibility of getting away from daily drudgery and quiet desperation—but, as West words the pertinent query, "get away to where?" The problem is one of abstraction, for the lure "is not some specific stretch of the untamed West but the *idea* of spontaneous movement into a generically western landscape."[15]

The second type of ad employs the most prepossessing aspects of the Western myth to sell everything from luggage to communications systems. To do so, however, it has to handle effectively what West sees as its most basic difficulty: "how to use the old to sell the new? And even tougher, how to invoke a vanished way of life to sell what has caused that way of life to vanish?" Advertisers have relied on several strategies in that respect: "blurring over distinctions between that imagined Golden Age and the present" (some new product does the same thing that pioneers of old did but does it better), claiming that the opportunities of the frontier are still out there, or resorting to a vocabulary that nebulously calls up pioneer traits (*courage, stamina,* and the like). Ads composed by such strategies, though, are only loosely connected to the realia of Western history and promise at most "a *feeling* of the pioneer hero's accomplishment and transformation."[16]

The third type of ad, like the others, depends on abstraction but, as West argues, carries it further, so that the Western-mythic attributes of what is being sold become identical with it. Customers moved to smoke the Marlboro Man's cigarettes or drink the Budweiser beer that cowboys guzzle at the end of a day's work are "literally breathing and swallowing the fantasy, making it a part of themselves"— mountains, sunset, the whole movie. Contradiction lurks in ads of this type, too, but not in a way that can't be turned to the advertiser's advantage, most notably in the case of very personal items like cosmetics and clothing, because it resides in the customers as well, in their "hoping to wear the myth" as a means of defining themselves: the appeal is to people "who want to feel advanced and in sync with the latest trends while in touch with virtues of a receding past, in the same way that Americans have always celebrated both the wilderness and the pioneer's conquest of it." The master of West-as-style advertising with this sort of come-on, West argues, has been Lauren, for "no one else has exploited traditional themes better while working so artfully with that balance between old and new" than that Bronx-born designer—whether you're talking about fragrances, wearables, and home furnishings or the man himself. And, as West points out, the more abstract the "western adland" of such advertising has become, the more versatile its myth has become as a marketing device. But, he warns, in pandering to the ambivalence of "a society that takes as its heroes men who destroy what has made them heroic," that myth enlarges its success at the cost of "disengaging what is being sold from the West as a tangible place or as a story with actual consequences."[17]

Ralphlaurenization, like television shows such as *Dallas* and *L.A. Law* in White's construal, has contributed greatly to reducing the postregional West "to something called life-style, a sort of cultural costume."[18] To some extent that costume is a matter of self-definition, an act through which a person, from the casual wannabe to the veteran professional Westerner despised by social critics in the tradition of Frank Waters, makes up and inhabits his or her own private West—a quasi-autistic act that precludes consciousness of the West as a tangible place.[19] That act isn't, however, simply one of the individual self: it's accomplished by a cultural process Stephen Tatum describes as "the draining out of historicity and the substitution of the image."[20] Doubtless, as he says, Western costumery, by "harmonizing connotations of leisure and work, elegance and ruggedness, the artificial and the natural, ... promotes an illusion of personal renewal"; but collectively such illusory renewal causes a real depletion, for through it "the 'natural' gets displaced by *representation*"—and that displacement is expressive of "the postmodern condition, a condition in which the inability to experience origins due to a pervasive immersion in *simulacra* has caused a loss of faith in any larger, grand, totalizing narrative explaining everyday life."[21] Especially everyday life in the West.

Once in the Saddle I Used to Go Gay: Redoing Rodeo

There are rules, and you have to discover them for yourself or make them up to meet new conditions. And this includes, as The Virginian and a surprising number of John Wayne pictures testify, learning the more civilized, softer rules traditionally thought of as feminine.

  Robert Murray Davis, *Playing Cowboys: Low Culture and High Art in the Western*

Imagine you're at a rodeo cowboys' reunion. Old-timers have gathered somewhere on the High Plains. Faces sun-cured, hands twisted like mesquite, legs stiff-hinged, they walk with a rock, arms cocked tight from a thousand throws, bellies folded over big buckles hard-won. They sit and spit in the thin air, eat grilled *cabrito*, swap tales around the campfire as night falls: some long-gone bronco, bulldogger, woman, bad break—nomads' dreams. Songs are sung. There's gruff talk about New Westers, cowboy chic, what rodeo has come to. Gradually a few diehards drift off to sleep under the stars. The rest head back to motels.

Like those men bound for beds in comfortable cubicles, rodeo itself has gotten softer in the postregional era—and otherwise changed in ways that don't please the diehards but may not be wholly adverse in what they portend. Growing in popularity during recent decades, postmodern rodeo—what with competitors trained in clinics, the proliferation of gay and Indian rodeos, women's participating more in roughstock events, computerized matching of competitors and animals, more rodeos in indoor arenas (the first being in Madison Square Garden in 1922), and such—has increasingly questioned, contradicted, attenuated, and inverted the values affirmed by traditional rodeo, ambiguous values grounded in the white-male ethos of taming the Western wild. Like New Western History—though less radically—postmodern rodeo has been not only revising its take on those values but retelling their stories, making up new rules for reenactment. The result is a sport that has strayed from its origins but also has begun in some ways to symbolize a more appropriate wild-tame dialectic for the West.

Its standardizations and stereotypes aside, rodeo has never been one thing. "Up from the dust gets a buster named Tucson" at the end of May Swenson's poem "Bronco Busting, Event #1."[1] But the buster's name might well be more ethnically flavored or gendered differently. The context might be a pull-out-all-the-stops Indian rodeo (too wild for sanctioning by the Professional Rodeo Cowboys Association [PRCA]), a prison rodeo, a black rodeo, a Mexican rodeo, you name it. The shindig, PRCA-sanctioned or not, might be happening in any one of hundreds of towns or cities in the West—and beyond—with more money in the purses all the time. Still, though, for some decades there has been a mainstream in all these doings, and it consists of the thousands of members of the PRCA.

In a survey of those members conducted a few years ago, Wayne S. Wooden and Gavin Ehringer found that they fall into four categories: "traditionalists" (25 percent), who favor "the cowboy lifestyle rather than the rigors of athletic training"; "weekend warriors" (35 percent), who are serious competitors but have other jobs; "professional athletes" (25 percent), who are full-time competitors; and "elite athletes" (15 percent), who are full-timers making a living from the sport. The data indicate that the vast majority of the members participate primarily to express "their desire to identify with the mythology and traditions of the American cowboy."[2] The top competitors, on the other hand, spend a lot of hours sitting in chartered jets, talking about union issues, meeting with the corporate sponsors for whom they serve as walking billboards, and training. Most of them come off as businessmen— think of world champion all-around cowboy Ty Murray, now a millionaire rancher.[3]

Across all categories, most PRCA cowboys have never worked cattle on a ranch, and many of them wear protective gear—vests, helmets, masks—in the arena. Patently, there's a new breed straddling the critters in the chutes.

You can array arguments impugning that breed and its brand of rodeo. That postmodern rodeo cowboys' disconnection from the ranch, however economically justifiable, represents a significant apostasy—the further abdication of life lived in nature. That more than ever before they're just entertainers habituated to danger. That the entertainment they practice is but a shadow of what it once was, which was but a shadow of real ranch work. That, as Larry McMurtry complains, it's "a kind of caricature of cowboying."[4] That, as his stronger gripe goes, "rodeo, as publicly promoted, . . . wants both the lie and the truth: to be both the Wild West, and yet steeped in family values."[5] That, as he shoots with more concentrated fire, rodeo has become too much indoor show business and that rodeo hands, unlike the glorious Casey Tibbs, "are—and have been—the suburbanites of the West."[6] No surprise, I guess, that in suburban Kansas the Johnson County Fairgrounds now hosts Rodeo Bible Camp.

Enough defects to burden the bed of a dual-wheel pickup. But there are hopeful signs in postmodern rodeo as well. They have to do with the changing role of women in rodeo, the flourishing of gay rodeo, and—most subtly and ironically—the increasing popularity of bull riding.

As Mary Lou LeCompte and others have shown, the story of women's participation in rodeo for over a hundred years has been a troubled one.[7] The trouble can be understood once we see "the rodeo man" the way Elizabeth Atwood Lawrence sees him: "as exemplifying culture," albeit ambiguously, and "exerting a controlling force over nature, which includes animals, women, and land, and whatever wild elements can be brought under his power."[8] Because of the rodeo man's desire to control women, their participation has been restricted. Even when you grant their fuller participation in a range of events prior to World War II, a situation that altered subsequently for a number of reasons, that's still the case.[9] Mostly they have served in what Wooden and Ehringer call "ceremonial and supportive roles" (rodeo queens, flag bearers, trick riders, and the like)[10] and as the sole competitors in barrel racing, an event McMurtry condemns as "almost surrealistically pointless, and thus the perfect vehicle for keeping the little ladies of the rodeo securely in their place."[11]

But the circumstances of rodeo women shifted in the late twentieth century, most dramatically when the Girls Rodeo Association, founded in 1948, was renamed the Women's Professional Rodeo Association (WPRA) in 1982 and when that organization then established the Professional Women's Rodeo Association (PWRA), a separate division for all-women events—the gamut of them, both timed and judged (roughstock)—in 1987. Memberships in the WPRA and PWRA don't rival those in the PRCA, and women don't compete with men as equals; but their prestige and purses have gone up, and rodeo has become less patriarchal as a consequence. Having women ride broncs and bulls in their own rodeos and in some PRCA-sanctioned rodeos signals the achievement of a modicum of the augmented tough-and-tender feminization requisite for a saner nature-culture balance in the postregional West. Further hope may lie in the fact that, opposite the trend of their male counterparts, as LeCompte's research shows, "more than 85 percent of professional cowgirls still come from the old cattle frontier" and "more than half of them [live] on ranches."[12]

Homosexuality in the Old West, where whites censured berdachism, is a subject you wouldn't want to bring up in a bar during Cheyenne Frontier Days and one on which the research is inconclusive. Stephen Tatum observes that "the literature of the cattle trade is filled with episodes of cowboys, geographically isolated from the female community during cattle drives and round-ups, acting out or assuming both male and female sexual roles."[13] And Blake Allmendinger argues, concerning Gold Rush prospectors, that, "rather than escaping from civilization, men who went west re-created it, assuming both 'masculine' and 'feminine' roles in homosocial frontier communities."[14] He is careful to note in his discussion of cowboys, however, that, though their cross-dressing and male-male dancing "might suggest that homosexual or homoerotic behavior was common out West," those practices "cannot be *equated* with these forms of behavior in the absence of textual historical proof"—of which, he admits, he's found none.[15] But there are, of course, all those flaking sepia photographs of chummy cowboys that seldom include women. Also, there are some classic Westerns (The Virginian and Shane, for example) suffused with homoerotic energy in which, to follow Allmendinger's breakdown, violent acts "always function cathartically, first dramatizing intimate, complex relations between heroes and villains, then climactically purging them, terminating relations that might have become homosexual by means of a deadly fist fight, shoot-out, or hanging."[16] Indeed, the Western film, in Lee Clark Mitchell's interpretation, is "a genre that allows us to gaze at men," men who become men by having the male body "beaten, distorted, and pressed out of shape so that it can paradoxically become what it already is"—a renewal associated with "a special landscape (the American West)."[17] In rodeo a similar transformation is associated with that landscape's surrogate, the arena.

Whatever hermeneutics you employ in sifting the historical record for precedents, gay rodeo has flourished in the West and elsewhere since the first one of its kind was put on in Reno, Nevada, in 1975. Like WPRA and PWRA rodeo, it has, while suffering the denunciation of many traditionalists, profited from postmodern tolerance in the broader culture—even more so. The International Gay Rodeo Association (IGRA), established in 1985, with its thousands of members (both men and women) and regional affiliates, is now larger than the rodeo women's organizations. Though variously changed in the decades since it began and become culturally woollier than anything the PRCA would ever sanction (what with campy events like the wild drag race, goat dressing, and steer decorating as well as the more conventional ones), gay rodeo, in Wooden and Ehringer's estimation, has stayed true to the goals of the IGRA, which "are 'to promote and nurture, through fellowship, the sport of rodeo within the gay community; to foster a positive image of gay cowboys and cowgirls within all communities; . . . and to participate in the preservation of our western heritage.'"[18] Laudable enough.

What's most laudable, however, is hinted by Darrell Yates Rist in his reflections on his experience at a gay rodeo in Denver. There, he says, he found men and women who were reclaiming a Western past they'd fled "because 'queers' were not allowed a part in it" and who taught him "the joy of wider possibilities" unknown to homosexuals who had rejected rural life and left for cities.[19] There's a bit of sexual insinuation in his phrasing, but otherwise—and more significantly—those possibilities concern heritage and not a straying from but a return, with a difference, to Western roots. As the IGRA's goals suggest, gay rodeo promotes rodeo as a sport, but it promotes also something the West needs that straight rodeo now neglects: what McMurtry calls "rodeo considered as community experience."[20] In addition, the spirit of the community seems to be one at least as much of cooperation as of competition and one that playfully accepts more than it stolidly controls nature and its "wild elements" (including the feminine)—exactly the spirit explored by painter Delmas Howe in his gay-oriented *Rodeo Pantheon* series, maybe most iconoclastically in his 1992 oil *The Education of the Mortals*, where cowboys in a wilderness setting are shedding their clothes to join naked male gods in unabashedly savoring the natural world.[21]

Bull riding doesn't permit such savoring, and its recently burgeoning Bull Riders Only popularity suggests the decadence of Romans who flocked to gawk at gladiatorial gore; but it suggests as well, with a little close revisionist reading, something more important than spectators' getting thrills and riders' getting their chickens scattered. Bull riding requires the youthful attitude illustrated by Diamond Felts in Annie Proulx's short story "The Mud Below," who "felt the bull in himself, hadn't yet discerned the line of inimical difference between roughstock and rider."[22] That is, to recall one of Lawrence's points, bull riding, more than any other rodeo event, asks for the rider's strong sense of identification with, connection to as well as disciplined distance from, the wildness engaged during the eight-second ride—a sense salutarily different from that nurtured by the Disneyfied West. Also, that ton of Brahma hybrid between the legs of the rider, whose fellow contestants may refer to him as a wolf or some similar form of wildlife, freights a load of complex symbology by virtue of associations with both male and female principles (so that the rider's "kissing the bull" has undertones not yet often deliberated around the chutes), both paternal and maternal qualities, or, as Jack Randolph Conrad describes the combination in his history of the bull's symbolism, "tremendous strength and great fertility."[23] While the inference might seem far-fetched, the popularity of bull riding may harbinger the possibility of a more equilibrated relation between Western culture and nature, one with the ballast of a redressing feminization.

Indeed, that possibility, less conceivable earlier and less noticeable without postmodern perspective, has been symbolically inherent in rodeo for some time. Bonney MacDonald detects intimations of it in the course of an analysis of Gretel Ehrlich's essay "Rules of the Game: Rodeo":

> Furthering her . . . revision of gender codes and mutually exclusive binaries, Ehrlich turns to the icon of the western rodeo—the very celebration, as Tompkins has argued, of western male dominance and female invisibility. Within this bastion of codified behavior, however, Ehrlich finds oppositions in play. . . . In fact, leading into her inverting of male and female stereotypes, Ehrlich suggests that the male riders—in their aeronautic balance on bucking horses and their high-flung ropes in team roping—are marked by "feminine grace.". . . By contrast, "[b]arrel racing is the . . . women's event. Where the men are tender in their movements, as elegant as if Balanchine had been their coach, the women are prodigies of Wayne Gretsky, all speed, bully, and grit."[24]

An embryonic awareness of the implications of such labile stereotypes informs John Huston's film The Misfits, which was released in 1961, during the West's passage from region to postregion. Shot in and around Reno, it's superficially a movie about mustangers, but beneath the surface, in Cheryll Glotfelty's well-reasoned interpretation, it "contrasts the Old West with the New and depicts the dilemma of characters who are caught in this transition." The most compelling turn in the plot occurs when the sensitive and compassionate young Chicago woman Roslyn Taber, played by Marilyn Monroe, finally persuades aging cowboy Gay Langland (that surname, meaning "long land," not a bad kenning for the West), played by Clark Gable, to give up mustanging. That turn and several related ones, some occurring during a rodeo scene central to the movie's meaning, indicate that "in the face of change the best response is to adapt and become new rather than to be inflexible and get old," a lesson, Glotfelty argues, "as applicable to our own time—the new New West, the postmodern West, the twenty-first-century West—as it was to the 1950s West depicted in The Misfits." Stated flatly, the lesson is "that it is time for the Old West to change its ways." Change them so that the future West perhaps prefigured by today's redone rodeo (even if such rodeo is only a redaction of "a simulation of a popular image of the Old West"), like the future West projected by Huston's film, "actually offers a more humane set of values toward nature, a less destructive path for men, and more choices for women."[25] A future West that, like the best rodeo, is controlled but also wild.

Las Vegas: Ambiguous Oasis

The desert could not be cultivated—it could be sodded and watered and tricked
up to look like an oasis. But in true Ozymandian style, the lesson remained—
Nature always won.
      Carol Muske-Dukes, "Ann Stanford: In Memoriam"

We're on Interstate 15, not long out of Barstow, California, driving northeast, while evening deepens, into the Great Basin, a tectonically unsteady slab of the West where, before glaciers waned and heat took over, valleys once were green with life and rivers fed lakes now dry. To borrow the title of Nelson Algren's collection of skid-row stories, we're headed for "the neon wilderness" of Las Vegas. ("Neon looks good in Nevada," though, McPhee tells us: "The tawdriness is refined out of it in so much wide black space.")[1] Also, as Raoul Duke, the drugged-up narrator of Hunter S. Thompson's 1971 gonzo-journalistic book on that city, tells a hapless hitchhiker he and Doctor Gonzo have picked up around here on this very highway, "'we're on our way to Las Vegas to find the American Dream.'" Or at least the form of it to be found in the postregional West in what he later warns "is not a good town for psychedelic drugs. Reality itself is too twisted."[2]

In a couple of hours we've blown in. Las Vegas, the fastest-growing city in the fastest-growing state in America. It looks like an oversize cruise ship adrift on sand. Celebrities and imitators of dead celebrities perform here. Here you can huddle safe from the desert's indefinite darkness in the cool and noisy comfort of perpetually bright and clockless casinos. Watch long-legged women strut or magicians spin illusions. And more. Always more.

From the beginning of the twentieth century, when it was only a railroad station built by copper magnate William Andrews Clark, Las Vegas (named by the Spanish for "the meadows" its artesian springs once supported) has been the product of what Timothy Egan terms "a melding of technology and sleaze." After sufficient aggrandizement, that melding made its Strip the most-visited destination in the West and Las Vegas itself "the ultimate Western city, the boomtown that never went bust, the something-for-nothing metropolis that blew itself up every few years, the land that welcomed people without a past because it would never have a past." And, as water usage and the interest of the intellectually chichi intensified in the late decades of that century, more: "Some elite architects, Robert Venturi among them, pronounced the city fabulous. It was anything goes, alive, electric, original, American! It was the frontier of urbanism. Forget those prune-faced Puritans and their miserable City on a Hill. . . . Forget Edward Abbey's apocalyptic fear of a bloated urban monster rising in the desert, a cancer of melahomas. Here was the new century city dream." Now, that new century under way, Las Vegas, bold as ever, still trumpets to all doubting Thomases that "you can bend the desert to your will. The West, after all, is about possibility."[3] So far, so, more or less, good.

There are numerous histories of Las Vegas, and all of them treat it as a place about possibility. That's what it was for the Mormons who tried and failed to settle the area in the 1850s. Maybe also for the Mexicans whose caravans traveled through it in the 1830s, maybe even for the Paiutes who depended on its water for hundreds of years before the trains at Clark's station did. That's what it was for local Nevadans who played up Hoover Dam as a tourist attraction and grew fat on a boom of military business during World War II. And that's what it was in the 1960s, by which time it had become what Richard White dubs, hands down, "the most bizarre creation" of the New West, "the place where a contrived 'Old West' self-consciously met the New West of Hollywood and southern California leisure"; where the garish Strip was marketed as "the 'Ultimate West'"; where "the older western fascination with gambling, chance, luck, and getting rich quick merged with the New West's picture of itself as a land of relaxation."[4] Egan expounds the city's history since around 1931, when table games were legalized, as that of a place that "started as a cowboy fantasy retreat" and then evolved—through successive generations of gangsters, teamsters, and corporation executives—into "the American Vatican for Vice, requiring grand ritual and show for pilgrims dressed like six-year-olds" (and, moreover, the appearance of being family-oriented enough to bring in gaggles of real six-year-olds as well as their vice-craving parents).[5]

What you learn from such perspectives is that possibility in Las Vegas, the city Hal K. Rothman calls "the prototype for entertainment tourism," is about a grotesque "malleability" that has been its survival stratagem from the heyday of its "ersatz frontier conception" in the 1940s on through the tropical frills of the 1950s and the more exotic themes—ancient Egypt, Camelot, Venice, and so on—ostended in the colossal resorts of recent decades. What wasn't very malleable through those stages of mutation, however, was the overarching emphasis on gambling, a profitable distraction Las Vegas made into "an offering of all things to all people." And all those things, from free drinks to high-dollar suites, function, just as Rothman says the original Western theme did, "as a mask for gambling."[6]

Since gambling in a broad sense has long been part of the Euro-American modus operandi in the West, it's not surprising that many of the contemporary Western venues for games of chance were once mining towns—and have present problems that echo similar ones in the past.[7] Still chief among all those venues, irrespective of competition from riverboat and Indian casinos around the country and from Atlantic City, Las Vegas, given its dedication to gambling and its isolation in the desert, might well be renamed, after one of its resorts, Treasure Island. Gambling is a wild indoor sport but one whose unpredictability is delimited for the house's margin, and the dizzying frenzy of it in Las Vegas has something to do, as Jean Baudrillard theorizes, with its affinity with that surrounding and reinforcing context:

"Gambling itself is a desert form, inhuman, uncultured, initiatory, a challenge to the natural economy of value, a crazed activity on the fringes of exchange. But it too has a strict limit and stops abruptly; its boundaries are exact, its passion knows no confusion."[8] That affinity suggests that Las Vegas has to do with possibility—and the risk attendant on its rigid laws—in a peculiarly Western way.

How so? Because in the gaudy artificiality of the casinos' bewildering space gambling can, as Elizabeth Raymond observes, "substitute for the nineteenth-century drive to dominate and control the natural world."[9] Because the hucksters who build and run those abstract wildernesses understand what Robert G. Athearn describes as "the possibilities of tapping the fantasy of the western bonanza, the hallowed belief that out in the wilds of the deserts or mountains, one could turn one's life around by panning the right gravel or turning the right card."[10] Because in Las Vegas casinos the acts of Western nature, like the women in Harte's stories, to follow Lee Clark Mitchell's gloss on them, "become equivalent to the game of poker itself: inscrutable, unpredictable, needing to be patiently read and dealt with carefully, invariably introducing the prospect that one may lose one's shirt in the encounter."[11]

Correlate with such figures of substitutional equivalence is the ambiguity, through incongruity or contradiction, of Las Vegas, a quality long associated with America's ambivalent hunger for Western wildness and given extravagant postmodern expression in this meretriciously beautiful but treacherous Cockaigne. Rothman sees that quality already starting to take hold during the 1930s, when, after the completion of their nearby famous dam, small-town Las Vegans "exalted the accomplishments of their culture, embracing the conquest of nature by industry and technology," but "also saw themselves as a symbol of the wide-open life."[12] By the early 1990s Las Vegas had become, in the words of David Spanier, "wonderful and awful simultaneously."[13] By the late 1990s, David Thomson, meditating on its "outrages of juxtaposition," its enshrinement of gambling in all its excitement and disappointment, its exhibition of the enchanting sort of "gruesome parody" represented by Caesars Palace, concluded that Las Vegas "teaches us the very startling lesson that Hell and Heaven may be the same place."[14] Now, in the twenty-first century, it has become, in Rothman and Mike Davis's assessment, a laboratory where diversified corporations experiment with ways "to integrate gaming with virtual reality and other interactive entertainment technologies," their aspiration thereby to emulate the kind of medleying that, on an urban-architectural scale, has made the Strip into "a Möbius Strip where casinos merge into malls into amusement parks into sports venues into residential subdivisions into casinos again." That aspiration is a derivative of the one that assembled the city as "the first 'arid metropolis,'" a conglomeration now fraught with mounting contradictions that Rothman and Davis compare to "a huge jumbo jet in which neither the pilot nor the crew, much less the passengers, have any idea of where it is ultimately headed or how high and far it can fly."[15]

This out-of-control situation paradoxically overseen by control freaks as compulsive as old Walt was—or Howard Hughes, one of the founding fathers of corporate Las Vegas—has arisen largely because of the disjunction between the unreal and the all-too-real. In his critique of the city, Norman M. Klein notices it everywhere, perhaps nowhere more poignantly, in terms of the wild-tame dialectic, than at the MGM Grand, where you find "animatronic replacements for animals that will soon be irreplaceable."[16] It's there in all the imagery of the Old World reconquering the New through reinventive replications of the decadent luxury of the former being built and rebuilt in the ruins of the latter. It's there predominantly in the way Las Vegas is, as Egan sums up its hubris, "not a city to match the setting, but a city to defy the setting."[17] Think of how the Colorado has been plundered, despite recycling, to supply water for the dream castles of Steve Wynn, one of the city's latest visionary developers and impresarios: for the waterfall at the Mirage, the moat at Treasure Island, the fountains at the Bellagio (where the Dunes was implosively razed). Pleasure domes rising and rising again from alluvium, their simulations maintained against nature's reality principle by hidden thickets of wire and computer chips. The virtual Vegas of airy casinos now available to Internet gamblers was always in the cards.

Thus, hand in hand with so many ersatzes goes etherealization. It's obvious enough in the fact that the service economy of Las Vegas now produces nothing but amusement without depth by a process whereby, in Klein's description, "the guest is transported directly into movie set design" and absorbed by the outward-expanding foreground.[18] Absorbed by the forced motion of the moving sidewalk at the airport, by the endless spinning of slot-machine wheels and roulette pans, by the omnipresent inward-sucking whirl of industrialized entertainment in what Zeese Papanikolas hails as "City of treadmills!" And the treadmills run in a space dominated by "the Sign," as he explains: "It looms above the landscape, immense, aggressive, insistent. . . . You consume the sign here, not that to which it points. Beyond the sign is metaphysical darkness." Which explanation prompts him to inquire, regarding this manifold of signifiers with vacuous referents, "Is this not, indeed, Utopia? Where the idea becomes the pure environment, a kind of gigantic bottle that shuts out anything but itself?"[19] Compared to the Las Vegas that old-timers remember, the world inside that bottle, in Thomson's more common parlance, is "automatic, bureaucratic, mass-market, perfumed, and anonymous." Naturally wild long ago, the place is now not even culturally wild for those who lived there fifty years back: "Gambling then was akin to fine old whiskey; today it's like Coca-Cola. Once upon a time, Nevada was a place for outcasts, adventurers, and tough godless men who believed in the whim of chance. Now, it's another kind of Disneyland."[20]

To put the matter another way, Las Vegas, the touristic fantasia that an Americanized and updated King Ludwig of Bavaria loosed in the desert might have devised, fills the role Neil Campbell attributes to it: "the postmodern New West's capital city." As such, it's an "oxymoronic dark wonderland of danger and promise," complete with any myth you wish. Seed crystal for the continuing spread of Lasvegasation, it "represents, in excess, the growth of the New West as a series of overlapping, often contradictory, phases from which emerges a complex space— city and desert, settled and transient, fragile and booming all at the same time."[21] Surfacy, rhizomatic, indeterminate, ironic in its authentic artificiality, Las Vegas embodies the postregional wild-tame dialectic at its zaniest pitch.[22]

But Campbell's dialectical pairs contain nervous-making modifiers: *transient*, *fragile*. Ever overgrowing and shorter on water, Las Vegas is playing against the house of nature (the *eco-* in *ecology* comes from the Greek *oîkos*, "house"), a house whose probabilities (forget possibilities) are more merciless than those electronically coded in slot machines. Ultimately, as all gamblers know or learn, the house wins. The only question is how long it will take.

Those who have studied Las Vegas closely have all arrived at much the same prognosis. Egan, for instance, acknowledges that, propelled by a skewed hunger for the wild, "everybody wants what Vegas has—lights, fantasy, the Fever [of gambling], and all you can eat for $8.95"—and he suspects that the city will get sufficient water to bear such pressure for a few decades; then, he predicts, it "will consume itself," decay into a ghost town, and finally be nothing but a ruin.[23] Papanikolas writes of how the city "could, over night, blow away, the rough magic of gangsters and hoteliers disappearing like the trembling lines of heat mirage."[24] Thomson, reminding such gamblers of the desert's patience, advises them to "know that if you play long enough, it gets back its money"—though he concedes that Las Vegas is "a city built in the spirit that knows its days are numbered."[25]

Has anyone really thought through what such handwriting on the wall means? Is Las Vegas the West's last big party for the American dream before nature levels it all into a junkyard? The rules in the heat-death game of thermodynamics are absolute. You can't win. You can't break even. You can't get out.

Or can you?

Weird Weird West: Roswell and Other Landing Sites

Aliens seems to be more prevalent in the West.
   Joel Achenbach, *Captured by Aliens: The Search for Life and Truth in a Very Large Universe*

My heart's wilderness must retain
a shadow, a longing, which nothing can disappoint.

If you've got a better theory, go for it!
My world of possibilities won't be tamed.
Lilace Mellin Guignard, "My Bigfoot Theory of Love"

During much of James C. Work's 1999 Western novel *Ride South to Purgatory*, an Arthurian story that takes place on the High Plains of the late 1870s, the protagonist, Pasque Pendragon, searches for a cyclopean and apparently invulnerable stranger who has challenged him to a duel. At one point in his quest he asks himself if the stranger might be "pure loco." "The West," after all, he ruminates, "was full of crazy lunatics."[1] Well, it was long before then. It still is, more than ever—partly just because of population growth, partly for other reasons. In the last half century or so the traditional conception of the West as a wild place has been, in many ways, radically revised by Cold War paranoia, suspicion about sites for secret scientific experimentation, beliefs about the spiritual potency of some locales, and other factors—until the postregion has become, more than anywhere else in the United States, a magnet and agar for an astounding variety of cultural and personal oddities.

What, for instance? Spectral gunfighters in Tombstone, Arizona. Aging hippies, artists, computer geeks, and others partying naked or in outlandish get-ups at the annual Burning Man Festival on Labor Day weekend in the Black Rock Desert in northwestern Nevada, a state whose Route 375 has been officially declared the Extraterrestrial Highway. UFO cults here and there. Any number of people whose coffee tables display the paraphernalia of polymorphous Western-flavored mysticism.

Most of the places that serve as foci for such weirdness are in the Southwest, where alien-invasion movies typically are set (a noteworthy exception is Steven Spielberg's 1977 film *Close Encounters of the Third Kind*, in which the alien landing transpires in northeastern Wyoming—still the West, though). That's a portion of the West whose "magical power" is stronger than and can mythologically transform "the overwhelmingly rationalist flavor of the military" there, according to Paula Gunn Allen: "the story of what some call 'the Roswell incident'; the rumors of otherworldly activity at a small military installation at Dulce, bordering Jicarilla Apache country; odd sightings near China Lake, Vandenberg, Manzano, and Kirtland; along with rumors circling around NORAD and the underground base in the Manzanos—all testify to the presence of the otherworldly in the very heart of the military's Southwest."[2] Roswell, New Mexico, is the best known of the places she mentions, so let's go there first; then to another Southwestern place of military-based myth, Area 51; and then on to some New Age haunts before heading north to wrap up our tour in Bigfoot country.

Now familiar enough to the American public to be the subject of bumper stickers ("The truth is out there") and television documentaries and the theme of a vodka ad ("Absolut Roswell"), Roswell made its debut as the icon of ufology in 1947. The incident that changed the town from ordinary to extraordinary concerned the manager of a ranch northwest of Roswell who witnessed an explosion on the night of July 4 of that year, found the wreckage of some unusual vehicle at the site of the explosion, and notified the local authorities. The army investigated, removed the crashed vehicle, reported that a flying saucer had been recovered—but later said the thing was a weather balloon. Thereafter the story gets indeterminate. There were—or weren't—bodies of aliens in the vehicle. The bodies were taken to various locations and studied. The aliens died—or didn't. The military may have learned from analyzing the debris of the craft how to make new high-tech materials. The truth was covered up and remains so.[3]

The incident occurred at the onset of the nuclear age, wasn't forgotten during the decades of the Cold War (a time of multitudinous UFO sightings), and put Roswell on the map as a destination for the UFO nuts, many in science-fictional costumes, who flock to the anniversary commemorations of the incident and visit the International UFO Museum and Research Center, browse through the Alien Zone gift shop, or just eat a snow cone topped with "alien juice." The most intriguing thing about the incident and similar ufological phenomena that attract such interest is that, for the most part, they all have to do with sparsely populated and relatively wild places—in the West. There seems to be a connection between the way Americans perceive UFOs and the way they perceive the postregional West. What is it?

Thomas E. Bullard, who has methodically studied UFO mythology, offers thoughts that may help us specify that connection. He notes that contemporary UFO beliefs take shape around "age-old mythic motifs" and concern "the unexpected and uncontrolled." Though skeptical about the ability of structuralist theory to show how myths reconcile cultural contradictions, he grants that it "highlights several unmistakable characteristics of the UFO myth" that make up the "conundrum of oppositions" presented by UFOs: "Exemplars of wonder and progress, they also pose the threat of invasion and the vague terror of alienness. Futuristic in design and the product of advanced civilization, they also mirror a bygone past of magic, angels, demons, and supernatural power." Furthermore, they "embody technology as both mastery of nature and soulless destroyer of life, symbolizing a love-hate dilemma that divides the two throbbing lobes of the modern mind." Also, the messages aliens have been communicating to postmodern abductees "have redirected from the nuclear fears characteristic of the 1950s contactee era to the ecological concerns prevalent over the last two decades"—at the same time that the myth has taken on a new aspect, an "ecological apocalypticism that looks for overpopulation and pollution to destroy a corrupt technological civilization, followed by an Arcadian society living in harmony with nature." Bullard's analysis yields a lace of associations that, in a manner no more linearly rational than the myth itself, translates into postmodern terms America's enduring ambivalent attitude toward the West—through which it's perceived as both a finite physical place and a limit-less state of mind, both the nation's silicon future and its Native past, both nature mastered and nature destroyed, and the like—and he observes that UFO stories of "final battles" recall, among other antecedents, Custer's defeat and that those expressing millenarian hopes for righting a world gone ecologically astray recall, among other antecedents, the Ghost Dance religion.[4]

Phil Patton's investigation of Area 51 conjures up similarly evocative associa-tions. Located in the desert northwest of Las Vegas, Area 51 designates a section of a four-million-acre government tract that contains a "secret test facility" and an air base and restricted airspace known as, "irresistibly, 'Dreamland.'" The U-2 spy plane was engineered there, as were the SR-71 Blackbird and the F-117 Stealth. Fed-eral officials deny its existence. Some UFO buffs claim to have seen flying saucers above it. Some contend that the Roswell-incident aliens and their craft are hidden in it. Some assume that aliens control it. From the beginning of its Cold War his-tory, Area 51 "was about mystery engendering fantasy," says Patton: "It was like one of those empty spaces in the unexplored interiors of continents that medieval cartographers had imaginatively supplied with dragons and other monsters." In that respect it's somewhat like what the West itself once was, as it is also by virtue of how its inaccessibility has made it a preserve for wildlife. In the extremity of its experimentation, Area 51 "is to technology what Las Vegas is to the everyday economy." Finally, most resonantly, the perimeter that circumscribes the place is, in Patton's explication, a "manifestation of our old friend the Frontier: the original settlement line, but also the New Frontier, the Last Frontier"—thus "the edge of the known" and "the launching point for all sorts of explorations."[5]

You can find other such manifestations in the postregional West—postmodern frontiers where the known and the unknown meet. The San Luis Valley, an expanse of land west of the Sangre de Cristo Range shared by southern Colorado and north-ern New Mexico, is one. There, at night, says David Perkins, "you might be treated to dazzling aerial displays of huge flaming fireballs, small dancing fireballs, flying triangles, bell-shaped objects, hybrid aircraft . . . and good old-fashioned flying saucers"; during the day you might "stumble upon the carcass of a freshly mutilated cow" (a phenomenon, seemingly the work of aliens, much in evidence of late). If you go to Crestone, Colorado, in the north of the valley and a few miles from the Great Sand Dunes National Monument (near which, Perkins reminds us, is what "some Native Americans call the sipapu, or point of emergence of their people from the underworld"), you'll be in the center of the "heart of weirdness," a town once dedicated to mining that has become "a thriving New Age Mecca," those who've made the hajj "drawn by 'a certain mystical vibration.'"[6]

The New Age movement, as Catherine L. Albanese informs us, incorporates an eclectic notion of "Amerindian immersion in nature," along with transcendental-ism and other isms, into its "religious syncretism."[7] The movement's "spiritual trekkers," as Allen dubs them, are certainly eclectic as to what they're seeking on their Southwestern treks to "all the spots deemed 'sacred.'" They visit the Santuario de Chimayó in northern New Mexico to get supernaturally curative dirt from a hole in the ground in one of the sacristies, take healing baths at Jemez Springs west of Los Alamos, and tune in to "a variety of 'vortexes' that surround Sedona, in northern Arizona." They also want to "chase UFOs, make offerings to Native gods, and wait to hear spirits sing and weep among the magnificent ruins of Chaco Canyon, Mesa Verde, Bandelier, and Canyon de Chelly."[8] Or they might prefer riding horseback not far from Georgia O'Keeffe's beloved Cerro Pedernal on a Jungian equestrian shamanic vision quest to cross an inner frontier into their shadow selves.[9] But where they all wind up, sooner or later, is Santa Fe.

The City Different is the cultic pivot in a state that's home to what Stephen Fox describes as "a stunning array of spiritual communities," many of which derive from countercultural goings-on there in the late 1960s that had ancestors in earlier Beat and bohemian experiments with lifestyle. To borrow from Patton's analogy, what Las Vegas is to the everyday economy Santa Fe is to everyday American culture. If, as Fox asserts, the religious composite of the New Age movement often "is mixed in such a way—at the lowest common denominator of meaning—that it functions as alternative Muzak in the Spiritual Mall," then Santa Fe is the atrium of that mall.[10]

The singing of New Age activities in all that dry blue is indeed different from the usual Muzak, for their general emphasis on alternativity suggests a constant crossing of frontiers between the usual and a desideratum beyond it: a past life, an entity on another planet, or a tunnel into the nth dimension reached through a channeler; knowledge of the future through a Tarot reading; the existential vibrancy that follows an aura cleansing and chakra alignment; and so forth. Santa Fe is the destination for postmodern Americans with a hunger for alternatives, an old motive for heading west. In this case they're interested in the supramundane wildness of a place, like Sedona as Patricia Nelson Limerick limns it, "where cosmic energies accumulate"—though she goes on to warn of one of the many guises of the Boone paradox: such places are also "where real estate agents congregate."[11] Santa Fe, like the whole West, is ever at risk of becoming the City Same.

But that hasn't happened yet. The roominess of the West still permits some abundance of alternative lifestyles and life-forms. The unpredictable hasn't been totally homogenized into predictability. Places culturally akin to Santa Fe dot the Southwest and, less densely but increasingly, more northerly states of the postregion as well, most intriguingly those, to borrow the title of Robert Michael Pyle's book on Sasquatch, "where Bigfoot walks."

"Something is definitely afoot in the forests of the Pacific Northwest," Pyle maintains. Whatever the Yeti-like Bigfoot, single or multiple, may be, "more and more people . . . believe that giant hairy monsters are present in our midst," he writes; and the purpose of his book—which carries a subtitle, *Crossing the Dark Divide*, suggestive of yet another frontier—is to answer the question of what that means. It's a question that leads him to learn of Bigfoot's precursors in stories from the Kwakiutl of British Columbia, to wrestle with disagreements between believers and skeptics, and to ponder the social-anthropological consignment of Bigfoot "to the category of archetypal myth: the contemporary expression of Beowulf's Grendel, the modern manifestation of the medieval Green Man—the wild counterpart to our domestic selves that all folk seem to need." It's therefore a question that leads to other questions—not of whether or not Bigfoot might physically exist but of "how our hearts are carried off by hairy monsters that may live only in our minds . . . and how much wildness will survive our rough handling of the land." For Pyle, Bigfoot "is one big metaphor—a model for wildness, the unknown."[12] A metaphor, in particular, for the Western wild that Americans need deeply even as they handle it roughly.

Paul Shepard has a cognate take on Bigfoot. He sees the creature as "a modern form of the Wild Man" on a globe where wilderness is endangered and ever shrinking. Responsible for that situation, we're now more wistful about such a form than fearful of it: "We camp and hike 'in nature,' as though emulating the . . . Wild Man of the past, an aspect of ourselves we cannot give up."[13]

Despite the variety of the weirdness I've discussed, it all involves something we cannot give up and are best able to keep only in the West. It has to do with how early travelers and settlers in the West celebrated its extremes in exaggerated accounts even as they fought with them. With the West as always what Neil Campbell calls "a place of encounter, a meeting place for differences."[14] With the West as a place of *l'homme différent*, Lucian Boia's term for what Boria Sax classifies as a being "usually located at the boundaries of the known world" that is exemplified by "Yetis, and aliens from outer space."[15] With the West, preeminently the Mars-like Great Basin, as a place where, by William L. Fox's tropology, "we still see aliens just off the edge of the map, those invisible inhabitants of terra incognita we call the Other, and with whom we collaborate to define ourselves" in a "void here on earth [that] is simply reminding us of the void out there" in the universe beyond.[16] With what Donald Snow argues is "perhaps the least understood imperative driving the late-twentieth-century 'resettling' of the American West: the quest for a spiritual life, which in modern terms probably means the opportunity to link together livelihood, personal growth, and the appreciation of wild nature."[17] Ultimately, what we cannot give up and are best able to keep only in the West has to do with a still-vital national trait captured in a generalization that preoccupied D. H. Lawrence in his *Studies in Classic American Literature* and that Philip Deloria, seeing it exemplified in New Agers' co-optation of Indian traditions, phrases as Americans' "wanting to savor both civilized order and savage freedom at the same time."[18]

The weirdness of the postregional West springs from fluid ligatures (to use a word that echoes the etymon of *religion*) that withstand disjunction: between here and there, now and then, world and otherworld, tame and wild.

The Last Best Craze: Madness in Montana

Through the warm dusk I drove
To blizzards sifting on the hissing stove,

And found no images of pastoral will,
But fear, thirst, hunger, and this huddled chill.
    J. V. Cunningham, "Montana Pastoral"

On April 20, 1995, the *Daily Oklahoman* carried the front-page headline "MORNING OF TERROR." The subheading read "City Struggles with Shock of Deadly Bombing." Below it, edge to edge on the newsprint, spread a smoke-filled photograph of what was left of the Alfred P. Murrah Federal Building.[1] An explosion the previous morning had torn away the front of it and brought about the collapse of floor on floor into a rubble of broken concrete, crooked steel, smashed bodies. The stratified cavity looked like the wall of an open-pit mine, and I wondered if any of the notorious antigovernment zanies in Montana were to blame.

My intuition turned out to be off in that I had the state wrong. The man who had parked the Ryder truck packed with ammonium nitrate and diesel fuel in front of the building was Timothy McVeigh, a psychopath, since executed, who had grown up in Pendleton, New York, and had moved around during and after his years in the U.S. Army but for sure wasn't a Montanan. Aside from geography, though, the earmarks were there, as the public found out after his arrest: he was a National Rifle Association member who spent hours cleaning his weapons, stockpiled food in preparation for some imminent social meltdown, was afraid of the feds (maliciously so after the 1993 Branch Davidian disaster), was interested in white supremacy, and so on. And he did have linkages to the geographical West (Kansas and Arizona) as well as to what Jonathan Raban, in his social history of eastern Montana, calls a "version of the West [that] seemed half boy-scout play-acting, half deadly paranoia, with some queer Bible-reading thrown into the mixture" and whose "leading figures—Bo Gritz, the Trochmann brothers, Randy Weaver, Timothy McVeigh—were like bad-blood descendants of the homesteaders," a "perverse legacy" of their hard-tried ancestors evident "in their resentment of government, their notion of property rights, their harping on self-sufficiency and self-defence, as in their sense of enraged Scriptural entitlement." In the midst of breast-beating over the fact that an American, not a Middle Eastern maniac, had brought terror to the heartland, Raban was told by a Montanan that "'any farm-kid could have done'" what McVeigh did.[2] The man was speaking of how the bomb was made—in part. But no Californian would have said that. Most Westerners from elsewhere wouldn't have. The truth of the statement, for my purpose here, lies in its suggestion that, because of his temperament, the kid on Raban's list from rural New York who did it might well have been from Montana.

That temperament, characteristic of many people in the state but not pandemic, has a history that refuses to become historical. Larry McMurtry says as much when he avers that Montana "remains closer to the frontier experience than any state except Alaska; the urge to reach for the Winchester when there's serious conflict still comes naturally to some."[3] An anecdote from William W. Bevis is also corroborative: while on a drive through the Danish countryside, his teenage daughter, a Montanan from birth, remarked to him that Denmark was different from her home state in that the stop signs didn't have bullet holes.[4] Montanans traditionally haven't liked to stop, haven't recognized the need for limits (even on highway speed), have clung to a habit of rapaciously plundering timber and metals from their seemingly inexhaustible outdoors, have gone their violent way through myriad battles—Indians and whites, cattlemen and rustlers, one copper king and another, liberal and conservative politicians, lumbermen and environmentalists, on and on. Montana, as Timothy Egan puts it, "has never learned to say no."[5] The result is that its culture is one of extremes as arresting as those of its weather. K. Ross Toole describes it as a state with cities "sprung almost literally from the raw wilderness" that "inspires strong reactions."[6]

Extremes produce serious conflicts, and serious conflicts produce strong reactions (like reaching for the Winchester)—conflicts, tense with obdurate values and grievances, like those between country and city, West and East, openness and fences, individualism and the rule of law, wolf-haters and wolf-lovers. And strong reactions are crazy-making, especially when they're compromised. So you get Montanans fanatically wed to the principle of self-reliance, Westerners writ large in that regard, who can't handle their against-the-grain dependence on the federal government, with the consequence, in John Taylor's assessment, that "the contradictions they are forced to internalize have made them hysterical."[7] You get survivalists high on backwoods Aryanism who go batty equipping themselves for an Armageddon that never happens. You get the Unabomber, Ted Kaczynski, holed up in his cabin in Lincoln, writing a manifesto in which he ranted against technology and industrial society and on behalf of wild nature and living solitarily within it while he was being, in Raban's words, "constantly mocked by the late-twentieth-century tourists who piled into Lincoln, at every season," with their fishing gear and guns and skis and off-road vehicles.[8] You get New Westers bent on Aspenizing Bozeman and

Three Forks at odds with locals sick of the influx of newcomers, their yuppified ways, and inflated housing prices.

Most of those conflicts can be arrayed in terms of a wild-tame opposition that in the last century or so—and especially in recent decades—has come to be biased toward the tame pole. "When Montana became a state in 1889," Roderick Nash observes, "civilization existed as tiny specks and thin strings along railways and a few roads. The matrix was wild; civilization, not wilderness, was fragile."[9] Now the converse is much the case. But the changeabout has been uncertain. The matrix is large and still has a lot of wildness to it, as a winter trip lengthwise through the state will prove; on the other hand, though, as McMurtry informs us with more comforting words than he shared earlier, "the ruthlessness and brutality that were common in the nineteenth-century west have generally been poeticized" there, "turned into pastoral."[10] Civilization may be less fragile now, but I wouldn't wait for its perfection in a state that havens fringe groups like the Freemen.

Mary Murphy sees many of Montana's wild-tame intertanglements as externalizations of the "divided consciousness" of a state in which the dominant "patriarchal values" are countered by "contrary voices," and her thinking about such division leads her to a subtle figuration of its complexity. She grants that Montana—by virtue of its openness, thin population, and natural splendor people can live close to—"is everything the phrase 'the Last Best Place' implies," but she finds that it also "is insular, racially homogeneous, often anti-intellectual, and increasingly xenophobic," very suspicious of outsiders: "While sipping their cappuccinos and lattes, Montanans complain about the influx of Californians and the changing sensibilities they import. Coffee becomes the metaphor for how complicated these issues are."[11] And resolving them may be almost as difficult as turning the coffee back into beans.

The resolution that's been effected to date favors etherealized iconicity. Thus Montana serves as the name for Pontiac's sturdy and fun-to-drive minivan; and Yellowstone National Park, which the state shares with Idaho and Wyoming, is becoming what Robert D. Kaplan describes as "a big, crowded theater," while Missoula becomes more cutely gentrified.[12] Which means that Montana's postregional economy is grounded in the service sector, with an accent on tourism, an industry that seeks to preserve, even as it undermines, the state's myths and natural charms. It means also that Montana's postmodern marketing has made the state what David Brooks calls "one of those places Where Life Is Honest and True" and therewith appealing to Brooks's affluent Bobos, or "bourgeois bohemians," who have constructed a "spiritualized Montana [that] feeds off the idea of Montana and the beauty of Montana while rarely touching the lower-middle-class grind of the actual state." Though Montana's bounteous space allows freedoms as well as delivers rigors, the place, he says, "is no loosey-goosey New Age wonderland"; but an upscaler can build a detached "Bobo Heaven" where Hell reigns for lots of Butants (inhabitants of polluted Butte) and others.[13] Many of the Bobos, however, don't stay a whole lot longer than tourists or have only second homes there, tendencies that contribute to making Montana into more a symbolic sanctuary for temporary escape than a substantive place for implanted dwelling of the kind Annick Smith, originally an outsider, writes about in her 1995 memoir *Homestead*.

The disconnection between a real Montana subject to the laws of nature and a spiritualized Montana spangled with romantic dreams is a story that's old, exemplarily Western, and by now sullenly satirical. It explains a repeating pattern of "illusion, disillusionment, endurance" Bevis finds in the history of Montana's settlers.[14] It has bearing on a generic pattern of mythic expectation giving way to bitterness and rage at being cheated. It's a story that helps us understand the failure and poverty and misery evidenced in Raban's observation that, out on the state's prairie, "for every surviving ranch, I passed a dozen ruined houses."[15] It throws light on why Sharman Apt Russell would say that "the romance of Montana continues to compel me, even as I distrust it."[16] And it should help us grasp why in Montana "the wilderness experience has become one of crying through an impossibly hopeful smile," according to Leslie Ryan: "Under the shroud of perpetual progress, in this relentlessly transformed place which we desired with such fury and into which we have hemmed ourselves, to cherish is to know the end, and each kiss says good-bye."[17]

But the place that receives such kisses is resilient. It has formidable power to reclaim its own. When the divinity the Blackfeet call Cold Maker marshals his forces and winter comes to West Yellowstone, those whom Kittredge styles "the cartoon tourists of summertime" are departed and the great park is nature's once again. This is the scene he paints:

> The cold is now sometimes terrible, and always there. Wind sculpts the frozen snow, and steam rises from the hot pools. The ice on Yellowstone Lake sings its music of tension, the coyotes answering back on clear nights. Elk wade in the Firehole, which is fed by hot springs, and feed on the aquatic life. This is winter in the high northern Rockies. Things have always been like this, except for the snowmobiles.[18]

After the cartoon tourists, snowmobilers, Bobos, survivalists, real-estate shysters, and all the rest have finally destroyed enough of Montana to destroy themselves, it will recover and entirely revert to nature. Then for more than a season things will be "like this."

Still, things might be different. How would we make them so, both in Montana and in the West at large? Bevis argues that we white Americans need a shift in how we look at nature, which for us has always been "an identity as well as a resource." That identity, moreover, has been a double one: "we are the people who use up nature, and we are the people who have a lot of it left." For a long time the contradiction between the reality of development and the romance of the wilderness didn't overly bother us. Now, though, we sense that nature in critical respects really can be used up. For good reason, Bevis says, such awareness holds a foreboding:

> We would like to think there is something beyond. And that is part of the enduring appeal of Montana, mountains, the West; they give the impression of a whole lot beyond, greater than us, out of our control. But in a short-term physical sense, that is no longer true. . . . Behind our anger at this news is our fear of an exploding population and technology that seems to have run "wild," in a cruel parody of that term's reversal over the last 400 years.

Motivated by fear of ourselves or otherwise, the shift in our way of looking at Western nature, he cautions, will have to eventuate in a more humble consciousness of its frangibility, of the limits to what we can take from it; revision of the nostalgic, utopian myths we have imposed on it; and committed engagement with, not avoidance of, the future, land planning, and a contentious society. The place to do that, Bevis concludes, is one "that knows what clean air and water are, a place that knows what a sweet world it is without too many people."[19]

At the same time, of course, I wouldn't want the West completely to repudiate its colorful cultural wildness. As Montanans figure out, I hope, how best to live in their Treasure State, I'd like to believe they'll not get too either/or–minded, that it'll still be possible to go to some little eatery for chicken-fried steak and read a sign on the wall not unlike the owner-signed one Bevis relishes in the Calf-A in Dell:

$250 REWARD
for enof information
on the party who stole
the old phonograph
so that I can shoot
the son of a bitch.[20]

Little Hassle on the Prairie: The Issue of Wise (Non)use

The way it's currently interpreted, wilderness is what's left over when you take out all the places where diverse life-forms can survive. The joke around here is that wilderness means "rock and ice."
    Leslie Ryan, "The Clearing in the Clearing"

Just east of Dodge City, a sign invites you to pull your car off Highway 50/56 and take in the view of gently rolling land to the south. If you can stand the stench. From the overlook, all you see, acre upon acre, is a feedlot.

Is the land aesthetic, let alone the land ethic, of the West now so screwy that somebody might seriously ask people driving by and pinching their noses to stop, hop out, and admire what's before them? Apparently.

The feedlot, that parody of a roundup, has come about through the economics of efficiency. It uglifies the land, but it's an inexpensive way to fatten cattle. You could graze cattle more expensively in Kansas's Tallgrass Prairie Preserve, and the beef would taste better; but then you wouldn't be leaving that area to a less domestic grass menagerie. Would more feedlots be a good idea, other considerations aside, because they would help relieve the grazing pressure on all the Western soil now trampled by cattle? If you want fewer feedlots and nicer steaks, should more of the federally owned land in the West, nearly half the total, be made available for grazing—and the fees for it lowered? In any case, isn't grazing preferable to subdividing? Such questions relate to issues of land use hotly debated in the West.

Most of those issues are subsumed by the overarching issue of the use of more or less untamed land. Examples of problems in the West, besides those of ranching, that fuel the issue come quickly to mind: increasing road access into wilderness areas and allowing them to serve as playgrounds for anglers and bicyclists or Golcondas for loggers; traffic congestion in Grand Canyon National Park; rapid sprawling of once-sleepy towns like Cornville, Arizona, golfers in tow, into their once-natural surroundings; corporate interest in exploiting imperfectly protected public wildlands like the natural-gas-rich Roan Plateau in northwestern Colorado or the twenty-two million Bureau of Land Management–controlled acres held in trust in Utah, where the gorgeous Kaiparowits Plateau could be excavated to harvest five billion tons of coal.[1]

The voices enlivening that issue began to rise in the 1960s and 1970s when the environmental movement was gaining momentum and legislation such as the Wilderness Act (1964), the National Environmental Policy Act (1969), and the Endangered Species Act (1973) were passed and the Environmental Protection Agency was created—and the cattle, mining, timber, and oil industries became apprehensive about being locked out of wilderness areas by Uncle Sam, their normally pliable landlord. The result was a Western backlash against environmentalism, and in counterpoint to it came the establishment of deep-ecology groups like Earth First! and, later, the Earth Liberation Front, whose vandalistic acts on behalf of nature's rights included sabotaging lumbering equipment, cutting barbed-wire fences, torching ski resorts. Eco-vigilant city slickers lined up against status-quo country curmudgeons. Quirky coalitions crystallized and splintered. Worry about the rape of the West met with get-out-of-the-way greed. Memberships in the Sierra Club, the Audubon Society, and the Wilderness Society swelled.

Such antagonisms, especially those about control of public rangeland, gave birth to the Sagebrush Rebellion of the late 1970s and early 1980s. Urban New Westers may have been repelled by the damage caused by overgrazing, but anti-urban Old Westers were intent on having dominion over what they regarded as local, not national, property—and not just for ranching. The rhetoric of privatization and economic growth abounded from participants in an insurgency Patricia Nelson Limerick describes as a "media event . . . in which Western businessmen lamented their victimization at the hands of the federal government and pleaded for the release of the public domain from its federal captivity." Satisfaction of that hunger for the wild was hindered by opposition, of course—from Western governors as well as environmentalists—but the tapering of the rebellion was hurried by an irony, as she explains: "Like many rebellions, this one foundered with success: the election of Ronald Reagan in 1980 and the appointment of James Watt as secretary of the interior meant that the much-hated federal government was now in the hands of two Sagebrush Rebels. It was not at all clear what the proper rebel response to the situation should be."[2] The victims couldn't play the victimization card. Watt's machinations to give the natural West away to ranchers, miners, lumberers, and drillers went agley.[3]

But by the 1990s the rebellion had shape-shifted into People for the West! and the more influential Wise Use movement. By a supreme catachresis, the name of the latter, as J. Baird Callicott and Michael P. Nelson point out, amounts to "a dissembling perversion of the credo of Gifford Pinchot." It's the verbal velvet glove on the reactionary fat fist of an agenda funded by corporate interests. Their propagandists, whose harping on the need to undo regulations that prevent exploitation appealed most strongly to ranchers, claimed to speak for ordinary Americans aggrieved by big government, but their aim wasn't to achieve some long-awaited political vindication but "to profit from the opening of wilderness areas."[4] Though that aim is still persistent, it's been impeded by a paradox Bruce Babbitt sees in Americans' sentiments about Western public lands, its inconsistency rooted in ambivalence toward the wild that's gradually becoming more affirmative in character: Wise Use arguments elicit sympathies attached to obstinate ideals (individualism, private property, hands-off government); yet in the regional and postregional West "public lands have remained largely intact, and the consensus for public ownership seems to grow with each generation."[5]

In 1960, in an attempt to resolve the conflicts over that ownership later prominent in the Wise Use movement, Congress passed the Multiple Use–Sustained Yield Act and perpetuated in contemporized terms a concept favored by Pinchot. It addressed primarily the polemics of forestry, but the multiple-use doctrine had broad implications for land use in the West. Utilizing land inclusively for recreation, lumbering, grazing, wildlife preservation, and so on sounds good in theory, but, as Babbitt states, it "has proven unworkable in practice."[6] An act that gave everything to everybody without informed standards and enforced priorities led to commercial abuse and solved nothing. Indeed, Gundars Rudzitis avers, it appears to have "contributed to a form of individual and corporate welfare."[7]

In any case, the multiple-use doctrine relies on a far-too-simple construction of wilderness that has intensified the polarization of positions on use. Its simplicity has made it attractive to members of the Wise Use movement, what with their belief in a social order that requires, in Jack Turner's list, "Christian revelation, pre-Darwinian science, pre-particle physics, and a model of reason as the maximization of utility," but that belief hasn't led to "a shared vision of the good."[8] The suitability of the doctrine in the West is wholly questionable. As applied there, William Kittredge tells us, it "has worked out, obviously, to be a sweet deal for the homefolks and an endless windfall for timber and mining corporations." They've gotten a lot—through low grazing fees, generous access to minerals, subsidization, and so forth—on the cheap. "But," he says, "all this is changing." New interests and new demographics are in the game: "Money men and power brokers are very much aware that the economic hot spots in the West are Reno (gambling), Las Vegas (gambling and defense), Salt Lake City (high-tech industry), Boise (computers), Aspen, Jackson Hole, and Santa Fe (amenities and recreation). Tourism and the educated are in the saddle." Tourists, however unacquainted with its realities, "come for the wilderness" and think the West should be protected, not clear-cut and dug up. The newcomers know that public lands belong to the public, and they "are going to prevail in the long run."[9] In such a situation, multiple use can't suffice, helps only to divide.

What to do, then? The West needs a doctrine of wise nonuse, and there's no paucity of ideas for how it might be worked up and implemented. Jim Robbins, writing of "the battle between New West and Old" over public domain, stresses that the two different worldviews involved demand "a new kind of vision that seeks a middle ground that might preserve the best of both"—by eco-sensitive development, balancing extraction and naturalness, wilderness restoration, and allied measures.[10] Others emphasize the importance of interconnected wildlife habitats, dominant-use areas, more diversified ranching enterprises, more holistic range-management practices, or conservation trusts to keep some private land protected from development (the sort of project being undertaken by the Sun Ranch in Montana and the Heritage Ranch in New Mexico). Still others are requesting more research, like that conducted by the Nevada Biodiversity Initiative, on how better to integrate public-lands management with planning for biological resources.[11] There's a general desire to move beyond dichotomizing that lumps adversaries into strip miners and tree huggers. Many, like Rudzitis, are asking for "a larger public discussion and debate on exactly how people want their public lands managed."[12]

What the interplay of such ideas, the give-and-take of discussion and debate, must come to is the recognition that much of the West belongs to all Americans, is an uncommon nature that should be reclaimed (etymologically, "called back"—in a sense foreign to the Bureau of Reclamation) for the commons. And we will have to abide by the lesson in Peggy Simson Curry's poem "Abandoned Irrigation Ditch" that "some land is best left to the hawk's thin shadow."[13]

That won't be easy. In the postregional era nonuse—letting the wild remain in its autonomous otherness as much as possible—is a proposition charged with ironies. In many respects Western nature now is wildlife management (as well as human-life management: restricted admittance to Yosemite, permit systems for white-water recreation, and the like), and we have yet fully to tackle the dilemma of what Paul S. Sutter terms "the affinity between environmental sentiment and consumerism" through which we've "constructed nature as consumers" so that "wilderness itself is a consumer ideal."[14] Thus ironies are compounded with complexities. Alone, single-species arguments for preservation don't wash anymore—with either Wise Users or savvy environmentalists. Ted Turner's ranches can never turn back the ecological hands of time: restorative rewilding is as intractably problematic as static preservation is impossible. The order of nature proceeds through barely fathomed intricacies of seeming disorder. Wilderness, Curt Meine apprises us, borrowing a phrase from Aldo Leopold, "has given 'definition and meaning' even to the lives of those most removed from, ignorant of, hostile towards, and oblivious to, its existence. This is a 'use' so all-encompassing that even we who choose to defend wilderness have difficulty comprehending it."[15] More and more of us know all this. The question that recurs throughout our learning is Gerontion's in T. S. Eliot's poem about that old man: "After such knowledge, what forgiveness?"[16] Very little if we don't act appropriately.

There's now a bookcase-bending library of literature on how, in light of the ironies and complexities of land use, we might act appropriately, but the agreement among the sources isn't yet close.[17] That'll take a while to fall out. In the meantime, there are don'ts and dos to which Westerners of all walks might be prepared, with intelligent and patient tutoring, to assent. We don't want the West's forests reduced to skull orchards of stumps. We don't want Western rivers to be nothing but concrete canals and sewers. We don't want Western cities to become abandoned Babylons. We don't want to make a final dust bowl, a radioactive Empty Quarter, a chemical-waste charnel house of the agricultural and desert West. We do want to eschew the push to overdevelop beautiful Western places because they're beautiful. We do want continually to reevaluate and revise the canons of environmentalism itself. We do want to limit the human population of the West. We do want what the *Atlas of the New West* acclaims as "a wilder vision" of living there, the top mandate of which is that "we must change the West from a landscape of development surrounding remaining pockets of naturalness into the reverse: limited development embedded in a geography of wildness."[18]

Beyond John Wayne: Bewildering Westerns and Wild Wild Texts

Postmodernism became what modernism was not. It emphasized pluralism instead of unity, many stories rather than one, deconstruction of the metanarrative, the reintroduction of older styles and alternative styles, contradiction, ambiguity.

> Joan M. Jensen, *One Foot on the Rockies: Women and Creativity in the Modern American West*

In the postregional era the imagery of the West, in all artistic media, has become more complex and diverse than ever before, and the elaboration of that imagery has gone on hand in hand with an uneasy cultural self-consciousness of the continuing and enlarging, even if more ethereal, significance of the West as a wild place. An index of such self-consciousness may be the number of Western movies, starting in the late 1950s, when America was in a frenzy of suburbanized estrangement from the natural West, that have titles containing the word *wild*: *Wild Is the Wind* (1957), *Wild Heritage* (1958), *The Wild and the Innocent* (1959), *The Wild Westerners* (1962), *The Wild Bunch* (1969), *Wild Women* (1970), *Wild Rovers* (1971), *The Wild McCullochs* (1975), *The Wild Wild West Revisited* (1979), *Wild Times* (1980), *Wild Horses* (1985), among others. Many of those films have conduced to a tendency for postmodern portrayals of the West to be revisionist, exposing suppressed or ignored contradictions and ambiguities in Euro-American attitudes toward Western wildness; following out their ironies through aesthetics, from tragically realistic to satirically surrealistic, of disillusionment; and questioning, toying with, or reversing the axiological polarity of the modern wild-tame dialectic—or maybe suggesting some resolution for it.

"No Western theme has been explored with greater frequency since the early 1960s than that of the passing of the frontier," observes John H. Lenihan regarding films in the vein of Ford's *The Man Who Shot Liberty Valance*—an observation corroborated by the number of films around that time and thereafter with the word *last* in their titles. As Ford's film testifies, even John Wayne Westerns, usually preaching the gospel of Manifest Destiny, were dragging ideological uncertainties into view; but *Lonely Are the Brave* (1962), *Hud* (1963), *The Last Picture Show* (1971), *Bite the Bullet* (1975), and other films would go further in dramatizing the contradictions and ambiguities of the civilized West, largely by how they stressed the tedium and dehumanization that had replaced frontier vitality or portrayed a turn-of-the-century West grappling with "middle-class blandness and conformity, technology (typically the automobile) that seemed more intrusive than purposeful, and often an oppressive corporate-legal establishment."[1] In Westerns released after 1970, as Jon Tuska notes, acknowledgment of conquest gone amiss informed stories, like *Man in the Wilderness* (1971), in which the ideology of a cocksure faith in technology "would occasionally be reversed, so instead the theme becomes that of preserving the wilderness in the face of the onslaught of technology."[2] A correlate reversal born of such acknowledgment, Richard White points out, may be found in Westerns released during and after the late 1960s: "'Savagery,' symbolized by outlaws or Indians, now became good, and 'civilization,' symbolized by the town or farmers or the U.S. Cavalry, now became either evil or weak."[3]

That sort of reversal conspicuously marks Sam Peckinpah's films, in which, as A. Carl Bredahl Jr. notes, the sterility and lawlessness of civilization are salient themes. In The Wild Bunch (1969), for instance, "Harrigan of the railroad and Mapache of the Federales are the representatives of law and order, but they are vicious and corrupt," in which situation the bunch's wildness "seems more an expression of frustrated internal energies than a destructive principle harmful to civilization." As for the violence of the film, Bredahl argues that the kind amply depicted in Peckinpah's work differs, at least in exposition, from that in Ford's: the latter occurs when white society acts on "the desire to wipe out resistance to the onrushing, enclosing civilization," whereas the former "is usually the result of cruelty that seems bent on destroying the natural world."[4] So, though the film's glorification of violence may be dubious, the wildness of the outlaws, opposing repression, is as positive as a thundershower on a dog day.

Other, later postmodern Westerns, however, would offer less-heartening disillusionment, incomplete or equivocal reversals. Robert Altman's McCabe and Mrs. Miller (1971)—set in a landscape "both harsh and beautiful, both unforgiving and fragile," as Michael Kowalewski describes it—concerns corporate exploitation, but it doesn't wind up being an anti-Western like Soldier Blue (1970) or Little Big Man (1970); instead, it proposes that "the 'real' West . . . may indeed have helped shape the national character—but in ways more ambiguous, irresolute, even dispirited than it may be convenient for most of us to remember."[5] In Michael Cimino's Heaven's Gate (1980), as Neil Campbell argues, the traditional expectations of the genre (about taming the land and such) are displaced, but the film's rethinking of them yields "no reconciliatory pattern healing oppositions that structure so many Westerns" and leaves the audience with a "lack of resolution [that] is the point."[6] Much the same is true of Unforgiven (1992), a film taut with tensions between savage and civilized impulses whose resolution is, in Fred Erisman's capsuling, "disturbingly ambivalent."[7]

Those effects typify films that aren't so much anti-Westerns as meta-Westerns, narrative commentaries on a genre that in its classic form, according to White, not only didn't "reconcile the contradictions between the premodern virtues of a western hero" and his efforts toward "saving a modern society that threatened those very virtues" (the crux that characteristically stalls the climactic resolution of the wild-tame dialectic) but often actually "flaunted those contradictions."[8] Meta-Westerns, however, critically take hold of them, and the result, as Christian Metz explains, is a Western cinema that has "passed from parody to contestation," with its anti-Western gestures, that in turn—most notably during the late 1960s in Italian Westerns like Sergio Leone's *Once upon a Time in the West* (1968)—"gives way to 'deconstruction': the entire film is an explication of the code and of its relation to history." What's experienced may still be a Western, but the genre "has passed from parody to critique."[9] With that passage the floodgates were opened, and there came a spate of attempts to problematize, demythologize, and remythologize the genre.

And so, in an era whose later years would see Franklin Mint collector plates and glass-belled sculptures that memorialized John Wayne, now a metaphysical force, looking anachronistically confident in his conquest of the wild, a revolution was under way. Films like Elliot Silverstein's *Cat Ballou* (1965) and Mel Brooks's *Blazing Saddles* (1974) subjected the genre's supporting mythology, in Robert G. Athearn's enumeration, to "abuse, ridicule, burlesquing, satire, and disdain."[10] Leone and Peckinpah, Lee Clark Mitchell observes, "both turned away from fixed generic assumptions, most prominently by turning the Western itself into a Mexican context, placing Anglo-American characters in a culturally alien setting rather than loose in wilderness space"—an abstract and vague setting in which the landscape and the town fold "into a single depressing symbolic entity, controverting the genre's traditional split between nature and culture, West and East, the wild and the civilized."[11] No surprise, therefore, that the genre's mythic West was increasingly transplanted into science fiction (where, as the opening words of the cult television show *Star Trek* announced, outer space is "the final frontier"—and the town is the starship *Enterprise*) and urban crime drama (where the hero wears his white hat ambiguously and deals with bottomless confusions of the wild and the civilized). No surprise, given such etherealization, that *Blazing Saddles* self-consciously but readily transferred the viewer alternately into and out of its put-down mythic world—that by the 1970s the Western already, as Thomas Schatz sketches its status then, "had become something of an end in itself, disconnected from its social and historical moorings," and its style "had outlived its substance: it had in fact become its substance."[12]

But still other reinventional turns were astir. In Milos Forman's *One Flew over the Cuckoo's Nest* (1975), much as in the Ken Kesey novel on which it was based, the New West, as Leslie Fiedler nails it, "was clearly defined: the West of Here and Now, rather than There and Then—the West of Madness," of psychiatric inner wilderness.[13] Robert Zemeckis's time-travel Western *Back to the Future, Part III* (1990), like many Westerns to come, was so allusively entangled with earlier films that its natural, as well as social and historical, moorings were no more than intertextual cinematic references. *Dances with Wolves* (1990), among several other films, revisited the issue of who was savage and who civilized in white–Indian conflicts of the previous century. During the 1990s a series of films, beginning with *Thelma & Louise* (1991) and including *The Ballad of Little Jo*, *Bad Girls*, and *The Quick and the Dead* (in which violence in Redemption is scheduled by the town clock), blurred the traditional contraposition of parlor and open country and portrayed their female protagonists as woolly and dangerous. In 1996 Jim Jarmusch's *Dead Man* told the tale of an Adamic nineteenth-century poet named William Blake (Johnny Depp) who travels west in search of regeneration and finds himself errant in an eerie, smoke-poisoned, Misrachian landscape, paradise untimely lost to surreal industrialism. In the same year Stephen Ives, who directed and co-produced (with Ken Burns) the eight-part 1996 PBS documentary *The West*, spoke in an interview of how it strives to go beyond the Western story "as either the conquest of savagery by 'civilization' or, more recently, as a catalog of cruelty and unbridled exploitation" and "to deal with complexity and ambivalence."[14]

Filmmakers haven't been the only postmodern artists dealing with the West's complexity and ambivalence. In the 1960s, as Richard W. Etulain recounts, "Photo Realism quickly took root on the West Coast," where metasticizing cities plentifully offered practitioners like Ralph Goings and Robert Bechtle scenes of the suburban quiet desperation that was their cup of tea. By the 1970s, land artists like Robert Smithson and Michael Heizer were busy creating Western earthworks, structures in the vein of Heizer's *Double Negative* (1969–70), that symbolically suggested "an open, balanced marriage between nature and man-made forms." At the same time a mixed-blood Luiseño abstract expressionist named Fritz Scholder (and then his protégé, T. C. Cannon, a Kiowa-Caddo artist) "utilized a bittersweet iconography to depict 'paradoxical Indians,' Native Americans caught in the tensions of alienation and assimilation, tradition and modernity." Such artists have continued to explore the intricacies and ironies of the postregional wild-tame dialectic, significantly re-patterning the kaleidoscope of "overlapping visions of the West as frontier, region, and postregion."[15]

No artists, though, have revised the image of the West more than its postregional writers. Taking off the blinders of idealization, they've tried assiduously to write it anew as a place, as a state of mind, and as an integration (or, at least, reconciliation) of the two. In that effort they have done and still do what real Western artists—all real artists—"are for," as William Kittredge puts it: "they help us *see*; they drive society through the process of coming to fresh recognitions."[16]

What those writers help us freshly recognize is, as Stephen Tatum characterizes it, "'the West' as a contact zone, a borderlands . . ., a topography of transitions instead of a stable place."[17] They help us rediscover it in terms of the "trialectics" of Edward W. Soja and ideas about spatiality he has adapted from Henri Lefebvre that afford a perspective in which space, as Campbell explains, "is not adequately defined by such statements as 'real, material space' or 'imagined, illusory space,' because our experience of it is precisely a combination or dialogized mixture of these effects." That perspective enables us to perceive the West without relying on restrictive binaries and understand how in the flux of all its borders and thresholds "it has always existed as both a region and more than region, as imagined dream-space as well as real, material space."[18] Postregional writers thus bring to us and bring us to a more multidimensional West than the regionalists wrote: their work may be, as Russell Martin says, "anchored in a place," but that place is much more than physical and, for many of them, "remains as strange in some ways as the country that Buffalo Bill encountered."[19]

The story those writers collectively write answers to some extent a need for what Timothy Egan calls "a common story, not a mythic one, not a plunderer's tidied-up view."[20] Common. Also, on the whole, more nonfictional. And, as Patricia Nelson Limerick remarks, more by writers native to the West whose work "has improved our chances of regional self-understanding" and "given non-Westerners a much more grounded and complicated picture of the West to contemplate."[21] A more diverse, multivoiced story of what, to generalize Scott P. Sanders's description of the Southwest, "is still today a gothic frontier, an unsettled mix of cultural and geological variety that exists in a fantastic place that lies somewhere between landscape and locale."[22] Slowly but surely more a story of home as well, of "where tensions are lived out," by Harold P. Simonson's definition, "the special place where connections and clarifications occur" that is itself "perhaps the only resolution any of us can know."[23]

The West as a place. "No one has done more than Texas author Larry McMurtry to popularize this new remythologized West," Etulain argues, citing some of his best novels, from *Horseman, Pass By* (1961) to *Buffalo Girls* (1990), as evidence that he "has depicted a complex, unheroic, gray West devoid of the Zane Grey–Louis L'Amour popular images."[24] But many others have lent a hand—Martin Cruz Smith, for example, in his novels *Nightwing* (1977) and *Stallion Gate* (1986), both thematized by blighted and eschatologically threatened landscapes.[25] More recently Annie Proulx, in her short story "The Governors of Wyoming," has evoked a postregional West of industrial usurpation—dams, mines, refineries, dirty rivers, dumps, on and on—in which the remaining ranchers "couldn't see their game was over."[26]

Indeed, some of those ranchers don't see their game that way at all and are intent on reinvigorating it. Particularly those who are cowboy poets, writers and performers who practice a post–Civil War song-related genre that has grown immensely popular since the first cowboy-poetry gathering at Elko, Nevada, in 1985. Their work, from the charming doggerel of S. Omar Barker to the more polished lines of Paul Zarzyski, celebrates, often with humor, what's left of a colorful and unsullied West; moreover, even though commercialized, it seeks to advance, in the opinion of Craig Miller, a "stewardship of nature" and imparts many cowboys' fresh recognition that "their cultural identity has come to depend upon a strong, close relationship with the natural environment."[27]

Thomas J. Lyon certainly was correct in his observation, cited earlier, that ethnic writers may not be interested in the Euro-American dialectic of civilization and wilderness, but some postregional ones are—perforce, given the mainstream Euro-American context in which they live.[28] It can be found, with differing cultural takes, in Chicano poet Gary Soto's collection *The Elements of San Joaquin* (1977) and N. Scott Momaday's novel *House Made of Dawn* (1968), among other works. It figures acutely in postmodern Native American literature, when present there, and tends to have the form of the conflict Andrew Smith finds in Chickasaw writer Linda Hogan's 1990 novel *Mean Spirit*: one between the distracting "shiny simulations" of Euro-American culture and the "original realities" of the natural world of Indian culture. If there's an imaginary resolution of the dialectic, it usually involves, as Hogan's title suggests, giving attention to those realities and healing through which "the mean spirits of chaos and disintegration for the Indian people are dynamically transformed into the mean spirit of the middle ground—the place where all contraries embrace and potential radiates from a newly recovered center."[29] Such balancing of bicultural claims through a homeward reconnection with place is a recurrent theme in contemporary literature by Native American women in the West—Navajo poet Luci Tapahonso, Muskogee poet Joy Harjo, and O'odham poet Ofelia Zepeda, for instance.

That theme of reconnection appears also in the work of postregional women writers in general, most of whom have been influenced by the feminism that's flourished since the 1960s and, through the awareness it affords, have contributed indispensably to revising the traditional Euro-American view of the West as a place of adventurous and competitive male conquest. In their commitment to such revisionism, they represent a sizable proportion of New Western writers who, as Sheila Ruzycki O'Brien argues, "recognize the complexity of western life." Her exemplum is Marilynne Robinson's 1981 novel *Housekeeping*, set in post–World War II northern Idaho, which has as its central characters "female drifters who do not try to dominate other characters or their environment" and who, unlike the women in classic Westerns, are motivated by "free spirits [that] chafe at the confines of civilization."[30] The Bitterroot Mountains may loom as a "psychic wilderness" those women don't face adequately, but for Annette Van Dyke the novel finally holds out a possibility at once postregional and pre-Euro-American: "that people can come to see themselves as part of the wild landscape, living in harmony with its powerful force, admitting that its magical force is also in them, rather than existing in opposition and separation."[31] It's a possibility investigated over and over in the short stories, poems, and personal essays gathered in the 1994 compilation *Circle of Women: An Anthology of Contemporary Western Women Writers*, whose editors, Kim Barnes and Mary Clearman Blew, announce that, through the work of writers like those included, there has emerged a vision of the Western experience that "draws on the self-reliance and courage of the old western mythology but sees greater strength in community, in making connections, in interdependence."[32] Look for it elsewhere too—in the poetry, for example, of Jane Candia Coleman and Laurie Wagner Buyer.

And in the recent memoirs by Western writers of all stripes, whose greatest challenge, according to Blew, herself a memoirist, "has been dismantling the western myth" in order to write about the West as home, as "a specific, carefully evoked place."[33] Not a new place to which they light out but, typically, an old place, one more of families than of solitaries, to which they return. Ivan Doig met that challenge in 1978 with *This House of Sky: Landscapes of a Western Mind*, which began his career as a writer who has furthered, in Etulain's words, "an enlarged postregional understanding of the clashes between nature and culture in the northern interior West."[34] That understanding arises through what Bredahl calls a story "of discovering and accepting 'place.'"[35] Kittredge met the challenge in 1992 with *Hole in the Sky: A Memoir*, in which he both disowns the Old Western exploitation of the environment and advocates a New Western conception of it that encourages reverence and care. Kathleen Norris met it in 1993 with *Dakota: A Spiritual Geography*, her account of dedicating herself to a specific place in the West as both a natural and a numinous home. So have many others since.

Researching in the revisionist mode of history inaugurated by works such as Wallace Stegner's *Beyond the Hundredth Meridian: John Wesley Powell and the Second Opening of the West* (1954) and Dee Brown's *Bury My Heart at Wounded Knee: An Indian History of the American West* (1970), New Western Historians too, of course, have been writing the West anew, leading us to fresh recognitions of it as a place. Lots of those historians, as Campbell says of Western photographer Mark Klett, have "rejected ... metanarrative in favour of micronarratives" in storying the West "as ambiguous, mobile, inhabited space."[36] The result of that partiality remains pretty much what Brian W. Dippie said it was in 1991: "new topics rather than a consistent new direction for western history, fragmentation rather than synthesis." He recommended as a remedy more myth analysis of the kind Richard Slotkin has done, for "the myth and the anti-myth are keys to the western past and the western present that can also unlock the American past and the American present"—a call for both synthesis and a resumption, with a difference, of metanarrative.[37] He may have overstated his case, though, because the major New Western Historians were already treating the West, as Etulain puts it, "more holistically than do most historians."[38] Nonetheless, given the extent to which other postregional writers have been rewriting the mythic West, I think Dippie's recommendation has been vindicated.

The West as a state of mind. The romantic myth still lives on but dominantly, except for the Western section at the bookstore, in ironic and satiric editions indebted to more complex literary treatments of the etherealized West that started in the 1960s and proceeded side by side with works penned to retell the actuality of the place. Joan Didion produced two novels, *Run River* (1963) and *Play It as It Lays* (1970), that portray California as, in Etulain's sketch, a "failed Eden" of "blighted landscapes" more emotional and moral than physical.[39] In his 1969 novel *Yellow Back Radio Broke-Down*, African American novelist Ishmael Reed wove a "surrealistic West," as Todd

F. Tietchen terms it, a "HooDoo West [that] often loses all coherent boundaries, placing it in stark contrast to the mythic frontier."⁴⁰ Michael Ondaatje's multigenre text *The Collected Works of Billy the Kid* (1970) presented an interiorized "gothic Western" in which, as Robert Murray Davis describes it, "the world is monstrous and unaccountable" and the hero's legend "defies clear resolutions into fact or myth."⁴¹

During the 1970s and 1980s, there were more such treatments, and they had broader appeal. In a series of plays, including *Buried Child* (1978) and *True West* (1980), Sam Shepard explored what Mark Busby interprets as "the two sides of the American myth: the hope and promise of the dream of regeneration on the American frontier and the recognition that the dream has often been violent and destructive, that it appears as a 'lie of the mind' continuing to entrap and destroy."⁴² In *Lonesome Dove* McMurtry reprised Don Quixote and Sancho Panza in a story, as ambiguous in its satirization of romance as Cervantes's seventeenth-century novel, that both monumentalizes and critiques that myth.⁴³ In 1984 Cormac McCarthy published *Blood Meridian; or, The Evening Redness in the West*, the first of his several novels about the Southwest as a land of multiple borders between civilization and wilderness, known and unknown, deceptive myth and imperiled reality, among other oppositions. Combining hallucinatory realism with allegorical romance, eliciting horror and fascination, the book dramatizes conquest as routinized genocide in a Daliesque space of baroque chaos and violence that regenerates nothing.⁴⁴ In 1987 Gloria Anzaldúa rewrote, from a postmodern Chicana viewpoint, traditional Anglo notions of such *zonas fronterizas* in her eclectic *corrido* of a book *Borderlands/La Frontera*.

The state-of-mind stops seemed to have all been pulled out by 1990, the year that saw the publication of David Thomson's novel *Silver Light*, a self-consciously cinematic text concocted from Western fictions that compounds and escalates the unreality of the etherealized frontier. Then in 1993 appeared William Gibson's *Virtual Light*, in which the natural landscape has been transmogrified into a dispersed science-fictional abstraction Campbell synopsizes as "the American West Coast, NoCal, run by global zaibatsu (multinational) culture as a world of 'mega-cities,' 'mirrored ziggurats,' gunships, climate control, and urban micropolitics, echoing films like *Blade Runner* and *Strange Days*."⁴⁵ And in 1995 Clyde Edgerton came out with *Redeye: A Western*, a narratively looped burlesque of standard Western mythology. By 2000 McMurtry could write confidently that the West of the writers assembled in his anthology *Still Wild: Short Fiction of the American West, 1950 to the Present* "is not so much the West of history or the West of geography as it is the West of the imagination: funny, gritty, isolate, searing, tragic, complex."⁴⁶

That McMurtry's table of contents has few names of Indian authors belies the fact that many such authors have proven themselves adept at dealing with the West of the imagination, writing its wildness Indian-style in short fiction and other genres, as a way of trying to make sense of and maybe even imaginarily mend the bicultural West they live in. The verbal strategies of that dealing can be traced back to works like D'Arcy McNickle's *The Surrounded*, one of only a handful of Indian novels published before the 1960s and in its symbolic delineation of cultural conflict a precursor of *House Made of Dawn*, the novel that, in Lyon's phrase, was the "bringer of the fire" that initiated a renaissance in Native American writing. Momaday's novel, like his poetry, drew on "dual literary legacies," and so did others' work in its wake. Thus, for instance, James Welch's novel *Winter in the Blood* (1974), saturated with his Blackfoot and Gros Ventre heritage, employs oral-storytelling techniques along with flashbacks, absurdist humor, "surreal dreams," and the like to communicate its bleak ironic tale—a kind of ancient-modern mergence Lyon sees at play in contemporary Indian poetry.[47] In 1978, however, Indian bicultural literature rose to a new level of intellectual ingenuity with the publication of mixed-blood Chippewa writer Gerald Vizenor's first novel, *Darkness in Saint Louis Bearheart*, a disruptive narrative that functions, according to Louis Owens, much as Menippean satire does: "to test and expose ideas and ideologues"—in a way, in this instance, that both positively re-imagines the Indian and "mocks the American myth with its sacrosanct westering journey into psychic and literal wilderness."[48]

Leslie Marmon Silko's 1977 novel *Ceremony*, a circular story structured by Laguna cosmology, reached that level in a text somewhat more popularly accessible than Vizenor's that, in Campbell's dissection, "combines feminist revisionism and 'postindian' restorying with New West issues such as loss, imperialism, hegemony, technology, education, and the land."[49] Moreover, it hinted at a mending of the split between reality and myth, the West as a place and the West as a state of mind, because, as Owens notes, its mythology "insists upon its actual simultaneity with and interpenetration into the events of the everyday, mundane world."[50] That's an insistence, old in Native traditions and basically stressing nothing more than a sensible correspondence, that recurs, in one cultural register or another, throughout postmodern nature writing about the West, even if not always centrally in the outpouring during the 1990s of bicultural remythologizing of the West represented by Vizenor's later works, Silko's stories and compendious anticolonial novel *Almanac of the Dead* (1991), mixed-blood Cherokee Thomas King's tricksterish novel *Green Grass, Running Water* (1993), Cherokee-Choctaw-Irish Owens's novels such as *Wolfsong* (1994), and Spokane–Coeur d'Alene Sherman Alexie's poetry and tragicomic novel *Reservation Blues* (1995)—with more yet to come.

The West as an integration of place and state of mind. A key player here is environmental history, a discipline whose legitimacy, as Dan Flores reminds us, "has been recognized only since the 1970s," but, he adds, its belated appearance as a study of the relations between people and nature "is one of the more intriguing seismic stirrings in academics in recent years."[51] Indeed, such history may be becoming *the* way of formally studying the Western past, but its writers are just some among the many writing in several genres whose work concerns environmentalism—so many that, Etulain estimates, "more postregionalists deal with this subject than any other."[52] Their approaches vary, but all of them question the concept of nature as a resource for unlimited exploitation and urge leaving it in a dynamic as undisturbed by human meddling as possible. In this respect, chief among that host are Western nature writers, from Edward Abbey to Ann Zwinger, whose literary output prompts Michael Kowalewski's argument that "the newly revived interest in nature writing may well be the most exciting development in the study of western American literature." A multitude of factors I've discussed have inspired "closer, more attentive accounts of natural environments in the West," and those accounts may make postregional nature writing the most exciting—and most important—development in the study of the West itself precisely because of their concern with how to achieve a closer fit between state of mind and place in what Kowalewski accentuates as "the complex interconnections between societal beliefs and biophysical processes."[53]

Much of recent Western nature writing thus exemplifies what Lawrence Buell terms "the motif of the (re)turn from the city to the rural place of cultural origin and spiritual centeredness." Tracing the presence of that motif in mainstream writing back to Thoreau's *Walden* and finding it running through works by Indian writers such as Momaday, Silko, and the mixed-blood Chippewa novelist Louise Erdrich, he concludes that it indicates a cross-cultural convergence on "a commitment to imagining a less technologized, less 'artificial' life."[54] In Western nature writing that commitment requires the articulation of a state of mind accordant not with an idealized West but with the biophysical place. Such writing, even if it focuses on environments less wild than, say, the most remote areas of the Humboldt-Toiyabe National Forest in Nevada, strives to communicate the momentousness of experiences like the metanoia of Locke Setman, the mixed-blood artist in Momaday's novel *The Ancient Child* (1989), who leaves the discontenting urban world of San Francisco, goes to Cradle Creek (the Oklahoma home of his Kiowa father's people), and has a vision through which he, as Owens puts it, "enters into the myth" that helps him become capable of "entering into a new and infinitely more profound relationship with the natural world."[55]

Now the misfit between the values of an Old Western mental space and the realities of a New Western empirical place has reached a crisis that echoes, with a more plaintive timbre, the postfrontier anxiety of a century ago. Alison Hawthorne Deming says as much in her declaration that "the old story of the West . . . is dead" and decidedly irrelevant to a postregion beset by predicaments besides a wild that no longer seems as dangerous to us as it once did and in which indeed "we long for our own wildness . . . and for the spiritual lessons wilderness can teach." She finds hope, though, in "the new story of the West [that] is just beginning to be written— part elegy to the past, part rage at its injustices; part imaginative retelling of the past so that we understand how our collective character has been formed."[56] And, in large part, I'd argue, rewriting of Western nature so that soon, as Lyon phrases his hope, there'll come a time when "a relation-seeing and complex view of existence replaces a simplistic or romantically abstract attention."[57] It's a view he sees expressed already in the work of Gary Snyder and William Stafford, poets who are both very much nature writers—specifically, in the former's *Turtle Island* (1974) and *Axe Handles* (1983) and in the latter's collections from *West of Your City* (1960) on.

Near the end of a 1990 essay on ecocriticism, the study of the relationship between literature and the biophysical environment, that was originally his past president's address at the 1989 meeting of the Western Literature Association, Glen A. Love offered these words:

> The most important function of literature today is to redirect human consciousness to a full consideration of its place in a threatened natural world. Why does nature writing, literature of place, regional writing, poetry of nature, flourish now—even as it is ignored or denigrated by most contemporary criticism? Because of a widely-shared sense—outside the literary establishment—that the current ideology which separates human beings from their environment is demonstrably and dangerously reductionist.[58]

Much has changed since then, for ecocriticism itself now flourishes; and, with the recent efforts of Rick Bass, Barry Lopez, Snyder, and many others, no literature has been doing a better job of fulfilling the function Love singles out than Western nature writing. Its authors continue to convince Lyon that "an alternative to the frontier mentality is finally beginning to be created."[59] They are first in rank among the many contemporary Western writers Erdrich praises because they "give us a glimpse of what the world could be like if humans learned the knack of just touching the edge of wildness—not conquering, but learning to walk the serene hem."[60] An edge that's not a frontier between civilized and savage, culture and nature, known and unknown, state of mind and material place, but a hem, a border where, to tweak Erdrich's metaphor, each is joined intimately yet lightly to the other, the wild-tame dialectic resolved—or even replaced—by a seam.[61]

Way Out Walden: Rewriting Western Nature

We started to tell stories of the people we knew and their relationships to the environment and Terry came back round to her interest in creating a literature that reactivates a sense of the ancestral, a vision that includes a strong sense of the animal.

"I think it's that: a wild response. It's remembering what we're connected to."
Ona Siporin, "Terry Tempest Williams and Ona Siporin:
A Conversation"

In 1795 a greenhorn named John Evans traveled up the Missouri as a member of a Spanish trading expedition led by James Mackay, formerly a Northwest Company man. When the party reached the Omahas, Mackay sent Evans on north overland to search for the same passage to the Pacific that Lewis and Clark would seek. Evans made charts and kept journals that would be useful to those explorers, but his own objective was to find the lost tribe of Welsh Indians fabled to exist in the New World. He got no further than the Mandans' villages, however, before he returned to St. Louis, disappointed that he had found no blue-eyed savages—though several decades later George Catlin would persuade himself, on the basis of the Mandans' vaguely biblical origin myth about a birchbark and a flood, that those people were indeed scions of immigrants from Wales.[1]

Donald A. Barclay, James H. Maguire, and Peter Wild read Evans's experience as a parable linking him and his exploratory fantasies, the kind that drew "other dreamers ever farther westward into the wilderness," to contemporary nature writers who, less deluded, "look more closely" and "see a ravaged landscape, a biotic holocaust" hellbent for ecocide. The good news is that those writers carefully record the Malthusian-technological mess we've made and by art and argument goad us to "begin living what is, paradoxically, the newest and oldest of all dreams: the dream of the earth."[2] Like John Muir, Aldo Leopold, J. Frank Dobie, Joseph Wood Krutch, and other predecessors, they look at the West ecologically but more closely so, and their cris de coeur arise from clearer, deeper knowledge of more desperate circumstances.

Postregional nature writing cranked up around 1970, the year of the first Earth Day, a milestone that betokened the culmination of what Max Oelschlaeger calls "a greening of consciousness in America." It was a greening that made us marvel at the exquisite systematization of the wild, brood on why we ever imposed simple ideas of order on it, and envision bioregional cultures. It let us know nature more ecocentrically, less egocentrically and anthropocentrically. It began the transformation of "the modern mind," with its rage to control the natural world, into "the postmodern mind," with its grasp of the need for wildness and its view, "both behind and ahead, to a world that might be, where humankind has rediscovered its fundamental co-relatedness with nature."[3]

Western nature writers, like Indian authors such as Linda Hogan and Louise Erdrich, have thus taken on what Thomas J. Lyon sees as "the struggle to heal the broken world," which demands the attentiveness to place, exemplified early in the postregional era by Edward Abbey's *Desert Solitaire: A Season in the Wilderness* (1968), that indexes "a change of paradigm from that of the frontier mind, which has its eyes, so to speak, on the far horizon." The struggle demands also a strong allegiance to wilderness, aggressive criticism of the social structures that threaten it and championship of alternatives to them, and often some humor to prevent an excess of green dogmatism and righteousness—all qualities typically found in the work of Abbey, Charles Bowden, Barry Lopez, and others. Humorous or not, though, the writing that forwards this struggle, Lyon stresses, "is not the scenic nature writing of earlier, more genteel times, but a serious enterprise"—and now and then, as in Terry Tempest Williams's *Refuge* or Rick Bass's *The Book of Yaak* (1996), a defense of the chain-saw-menaced Montana valley where he lives, tragically passionate.[4] Indeed, as Scott Slovic points out, *The Book of Yaak*, along with many of Bass's magazine articles and his later book *Fiber* (1998), signals that nature writing recently has shifted from using "the pastel language" of acquiescence to environmental ruination (as exemplified by John Nichols's *The Last Beautiful Days of Autumn* [1982]) to a "screeching along the border of language where the story of potential loss becomes a plea."[5]

Slovic sees this new nature writing as having a hand in "the evolving discourse of warning and nostalgia, of love and loss."[6] Through its efforts toward restor(y)ing nature in America, most of that nature Western, it's giving rise to an industry of essays and poems and books, books about books, catalogues of books, journals and magazines (with names like *Terra Nova* and *Wild Earth*), videos, symposia and conferences all over the West. Practically every Westerner who's had a backyard epiphany seems to be turning it into text and networking with others who do the same. So we have a market-driven plague of green textuality, nature commodified by words.

Western nature writing is now rife with such ironies. According to Frank Stewart in his history of nature writing, most Americans feel a "lack of ease" with other creatures, because of which "we feel neither entirely one with them nor entirely separate." Nature writers, he argues, "have become increasingly important to us because they struggle, in memorable language, to resolve the deep issue of this in-betweenness, a resolution crucial to the physical and spiritual survival of our world."[7] They're trying to use a language that differentiates us from the rest of nature (makes us two with it, as Woody Allen would say) as a means of uniting us with it. Words are bookish, say the disparagers, and nature is no book. Nature writing, Paul Shepard argues, "nourishes the view of nature as esthetic abstraction" and "captivates its readers with a spurious substitute for experience in the natural world"—an etherealization that, he admits, some writers (mostly Western, I think) curtail by "an antiwriting against the seductive illusions of the 'beauty' of nature."[8] Supporters, on the other hand, say nature writing returns its readers to nature with heightened senses and versant appreciation. Disparagers say nature writers are apt to be self-absorbed, to suffocate their subjects with sentiment. Supporters say nature writers at their best unobtrusively reveal the otherness of nature in relation to themselves. For their own part, nature writers concede that telling about the wild can be at odds with saving it, let alone resolving the issue of in-betweenness—ecotourists are always eager to descend on some new location. If you bill it, they will come.

All that granted, Western nature writers are willing to risk their subject's being verbally aestheticized or loved to death. So, moving beyond grieving and some-times stopping just short of green fascism, they're devoted to advocacy, whether in the reasoned voice that was Wallace Stegner's style or through the Dionysian persona that was Abbey's. Either way, they mean to lead their readers out of bad ecological habits. They're people with fire in their bellies, a matter in which Bass was instructed by Doug Peacock while they were looking for grizzlies in the San Juans in fall 1990: "Once, when I asked him why he thinks so many writers cross over into what's called nature writing, he said succinctly that nature is a way to 'al-leviate nightmares.' Literature is about passion, he said, and it follows that writers and others are going to be passionate about objects and places of great beauty. 'No-body ever got lyrical or mournful over a busted thermostat.'"[9] If they see that beauty threatened by forces from the world of the thermostat, their passion turns advoca-tive—nowhere more vehemently than in the 1996 anthology *Testimony: Writers of the West Speak on Behalf of Utah Wilderness*, which was compiled by Williams and Stephen Trimble and presented, in its first edition, to Congress.[10] Whatever the members of that parliament of fools gleaned from the book, most of its readers have gotten what its contributors (Bass, William Kittredge, Lopez, John McPhee, T. H. Watkins, and many others) have been creating for years: literature that is, as Glen A. Love has it, "the clearest and most direct antidote to the presumption of human dominance and control."[11]

Given that antidotal counteraction, it's remarkably ironic (unless you accept flatly the premise that all writing is nature writing) that postmodern nature writ-ing includes cities in its province, places bashed by traditional nature writers that would seem to be its anti-territory. Arguably Eastern in origin, urban nature writing has spread into the West. Peter Friederici, one of its practitioners and a Chicagoan now living in the Southwest, propounds the postulate of such writing: "American suburbs, with their piecemeal grid of grass and asphalt, are becoming an increas-ingly accurate model of the ecological state of the entire country, and indeed the world." What's necessary in that circumstance is unvarnished realism: "If we wish to learn how our lives are mirrored in the natural world—and I would argue that our future well-being, physical and psychological, depends on such learning—we are going to have to do it in landscapes like the suburbs," which are flush with "remnants of wildness" from weeds to coyotes and skunks to "the wildness within us" still.[12] For writers who would advance that learning, the contemporary city, even with many of its traditional functions "dematerialized, transferred to virtual forms like telecommuting and cyber-everything," is, as Emily Hiestand attests, "a place on a continuum with fields and cedar forests and tundras, a place with its own authentic nature."[13] Jennifer Price, a native of the Southwest, says she "had never planned to become a Thoreau of the mall" but nonetheless began to examine the contradictory relations between "the Nature I loved as Out There" and its role "In Here," in the city, which seems only to destroy it. Finally, she "joined the proliferating calls to reenvision the spaces we inhabit as places where people must use nature. I even moved to Los Angeles."[14] She's far from alone in that attempt to understand more subtly nature in the Western city.[15]

But the most important evolvement in postregional nature writing is the increasing number of women doing it—and doing it with a difference. Anyone who has heard Pattiann Rogers read her poem "Rolling Naked in the Morning Dew," with its exulting "In the magical powers of dew on the cheeks / And breasts of Lillie Langtry,"[16] must at least suspect that women may be revolutionizing Western nature writing, poetry and prose alike, and that the old ideology of the white-male dominance of nature (and women and otherness) may be slipping like a hiker hoofing in Front Range scree. "An unprecedented boom in western women's writing is afoot," writes Krista Comer, and one of its traits is a revisionist feminism that sets store by an empowering, rather than an oppressive or combative, relationship with the land and critiques "the legacy of western environmental exploitation."[17] Heirs to a bequest of nature writing initiated by women such as Susan Fenimore Cooper, whose studious *Rural Hours* was published in 1850, and Isabella Bird, whose *A Lady's Life in the Rocky Mountains* was published in 1879, feminist nature writers tend to validate John P. O'Grady's assumption "that 'the wild' is erotic space."[18] That's extravagantly true for Williams, as evidenced by her *Desert Quartet* (1995), *Leap* (2001), and *Red: Passion and Patience in the Desert* (2001), but it holds for other feminist Western nature writers as well.[19]

Whether they experience the wild erotically or not, Western women nature writers typically communicate what Lorraine Anderson calls "a feminine way of being in relationship to nature." That way, illustrated by Rogers, Williams, Gretel Ehrlich, and other Westerners, "is caring rather than controlling; it seeks harmony rather than mastery; it is characterized by humility rather than arrogance, by appreciation rather than acquisitiveness."[20] No matter that it may incorporate the problematic personification of nature as a woman, such writers are addressing the neglect of that way with vigor.[21]

So much nature writing has inspired the burgeoning of a secondary industry, the ecocriticism I mentioned earlier. A field of inquiry that draws on the methodologies of both literary criticism and environmental studies, it had some unlicensed practitioners before the founding of the Association for the Study of Literature and Environment in 1992, but that founding, largely the accomplishment of members of the Western Literature Association, gave it an imprimatur, a professional home base, and soon a journal, *Interdisciplinary Studies in Literature and Environment*, along with regular conferences. Since then much of its energy has been directed toward Western literature, particularly nature writing, with focal attention on the central interest of most of that literature: the interrelations of nature and culture, wild and civilized, country and city.[22]

Western nature writing and the ecocriticism that midwifes its deepest significance are leading participants in a broadening attempt to redefine all human-non-human interplay in terms of a more open and flexible dialectic. As Barney Nelson shows through the prickly arguments of her 2000 book *The Wild and the Domestic: Animal Representation, Ecocriticism, and Western American Literature*, it's a project that entails investigating the inosculations of realms that ultimately are as inseparable as the title of Peter Goin's 1996 book *Humanature* suggests. It entails rectifying the privileging of conquest over concord, abstract distance over sensory immediacy. It entails comprehending the degree to which, by a wisdom in us not entirely conscious, "wild nature," as Love puts it, "has replaced the traditional middle state of the garden and the rural landscape as the locus of stability and value, the seat of instruction," a locus whose "key terms . . . in the past were *simplicity* and *permanence*" but "have shifted in an ecologically-concerned present to *complexity* and *change*."[23] In the desert West, that project entails, to quote the title of a 2001 collection of contemporary Southwestern environmental literature Slovic edited, *Getting Over the Color Green*—that is, ceasing to affix to arid land expectations more suited to high-rainfall biomes.[24] It entails acknowledging about such a place, however alien it may seem to us (an involute preoccupation of Abbey's in *Desert Solitaire*), that "its silence and space," as Reg Saner advises in one of his essays on the Anasazi, for whom stretches of the high-desert Southwest were once home, "are unimprovable."[25] It entails not avoiding the postregion's most harshly and delicately beautiful places but acting in a certain way while we are there, as Gary Snyder tells us in a teacher's voice:

To climb these coming crests
one word to you, to
you and your children:

stay together
learn the flowers
go light[26]

The Wild Woman in the Outback:
Postregional Cowgirls

They said the girl had surely become one of the wild horses at last.
Paul Goble, *The Girl Who Loved Wild Horses*

On December 10, 1910, Giacomo Puccini's *La Fanciulla del West* premiered at the Metropolitan Opera in New York. Based on David Belasco's *The Girl of the Golden West*, a play recalling his father's experiences as a gold miner that had premiered in 1905 in Pittsburgh, that grand opera, the first with an American theme, has as its principal a woman named Minnie, the comely keeper of a saloon in a miners' camp during the Gold Rush. Apart from her obvious charms, the most interesting thing about Minnie is the realism of her personality. She's a bundle of all-too-human contradictions: vulnerable passion and stalwart determination, gentleness and toughness, sociability and independence. To Puccini's credit—and Belasco's—she's a more psychologically compelling Western heroine than the cross-dressing Amazons of earlier dime novels or the fainting flowers of later movies. A woman who lives alone, since the death of her father, in a cabin halfway up a mountain (at least until she falls in love and heads elsewhere) and who schools her customers in the Bible even as she provides them with a hangout for drinking and gambling, Minnie is much more like many actual Western women of the nineteenth century than she is like the stereotypes that have long represented them—especially in how she relates to the tame and the wild.

We know that now because of the revisionist history of Western women that started in the 1970s, history long delayed by the traditional emphasis on the conquest and settlement of the West as masculine narratives structured by a male mythology that, for many postregionalist historians, "had to be challenged, even destroyed," Richard W. Etulain argues, "if women's experiences in the American West were to be understood"—just as it had to be likewise treated to allow "for new, more realistic interpretations of the environment."[1] During and after that decade there appeared study upon study that refuted such mythology and pieced together stories of women—mostly Anglo but also Hispanic, Asian, African American, and Native American—every bit as complex as Minnie, among them these: Julie Roy Jeffrey's *Frontier Women: The Trans-Mississippi West, 1840–1880* (1979), Sandra L. Myres's *Westering Women and the Frontier Experience, 1800–1915* (1982), Glenda Riley's *The Female Frontier: A Comparative View of Women on the Prairie and the Plains* (1988), Peggy Pascoe's *Relations of Rescue: The Search for Female Moral Authority in the American West, 1874–1939* (1990), and Linda Peavy and Ursula Smith's *Pioneer Women: The Lives of Women on the Frontier* (1996), as well as anthropologically oriented collections such as Laura F. Klein and Lillian A. Ackerman's *Women and Power in Native North America* (2000) and literary-critical studies such as Janet Floyd's *Writing the Pioneer Woman* (2002).

From all that rewriting we've learned a lot about the preconceptions pioneering women brought to the West, how they adapted or failed to adapt to unfamiliar conditions as those preconceptions dissolved in daily ordeals, the extent to which they retained Eastern models of behavior, how much gender determined or colored their experiences, on and on—even as stereotypes of them (the weary frontier wife, the passive sufferer, the Christianizing saint, and the like) have persisted in American culture at large. Yet there's a plethora of questions regarding the history of Western women, even women of the regional and postregional eras, that remain to be answered. The most pertinent one here, foregrounded by Glenda Riley and bristling with ties to other questions, "is the way(s) western women conceive of, and utilize, their environment." "We know," she says, "that many women supported the activities of John Muir, joined Muir's expeditions, encouraged the development of a national-park concept, and formed naturalists' clubs, but we know little about their role in the Sierra Club, in Greenpeace, and other environmental-reform movements." She goes on to ask if Western women tend to be more conservationists or trash-producing consumers, how much women native to the West differ in their relationship to its environment from women recently arrived there, whether Western women generally share "an outdoor aesthetic" that shapes their thinking about environmental issues or have a great variety of attitudes—across ages, races, and so on—"that would belie the concept of a unified western women's view of the environment."[2] Further research doubtless will show such variety to be the case. In the nineteenth century, Euro-American Western women didn't have a uniform view of the environment. Nor do they in the twenty-first. But you can distinguish a wide, if not all-inclusive, pattern of historical change in their attitude toward the natural West, and it's a pattern that may have crucial implications for the postregion's future.

Those women, as a rule, were as complicit in advancing the frontier as Native American women, some of them warriors, were in resisting its progress.[3] From the research of feminist scholars such as Annette Kolodny and Nina Baym, Lawrence Buell infers that, because of the hardships pioneer women faced, "many of them . . . aspired not to be freed from civic restraint but to see nature civilized."[4] And Patricia Nelson Limerick notes that their history and the history of Indian wars "are very much intertwined," that pioneer women (like women on the other side) could act as "powerful forces in demanding revenge and retaliation" and were, furthermore, "members of a civilian invading force and beneficiaries of the subordination of the natives."[5] They had a vested interest in Manifest Destiny.

More daedal intertwinings of that sort can be discovered once you overcome, in Limerick's droll apposition, "the 'Bride Comes to Yellow Sky' notion of the woman as the civilizer." Helpful in that task, she suggests, would be the reading of Raymond Chandler's Philip Marlowe novels with attention to his female characters. Not simply madonnas, whores, or schoolteachers, they're "capable of starting the shooting as well as stopping it. . . . They can be forces of wilderness, as well as forces fighting back wilderness."[6] They can be and were like Calamity Jane, Cattle Kate, Belle Starr, Poker Alice.[7] Or Carry Nation. Or Annie Oakley, born Phoebe Anne Mozee on a farm in Ohio, who escaped from childhood poverty and abuse to become a peerless wing shot in Buffalo Bill's Wild West and, in Riley's summary of the impact of her unassuming persona, "burned into the public mind a vision of the archetypal western woman—daring, beautiful, and skilled."[8] Or maybe one of the many women, Oakley's contemporaries, who, as Riley introduces us to them in her 1999 book *Women and Nature: Saving the "Wild" West*, weren't the degraded gun-toting heroines of dime novels or the trapped wives or doomed saloon girls of nickelodeon movies but women on the way to getting the right to vote before their Eastern sisters would, women outdoors unintimidated by wild nature, enjoying it, wanting to protect it.[9]

Albert B. Tucker contends that "the pretty girl" in B Westerns "was independent unless she chose, for her own reasons, to let the cowboy hero help her."[10] That's questionable. But her real-life counterpart, in many instances, may well have been. She sure was if she was a real cowgirl, like one of the members of the Wild Women of the Frontier from Meriden, Kansas, I saw riding horseback (*not* side-saddle) in a parade some years ago—whoop-it-up women. Women Teresa Jordan terms the "more adventurous sisters" of prairie madonnas and temperamental kin to "wild, outrageous women" such as Belle Starr[11]—but with Oakley as their paragon. They're the Marlboro Women whose nonfiction can be read in the 1997 collection *Leaning into the Wind: Women Write from the Heart of the West*, edited by Linda Hasselstrom, Gaydell Collier, and Nancy Curtis (literary ranchwomen all), a book that makes clear that Western women's independent spirit has always derived from their connections to nature and its animals—to wind and the weather it fetches, sun and moon, pines, birds, horses, piglets, wild and domestic blurred together like birth and death. There are now more cowgirls of one type or another, with or without cattle, than ever before partly, of course, because the West has grown in population but also because a lot of women have stopped biding some more propitious time (and, as we'll see, gotten proactive). The reason for that biding had and still has everything to do with the ideology of dependency behind B Westerns, with how men see women.

"The imagined West that has gripped American consciousness has been, on the whole, an overwhelmingly masculine West," Richard White safely observes. However, he adds, its masculinity is odd, "because it reverses the usual symbolism that identifies men with culture and women with nature." To accomplish that, its stories "strip white women of the sexuality that usually marked them as natural," a process that also denies them "access to the premodern virtues the West supposedly embodies." If the women in the stories initially reject those virtues, they usually come around to accepting them—though they still don't really have access to them—as superior to their own values. So the schoolteacher marries the hero, and their union symbolically brings about "the reconciliation of the premodern West and the new civilized West"—apparently to the man's advantage. Messing with that formula in late-modern Westerns made *Shane* (with its extramarital yearnings) a bit of a study in sexual frustration and *Johnny Guitar* (with its butch leading women) a bit of "a

Photograph, printed by Gilbert & Bacon, of Annie Oakley taken in Philadelphia (circa 1889): the archetypal Western woman. (P.69.1164. Buffalo Bill Historical Center, Cody, Wyoming.)

conventional Western in drag." By now, though, as a number of postmodern Westerns (*Bad Girls, Even Cowgirls Get the Blues, The Ballad of Little Jo*, and others) demonstrate, "a feminist imagining of the western past," as White concludes, "has already begun."[12] Those movies also suggest that the symbolism is reversing again, that Western women are seeing themselves (even if some men can't) as more independent, and that they have more access to those premodern virtues based in nature.

But the whole endeavor has been and remains uphill. The nineteenth-century Western white man's image of the white woman seems to have been determined, to borrow phrasing from Lee Clark Mitchell's discussion of Harte's stories, by "ideological tension" concerning "male control" and "a continuing (and mysterious) threat to masculine self-construction."[13] Robert G. Athearn tells us that few American men of the 1920s wanted to hear a message well documented by then: "Pioneer women were always at least as tough and resilient as their men."[14] One sentence written by Larry McMurtry in the late 1960s says much about the rural Western male's attitude toward women at the time: "Sex is still a word to freeze the average Texan's liver, particularly if the Texan is over forty and his liver not already pickled."[15] On the other hand, as he wrote in the early 1970s, the cowgirl as idealized by the Miss Rodeo America contest persuasively warrants the argument that "the men of the West don't consider women good for anything but bedding down with."[16] To a great extent that slippery attitude mirrors that of such men toward Native peoples in that both reveal a double-edged desire for otherness to be kept in subjugation, nature subject to their will, wildness in check—and fear of the opposite.

That fear. Tom Pilkington illuminates it in his afterword to R. G. Vliet's 1974 novel *Rockspring*, the story, set in the Nueces River valley during the 1830s, of an adolescent Anglo girl named Jensie who is kidnapped by three men, two Mexicans and an Indian. At first, raped and desperate, she wants to die, but gradually she "is ineluctably changed by her experiences in the wilderness. She tastes the wild, and it is sweet." By the same token, though, the girl is now "unfit for civilization," more so because she's pregnant by one of the men. Thus, by the end of the story, when she's in some sense rescued, Jensie has assumed "the taint . . . of 'the marginalized Other,'" an outcome on which Pilkington expatiates: "In white society she will always be identified with the forces of savagery. . . . The fear that Jensie, and others like her, provoked in frontier white males was a fear of their own attraction to darkness, wildness, savagery; at bottom it was a fear of uncontrolled female sexuality."[17]

Small wonder, then, that the Victorian love manuals and tracts Stan Steiner surveys are so full of warnings about "the primitive evil of a woman's lovemaking" and that "the later immigrants to the West brought these ideas with them." While, as he grants, "the reality of life on the prairies and in the mountains . . . did not easily bend itself to fit these male myths," they nevertheless, "in time, became the reality, and the reality began to resemble the myths"—and Western women often were "fitted into the masculine stays and mental corsets of the women of the East."[18]

That constraining surely was abetted by a historical collaterality Irene Klaver discusses:

> The rise of the concept of wilderness coincides with the first serious thematization of the unconscious, the mental equivalent of wild land, and an obses-

sion with sexuality, its bodily equivalent. Since modernity is fundamentally a patriarchal development, the main focus of the thematization of sexuality is on woman's body. Woman, like wilderness, figures as an abstract ideal who channels profoundly ambivalent emotions: as the mysterious other, she is uncontrollable but utterly desirable, and at the same time she is an other to be conquered and domesticated.

If the woman breaks out of this paradigm to assume some traditionally male role, she becomes undesirable. In a like way, Klaver argues, "when nature breaks out of the imagery of wilderness, it loses its imputed magic and is reduced to a mere resource, rather than being a regenerative source."[19] That breaking out involves moving into a bad fit with masculinized culture that begets, as an extreme consequence, to borrow the title of Sandra M. Gilbert and Susan Gubar's 1979 study of female writers in the nineteenth century, "the madwoman in the attic."[20] And, correlatively, polluted wilderness.

Recently, however, women, Western women all the more, have been breaking out of that paradigm by moving, contrary to the conventional way, into what they're discovering is a good fit with nature feminized on their terms that begets, as an extreme consequence, the wild woman in the outback. And, correlatively, wilderness valued once more as a regenerative source. This wild woman isn't the one of medieval legend who, according to Hayden White, "was supposed to be surpassingly ugly" but "could appear as the most enticing of women, revealing her abiding ugliness only during sexual intercourse."[21] That monstrosity, like her similars in other times, was invented by men, as Sharon W. Tiffany and Kathleen J. Adams adroitly argue, to "perpetuate male supremacy."[22] The new wild woman may still stir ambivalent emotions in men, but she's not bestially uncontrollable. Like the captivity victim converted by savages, she's changed from what she was (supposed to be) in the old paradigm but in a manner she and her sisters, as well as their wisehearted male and female sympathizers, find salubrious.

In the vanguard of those wild women are ecofeminists, whose basic beliefs Max Oelschlaeger conveniently tabulates:

Mother Earth is a nurturing home for all life and should be revered and loved as in premodern (Paleolithic and archaic) societies.

Ecosystemic malaise and abuse is rooted in androcentric concepts, values, and institutions.

Relations of complementarity rather than superiority between culture and nature, the human and nonhuman, and male and female are desirable.

The many problems of human relations, and relations between the human and nonhuman worlds, will not be resolved until androcentric institutions, values, and ideology are eradicated.[23]

Some may be tempted to dismiss one or more of those beliefs (or their corollaries for, say, resourcism) as qualified for inclusion among the six impossible things the White Queen in Lewis Carroll's *Through the Looking-Glass* is able to believe before breakfast, but ecofeminists have the correct heading toward needed adjustments to the wild-tame dialectic.

Such beliefs imply reversal or, at least, major rewriting of the male recovery narrative. If acted upon too radically or narrowly, they'll lead to nothing more than rancorous defeatism. If acted upon patiently and broad-mindedly, however, they may be of great help to Westerners who would like to save their world from their own foolishness. If acted upon, that is, in the disposition of what Sharman Apt Russell calls "the green woman, an elusive dryad hidden in our hardened modern selves," an ultimate cowgirl in whose credo, for Westerners who call her out in themselves, there's realistic advice to heed: "Land health is the bottom line. . . . I believe in wilderness and large expanses of wildlife habitat because wilderness and wildlife have an intrinsic right to exist. . . . I believe in a biodiversity of myth."[24]

In 1994 Donald Worster noticed "the increasing role of women in this debate over wild things, a role that may alter significantly the issues and the manner of their discussion" since "modern women may represent a fresh perspective on the human-animal relation."[25] Ample evidence of the truth of that optative prophecy is supplied by the dozens of women whose writings appear in the 1998 collection *Intimate Nature: The Bond between Women and Animals*, edited by Linda Hogan, Deena Metzger, and Brenda Peterson. It's a collection that validates the editors' contentions that "we are witnessing a return to respect for the natural world and the authority of wildness," that women have been crucial in reestablishing such an attitude, and indeed that the book's literary and scientific contributors, a number of them Westerners, have been "transformative" in that reestablishment "because our approach to relationship has been different from that of men. What women have brought into the equation is a respect for feeling and empathy as tools to create intimate bonds of connection." The origins of that respect, they speculate, may be both biological and historical: "Perhaps it is our own bodies that remind us that we, too, are animal. . . . Perhaps it is because, like animals, we have so often been cherished at the same time we have been hated."[26] The male Old West that was, as some cowman once said, hell on horses and women (however much both were ambivalently cherished) many women are now determined to make into a more female New West that's heaven for horses—and other animals, including women.[27]

Stay with the horses awhile. Some of those women in the postregional West are as obsessed with horses as famous Montana rodeo cowgirl Fannie Sperry Steele was in the regional era, but their way of relating to them is older than the Old West. They believe that wild horses should be left wild, by and large, and that any untrained horse to be ridden should be not forced into obedience but "gentled" by a slow building of trust and rapport between horse and rider, by thinking and feeling with and not against the animal's instincts.[28] They don't want to sit atop a subservient symbol of patriarchy: when they ride, they want, as one of Peggy Simson Curry's poems avows, to "clasp / Between my thighs the power of all creation."[29] They wish the West had been gentled and not conquered in the first place. They understand, in Neila C. Seshachari's words, "how many of our environmental crises have psychosexual roots," and they're interested in "a psychic wholeness" formed from "the infusion of the so-called feminine into the patriarchal masculine."[30] Georgia O'Keeffe's severe blacks and whites *and* terrene colors, rams' heads *and* hollyhocks, buck horns *and* cow pelvises, starkly geometrical walls and crosses and towers *and* mammiform hills and vulval shells and flowers. The yin-yang harmony of almost any cowgirl painting by Donna Howell-Sickles.

As Dorothy M. Johnson's *Some Went West* affirms, women did go west in earlier years. Quite a few more did in later years. Scads more have done so in recent years. And not just to suffer Didion-esque ennui in pseudo-ranchy subdivisions or die comfortably in retirement communities but to discover for themselves the reasons for Mary Austin's love of the West's landscape and what Cynthia Taylor terms "her insistence that women belong in it."[31] They're looking to go wild—*wild*, as Clarissa Pinkola Estés clarifies, in the sense of living "a natural life, one in which the *criatura*, creature, has innate integrity and healthy boundaries."[32]

Leslie Ryan recalls that by the time she'd finished college she "was living almost completely in my head . . . and hardly knew if or why I was alive." But, she tells us, "my body had better sense. She spoke up from under the bed, where I'd kept her locked up like a caged animal and had fed her only scraps for years. She said, 'Get outside.'" So Ryan went to the desert of southern Idaho. There she worked with troubled teenagers in a wilderness-therapy program and learned that a woman "has power within herself and through her connection with the natural world, not power over them."[33]

Thus empowered, Western women wed to the wild relish traveling into untamed places on their own. Among those women is Susan Ewing. In one of her essays she writes, "I sing along with the Sweethearts of the Rodeo, accelerating westbound out of Bozeman. Behind the seat in my little pickup are chains for all four tires, an emergency sleeping bag, my rifle and my knife. And of course my purse, which looks as if it got on the wrong bus. Feeling like a wolf in sheep's clothing (in polar fleece, actually), I sip a double cappuccino and think about antelope meat. . . . I find myself hungry to be out." Later, before her adventure in subfreezing backcountry really begins, she informs us she has "a picture postcard of Annie Oakley on the dashboard for good luck."[34] Maybe she's not entirely on her own.

In 1993 the Bradford Exchange advertised a limited-edition porcelain plate, titled "Soul Mates," graced with the representation, so ran the pitch, of "A CHEROKEE PRINCESS . . . IN THE COMPANY OF HER SPIRIT GUARDIAN—A MAGNIFICENT TIMBER WOLF" (and a pup too, for cuteness)—that "CAPTURES THE BOND BETWEEN THE CHEROKEE AND NATURE" off

Donna Howell-Sickles, The Grove (1986): *the yin-yang harmony of masculine and feminine.* (Courtesy of Donna Howell-Sickles.)

in "A WORLD OF BEAUTY, PASSION, AND MYSTICISM—A WORLD LONG VANISHED BUT ONE THAT YOU CAN NOW SHARE."[35] Or you can share one a little closer to wild-woman reality through Grey, the dreamy young medicine woman in N. Scott Momaday's novel *The Ancient Child*: "When she thought of the things that remarked her essential life, she did not think of numbers or graphs or blueprints or print upon a page. She thought of hawks and horses, the sun rising, and clouds bursting with rain."[36] Closer still might be Ron Hansen's vignette of Leslie Marmon Silko as a thoroughly postmodern Minnie who "lives in the rugged foothills above Tucson, Arizona, where she holds a weekly poker game and tries out her extensive pistol collection on a stash of empty bottles from the finest wineries in Bordeaux."[37] Close enough.

The Return of the Native: Reclaiming Identities

> Yet there is a tremendous schizophrenia among non-Indians regarding the Indian image, since so many people want to claim Indian blood. It is the nobility and authenticity of nature that they see in Indians and want—they want to be pure and natural.
>
> Vine Deloria Jr., *Red Earth, White Lies: Native Americans and the Myth of Scientific Fact*

The once dominantly white-male West to which women have been returning naturally is also the West to which Indians have been returning culturally. The postmodern Ghost Dance for bootstrapping themselves back began in the 1960s with a swirl of events through which Indians sought to reclaim their identities and the places that spiritually informed them—and through which whites once again came to see Indians as Noble Savages. In 1961 the National Indian Youth Council was established, followed in 1968 by the founding of United Native Americans and the more politically influential American Indian Movement (AIM). Acutely aware that the massive postwar relocation undertaken by the Bureau of Indian Affairs (BIA) was meant to terminate tribes, urbanize their members, and sell their reservation lands (portions of which President Richard Nixon would later restore), many Indians dug in their heels or became militantly activist. In the Pacific Northwest in the mid-1960s they strove to preserve fishing rights granted by treaties being flagrantly violated. In the late 1960s, protests over other treaty violations, inequities, and brutalities occurred around the country. The capstone happening of the decade in that regard was the Indian invasion of Alcatraz, the vacant island prison in San Francisco Bay, in November 1969. The phalanx of two hundred, which in changing makeup would occupy the site for nearly two years, maintained that a Sioux treaty entitled them to it and, as Vine Deloria Jr. recalls, "issued a proclamation asking for title to the island so it could be used for a spiritual center, university, and social service center" and, ironically, "compared Alcatraz to most Indian reservations: no water, no good housing, land unfit for cultivation, no employment; in short, a prison."[1] In the same year Deloria's *Custer Died for Your Sins: An Indian Manifesto* was published.

That book, which prepared a readership for Dee Brown's *Bury My Heart at Wounded Knee* and Deloria's *God Is Red: A Native View of Religion* (1972), helped set the stage for more protests and occupations as well as white plunderings of Indian burial grounds (sometimes with good, if ignorant, intentions) and murders of Indians. In November 1972 Indians seized the BIA headquarters in Washington and rampaged through its offices, after which offense, as Deloria tells us, "the public was in favor of the Indians" and didn't want them prosecuted. Then in February 1973 AIM members engineered the most conspicuous Indian event of the twentieth century, now as commemorated as its namesake massacre of 1890: armed Sioux and their adherents took over the village of Wounded Knee on the Pine Ridge Reservation in southwestern South Dakota. Their two-month occupation was a sympathy-gathering protest about the nation's treatment of Indians, and it made a media splash. It made also a bloody story Deloria calls "both tragic and comic," as did ensuing episodes—the trial for high crimes of the occupation's leaders in 1974, the killing of two FBI agents west of Pine Ridge in 1975, Leonard Peltier's controversial conviction as their killer, and so forth. But through all that tragicomedy, Deloria argues, "a different sense of Indian identity was born."[2]

That sense arose from a refreshed consciousness of nature, at the time evident in the West and American society in general but peculiarly exigent in Indian country, a causal tie Deloria alludes to in his discussion of the meaning, beyond disputes over rights and reservation boundaries, of the Indian protests of the late 1960s and early 1970s: "At the bottom of everything, I believed then and continue to believe, is a religious view of the world that seeks to locate our species within the fabric of life that constitutes the natural world. . . . As long as Indians exist there will be conflict between the tribes and any group that carelessly despoils the land and the life it supports." Those protests, he says, helped many become "alerted to the ecological meltdown we face" and inspired "revivals of ancient ceremonies" that might lead to what he foresees as "a final effort to renew the earth and its peoples—hoofed, winged, and others."[3]

The difference in the Indians' sense of identity, in terms of the meaning Deloria considers, may be discerned more readily in the protest of several dozen Lakotas who took possession of a valley in the Black Hills National Forest near Rapid City, South Dakota, in April 1981 and held it till almost the end of the decade. In contrast to the Wounded Knee occupation, this one was peaceful, and it was backed not only by AIM but also by the Black Hills Alliance. The latter, as Donald Worster explains, was "an environmental group formed in 1979 to forestall the invasion of the mountains and nearby plains by some of the nation's largest energy and mining companies," and it included environmental activists and white farmers and ranchers as well as Indians, none of whom wanted the area reduced to desolation far worse than what gold crazies had created a century before, when the Indians had been governmentally swindled out of that land. So, in the ensuing court hearings about restoring the Black Hills to the Lakota people, ecological argument bolstered what became fundamentally a spiritual position: those hills "were a 'sacred space'" bound up with the past, like the Taos' Blue Lake and surrounding forest Congress had restored to them in 1970. But here's the crux, according to Worster, and it has everything to do with a change in the Indians' sense of identity apparent in their land disputes during the 1980s and subsequently: "What is going on among the Lakota is not so much the presentation of a legal case for sacredness as it is the awakening of a new or revitalized religion" by means of which they "are trying to invest . . . with high numinosity" a mountain range that, if restored, they've pledged to tend "with 'respect for nature.'"[4] A happy possibility in the despoiled West—and not only for Indians out to affirm who they are.

That affirmation was pan-Indian and well under way in the 1980s and still carries on apace by various visions and revisions, moves and countermoves. It has been aided by an explosion of ethnohistorical interest in Indians. By tribal histories written by Indians. By rewritten war history. By the unprecedented revenues generated by tribal casinos. By enlarged Indian sovereignty over Indian matters. By a renaissance in Indian literature and other arts. By the 2004 opening of the Smithsonian's National Museum of the American Indian. And by other benefits. All of them concern Indians' rediscovery of their identity in relation to the natural environment.

Reginald Horsman offers the idea, in his overview of Indians' "search for a usable Indian past," that the story of that past "can be seen as a type of environmental history." Indeed, he attests, "the approach that links Indians firmly with their environment is one that finds much favor among the Native Americans themselves."[5] That's an anticipatable response from people whose past figures vitally in the present and whose environment—in the main, tens of millions of Western acres of reservation land—is all somehow sacred. Despite a degree of urbanization (though not the retribalization that has been its ironic by-product), languages dying out, alcoholism, poverty, gangs, unemployment, suicide epidemics, lost squabbles over water, and the other scourges of reservation life, that past and that land remain interwoven. They may be becoming more so.[6]

The casinos now run by over two hundred tribes in more than half the states, a multibillion-dollar enterprise, had their humble origin in 1979 when Florida's Seminoles stumbled on what Patricia Nelson Limerick terms "a new use of Indian territory": high-stakes bingo.[7] A few years later a hundred-odd reservations were taking economic advantage of their status as nations within the nation of the

United States—and therefore bodies exempt from both state gambling prohibitions and income tax. After the bingo palaces came the casinos. They popped up all over the West, with names like Cities of Gold and Desert Diamond. Though not yet the growing threat they are now to the profitability of the casino-hotels in Las Vegas, they were turning the tables on white culture. They generated capital, raised employment, and constituted a far more defensible use of Indian territory than, say, nuclear-waste disposal, an expedient entertained by the Skull Valley Gosiutes and other tribes. And, besides, there were ancient traditions of gambling, sometimes as a sacred activity (and sometimes with very high stakes), in Indian cultures.[8]

"By the turn of the century, abandoned casinos may well join the disused factories and empty motels that already blight the landscape around many reservation towns," wrote Fergus M. Bordewich in his 1996 book *Killing the White Man's Indian: Reinventing Native Americans at the End of the Twentieth Century*.[9] He was pondering the imminence of gambling-market saturation, and he's been proven wrong; but it is true that most Indian casinos have encountered problems, fiscal and otherwise, that may forebode a slightly grayer future than was once looked forward to. Still, whatever problems—or evils—you may associate with those casinos, they continue to serve as Indian social centers and sites of retribalization.[10] At least some of the money earned has been spent quite advantageously—for example, in buying land that's thereby saved from white depredations. To a remarkable extent Indian-casino gambling functions in reality much as, according to Kristan Sarvé-Gorham, it does in Louise Erdrich's fiction: "as a unifying factor . . ., for, through gaming proceeds, the land has been—and will again be—restored." With such restoration, by a propitious logic, "the people will be renewed."[11]

Gambling thus plays a role in what Bordewich calls "the sovereignty movement." That movement bears the hope—through political, economic, and cultural opportunities—"for peoples who have been flattened out into cliché and myth to regain dimension and to shape an identity that is simultaneously more traditional and more modern, more conscious of history and less dominated by it, and, ultimately, both more Indian and more American." In his most optimistic mood Bordewich foresees the possibility that regenerate tribes "will have a direct and unpredictable impact on many communities, and not only in the lightly populated West." He believes that that impact, however upsetting, will be constructive, just as Indians' campaigns to protect their sacred lands already have been in that they "challenge other Americans to think more profoundly about the nature of the earth and the consequences of our actions upon it."[12] That impact won't fulfill the prophecy of El Feo, one of the Indian leaders in Leslie Marmon Silko's *Almanac of the Dead*, that "tribal people would retake the Americas" since that "was what earth's spirits wanted: her indigenous children who loved her and did not harm her."[13] But it will change some thinking.

Indians' furthering of their sovereignty has required and will continue to require not only money but also education, through both tribal schools and programs of indigenous-nations studies in mainstream institutions, that enables them to balance adaptively tradition and postmodernity. Such balancing, as Chippewa activist Winona LaDuke stresses in her 1999 book *All Our Relations: Native Struggles for Land and Life*, involves resistance to environmental and cultural degradation as well as a quest for richer unity within and between natural and cultural realms. It involves nurturing those aspects of Indian identity that have persisted against white acculturative pressures as well as dealing with novel "identitarian concerns," as Arnold Krupat terms them.[14] It involves also, in N. Scott Momaday's phrasing, both leveraging the willingness of "the contemporary white American . . . to assume responsibility for the Indian" and defusing his unwillingness "to divest himself of the false assumptions which impede his good intentions."[15]

That last project calls for defying overdetermined stereotypes and putting forward more accurate, vibrant, and complex imagery of the Indian, often ironically. Sculptures such as Luis Jiménez's *End of the Trail (with Electric Sunset)* pursue that double goal, as do the antimascot pieces by Spokane installation artist Charlene Teters, the in-your-face presentations of Luiseño-Diegueño multimedia performance artist James Luna, and a steady flow of recent films made by and starring Indians. So do the literary works of James Welch, Sherman Alexie, Louis Owens, Joy Harjo, and others, and the deromanticizing paintings of artists such as Fritz Scholder and T. C. Cannon, who, as William H. Goetzmann and William N. Goetzmann note, "have brought the contemplation of the Indian experience into the art gallery, demanding that the viewer explore with the artist the multifarious threads of his influence, and begin to understand the history of the West from his point of view."[16] So does the literary criticism of Kenneth Lincoln, who investigates how Native American and white poetic traditions have merged and given rise to "an *earth-minded* aesthetics."[17] So does Thomas King's wily satirization of dam-building American culture in *Green Grass, Running Water* or the finespun argument by which Gerald Vizenor shows that "native survivance [active, renewing continuance] is a sense of presence, but the true self is visionary" and "an ironic consciousness, the cut of a native trickster."[18]

Such efforts relate to Indian identity, and that, of course, is an issue of place. Tribalism, like environmentalism, as William E. Bevis points out, is a movement that bucks what he calls "the culture of liquidity," the production of a "capitalist modernity [that] seeks to create a kind of no-place center, compared to which all 'places' or 'regions' are marginal." Liquidity, pushing mobility, commodification, and abstraction, "cannot confer identity," but tribalism, which underscores the importance of place, can.[19] For most Indians place means the West, which in both their literature and their daily lives, by Philip Burnham's formulation, "represents, as it once did for Turner, a cutting edge of identity."[20]

"The native has literally 'returned,'" Burnham announces. Returned to the West. "Indian peoples were, after all," he says, "the first to see the West—many of them on their way somewhere else—in the prehistorical migration that traversed the Americas thousands of years ago. Within historical memory, only the West has been deemed large enough to hold what remains of aboriginal America." The deeming still rings true. Those peoples aren't vanishing, and they "have started to reinvent their identity in the paradigm popularly known as the 'American mosaic.'" What ties together all the recent Indian writing that both assists and symbolizes that reinvention, he speculates, solidly, "is a link to the land, to the wide open West and places rural."[21]

So the return of the native is a turn to nature, but it's also a turn from something; and that double act is loaded with irony. Here, in Owens's words, is its main premise: "The evolving myth of America . . . demanded the presence of the Indian in the dark heart of the continent as the mirroring 'other.'" It was demanded because without the Indian "the threat to the white psyche would remain unacceptably disembodied and amorphous, internalized and unsignified." The Indian therewith became an external embodiment of wilderness that threatened white identity even as it contrastively defined it. Now, though, the challenge to identity "arises not out of the pure 'otherness' of wilderness but rather out of the immanently present landscape of a ravaged post-industrial world." That situation is powerfully poignant for Indians. Speaking of Vizenor's mixed-blood characters but by extension their real-life counterparts as well, Owens comments that they "find themselves in a position paradoxically similar to that of present-day Romans: they inhabit a world of ruins that testify to past greatness." The difference is that the Romans' ruins are more strictly cultural. "It is ironic, however," he thus observes, "that for Native Americans the existing monuments to an ideal past consist of mountains, rivers, and trees—topographical tropes of a seemingly lost coherence and identity-conferring order."[22] But the coherence and order are being recovered. Even when only a few students from Haskell Indian Nations University in Lawrence, Kansas, walk to the nearby Medicine Wheel, an earthwork quartered circle formed by stones and paths that symbolizes the interjoining of all life, they turn, for all of us, to those qualities and verify the possibility of rebuilding ruins. As Ray Pierotti says, "'it's a place of spiritual significance . . . where they go to re-establish their connections with wildness and with nature.'"[23] If they're motivated by a sense of the past, it's not nostalgic; and in their going they're turning from a postindustrial world that would callously put a highway through the wetlands stretching out from that consecrated center.

This line of thought quickly leads to the acknowledgment of a profoundly ironic convergence: in the postmodern world and particularly in the postregional West, with regard to what challenges identity and what in more or less salvageable ruins confers it, Indian and non-Indian Americans, as many of the latter have come to realize, are in the same boat. With that realization has come the widespread belief that Indians, with their cultures seated in wild nature instead of adrift in postindustrial artifice, represent a larger awareness of the self in connection with its environment, a less fragmented past, a more sustainable future. It's a belief that began taking shape in the late 1940s, as Robert F. Berkhofer Jr. notes, when white writers and intellectuals "increasingly looked to the experiences of other peoples to criticize their own society" and "employed the Indian as a symbol for a more humane way of life."[24] It gathered strength through later anti-Custerism and other countercultural trends. By the end of the century, as the census figures from 1990 and 2000 disclose, more Americans were identifying themselves as Indians. Those new identifications may or may not have been rationalized by real blood quanta from one tribe or another, but they certainly indicate that, as Burnham sums up the vogue, "it has become chic to be 'Indian.'"[25] And *Indian country*, once so negative in its connotations, has become what rhetoricians call a god term.

But wannabeism, however sincere, can't avoid—though it can modify—the enigmas of Indian otherness, which is contrived by a centuries-old strategem Owens analyzes as follows: "European America holds a mirror and a mask up to the Native American. The tricky mirror is that Other presence that reflects the Euramerican consciousness back at itself, but the side of the mirror turned toward the Native is transparent, letting the Native see not his or her own reflection but the face of the Euramerican beyond the mirror." This "fabricated 'Indian'" may, I'd argue, turn to nature to find a reflection but through the two-way mirror will now see, more and more, only a wannabe who is the latest manifestation of "America's obsession with first constructing the Indian as Other and then inhabiting that constructed Indianness as fully as possible."[26] The wannabe, like other Euro-Americans, will, as Bordewich puts it, "often see little more than the distorted reflection of . . . fears, fancies, and wistful longings."[27]

Fewer fears now, mostly enhanced incompatible fancies and longings—the hunger for the untamed West once again. Nor is the mediation that composes otherness yet interrupted, for the Indian's mask is apt to be that of the ecological mystic, a twenty-first-century revision of the image, on a 1970s poster, of the Cherokee actor Iron Eyes Cody, unrestrained by standard Indian stoicism, weeping over what white pollution has done to the natural world with which he's associated.[28] Wannabes, like Westerners in general by the diagnosis of David H. Getches, thus "suffer a kind of schizophrenia about Indians." The pandemic version is distinguished by a conflict between resentment of Indians' ownership of "coveted resources in the West" and gladness "that there are still Indians here, a romantic reminder of people living close to the earth, a colorful culture with enviable traditions." The wannabes' version is marked by a conflict between two desires: for Indians to conform to an accessible (and accessorizable) iconicity of Indianness and for them to be as they are on their own terms, people who intuit "the interrelatedness of everything in our environment."[29]

The first desire revved up in the late 1960s when America was experiencing what Leslie Fiedler in 1968 saw as "a genuine hunger for the West." It was a hunger that many of the hungry felt as an itch "to go Native." Some have followed his counsel that hallucinogens found in nature (marijuana, peyote, and the like) "are our bridge to—even as they are gifts from—the world of the Indian."[30] More have entered the Western Indian world by a New Age path, casually co-opting Indian spiritual traditions—much to the indignation or, at least, irritated amusement of numerous tribes. Such wannabes, deluded cultists or profiteering hucksters, make medicine wheels and undertake vision quests, sometimes with the help of Indians who are willing to prostitute their heritage.[31]

New Agers' use of pseudo–Native American spirituality in their transcendentalizing of nature has led to more commodification and etherealization of the Indian. Though the fascination with it ebbed some in the 1980s, as S. Elizabeth Bird observes, "the Indian 'wanna-be' phenomenon was gaining momentum, with the fascination rising again in the 1990s, this time in a more mainstream, ecologically minded form." The result was that, "as never before, Indians were chic—mystical, wise, earth-loving, and tragic. New Age culture appropriated Indian religious practices, clothing, music, and myths, while Indian-inspired art and design became all the rage."[32] New Age stores sold statuettes of Kokopelli and Native American flutes whose notes stimulated daydreams of spirit-suffused desert spaces. Soon the Umatillas in Oregon were selling their culture to German tourists, and a little clicking on the Internet could put you in possession of the e-mail address of a realtor with Pueblo ruins for sale. New castings of old stereotypes were everywhere, and yet those who were playing Indian wanted, in Philip Deloria's phrase, "to encounter the authentic amidst the anxiety of urban industrialism and postindustrial life." However understandable that playing might be, it meant what it still means: consuming Indian cultures; building identities "not around synthesis and transformation, but around unresolved dualities"; and engaging not in Indian realities but in "an exercise in distance, abstraction, and cultural imagination."[33]

The second of the wannabes' desires has intensified more slowly, but it may slowly be gaining the upper hand. That desire knows what some whites surely knew in the 1850s and Roy Harvey Pearce knew when the postregional era was just under way: Horatio Greenough's The Rescue "epitomizes the perils not only of the American wilderness, but of American civilization."[34] That desire knows, as Gundars Rudzitis suggests, that "perhaps, finally, we are ready to admit that there is much we can learn from Native Americans about how we can live with the wilderness that still remains in the American West."[35] It knows that we non-Indians can't learn what such living requires until we're able to see Indians as they are, which blessing, though difficult to achieve, would let us behold the reward Bordewich promises: "a far richer tapestry of life than our fantasies ever allowed."[36]

That tapestry might inspire us not to try to copy Indians' spirituality but to adopt and adapt their religiousness (both reverence and, etymologically, connectedness) toward nature. Then we could be not who we want to be but who we *ought* to be: beings who accept their ecological responsibilities. Then we, Indians and non-Indians together, might transform the wild-tame dialectic that divides us by differences reconciled only facilely or never at all into what Bordewich describes as "an embrace that permits neither consummation nor release, but that is, nonetheless, full of hope."[37] Then truly we would all be, to borrow the title of a 1997 Native American symposium in Oklahoma City, remembering our future.

Break on Through to the Other Side:
The Postmodern Frontier Imperative

Whether geographically or more symbolically, we Americans see ourselves on the frontier, . . . doggedly pursuing Jefferson's almost mystical grail of "Happiness" wherever it might lead us. . . . If we Americans are not on the edge of the unknown, not in the process of becoming, not on the "cutting edge," we somehow see ourselves as having failed.
    Ken Burns, "On the Edge of the Unknown"

In 1996 I ran across two news items that spoke volumes about the persistence of America's need for frontiers.

The first item was a report by Julia Prodis on the perils of life in Tombstone. Things had been antsy there since 1992, when some locals, with the help of the National Rifle Association, got the so-called Virgil Earp Law, which forbade the carrying of guns in the city limits, repealed. The last four years had been punctuated by unnerving incidents, often alcohol-related, involving loaded side arms: joke stickups, a staged gunfight turned suddenly actual, a fast-draw artist's shooting himself in the ass, on and on. Armed tourists strolled through the town's mock-up of the O.K. Corral, lost in revery.[1]

The second item was a piece by Zoë Ingalls that concerned an art workshop offered by the University of New Mexico. Conducted at the D. H. Lawrence Ranch north of Taos, Mythological Adventuring was a course designed to help its enrollees break out of ingrained artistic habits by way of exercises that forced each student to become conscious of how he or she "frames his or her reality" and then progress beyond the accustomed frame. One student's testimony regarding such an exercise made clear the pedagogical thrust of the workshop: "'It was a great exercise to get you out of doing the same thing and out of doing what you know,' says Sandra K. Wilson, a senior majoring in art and psychology. 'Everybody got to that point of frustration and then switched. It's a pretty good metaphor for this class—pushing yourself through to the other side.'"[2]

The first item is about going backward to a past frontier; the second, about going forward to a future frontier. Both have to do with the experience of a threshold between ordinary order and something else. The pursuit of Frontierland and the pursuit of Tomorrowland aren't identical; but they are two sides of the same coin. Both manifest what I call the frontier imperative (a word closely related to *empire*), the press to meet a limen at once novel and recollective, forever already left behind for another. An American addiction, the frontier imperative subsumes what Richard Slotkin calls "the imperatives enjoined on us by our role in the [Frontier] Myth."[3] To borrow language from a Wallace Stevens poem, that imperative arises from the hunger for "more" stoked by America's "never-resting mind," its telos kept protean by an irony: "The imperfect is our paradise."[4] Up to a point.

That imperative, now grown complex in its figurations, was once expressed in seemingly straightforward metaphors. "The skill and resourcefulness demanded by the early cars and old roads made every highway a new frontier," Roderick Nash says of American automotive travel a century ago.[5] The new Indians on a frontier expanding conceptually were unwelcome immigrants, Bolsheviks, then Black Shirts, Huns, Japs. In the early 1930s Henry A. Wallace, Franklin Roosevelt's secretary of agriculture, touted a new frontier in farming through more supportive federal policies. By 1960, however, the notion of frontier had become so stretchy that John Kennedy, accepting the Democratic nomination for president in Los Angeles, spoke of a New Frontier that encompassed all manner of political, economic, military, scientific, and technological subfrontiers—proving already true what Timothy Egan would assert of that Byzantine city almost four decades later: "Yes, the West ends here. But the frontier begins."[6] Still, though, most Americans translated Kennedy's multiplex frontier, with its lofty goals, into the terms that made the most suitable sense historically and mythically: spatial. In the 1960s, outer space would be the new wilderness, the empyrean West into which America would advance, and astronauts would be its cowboys.

The next president to speak his convictions in frontier metaphors, though more backward- than forward-looking ones, was Reagan. The rhetoric of his agenda projected him, in Michael S. Kimmel's portrayal of him in 1987, during his second term, as "the country's most obvious cowboy-president," a Strangelove-like remake of the sort of Westerner he'd once played in movies: "Reagan sits tall in the saddle, riding roughly over the environment, Central America, Grenada, toward the gunfight at the nuclear arsenal, the ultimate test of the modern cowboy's mettle."[7] By the end of his presidency, there was hardly a politician around who hadn't made some oratorical use of frontier metaphors. By now, after so much employment, the idea of the frontier, as Patricia Nelson Limerick argues, is indeed "capable of sudden twists and shifts of meaning," but her research—which took as data some four thousand headlines using the words *frontier* and *pioneer* that appeared between 1988 and 1993—shows a consistent leaning in the domain of its reference: "the American public has genuinely and completely accepted, ratified, and bought the notion that the American frontiering spirit, sometime in the last century, . . . made a definitive relocation from territorial expansion to technological and commercial expansion."[8]

Well, maybe not completely, what with America's worldwide network of fortified outposts and eccentric entrepreneurial schemes—for mining asteroids, for example, or building a lunar theme park on the moon—with a territorial dimension, as well as a program for exploring the outer planets of the solar system that has been christened New Frontiers.[9] Still, such relocation illustrates cogently the continuing pervasion and etherealization of the frontier as an American obsession.

Frederick Jackson Turner foretold that the geographical frontier so significant for America's selfhood would be tropologically transplanted and propagated in other spheres and therefore survive indefinitely. He'd have understood the impetus behind the effusive pronouncement about outer space voiced in 1989 by as redoubtable a Westerner as Louis L'Amour that "there are endless frontiers out there, each one difficult, each one offering fresh discoveries, unexpected challenges, and rewards beyond belief."[10] Turner knew in his own way what Slotkin later would explicate: that through myth "the past is made metaphorically equivalent to the present."[11]

In 1958, Beat poet Lawrence Ferlinghetti wrote of "waiting / for the discovery / of a new symbolic western frontier."[12] Well, he didn't have to wait long, and plenty of such frontiers had already been discovered. "Frontier settings," as David Mogen, Scott P. Sanders, and Joanne B. Karpinski remind us, were being "adapted to current literary needs, as self-consciously constructed symbolic environments" of various kinds.[13] "The tendency to practice symbolic frontiersmanship," Larry McMurtry argues, "might almost be said to characterize the twentieth century Texan, whether he be an intellectual, a cowboy, a businessman, or a politician."[14] In his symbological study of American cities, Yi-Fu Tuan notes that by 1965 "no less than 183 cities boast the title 'Gate' or 'Gateway,'" often thereby associating themselves with westward migration, one of them, Titusville, Florida, trumping all the rest in symbolic-frontier éclat by proclaiming itself "the Gateway to the Galaxies."[15] Even when the ideology of the frontier was out of favor with New Western Historians, more and more people were seeing the world through frontier-colored glasses.

Which prevalence bolsters Cheryl Lester's argument that "Turner was astute in suggesting that the disappearance of the mythical frontier was not bound to terminate the 'incessant expansion' that began in the age of conquest" because we've witnessed a "proliferation of new frontiers," cyberspace being the most recent.

Indeed, that frontier, with its virtual range ridden by digital outlaws no further away than the monitor screen, lends special plausibility to her impression that through such proliferation "the unfamiliar and the upside-down have been drawn closer and closer to home."[16] In her analysis of how the frontier has undergone a transition from landscape to mindscape, Linda Kintz writes of the evolution of the "internal frontier," an "ironic postmodern terrain" she further describes as "abstract, the digitalized speculative terrain of economic growth."[17]

However that ethereal frontier shows up, it's a space, like its prototype in Stan Steiner's characterization, with "an edge" and thus, in comparison to the space left behind, one where "there is much more contradiction—there's much more tragedy and paradox, and irony."[18] Think of Lyndon Johnson's ambiguous Vietnamese frontier. Or the intermeshing of realities and unrealities in the Frontierland that was Reagan's presidency, during which rightist visions of a clean, well-lighted nation blurred into what Rebecca Solnit says "the American idea of a nuclear Armageddon" is really about: "the preservation and reinvention of the frontier" as a place "for a new beginning of lawlessness, chaos, every man for himself."[19] Or the latter-day frontiers that served as settings for television series like Dallas and Dynasty that flourished in the 1980s and featured heroes who were, as Blake Allmendinger observes, at once ruthless villains whose "plundering of the West was deplorable" and triumphant enterprisers invariably made wealthy by that plundering.[20] Or the "last frontier," which we plot to ransack more even as we reserve it, that we've made of Alaska as recompense for our devastation of the lower forty-eight states and their indigens, as Susan Kollin alleges in her 2001 study Nature's State: Imagining Alaska as the Last Frontier. It's fair to say, with David Mogen, that our frontier mythology "still . . . expresses an ambivalent sense of destiny."[21]

In 1968 Leslie Fiedler asserted that, "by and large, we have used up the mythological space of the West." And he asked the pendent question: "Can we reestablish the West anywhere at all, then?" In the fashion of the time, he thought about the moon or Mars as a future West, and he raised the issue of what "hostile aliens" would play what he insisted was the mythically requisite role of Indians in an extraterrestrial New World.[22]

Fiedler believed that Americans couldn't shake their classical frontier mythology, whatever its alteration, or the ambivalent sense of destiny it expressed. Many agreed with him. But others were beginning to consider reconstituting the West not in a new mythological space but in the old real space where it had been all along. If they had an inkling of a different myth, it was not of one that entices with yet another "false pastoral," as Slotkin puts it, but of one "that allows us to see our history as an ecological system . . . bound together by patterns of struggle and accommodation."[23] They were becoming profoundly cognizant of the desperate irony of westering impelled by the frontier imperative in a postmodern world where Nash's travelers, as Reg Saner later would elucidate, were still on the road—be it concrete interstate or rocket trajectory or information superhighway—and still missing the point, more than ever:

> Even at a standstill you can feel it inside you: the road as verge, as threshold, making "destination" a mere pretext for the real business of going to meet it. . . . The Hopi roved a long while, looking for the center place; Zuñi likewise, in search of "the middle." Anasazi wanderings, petroglyphed, spiral in toward a center: both a place and a discovery of self. But for many of us four-wheeled, non-Native Americans, isn't it true that our "center" and best mode of being is motion? Whose aim is less a place than simply the horizon.[24]

By now some of us Americans have come to suspect the truth of Annette Kolodny's argument, in 1975, that the disappointment of successive frontiers' not leading to "an ambience of total gratification" has indeed caused frustration and anger, one of whose expressions has been "the single-minded destruction and pollution of the continent."[25] The lessons of symbolic Wests bid us learn to live in and steward the real West, let it be our "middle" landscape, our center, not the next place there but this place here. That's the *new* frontier imperative. It urges us, like those art students at the D. H. Lawrence Ranch, to stop "doing the same thing"—but not by breaking through to the other side, which is the same thing once again, rather by spiraling in, a principle Kim Addonizio and Dorianne Laux may understand much as the Anasazi did: "Every landscape is a frontier, a place of energy and discovery for the people who inhabit it. It can also be a gateway into our internal and emotional lives."[26] That place is imperfect and lacks the total gratification of dreams, but it's one we might stay in—and discover to be sufficient.

Wildfire: A Taste of Authenticity

> As all of us looked on
> you stormed in solitude,
> you shrugged and shook aside
> what we called beautiful
> as if none of us were here.
>   John Daniel, "To Mt. St. Helens"

On the morning of May 4, 2000, a National Park Service crew started a prescribed burn on Cerro Grande, a hill southwest of Los Alamos, New Mexico, and on the northern edge of Bandelier National Monument. It was a preemptive measure intended to rid the area of thick, dry overgrowth just waiting for summer lightning to ignite a firestorm. Wind velocity was low. Professionals were in charge. Before noon, though, the fire had leaped a safety line. More personnel were brought in. The fire spread northwest, kept on spreading. By the next day the initially controlled had turned into the totally wild. Soon slurry bombers were taking off from Albuquerque, sixty-odd miles south, in a smoke-scented haze. Thousands of residents from Los Alamos and nearby communities were evacuated; they moved into motels along Highway 84/285, got by on makeshift meals, watched the news. On May 10 the fire swept into Los Alamos, consuming over two hundred houses. Dozens of buildings at the Los Alamos National Laboratory were destroyed or damaged, none, apparently, holding hazardous materials. The fire was not contained until late July. Once the blazing present had become the charred past, some fifty thousand acres of forest on Indian and federal land lay blackened. Statewide that year other fires had burned almost half a million acres.[1] West-wide that year the Cerro Grande fire was just a drop in the bucket of pyric cataclysms.

Early the following spring Dave Fox, a cousin of mine and owner of the town's sole department store as well as a plant nursery, gave me a tour of the burned area. He recounted how La Niña drought had primed the land for what had happened. He showed me a spot where the fire had been stopped just yards from a National Laboratory edifice surrounded by fence topped with razor wire—might be something hazardous in there, I thought. He said lots of elk had died in the fire. Grasses and wildflowers were taking hold at the lower elevations, but higher up, he explained, they'd be slower to appear. The cottonwoods would come back in a hurry, but the return of the pines would require a human lifetime.

"The odor of burning juniper," Edward Abbey raves, "is the sweetest fragrance on the face of the earth. . . . One breath of juniper smoke, like the perfume of sagebrush after rain, evokes in magical catalysis, like certain music, the space and light and clarity and piercing strangeness of the American West. Long may it burn."[2] He writes only of a campfire, but his statement resonates on a larger scale: fire (its smoke fragrant or not) indexes the whole authentic West, and "it"—juniper, ponderosa, much of that West—will burn long. That's the *nature* of the place. Control will always be difficult, even deadly—in 1948 Aldo Leopold died of a heart attack while helping neighbors fight a grass fire, a better end than that suffered by the smoke jumpers who perished in the Mann Gulch fire in Montana the next year and by many other firefighters since. We fight fire in the West as we once fought Indians, in either case a final suppression of all dangerous wildness (for which fire serves as a synecdochic sign) the aim of our ignorant taming. We've forgotten some basics of which Richard Manning isn't shy in reminding us: "Nature keeps order not with laws, justice, and right, but with predator, prey, fire, and wind. . . . We were not there when nature laid the earth's foundations. Our every attempt to replace them with our own has backfired."[3] We discriminate between lightning-triggered and anthropogenic wildfires (and tend to treat them differently), but nature doesn't.[4] Because of those replacements and such niceties of discrimination, we have made tinder of half our federal forests, not grasped (except when, say, we use it in the spring to replenish the prairie's nutrients and stimulate new growth) that fire is an integral process of Western ecosystems, built too many residences on urban-wildland interfaces prone to burn, allowed exotic species of plants to prevent the thriving of native ones better adapted to fire, encouraged or ignored tree densities and ladder fuels ideal for fast-propagating crown fires, meddled with our meddlings till in any given summer all the West seems to bloom with flame at once.[5]

Fire is one aspect of the authentic West, the real thing, but there are others.

Drought, the condition of fire: an ocean current off the coast of Ecuador cyclically extends south, and the West eats more dust than, as we're wont to say, usual; the snowpacks shrink. The more we plow and graze and subdivide the West, the more we stifle its rivers and pump its nonrenewing groundwater, the more we foster ecological backlash and rush our hydraulic empire's Mesopotamian twilight. Dry wells number in the thousands. Too many Westerners live by the illusion that, even if the rivers get tapped out, there's boundless water down in a mysterious somewhere underfoot.[6]

Desert, the land long-drawn-out drought makes, the anvil on which the Hephaestan sun hammers the shapes that conform to its intensity. And, as Bruce Berger warns, "part of the desert's intensity is its ability to startle," which, like a diamondback rattling and coiled for a strike, should keep us mindful "of one of life's great premises—that there is always a present tense one can't quite prepare for."[7] Reg Saner offers brusquer advice to anyone who'd see the xeriscape of the desert as other than what it is: there, he says, "you become either a realist or a set of bleached bones."[8]

Snow, often in the form of a blinding storm, sudden and trapping enough in Western mountains to drive even well-equipped postmodern Donners to loathsome dining. A white nothingness that owns much of the West in winter, it melts in spring into vital water—but maybe in the form of a flood.

And, come spring, water, in some parts, gets whipped into the updraft of a tornado, a pythonic typhoon over land, reviving the knowledge that the West lies between the Mississippi and the Pacific, two fluctuant leviathans that don't take us into account any more than do the earthquakes, born of the planet's fractured exoskeleton, that can happen in other parts at any time.

Such truth has been told before. "Western writing," James K. Folsom assures us, "contains a long tradition of 'telling it like it is,' habitually debunking the pretensions of Western myth on the basis of the hard facts of Western life."[9] In recent years Donald Worster has continued that tradition by exposing the reckless vanity of trying to dominate Western nature. So has Gary Short in writing of "the distance that becomes time" in a Nevada where "the windshield / can't hold all the sky."[10] So has Joseph Kanon in his 1997 novel Los Alamos, in a passage where the protagonist,

Michael Connolly, takes in the canyoned Pajarito Plateau: "This was the West he had always imagined and never seen, . . . land that seemed to exist at the beginning of time, monumental, so resistant to man that it found its beauty in geology, as if vegetation were a hapless afterthought."[11] So has Larry McMurtry in writing that "I still feel drawn to the stretch of country between Laredo and the sea, but drawn to it ambivalently. I've never been comfortable there: it's a hard, scary land."[12] Those writers portray the West in a way that makes graphic what Jane Hirshfield calls "the chilling nonnegotiability of the wild."[13] They present the West as a place that, spiritual or not, is unforgiving, a vastitude where, as in Walter Van Tilburg Clark's 1943 short story "The Indian Well," wildlife quickly retakes forsaken human space. Where the center of Yellowstone—with its geysers, hot springs, mudpots, and fumaroles—consists of a huge caldera, a basin extending over more than a thousand square miles and rising with magmatic heat, that someday, maybe soon, will swell until it must erupt.

The West like it is is the West where, Louis L'Amour allows, "gunfights were rare, raids by horse thieves rare, but hard work was every day."[14] It's the West where we have no more control over outer nature than we have over the hermetic wilderness of our internal organs. Where names such as Death Valley and Hell's Half Acre warn of vicissitudes never experienced by computer-in-the-cabineers. Where things are thorny, heavy, dug-in, capable of unhinging the many who lived and toiled there before cities lured them away from the land. Where the rate of suicide (mostly by guns, with overdoses of alcohol and other drugs running a close second) now exceeds that of anywhere else in the United States—for reasons that aren't entirely clear, though some surely relate to failure in adjusting to the realities of the West, which place often is, to borrow phrases from Victor Davis Hanson, "dreams without fields" but is also "fields without dreams."[15]

Those two spheres correspond to what Patricia Nelson Limerick terms, respectively, "the Fake West" and "the Real West," the pair "virtually Siamese twins sharing the same circulatory system."[16] The first, however, tends to be delusional, turning its back on the second by a process McMurtry calls "the dissolving of context," a denial "fundamental to the romanticizing of the West."[17] With that dissolving comes forgetting—until the mythic text of the West accords little with the substantiality of its original context. Yet, of course, that other West to which we have trouble attending doesn't go away; so in lucid moments we catch ourselves in a tragic awareness of how, as Gary Lease puts it, "the relationship between human cultural production and the biophysical world may be dangerously skewed."[18]

Dangerously, thereby, the twins remain joined. Because they're still joined, distinguishing the Real West is a catchy proposition. Virginia Scharff asks the pertinent question here: "What does the authentic West look like anyway?" She answers that "it looks much like whatever West we happen to have"—a place that never was moored enough to prevent its being lifted into myth.[19] John Wesley Powell, for all his objectivity, couldn't thoroughly precipitate the matter of the West from the mind-matter solution. Any quest for realism has been complicated also by our ambivalently metaphorizing the West, like nature generally, in binaries Yi-Fu Tuan summarizes as "home and tomb, Eden and jungle, mother and ogre, a responsive 'thou' and an indifferent 'it.'"[20] Our most harebrained conceptions of the West— for example, that of the landscape as an agricultural machine—have proven disastrously mismatched with actuality, but even one of the most compelling, Nebraska ecologist Frederic Edward Clements's idea that its natural systems regularly develop toward equilibrated climax communities, turned out, decades ago, to be, in William Cronon's words, "far more metaphorical than real."[21] In writing *Young Men and Fire*, his account of the Mann Gulch tragedy, Norman Maclean "set for the book a rigid standard of truth, and . . . detachment," Manning notes, and yet throughout his text "the fire is demonized" till finally it's similized as a cancerous nuclear explosion—and the reader not helped "to understand that fire is not evil but necessary."[22]

Our inability to separate the twins has left us open to "the humbug" that Zeese Papanikolas sees as the modern incarnation of the Native Americans' trickster. "For us, the latter-day Americans," he argues, the humbug "represents the fluid, teasing spectacle not of what is, but what is possible"—or *seems*, in the shape of "pseudo-utopias," to be possible.[23] Duped by it, we discount aridity, overgraze, exterminate animals we don't like, defy geology, repair and backpedal and cobble— whatever it takes to keep the follies rolling. In that regard, California is an extreme example, though not by much, of how we postregional Westerners, as Papanikolas rebukes us, "have forgotten nature" and so "go on building our public buildings and nuclear power plants on the fault line and watering our patches of lawn during the scorching years of drought and watching our houses slip off the cliffsides when the rains come, which they always sooner or later do." All of which bespeaks, in tightening implications, "discontinuity, fragmentation, even alienation. From geography. From history. From one another."[24]

A gauge of our alienation from nature is the hurdles we encounter in trying to capture it in our customary languages, verbal and otherwise, the extent to which, however entangled in their nets, it retains its autonomy. But it *is*, nonetheless, entangled, deeply. So, separating the twins may not be feasible. Given that, we'd better have a more complete understanding of their interrelationship. And that calls for what Scott Hermanson delineates as "a realignment of the categories we use to define nature," a way of interpreting it that lets us recognize the extent to which we've erased it from our lives or criminalized it as the cause of fires, floods, and the like. In Mike Davis's *City of Quartz: Excavating the Future of Los Angeles* (1990) and *Ecology of Fear: Los Angeles and the Imagination of Disaster* (1998), Hermanson discerns an indication of that realignment in his use of a language that clarifies "the infinite interpenetration between the wild and the civilized."[25] Hermanson argues that such a language, still evolving, is absolutely essential; if we mythopoeic creatures have to live in the scramble of truth and myth, then we need to know more of both. "In the writings of and about cowboys," Richard Hutson tells us, "figures who claim to be 'real' cowboys also claim to be the last cowboy."[26] Someday one of them will be, but the real West is already the last West.

Discussing the "full-scale Sir Walter Scottification of the West," Leslie Fiedler theorizes that it "could not occur until the myth of the West had become a source of nostalgia rather than hope—a way of defining the Other Place rather than This Place, where we once were rather than where we go from here." Which is to say, it was well under way during the early throes of postfrontier anxiety:

> At that point, no one in the East seemed any longer to remember, and no one in the actual West (just beginning to contemplate tourism as a major industry) cared to remind them, that it was gunslingers and pimps, habitual failures and refugees from law and order, as well as certain dogged pursuers of a dream, who had actually made the West—not Ivanhoes in chaps. . . . No wonder the myth had to be immunized against reality, more and more narrowly localized in time and space—to keep anyone from making comparisons with a world he knew at first hand.[27]

There were, of course, larger reasons for immunization and localization (and etherealization)—not just who had made the West but also what they had done to Indians and to the land they inhabited—but we no longer have the luxury of applying such procedures wholesale to protect ourselves from the historical West. Nor from the present biophysical West, This Place, a here from which we can no longer go, a context we must try to reintegrate.

Can the real West survive our dissolution of it? Yes, it can. And will. With us or without us. Better, for us, with us. New metaphors for nature's nonlinear dynamism will help, as will our learning not to perceive nature as some umbral otherness we must force to obey our bright wishes but to admit, as John Sandlos reminds us Coyote myths do, "the possibility and inevitability of wild and unpredictable behavior" and "regard the world as a Trickster-phenomenon" (but not of the humbug sort)—maybe even with a sense of humor.[28] The broad goal should be one Limerick proposes: "to get humanity's role in nature back to the right size, neither too big nor too small, neither too powerful nor too powerless."[29] To help us remember we didn't "conquer" the West and never will, we need to meet anew its obdurate deserts and immovable mountains to which we, like other crowded life-forms, are fleeing in search of openness. Or perhaps, as David Rothenberg exhorts (with a final caveat about balance), the sea that sculpts the outermost edge of the West and once covered land now so liable to fire:

On the coast, in the storm, we are running on the sand, trying to beat the tides. The rush of wind. The sound. The close inhospitability of it all. The immediacy of the wild that is both frightening and exhilarating is the old aesthetic category of the sublime. . . . You must put your life on the line to discover the wild. You must not be afraid to doubt, to throw away all presuppositions if they hold experience back. It may not be good for you, but it will encourage the wild. And this wild isn't everything; no, it harbors, along with creation, total annihilation if we lose all control.[30]

Auténtico.

To adapt one of Octavio Paz's trenchant aphorisms about the United States and Mexico, Euro-Americans haven't looked for the West in the West: they have looked for whatever obsessed them—and found it there. Now they need to look for something else.

Hunger for the Wild: Finding a True Western Heritage

The primeval wilderness—which some people now believe to have vanished from the planet Earth—is a recurring interest in the story. But the main interest . . . will be traces of wildness (a quality, not a terrain), along with experiences of freedom, abundance, the sense of being alive, the feeling of being connected with something elemental—with the spirit of a place, perhaps, or with the entire universe.

> Melanie L. Simo, *Forest and Garden: Traces of Wildness in a Modernizing Land, 1897–1949*

In November 1934 a twenty-year-old artist named Everett Ruess walked out of Escalante, Utah, and headed into the labyrinthine canyonlands southeast of town. He had two burros, a stock of food, and the intention of not returning to civilization soon. He'd wandered through the trackless West before, but not for weeks on weeks. By February his parents were frantic with worry. In the spring, search parties found the burros, candy wrappers and such, footprints, and an inscription in sandstone at the base of a door in an Anasazi ruin: "NEMO 1934." But the young man who had scratched the Latin word for "no one" and that date had disappeared for good into what John P. O'Grady calls "the utterly wild."[1]

While we'll never know exactly what happened to Ruess in those stony distances, we do have some comprehension of—or.intelligent speculation about—why he left a comfortable home in Hollywood and a professional career as a painter and went into them alone. After studying his journals and letters, Bruce Berger concludes that he was "a born ecstatic" whose later teenage years were marked by carelessness as well as a "hunger for life" because of which he braved the country near the confluence of the Escalante and the Colorado "simply to relish it, to absorb it, and to shape that love in the arts."[2] O'Grady, drawing on those and other sources, is also illuminative, though more psychologically theoretical. According to him, Ruess undertook a pilgrimage in search of "a sense of his identity" he couldn't find in the noise and sordidness of urban society. He sought a "wild within . . . inseparable from the wild without," crossed a threshold into enrapturing "strange territories," and committed "an abandonment." He fashioned for himself a rite of passage, "but he lacked the guidance, the cultural framework, that provides the context for successful passage."[3] He entered the wild to be renewed, to become someone new, but he wound up being only *nemo* doomed in his freedom, without an appropriate community to which to return, people who could better appreciate what he was about. Had he come from a world less "civilized," his hunger might have led him to rebirthing beauty and back and not west of everything.

Few Americans would go on a pilgrimage like Ruess's, but something—abstracted, virtualized, displaced—of what transported him is more and more in evidence. Our forebears felt the pull of wildness, even as they cursed it; we, however, may not always recognize that pull, given its many gradations, even as more of us acknowledge its importance. Tired of deadening routines, television-news hysteria, trivial jobs, we spike our lives with intimations of the Western wild: keep gray wolves as pets; join Wilderness Watch; eat buffalo burgers, antelope steaks, and other wild meat from outdoor grills; decorate our shelves with pseudo-Indian knickknacks; hang our walls with John Nieto prints of coyotes; visit dude ranches; hike in the Rockies; maybe participate in one of the many expurgated rendezvous so popular since the early 1970s.

Even in the most audacious of those doings, though, the old ambivalence, along with its natural-cultural mismatches, tends to sneak in. Not only in our wearing voguish Gore-Tex and Lycra outfits but in our whole approach. Berger argues that there may be no more loners like Ruess since now "most hardened desert rats run in a pack, plan ahead like accountants, and have honed their trips to rituals that may say more about themselves than the barrens through which they pass." They carry survival manuals, cell phones, zip-lock bags of choice grinds of coffee, dehydrated delicacies, goose-down sleeping bags, nylon tents, compressed gas for cooking. Each, Berger says of their making camp, "has his own touch at domesticating the wild, . . . as he turns his piece of the wilderness into the great indoors."[4] Such meticulous adventurers, as David Brooks remarks of "bourgeois bohemian" or "Bobo" naturalists, are prone to "go into nature to behave unnaturally."[5] Postmoderns often labor to tame the very untamed they long for, failing to experience what Yi-Fu Tuan calls "nature as impact" because their "'escape to nature' is a cultural undertaking, a covered-up attempt to 'escape from nature.'"[6]

Not always, however. Some Americans are getting wise to that paradox, trying to evade it. They really want to go back to nature and not back to the hotel. They want to be in the presence of animals that will help them feel how the natural world is alive with lives templated by DNA near in coding to their own and not just scenic and cute. They want out of the drab, terrorized mental ward of a world where, as Jim Harrison pegs it, "the buzz of the airport metal detector is more familiar than the sound of the whippoorwill or coyote" and "our essential and hereditary wildness slips, crippled, into the past."[7]

If those Americans want all that enough, they may go far away to Iceland or Tibet or New Zealand; but usually they go to the West, where Americans have always gone, in fact or fantasy, when endeavoring to flee civilization's superfluous commotion and enter the space of fundamental energies. That space, as Gretel Ehrlich says, "can heal what is divided and burdensome in us" and is an expanse "we might also learn how to carry . . . inside ourselves in the effortless way we carry our skins."[8] For latter-day Puritans, learning to carry such space in that way takes philosophical revamping and a specific preparedness—first off, acceptance of C. L. Rawlins's bottom-line creed about caring for the West: "What we've been fighting for isn't places but our souls."[9] Only by saving them can we save the places.

Those souls aren't the gaseous, otherworldly spooks the original Puritans sulked about. Soul as Rawlins uses the word means something more like *querencia* ("homing instinct"). You sense its action in Diana Ossana's 1999 short story "White Line Fever," in a scene where the protagonist, a woman named Tucker whose husband has left her, is driving west from Clovis, New Mexico, through the openness of plains dotted with yucca and sage and suddenly is "overwhelmed with a feeling of belonging," her eyes full of tears from "a powerful emotion that recurred many times, whenever she drove west."[10] This soul is an elemental internal presence that craves conversation with its external counterpart, what Jack Turner calls "the reciprocity between the wild in nature and the wild in us," a mutuality that can't be accomplished by thinking of nature as a problem or a commodity, by reading nature writing or ecotouring or viewing the cinematic West—but only by going out there and giving the patient time to let the heart-to-heart talk start getting the relationship right.[11] Even if you're on a highway.

Relation is everything. A feeling of belonging, of being a part of and not apart from the chamisa and pines and wolves and deer. Letting the wide country recharge us. Letting the grizzly wild, danger and all, take away—as Doug Peacock swears it can—"the burden of dominion."[12] Letting its emptiness fill us. Letting its fullness empty us. Letting it teach us what being civilized, for both good and ill, polio vaccine and thermonuclear bombs, means. Letting it teach us to follow its genius.

"To resolve the dichotomy of the civilized and the wild," Gary Snyder submits, "we must first resolve to be whole." As to "the final meaning of 'wild'" in that resolution, he's more Buddhistic: "Those who are ready for it will come to it."[13] How be ready? How resolve? We could begin by partaking of the "pleasures in ruin" Reg Saner finds can be experienced among the thousand-year-old mud-mortared walls scattered on the Colorado Plateau. They are many. Here's one: "Through Anasazi vestiges, we perhaps pay our respects to what's missing in us, thus honoring those ancient ones (a bit ruefully?) as a people able to live out lives undivided from themselves," which "we need their help even to imagine." Here's another, a grounding moment on a June evening near where Saner had pitched his tent on the rim of Dark Canyon in southeastern Utah, about fifty miles, as the raven flies, from where Ruess had disappeared over six decades earlier: "Red rock, creamy cloud, blue sky. Desert stillness like some wordless dream-voice telling a sleeper who he really is. Then low sun through manzanita foliage and curl-leaf mahogany slowly made their leaves translucent, while smearing that entire bush-stippled rim in green-gold. I was just standing there, admiring, when my own voice surprised me by murmuring aloud and to no one, 'I'm home.'"[14]

Fear and Loathing in Santa Fe: Meatspace or Virtual Reality?

The Virginian walked in open air with thoughts disturbed. "I am of two minds about one thing," he said to himself uneasily.
  Owen Wister, *The Virginian: A Horseman of the Plains*

In expensive northeastern Santa Fe, atop a hill above Hyde Park Road, sits a sanctum for collaborative, interdisciplinary, and computer-based creativity known as the Santa Fe Institute. It's a rambling house, once owned by a diplomat, refurbished to accommodate clutches of computers and interactions among a changing population of innovative researchers in fields as diverse as biology, physics, urban planning, economics, you name it. Less materially, it's a symposium that began in 1984 and has since grown ever more animated in its investigation of complex systems, emergent behavior, chaos. Which means that the institute has become the global academy (how appropriate that it's in the American West) for the study of wildness as variously manifested, the overt messiness of the universe, and the underlying order that gives rise to it. Which means trying to decipher and simplify the complicated, understand how it derives from some more elementary—and maybe, after enough luminaries have puzzled till their puzzlers are sore, ultimate—substrate. Which means constant computer simulation of all kinds of processes, including those of life itself—and thus cooking up artificial life (also known, with a cautionary negativity in the prefix, as "alife"), abstract biological systems generated by algorithms that instantiate theories about how such things work.[1]

It could be argued that Santa Fe is the perfect setting for these goings-on. The city is passionately interested in and closely integrated with its natural environment, and yet over the past century it also has become detached from that environment and turned into (depending on whom you query on the matter) a quaint fantasy re-creation of itself, a multicultural hall of mirrors, a myth (and a victim of that myth), Santa Feyness, Info Mesa, a faux-adobe Brigadoon, a toy-West island in a sea of drug smuggling and poverty, a quasi-natural utopia trying simultaneously to freeze-frame and fast-forward its history. With its ordinance-mandated architectural homogeneity, the place has endeavored to uphold its reputation as, in Patricia Nelson Limerick's words, "one of a number of settings designed and built to convince visitors that they were having an authentic and genuine Western experience."[2] Santa Fe's image, according to Devon Jackson, "has in the past three decades become inseparable from its identity. 'Santa Fe' has been packaged and repackaged, marketed, and commodified so often and so aggressively that it's virtually impossible to distinguish 'Santa Fe' from Santa Fe."[3] From its beginnings as a tourist trap, says Hal K. Rothman, speaking of the city as if it were a computer program, "Santa Fe had been scripted to create an ambience of Otherness without eliminating the pleasures industrial life made possible"—more roughing it in style.[4] No surprise that it's now the e-Western destination of choice for many Bobos, perhaps the city they deserve.

"Santa Fe" may be the inferable consequence of a postmodern America where children have virtual pets and play butt-numbing video games. Gary Paul Nabhan reports, on the basis of interviews conducted in the early 1990s, that the majority of children from four different cultures in the Sonoran Desert (Mexican, Anglo, Yaqui, and O'odham) "had seen more animals on television and in the movies than they had personally seen in the wild"—a datum that justifies his judgment that "we have arrived at a new era in which ecological illiteracy is the norm."[5] It's an era in which "what we call the world," as Sven Birkerts sees it, "is more likely than not that obscure third thing, a gelid sort of extrusion not much characterized by nature or even by things, but rather by electronic communications, media images and devices, and a vast circulatory system of mass-produced goods felt by a great many of us to be indispensable. There is no clear *other* now, no obvious not-I." The response to this tertium quid often is a further withdrawal from nature he metaphorizes as a B-Western gesture: "the self, overwhelmed and frightened, unable to get its bearings, circles the wagons."[6]

There aren't many rays of hope in this situation, but one of them, ironically, emanates from the Santa Fe Institute; for what we're learning from the research being done in that citadel of simulation is that what's *really* indispensable, to self and other alike, may be impossible to duplicate. You can model childhood brain development, evolutionary adaptation, or the origin of life until the cows come home, but the output won't be quite the thing itself, only the sequel of a theory. In the course of the modeling, though, your thinking about what is modeled may change. That's precisely what's happening, and the upshot, as Daniel B. Botkin explains, is auspicious: "Nature as wilderness, the out-there that has played such an important role in western ideas throughout the centuries, seems now fundamentally different from what it seemed before. Wilderness is a nature of chance and complexities that we need no longer fear as unknowable or unpredictable. Strangely, that most novel of our tools, the computer, is helping us grasp what we have feared to seek."[7] If that comprehension is lessening our fear, it's also cluing us that nature, in Frieda Knobloch's words, can "no longer be considered masterable in the old exploitative ways."[8] Even if, given what we now know of "a new *ecology of chaos*," as Donald Worster calls it, "we cannot love nature quite so easily as Muir did," there's no small measure of cheer in the fact that "we have discovered more reason than ever to respect it."[9] Certainly, we have discovered more reason than ever to dispute the notion that the New West, to borrow Tom Mix's dictum about the Old West, is whatever you want it to be.

From the standpoint of eternity, the West is still mostly what it wants to be, our wishes be damned, and what it wants to be is not virtual reality but meatspace, what you have after you pull the plug on the computer, what Rick Bass calls "hard reality," the natural wholeness he savors while searching for grizzlies in the San Juan Mountains, where he watches Doug Peacock "gathering fistfuls of orange chanterelles late in the autumn, not with any special electronic glove but barehanded." Bass is utterly skeptical of any claim by virtual-reality buffs that they can change the essentials of nature. "We can change only the perception of these things," he argues and offers uncommon sense: "Nature, and the original system that created us, must always remain somehow with us, the bedrock."[10]

That being the case and the history of the West being what it is, we need to change our perception of the postregion itself, draw significance (especially the virtual reality we speak of as myth) into line with fact, bring the dream politics of economy into consonance with the realpolitik of ecology. For the Virginian, as he muses to Molly on their honeymoon, to be responsible means, regardless of his strong desire to the contrary, not to "mix with the whole thing" of Western nature; for us, though, to be responsible means very much to mix with it, to reach an atonement of nature and culture, savage and civilized, all the oppositions that still inform the destructive ambivalence of the Western wild-tame dialectic.

Conclusion: Some New Vision:
Resolving the Western Paradox

Unless Americans, and all human beings, can learn to imagine themselves as intimately and inextricably related to every aspect of the world they inhabit, with the extraordinary responsibilities such relationship entails—unless they can learn what the indigenous peoples of the Americas knew and often still know—the earth simply will not survive. A few square miles of something called wilderness will become the sign of failure everywhere.
    Louis Owens, "The American Indian Wilderness"

Over half a century ago, in his critique of Frederick Jackson Turner's essay "The Significance of the Frontier in American History," Henry Nash Smith highlighted a salient problem when he pointed out the disadvantages, to the literature and history of the West, of having to interpret the region in terms of "the paired but contradictory ideas of nature and civilization": the idea of nature "tended to cut the region off from the urban East and from Europe," and the idea of civilization "imposed on Westerners the stigma of social, ethical, and cultural inferiority." The latter was especially distressing because it "implied that America in general, and the West *a fortiori*, were meaningless except in so far as they managed to reproduce the achievements of Europe." He concluded that "a new intellectual system was requisite" for avoiding this interpretive entrapment.[1] He, for all his ingenuity, didn't quite put it together, however; nor do we have it yet—though impressive groundwork has been laid.

In the late 1990s Donald Worster saw the problem in terms of "a deep contradiction," inherited from the nineteenth century, in the American attitude toward land: "On the one hand, a romantic love of wilderness, hungry for natural beauty and natural freedom and insisting on the intrinsic worth and value of the nonhuman, pushed us toward a change in consciousness; on the other hand, a utilitarian devotion to intensively managing and using land, which justified itself in the name of wealth and progress, resisted change." He found commendably cheering a new movement of artists (specifically artists, like photographer Terry Evans, intent on enriching perceptions of the Western prairie) who want to find middle ground between those two inclinations; but he concluded that "we have not yet resolved this contradiction, either in our private feelings or in our public policies, and it is unlikely we ever will."[2]

I'm not that pessimistic—not yet, anyway. Neither was Worster in 1992 when he argued that the West's only "spiritual claim to uniqueness," what he called the "Western Paradox," was its attachment to two dreams subsumed by the wild-tame dialectic—"one of a life in nature, the other with machines; one of a life in the past, the other in the future"—and declared, acknowledging the complexity of the postregional West, that transcending the paradox or at least resolving it through "some new vision" wasn't improbable but would take a while. He expressed the hope that that vision of the West "will, in a thoughtful way, incorporate what was most noble in its old visions, leaving out the base excesses," and "suggest how we can occupy this place without consuming it or letting it consume us."[3] However else it differs from the old visions, the new one will have to take as its starting premise what Hillel Schwartz calls "the missing piece of our puzzle" in this time of ecological disorientation and danger: the unambivalent admission that "it is our essence to be at once wild and cultivated."[4]

Denial or, more often, equivocal avowal of that double essence caused America typically to make of its wildness—long west of where white settlement was thickening—a Jungian shadow it has labored to banish with all the vanquishing apparatus of its hubristic civilization. But that wildness (undeveloped land, Indians, buffalo, wolves, almost anything not conforming to European ideals) refuses to stay gone. It returns, to whatever degree indirectly, in reveries about the beauty of the natural West, in the values embedded in Western paintings, in rituals performed in Westerns in popular media, and in the habits of ordinary language, always recalling what we undid or hid, rode and built over, and hunger for—more desperately now, as selves beneath our scurrying selves know, than in the past. It tells us, if we attend, of the different West that Álvar Núñez Cabeza de Vaca intuited and even, for a time and in his own way, experienced.

A different West, the West that might have been and still might come to pass—what, to sum up, would it be?

A different West would be a place people continue to explore and discover anew, one whose "ironic society," as William Kittredge terms it, "is making itself up in a sometimes quite self-reflexive way"—toward "learning a skill: how to live in paradise."[5]

A different West would be a place of roots as well as routes, a place where people are sticking and protecting instead of escaping and exploiting.[6]

A different West would be a place where nature and culture are bound together in a fluent give-and-take; the traditional wild-domestic dichotomy (and its clichés of the masculine and the feminine) has been deconstructed; and people have broken the mental manacles of outdated metaphors of the organic and the mechanical.[7]

A different West would be a place where complexity is celebrated rather than delusively reduced; people have reframed their ideas of wilderness to expect the unexpected; and the human stance in the universe is defined by the graces of poised interrelation the Navajos honor as hózhó.

A different West would be a place where people are no longer torn between refined amenities and primitive vitalities but, as Bonney MacDonald puts it, have abandoned "tropes of opposition for those of synthesis, interface, and balance" and adapted to "a middle region of interchange."[8]

A different West would be a place with a mythos that reveals rather than veils truth, features the community (human and otherwise) as much as the individual, has a fallible but inspiring hero of the kind Patricia Nelson Limerick praises as "sustainable,"[9] and teaches the Westerner facing the natural world not to fixate on "making my mark" but always to ask what Brenda Peterson tells us should be the primary question: "how do I fit in?"[10]

A different West would be a place with an ethic not of pillage but of nurturance, one that defines "a new relation to nature and a new technics" that, as Worster advises, will require going with nature's grain rather than being enslaved by "the tyranny of instrumentalist reasoning."[11]

A different West would be a place where people hold dear the gift "trickster the culture hero" gives, according to Lewis Hyde: "the flexibility to endure."[12]

A different West would be a place where people exercise that trickster's sense of humor in dealing accommodatively with its wildness—apropos of which sine qua non I offer an anecdote from Gretel Ehrlich, itself a small cultural history, that's about a friend of hers whose transmission froze while he was in a bar on one fiercely cold Wyoming night: "The only gear that worked was reverse so he drove the eight miles home backward through two towns and up the hill past the hospital, waving at astonished onlookers all the way. When his wife accused him of drunkenness he said, 'I just got tired of looking at things the same old way.'"[13]

Maybe we have, too.

> We build our experience of nature as a kind of palimpsest, a blurred record of many passings. Personal memories, family histories, myths and dreams and tales, language itself, even the ancient body-knowledge coded into legs and lungs and cells: these make strata uncounted, sweet as baklava, rich as meadows, persistent as bedrock.
>
> All of it makes wildness: that pattern of patterns that we will never fully grasp. It grasps us, though, and gives us a shake, a hug, a death grip, an embrace. That's wild.
>
> David Oates, Introduction, *Paradise Wild: Reimagining American Nature*

Notes

PREFACE: A CONFERENCE IN RENO

1. This conference in more recent years has gone by a tamer name: the North American Interdisciplinary Conference on Environment and Community.

2. This impression was subsequently confirmed by a search of pertinent sources. Even as comprehensive a researcher's vade mecum as *Researching Western History: Topics in the Twentieth Century*, ed. Gerald D. Nash and Richard W. Etulain (Albuquerque: University of New Mexico Press, 1997), doesn't discuss the possibility of this sort of synthetic study.

3. Brooke Williams, "The Barbarian Link," in *Wilderness Tapestry: An Eclectic Approach to Preservation*, ed. Samuel I. Zeveloff, L. Mikel Vause, and William H. McVaugh (Reno: University of Nevada Press, 1992), pp. 8, 12.

4. Bill McKibben, "*Walden* Revisited," review of *Walden*, by Henry David Thoreau, *Double-Take*, Spring 1997, p. 128.

5. Elizabeth Atwood Lawrence, *Rodeo: An Anthropologist Looks at the Wild and the Tame* (Knoxville: University of Tennessee Press, 1982), p. 227.

6. Frederick Turner, *Beyond Geography: The Western Spirit against the Wilderness* (1980; reprint ed., New Brunswick, NJ: Rutgers University Press, 1992), p. xiv.

INTRODUCTION: A WILDE WESSTE

1. Donald Worster, *Under Western Skies: Nature and History in the American West* (New York: Oxford University Press, 1992), pp. 237, 231.

2. *The Oxford English Dictionary*, s.v. "wild." The etymology and semantics of *wild* and related words have been subjects of considerable research. A good deal of it comes into play *passim* in Max Oelschlaeger's *The Idea of Wilderness: From Prehistory to the Age of Ecology* (New Haven, CT: Yale University Press, 1991), which investigates the "long and tangled history of the idea of wilderness that begins with the ancient Sumerians and Egyptians (c. 3000 B.C.E.)"; notice especially his mention of the Hebrew word *midbar*, which is used in the Bible to refer to both "wilderness as a place of refuge" and "wilderness as a place that civilized people avoid" (pp. 30, 356). See also Gary Snyder's essay "The Etiquette of Freedom" in his collection *The Practice of the Wild* (New York: North Point Press, 1990), pp. 3–24, and Jay Hansford C. Vest, "Will-of-the-Land: Wilderness among Primal Indo-Europeans," *Environmental Review* 9 (1985): 323–29.

3. *Oxford English Dictionary*, s.v. "wild."

4. James H. Maguire, Introduction to Part 1: Encountering the West, *A Literary History of the American West*, ed. J. Golden Taylor et al. (Fort Worth: Texas Christian University Press, 1987), p. 4.

5. Ibid., p. 5.

6. Rita Parks, *The Western Hero in Film and Television: Mass Media Mythology* (Ann Arbor, MI: UMI Research Press, 1982), pp. 12, 17.

7. Richard C. Poulsen, *The Landscape of the Mind: Cultural Transformations of the American West* (New York: Lang, 1992), pp. 27, 28. Poulsen deals more extensively with the West as a place of direction in his *Misbegotten Muses: History and Anti-History* (New York: Lang, 1988), and, as he acknowledges, his treatment of westward movement as motion against chaos is indebted in part to Claude Lévi-Strauss—see the latter's *Tristes Tropiques* (New York: Atheneum, 1975), p. 122.

8. William Cronon, "The Trouble with Wilderness; or, Getting Back to the Wrong Nature," in *Uncommon Ground: Rethinking the Human Place in Nature*, ed. William Cronon (New York: Norton, 1995), p. 88.

9. Simon Schama, *Landscape and Memory* (New York: Vintage Books, 1996), p. 10.

10. Poulsen, *Landscape of the Mind*, p. 22. See also Denis Cosgrove, "Habitable Earth: Wilderness, Empire, and Race in America," in *Wild Ideas*, ed. David Rothenberg (Minneapolis: University of Minnesota Press, 1995), pp. 27–30.

11. Richard Slotkin, *Regeneration through Violence: The Mythology of the American Frontier, 1600–1860* (1973; reprint ed., New York: HarperPerennial, 1996), pp. 7, 6.

12. David Daly and Joel Persky, *The West and the Western*, a special issue of *Journal of the West* 29, no. 2 (April 1990): 8–9.

13. Roland Barthes, *Mythologies*, trans. Annette Lavers (New York: Hill and Wang, 1972), p. 143.

14. Claude Lévi-Strauss, *The Savage Mind* (Chicago: University of Chicago Press, 1966), p. 135.

15. Daly and Persky, *West and the Western*, p. 10.

16. Henry Nash Smith, Preface to the Twentieth Anniversary Printing, *Virgin Land: The American West as Symbol and Myth* (1950; reprint ed., Cambridge, MA: Harvard University Press, 1970), p. viii.

17. Stephen Tatum, "The Problem of the 'Popular' in the New Western History," in *The New Western History: An Assessment*, ed. Forrest G. Robinson, a special issue of *Arizona Quarterly* 53, no. 2 (Summer 1997): 184.

18. Smith, Preface, pp. ix–x.

19. Winifred Gallagher, *The Power of Place: How Our Surroundings Shape Our Thoughts, Emotions, and Actions* (New York: Poseidon Press, 1993), p. 221.

20. Ibid., pp. 221, 222.

21. Slotkin, *Regeneration through Violence*, p. 86.

22. Smith, *Virgin Land*, pp. 78, 79.

23. Herman Melville, *Moby-Dick*, ed. Harrison Hayford and Hershel Parker (New York: Norton, 1967), pp. 169, 165.

24. Elizabeth Atwood Lawrence, *Rodeo: An Anthropologist Looks at the Wild and the Tame* (Knoxville: University of Tennessee Press, 1982), pp. 270–71.

25. Tatum, "Problem of the 'Popular,'" pp. 166, 167. The quotation from Limerick is from her essay "The Adventures of the Frontier in the Twentieth Century," in *The Frontier in American Culture: An Exhibition at the Newberry Library, August 26, 1994–January 7, 1995: Essays by Richard White and Patricia Nelson Limerick*, ed. James R. Grossman (Berkeley: University of California Press, 1994), p. 70.

26. Richard Slotkin, "Myth and the Production of History," in *Ideology and Classic American Literature*, ed. Sacvan Bercovitch and Myra Jehlen (New York: Cambridge University Press, 1986), pp. 85–86.

27. F. Scott Fitzgerald, "The Crack-Up," in *The Art of the Personal Essay: An Anthology from the Classical Era to the Present*, selected and with an introduction by Phillip Lopate (New York: Anchor Books, 1994), p. 520.

28. Elliott West, "Stories," in *The Way to the West: Essays on the Central Plains* (Albuquerque: University of New Mexico Press, 1995), pp. 138, 137.

29. Richard Slotkin, *Gunfighter Nation: The Myth of the Frontier in Twentieth-Century America* (1992; reprint ed., New York: HarperPerennial, 1993), p. 5.

30. Gerald D. Nash, *Creating the West: Historical Interpretations, 1890–1990* (Albuquerque: University of New Mexico Press, 1991), pp. 272, 274.

PART ONE: A BRIEF HISTORY OF WILD

The Prehuman West

1. SueEllen Campbell, "Pristine," in *Bringing the Mountain Home* (Tucson: University of Arizona Press, 1996), pp. 24, 25.

2. Donald Worster, *An Unsettled Country: Changing Landscapes of the American West* (Albuquerque: University of New Mexico Press, 1994), p. 1.

3. Ibid., p. 2.

4. Ibid., p. xi.

5. Nancy Vogel, "Deep Time and Space out West: The Fossil Trilogy by Kathryn Lasky and the Sternberg Museum of Natural History," *Heritage of the Great Plains* 29, no. 1 (Spring–Summer 1996): 26.

6. William Heyen, "Before," *TriQuarterly* 93 (Spring–Summer 1995): 158.

7. Donald Worster, "A Tapestry of Change: Nature and Culture on the Prairie," in *The Inhabited Prairie*, by Terry Evans (Lawrence: University Press of Kansas, 1998), p. xi.

8. Ibid., p. xv.

9. Douglas Preston, "Footprint of History: Currents of the Centuries Ebb and Flow in Clayton," *New Mexico Magazine*, September 1997, p. 39.

10. Michael Tincher, "Río Grande Rift: And the Earth Did Move," *New Mexico Magazine*, November 1997, pp. 42, 46.

11. Tony Hillerman, "In the Heart of Navajo Country," reprint of a March 1975 article then entitled "New Mexico's Navajoland: The Very Heart of Our Land," *New Mexico Magazine*, July 1997, p. 27.

12. Halka Chronic, *Roadside Geology of New Mexico* (Missoula, MT: Mountain Press, 1987), p. 28.

13. Campbell, *Bringing the Mountain Home*, pp. 74, 101.

14. John McPhee, *Rising from the Plains* (New York: Noonday Press, 1991), p. 51.

15. John McPhee, *Basin and Range* (New York: Noonday Press, 1990), pp. 22, 23.

16. John McPhee, *Assembling California* (New York: Noonday Press, 1994), pp. 5–6.

Native Nature

1. The Bering-land-bridge theory of those forebears' immigration is widely accepted, but there is reason to be skeptical about it—see, for example, Sasha Nemecek, "Who Were the First Americans?" *Scientific American*, September 2000, pp. 80–87. Vine Deloria Jr. has been a witty critic of the theory—see his *Red Earth, White Lies: Native Americans and the Myth of Scientific Fact* (1995; reprint ed., Golden, CO: Fulcrum, 1997), pp. 67–91. Also, the time of those forebears' arrival is a matter of debate—see J. M. Adovasio with Jake Page, *The First Americans: In*

Pursuit of Archaeology's Greatest Mystery (New York: Random House, 2002). A synoptic discussion of such controversies, along with summaries of alternative origin stories from several Indian tribes, may be found in Colin G. Calloway's *One Vast Winter Count: The Native American West before Lewis and Clark* (Lincoln: University of Nebraska Press, 2003), pp. 25–33.

2. George R. Stewart, *Names on the Land: A Historical Account of Place-Naming in the United States* (Boston: Houghton Mifflin; 1958), p. 9. Indian place-naming is a fairly sophisticated and time-sensitive process, as may be seen in Keith H. Basso's discussion of it in his *Wisdom Sits in Places: Landscape and Language among the Western Apache* (Albuquerque: University of New Mexico Press, 1996), esp. pp. 3–35. Also, concerning Tapahonso's statement, see Andrew Light, "Urban Wilderness," in *Wild Ideas*, ed. David Rothenberg (Minneapolis: University of Minnesota Press, 1995), in which he claims that "no word in any indigenous North American language has been identified as meaning what Europeans or Euro-Americans take to mean 'wilderness'" (p. 198). While some indigenous languages have terms for "wildness" of a sort, they don't mean what the English word typically means and tend to carry only positive connotations. For discussion of an example, from the Piman-speaking O'odham, see Gary Paul Nabhan, "Cultural Parallax in Viewing North American Habitats," in *Reinventing Nature? Responses to Postmodern Deconstruction*, ed. Michael E. Soulé and Gary Lease (Washington, DC: Island Press, 1995), p. 96. Also relevant is Angie Debo's observation that the name *Seminole*, denoting the tribe that separated from the Creek Confederacy in the eighteenth century and migrated to Florida, comes from a Creek word meaning, by her definition, "'wild,' or 'those who camp at a distance'" (*A History of the Indians of the United States* [Norman: University of Oklahoma Press, 1970], p. 10)—though she doesn't go on to say that the present form of the word was influenced by the Spanish word *cimarrón*, meaning "runaway" or "fugitive."

3. Richard White, *"It's Your Misfortune and None of My Own": A New History of the American West* (Norman: University of Oklahoma Press, 1991), pp. 3, 212, 4, 213. According to Stephen J. Pyne, in his *Fire in America: A Cultural History of Wildland and Rural Fire* (Princeton, NJ: Princeton University Press, 1982), "Indian fire practices . . . were enormously powerful as landscape modifiers" and illustrative of how fire exists, like wilderness, as a "cultural and natural hybrid" (pp. 17, 18). Corroborating the aptness of Pyne's concept of hybridization here is Light's argument that for Native Americans "the 'wilderness' was a part of everyday life"—so much so, he speculates, that "the 'absence of the wild' for Native Americans may have a . . . coherent material base" in their extensive cultivation of land ("Urban Wilderness," pp. 200, 199). Concerning the extent of such intervention at various times in North American bioregions, Western and otherwise, see William Cronon, *Changes in the Land: Indians, Colonists, and the Ecology of New England* (New York: Hill and Wang, 1983); *Before the Wilderness: Environmental Management by Native Californians*, ed. Kat Anderson and comp. Thomas C. Blackburn (Menlo Park, CA: Ballena Press, 1993); William M. Denevan, "The Pristine Myth: The Landscape of the Americas in 1492," *Annals of the Association of American Geographers* 82 (1992): 369–85; Gary Paul Nabhan, *Enduring Seeds: Native American Agriculture and Wild Plant Conservation* (San Francisco: North Point Press, 1989); and *Wilderness and Political Ecology: Aboriginal Influences and the Original State of Nature*, ed. Charles E. Kay and Randy T. Simmons (Salt Lake City: University of Utah Press, 2002).

4. Roderick Nash, Preface to the Third Edition, *Wilderness and the American Mind*, 3rd ed. (New Haven, CT: Yale University Press, 1982), pp. xiii, xiv.

5. Ibid., p. xvi.

6. See Ian Frazier, *Great Plains* (New York: Penguin Books, 1990), p. 83.

7. See Michael Richie, "Valley of Fires," *New Mexico Magazine*, January 1998, p. 21.

8. See Frazier, *Great Plains*, p. 84. See also *Pleistocene and Recent Environments of the Central Great Plains*, ed. Wakefield Dort Jr. and J. Knox Jones Jr. (Lawrence: University Press of Kansas, 1970).

9. N. Scott Momaday, "A First American Views His Land," in *The Man Made of Words: Essays, Stories, Passages* (New York: St. Martin's Press, 1997), pp. 30–31.

10. Ibid., pp. 31, 32.

11. Aldo Leopold, *"A Sand County Almanac" and "Sketches Here and There"* (1949; reprint ed., New York: Oxford University Press, 1989), p. 177.

12. Richard Rhodes, "The Killing of the Everglades," *Playboy*, January 1972, p. 114.

13. Carolyn Merchant, "Reinventing Eden: Western Culture as a Recovery Narrative," in *Uncommon Ground: Rethinking the Human Place in Nature*, ed. William Cronon (New York: Norton, 1995), p. 144. A fuller sense of these and related differences between Indians and Europeans may be gained by reading Daniel K. Richter's *Facing East from Indian Country: A Native History of Early America* (Cambridge, MA: Harvard University Press, 2001).

14. Catherine L. Albanese, *Nature Religion in America: From the Algonkian Indians to the New Age* (Chicago: University of Chicago Press, 1990), pp. 17, 21, 23. For an overview of the collective mythological tradition that underlies these shared assumptions, see David Leeming and Jake Page, *The Mythology of Native North America* (Norman: University of Oklahoma Press, 2000).

15. See Peggy V. Beck, Anna Lee Walters, and Nia Francisco, *The Sacred: Ways of Knowledge, Sources of Life*, redesigned ed. (Tsaile, AZ: Navajo Community College Press, 1992), pp. 93, 67–68.

16. Gary Short, "Shoshonean," in *Flying over Sonny Liston* (Reno: University of Nevada Press, 1996), p. 47.

17. Richard C. Poulsen, *The Landscape of the Mind: Cultural Transformations of the American West* (New York: Lang, 1992), pp. 48, 49, 50. For a more extensive treatment of Indians' relation to the whole of nature, see J. Donald Hughes, *American Indian Ecology*, 2nd ed. (El Paso: Texas Western Press, 1998).

18. Vine Deloria Jr., *God Is Red: A Native View of Religion*, updated ed. (Golden, CO: Fulcrum, 1994), pp. 81, 83, 82.

19. Poulsen, *Landscape of the Mind*, p. 49. Shepard Krech's *The Ecological Indian: Myth and History* (New York: Norton, 1999) argues fairly convincingly against the European view of Native Americans as noble preservationists and endeavors to present them as people who, from the Pleistocene on, very much left their traces on the land.

20. Martin W. Lewis, "Environmental History Challenges the Myth of a Primordial Eden," *Chronicle of Higher Education*, 4 May 1994, p. A56. See also Lewis's *Green Delusions: An Environmentalist Critique of Radical Environmentalism* (Durham, NC: Duke University Press, 1992) as well as Paul S. Martin's *The Last 10,000 Years: A Fossil Pollen Record of the American Southwest* (Tucson: University of Arizona Press, 1963), the book that initiated debate concerning Native American responsibility for the extinction of numerous animal species.

21. Nabhan, "Cultural Parallax," pp. 87, 89, 94–95, 93. A summary of the principal positions in the debate in the wake of Martin's thesis may be found in Kate Wong, "Mammoth Kill," *Scientific American*, February 2001, p. 22. Deloria's argument against Martin's thesis may be found in his *Red Earth, White Lies*, pp. 99–112, where he ridicules what he sees as its ideological bias and questionable scientific objectivity. Also relevant here is Calloway's

discussion of Martin's thesis and what we know of Paleo-Indian hunting practices—see his *One Vast Winter Count*, pp. 33–44.

22. Simon Schama, *Landscape and Memory* (New York: Vintage Books, 1996), p. 7.

23. Gundars Rudzitis, *Wilderness and the Changing American West* (New York: Wiley, 1996), p. 58.

24. Steven R. Simms, "Wilderness as a Human Landscape," in *Wilderness Tapestry: An Eclectic Approach to Preservation*, ed. Samuel I. Zeveloff, L. Mikel Vause, and William H. McVaugh (Reno: University of Nevada Press, 1992), pp. 188, 185, 187, 191. See also Simms's *Behavioral Ecology and Hunter-Gatherer Foraging: An Example from the Great Basin* (Oxford, UK: B.A.R., 1987). Two other studies that significantly qualify commonplaces about the Indian's "harmony with nature" are Leland C. Bemont, *Bison Hunting at Cooper Site: Where Lightning Bolts Draw Thundering Herds* (Norman: University of Oklahoma Press, 1999), and Christy G. Turner II and Jacqueline A. Turner, *Man Corn: Cannibalism and Violence in the Prehistoric American Southwest* (Salt Lake City: University of Utah Press, 1999). Henry F. Dobyns's phrase may be found in his *Their Number Become Thinned: Native American Population Dynamics in Eastern North America* (Knoxville: University of Tennessee Press, 1983), p. 8.

25. Donald Worster, *An Unsettled Country: Changing Landscapes of the American West* (Albuquerque: University of New Mexico Press, 1994), pp. 66, 67, 68. As Worster acknowledges in detail, his data are taken from Ernest Thompson Seton's multivolume work *Lives of Game Animals* (Garden City, NY: Doran, 1929). Worster mentions (pp. 129–30, n. 15) several supplementary sources of documentation on animal declines, all of which I'd recommend. See also Andrew C. Isenberg, *The Destruction of the Bison: An Environmental History, 1750–1920* (New York: Cambridge University Press, 2000), a more recent study that considers the gamut of factors besides rapacious white hunting that contributed to the extraordinary reduction of the bison's population, which at its height, Isenberg proposes, had passed the point of stable sustainability.

26. T. H. Watkins, "The Travels of Turner," in Frederick Turner, *Beyond Geography: The Western Spirit against the Wilderness* (1980; reprint ed., New Brunswick, NJ: Rutgers University Press, 1992), p. xxi.

27. Ibid., p. xxiii.

28. Donald Johanson, review of *Becoming Human: Evolution and Human Uniqueness*, by Jan Tattersall, *Scientific American*, March 1998, p. 103.

29. Zeese Papanikolas, *Trickster in the Land of Dreams* (Lincoln: University of Nebraska Press, 1995), pp. 8, 41.

30. The quotation is attributed to Montezuma in Stan Steiner, "None of Us Is Native," in *The Waning of the West*, ed. Emily Skretny Drabanski (New York: St. Martin's Press, 1989), p. 131. The reader should be aware that such attributions are often spurious (though I certainly have no special reason to believe that this one might be). For a pithy account of the problems entailed in reports of what Indians have "said," see Jill Lepore, "Wigwam Words," *American Scholar* 70, no. 1 (Winter 2001): 97–108.

PART TWO: FROM THE 1530S TO THE 1840S: THE WEST AS WASTE AND PROMISED LAND

Prelude and Overview

1. Richard W. Etulain, *Re-imagining the Modern American West: A Century of Fiction, History, and Art* (Tucson: University of Arizona Press, 1996), p. xviii. For further discussion of

such visions, see Loren Baritz, "The Idea of the West," *American Historical Review* 66 (1961): 618–40.

2. Leonard Lutwack, *The Role of Place in Literature* (Syracuse, NY: Syracuse University Press, 1984), pp. 144, 145.

3. Ibid., pp. 177, 178–79.

4. Ibid., pp. 179, 180.

5. Roderick Nash, Preface to the Third Edition, *Wilderness and the American Mind*, 3rd ed. (New Haven, CT: Yale University Press, 1982), p. xi.

6. T. H. Watkins, "The Travels of Turner," in Frederick Turner, *Beyond Geography: The Western Spirit against the Wilderness* (1980; reprint ed., New Brunswick, NJ: Rutgers University Press, 1992), p. xxii.

7. Turner, *Beyond Geography*, p. 255.

8. See Lynn White Jr., "The Historical Roots of Our Ecological Crisis," in *The Ecocriticism Reader: Landmarks in Literary Ecology*, ed. Cheryll Glotfelty and Harold Fromm (Athens: University of Georgia Press, 1996), pp. 3–14. This influential and mostly persuasive essay, which originally appeared in *Science* 155 (1967): 1203–7, is not without its critics. See, for example, Max Oelschlaeger, "Wilderness, Civilization, and Language," in *The Wilderness Condition: Essays on Environment and Civilization*, ed. Max Oelschlaeger (San Francisco: Sierra Club Books, 1992), pp. 283–85.

9. N. Scott Momaday, "The American West and the Burden of Belief," in *The Man Made of Words: Essays, Stories, Passages* (New York: St. Martin's Press, 1997), p. 91.

10. Donald A. Barclay, James H. Maguire, and Peter Wild, Introduction, *Into the Wilderness Dream: Exploration Narratives of the American West, 1500–1805*, ed. Donald A. Barclay, James H. Maguire, and Peter Wild (Salt Lake City: University of Utah Press, 1994), p. xii.

11. Henry Nash Smith, *Virgin Land: The American West as Symbol and Myth* (1950; reprint ed., Cambridge, MA: Harvard University Press, 1970), p. 12.

12. J. Hector St. John de Crèvecoeur, *Letters from an American Farmer*, ed. Warren Barton Blake (New York: Dutton, 1957), pp. 49, 48, 208.

13. Winifred Gallagher, *The Power of Place: How Our Surroundings Shape Our Thoughts, Emotions, and Actions* (New York: Poseidon Press, 1993), p. 222.

Conquistadors and Colonizers: The Spanish Encounter with Unbridled Wilderness

1. Roderick Nash, *Wilderness and the American Mind*, 3rd ed. (New Haven, CT: Yale University Press, 1982), pp. 25, 26. The fairway-rough metaphor analogizes also what Denis Cosgrove, drawing on Peter Hulme's *Colonial Encounters: Europe and the Native Caribbean, 1492–1797* (London: Routledge, 1986), distinguishes as the "two discourses of wilderness" between which "Europe's reading of the New World was . . . stretched" from the Homeric epics on: one concerns the Arawaks, "an innocent, childlike people inhabiting the islands of the Western Ocean during the Golden Age of harmony with the natural world"; the other concerns the Caribs, "scarcely human wild warriors and cannibals bent on conquering, enslaving, and (where appropriate) eating the gentle Arawaks" ("Habitable Earth: Wilderness, Empire, and Race in America," in *Wild Ideas*, ed. David Rothenberg [Minneapolis: University of Minnesota Press, 1995], p. 30). Seen in these terms, the promoters of the New World were highlighting the discourse of the Arawaks and ignoring or suppressing that of the Caribs. Such discourses contributed much to the post-Columbian fabrication of an unreal America—see Edmundo O'Gorman, *The Invention of America: An Inquiry into the Historical Na-*

ture of the New World and the Meaning of Its History (Bloomington: Indiana University Press, 1961).

2. Nash, *Wilderness and the American Mind*, p. 26.

3. SueEllen Campbell, "The Rare," in *Bringing the Mountain Home* (Tucson: University of Arizona Press, 1996), p. 99.

4. See Frederick Turner, *Beyond Geography: The Western Spirit against the Wilderness* (1980; reprint ed., New Brunswick, NJ: Rutgers University Press, 1992), p. 118–43. Turner's main sources are Samuel Eliot Morison, *Admiral of the Ocean Sea: A Life of Christopher Columbus* (Boston: Little, Brown, 1942); Bartolomé de las Casas, *History of the Indies*, ed. and trans. Andrée Collard (New York: Harper and Row, 1971); and *The Four Voyages of Christopher Columbus: Being His Own Log-Book, Letters and Dispatches with Connecting Narrative Drawn from the Life of the Admiral by His Son Hernando Colón and Other Contemporary Historians*, ed. and trans. J. M. Cohen (Baltimore: Penguin Books, 1969).

5. Turner, *Beyond Geography*, p. 130.

6. Ibid., pp. 131.

7. Ibid., pp. 136, 139, 143, 142.

8. Tzvetan Todorov, *The Conquest of America: The Question of the Other*, trans. Richard Howard (New York: Harper and Row, 1984), pp. 49–50.

9. Carla Mulford, "Colonial Period: To 1700," *The Heath Anthology of American Literature*, ed. Paul Lauter et al., 2nd ed., 2 vols. (Lexington, MA: Heath, 1994), 1: 8.

10. Stephen Greenblatt, *Marvelous Possessions: The Wonder of the New World* (Chicago: University of Chicago Press, 1991), p. 14.

11. Lawrence Weschler, *Mr. Wilson's Cabinet of Wonder* (New York: Vintage Books, 1995), pp. 81, 80. For several discussions of how dramatically information and images disseminated by the conquistadors reshaped European thinking, specifically about the West, see *The Mapping of the Entradas into the Greater Southwest*, ed. Dennis Reinhartz and Gerald D. Saxon (Norman: University of Oklahoma Press, 1998).

12. Greenblatt, *Marvelous Possessions*, p. 9.

13. Turner, *Beyond Geography*, p. 146. In order to survive, the Indians learned to resist Spanish domination more and more cannily as time passed; for examples of their strategies, see Gary Clayton Anderson, *The Indian Southwest, 1580–1830: Ethnogenesis and Reinvention* (Norman: University of Oklahoma Press, 1999), and Andrew L. Knaut, *The Pueblo Revolt of 1680: Conquest and Resistance in Seventeenth-Century New Mexico* (Norman: University of Oklahoma Press, 1997).

14. Stephen Tatum, "Topographies of Transition in Western American Literature," *Western American Literature* 32 (1998): 341.

15. Frederick Turner, "Visions of the Pacific," in *Of Chiles, Cacti, and Fighting Cocks: Notes on the American West* (1990; expanded reprint ed., New York: Owl Books, 1996), pp. 267–68.

16. Zeese Papanikolas, *Trickster in the Land of Dreams* (Lincoln: University of Nebraska Press, 1995), p. 45.

17. David J. Weber, *The Spanish Frontier in North America* (New Haven, CT: Yale University Press, 1992), p. 10.

18. Ibid., pp. 12, 48, 312. Concerning later Spanish explorers' indifference to the beauty of the Grand Canyon, see Stephen J. Pyne, *How the Canyon Became Grand: A Short History* (New York: Viking, 1998), pp. 15–22.

19. Richard White, *"It's Your Misfortune and None of My Own": A New History of the American West* (Norman: University of Oklahoma Press, 1991), p. 5. For an extended account of Cabeza de Vaca's adventure, see Paul Schneider, *Brutal Journey: The Epic Story of the First Crossing of North America* (New York: Holt, 2006).

20. Patricia Nelson Limerick, *The Legacy of Conquest: The Unbroken Past of the American West* (New York: Norton, 1987), p. 223.

21. John Murray, review of *The West: An Illustrated History*, by Geoffrey C. Ward, *Bloomsbury Review* 16, no. 5 (September–October 1996): 26. For an English translation of *La Relación*, see *The Account: Álvar Núñez Cabeza de Vaca's "Relación*," trans. Martin A. Favata and José B. Fernández (Houston: Arte Público Press, 1993).

22. Papanikolas, *Trickster in the Land of Dreams*, pp. 46, 48.

23. Turner, *Beyond Geography*, pp. 254, 253.

24. Richard Slotkin, *Regeneration through Violence: The Mythology of the American Frontier, 1600–1860* (1973; reprint ed., New York: HarperPerennial, 1996), pp. 35–36, 37. As Slotkin's discussion of Cabeza de Vaca suggests, there were surely negative aspects to his self-division. Todorov, for instance, interprets Cabeza de Vaca, in contrast to Columbus, as a man able "to experience difference in equality," but he also sees him as one who, "without becoming an Indian, . . . was no longer quite a Spaniard"—and thus doubly an "exile" (*Conquest of America*, p. 249).

25. Weber, *Spanish Frontier in North America*, pp. 18, 22.

26. Ibid., p. 23.

27. Papanikolas, *Trickster in the Land of Dreams*, pp. 49, 50.

28. Richard C. Poulsen, *The Landscape of the Mind: Cultural Transformations of the American West* (New York: Lang, 1992), p. 29.

29. Papanikolas, *Trickster in the Land of Dreams*, pp. 54, 55. Pedro de Castañeda's "Narrative" as well as other accounts of the expedition are included in *Narratives of the Coronado Expedition, 1540–1542*, ed. and trans. George P. Hammond and Agapito Rey (Albuquerque: University of New Mexico Press, 1940).

30. Tatum, "Topographies of Transition," p. 312.

31. Ray Allen Billington, *Land of Savagery, Land of Promise: The European Image of the American Frontier in the Nineteenth Century* (New York: Norton, 1981), p. 2.

32. William H. Goetzmann, *Exploration and Empire: The Explorer and the Scientist in the Winning of the American West* (1966; reprint ed., Austin: Texas State Historical Association, 1993), p. xii.

33. White, *"It's Your Misfortune and None of My Own,"* p. 213.

The Antipode of Paradise: William Bradford and the Hatred of Wilderness

1. Roderick Nash, *Wilderness and the American Mind*, 3rd ed. (New Haven, CT: Yale University Press, 1982), p. 6.

2. William Bradford, *Of Plymouth Plantation, 1620–1647*, ed. Samuel Eliot Morison (New York: Knopf, 1953), p. 62. The text has, of course, been modernized.

3. Nash, *Wilderness and the American Mind*, p. 25.

4. John Winthrop, "A Modell of Christian Charity," in *The Heath Anthology of American Literature*, ed. Paul Lauter et al., 2nd ed., 2 vols. (Lexington, MA: Heath, 1994), 1: 233. The city Winthrop conceived was never meant to be a city in the modern sense but more a place

defined by the rural-agrarian middle landscape. As Yi-Fu Tuan argues, "the Puritan's 'City on a Hill' shared the farmer's values and accepted his cosmos; and it was far from the Puritan's mind to translate these values into urban life styles and design" (*Topophilia: A Study of Environmental Perception, Attitudes, and Values* [1974; reprint ed., New York: Columbia University Press, 1990], p. 194).

5. Nash, *Wilderness and the American Mind*, p. 35.

6. Tuan, *Topophilia*, p. 110.

7. Nash, *Wilderness and the American Mind*, p. 24. Hans Huth observes that "even the earliest descriptions of the virgin land contain passages indicating that some of the newcomers felt that the new country was actually a pleasant place," but he dismisses them as "more or less stylized accounts" intended to attract more settlers or sponsors for colonial enterprises and implies that utilitarian repugnance was the more characteristic response (*Nature and the American: Three Centuries of Changing Attitudes*, new ed. [Lincoln: University of Nebraska Press, 1990], p. 4).

8. Catherine L. Albanese, *Nature Religion in America: From the Algonkian Indians to the New Age* (Chicago: University of Chicago Press, 1990), p. 35.

9. Paul Shepard, *The Others: How Animals Made Us Human* (Washington, DC: Shearwater Books, 1996), pp. 223, 227.

10. Richard Slotkin, *Regeneration through Violence: The Mythology of the American Frontier, 1600–1860* (1973; reprint ed., New York: HarperPerennial, 1996), pp. 58, 59, 63.

11. Ibid., pp. 63, 64, 38.

12. Frederick Turner, *Beyond Geography: The Western Spirit against the Wilderness* (1980; reprint ed., New Brunswick, NJ: Rutgers University Press, 1992), p. 233.

13. Ibid., pp. 235, 236. See also Richard VanDerBeets, "The Indian Captivity Narrative as Ritual," *American Literature* 43 (1972): 548–62.

14. Turner, *Beyond Geography*, pp. 236, 238.

15. An illustrative collection of later captivity narratives is *Captured by the Indians: 15 Firsthand Accounts, 1750–1870*, ed. Frederick Drimmer (1961; reprint ed., New York: Dover, 1985). We have no accurate figures for how many whites went native from the beginning of Jamestown on, but Kirkpatrick Sale conjectures in his discussion of that settlement's rough census of 1625 that there alone "an embarrassingly high number of good Englishmen decided to become good Indians" (*The Conquest of Paradise: Christopher Columbus and the Columbian Legacy* [New York: Knopf, 1990], p. 271).

16. David Mogen, "Wilderness, Metamorphosis, and Millennium: Gothic Apocalypse from the Puritans to the Cyberpunks," in *Frontier Gothic: Terror and Wonder at the Frontier in American Literature*, ed. David Mogen, Scott P. Sanders, and Joanne B. Karpinski (Rutherford, NJ: Fairleigh Dickinson University Press, 1993), pp. 97, 94, 96, 97.

17. Carolyn Merchant, "Reinventing Eden: Western Culture as a Recovery Narrative," in *Uncommon Ground: Rethinking the Human Place in Nature*, ed. William Cronon (New York: Norton, 1995), pp. 133, 136.

18. Ibid., p. 137.

19. Ibid., p. 141. Merchant's analysis is on pp. 140–41. See also Vladimir Propp, "Morphology of the Folktale," *International Journal of American Linguistics* 24, no. 4 (October 1958): 46–48.

20. Richard C. Poulsen, *The Landscape of the Mind: Cultural Transformations of the American West* (New York: Lang, 1992), pp. 43, 45, 46.

21. In this connection see Gesa Mackenthun, *Metaphors of Dispossession: American Beginnings and the Translation of Empire, 1492–1637* (Norman: University of Oklahoma Press, 1997).

22. Turner, *Beyond Geography*, pp. 203, 205. This is the classical, as opposed to Romantic, view of the Wild Man, in correspondence with which, according to Andrew Light, savages are considered so driven by their passions that even outside the wilderness they "are still wild because of the 'cognitive' wilderness within them" ("Urban Wilderness," in *Wild Ideas*, ed. David Rothenberg [Minneapolis: University of Minnesota Press, 1995], p. 196). It's a view that surely makes domestication disputable, which it would be long after the Puritans' time. See also E. M. W. Tillyard, *The Elizabethan World Picture* (London: Chatto and Windus, 1943).

23. Turner, *Beyond Geography*, pp. 211, 228.

24. Lawrence Buell, *The Environmental Imagination: Thoreau, Nature Writing, and the Formation of American Culture* (Cambridge, MA: Belknap Press, 1995), pp. 70, 60. See also Leo Marx, *The Machine in the Garden: Technology and the Pastoral Ideal in America* (New York: Oxford University Press, 1964), p. 42, and Alan Heimert, "Puritanism, the Wilderness, and the Frontier," *New England Quarterly* 26 (1953): 361–82.

25. Slotkin, *Regeneration through Violence*, pp. 178–79.

26. Ibid., p. 179.

27. Ibid.

28. Albanese, *Nature Religion in America*, pp. 37, 40. As Ray Allen Billington argues, during the seventeenth century "Europe's image-makers" pictured "good" Indians, modeled on the amiable Arawaks whom Columbus encountered, as well as "bad" ones, modeled on the execrable Caribs, but the image of the Indian as "Nature's nobleman" was quashed for a while by "shudderingly realistic" reports from across the Atlantic (*Land of Savagery, Land of Promise: The European Image of the American Frontier in the Nineteenth Century* [New York: Norton, 1981], pp. 5, 6).

29. Nash, *Wilderness and the American Mind*, p. 37.

30. Richard Rodriguez, "True West," in *The Anchor Essay Annual: The Best of 1997*, ed. Phillip Lopate (New York: Anchor Books, 1997), p. 322.

31. Light nicely clarifies the interlinks among separateness, innocence, superiority, and domination in his propositional summary of the "classical position" on the wilderness—see "Urban Wilderness," p. 197.

32. Albanese, *Nature Religion in America*, pp. 42, 45. It's true, of course, as Tuan says, that Mather "showed the same ambivalence toward the waste lands that we can find in the Old and New Testaments," but I'd argue that anybody "who would speak seriously of demons and dragons in the forests" favored a bleak view of them (*Topophilia*, p. 110). In regard to Edwards, Albanese doubtless would agree with Huth that he, "in spite of his deeply poetic nature, could not completely disengage himself from the line of Puritan thinking" (*Nature and the American*, p. 7). A number of sources that bear on such conflicts in the European attitude toward nature in the eighteenth century are mentioned in Billington's bibliographical notes—see his *Land of Savagery, Land of Promise*, pp. 334–36.

33. Richard Rhodes, "The Killing of the Everglades," *Playboy*, January 1972, pp. 281, 282.

34. Rodriguez, "True West," pp. 329, 330.

35. Robert Frost, "The Gift Outright," in *The Poetry of Robert Frost*, ed. Edward Connery Lathem (New York: Holt, Rinehart and Winston, 1969), p. 348. For additional critique of the poem in this vein, see George B. Handley's "A Postcolonial Sense of Place and the Work

of Derek Walcott," *Interdisciplinary Studies in Literature and Environment* 7, no. 2 (Summer 2000): 6.

36. Zeese Papanikolas, *Trickster in the Land of Dreams* (Lincoln: University of Nebraska Press, 1995), pp. 16, 35.

37. See T. M. Barkley, *Field Guide to the Common Weeds of Kansas* (Lawrence: University Press of Kansas, 1983), p. vii.

38. A. Carl Bredahl Jr., *New Ground: Western American Narrative and the Literary Canon* (Chapel Hill: University of North Carolina Press, 1989), pp. 33, 34.

39. Ibid., pp. 34, 35.

40. Nash, *Wilderness and the American Mind*, pp. xvi, 33.

41. Ibid., pp. xvii, 43.

Ravage through the Garden: The Wild according to Boone, Lewis and Clark, and Crockett

1. Richard White, "'Are You an Environmentalist or Do You Work for a Living?' Work and Nature," in *Uncommon Ground: Rethinking the Human Place in Nature*, ed. William Cronon (New York: Norton, 1995), pp. 175–76.

2. *Encyclopedia of the American West*, ed. Charles Phillips and Alan Axelrod (New York: Simon and Schuster Macmillan, 1996) s.v. "Boone, Daniel."

3. William Carlos Williams, "The Discovery of Kentucky," in *In the American Grain* (1925; reprint ed., New York: New Directions, 1956), pp. 130, 131, 136. Predictably, D. H. Lawrence "found Williams's conception compelling," as John Mack Faragher remarks in his *Daniel Boone: The Life and Legend of an American Pioneer* (New York: Holt, 1992), p. 341; but Lawrence ignored the extent to which the real Boone wasn't free of what he calls "the Puritan way," which involves "gutting the great continent in frenzies of mean fear" ("American Heroes," *Nation*, 14 April 1926, p. 413).

4. Williams, "Discovery of Kentucky," pp. 137, 138.

5. Richard Slotkin, *Regeneration through Violence: The Mythology of the American Frontier, 1600–1860* (1973; reprint ed., New York: HarperPerennial, 1996), pp. 268–69. Some recent historians would argue that what Boone "made the wilderness safe for" was industrialization—see, for example, Stephen Aron, *How the West Was Lost: The Transformation of Kentucky from Daniel Boone to Henry Clay* (Baltimore: Johns Hopkins University Press, 1996).

6. Slotkin, *Regeneration through Violence*, p. 272.

7. Ibid., pp. 272, 273, 274, 277.

8. Ibid., pp. 281, 284.

9. Ibid., p. 293.

10. Ibid., pp. 294, 301, 300, 301. While it seems inarguable, as Annette Kolodny says, that "the West was a woman, and to it belonged the hope of rebirth and regeneration," that identification has never been unambiguous—nor has the "metaphor of the land-as-woman" itself, for, as she explains, implicit in it "was both the regressive pull of maternal containment *and* the seductive invitation to sexual assertion" (*The Lay of the Land: Metaphor as Experience and History in American Life and Letters* [Chapel Hill: University of North Carolina Press, 1975], pp. 136, 67).

11. Slotkin, *Regeneration through Violence*, pp. 309, 310.

12. Ibid., p. 311.

13. Henry Nash Smith, *Virgin Land: The American West as Symbol and Myth* (1950; reprint ed., Cambridge, MA: Harvard University Press, 1970), pp. 51, 52.

14. Lord Byron, *Don Juan*, canto 8, stanzas 63, 61. Byron's Boone resembles Filson's in that, as Ray Allen Billington characterizes the latter, he "was the logical counterpart of the Noble Savage then so popular" (*Land of Savagery, Land of Promise: The European Image of the American Frontier in the Nineteenth Century* [New York: Norton, 1981], p. 153).

15. Smith, *Virgin Land*, pp. 52, 53, 54, 53.

16. Ibid., pp. 61, 58. Faragher observes that "Cooper's saga is permeated by the conflict between natural freedom and civilized restraint" and that, while he believed "in the development of the country," his "ambivalence about progress spoke to a deeply felt regret about the loss of wilderness as an imagined place of unbound freedom" (*Daniel Boone*, pp. 332, 333).

17. Regarding that shift of mood in general and, *passim*, Boone in particular, see *The Frontier Re-examined*, ed. John Francis McDermott (Urbana: University of Illinois Press, 1967).

18. Leonard Lutwack, *The Role of Place in Literature* (Syracuse, NY: Syracuse University Press, 1984), p. 175.

19. Frederick Turner, *Beyond Geography: The Western Spirit against the Wilderness* (1980; reprint ed., New Brunswick, NJ: Rutgers University Press, 1992), p. 260.

20. Patricia Nelson Limerick, *The Legacy of Conquest: The Unbroken Past of the American West* (New York: Norton, 1987), p. 90.

21. Faragher, *Daniel Boone*, pp. 351, 362.

22. David Daly and Joel Persky, *The West and the Western*, a special issue of *Journal of the West* 29, no. 2 (April 1990): 41.

23. William H. Goetzmann and William N. Goetzmann, *The West of the Imagination* (New York: Norton, 1986), pp. xiii, xii, xiii.

24. Catherine L. Albanese, *Nature Religion in America: From the Algonkian Indians to the New Age* (Chicago: University of Chicago Press, 1990), p. 66.

25. Concerning Jefferson's belief in farmers as chosen people, as well as his detestation of the mobs who live in cities, see his *Notes on the State of Virginia*, ed. William Peden (Chapel Hill: University of North Carolina Press, 1955), pp. 164–65. His pastoral idealism stands sharply in contrast to the political maneuvering connected with the expedition in which he became embroiled—on which topic, see Laurie Winn Carlson, *Seduced by the West: Jefferson's America and the Lure of the Land beyond the Mississippi* (Chicago: Dee, 2003).

26. Albanese, *Nature Religion in America*, pp. 64, 65, 66, 67, 69, 70.

27. The idea of the sublime current in Jefferson's time, partly indebted to Edmund Burke's study *A Philosophical Enquiry into the Origin of Our Ideas of the Sublime and Beautiful* (1757), was of a mood, involving awe or even terror as much as an admiration of beauty, stimulated by a sense of vastness, obscurity, power, and the like—a range of qualities readily associated with an unruly wilderness but less so with one under control.

28. Winifred Gallagher, *The Power of Place: How Our Surroundings Shape Our Thoughts, Emotions, and Actions* (New York: Poseidon Press, 1993), p. 222. "From the birth of the republic," Wilbur R. Jacobs asserts, apropos of Jefferson's attitude, "there was an ambivalence about appreciating and protecting nature or exploiting the land" (*The Fatal Confrontation: Historical Studies of American Indians, Environment, and Historians* [Albuquerque: University of New Mexico Press, 1996], pp. 17–18).

29. Lawrence Buell, *The Environmental Imagination: Thoreau, Nature Writing, and the Formation of American Culture* (Cambridge, MA: Belknap Press, 1995), pp. 269, 270.

30. John R. Stilgoe, *Common Landscape of America, 1580 to 1845* (New Haven, CT: Yale University Press, 1982), pp. 106–7. Concerning the ideological implications of disjunctive and

unstable intersections between land as mapped and land as experienced, with reference to the writings of Jefferson and others, see Thomas Hallock, *From the Fallen Tree: Frontier Narratives, Environmental Politics, and the Roots of a National Pastoral, 1749–1826* (Chapel Hill: University of North Carolina Press, 2003).

31. Rita Parks, *The Western Hero in Film and Television: Mass Media Mythology* (Ann Arbor, MI: UMI Research Press, 1982), p. 7.

32. John Logan Allen, *Passage through the Garden: Lewis and Clark and the Image of the American Northwest* (Urbana: University of Illinois Press, 1975), pp. xiii, xxiv.

33. They perused a great deal of other written "lore" relevant to the expedition, of course, including, most notably, seventeenth- and eighteenth-century chronicles and reports, in which "the garden concept was reinforced," from "French missionaries, adventurers, soldiers, and fur traders [who] had sought to find a water passage to the Pacific" (Allen, *Passage through the Garden*, pp. 3, 2).

34. Goetzmann and Goetzmann, *West of the Imagination*, p. 7.

35. See the footnote on Sacagawea's role in *The Journals of Lewis and Clark*, ed. John Bakeless (New York: Mentor, 1964), p. 211. On the whole matter of the expedition's reliance upon Indian assistance for survival as well as success, see James P. Ronda, *Lewis and Clark among the Indians* (Lincoln: University of Nebraska Press, 1984).

36. Allen, *Passage through the Garden*, p. 395.

37. William H. Goetzmann, *Exploration and Empire: The Explorer and the Scientist in the Winning of the American West* (1966; reprint ed., Austin: Texas State Historical Association, 1993), p. 8.

38. Ibid. The report, edited by Nicholas Biddle, was published in 1814 as, to use the short form of the title, *The Journals of the Expedition under the Command of Capts. Lewis and Clark*.

39. Stephen E. Ambrose, *Undaunted Courage: Meriwether Lewis, Thomas Jefferson, and the Opening of the American West* (New York: Touchstone, 1997), pp. 139, 152, 150.

40. *The Journals of the Lewis and Clark Expedition*, ed. Gary E. Moulton, vol. 2 (Lincoln: University of Nebraska Press, 1986), pp. 330, 346. Donald Jackson stresses that Lewis and Clark "were army men going by the book" and that those in their group who had had military experience understood well that "the importance of whiskey to the morale of the men" was such that stealing it, apart from any other infraction, could lead to a court-martial and the lash (*Thomas Jefferson and the Stony Mountains: Exploring the West from Monticello* [Urbana: University of Illinois Press, 1981], pp. 164, 168).

41. *Journals of the Lewis and Clark Expedition*, ed. Moulton, 2: 428.

42. Of asperities of all sorts there were many, starting, most tryingly, with the wretched winter of 1804–05; yet none of them definitively "create[d] an image of harshness or hostility for Lewis and Clark, and the strength of the garden image did not diminish" (Allen, *Passage through the Garden*, p. 201)—such was the power of "the geography of the mind" to maintain their double awareness of the wilderness.

43. Ambrose, *Undaunted Courage*, pp. 213, 216.

44. Donald A. Barclay, James H. Maguire, and Peter Wild, Epilogue, *Into the Wilderness Dream: Exploration Narratives of the American West, 1500–1805*, ed. Donald A. Barclay, James H. Maguire, and Peter Wild (Salt Lake City: University of Utah Press, 1994), p. 383.

45. Richard White, *"It's Your Misfortune and None of My Own": A New History of the American West* (Norman: University of Oklahoma Press, 1991), p. 119.

46. White, "Are You an Environmentalist?" p. 176.

47. Richard W. Etulain, *Re-imagining the Modern American West: A Century of Fiction, History, and Art* (Tucson: University of Arizona Press, 1996), pp. xxii, xxi.

48. Richard C. Poulsen, *The Landscape of the Mind: Cultural Transformations of the American West* (New York: Lang, 1992), pp. 74, 76, 77.

49. Donald Worster, *Under Western Skies: Nature and History in the American West* (New York: Oxford University Press, 1992), pp. 83, 86. The quotation from Clark is from *The Journals of Lewis and Clark*, ed. Bernard DeVoto (Boston: Houghton Mifflin, 1953), p. 14.

50. Thomas J. Lyon, "The Nature Essay in the West," in *A Literary History of the American West*, ed. J. Golden Taylor et al. (Fort Worth: Texas Christian University Press, 1987), pp. 222, 223.

51. *The Journals of the Lewis and Clark Expedition*, ed. Gary E. Moulton, vol. 4 (Lincoln: University of Nebraska Press, 1987), pp. 67, 66, 67.

52. Ibid., p. 78.

53. Ibid., p. 227. Lewis got the taxonomy wrong, however; as Moulton notes, the fox mentioned is "not a distinct species . . ., but a cross fox, a color phase of the red fox, *Vulpes vulpes*" (p. 243). Also, Lewis's construing the landscape in somewhat Greco-Roman terms wasn't unusual. Barbara Novak explains that "the opposition between Europe's antiquity and their own wilderness had given Americans an alternative past," a "natural antiquity" whose brief tradition sometimes drew on the longer one of "cultivated antiquity"—to the extent that "the resulting mixture of themes, associations, and conventions even now tends to defy disentanglement" (*Nature and Culture: American Landscape and Painting, 1825–1875*, rev. ed. [New York: Oxford University Press, 1995], p. 145).

54. Donald Worster, *An Unsettled Country: Changing Landscapes of the American West* (Albuquerque: University of New Mexico Press, 1994), p. 60.

55. Barry Lopez, "Renegotiating the Contracts," *Parabola: Myth and the Quest for Meaning* 8, no. 2 (Spring 1983): 15–16.

56. Worster, *Unsettled Country*, p. 60.

57. Ibid., p. 61.

58. Ibid., p. 62.

59. With respect to that mass, see *Journals of the Lewis and Clark Expedition*, ed. Moulton, 2: 242–43. In essentials, Lewis and Clark subscribed to Jefferson's chain-of-being philosophy, by which, as Jackson summarizes it, "all natural creations were thought to be links in an unbroken chain, from the mineral to the human being" (*Thomas Jefferson and the Stony Mountains*, p. 29)—humans at the top, wildlife a ways down the line. See also Charles A. Miller's discussion of this model in his *Jefferson and Nature: An Interpretation* (Baltimore: Johns Hopkins University Press, 1988), p. 52.

60. *Journals of the Lewis and Clark Expedition*, ed. Moulton, 4: 219.

61. Worster, *Unsettled Country*, p. 62.

62. Ambrose, *Undaunted Courage*, p. 55.

63. Allen, *Passage through the Garden*, p. 4.

64. Ambrose, *Undaunted Courage*, p. 346.

65. Ibid., p. 347.

66. Jackson opines that, "could Jefferson have chosen his own timetable, the policy might have worked, especially if he also could have controlled the temperament and unabating land hunger of the American people" (*Thomas Jefferson and the Stony Mountains*, p. 218)—a large order.

67. Ambrose, *Undaunted Courage*, pp. 347, 348. Jefferson studied and admired Native cultures, but he hardly opposed their being dismantled in the name of westward expansion—an ambivalence that gave rise to destructive problems in the application of his Indian policy, all of which are scrutinized by Anthony F. C. Wallace in his *Jefferson and the Indians: The Tragic Fate of the First Americans* (Cambridge, MA: Belknap Press, 1999).

68. John R. Milton, *The Novel of the American West* (Lincoln: University of Nebraska Press, 1980), p. 72.

69. Frank Bergon, "The Journals of Lewis and Clark: An American Epic," in *Old West–New West: Centennial Essays*, ed. Barbara Howard Meldrum (Moscow: University of Idaho Press, 1993), pp. 143, 144.

70. J. Golden Taylor, "Across the Wide Missouri: The Adventure Narrative from Lewis and Clark to Powell," in *Literary History of the American West*, ed. Taylor et al., p. 71.

71. Kolodny, *Lay of the Land*, p. 67. A germane collection of essays on Jefferson's West and its future is *Thomas Jefferson and the Changing West: From Conquest to Conservation*, ed. James P. Ronda (Albuquerque: University of New Mexico Press; St. Louis: Missouri Historical Society Press, 1997).

72. Ambrose, *Undaunted Courage*, p. 483. See also Carlson, *Seduced by the West*, pp. 168–87.

73. Faragher, *Daniel Boone*, pp. 335–36.

74. Albanese, *Nature Religion in America*, p. 75.

75. Ibid., p. 74.

76. Richard Slotkin, *The Fatal Environment: The Myth of the Frontier in the Age of Industrialization, 1800–1890* (New York: Atheneum, 1985), p. 169.

77. Slotkin, *Regeneration through Violence*, p. 125.

78. Albanese, *Nature Religion in America*, p. 75.

79. Ibid., pp. 75, 78.

80. "The Ballad of Davy Crockett," rec. 1954, on vol. 2 of *The Disney Collection*, Walt Disney Records, audiocassette 60817-0, 1991. Faragher rightly suspects that Fess Parker's playing the role of Crockett in Disney's 1950s Crockett series and then "replaying" that role as Boone in its 1960s Boone series "is largely responsible for the persistent popular confusion that exists today between these two frontier heroes" (*Daniel Boone*, p. 339)—a confusion that says worlds about the public's ignorance of the range and complexity of attitudes toward the Western wild that have shaped its history.

81. Carroll Smith-Rosenberg, "Davy Crockett as Trickster: Pornography, Liminality, and Symbolic Inversion in Victorian America," in *Disorderly Conduct: Visions of Gender in Victorian America* (1985; reprint ed., New York: Oxford University Press, 1986), pp. 92, 93, 101, 107.

Mountain Men and Other Explorers: The Vanguard of Western Exploitation

1. Howard R. Lamar, "An Overview of Westward Expansion," in *The West as America: Reinterpreting Images of the Frontier, 1820–1920*, ed. William H. Truettner (Washington, DC: Smithsonian Institution Press, 1991), p. 3.

2. Ibid., p. 1.

3. Ian Frazier, *Great Plains* (New York: Penguin Books, 1990), p. 176. For accounts, true and otherwise, of that woolly lifeway, see *A Rendezvous Reader: Tall, Tangled, and True Tales of the Mountain Men, 1805–1850*, ed. James H. Maguire, Peter Wild, and Donald A. Barclay (Salt Lake City: University of Utah Press, 1997), and David Dary, *Seeking Pleasure in the Old West* (Lawrence: University Press of Kansas, 1995), pp. 22–33.

4. Winfred Blevins, *Dictionary of the American West* (New York: Facts on File, 1993), s.v. "mountain man."

5. See, for example, Richard White, *"It's Your Misfortune and None of My Own": A New History of the American West* (Norman: University of Oklahoma Press, 1991), pp. 46–47, and Elliott West, *The Contested Plains: Indians, Goldseekers, and the Rush to Colorado* (Lawrence: University Press of Kansas, 1998), pp. 80–81. A classic treatment of the workings of the fur trade is Hiram Martin Chittenden, *The American Fur Trade of the Far West: A History of the Pioneer Trading Posts and Early Fur Companies of the Missouri Valley and the Rocky Mountains and of the Overland Commerce with Santa Fe*, 2 vols. (1902; reprint ed., Stanford, CA: Academic Reprints, 1954). For a more ecologically oriented study, see Mari Sandoz, *The Beaver Men: Spearheads of Empire* (New York: Hastings House, 1964).

6. Richard Slotkin, *Regeneration through Violence: The Mythology of the American Frontier, 1600–1860* (1973; reprint ed., New York: HarperPerennial, 1996), p. 417.

7. William H. Goetzmann, *Exploration and Empire: The Explorer and the Scientist in the Winning of the American West* (1966; reprint ed., Austin: Texas State Historical Association, 1993), pp. 106, 107.

8. Ray Allen Billington, *Land of Savagery, Land of Promise: The European Image of the American Frontier in the Nineteenth Century* (New York: Norton, 1981), p. 162.

9. Goetzmann, *Exploration and Empire*, pp. 107, 108.

10. White, *"It's Your Misfortune and None of My Own,"* pp. 47–48.

11. Relevant here is James P. Ronda's designation of South Pass as a place, like others in the West, "more dream and idea than precisely located point on the map," one that elicited the complex spectrum of emotions—"anticipation, anxiety, expectation, disappointment, and jubilation"—that figured in the "often painful tension between moving on and staying put" ("Dreaming the Pass: The Western Imagination and the Landscape of South Pass," in *The Big Empty: Essays on Western Landscapes as Narrative*, ed. Leonard Engel [Albuquerque: University of New Mexico Press, 1994], pp. 8, 18, 22).

12. Osborne Russell, *Journal of a Trapper*, ed. Aubrey L. Haines (Lincoln: University of Nebraska Press, 1965), p. 46.

13. J. Golden Taylor, "Across the Wide Missouri: The Adventure Narrative from Lewis and Clark to Powell," in *A Literary History of the American West*, ed. J. Golden Taylor et al. (Fort Worth: Texas Christian University Press, 1987), p. 82.

14. West, *Contested Plains*, p. 183.

15. Richard C. Poulsen, *The Landscape of the Mind: Cultural Transformations of the American West* (New York: Lang, 1992), pp. 59, 60, 70.

16. Ibid., pp. 71, 77, 78.

17. William H. Truettner, "Ideology and Image: Justifying Westward Expansion," in *West as America*, ed. Truettner, p. 42.

18. Goetzmann, *Exploration and Empire*, pp. 144, 145.

19. Thomas J. Lyon, "The Nature Essay in the West," in *Literary History of the American West*, ed. Taylor et al., p. 228.

20. Henry Nash Smith, *Virgin Land: The American West as Symbol and Myth* (1950; reprint ed., Cambridge, MA: Harvard University Press, 1970), pp. 84, 85, 86, 88, 89.

21. Alex Nemerov, "'Doing the "Old America"': The Image of the American West, 1880–1920," in *West as America*, ed. Truettner, p. 328.

22. David Daly and Joel Persky, *The West and the Western*, a special issue of *Journal of the West* 29, no. 2 (April 1990): 41. A balanced study of Carson's relations with Indians as his

sympathies and allegiances played back and forth between them and his own people is Tom Dunlay's *Kit Carson and the Indians* (Lincoln: University of Nebraska Press, 2000), which concludes that he "lived most of his life, physically and psychologically, in the middle ground," a place that proved increasingly insecure for him (p. 458).

23. Goetzmann, *Exploration and Empire*, pp. 148, 153, 155.

24. Richard Dankleff, "California," in *Westerns* (Corvallis: Oregon State University Press, 1984), p. 84.

25. Zenas Leonard, *Narrative of the Adventures of Zenas Leonard*, ed. Milo Milton Quaife (1934; reprint ed., Lincoln: University of Nebraska Press, 1978), p. 154.

26. Goetzmann, *Exploration and Empire*, p. 181. For an extended discussion of Long's several expeditions, including that of 1820, and the changes they wrought in the image of the West, see Roger L. Nichols and Patrick L. Halley, *Stephen Long and American Frontier Exploration* (1980; reprint ed., Norman: University of Oklahoma Press, 1995).

27. Goetzmann, *Exploration and Empire*, pp. 198, 231.

28. Lamar, "Overview of Westward Expansion," p. 1.

29. Frederick Turner, *Beyond Geography: The Western Spirit against the Wilderness* (1980; reprint ed., New Brunswick, NJ: Rutgers University Press, 1992), p. 258.

30. William H. Goetzmann and William N. Goetzmann, *The West of the Imagination* (New York: Norton, 1986), p. 82.

31. Lyon, "Nature Essay in the West," p. 229.

32. J. C. Frémont, *Report of the Exploring Expedition to the Rocky Mountains in the Year 1842, and to Oregon and North California in the Years 1843–'44* (Washington, DC: U.S. Congress, 1845), p. 66.

33. Lyon, "Nature Essay in the West," p. 262.

34. Goetzmann, *Exploration and Empire*, p. 257.

35. See John Tallmadge, "Toward a Natural History of Reading," *Interdisciplinary Studies in Literature and Environment* 7, no. 1 (Winter 2000): 39–42, especially his discussion of King's descriptions "as combinations of physiographic fact and cultural artifact" (p. 42).

36. Donald Worster unearths considerable "ambivalence and contradiction" in Powell's attitude toward the natural West, noting, for instance, that "he called for . . . transforming the arid lands into an agricultural empire, though at the same time he extolled the wilderness and criticized ruthless corporations" (*A River Running West: The Life of John Wesley Powell* [New York: Oxford University Press, 2001], p. xi).

37. See Goetzmann, *Exploration and Empire*, pp. 496, 498.

38. Lyon, "Nature Essay in the West," p. 233. Despite Dutton's efforts to avoid his culture's categories of perception and expression, he "could not resist," as Worster notes, "trying to pull the canyon into some more familiar, cultural frame of reference," and so he drew on "ancient pagan religions" and the names of well-known scientists for his non-Christian christenings (*River Running West*, pp. 326, 327); thus came about Vishnu's Temple, Darwin Plateau, and the like.

39. Goetzmann and Goetzmann, *West of the Imagination*, pp. 12, 103.

40. Barbara Novak, *Nature and Culture: American Landscape and Painting, 1825–1875*, rev. ed. (New York: Oxford University Press, 1995), pp. 4, 5.

41. Goetzmann, *Exploration and Empire*, pp. 187, 191.

42. Julie Schimmel, "Inventing 'the Indian,'" in *West as America*, ed. Truettner, pp. 149, 154.

43. Ibid., pp. 154, 155.

44. See Hans Huth, *Nature and the American: Three Centuries of Changing Attitudes*, new ed. (Lincoln: University of Nebraska Press, 1990), pp. 134–36, for a discussion of Catlin's visionary commitment to preserving "the primeval glories of nature" (p. 134) toward whose end he was paradoxically laboring.

45. Goetzmann and Goetzmann, *West of the Imagination*, p. 68.

46. See Nancy K. Anderson, "'The Kiss of Enterprise': The Western Landscape as Symbol and Resource," in *West as America*, ed. Truettner, p. 254.

47. Alexis de Tocqueville, *Journey to America*, rev. and augm. ed., trans. George Lawrence, ed. J. P. Mayer (Garden City, NY: Anchor Books, 1971), pp. 399–400, 399. Such thoughts and feelings weren't unusual among early artists of the West, whose writings, as may be seen in *Different Travellers, Different Eyes: Artists' Narratives of the American West, 1820–1920*, ed. Peter Wild, Donald A. Barclay, and James H. Maguire (Fort Worth: Texas Christian University Press, 2001), sometimes express sentiments that contrast strongly to those expressed in their paintings.

48. Huth, *Nature and the American*, p. 141.

49. Lee Clark Mitchell, *Westerns: Making the Man in Fiction and Film* (Chicago: University of Chicago Press, 1996), pp. 64, 71.

50. Goetzmann and Goetzmann, *West of the Imagination*, p. 182.

51. Novak, *Nature and Culture*, p. 151.

52. Taylor, "Across the Wide Missouri," p. 95.

53. A. Carl Bredahl Jr., *New Ground: Western American Narrative and the Literary Canon* (Chapel Hill: University of North Carolina Press, 1989), pp. 36, 42. Given the sensibility dominant in Parkman's book, it's not surprising that he, like other writers of his day, betrays "uncertainty about the character of the West" as either a desert or the Promised Land (Huth, *Nature and the American*, p. 131)—nor is it surprising that in his later works he celebrates the subjugation of the Indian.

54. Hal K. Rothman, *Devil's Bargains: Tourism in the Twentieth-Century West* (Lawrence: University Press of Kansas, 1998), pp. 32, 35, 40.

55. Oakley Hall, *Separations* (Reno: University of Nevada Press, 1997), pp. 101, 225.

56. Jack Turner, "Economic Nature," in *The Abstract Wild* (Tucson: University of Arizona Press, 1996), p. 55. The standard work on the surveys and how they redescribed the West is Richard A. Bartlett's *Great Surveys of the American West* (1962; reprint ed., Norman: University of Oklahoma Press, 1980). See also Richard Manning's discussion of Powell and his frustrations in opposing the rectilinear dicing up of Western land in his *Grassland: The History, Biology, Politics, and Promise of the American Prairie* (New York: Viking, 1995), pp. 106–9.

57. Angie Debo, *A History of the Indians of the United States* (Norman: University of Oklahoma Press, 1970), p. 4.

58. White, *"It's Your Misfortune and None of My Own,"* p. 212.

59. Frank Waters, *The Colorado* (New York: Farrar and Rinehart, 1946), p. 275.

60. T. S. Eliot, "Little Gidding," in *Collected Poems, 1909–1962* (San Diego: Harcourt Brace Jovanovich, 1963), p. 208.

Inventing the Indian: The Noble Savage

1. Frederick Turner, *Beyond Geography: The Western Spirit against the Wilderness* (1980; reprint ed., New Brunswick, NJ: Rutgers University Press, 1992), p. 209.

2. Elliott West, *The Contested Plains: Indians, Goldseekers, and the Rush to Colorado* (Lawrence: University Press of Kansas, 1998), p. 17.

3. Ray Allen Billington, *Land of Savagery, Land of Promise: The European Image of the American Frontier in the Nineteenth Century* (New York: Norton, 1981), pp. 9, 13. There's ample evidence that, regardless of the fashionability of that revolt, much difference and ambivalence of opinion flourished, a point made by Robert Berkhofer Jr. in *The White Man's Indian: Images of the American Indian from Columbus to the Present* (1978; reprint ed., New York: Vintage Books, 1979), where he argues, for instance, that John Locke's opposition to Thomas Hobbes's "equating nature with a state of war" is indicative of "the ambivalence of imagery" that English social philosophers associated with the generic Native American (p. 22).

4. It's wise to remember in any discussion of white people's inventing images of "wild" Indians that Indians invented images of "civilized" white people, too. Though it's beyond my scope in this book, a full-blown typological study of those images, never undertaken as far as I know, ought to be done. Such a study would help us understand how all along, to borrow from Berkhofer, "both sides [have] exhibited behavior that confirmed previous stereotypes of each other" (*White Man's Indian*, p. 18).

5. Geoffrey Symcox, "The Wild Man's Return: The Enclosed Vision of Rousseau's Discourses," in *The Wild Man Within: An Image in Western Thought from the Renaissance to Romanticism*, ed. Edward Dudley and Maximillian E. Novak (Pittsburgh, PA: University of Pittsburgh Press, 1972), pp. 224, 244. On Columbus's contribution to the Noble Savage myth—and his subsequent dubiety about the nobility of the Indians he encountered—see Tzvetan Todorov, *The Conquest of America: The Question of the Other*, trans. Richard Howard (New York: Harper and Row, 1984), pp. 39–40.

6. Hayden White, "The Forms of Wildness: Archaeology of an Idea," in *Wild Man Within*, ed. Dudley and Novak, p. 28.

7. James K. Folsom, "Precursors of the Western Novel," in *A Literary History of the American West*, ed. J. Golden Taylor et al. (Fort Worth: Texas Christian University Press, 1987), p. 143.

8. Symcox, "Wild Man's Return," p. 227.

9. Richard Slotkin, *Regeneration through Violence: The Mythology of the American Frontier, 1600–1860* (1973; reprint ed., New York: HarperPerennial, 1996), pp. 203, 204, 205.

10. Roy Harvey Pearce, *Savagism and Civilization: A Study of the Indian and the American Mind* (Baltimore: Johns Hopkins Press, 1967), pp. 48, 138, 179.

11. Lawrence Buell, *The Environmental Imagination: Thoreau, Nature Writing, and the Formation of American Culture* (Cambridge, MA: Belknap Press, 1995), p. 21.

12. Richard C. Poulsen, *The Landscape of the Mind: Cultural Transformations of the American West* (New York: Lang, 1992), p. 37.

13. Gary B. Nash, "The Image of the Indian in the Southern Colonial Mind," in *Wild Man Within*, ed. Dudley and Novak, pp. 60, 61.

14. Ibid., p. 79.

15. Pearce, *Savagism and Civilization*, p. 232.

16. Roderick Nash, *Wilderness and the American Mind*, 3rd ed. (New Haven, CT: Yale University Press, 1982), p. 65.

17. West, *Contested Plains*, p. 187.

18. Julie Schimmel, "Inventing 'the Indian,'" in *The West as America: Reinterpreting Images of the Frontier, 1820–1920*, ed. William H. Truettner (Washington, DC: Smithsonian Institution Press, 1991), p. 157.

19. Pearce, *Savagism and Civilization*, pp. 48–49.

20. Patricia Nelson Limerick, *The Legacy of Conquest: The Unbroken Past of the American West* (New York: Norton, 1987), p. 190.

21. Peter L. Thorslev Jr., "The Wild Man's Revenge," in *Wild Man Within*, ed. Dudley and Novak, pp. 285, 284.

22. See William H. Goetzmann, *Exploration and Empire: The Explorer and the Scientist in the Winning of the American West* (1966; reprint ed., Austin: Texas State Historical Association, 1993), p. 628. The picture flirts with the centuries-old iconography of America (in this case, the West) as an Indian maiden.

23. N. Scott Momaday, "The Morality of Indian Hating," in *The Man Made of Words: Essays, Stories, Passages* (New York: St. Martin's Press, 1997), p. 58.

24. The reader should keep in mind the difference between the term *Romantic* (with an uppercase r), which refers to a multifaceted movement against neoclassicism, and the term *romantic* (with a lowercase r), which—though it has other applications in my text—I use in this context to refer figuratively to the romance, here a historical one in which the Indian plays a decidedly antagonistic role. The semantic fields of the two terms may overlap, of course.

Trails and Trials: The Inroads of Commerce

1. Bryan J. Wolf, "How the West Was Hung; or, When I Hear the Word 'Culture' I Take Out My Checkbook," *American Quarterly* 44 (1992): 437.

2. Gundars Rudzitis, *Wilderness and the Changing American West* (New York: Wiley, 1996), p. 124.

3. William G. Robbins, *Colony and Empire: The Capitalist Transformation of the American West* (Lawrence: University Press of Kansas, 1994), pp. x, xii.

4. Richard White, "Trashing the Trails," in *Trails: Toward a New Western History*, ed. Patricia Nelson Limerick, Clyde A. Milner II, and Charles E. Rankin (Lawrence: University Press of Kansas, 1991), p. 28.

5. See *The Oxford English Dictionary*, s.v. "commerce."

6. David Dary, *Entrepreneurs of the Old West* (New York: Knopf, 1986), pp. ix, 10.

7. Zebulon Montgomery Pike, *The Journals of Zebulon Montgomery Pike*, ed. Donald Jackson, 2 vols. (Norman: University of Oklahoma Press, 1966), 2: 28.

8. Dary, *Entrepreneurs of the Old West*, p. 12.

9. Frederick Turner, *Beyond Geography: The Western Spirit against the Wilderness* (1980; reprint ed., New Brunswick, NJ: Rutgers University Press, 1992), p. 279.

10. Ibid., p. 282.

11. Larry McMurtry, *Dead Man's Walk* (New York: Simon and Schuster, 1995), pp. 82, 79.

12. Dary, *Entrepreneurs of the Old West*, p. 18. See also Dary's *The Santa Fe Trail: Its History, Legends, and Lore* (New York: Knopf, 2000), in which he discusses, among other matters, not only Anglos' trading in Santa Fe but also Mexicans' trading in Missouri and further east, even in Europe.

13. Howard R. Lamar, "An Overview of Westward Expansion," in *The West as America: Reinterpreting Images of the Frontier, 1820–1920*, ed. William H. Truettner (Washington, DC: Smithsonian Institution Press, 1991), p. 10.

14. Josiah Gregg, *Commerce of the Prairies*, ed. Max L. Moorhead (Norman: University of Oklahoma Press, 1954), pp. 14, 15, 16, 23, 29.

15. Donald Worster, *Under Western Skies: Nature and History in the American West* (New York: Oxford University Press, 1992), pp. 3–4.

16. Gregg, *Commerce of the Prairies*, p. 362.

17. Richard C. Poulsen, *The Landscape of the Mind: Cultural Transformations of the American West* (New York: Lang, 1992), pp. 33, 34.

18. Gregg, *Commerce of the Prairies*, pp. 328–29, 330.

19. Lamar, "Overview of Westward Expansion," p. 12.

20. See White, "Trashing the Trails," p. 26.

21. Elizabeth Johns, "Settlement and Development: Claiming the West," in *West as America*, ed. Truettner, p. 218.

22. Elliott West, *The Contested Plains: Indians, Goldseekers, and the Rush to Colorado* (Lawrence: University Press of Kansas, 1998), pp. 215, 225. For background on the impact of stage travel and freighting, see Ralph Moody, *Stagecoach West* (1967; reprint ed., Lincoln: University of Nebraska Press, 1998), and Henry P. Walker, *The Wagonmasters: High Plains Freighting from the Earliest Days of the Santa Fe Trail to 1880* (Norman: University of Oklahoma Press, 1966).

23. Dee Brown, *The American West* (New York: Touchstone, 1995), p. 59.

24. Poulsen, *Landscape of the Mind*, pp. 84–85, 86, 89.

25. West, *Contested Plains*, pp. 117, 129.

26. White, "Trashing the Trails," p. 39.

27. David Binkley, quoted in Jan Biles, "From Ritual to Retail: Fred Harvey Company Helps Invent the Image of Southwestern Art," *Lawrence Journal-World*, 2 November 1997, p. 1D. For a collection of discussions pertinent to this ritual-to-retail transformation, see the symposium volume prepared in connection with the exhibition, *The Great Southwest of the Fred Harvey Company and the Santa Fe Railway*, ed. Marta Weigle and Barbara A. Babcock (Phoenix, AZ: Heard Museum, 1996).

28. Richard Dankleff, "Route 56," in *Westerns* (Corvallis: Oregon State University Press, 1984), p. 47.

29. Gary Snyder, "On the Path, off the Trail," in *The Practice of the Wild* (New York: North Point Press, 1990), p. 154.

PART THREE: FROM THE 1840S TO THE 1890S: THE WEST AS FRONTIER
Prelude and Overview

1. Richard Slotkin, *The Fatal Environment: The Myth of the Frontier in the Age of Industrialization, 1800–1890* (New York: Atheneum, 1985), pp. 37, 40. For a fuller treatment of the West as multiple frontiers, see Robert V. Hine and John Mack Faragher's synthesizing revisionist study *The American West: A New Interpretive History* (New Haven, CT: Yale University Press, 2000).

2. David Mogen, "Wilderness, Metamorphosis, and Millennium: Gothic Apocalypse from the Puritans to the Cyberpunks," in *Frontier Gothic: Terror and Wonder at the Frontier in American Literature*, ed. David Mogen, Scott P. Sanders, and Joanne B. Karpinski (Rutherford, NJ: Fairleigh Dickinson University Press, 1993), p. 106.

3. Concerning the development of the optimistic ideals that motivated the enlarging settlement of the West, see William H. Goetzmann, *When the Eagle Screamed: The Romantic Horizon in American Expansionism, 1800–1860* (1966; reprint ed., Norman: University of Oklahoma Press, 2000).

4. Christopher A. Conte, review of *Environment and History: The Taming of Nature in the USA and South Africa*, by William Beinart and Peter Coates, *Western Historical Quarterly* 28 (1997): 246.

5. Richard Slotkin, *Gunfighter Nation: The Myth of the Frontier in Twentieth-Century America* (1992; reprint ed., New York: HarperPerennial, 1993), pp. 11, 12, 14.

6. Richard White, *"It's Your Misfortune and None of My Own": A New History of the American West* (Norman: University of Oklahoma Press, 1991), p. 620.

7. Walter Crockett to Dr. Black, 15 October 1853, University of Washington Library. The letter is quoted, without notation of a specific collection or depository, in Richard White, "Trashing the Trails," in *Trails: Toward a New Western History,* ed. Patricia Nelson Limerick, Clyde A. Milner II, and Charles E. Rankin (Lawrence: University Press of Kansas, 1991), p. 33.

8. Gerald F. Kreyche, *Visions of the American West* (Lexington: University Press of Kentucky, 1989), p. 5.

9. Ibid.

10. For a broad consideration of sweeping change, technological and otherwise, in the late-nineteenth-century West, see Rodman W. Paul, *The Far West and the Great Plains in Transition, 1859–1900* (New York: Harper and Row, 1988).

Settlement and Its Discontents

1. William Cullen Bryant, "The Prairies," in *Poetical Works of William Cullen Bryant* (New York: Appleton, 1882), pp. 130, 133.

2. Elliott West, *The Contested Plains: Indians, Goldseekers, and the Rush to Colorado* (Lawrence: University Press of Kansas, 1998), p. 46.

3. Rita Parks, *The Western Hero in Film and Television: Mass Media Mythology* (Ann Arbor, MI: UMI Research Press, 1982), pp. 10, 11. Though Parks's point is well taken, it's nevertheless true that many Easterners and, especially, Europeans held the pioneers in high esteem as champions of civilization; there was more ambivalence than she allows. The result, as Ray Allen Billington notes, "was a dual image of the pioneer farmer that persisted for most of the nineteenth century" (*Land of Savagery, Land of Promise: The European Image of the American Frontier in the Nineteenth Century* [New York: Norton, 1981], p. 176).

4. Frederick Turner, *Beyond Geography: The Western Spirit against the Wilderness* (1980; reprint ed., New Brunswick, NJ: Rutgers University Press, 1992), pp. 261–62. Citing examples of European visitors' amazement at how fast the pioneers transformed the land, Billington offers several eye-opening juxtapositions, among them this one: "So hurried was the transformation that . . . visitors could step from an untamed forest into a store stocked with silks from Paris" (*Land of Savagery, Land of Promise,* p. 179).

5. Francis Parkman, quoted in Wilbur R. Jacobs, "Francis Parkman's Oration 'Romance in America,'" *American Historical Review* 68 (1963): 696. Jacobs found the original manuscript of Parkman's oration "lodged among his papers in the Harvard College Library" (p. 692).

6. Roderick Nash, *Wilderness and the American Mind,* 3rd ed. (New Haven, CT: Yale University Press, 1982), p. 99.

7. Matilda Armstrong Steele, quoted in Joanna L. Stratton, *Pioneer Women: Voices from the Kansas Frontier* (New York: Touchstone, 1982), p. 100.

8. Walter McDonald, "Steeples and Deep Wells," in *Where the Skies Are Not Cloudy* (Denton: University of North Texas Press, 1993), p. 7.

9. Lawrence Buell, *The Environmental Imagination: Thoreau, Nature Writing, and the Formation of American Culture* (Cambridge, MA: Belknap Press, 1995), p. 57.

10. Richard C. Poulsen, *The Landscape of the Mind: Cultural Transformations of the American West* (New York: Lang, 1992), p. 115.

11. The settler's position on agricultural intervention in the natural world is made clear in an old joke about a preacher who looks over a prosperous farmer's spread and compliments him on how he and the Lord have done such a fine job of growing corn, raising hogs, and such, pushing the farmer to lose his patience and counter, "Listen, preacher, you should've seen this place when God was runnin' it all by Himself!"

12. In his discussion of late-nineteenth-century California settlers' "attempt to graft a midwestern society onto the most Western of states," Timothy Egan tells of how they brought "gables and picket fences to a place where people lived more comfortably behind mud and mortar," among other examples of architectural impositions (*Lasso the Wind: Away to the West* [New York: Knopf, 1998], p. 239).

13. Poulsen, *Landscape of the Mind*, p. 34. I agree with Hans Huth that the ax (broadax and otherwise) became "accepted as the appropriate symbol of the early American attitude toward nature" (*Nature and the American: Three Centuries of Changing Attitudes*, new ed. [Lincoln: University of Nebraska Press, Bison Books, 1990], p. 2), but I'd argue that the plow is the more appropriate symbol of the early Western American attitude.

14. Richard White, *"It's Your Misfortune and None of My Own": A New History of the American West* (Norman: University of Oklahoma Press, 1991), pp. 181, 184.

15. Frieda Knobloch, *The Culture of Wilderness: Agriculture as Colonization in the American West* (Chapel Hill: University of North Carolina Press, 1996), pp. 2, 3. A number of Mary Hallock Foote's drawings illuminate both Knobloch's discussion here and mine earlier in this chapter—see, for instance, *The Coming of Winter* (1989), with its schematic (but unstable) division between culture and nature and its ominous clarity about the incompleteness of the latter's transformation into the former.

16. Knobloch, *Culture of Wilderness*, p. 5.

17. Ibid., p. 8. Concerning Annette Kolodny's argument, see her book *The Land before Her: Fantasy and Experience of the American Frontiers, 1630–1860* (Chapel Hill: University of North Carolina Press, 1984).

18. George Berkeley, "Verses on the Prospect of Planting Arts and Learning in America," in *Eighteenth Century Poetry and Prose*, 2nd ed., ed. Louis I. Bredvold, Alan D. McKillop, and Lois Whitney (New York: Ronald Press, 1956), p. 308.

19. West, *Contested Plains*, pp. 326, 325, 326. This illusion often merged with one furthered by promoters, that the West had already been tamed—concerning which, see David M. Wrobel, *Promised Lands: Promotion, Memory, and the Creation of the American West* (Lawrence: University Press of Kansas, 2002).

20. Carolyn Merchant, "Reinventing Eden: Western Culture as a Recovery Narrative," in *Uncommon Ground: Rethinking the Human Place in Nature*, ed. William Cronon (New York: Norton, 1995), pp. 142, 147.

21. Oakley Hall, *Separations* (Reno: University of Nevada Press, 1997), p. 204. Cf. Barbara Novak's observation that in Thomas Cole's paintings "the cut stump suggests a new iconology of progress and destruction" (*Nature and Culture: American Landscape and Painting, 1825–1875*, rev. ed. [New York: Oxford University Press, 1995], p. 161).

22. Patricia Nelson Limerick, "The Shadows of Heaven Itself," in *Atlas of the New West: Portrait of a Changing Region*, ed. William E. Riebsame et al. (New York: Norton, 1997), pp. 152–53.

23. John Ise, "Pioneering Life in Western Kansas," in *Economics, Sociology and the Modern World: Essays in Honor of T. N. Carver*, ed. Norman E. Himes (Cambridge, MA: Harvard University Press, 1935), p. 143.

24. Helen Vendler, *Seamus Heaney* (Cambridge, MA: Harvard University Press, 1998), p. 26.

To California Go: The Thar in Them Thar Hills

1. See Michael P. Malone, *The Battle for Butte: Mining and Politics on the Northern Frontier, 1864–1906* (Seattle: University of Washington Press, 1981).

2. J. E. Cirlot, *A Dictionary of Symbols*, trans. Jack Sage (New York: Philosophical Library, 1962), s.v. "gold."

3. John Wilmerding, "The Luminist Movement: Some Reflections," in *American Light: The Luminist Movement, 1850–1875*, ed. John Wilmerding (New York: Harper and Row; Washington, DC: National Gallery of Art, 1980), pp. 96, 97.

4. Elliott West, *The Contested Plains: Indians, Goldseekers, and the Rush to Colorado* (Lawrence: University Press of Kansas, 1998), pp. 97–98, 336.

5. Richard Rodriguez, "True West," in *The Anchor Essay Annual: The Best of 1997*, ed. Phillip Lopate (New York: Anchor Books, 1997), p. 329.

6. Gary Snyder, "What Happened Here Before," in *Turtle Island* (New York: New Directions, 1974), p. 78.

7. Michael Kowalewski, Introduction, *Gold Rush: A Literary Exploration*, ed. Michael Kowalewski (Berkeley, CA: Heyday Books, 1997), p. xiv.

8. Malcolm J. Rohrbough, *Days of Gold: The California Gold Rush and the American Nation* (Berkeley: University of California Press, 1997), p. 9. Soon the Indians, who sometimes competed with whites in panning for gold, would be exploited, displaced, and killed ruthlessly.

9. Snyder, "What Happened Here Before," p. 79.

10. Leonard Lutwack, *The Role of Place in Literature* (Syracuse, NY: Syracuse University Press, 1984), p. 149.

11. Reverend Randall Hobart and Elmon S. Camp, quoted in *The Gold Rush: Letters from the Wolverine Rangers to the "Marshall, Michigan, Statesman," 1849–1851* (Mount Pleasant, MI: Cumming Press, 1974), pp. 123, 138, 145. Accounts of the difficulties encountered in traveling to the gold fields may be found in *Journals of Forty-Niners: Salt Lake to Los Angeles*, ed. LeRoy R. Hafen and Ann W. Hafen (Lincoln: University of Nebraska Press, 1998). The entire cycle of the rush is documented, mostly through the diary and letters of William Swain, in J. S. Holliday, *The World Rushed In: The California Gold Rush Experience* (1981; reprint ed., Lawrence: University Press of Kansas, 2002). The culturally bewildered world in and around the mining camps has been repeatedly portrayed novelistically in the last century and a half, beginning with John Rollin Ridge's *The Life and Adventures of Joaquín Murieta, the Celebrated California Bandit* (1854; reprint ed., Norman: University of Oklahoma Press, 1955). A recent example is Naida West's *River of Red Gold* (Rancho Murieta, CA: Bridge House Books, 1996). One of the best historical studies of that world is Susan Lee Johnson's *Roaring Camp: The Social World of the California Gold Rush* (New York: Norton, 2000). A classic, if dated, study that provides broad background on this rush and others in the West is William S. Greever's *Bonanza West: The Story of the Western Mining Rushes, 1848–1900* (1963; reprint ed., Moscow: University of Idaho Press, 1986).

12. See David Goodman, *Gold Seeking: Victoria and California in the 1850s* (Stanford, CA: Stanford University Press, 1994), pp. xxviii–xxix.

13. Bayard Taylor, *Eldorado; or, Adventures in the Path of Empire* (1850; reprint ed., New York: Knopf, 1949), pp. 87–88, 44.

14. Goodman, *Gold Seeking*, p. 206.

15. Rohrbough, *Days of Gold*, pp. 10, 11, 12, 15.

16. John McPhee, *Assembling California* (New York: Noonday Press, 1994), p. 59. Charles Nahl's 1872 oil *Sunday Morning in the Mines* offers a corroborative depiction of miner rowdiness. It features drinking, an unruly poker game, gunplay, horse racing, even (at the far right) a somewhat homoerotic laundering scene—though elsewhere in the picture one man is reading the Bible and another diligently writing a letter home. On the whole, then, Nahl's scene is ambivalent, "a synthesis," as Tara Penry notes, "with dissolute men in the vast, uncivilized spaces of the West on the left-hand side . . . and hard-working, home-loving miners . . . on the right" ("Manly Domesticity on the Gold Rush Frontier: Recovering California's Honest Miner," *Western American Literature* 38 [2004]: 331).

17. Bill Barich, *Big Dreams: Into the Heart of California* (New York: Pantheon Books, 1994), pp. 167–68.

18. Goodman, *Gold Seeking*, pp. xiv, xvii.

19. Kowalewski, Introduction, p. xvii.

20. Ibid., pp. xix, xx.

21. John Muir, *The Mountains of California*, 2 vols. (1894; reprint ed., Boston: Houghton Mifflin, 1916), 2: 62, 63. Muir was not without ambivalence in his portrayal of miners—see Nicolas Witschi's "John of the Mines: Muir's Picturesque Rewrite of the Gold Rush," *Western American Literature* 34 (1999): 316–43, which shows how, in some of his writings, though "unambiguous in his contempt for the methods and side effects of mineral extraction," Muir nonetheless "naturalizes not only the figures and relics of the Gold Rush but the Gold Rush itself" (pp. 320, 330). Twain too isn't free of ambivalence: though he marks well the damages of mining in *Roughing It* (and rails against the tawdry materialism associated with it in *The Gilded Age* [1873]), "the expectation of a sudden bonanza remained dear to his heart" (Richard Slotkin, *The Fatal Environment: The Myth of the Frontier in the Age of Industrialization, 1800–1890* [New York: Atheneum, 1985], p. 519). And Harte isn't consistent in his depiction of mining as degrading; for instance, in his story "The Luck of Roaring Camp," first published in 1868, ten years before *The Story of a Mine*, he portrays the early California miners, in Blake Allmendinger's convincing against-the-grain interpretation, not as "conquering the land" but as existing "with mother nature, metaphorically, in a domestic copartnership"—so that the story became popular, in part, "because it justified Manifest Destiny" (*Ten Most Wanted: The New Western Literature* [New York: Routledge, 1998], pp. 72, 77).

22. Richard White, *"It's Your Misfortune and None of My Own": A New History of the American West* (Norman: University of Oklahoma Press, 1991), pp. 232–33.

23. McPhee, *Assembling California*, pp. 64–65. He doesn't cite the source of his quotation from Silliman.

24. William Shakespeare, *The Taming of the Shrew*, act 5, scene 2, lines 142–43.

25. See Goodman, *Gold Seeking*, p. xxiii, where he discusses and documents the background for this less romantic reconsideration of mining frontiers.

26. See Bernard DeVoto, "The West: A Plundered Province," *Harper's*, August 1934, pp. 355–64.

27. Anne F. Hyde, "Round Pegs in Square Holes: The Rocky Mountains and Extractive Industry," in *Many Wests: Place, Culture, and Regional Identity*, ed. David M. Wrobel and Michael C. Steiner (Lawrence: University Press of Kansas, 1997), p. 104.

28. John Muir, *Steep Trails* (Boston: Houghton Mifflin, 1918), p. 203.

29. Lutwack, *Role of Place in Literature*, p. 148.

30. Goodman, *Gold Seeking*, pp. 105, 136, 147.

31. Ibid., pp. 139, 147.

32. Hyde, "Round Pegs in Square Holes," p. 110. A book that goes a long way toward answering Hyde's concluding call is Gary Ferguson, *The Great Divide: The Rocky Mountains in the American Mind* (New York: Norton, 2004).

33. Aldo Leopold, Foreword, *"A Sand County Almanac" and "Sketches Here and There"* (1949; reprint ed., New York: Oxford University Press, 1989), p. ix.

34. Rohrbough, *Days of Gold*, pp. 291, 293.

35. Earle Labor, "Jack London," in *A Literary History of the American West*, ed. J. Golden Taylor et al. (Fort Worth: Texas Christian University Press, 1987), pp. 384, 385, 386.

36. Robert Service, "The Spell of the Yukon," in *"The Shooting of Dan McGrew" and Other Poems* (New York: Dover, 1993), pp. 1, 2.

37. Zeese Papanikolas, *Trickster in the Land of Dreams* (Lincoln: University of Nebraska Press, 1995), pp. 60, 66.

38. In this connection, see Carolyn Merchant, *Green versus Gold: Sources in California's Environmental History* (Washington, DC: Island Press, 1998).

39. Barich, *Big Dreams*, p. 7.

Reinventing the Indian: The Red Devil

1. Richard F. Burton, *The City of the Saints, and across the Rocky Mountains to California* (New York: Harper and Brothers, 1862), pp. 102, 105, 106, 107, 106. On the Indian's eye, see also Richard C. Poulsen, *The Landscape of the Mind: Cultural Transformations of the American West* (New York: Lang, 1992), pp. 46–47, where he discusses it as "a moral revelator" betraying "stealth and snakelike craft" (p. 47).

2. Jill Lepore, "Wigwam Words," *American Scholar* 70, no. 1 (Winter 2001): 98. Even when the Indian's speech was considered eloquent, that was so, according to Lepore, "only when his words were translated into English" in renderings that were "apt to be poetic and metaphorical" (pp. 98–99).

3. Robert F. Berkhofer Jr., *The White Man's Indian: Images of the American Indian from Columbus to the Present* (1978; reprint ed., New York: Vintage Books, 1979), pp. 27, 28.

4. Poulsen, *Landscape of the Mind*, p. 54.

5. Donald Worster, *An Unsettled Country: Changing Landscapes of the American West* (Albuquerque: University of New Mexico Press, 1994), p. 70.

6. Peter L. Thorslev Jr., "The Wild Man's Revenge," in *The Wild Man Within: An Image in Western Thought from the Renaissance to Romanticism*, ed. Edward Dudley and Maximillian E. Novak (Pittsburgh, PA: University of Pittsburgh Press, 1972), p. 285.

7. William H. Truettner, "Ideology and Image: Justifying Westward Expansion," in *The West as America: Reinterpreting Images of the Frontier, 1820–1920*, ed. William H. Truettner (Washington, DC: Smithsonian Institution Press, 1991), p. 44. See Richard Drinnon, *Facing West: The Metaphysics of Indian-Hating and Empire-Building* (1980; reprint ed., Norman: University of Oklahoma Press, 1997), for a fuller discussion of the connections between racism and colonialism in westward expansion. Indians weren't the only group subject to white demonization and hatred, of course; so were Asians, especially Chinese, and others. Even some

whites were, with concomitant savagery-civilization ironies, as Blake Allmendinger shows in a chapter on anti-Mormon literature in his *Ten Most Wanted: The New Western Literature* (New York: Routledge, 1998), pp. 51–64.

8. Berkhofer, *White Man's Indian*, pp. 147, 148. As Ray Allen Billington reminds us, with the waning of Romanticism there were plenty of white depredations against Indians short of outright killing since they often were cheated in trade, "besotted . . . with whiskey," raped, and otherwise abused in ways that "left a residue of hatred that turned the kindliest Indian into a savage barbarian" (*Land of Savagery, Land of Promise: The European Image of the American Frontier in the Nineteenth Century* [New York: Norton, 1981], p. 108).

9. Julie Schimmel, "Inventing 'the Indian,'" in *West as America*, ed. Truettner, pp. 167–68.

10. Poulsen, *Landscape of the Mind*, p. 40.

11. Frederick Turner, *Beyond Geography: The Western Spirit against the Wilderness* (1980; reprint ed., New Brunswick, NJ: Rutgers University Press, 1992), p. 282.

12. The kind and extent of atrocities committed by Chivington's soldiers at Sand Creek is a matter of some debate, but there's a good deal of testimony about particular offenses, as Stan Hoig, among others, has shown—see his study *The Sand Creek Massacre* (Norman: University of Oklahoma Press, 1961). A more recent, multigenre account is Bruce Cutler's *The Massacre at Sand Creek: Narrative Voices* (Norman: University of Oklahoma Press, 1995), a work that compels the reader to move outside any single, white perspective on actions taken against Indians and see them as complex events replete with ambiguities and ironies concerning savagery and civilization.

13. See Richard Slotkin, *The Fatal Environment: The Myth of the Frontier in the Age of Industrialization, 1800–1890* (New York: Atheneum, 1985), esp. pp. 435–532, for an extended treatment of the significance of Custer's Last Stand for the redefining of late-nineteenth-century frontier mythology. As a result of that battle, Slotkin says, there was an "indigestible paradox": "it was as if the perennial scenario of American history had been reversed: red stood and white fell, civilization perished and recoiled and savagery went forward" (p. 10). For a Native American examination of the event, its background, and its aftermath of intense mythic heroizing and demonizing, see James Welch with Paul Stekler, *Killing Custer: The Battle of the Little Bighorn and the Fate of the Plains Indians* (New York: Norton, 1994).

14. See Richard White, *"It's Your Misfortune and None of My Own": A New History of the American West* (Norman: University of Oklahoma Press, 1991), pp. 104–8, for further discussion of such examples.

15. *Bismarck Tribune*, 6 July 1876, p. 1.

16. Robert M. Utley, *The Lance and the Shield: The Life and Times of Sitting Bull* (New York: Holt, 1993), pp. 175, 176. In Slotkin's similar formulation, Sitting Bull "is the 'model savage,' . . . and the treatment envisioned for Sitting Bull becomes a generalized response to 'savagery' of all kinds" (*Fatal Environment*, p. 459).

17. Ian Frazier, *Great Plains* (New York: Penguin Books, 1990), p. 41. See also Angie Debo, *A History of the Indians of the United States* (Norman: University of Oklahoma Press, 1970), pp. 289–94, and Michael Hittman, *Wovoka and the Ghost Dance*, exp. ed., ed. Don Lynch (Lincoln: University of Nebraska Press, 1997).

18. Turner, *Beyond Geography*, pp. 291, 292.

19. Larry McMurtry, *Comanche Moon: A Novel* (New York: Simon and Schuster, 1997), p. 78.

An Animal Holocaust: Wildlife Management in the Old West

1. John G. Neihardt, Black Elk Speaks: Being the Life Story of a Holy Man of the Oglala Sioux (1932; reprint ed., Lincoln: University of Nebraska Press, Bison Books, 1961), p. xv.

2. Ibid., p. 9.

3. Donald Worster, An Unsettled Country: Changing Landscapes of the American West (Albuquerque: University of New Mexico Press, 1994), p. 55.

4. Ibid., pp. 56, 57.

5. Ibid., pp. 65, 85, 72, 90.

6. Richard C. Poulsen, The Landscape of the Mind: Cultural Transformations of the American West (New York: Lang, 1992), p. 30.

7. Elliott West, The Contested Plains: Indians, Goldseekers, and the Rush to Colorado (Lawrence: University Press of Kansas, 1998), pp. 161, 162.

8. Eugene D. Fleharty, Wild Animals and Settlers on the Great Plains (Norman: University of Oklahoma Press, 1995), pp. 3, 4, 6. The two newspaper accounts quoted by Fleharty are from, respectively, the Osborne County Farmer, 6 July 1877, and the Ellsworth Reporter, 15 August 1872. On the multiplex symbology of the "hateful rattlesnake" when the Great Plains were rapidly being transformed from a tallgrass wild into geometrized fields, see Steven Trout, "Seeing the Rattlesnake in Willa Cather's My Ántonia," Interdisciplinary Studies in Literature and Environment 12, no. 1 (Winter 2005): 99–114.

9. Fleharty, Wild Animals and Settlers, p. 294. Background on growing Euro-American opposition to the destruction of wild animals during the nineteenth century may be found in Keith Thomas, Man and the Natural World: Changing Attitudes in England, 1500–1800 (1983; reprint ed., New York: Oxford University Press, 1996).

10. Scott Cummins, Reminiscences of the Early Days, in Musings of the Pilgrim Bard: A Book of Poems (Wichita, KS: Eagle Press, 1903), pp. 253–54. I have no special reason to doubt the veracity of Cummins's account here, but I should note that Joseph Barrell in The Red Hills of Kansas: Crossroads of Plant Migrations (Rockford, IL: Natural Land Institute, 1975) states that the summit of what he terms "Flowerpot Mound" is "inaccessible to large grazing animals" (p. 9). Having seen that flat-topped and scarped hill, I tend to agree with him. On the other hand, I'd concede that the presence of a buffalo on its plateau is improbable rather than impossible and that maybe that's why Cummins was surprised to see one there.

11. Richard Slotkin, Regeneration through Violence: The Mythology of the American Frontier, 1600–1860 (1973; reprint ed., New York: HarperPerennial, 1996), pp. 412, 413.

12. Conger Beasley Jr., "The Killing Grounds: Nineteenth-Century Destruction of Native Animal Species," Forty-fifth Annual Conference on Composition and Literature, University of Kansas, Lawrence, 13 October 1997, pp. 1, 13.

13. Ibid., pp. 14, 17. See also SueEllen Campbell's discussion of the gluttonous dinners eaten by a Great Plains hunting party of wealthy New Yorkers hosted by General Philip Sheridan in 1871, where she finds that the rhetoric of a meat-rich menu suggests that the participants' "armor of civilization" betrays their fear of "being overcome by their own hidden wildness, their animal selves"—an insight that anticipates her later remark that Euro-Americans' consumption of staple Indian food involved "fear of," as well as "desire for, becoming as 'wild' as they considered the Native Americans to be" ("Feasting in the Wilderness: The Language of Food in American Wilderness Narratives," American Literary History 6 [1994]: 4, 5, 7).

14. Beasley, "Killing Grounds," pp. 19, 21, 25. It should be remembered that, though by the late 1850s Americans' interest in hunting was amplified by the romance of migration into the West, a place much associated with hunting in the popular press, "at no time in the mid-nineteenth century did hunting become completely accepted"—and indeed, moral issues aside, was mocked by many as "simply a waste of money" (Michael A. Bellesiles, *Arming America: The Origins of a National Gun Culture* [New York: Knopf, 2000], p. 340).

15. See William H. Goetzmann and William N. Goetzmann, *The West of the Imagination* (New York: Norton, 1986), p. 262.

16. The number of buffalo then remaining, like the number of them before the white slaughter began (fifty million? forty? sixty?), can only be estimated, of course, but the order of magnitude, in both cases, is surely accurate. The status of the remaining animals as "wildlife" is debatable, though it may well be true, as William Kittredge claims, without documentation, that "the last wild ones" were shot in 1886, south of Jordan, Montana, by William T. Hornaday, at the time chief taxidermist for the National Museum, "for display in the Smithsonian," which was "his nineteenth-century way of preserving the last wild buffalo" (*Who Owns the West?* [San Francisco: Mercury House, 1996], p. 119).

17. Jane Tompkins, *West of Everything: The Inner Life of Westerns* (New York: Oxford University Press, 1992), pp. 187, 188.

18. Patricia Nelson Limerick, *The Legacy of Conquest: The Unbroken Past of the American West* (New York: Norton, 1987), p. 314.

19. Richard Dankleff, "Buffalo," in *Westerns* (Corvallis: Oregon State University Press, 1984), p. 37.

20. Frederick Turner, "Wind on the Buffalo Grass," in *Of Chiles, Cacti, and Fighting Cocks: Notes on the American West* (1990; exp. reprint ed., New York: Owl Books, 1996), pp. 97, 99.

21. "Horse-killing Suspects Nabbed," *Lawrence Journal-World*, 14 January 1999, p. 6A.

In without Knocking: The Cowboy as Wild Man

1. "Horse-killing Suspects Nabbed," *Lawrence Journal-World*, 14 January 1999, p. 6A.

2. William H. Goetzmann and William N. Goetzmann, *The West of the Imagination* (New York: Norton, 1986), pp. 272–73.

3. The scene isn't *too* overstated, given the tenor of events in the cow towns at their wildest—for examples, see Nyle H. Miller and Joseph W. Snell, *Why the West Was Wild: A Contemporary Look at the Antics of Some Highly Publicized Kansas Cowtown Personalities* (Topeka: Kansas State Historical Society, 1963).

4. Stephen Tatum, "The Problem of the 'Popular' in the New Western History," in *The New Western History: An Assessment*, ed. Forrest G. Robinson, a special issue of *Arizona Quarterly* 53, no. 2 (Summer 1997): 154.

5. Barre Toelken, "Folklore in the American West," in *A Literary History of the American West*, ed. J. Golden Taylor et al. (Fort Worth: Texas Christian University Press, 1987), p. 45. Toelken says in a note that the text and tune of the song were collected by him "from Lewis Gordon at Logan, Utah, December 1955" (p. 64). Various expressions of this ambivalent close-but-dominating relation turn up in many cowboy songs, songs that Robert G. Weiner argues "reflect an oral tradition among western ranch hands that both glorified and condemned the natural environment in which they lived" ("Cowboy Songs and Nature in the Late Nineteenth Century," in *The Cowboy Way: An Exploration of History and Culture*, ed. Paul H. Carlson [Lubbock: Texas Tech University Press, 2000], p. 152).

6. Lawrence Clayton and Kenneth W. Davis, Introduction, *Horsing Around: Contemporary Cowboy Humor*, ed. Lawrence Clayton and Kenneth W. Davis (Detroit: Wayne State University Press, 1991), p. 19.

7. See Richard Grant, "Cocaine Cowboys," *Details*, November 1998, pp. 134–48.

8. Richard W. Slatta, *Cowboys of the Americas* (New Haven, CT: Yale University Press, 1990), pp. 11, 20.

9. Richard C. Poulsen, *The Landscape of the Mind: Cultural Transformations of the American West* (New York: Lang, 1992), pp. 87, 94, 99. Whole shelves of books deal with the real cowboy and his world. In this chapter and elsewhere I cite a number of them, but here are the titles of a couple of others I'd recommend as well: Richard W. Slatta, *Comparing Cowboys and Frontiers* (Norman: University of Oklahoma Press, 1997), and Philip Ashton Rollins, *The Cowboy: An Unconventional History of Civilization on the Old-Time Cattle Range*, rev. ed. (Norman: University of Oklahoma Press, 1997).

10. Donald Worster, *Under Western Skies: Nature and History in the American West* (New York: Oxford University Press, 1992), pp. 41, 45.

11. Paul Shepard, *The Others: How Animals Made Us Human* (Washington, DC: Shearwater Books, 1996), pp. 206, 221.

12. Scott Cummins, "The Maid of Barber," in *Musings of the Pilgrim Bard: A Book of Poems* (Wichita, KS: Eagle Press, 1903), p. 180.

13. Jane Tompkins, *West of Everything: The Inner Life of Westerns* (New York: Oxford University Press, 1992), p. 132.

14. Owen Wister, *The Virginian: A Horseman of the Plains* (1929; reprint ed., Lincoln: University of Nebraska Press, 1992), p. 434.

15. Ibid., pp. xviii, xix, 19, 10, 11, 10, 425–26, 425.

16. Thomas McGuane, Introduction, *The Virginian*, by Wister, p. x.

17. Robert Murray Davis, *Playing Cowboys: Low Culture and High Art in the Western* (Norman: University of Oklahoma Press, 1992), pp. 21, 24, 27–28. The Virginian might be interpreted as functioning to reconcile another opposition, that between male and female (which may implicate that between black and white as well), relevant to my discussion of his wild-tame character—see, in this connection, Blake Allmendinger's analysis of transgressive same-sex love in Wister's novel in his *Ten Most Wanted: The New Western Literature* (New York: Routledge, 1998), pp. 154–55, 157–58.

18. Zeese Papanikolas, *Trickster in the Land of Dreams* (Lincoln: University of Nebraska Press, 1995), pp. 73, 77.

19. See Umberto Eco, *The Role of the Reader: Explorations in the Semiotics of Texts* (Bloomington: Indiana University Press, 1979), pp. 214–15.

20. See William W. Savage Jr., *The Cowboy Hero: His Image in American History and Culture* (Norman: University of Oklahoma Press, 1979), as well as Michael L. Johnson, *New Westers: The West in Contemporary American Culture* (Lawrence: University Press of Kansas, 1996), pp. 264–69.

21. Henry Nash Smith, *Virgin Land: The American West as Symbol and Myth* (1950; reprint ed., Cambridge, MA: Harvard University Press, 1970), p. 109.

22. Gretel Ehrlich, "About Men," in *The Solace of Open Spaces* (New York: Penguin Books, 1986), p. 49.

23. David Daly and Joel Persky, *The West and the Western*, a special issue of *Journal of the West* 29, no. 2 (April 1990): 29. In this vein, Ray Allen Billington observes that, in the 1880s and

1890s, European fiction concerning the West portrayed the cowboy as a progress-furthering Hector who prefigured "the lone avenger with muscles of steel and heart of gold, quick to kill bad men whether red or white, but staunchly committed to the laws of decency that governed civilized men" (*Land of Savagery, Land of Promise: The European Image of the American Frontier in the Nineteenth Century* [New York: Norton, 1981], p. 173).

24. Robert G. Athearn, *The Mythic West in Twentieth-Century America* (Lawrence: University Press of Kansas, 1986), p. 25.

25. Marilynne Robinson, "Hearing Silence: Western Myth Reconsidered," in *Northern Lights: A Selection of New Writing from the American West*, ed. Deborah Clow and Donald Snow (New York: Vintage Books, 1994), p. 59.

26. Larry McMurtry, "How the West Was Won or Lost," *New Republic*, 22 October 1990, p. 38.

27. Dayton Duncan, *Out West: An American Journey* (New York: Viking, 1987), pp. 312, 313.

28. Sharman Apt Russell, *Kill the Cowboy: A Battle of Mythology in the New West* (Reading, MA: Addison-Wesley, 1993), p. 3.

29. Sara L. Spurgeon, "'Pledged in Blood': Truth and Redemption in Cormac McCarthy's *All the Pretty Horses*," *Western American Literature* 34 (1999): 25, 29.

30. Ibid., pp. 36, 37, 39. Concerning Annette Kolodny's codification of the pastoral paradox, see her book *The Lay of the Land: Metaphor as Experience and History in American Life and Letters* (Chapel Hill: University of North Carolina Press, 1975), p. 46.

31. J. E. Cirlot, *A Dictionary of Symbols*, trans. Jack Sage (New York: Philosophical Library, 1962), s.v. "wild man."

32. Hayden White, "The Forms of Wildness: Archaeology of an Idea," in *The Wild Man Within: An Image in Western Thought from the Renaissance to Romanticism*, ed. Edward Dudley and Maximillian E. Novak (Pittsburgh, PA: University of Pittsburgh Press, 1972), p. 31.

33. Henry D. Thoreau, *The Maine Woods* (1864; reprint ed., Boston: Houghton Mifflin, 1889), p. 70.

34. Simon Schama, *Landscape and Memory* (New York: Vintage Books, 1995), p. 571. Thoreau's eventual resolution of his ambivalence may suggest how that of the cowboy—and therefore perhaps that of the Western mind-set he embodies—could be resolved. He accomplished it by developing "an evolutionary perspective on nature" that allowed him to know all of it as "virtually a living continuum" and thus to harmonize "the positive side of the wilderness" with its "negative and foreboding" side (Max Oelschlaeger, "Wilderness, Civilization, and Language," in *The Wilderness Condition: Essays on Environment and Civilization*, ed. Max Oelschlaeger [San Francisco: Sierra Club Books, 1992], p. 281).

35. Savage, *Cowboy Hero*, pp. 30, 31. Gary McMahan has expressed the same afterlife hope in a poem—see "The Two Things in Life That I Really Love," in *New Cowboy Poetry: A Contemporary Gathering*, ed. Hal Cannon [Layton, UT: Peregrine Smith Books, 1990], p. 39).

36. John Keats, "Ode on a Grecian Urn," in *Keats: Poetical Works*, ed. H. W. Garrod (London: Oxford University Press, 1956), p. 210.

Romancing the Gun: Outlaws and Man-Killers in Helldorado

1. Stephen Tatum, *Inventing Billy the Kid: Visions of the Outlaw in America, 1881–1981* (1982; reprint ed., Tucson: University of Arizona Press, 1997), p. 55.

2. Pat F. Garrett, *The Authentic Life of Billy, the Kid, the Noted Desperado of the Southwest, Whose*

Deeds of Daring and Blood Made His Name a Terror in New Mexico, Arizona and Northern Mexico (1882; reprint ed., Norman: University of Oklahoma Press, 1954), p. 156.

3. Michael A. Bellesiles, *Arming America: The Origins of a National Gun Culture* (New York: Knopf, 2000), pp. 17, 5, 353. As I noted, some of Bellesiles's sources and methodology have been subjects of debate. An overview of the controversy may be found in Danny Postel, "Did the Shootouts over 'Arming America' Divert Attention from the Real Issues?" *Chronicle of Higher Education*, 1 February 2002, pp. A12–15. Postel quotes historian Edmund S. Morgan, who earlier reviewed the book favorably ("In Love with Guns," *New York Review of Books*, 19 October 2000, pp. 30–32) and "calls some of the accusations against Mr. Bellesiles's book 'pretty incriminating,'" to the effect that, all the same, "it would be 'difficult to disprove' the book's central contention—that the gun culture in America really took hold only after the Civil War" (p. A15).

4. Bellesiles, *Arming America*, pp. 9, 14, 15, 14.

5. Ibid., pp. 430, 378, 344, 364.

6. Ibid., p. 15.

7. Stephen Crane, "The Bride Comes to Yellow Sky," in *Prose and Poetry of the American West*, ed. James C. Work (Lincoln: University of Nebraska Press, 1990), p. 287.

8. Elliott West, *The Contested Plains: Indians, Goldseekers, and the Rush to Colorado* (Lawrence: University Press of Kansas, 1998), p. 49.

9. Soon enough, Indians in the West would have guns of one kind or another—Eastern Indians had a good number of them by the mid-eighteenth century—but never as many as whites, especially the military, had.

10. Wallace Stevens, "Anecdote of the Jar," in *The Palm at the End of the Mind: Selected Poems and a Play by Wallace Stevens*, ed. Holly Stevens (New York: Vintage Books, 1972), p. 46.

11. Jane Tompkins, *West of Everything: The Inner Life of Westerns* (New York: Oxford University Press, 1992), pp. 193, 194.

12. Robert Bringhurst, "The Beauty of the Weapons," in *The Beauty of the Weapons: Selected Poems, 1972–82* (1982; reprint ed., Port Townsend, WA: Copper Canyon Press, 1985), p. 19.

13. James C. Work, Introduction, *Gunfight! Thirteen Western Stories*, ed. James C. Work (Lincoln: University of Nebraska Press, 1996), p. xvi.

14. Jack Schaefer, *Shane* (1949; reprint ed., New York: Bantam Books, 1983), p. 101.

15. David Daly and Joel Persky, *The West and the Western*, a special issue of *Journal of the West* 29, no. 2 (April 1990): 29.

16. Jonathan Holden, *Guns and Boyhood in America: A Memoir of Growing Up in the 50s* (Ann Arbor: University of Michigan Press, 1997), p. 26.

17. Work, Introduction, p. xvii.

18. West, *Contested Plains*, p. 55.

19. Holden, *Guns and Boyhood in America*, p. 24.

20. Raymond Carver, "Wes Hardin: From a Photograph," in *Fires: Essays, Poems, Stories* (New York: Vintage Books, 1984), p. 91. Carver's poem, based on a postmortem photo, may romanticize Hardin's hand; in the well-known 1871 studio photo of him, it looks somewhat chubby and coarse. Albeit a creature of culture, in some sense, the much-feared Hardin seems to have been equally just a violent force of nature, which is pretty much the way Brice McGinnis portrays him in his *Reflections in Dark Glass: The Life and Times of John Wesley Hardin* (Denton: University of North Texas Press, 1996).

21. N. Scott Momaday, "A Prospector Catches Sight of Him in the Doña Anas," in "The Strange and True Story of My Life with Billy the Kid," in *In the Presence of the Sun: Stories and Poems* (New York: St. Martin's Press, 1992), p. 54.

22. Roger D. McGrath, *Gunfighters, Highwaymen, and Vigilantes: Violence on the Frontier* (Berkeley: University of California Press, 1984), pp. 271, 264. See also Kent Ladd Steckmesser, *The Western Hero in History and Legend* (Norman: University of Oklahoma Press, 1965), and Joseph G. Rosa, *The Gunfighter: Man or Myth?* (Norman: University of Oklahoma Press, 1968).

23. McGrath, *Gunfighters, Highwaymen, and Vigilantes*, pp. 265, 262, 263, 264, 270. See also Frank Richard Prassel, *The Western Peace Officer: The Legacy of Law and Order* (Norman: University of Oklahoma Press, 1972); W. Eugene Hollon, *Frontier Violence: Another Look* (New York: Oxford University Press, 1974); and W. H. Hutchinson, "Wilding the Tame West," *Westways*, February 1978, pp. 21–22, 80. As regards imaginative wilding toward the end of the nineteenth century, Robert F. Berkhofer Jr. observes that in dime novels "the savagery of the hero at times came to resemble that of the villain" (*The White Man's Indian: Images of the American Indian from Columbus to the Present* [1978; reprint ed., New York: Vintage Books, 1979], p. 100), and Ray Allen Billington finds that European image-makers, who previously "had pictured the West as a land of both opportunity and savagery, . . . would now picture it solely as a land where civilization had surrendered to barbarism, where justice was carried in holsters rather than in books" (*Land of Savagery, Land of Promise: The European Image of the American Frontier in the Nineteenth Century* [New York: Norton, 1981], p. 267).

24. Ian Frazier, *Great Plains* (New York: Penguin Books, 1990), p. 151.

25. McGrath, *Gunfighters, Highwaymen, and Vigilantes*, p. 269.

26. Richard White, *"It's Your Misfortune and None of My Own": A New History of the American West* (Norman: University of Oklahoma Press, 1991), pp. 351, 328–29. For some further discussion of the relations between violence and the Western social order, see William R. Handley, *Marriage, Violence, and the Nation in the American Literary West* (Cambridge: Cambridge University Press, 2002).

27. White, *"It's Your Misfortune and None of My Own,"* p. 332.

28. Perhaps the most intriguing example of a gunfighter with this sort of split personality is John Henry ("Doc") Holliday, a paradoxical man of genteel rearing and frail constitution who cultivated the image of himself as a wild-man gambler and gunfighter and was finally in fact as much law-abiding gentleman as outlaw murderer—see Karen Holliday Tanner, *Doc Holliday: A Family Portrait* (Norman: University of Oklahoma Press, 1998), and Pat Jahns, *The Frontier World of Doc Holliday* (1973; reprint ed., Lincoln: University of Nebraska Press, 1998).

29. Cormac McCarthy, *Cities of the Plain* (New York: Knopf, 1998), p. 185.

30. See Merrill Lindsay, *One Hundred Great Guns: An Illustrated History of Firearms* (New York: Walker, 1967), pp. 143–77 passim.

31. McGrath, *Gunfighters, Highwaymen, and Vigilantes*, p. 265.

32. Kent L. Steckmesser, "Lawmen and Outlaws," in *A Literary History of the American West*, ed. J. Golden Taylor et al. (Fort Worth: Texas Christian University Press, 1987), pp. 119, 130.

33. McGrath, *Gunfighters, Highwaymen, and Vigilantes*, p. 270.

34. N. Scott Momaday, "New Mexico: Passage into Legend," in *The Man Made of Words: Essays, Stories, Passages* (New York: St. Martin's Press, 1997), p. 157.

35. Richard Dankleff, "The Legend," in *Westerns* (Corvallis: Oregon State University Press, 1984), p. 40. The legend of Wyatt Earp has undergone a good deal of critical scrutiny in re-

cent years, all of which shows him to have been a man of many contradictory wild and tame aspects, not the simple antitype of Clay Allison—see, for example, Paula Mitchell Marks, *And Die in the West: The Story of the O.K. Corral Gunfight* (New York: Morrow, 1989), and Allen Barra, *Inventing Wyatt Earp: His Life and Many Legends* (New York: Carroll and Graf, 1998).

36. Christine Bold, "Malaeska's Revenge; or, The Dime Novel Tradition in Popular Fiction," in *Wanted Dead or Alive: The American West in Popular Culture*, ed. Richard Aquila (Urbana: University of Illinois Press, 1996), p. 27.

37. Eugene Weber, "The Ups and Downs of Honor," *American Scholar* 68, no. 1 (Winter 1999): 82. That provision, in a certain variation, is apparently what, by a bizarre Western theology, allows for the redemption into Heaven of both Hickok and three other gunfighters (Jesse James, Billy the Kid, and Doc Holliday) in the 1999 TBS made-for-television movie *Purgatory*.

38. Marilynne Robinson, "Hearing Silence: Western Myth Reconsidered," in *Northern Lights: A Selection of New Writing from the American West*, ed. Deborah Clow and Donald Snow (New York: Vintage Books, 1994), p. 63.

39. John Cawelti, *The Six-Gun Mystique*, 2nd ed. (Bowling Green, OH: Bowling Green State University Popular Press, 1984), pp. 65, 66, 68.

40. Ibid., pp. 72, 73.

41. Ibid., pp. 83, 84. Similarly, Berkhofer argues that, just as "the earliest . . . White frontiersmen . . . were as doomed to disappear as the savages they replaced," so were the gunfighters (they "possessed too little 'Whiteness' and too much savagery to survive beyond a certain point")—in each case by "an ideology of social progress" that "reconciled the ambivalent images of nature, the Indian, and the frontier" by postulating "the inevitable evolution of the frontier from savagery to civilization" (*White Man's Indian*, pp. 92, 94, 92).

42. Cawelti, *Six-Gun Mystique*, pp. 87, 88. Cf. D. H. Lawrence's judgment that "the essential American soul is hard, isolate, stoic, and a killer" (*Studies in Classic American Literature* [New York: Seltzer, 1923], p. 92).

43. Edward Dorn, *Slinger* (Berkeley, CA: Wingbow Press, 1975), n. pag.

44. Tatum, *Inventing Billy the Kid*, pp. x, 10.

45. Ibid., pp. 10, 41.

46. Ibid., pp. 46, 57.

47. Ibid., pp. 65, 66, 135, 163. See also Jack Nachbar, "Riding Shotgun: The Scattered Formula in Contemporary Western Movies," in *Focus on the Western*, ed. Jack Nachbar (Englewood Cliffs, NJ: Prentice-Hall, 1974), pp. 101–12.

48. Michael Ondaatje, *The Collected Works of Billy the Kid* (1970; reprint ed., New York: Vintage International, 1996), p. 84.

49. Tatum, *Inventing Billy the Kid*, pp. 65, 195.

50. Harry Berger Jr., "Naïve Consciousness and Culture Change: An Essay in Historical Structuralism," *Bulletin of the Midwest Modern Language Association* 6, no. 1 (Spring 1973): 35.

51. Tatum, *Inventing Billy the Kid*, p. 196.

(En)closing the Frontier

1. Thomas J. Lyon, "Introduction: The Conquistador, the Lone Ranger, and Beyond," in *The Literary West: An Anthology of Western American Literature*, ed. Thomas J. Lyon (New York: Oxford University Press, 1999), pp. 1, 2.

2. Harold P. Simonson, *Beyond the Frontier: Writers, Western Regionalism and a Sense of Place* (Fort Worth: Texas Christian University Press, 1989), p. 2.

3. John Steinbeck, *The Red Pony* (1945; reprint ed., New York: Bantam Books, 1955), p. 91. This novella—in four episodes, one of them "The Leader of the People"—was originally part of Steinbeck's 1938 short-story collection *The Long Valley*.

4. Robert Frost, "The Oven Bird," in *The Poetry of Robert Frost*, ed. Edward Connery Lathem (New York: Holt, Rinehart and Winston, 1969), p. 120.

5. Donald Worster, "A Tapestry of Change: Nature and Culture on the Prairie," in Terry Evans, *The Inhabited Prairie* (Lawrence: University Press of Kansas, 1998), pp. xii, xiii.

6. Ibid., pp. xiv, xv, xvi, xvii.

7. Stephen Tatum, "Topographies of Transition in Western American Literature," *Western American Literature* 32 (1998): 346, 347.

8. James C. Work, Introduction to Part 2: The Mythopoeic Period, 1833–89, *Prose and Poetry of the American West*, ed. James C. Work (Lincoln: University of Nebraska Press, 1990), p. 91.

9. See Rainer Maria Rilke, "The Panther," in *Selected Poems of Rainer Maria Rilke*, trans. Robert Bly (New York: Harper and Row, 1981), p. 139. Cf. a passage from Richard Manning that thematically interrelates Lyon, Worster, Tatum, Jefferson, Work, and Rilke: "in flight, one need not look hard for Jefferson's grid. The wheat fields and cornfields lay out to the horizon like tiles. This is the obvious and squared face of the land that was once nothing more than an abstraction, a simple idea in the head of a man who never saw the place. All of the West is locked in a grid. The mask has become the face" (*Grassland: The History, Biology, Politics, and Promise of the American Prairie* [New York: Viking, 1995], p. 109).

10. Richard White, *"It's Your Misfortune and None of My Own": A New History of the American West* (Norman: University of Oklahoma Press, 1991), p. 236.

11. See David Dary, *Seeking Pleasure in the Old West* (Lawrence: University Press of Kansas, 1995), pp. 224–57.

12. Frederick Turner, *Beyond Geography: The Western Spirit against the Wilderness* (1980; reprint ed., New Brunswick, NJ: Rutgers University Press, 1992), pp. 262–63. In his discussion of the role of the railroad in the sudden post–Civil War economic development of the West, Donald Worster metaphorizes the latter in terms of the former, describing how it "had roared across the region in a cloud of smoke and ash," propelled by "a hunger that could not be satisfied" (*A River Running West: The Life of John Wesley Powell* [New York: Oxford University Press, 2001], p. 468). For another perspective on what that rail-mounted hunger was about, see Stephen E. Ambrose's *Nothing Like It in the World: The Men Who Built the Transcontinental Railroad, 1863–1869* (New York: Simon and Schuster, 2000).

13. William H. Truettner, "Ideology and Image: Justifying Westward Expansion," in *The West as America: Reinterpreting Images of the Frontier, 1820–1920*, ed. William H. Truettner (Washington, DC: Smithsonian Institution Press, 1991), pp. 31. Also, see Richard Slotkin, *The Fatal Environment: The Myth of the Frontier in the Age of Industrialization, 1800–1890* (New York: Atheneum, 1985), pp. 41–45.

14. Truettner, "Ideology and Image," p. 32.

15. In his discussion of cultural mythology as a device "for reconciling ambivalent ideologies" in the 1850s, Slotkin considers in some detail how railroad promoters used agrarian imagery to suggest "a benign and productive association between the order of industrialism and the ambitions of the yeoman farmer" by invoking "a fable of history, in which the remnant of wilderness, the plowed fields, and the steaming locomotive represent progressive stages of development" (*Fatal Environment*, pp. 213, 214, 215).

16. White, *"It's Your Misfortune and None of My Own,"* pp. 627, 630. Audrey Goodman notes, in agreement with White, that, while paintings represented an impressive imaginative West, "landscape photographs seemed to present a West of magnificent wild fact," typically one, like the Southwest as portrayed in Charles Lummis's books in several genres during the 1890s, rendered as "exotic but unthreatening" (*Translating Southwestern Landscapes: The Making of an Anglo Literary Region* [Tucson: University of Arizona Press, 2002], pp. 70, 3).

17. Barbara Novak, *Nature and Culture: American Landscape and Painting, 1825–1875*, rev. ed. (New York: Oxford University Press, 1995), pp. 180, 166, 167, 168, 169, 166. Novak's discussion, as she acknowledges, is indebted to ideas from Perry Miller (see, particularly, his *Errand into the Wilderness* [1956; reprint ed., New York: Harper Torchbooks, 1964]) and Leo Marx (see his *The Machine in the Garden: Technology and the Pastoral Ideal in America* [New York: Oxford University Press, 1964]).

18. Hal K. Rothman, *Devil's Bargains: Tourism in the Twentieth-Century American West* (Lawrence: University Press of Kansas, 1998), p. 39. See also Chris Rojek, *Ways of Escape: Modern Transformations in Leisure and Travel* (Lanham, MD: Rowman and Littlefield, 1993), pp. 185–86.

19. See Henry D. McCallum and Frances T. McCallum, *The Wire That Fenced the West* (Norman: University of Oklahoma Press, 1965), pp. 31–33, for an account of how the Gliddens invented the wire.

20. Donald Worster, *Under Western Skies: Nature and History in the American West* (New York: Oxford University Press, 1992), pp. 249, 250. Concerning Walter Prescott Webb's argument about fencing, see his *The Great Plains* (Boston: Ginn, 1931), pp. 316–17.

21. Worster, *Under Western Skies*, pp. 251, 250. Also, see Alan Krell, *The Devil's Rope: A Cultural History of Barbed Wire* (London: Reaktion Books, 2003), a global investigation of barbed wire as "an instrument of domination."

22. See McCallum and McCallum, *Wire That Fenced the West*, pp. 234–35, 242–43, 250–52, 259–60, 266–67.

23. Richard C. Poulsen, *The Landscape of the Mind: Cultural Transformations of the American West* (New York: Lang, 1992), pp. 100, 120.

24. David Daly and Joel Persky, *The West and the Western*, a special issue of *Journal of the West* 29, no. 2 (April 1990): 24–25.

25. William Stafford, "For the Grave of Daniel Boone," in *Stories That Could Be True: New and Collected Poems* (New York: Harper and Row, 1977), p. 143. The poem is reprinted from Stafford's 1966 collection *The Rescued Years*.

26. Turner, *Beyond Geography*, pp. 296, 297.

27. See Joseph G. Rosa and Robin May, *Buffalo Bill and His Wild West: A Pictorial Biography* (Lawrence: University Press of Kansas, 1989), p. 183—where, incidentally, there's a photograph of Cody anachronistically "at the wheel of an 'Atlas' automobile ca. 1907."

28. Turner, *Beyond Geography*, p. 299. Denver, as a "city beneath a hill" that gold built, might be seen also as an ironic realization of John Winthrop's more spiritual dream of transformed wilderness.

29. White, *"It's Your Misfortune and None of My Own,"* p. 391.

30. Carl Abbott, *The Metropolitan Frontier: Cities in the Modern American West* (Tucson: University of Arizona Press, 1993), p. xvii.

31. A recent book that tells much the same pictorial story is James R. Shortridge's *Our Town on the Plains: J. J. Pennell's Photographs of Junction City, Kansas, 1893–1922* (Lawrence: University Press of Kansas, 2000). The startling multiplication of power lines in Pennell's

photographs tells a story in itself, one repeated all over the West in the years before and after the turn of the century, as Thomas Parke Hughes shows in his *Networks of Power: Electrification in Western Society, 1880–1930* (Baltimore: Johns Hopkins University Press, 1983).

32. Elliott West, *The Contested Plains: Indians, Goldseekers, and the Rush to Colorado* (Lawrence: University Press of Kansas, 1998), p. 109.

33. Jon Roush, "Square Places, Round Wholes," in *Northern Lights: A Selection of New Writing from the American West*, ed. Deborah Clow and Donald Snow (New York: Vintage Books, 1994), p. 24.

34. Ibid., pp. 23, 24, 25.

PART FOUR: FROM THE 1890S TO THE 1960S: THE WEST AS REGION
Prelude and Overview

1. David Río, "Basques in the International West: An Interview with Frank Bergon," *Western American Literature* 36 (2001): 62–63.

2. Harold P. Simonson, *Beyond the Frontier: Writers, Western Regionalism and a Sense of Place* (Fort Worth: Texas Christian University Press, 1989), pp. 56, 55.

3. David M. Wrobel, *The End of American Exceptionalism: Frontier Anxiety from the Old West to the New Deal* (Lawrence: University Press of Kansas, 1993), pp. 3, 4, 5.

4. Robert G. Athearn, *The Mythic West in the Twentieth Century* (Lawrence: University Press of Kansas, 1986), pp. 10, 11.

5. Patricia Nelson Limerick, "Layer upon Layer of Memory in the American West," *Chronicle of Higher Education*, 3 March 2000, p. B6. The list quoted here is a condensed version of the one that appears in her *Something in the Soil: Legacies and Reckonings in the New West* (New York: Norton, 2000), pp. 23–26.

6. Richard W. Etulain, *Re-imagining the Modern American West: A Century of Fiction, History, and Art* (Tucson: University of Arizona Press, 1996), pp. 79, xxviii, 80.

7. See William Cronon, *Nature's Metropolis: Chicago and the Great West* (New York: Norton, 1991), p. xix, where he explains that, since "the boundary between human and nonhuman, natural and unnatural, is profoundly problematic," he has "tried to reduce confusion" about the references of such words "by resorting to the Hegelian and Marxist terms 'first nature' (original, prehuman nature) and 'second nature' (the artificial nature that people erect atop first nature)."

8. Hal K. Rothman, *Devil's Bargains: Tourism in the Twentieth-Century American West* (Lawrence: University Press of Kansas, 1998), pp. 21, 41–42, 47, 48. See also Cronon, *Nature's Metropolis*, pp. 56–57, 265–67. Notice that Rothman is modifying the meanings of the terms "first nature" and "second nature" as used by Cronon.

9. Donald Worster, *A River Running West: The Life of John Wesley Powell* (New York: Oxford University Press, 2001), pp. 572, 573.

10. Carol Steinhagen, "Dangerous Crossings: Historical Dimensions of Landscape in Willa Cather's *My Ántonia*, *The Professor's House*, and *Death Comes for the Archbishop*," *Interdisciplinary Studies in Literature and Environment* 6, no. 2 (Summer 1999): 66.

11. Richard Slotkin, *The Fatal Environment: The Myth of the Frontier in the Age of Industrialization, 1800–1890* (New York: Atheneum, 1985), p. 531.

12. John D. Dorst, *Looking West* (Philadelphia: University of Pennsylvania Press, 1999), pp. 102, 103.

13. Max Oelschlaeger, *The Idea of Wilderness: From Prehistory to the Age of Ecology* (New Haven, CT: Yale University Press, 1991), p. 4.

14. Gene M. Gressley, "Regionalism and the Twentieth-Century West," in *The American West: New Perspectives, New Dimensions*, ed. Jerome O. Steffen (Norman: University of Oklahoma Press, 1979), pp. 204–5.

15. Ibid., p. 202.

16. This list is partly indebted to Richard W. Etulain's "Chronology," in *A Literary History of the American West*, ed. J. Golden Taylor et al. (Fort Worth: Texas Christian University Press, 1987), pp. xxiv–xxvi.

Ending the Indian: Civilization (f)or Extinction

1. Richard Slotkin, *Regeneration through Violence: The Mythology of the American Frontier, 1600–1860* (1973; reprint ed., New York: HarperPerennial, 1996), p. 363.

2. Richard White, *"It's Your Misfortune and None of My Own": A New History of the American West* (Norman: University of Oklahoma Press, 1991), pp. 622, 623.

3. For a discussion of all such wide-ranging attitudes and their implications for governmental policy, see Brian W. Dippie, *The Vanishing American: White Attitudes and U.S. Indian Policy* (Middletown, CT: Wesleyan University Press, 1982).

4. Ray Allen Billington, *Land of Savagery, Land of Promise: The European Image of the American Frontier in the Nineteenth Century* (New York: Norton, 1981), pp. 139, 142, 144.

5. Concerning the proliferation of such questions during the post-Revolutionary period and their prevalence thereafter, see Susan Scheckel, *The Insistence of the Indian: Race and Nationalism in Nineteenth-Century American Culture* (Princeton, NJ: Princeton University Press, 1998).

6. Elliott West, *The Contested Plains: Indians, Goldseekers, and the Rush to Colorado* (Lawrence: University Press of Kansas, 1998), pp. 272, 335.

7. Robert F. Berkhofer Jr., *The White Man's Indian: Images of the American Indian from Columbus to the Present* (New York: Vintage Books, 1979), pp. 148, 149, 152, 153.

8. Larry McMurtry, *Walter Benjamin at the Dairy Queen: Reflections at Sixty and Beyond* (New York: Simon and Schuster, 1999), p. 82.

9. Susan Hegeman, "Landscapes, Indians, and Photography in the Age of Scientific Exploration," in *The Big Empty: Essays on Western Landscapes as Narrative*, ed. Leonard Engel (Albuquerque: University of New Mexico Press, 1994), pp. 52, 56, 57, 61–62, 71.

10. For a study of this process in the visual and verbal representations of Southwestern Indians in the late nineteenth and early twentieth centuries, see Leah Dilworth, *Imagining Indians in the Southwest: Persistent Visions of a Primitive Past* (Washington, DC: Smithsonian Institution Press, 1996).

11. Regarding this last category, see *Hollywood's Indian: The Portrayal of the Native American in Film*, ed. Peter C. Rollins and John E. O'Connor (Lexington: University Press of Kentucky, 1998), and Jacquelyn Kilpatrick, *Celluloid Indians: Native Americans and Film* (Lincoln: University of Nebraska Press, 1999).

12. Barbara A. Davis, *Edward S. Curtis: The Life and Times of a Shadow Catcher* (San Francisco: Chronicle Books, 1985), p. 31.

13. William H. Goetzmann and William N. Goetzmann, *The West of the Imagination* (New York: Norton, 1986), p. 229.

14. Berkhofer, *White Man's Indian*, p. 102.

15. Goetzmann and Goetzmann, *West of the Imagination*, p. 234.

16. N. Scott Momaday, "The Morality of Indian Hating," in *The Man Made of Words: Essays, Stories, Passages* (New York: St. Martin's Press, 1997), p. 59.

17. Kerwin Lee Klein, *Frontiers of Historical Imagination: Narrating the European Conquest of Native America, 1890–1990* (Berkeley: University of California Press, 1997), p. 1.

18. Roy Harvey Pearce, *Savagism and Civilization: A Study of the Indian and the American Mind* (Baltimore: Johns Hopkins Press, 1967), p. 127, 168, 74.

19. Julie Schimmel, "Inventing 'the Indian,'" in *The West as America: Reinterpreting Images of the Frontier, 1820–1920*, ed. William H. Truettner (Washington, DC: Smithsonian Institution Press, 1991), pp. 169, 173.

20. Patricia Nelson Limerick, *Something in the Soil: Legacies and Reckonings in the New West* (New York: Norton, 2000), p. 61.

21. Roderick Nash, *Wilderness and the American Mind*, 3rd ed. (New Haven, CT: Yale University Press, 1982), pp. 143–44. For a broad study of this reversal, see Sherry L. Smith, *Reimagining Indians: Native Americans through Anglo Eyes, 1880–1940* (New York: Oxford University Press, 2000).

22. Momaday, "Morality of Indian Hating," p. 69.

23. Angie Debo, *A History of the Indians of the United States* (Norman: University of Oklahoma Press, 1970), p. 166. For an account of Lame Bull's request, see John C. Ewers, *The Blackfeet: Raiders on the Northwestern Plains* (Norman: University of Oklahoma Press, 1958), pp. 222–23.

24. Berkhofer, *White Man's Indian*, p. 165.

25. Pearce, *Savagism and Civilization*, p. 239.

26. See Debo, *History of the Indians*, p. 294.

27. On reservations as zoos, see Paul Shepard, *The Others: How Animals Made Us Human* (Washington, DC: Shearwater Books, 1996), pp. 233–34.

28. Billington, *Land of Savagery, Land of Promise*, pp. 125, 127.

29. Frederick Turner, *Beyond Geography: The Western Spirit against the Wilderness* (1980; reprint ed., New Brunswick, NJ: Rutgers University Press, 1992), p. 286.

30. Debo, *History of the Indians*, p. 311.

31. Ibid., pp. 299, 300.

32. White, *"It's Your Misfortune and None of My Own,"* p. 111.

33. Patricia Nelson Limerick, *The Legacy of Conquest: The Unbroken Past of the American West* (New York: Norton, 1987), p. 186.

34. See Donald Worster, *A River Running West: The Life of John Wesley Powell* (New York: Oxford University Press, 2001), p. 542.

35. Schimmel, "Inventing 'the Indian,'" p. 182. See also Moreland L. Stevens, *Charles Christian Nahl: Artist of the Gold Rush, 1818–1878* (Sacramento: E. B. Crocker Art Gallery, 1976), p. 136. Cf. Ben Wittick's photograph *Tzashima and Her Husband, Governor of Laguna, Laguna Pueblo, ca. 1885*, in which the subjects are posed, with a fierce tension of estrangement, before a painted backdrop featuring a Victorian mansion and its grounds that doesn't spread wide enough to conceal the studio behind it. For a reproduction and discussion of the picture, see Audrey Goodman, *Translating Southwestern Landscapes: The Making of an Anglo Literary Region* (Tucson: University of Arizona Press, 2002), pp. 79, 76–77.

36. David Wallace Adams, *Education for Extinction: American Indians and the Boarding School Experience, 1875–1928* (Lawrence: University Press of Kansas, 1995), p. 336. For a full history

of those relations in the context of education, see Jon Reyhner and Jeanne Eder, *American Indian Education: A History* (Norman: University of Oklahoma Press, 2004).

37. Debo, *History of the Indians*, p. 288.

38. Adams, *Education for Extinction*, pp. 335, 336.

39. Ibid., pp. 337, 336.

40. Momaday, "Morality of Indian Hating," p. 71.

41. See Donald L. Fixico, *Termination and Relocation: Federal Indian Policy, 1945–1960* (Albuquerque: University of New Mexico Press, 1986).

42. Debo, *History of the Indians*, pp. 7, 8.

43. White, "*It's Your Misfortune and None of My Own*," p. 441.

44. Historically relevant here is Peter Iverson's study of a traditional Indian strategy for remaining Native, *When Indians Became Cowboys: Native Peoples and Cattle Ranching in the American West* (Norman: University of Oklahoma Press, 1994), which deals with some Indians' choice of ranching over the farming recommended by the BIA, an opting for the relatively "wilder" of two lifeways that's at once adjustive and resistive.

Thou Art Lost and Gone Forever: Postfrontier Anxiety and the Recall of the Wild

1. William Cronon, "The Trouble with Wilderness; or, Getting Back to the Wrong Nature," in *Uncommon Ground: Rethinking the Human Place in Nature*, ed. William Cronon (New York: Norton, 1995), p. 71.

2. Richard Slotkin, *Gunfighter Nation: The Myth of the Frontier in Twentieth-Century America* (1992; reprint ed., New York: HarperPerennial, 1993), p. 4.

3. See David M. Wrobel, *The End of American Exceptionalism: Frontier Anxiety from the Old West to the New Deal* (Lawrence: University Press of Kansas, 1993), p. viii.

4. Roderick Nash, Introduction, *The Call of the Wild, 1910–1916*, ed. Roderick Nash (New York: Braziller, 1970), pp. 2, 3.

5. Leonard Lutwack, *The Role of Place in Literature* (Syracuse, NY: Syracuse University Press, 1984), p. 168.

6. Cronon, "Trouble with Wilderness," pp. 77, 78.

7. Carolyn Merchant, "Reinventing Eden: Western Culture as a Recovery Narrative," in *Uncommon Ground*, ed. Cronon, p. 153.

8. Michael S. Kimmel, "The Cult of Masculinity: American Social Character and the Legacy of the Cowboy," in *Beyond Patriarchy: Essays by Men on Pleasure, Power, and Change*, ed. Michael Kaufman (New York: Oxford University Press, 1987), pp. 241, 240, 244.

9. Ann Lundberg, "John Muir and Yosemite's 'Castaway Book': The Troubling Geology of Native America," *Western American Literature* 36 (2001): 26, 35, 48, 36.

10. Nash, Introduction, pp. 3–4, 8, 11, 3, 9, 13, 14. Other manifestations of Nash's "compulsive urge" are the subject of Melanie L. Simo's *Forest and Garden: Traces of Wildness in a Modernizing Land, 1897–1949* (Charlottesville: University of Virginia Press, 2003).

11. Nash, Introduction, p. 14.

12. Richard White, "*It's Your Misfortune and None of My Own*": A New History of the American West (Norman: University of Oklahoma Press, 1991), p. 620.

13. Richard Slotkin, *The Fatal Environment: The Myth of the Frontier in the Age of Industrialization, 1800–1890* (New York: Atheneum, 1985), p. 41.

14. David Teague, "A Paradoxical Legacy: Some New Contexts for John C. Van Dyke's *The Desert*," *Western American Literature* 30 (1995): 171, 172.

15. Susan Stewart, *On Longing: Narratives of the Miniature, the Gigantic, the Souvenir, the Collection* (Baltimore: Johns Hopkins University Press, 1984), pp. 23, 142, 143, 23, 150.

16. Renato Rosaldo, *Culture and Truth: The Remaking of Social Analysis* (Boston: Beacon Press, 1989), pp. 69, 70.

17. Lee Clark Mitchell, *Westerns: Making the Man in Fiction and Film* (Chicago: University of Chicago Press, 1996), p. 97.

18. Larry McMurtry, *Walter Benjamin at the Dairy Queen: Reflections at Sixty and Beyond* (New York: Simon and Schuster, 1999), pp. 88, 189.

19. Gerald D. Nash, *Creating the West: Historical Interpretations, 1890–1990* (Albuquerque: University of New Mexico Press, 1991), p. 264.

20. McMurtry, *Walter Benjamin at the Dairy Queen*, p. 197.

21. Harold McCracken, Introduction, *Frederic Remington's Own West*, ed. Harold McCracken (New York: Dial Press, 1960), p. 7.

22. Richard W. Etulain, *Re-imagining the Modern American West: A Century of Fiction, History, and Art* (Tucson: University of Arizona Press, 1996), p. 59.

23. Alex Nemerov, "'Doing the "Old America"': The Image of the American West, 1880–1920," in *The West as America: Reinterpreting Images of the Frontier, 1820–1920*, ed. William H. Truettner (Washington, DC: Smithsonian Institution Press, 1991), p. 290.

24. Ibid., pp. 294–95, 321.

25. William H. Truettner, "Ideology and Image: Justifying Westward Expansion," in *West as America*, ed. Truettner, p. 39.

26. See William H. Goetzmann and William N. Goetzmann, *The West of the Imagination* (New York: Norton, 1986), p. 270, where, without formal citation, they attribute to Brian Dippie the opinion that Russell "probably never witnessed a buffalo hunt, and if he did, it was not in the traditional Indian manner."

27. Kate F. Jennings, *Remington and Russell and the Art of the American West* (New York: Smithmark, 1993), p. 80.

28. Etulain, *Re-imagining the Modern American West*, pp. 65, 66.

29. See Goetzmann and Goetzmann, *West of the Imagination*, p. 275.

30. Joni L. Kinsey, "Viewing the West: The Popular Culture of American Western Painting," in *Wanted Dead or Alive: The American West in Popular Culture*, ed. Richard Aquila (Urbana: University of Illinois Press, 1996), pp. 257, 258.

31. Goetzmann and Goetzmann, *West of the Imagination*, pp. 283, 282.

32. America wasn't the only country that wanted such a West. In "Theorizing the Western," an essay review of several studies of the genre, Susan Kollin reminds us that Karl May (1842–1912), the prolific German writer of Westerns much read by Adolf Hitler, was strongly influenced by James Fenimore Cooper, "whose idealization of the 'wild' was easily grafted onto German cultural concerns in the twentieth century" (*Western American Literature* 34 [1999]: 241).

33. Etulain, *Re-imagining the Modern American West*, p. xx.

34. Barre Toelken, "Folklore in the American West," in *A Literary History of the American West*, ed. J. Golden Taylor et al. (Fort Worth: Texas Christian University Press, 1987), p. 50.

35. Richard C. Poulsen, *The Landscape of the Mind: Cultural Transformations of the American West* (New York: Lang, 1992), pp. 17, 30. On the whole matter of marketing Western nostalgia, see Christine Bold, *Selling the Wild West: Popular Western Fiction, 1860 to 1960* (Blooming-

ton: Indiana University Press, 1987); Marcus Klein, *Easterns, Westerns, and Private Eyes: American Matters, 1870–1900* (Madison: University of Wisconsin Press, 1994); and G. Edward White, *The Eastern Establishment and the Western Experience: The West of Frederic Remington, Theodore Roosevelt, and Owen Wister* (New Haven, CT: Yale University Press, 1968).

36. Nash, Introduction, p. 1.

37. Jack London, *The Call of the Wild* (New York: Tor, 1990), p. 105.

38. Nash, Introduction, p. 2.

39. Ibid., p. 3. The increasing currency of the word *conservation* correlates with a change in attitude toward wilderness that's accompanied by a change in the metaphors used to describe it, a change Kaye E. Adkins traces in her doctoral dissertation, "Paradise Renamed: Context and the Metaphoric Reconstruction of American Wilderness, 1872–1916" (University of Kansas, 1998), which "reveals a gradual shift in metaphors from an emphasis on wilderness as wasteland or as warehouse to alternate depictions of wilderness as a physical and spiritual healer, as Paradise, as a house of worship, as a garden, as a farm, and as domestic space" (p. iii).

40. Ray Allen Billington, *Land of Savagery, Land of Promise: The European Image of the American Frontier in the Nineteenth Century* (New York: Norton, 1981), p. 313.

41. Frederick Turner, *Beyond Geography: The Western Spirit against the Wilderness* (1980; reprint ed., New Brunswick, NJ: Rutgers University Press, 1992), p. 272.

42. Cronon, "Trouble with Wilderness," pp. 78, 79.

43. Catherine L. Albanese, *Nature Religion in America: From the Algonkian Indians to the New Age* (Chicago: University of Chicago Press, 1990), p. 107.

44. Roderick Nash, *Wilderness and the American Mind*, 3rd ed. (New Haven, CT: Yale University Press, 1982), p. 160.

45. Wrobel, *End of American Exceptionalism*, p. 97.

Long Live the Weeds and the Wilderness Yet: Preserving the West

1. Hal K. Rothman, *Devil's Bargains: Tourism in the Twentieth-Century American West* (Lawrence: University Press of Kansas, 1998), p. 50.

2. Ibid., pp. 119, 120. Concerning Roosevelt's contradictoriness, Howard R. Lamar remarks that "he somehow managed to be both the symbol of a corporate, industrial, urban America and an America that harked back to an older, western frontier-oriented nation" ("An Overview of Westward Expansion," in *The West as America: Reinterpreting Images of the Frontier, 1820–1920*, ed. William H. Truettner [Washington, DC: Smithsonian Institution Press, 1991], p. 22). As Roderick Nash sums him up, "East and West, city and country, the machine and the garden—in Roosevelt they existed in delicate balance" (Introduction, *The Call of the Wild, 1910–1916*, ed. Roderick Nash [New York: Braziller, 1970], p. 8).

3. Michael P. Branch, "'Angel Guiding Gently': The Yosemite Meeting of Ralph Waldo Emerson and John Muir, 1871," *Western American Literature* 32 (1997): 132, 133. In regard to Muir's agreements and disagreements with Pinchot over issues of preservation, see Melanie L. Simo, *Forest and Garden: Traces of Wildness in a Modernizing Land, 1897–1949* (Charlottesville: University of Virginia Press, 2003), pp. 4–8.

4. See Frederick Turner, *Rediscovering America: John Muir in His Time and Ours* (New York: Viking, 1985).

5. Simon Schama, *Landscape and Memory* (New York: Vintage Books, 1996), pp. 7, 189, 7, 9. The material quoted from Adams is from a letter to Newton Drury, January 22 1952, and a

letter to David Brower, 15 February 1956, in Ansel Adams, *Our National Parks*, ed. Andrea G. Stillman and William A. Turnage (Boston: Little, Brown, 1992), pp. 113, 117.

6. Catherine L. Albanese, *Nature Religion in America: From the Algonkian Indians to the New Age* (Chicago: University of Chicago Press, 1990), p. 95.

7. Ansel Adams, *Yosemite and the Range of Light* (Boston: New York Graphic Society Books, 1979), p. 12.

8. Therese Lichtenstein, *Master of Light: Ansel Adams and His Influences* (New York: Todtri, 1997), pp. 7, 8, 9, 8. The disappointment comes about not only because of the paradisal anticipations Adams stirs up but also because his photographs—like those of his predecessors such as William H. Jackson, Timothy O'Sullivan, and Carleton E. Watkins—have what Joni L. Kinsey describes as an "ability to convey an undeniable reality about the West's exotic landscapes"; indeed, it was the "implicit veracity" of such photography "that made it seem a reliable witness to viewers far removed from the places and subjects portrayed"—so much so that "it could be said that it was principally through photography that Americans came to know the national parks and that the medium is still one of the most important means by which we enjoy them today" ("Viewing the West: The Popular Culture of American Western Painting," in *Wanted Dead or Alive: The American West in Popular Culture*, ed. Richard Aquila [Urbana: University of Illinois Press, 1996], pp. 248, 249). Concerning the ambiguities of visitors' relationships to the parks as canonized art, see Scott Herring, *Lines on the Land: Writers, Art, and the National Parks* (Charlottesville: University of Virginia Press, 2004).

9. Timothy Egan, *Lasso the Wind: Away to the New West* (New York: Knopf, 1998), p. 176. The extent to which Yellowstone attracted national interest not just by virtue of its beauties but as well by how its name (from the French "Roche Jaune, which first surfaced in 1795," Egan notes [p. 173]) subtly suggested the presence of gold makes for an interesting question.

10. Richard White, *"It's Your Misfortune and None of My Own": A New History of the American West* (Norman: University of Oklahoma Press, 1991), pp. 410, 411. Issues about nationalism and the park system are treated *passim* in any number of books, among them the following: Stephen J. Pyne, *How the Canyon Became Grand: A Short History* (New York: Viking, 1998); Hans Huth, *Nature and the American: Three Centuries of Changing Attitudes*, new ed. (Lincoln: University of Nebraska Press, 1990), esp. pp. 148–212; John C. Miles, *Guardians of the Parks: A History of the National Parks and Conservation Association* (Bristol, UK: Taylor and Francis, 1995); Paul Schullery and Lee Whittlesey, *Myth and History in the Creation of Yellowstone National Park* (Lincoln: University of Nebraska Press, 2003); and Richard Grusin, *Culture, Technology, and the Creation of America's National Parks* (New York: Cambridge University Press, 2004).

11. William Cronon, "The Trouble with Wilderness; or, Getting Back to the Wrong Nature," in *Uncommon Ground: Rethinking the Human Place in Nature*, ed. William Cronon (New York: Norton, 1995), pp. 76–77.

12. Denis Cosgrove, "Habitable Earth: Wilderness, Empire, and Race in America," in *Wild Ideas*, ed. David Rothenberg (Minneapolis: University of Minnesota Press, 1995), p. 36.

13. Richard Rhodes, "The Killing of the Everglades," *Playboy*, January 1972, p. 281.

14. Samuel I. Zeveloff, L. Mikel Vause, and William H. McVaugh, "A Multidimensional Mandate for Wilderness Preservation," in *Wilderness Tapestry: An Eclectic Approach to Preservation*, ed. Samuel I. Zeveloff, L. Mikel Vause, and William H. McVaugh (Reno: University of Nevada Press, 1992), p. 4.

15. Ibid., pp. 4, 5.

16. In a review of Robert L. Dorman's *A Word for Nature: Four Pioneering Environmental Advocates, 1845–1913*, Hillel Schwartz contends that both utilitarian conservationists like John Wesley Powell and George Perkins Marsh and preservationists like Thoreau and Muir "had to manage a Niagara Falls trapeze act between utilitarian and moral-aesthetic categories" and that "each blurred the distinctions so that he could argue that self-interest demanded of every human being a serious interest in the welfare of swamps, streams, rivers, fields, forests, and mountains around them" (*Journal of Unconventional History* 10, no. 2 [Winter 1998]: 75).

17. Keith Thomas, *Man and the Natural World: Changing Attitudes in England, 1500–1800* (1983; reprint ed., New York: Oxford University Press, 1996), p. 302.

18. See Donald Worster, *A River Running West: The Life of John Wesley Powell* (New York: Oxford University Press, 2001), p. 484.

19. On disputes with Indians over national parks, see Robert H. Keller and Michael F. Turek, *American Indians and National Parks* (Tucson: University of Arizona Press, 1998). On the ideology of—and practices employed in—culturally shaping parks that gave rise to such disputes, see Stephen A. Germic, *American Green: Class, Crisis, and the Deployment of Nature in Central Park, Yosemite, and Yellowstone* (Lanham, MD: Lexington Books, 2001).

20. Rothman, *Devil's Bargains*, p. 80.

21. Alison Byerly, "The Uses of Landscape: The Picturesque Aesthetic and the National Park System," in *The Ecocriticism Reader: Landmarks in Literary Ecology*, ed. Cheryll Glotfelty and Harold Fromm (Athens: University of Georgia Press, 1996), pp. 53–54, 64. An excellent study of how processes such as aestheticization have conceptually imprisoned nature is Neil Everden, *The Social Creation of Nature* (Baltimore: Johns Hopkins University Press, 1992).

22. Barbara Novak, *Nature and Culture: American Landscape and Painting, 1825–1875*, rev. ed. (New York: Oxford University Press, 1995), p. 159.

23. Kenneth R. Olwig, "Reinventing Common Nature: Yosemite and Mount Rushmore—A Meandering Tale of a Double Nature," in *Uncommon Ground*, ed. Cronon, pp. 382, 388, 384, 401, 402.

24. Sharman Apt Russell, *Kill the Cowboy: A Battle of Mythology in the New West* (Reading, MA: Addison-Wesley, 1993), p. 197.

25. Patricia Nelson Limerick, *The Legacy of Conquest: The Unbroken Past of the American West* (New York: Norton, 1987), pp. 311, 309, 310. Such weaknesses obtain even in managing relatively limited situations, such as that of a free-ranging herd of buffalo, the management of which, Peter A. Coates says, "is arguably as much of an oxymoron as the management of wilderness" ("Improving on 'A Paradise of Game': Ecological Impacts, Game Management, and Alaska's Buffalo Transplant," *Western Historical Quarterly* 28 [1997]: 157). Also, the ecological senselessness of national parks resulted from scientifically unsophisticated aesthetic considerations as well as from political ones. In that connection, Thomas R. Cox draws attention to Alfred Runte's argument that, as Cox summarizes it (from Runte's *National Parks: The American Experience* [Lincoln: University of Nebraska Press, 1979], pp. 108–10, 118–40), the boundaries of Yellowstone are thus senseless because its founders were so thoroughly "directed . . . toward simply saving spectacular scenery" ("Research Opportunities in Twentieth-Century Western History: Natural Resources and Environment," in *Researching Western History: Topics in the Twentieth Century*, ed. Gerald D. Nash and Richard W. Etulain [Albuquerque: University of New Mexico Press, 1997], p. 30).

26. Stephen J. Pyne, *Fire in America: A Cultural History of Wildland and Rural Fire* (Princeton, NJ: Princeton University Press, 1982), p. 17.

27. Gundars Rudzitis, *Wilderness and the Changing American West* (New York: Wiley, 1996), pp. 20, 51.

28. Patricia Nelson Limerick, *Something in the Soil: Legacies and Reckonings in the New West* (New York: Norton, 2000), pp. 173, 174, 175.

29. Roderick Nash, *Wilderness and the American Mind*, 3rd ed. (New Haven, CT: Yale University Press, 1982), p. 316.

30. Timothy Egan, "Story of a Hole in the Ground," review of *How the Canyon Became Grand: A Short History*, by Stephen J. Pyne, *New York Times Book Review*, 20 September 1998, p. 28.

31. Rothman, *Devil's Bargains*, p. 151. With respect to the impact of road building and automobiles on American wilderness during the interwar years, especially in the West, as well as how awareness of that impact motivated the organization in 1935 of the Wilderness Society, whose advocacies climaxed in the passage of the Wilderness Act of 1964, see Paul S. Sutter, *Driven Wild: How the Fight against Automobiles Launched the Modern Wilderness Movement* (Seattle: University of Washington Press, 2002).

32. Robert G. Athearn, *The Mythic West in Twentieth-Century America* (Lawrence: University Press of Kansas, 1986), p. 216.

33. Wallace Stegner, "Wilderness Letter," in *The Sound of Mountain Water* (New York: Doubleday, 1969), pp. 145, 148, 153.

34. Irene Klaver, "Silent Wolves: The Howl of the Implicit," in *Wild Ideas*, ed. David Rothenberg (Minneapolis: University of Minnesota Press, 1995), p. 124.

35. William Fox, *Driving by Memory* (Albuquerque: University of New Mexico Press, 1999), p. 27.

36. Yi-Fu Tuan, *Topophilia: A Study of Environmental Perception, Attitudes, and Values* (1974; reprint ed., New York: Columbia University Press, 1990), p. 112.

37. William H. Truettner, "Ideology and Image: Justifying Westward Expansion," in *West as America*, ed. Truettner, p. 48. Even as Moran was painting *The Grand Canyon of the Yellowstone* (1872), concessionaires' capitalistic commodification of the place into idealized roadside attractions, an enterprise later supported by the National Park Service, was beginning—see Mark Daniel Barringer, *Selling Yellowstone: Capitalism and the Construction of Nature* (Lawrence: University Press of Kansas, 2002).

Wild West Shows, Rodeos, and Dude Ranches: Wildness as Specious Spectacle, Ritual Reenactment, and Tenderfoot Travesty

1. Paul Reddin, *Wild West Shows* (Urbana: University of Illinois Press, 1999), p. 219.

2. L. G. Moses, *Wild West Shows and the Images of American Indians, 1883–1933* (Albuquerque: University of New Mexico Press, 1996), pp. 15, 17.

3. Reddin, *Wild West Shows*, p. 3.

4. Ibid., pp. 14, 17, 18.

5. See Joseph G. Rosa and Robin May, *Buffalo Bill and His Wild West: A Pictorial Biography* (Lawrence: University Press of Kansas, 1989), pp. 71–72.

6. Reddin, *Wild West Shows*, pp. 220–21, 223, 224. The characterization of Wild West shows as mythologizing spectacles could be applied as well to many contemporaneous theatrical productions about the frontier, some of which, of course, starred Cody—see Roger A. Hall's *Performing the American Frontier, 1870–1906* (New York: Cambridge University Press, 2001).

7. Ian Frazier, *Great Plains* (New York: Penguin Books, 1990), p. 182.

8. Jane Tompkins, *West of Everything: The Inner Life of Westerns* (New York: Oxford University Press, 1992), pp. 198, 199, 200.

9. Moses, *Wild West Shows and the Images of American Indians*, pp. 1, 8. Regarding the role of the powwow in forging Indian identity, see Clyde Ellis, *A Dancing People: Powwow Culture on the Southern Plains* (Lawrence: University Press of Kansas, 2003).

10. John D. Dorst, *Looking West* (Philadelphia: University of Pennsylvania Press, 1999), pp. 31, 32, 33, 32, 34. For a more detailed history of Cody's relationship with Sitting Bull, see Bobby Bridger, *Buffalo Bill and Sitting Bull: Inventing the Wild West* (Austin: University of Texas Press, 2002).

11. N. Scott Momaday, "The American West and the Burden of Belief," in *The Man Made of Words: Essays, Stories, Passages* (New York: St. Martin's Press, 1997), pp. 98, 106.

12. Henry Nash Smith, *Virgin Land: The American West as Symbol and Myth* (1950; reprint ed., Cambridge, MA: Harvard University Press, 1970), p. 108.

13. Richard White, "Frederick Jackson Turner and Buffalo Bill," in *The Frontier in American Culture: An Exhibition at the Newberry Library, August 26, 1994–January 7, 1995: Essays by Richard White and Patricia Nelson Limerick*, ed. James R. Grossman (Berkeley: University of California Press, 1994), pp. 11, 29, 35.

14. Rita Parks, *The Western Hero in Film and Television: Mass Media Mythology* (Ann Arbor, MI: UMI Research Press, 1982), p. 4, 65.

15. Joy S. Kasson, *Buffalo Bill's Wild West: Celebrity, Memory, and Popular History* (New York: Hill and Wang, 2000), pp. 13, 272, 273.

16. Ibid., pp. 273, 18.

17. Richard Slotkin, *Gunfighter Nation: The Myth of the Frontier in Twentieth-Century America* (1992; reprint ed., New York: HarperPerennial, 1993), pp. 63, 77.

18. Reid Badger, *The Great American Fair: The World's Columbian Exposition and American Culture* (Chicago: Nelson Hall, 1979), pp. 125, 126, 127.

19. Slotkin, *Gunfighter Nation*, pp. 81, 86.

20. Ibid., p. 87.

21. Moses, *Wild West Shows and the Images of American Indians*, pp. 275, 276. For an extended and provocative discussion of the cultural significance of Cody and his show that bears on several of my points, see Louis S. Warren, *Buffalo Bill's America: William Cody and the Wild West Show* (New York: Knopf, 2005).

22. Michael Allen, *Rodeo Cowboys in the North American Imagination* (Reno: University of Nevada Press, 1998), p. 16. The reader interested in further history of early rodeo might consult the following sources: Kristine Fredriksson, *American Rodeo: From Buffalo Bill to Big Business* (College Station: Texas A&M University Press, 1985), pp. 4–20; Richard W. Slatta, *Cowboys of the Americas* (New Haven, CT: Yale University Press, 1990), pp. 209–14; Mary Lou LeCompte, *Cowgirls of the Rodeo: Pioneer Professional Athletes* (Urbana: University of Illinois Press, 1993), pp. 6–16; and Wayne S. Wooden and Gavin Ehringer, *Rodeo in America: Wranglers, Roughstock, and Paydirt* (Lawrence: University Press of Kansas, 1996), pp. 7–16.

23. Allen, *Rodeo Cowboys*, pp. 22, 17.

24. Elizabeth Atwood Lawrence, *Rodeo: An Anthropologist Looks at the Wild and the Tame* (Knoxville: University of Tennessee Press, 1982), p. 267.

25. Beverly J. Stoeltje, "Rodeo: From Custom to Ritual," *Western Folklore* 48, no. 3 (July 1989): 245, 248.

26. Allen, *Rodeo Cowboys*, pp. 26, 33, 34, 35.

27. Lawrence, *Rodeo*, pp. 5, 7, 11, 269.

28. Allen, *Rodeo Cowboys*, pp. 5, 14, 6, 7, 12. The art-life conundrum Allen articulates gets more tangled when you take into account the fact that, during the pronounced dip in the cattle market in the 1880s and 1890s, "displaced cowboys . . . preserved their past on printed pages" by becoming "professional poets" as well as artists in other media—a trend that certainly continued past the end of the nineteenth century (Blake Allmendinger, *The Cowboy: Representations of Labor in an American Work Culture* [New York: Oxford University Press, 1992], pp. 9, 10).

29. Lawrence, *Rodeo*, pp. 189, 195.

30. Ibid., p. 197.

31. Stoeltje, "Rodeo: From Custom to Ritual," p. 254.

32. Hal K. Rothman, *Devil's Bargains: Tourism in the Twentieth-Century American West* (Lawrence: University Press of Kansas, 1998), p. 142.

33. Robert G. Athearn, *The Mythic West in Twentieth-Century America* (Lawrence: University Press of Kansas, 1986), p. 140.

34. Patricia Nelson Limerick, "Seeing and Being Seen: Tourism in the American West," in *Over the Edge: Remapping the American West*, ed. Valerie J. Matsumoto and Blake Allmendinger (Berkeley: University of California Press, 1999), p. 21.

35. Ibid.

36. Athearn, *Mythic West*, p. 137.

37. The origin of the word *dude* is a matter of disagreement, but it may well have come about through rural Westerners referring to the urban clothes, *duds*, of Easterners.

38. Athearn, *Mythic West*, p. 139.

39. Rothman, *Devil's Bargains*, pp. 115, 117, 116.

40. Fred Erisman, "The Enduring Myth and the Modern West," in *Researching Western History: Topics in the Twentieth Century*, ed. Gerald D. Nash and Richard W. Etulain (Albuquerque: University of New Mexico Press, 1997), p. 176.

41. Rothman, *Devil's Bargains*, p. 118.

42. "Western Adventures," advertisement, *American Cowboy*, July–August 1997, p. 91.

Dust Bowl: The Great American Desert with a Vengeance

1. Ernie Pyle, "Boom and Bust," in *Eyewitness to the American West: From the Aztec Empire to the Digital Frontier in the Words of Those Who Saw It Happen*, ed. David Colbert (New York: Viking, 1998), p. 297.

2. William Allen White, "Wagons East!" in *Eyewitness to the American West*, ed. Colbert, p. 205.

3. Elliott West, *The Contested Plains: Indians, Goldseekers, and the Rush to Colorado* (Lawrence: University Press of Kansas, 1998), p. 330.

4. Wallace Stegner, "Thoughts in a Dry Land," in *Where the Bluebird Sings to the Lemonade Springs: Living and Writing in the West* (1992; reprint ed., New York: Penguin Books, 1993), p. 46.

5. Wallace Stegner, "Living Dry," in *Where the Bluebird Sings*, pp. 57–58, 75.

6. Donald Worster, *Under Western Skies: Nature and History in the American West* (New York: Oxford University Press, 1992), pp. 94, 96. In an innovative essay on how historical narratives try to find the meaning of events through culturally constructed plots ("A Place for Stories: Nature, History, and Narrative," *Journal of American History* 78 [1992]: 1347–76), William Cronon discusses Worster's *Dust Bowl* as one of several declensionist versions of a story that

others, in competing narratives, tell in happier ways, with ascending plots; but, whatever their cogency in the past, the latter, with their unfounded optimism, now strain credibility to the breaking point.

7. Worster, *Under Western Skies*, pp. 98, 99, 100, 103.

8. Walter Prescott Webb, *The Great Plains* (1931; reprint ed., Lincoln: University of Nebraska Press, 1981), p. 376.

9. Blake Allmendinger, *Ten Most Wanted: The New Western Literature* (New York: Routledge, 1998), p. 144.

10. Donald Worster, *An Unsettled Country: Changing Landscapes of the American West* (Albuquerque: University of New Mexico Press, 1994), p. 103.

11. Frieda Knobloch, *The Culture of Wilderness: Agriculture as Colonization in the American West* (Chapel Hill: University of North Carolina Press, 1996), p. 16.

12. Stephanie Sarver, "William Ellsworth Smythe's Drama of Reclamation," *Western American Literature* 31 (1996): 224, 215, 216, 225. Concerning Smythe's success in promoting his democratic vision of an irrigated West—which would turn out, ironically, to be more what Sarver labels "an hydraulic empire" (p. 225)—see Donald Worster, *Rivers of Empire: Water, Aridity, and the Growth of the American West* (1985; reprint ed., New York: Oxford University Press, 1992), pp. 118–21.

13. William H. Goetzmann and William N. Goetzmann, *The West of the Imagination* (New York: Norton, 1986), p. 381.

14. Ian Frazier, *Great Plains* (New York: Penguin Books, 1990), pp. 196, 197.

15. Ibid., p. 199.

16. Richard White, *"It's Your Misfortune and None of My Own": A New History of the American West* (Norman: University of Oklahoma Press, 1991), p. 522.

17. Gene M. Gressley, "Regionalism and the Twentieth-Century West," in *The American West: New Perspectives, New Dimensions*, ed. Jerome O. Steffen (Norman: University of Oklahoma Press, 1979), p. 208. Americans have a history of failing to learn such lessons well, as John Opie shows in "Frontier History in Environmental Perspective," pp. 9–34 of the same volume.

18. Curt Meine, "The Utility of Preservation and the Preservation of Utility: Leopold's Fine Line," in *The Wilderness Condition: Essays on Environment and Civilization*, ed. Max Oelschlaeger (San Francisco: Sierra Club Books, 1992), p. 162.

19. Hans Huth, *Nature and the American: Three Centuries of Changing Attitudes*, new ed. (Lincoln: University of Nebraska Press, 1990), p. 193. On the ongoing and worsening problems of trying to make farmland into a machine, see *Fatal Harvest: The Tragedy of Industrial Agriculture*, ed. Andrew Kimbrell (Washington, DC: Island Press, 2002).

20. Worster, *Unsettled Country*, pp. 23, 101, 103.

21. Ibid., pp. 110, 120.

22. In this connection, see Randal S. Beeman and James A. Pritchard, *A Green and Permanent Land: Ecology and Agriculture in the Twentieth Century* (Lawrence: University Press of Kansas, 2001), much of which, in its consideration of alternative agricultural theories and practices, is germane to the post–Dust Bowl West, and Willard W. Cochrane, *The Curse of American Agricultural Abundance: A Sustainable Solution* (Lincoln: University of Nebraska Press, 2003).

23. Richard Manning, *Grassland: The History, Biology, Politics, and Promise of the American Prairie* (New York: Viking, 1995), pp. 267, 268.

24. Ibid., pp. 268, 270.

25. Wes Jackson, "Becoming Native to This Place," Twenty-eighth Annual Meeting of the Western Literature Association, Wichita, Kansas, October 8, 1993.

Re-imagining the Wildness: Modern Mediations

1. Larry McMurtry, "Notes on Rodeo: Occasioned by the Arena Photography of Louise L. Serpa," in Louise L. Serpa, *Rodeo* (New York: Aperture Foundation, 1994), p. 83.

2. Anne F. Hyde, "Cultural Filters: The Significance of Perception," in *A New Significance: Re-envisioning the History of the American West*, ed. Clyde A. Milner II (New York: Oxford University Press, 1996), pp. 192, 193.

3. Ibid., pp. 195, 197.

4. David Mogen, Scott P. Sanders, and Joanne B. Karpinski, Introduction, *Frontier Gothic: Terror and Wonder at the Frontier in American Literature*, ed. David Mogen, Scott P. Sanders, and Joanne B. Karpinski (Rutherford, NJ: Fairleigh Dickinson University Press, 1993), p. 15. They also note that the gothicism associated with the wilderness encountered makes it "a profoundly American symbol of an ambiguous relationship to the land" and "results when the epic moment passes, and a peculiar rift in history develops and widens into a dark chasm that separates what is now from what has been" (pp. 20, 16).

5. Barbara Allen, "Shaping and Being Shaped by the Land: The Western Landscape in Oral Narrative," in *The Big Empty: Essays on Western Landscapes as Narrative*, ed. Leonard Engel (Albuquerque: University of New Mexico Press, 1994), p. 107.

6. Forrest G. Robinson, *Having It Both Ways: Self-subversion in Western Popular Classics* (Albuquerque: University of New Mexico Press, 1993), p. 37.

7. Roderick Nash, *Wilderness and the American Mind*, 3rd ed. (New Haven, CT: Yale University Press, 1982), p. 77.

8. Robert G. Athearn, *The Mythic West in Twentieth-Century America* (Lawrence: University Press of Kansas, 1986), p. 165. See also Stephen Tatum's psychoanalytic characterization of this pull in his "Topographies of Transition in Western American Literature," *Western American Literature* 32 (1998): 319–23.

9. Thomas J. Lyon, "The Literary West," in *The Oxford History of the American West*, ed. Clyde A. Milner II, Carol A. O'Connor, and Martha A. Sandweiss (New York: Oxford University Press, 1994), p. 708.

10. A. Carl Bredahl Jr., *New Ground: Western American Narrative and the Literary Canon* (Chapel Hill: University of North Carolina Press, 1989), p. 43.

11. John R. Milton, *The Novel of the American West* (Lincoln: University of Nebraska Press, 1980), p. xiv. For his more detailed outline of the differences between Western and Eastern fiction, see pp. 57–60.

12. While I understand the critical rationale behind Leslie A. Fiedler's dictum that the Indian is the sine qua non of the wilderness confronted in this master-narrative, I don't agree with his opinion that "tales set in the West seem to us not quite Westerns, unfulfilled occasions for myth rather than myth itself, when no Indian . . . appears in them" (*The Return of the Vanishing American* [New York: Stein and Day, 1968], p. 24).

13. Lyon, "Literary West," p. 712. For some examples, see *Reading the West: An Anthology of Dime Westerns*, ed. Bill Brown (Boston: Bedford Books, 1997).

14. Athearn, *Mythic West*, p. 160.

15. Jane Tompkins, *West of Everything: The Inner Life of Westerns* (New York: Oxford University Press, 1992), pp. 14, 15, 45, 44. My suggestion that the Western satisfies a hunger for

adventurous meaning isn't facetious. In an insightful study of several Westerns, as well as N. Scott Momaday's *The Man Made of Words*, Susan J. Rosowski argues that "the language of the West is as wild and lawless as the country, for there, words—like individuals—have the potential to be anything at all" ("The Western Hero as Logos; or, Unmaking Meaning," *Western American Literature* 32 [1997]: 271).

16. William Bloodworth, "Writers of the Purple Sage: Novelists and the American West," in *Wanted Dead or Alive: The American West in Popular Culture*, ed. Richard Aquila (Urbana: University of Illinois Press, 1996), pp. 45, 62, 65.

17. Thomas J. Lyon, "Introduction: The Conquistador, the Lone Ranger, and Beyond," in *The Literary West: An Anthology of Western American Literature* (New York: Oxford University Press, 1999), p. 7.

18. Lee Clark Mitchell, *Westerns: Making the Man in Fiction and Film* (Chicago: University of Chicago Press, 1996), p. 27. Discussing the Western hero and his two worlds, Mitchell argues on the same page that "the Western is a form committed not to *resolving* these incompatible worlds but to *narrating* all those contradictions involved in what it means to be a man, in a way that makes them seem less troubling than they are"—an argument in response to Martin Pumphrey's analysis of the "most familiar narrative moments" in the filmic Western: "When examined, those moments—the refusal to draw first, the gentlemanly kindnesses, the glass of milk or soda pop in the saloon—reveal an ideal of masculinity founded on fundamental contradictions. Heroes must be *both* dominant and deferential, gentle and violent," and so on—they "must bridge, that is, not simply the division between savagery and civilization but the anxiously guarded (ambiguously experienced) frontier between the two worlds usually coded as masculine and feminine" ("The Western: A Cultural and Historical Dictionary," s.v. "masculinity," in *The BFI Companion to the Western*, ed. Edward Buscombe [New York: Atheneum, 1988], p. 181).

19. Russell Martin, Introduction, *Writers of the Purple Sage: An Anthology of Recent Western Writing*, ed. Russell Martin and Marc Barasch (New York: Viking, 1984), pp. x, xi–xii.

20. Lyon, "Literary West," p. 721.

21. Lyon, "Introduction," pp. 9, 10.

22. James C. Work, Introduction to Part 4: The Neowestern Period, 1915–Present, *Prose and Poetry of the American West*, ed. James C. Work (Lincoln: University of Nebraska Press, 1990), p. 627.

23. Athearn, *Mythic West*, pp. 162, 171.

24. Fred Erisman, "The Enduring Myth and the Modern West," in *Researching Western History: Topics in the Twentieth Century*, ed. Gerald D. Nash and Richard W. Etulain (Albuquerque: University of New Mexico Press, 1997), p. 177.

25. Blake Allmendinger, *Ten Most Wanted: The New Western Literature* (New York: Routledge, 1998), pp. 42–43, 50.

26. Mitchell, *Westerns*, pp. 79, 75.

27. Patrick D. Morrow, "Bret Harte, Mark Twain, and the San Francisco Circle," in *A Literary History of the American West*, ed. J. Golden Taylor et al. (Fort Worth: Texas Christian University Press, 1987), pp. 351, 352.

28. Relevant here is Lawrence Howe's contention that *Huckleberry Finn* "ironizes the ideal return to nature" (*Mark Twain and the Novel: The Double-Cross of Authority* [Cambridge: Cambridge University Press, 1998], p. 75).

29. Allmendinger, *Ten Most Wanted*, pp. 121, 106, 117, 120.

30. Lyon, "Literary West," p. 722. As he says on the same page, Crane was "attracted to the mythology" of romance but was also "subvertingly conscious of the attraction."

31. Richard W. Etulain, *Re-imagining the Modern American West: A Century of Fiction, History, and Art* (Tucson: University of Arizona Press, 1996), p. 24.

32. Lyon, "Literary West," p. 715.

33. Stephen Tatum, "The Problem of the 'Popular' in the New Western History," in *The New Western History: An Assessment*, ed. Forrest G. Robinson, a special issue of *Arizona Quarterly* 53, no. 2 (Summer 1997): 175, 179.

34. Robert Brophy, "Robinson Jeffers," in *Literary History of the American West*, ed. Taylor et al., pp. 409, 410, 411.

35. Thomas J. Lyon, "Revisionist Western Classics," in *Reading the West: New Essays on the Literature of the American West*, ed. Michael Kowalewski (Cambridge: Cambridge University Press, 1996), p. 150.

36. Fiedler, *Return of the Vanishing American*, p. 147.

37. Harold P. Simonson, *Beyond the Frontier: Writers, Western Regionalism and a Sense of Place* (Fort Worth: Texas Christian University Press, 1989), p. 13.

38. Charles L. Adams, "Frank Waters," in *Literary History of the American West*, ed. Taylor et al., pp. 935, 943.

39. Lyon, "Revisionist Western Classics," pp. 154, 155.

40. For an extended discussion of Boone Caudill's ironic relation to the wilderness, see Paul T. Bryant, "External Characterization in *The Big Sky*," *Western American Literature* 31 (1996): 195–210.

41. Lyon, "Literary West," p. 715.

42. Forrest G. Robinson, *Having It Both Ways*, p. 93. Moreover, while it may be true in some sense that the civilized community Shane defends is, as Robinson argues, "all, in short, that he is not" (p. 84), it's also true, more complexly, that he shows through his self-less and chivalric motives "signs of a nobility" that distinguish him as "an aristocrat of violence, an alien from a more glamorous world, who is better than those he helps" (Richard Slotkin, *Gunfighter Nation: The Myth of the Frontier in Twentieth-Century America* [1992; reprint ed., New York: HarperPerennial, 1993], p. 400).

43. Lyon, "Literary West," p. 715.

44. On *In Cold Blood* as a complex example of queer-frontier literature, see Allmendinger, *Ten Most Wanted*, pp. 160–70.

45. See, for instance, Annette Kolodny, *The Lay of the Land: Metaphor as Experience and History in American Life and Letters* (Chapel Hill: University of North Carolina Press, 1975), pp. 71–72.

46. Lyon, "Literary West," p. 725.

47. *Slogum House*, set in two fictitious counties on the Niobrara River in northwestern Nebraska around the turn of the century, is extraordinarily arresting in its revisionism because of its portraying a woman, Regula Haber Slogum (known as Gulla), as a villain, thus turning on its head the commonplace of woman as civilizer of the West. Gulla, Glenda Riley notes, "defied every western convention of the times—and, in doing so, probably . . . perplexed a goodly number of readers" among Americans who typically "thought of the West as female, a ripe, fertile source of abundance often defiled by rapacious men" and didn't know that "women pillaged it as well" ("Mari Sandoz's *Slogum House*: Greed as Woman," *Great Plains Quarterly* 16 [1996]: 35).

48. Susan J. Rosowski, "Molly's Truthtelling; or, Jean Stafford Rewrites the Western," in *Reading the West*, ed. Kowalewski, pp. 158, 159.

49. James C. Work, "Dorothy Johnson (1905–84)," in *Prose and Poetry of the American West*, ed. Work, p. 507. He acknowledges his indebtedness for this formulation to Barbara Howard Meldrum's consideration of Johnson and the "wild pastoral" ("Dorothy M. Johnson's Short Fiction: The Pastoral and the Uses of History," *Western American Literature* 17 [1982]: 214).

50. Lyon, "Introduction," p. 12.

51. Everett A. Gillis, "Oliver La Farge," in *Literary History of the American West*, ed. Taylor et al., p. 570.

52. Athearn, *Mythic West*, p. 167.

53. Thomas J. Lyon, "The Nature Essay in the West," in *Literary History of the American West*, ed. Taylor et al., pp. 240, 239.

54. Larry McMurtry, "Southwestern Literature?" in *In a Narrow Grave: Essays on Texas* (1968; reprint ed., New York: Touchstone, 1989), pp. 31, 35–36.

55. Lyon, "Nature Essay in the West," p. 253.

56. Ibid., p. 251.

57. Glen A. Love, "Revaluing Nature: Toward an Ecological Criticism," in *The Ecocriticism Reader: Landmarks in Literary Ecology*, ed. Cheryll Glotfelty and Harold Fromm (Athens: University of Georgia Press, 1996), p. 233.

58. Lyon, "Introduction," pp. 7, 8.

59. I acknowledge here, without pursuing the matter, that there are, in Rob L. Stacy's words, many "ethical, political, and metaphysical complexities involved in the paradoxical term 'nature writing,' with 'nature' signifying the acultural, non-human, and 'writing' signifying 'culture' and human presence" (review of *Dramas of Solitude: Narratives of Retreat in American Nature Writing*, by Randall Roorda, *Interdisciplinary Studies in Literature and Environment* 8, no. 2 [Summer 2001]: 286).

60. Donald Worster, *Under Western Skies: Nature and History in the American West* (New York: Oxford University Press, 1992), p. 27.

61. See Earl Pomeroy, "Toward a Reorientation of Western History: Continuity and Environment," *Mississippi Valley Historical Review* 41 (1955): 579–600, and *The Pacific Slope: A History of California, Oregon, Washington, Idaho, Utah, and Nevada* (New York: Knopf, 1965), and Howard R. Lamar, *The Far Southwest, 1846–1912: A Territorial History* (New Haven, CT: Yale University Press, 1966).

62. Kerwin Lee Klein, *Frontiers of Historical Imagination: Narrating the European Conquest of North America, 1890–1990* (Berkeley: University of California Press, 1997), pp. 8, 244, 245.

63. William H. Goetzmann and William N. Goetzmann, *The West of the Imagination* (New York: Norton, 1986), p. 323.

64. Nancy K. Anderson, "'The Kiss of Enterprise': The Western Landscape as Symbol and Resource," in *The West as America: Reinterpreting Images of the Frontier, 1820–1920*, ed. William H. Truettner (Washington, DC: Smithsonian Institution Press, 1991), p. 281.

65. Alex Nemerov, "'Doing the "Old America"': The Image of the American West, 1880–1920," in *West as America*, ed. Truettner, p. 330.

66. Patricia Janis Broder, *The American West: The Modern Vision* (Boston: Little, Brown, 1984), pp. 9, 150, vii, viii, 9, 92.

67. Etulain, *Re-imagining the Modern American West*, p. 119.

68. Ibid., p. 122.

1. Michael T. Marsden and Jack Nachbar, "The Modern Popular Western: Radio, Television, Film and Print," in *A Literary History of the American West*, ed. J. Golden Taylor et al. (Fort Worth: Texas Christian University Press, 1987), p. 1265.

2. Guy Vanderhaeghe, *The Englishman's Boy* (New York: Picador USA, 1998), pp. 107–8.

3. Robert G. Athearn, *The Mythic West in Twentieth-Century America* (Lawrence: University Press of Kansas, 1986), pp. 182, 189.

4. Rita Parks, *The Western Hero in Film and Television: Mass Media Mythology* (Ann Arbor, MI: UMI Research Press, 1982), p. 77.

5. See, for example, William K. Everson, *A Pictorial History of the Western Film* (Secaucus, NJ: Citadel Press, 1969), pp. 5–8, and Jon Tuska, *The American West in Film: Critical Approaches to the Western* (Westport, CT: Greenwood Press, 1985), pp. 23–37.

6. Will Wright, *Sixguns and Society: A Structural Study of the Western* (Berkeley: University of California Press, 1975), p. 15.

7. Ibid., pp. 49, 57.

8. Ibid., p. 57.

9. Jim Kitses, *Horizons West: Anthony Mann, Budd Boetticher, Sam Peckinpah: Studies of Authorship within the Western* (Bloomington: Indiana University Press, 1970), pp. 11, 12.

10. Wright, *Sixguns and Society*, p. 57.

11. Ibid., pp. 59, 69.

12. Ibid., pp. 74, 82, 84.

13. Ibid., pp. 86, 122.

14. Ibid., pp. 187, 189, 191, 190.

15. Athearn, *Mythic West*, p. 184.

16. Parks, *Western Hero in Film and Television*, p. 58.

17. Thomas Schatz, "The Western," in *Handbook of American Film Genres*, ed. Wes D. Gehring (New York: Greenwood Press, 1988), pp. 31, 28, 29, 30.

18. John G. Cawelti, *The Six-Gun Mystique*, 2nd ed. (Bowling Green, OH: Bowling Green State University Popular Press, 1984), p. 106.

19. Joy S. Kasson, *Buffalo Bill's Wild West: Celebrity, Memory, and Popular History* (New York: Hill and Wang, 2000), p. 269.

20. Robert F. Berkhofer Jr., *The White Man's Indian: Images of the American Indian from Columbus to the Present* (New York: Vintage Books, 1979), p. 98.

21. Blake Allmendinger, *Ten Most Wanted: The New Western Literature* (New York: Routledge, 1998), p. 159.

22. David Daly and Joel Persky, *The West and the Western*, a special issue of *Journal of the West* 29, no. 2 (April 1990): 53.

23. Tuska, *American West in Film*, p. 37.

24. Czeslaw Milosz, "On the Western," in *Visions from San Francisco Bay*, trans. Richard Lourie (New York: Farrar, Straus and Giroux, 1982), pp. 58, 60.

25. Stan Steiner, "Real Horses and Mythic Riders," in *The Waning of the West*, ed. Emily Skretny Drabanski (New York: St. Martin's Press, 1989), pp. 93, 94.

26. Christian Metz, *Language and Cinema*, trans. Donna Jean Umiker-Sebeok (The Hague: Mouton, 1974), p. 151.

27. William H. Goetzmann and William N. Goetzmann, *The West of the Imagination* (New York: Norton, 1986), pp. 305–6.

28. Vanderhaeghe, *Englishman's Boy*, p. 60.

29. Jesús Martínez-Saldaña, "La Frontera del Norte," in *Over the Edge: Remapping the American West*, ed. Valerie J. Matsumoto and Blake Allmendinger (Berkeley: University of California Press, 1999), p. 376.

30. Lee Clark Mitchell, *Westerns: Making the Man in Fiction and Film* (Chicago: University of Chicago Press, 1996), p. 162.

31. Philip French, *Westerns: Aspects of a Movie Genre*, rev. ed. (New York: Oxford University Press, 1977), pp. 107, 106.

32. Jane Tompkins, *West of Everything: The Inner Life of Westerns* (New York: Oxford University Press, 1992), pp. 70, 81, 93, 101.

33. Stephen Tatum, "The Classic Westerner: Gary Cooper," in *Shooting Stars: Heroes and Heroines of Western Film*, ed. Archie P. McDonald (Bloomington: Indiana University Press, 1987), pp. 61, 83. Interesting in regard to Cooper's opposing traits is the fact that, as Tatum notes, in his first movies he played not only a cowboy but also "an Indian or an outlaw"—as is the fact that this man who lived professionally by the classic Western formula, albeit one "subject to intensive revision," in 1961 "narrated an NBC television documentary entitled 'The Real West'" (pp. 66, 83, 61).

34. Garry Wills, *John Wayne's America: The Politics of Celebrity* (New York: Simon and Schuster, 1997), pp. 30, 45, 52, 88, 130, 261, 205, 221, 301, 288, 313.

35. Ibid., p. 250.

36. James K. Folsom, "Gothicism in the Western Novel," in *Frontier Gothic: Terror and Wonder at the Frontier in American Literature*, ed. David Mogen, Scott P. Sanders, and Joanne B. Karpinski (Rutherford, NJ: Fairleigh Dickinson University Press, 1993), p. 29.

37. A. Carl Bredahl Jr., *New Ground: Western American Narrative and the Literary Canon* (Chapel Hill: University of North Carolina Press, 1989), p. 150. Richard Slotkin more radically interprets the epilogue, probably justifiably, as the completion of the film's "ironic undoing of the progressive myth of the frontier," so that we're left with a hopeless civilization on one side of it and a dream of freedom, perhaps unrealizable, on the other ("John Ford's *Stagecoach* and the Mythic Space of the Western Movie," in *The Big Empty: Essays on Western Landscapes as Narrative*, ed. Leonard Engel [Albuquerque: University of New Mexico Press, 1994], p. 279).

38. Peter Wollen, *Signs and Meaning in the Cinema* (London: Secker and Warburg, 1969), p. 96.

39. Ronald L. Davis, *John Ford: Hollywood's Old Master* (Norman: University of Oklahoma Press, 1995), p. 192. Wollen's reading of the film may have been prompted in part by the extent to which it highlights Tombstone's "tentative progress toward a progressive society" (Fred Erisman, "The Enduring Myth and the Modern West," in *Researching Western History: Topics in the Twentieth Century*, ed. Gerald D. Nash and Richard W. Etulain [Albuquerque: University of New Mexico Press, 1997], p. 167); but such progress is subject throughout the film to a question Earp asks early on, as Bredahl seems to suggest: "The movie's setting emphasizes the fragile nature of the town within the enormity of surrounding wilderness, but physical wilderness is of minor concern. Earp's question—'What kind of a town is this?'—asks about human wilderness and the need for culture (Shakespeare), women (Clementine), churches, and effective law enforcement" (*New Ground*, p. 151).

40. Bredahl, *New Ground*, pp. 151, 152.

41. Davis, *John Ford*, pp. 214, 215.

42. Bredahl, *New Ground*, p. 153.

43. Richard Hutson, "Sermons in Stone: Monument Valley in *The Searchers*," in *Big Empty*, ed. Engel, p. 203.

44. Donald Worster, *An Unsettled Country: Changing Landscapes of the American West* (Albuquerque: University of New Mexico Press, 1994), p. x.

45. Mitchell, *Westerns*, pp. 23–24.

46. Bredahl, *New Ground*, pp. 154, 155.

47. Kitses, *Horizons West*, p. 13. For additional studies of this biographical-cultural trajectory, see Scott Eyman, *Print the Legend: The Life and Times of John Ford* (New York: Simon and Schuster, 1999), and Joseph McBride, *Searching for John Ford: A Life* (New York: St. Martin's Press, 2001).

48. Marsden and Nachbar, "Modern Popular Western," pp. 1269, 1267–68, 1269.

49. Richard Misrach, "Exceeding the Carrying Capacity of the West: An Artist's Perspective," in *A Society to Match the Scenery: Personal Visions of the Future of the American West*, ed. Gary Holthaus, Patricia Nelson Limerick, Charles F. Wilkinson, and Eve Stryker Munson (Niwot: University Press of Colorado, 1991), p. 135. Concerning Jean Baudrillard's concept of simulacra, see his *Simulacra and Simulation*, trans. Sheila Faria Glaser (Ann Arbor: University of Michigan Press, 1994). Also relevant here is Rebecca Solnit's *River of Shadows: Eadweard Muybridge and the Technological Wild West* (New York: Viking, 2003), a study of how, from the 1870s on, the West was turned, California-style, into the well-controlled imagery that would define Western movies and a technologically reconstituted region.

Derricks, Dams, Bombs, and Such: A Walk on the Dark Side of the West

1. Peggy Simson Curry, "Old Cowboy," in *Summer Range* (Story, WY: Dooryard Press, 1981), p. 32.

2. Richard White, *"It's Your Misfortune and None of My Own": A New History of the American West* (Norman: University of Oklahoma Press, 1991), p. 396.

3. Donald Worster, *A River Running West: The Life of John Wesley Powell* (New York: Oxford University Press, 2001), p. 488.

4. Roderick Nash, Introduction, *The Call of the Wild, 1900–1916*, ed. Roderick Nash (New York: Braziller, 1970), p. 15.

5. Donald C. Jackson, *Building the Ultimate Dam: John S. Eastwood and the Control of Water in the West* (Lawrence: University Press of Kansas, 1995), p. 6.

6. White, *"It's Your Misfortune and None of My Own,"* pp. 523, 524.

7. See *Atlas of the New West: Portrait of a Changing Region*, ed. William E. Riebsame et al. (New York: Norton, 1997), pp. 84–86.

8. Bruce Babbitt, "Public Use and the Future of the Federal Lands," in *A Society to Match the Scenery: Personal Visions of the Future of the American West*, ed. Gary Holthaus, Patricia Nelson Limerick, Charles F. Wilkinson, and Eve Stryker Munson (Niwot: University Press of Colorado, 1991), p. 165.

9. Donald Worster, *An Unsettled Country: Changing Landscapes of the American West* (Albuquerque: University of New Mexico Press, 1994), p. 44.

10. Joseph E. Stevens, *Hoover Dam: An American Adventure* (Norman: University of Oklahoma Press, 1988), pp. vii, viii, 244, 266, 265. To get a sense of the region-altering significance of the Hoover and other dams and building projects during the New Deal and in its wake, see Donald E. Wolf, *Big Dams and Other Dreams: The Six Companies Story* (Norman: University of Oklahoma Press, 1996).

11. Simon Schama, *Landscape and Memory* (New York: Vintage Books, 1996), p. 396.

12. Donald Worster, *Under Western Skies: Nature and History in the American West* (New York: Oxford University Press, 1992), pp. 66, 78.

13. Katie Lee, *All My Rivers Are Gone: A Journey of Discovery through Glen Canyon* (Boulder, CO: Johnson Books, 1998), pp. 243, 247, 249. On the negative consequences of the dam, see also Russell Martin, *A Story That Stands Like a Dam: Glen Canyon and the Struggle for the Soul of the West* (1998; reprint ed., Salt Lake City: University of Utah Press, 2000); Ann Haymond Zwinger, *Down Canyon: A Naturalist Explores the Colorado River through the Grand Canyon* (Tucson: University of Arizona Press, 1995), passim; and Daniel J. Philippon, "Edward Abbey's Remarks at the Cracking of Glen Canyon Dam," *Interdisciplinary Studies in Literature and Environment* 11, no. 2 (Summer 2004): 161–66.

14. See Michael P. Collier, Robert H. Webb, and Edmund D. Andrews, "Experimental Flooding in Grand Canyon," *Scientific American*, January 1997, pp. 82–89.

15. Jackson, *Building the Ultimate Dam*, p. 7.

16. Roderick Nash, *Wilderness and the American Mind*, 3rd ed. (New Haven, CT: Yale University Press, 1982), p. 237.

17. Donald Worster, *Rivers of Empire: Water, Aridity, and the Growth of the American West* (1985; reprint ed., New York: Oxford University Press, 1992), p. 311.

18. Wallace Stegner, "Striking the Rock," in *Where the Bluebird Sings to the Lemonade Springs: Living and Writing in the West* (1992; reprint ed., New York: Penguin Books, 1993), pp. 78, 85, 98.

19. Bruce Berger, "Art Deco Mirage," in *The Telling Distance: Conversations with the American Desert* (1991; reprint ed., Tucson: University of Arizona Press, 1997), p. 212.

20. Timothy Egan, *Lasso the Wind: Away to the New West* (New York: Knopf, 1998), p. 246.

21. William Kittredge, *Who Owns the West?* (San Francisco: Mercury House, 1996), p. 118. For further historical treatments of the kind of conflicts over dams I've been discussing, see *Fluid Arguments: Five Centuries of Western Water Conflict*, ed. Char Miller (Tucson: University of Arizona Press, 2001).

22. White, *"It's Your Misfortune and None of My Own,"* p. 497.

23. Stan Steiner, "When the Bomb Fell on New Mexico," in *The Waning of the West*, ed. Emily Skretny Drabanski (New York: St. Martin's Press, 1989), pp. 225, 228, 229, 230–31.

24. Ibid., p. 231.

25. David Thomson, *In Nevada: The Land, the People, God, and Chance* (New York: Knopf, 1999), pp. 227, 226, 227.

26. See Steiner, "When the Bomb Fell on New Mexico," pp. 223–24.

27. Richard Rhodes, *The Making of the Atomic Bomb* (New York: Touchstone, 1988), p. 451.

28. Richard Misrach with Myriam Weisang Misrach, *Bravo 20: The Bombing of the American West* (Baltimore: Johns Hopkins University Press, 1990), p. xiii.

29. William Stafford, "At the Bomb Testing Site," in *Stories That Could Be True: New and Collected Poems* (New York: Harper and Row, 1977), p. 41.

30. Gary Short, "Near the Bravo 20 Bombing Range," in *Flying over Sonny Liston* (Reno: University of Nevada Press, 1996), p. 9.

31. See *Atlas of the New West*, ed. Riebsame et al., p. 134. I'm aware of the polemics over this atlas, with its somewhat restrictive cartographical criteria—see, for example, the reactions to it in "Forum: *Atlas of the New West*," *Pacific Historical Review* 67 (1998): 379–420—but it's accurate in the essentials of its data.

32. Reg Saner, "Technically Sweet," in *The Four-cornered Falcon: Essays on the Interior West and the Natural Scene* (Baltimore: Johns Hopkins University Press, 1993), p. 78.

33. Berger, Introduction, *Telling Distance*, p. 3.

34. Tad Bartimus and Scott McCartney, *Trinity's Children: Living along America's Nuclear Highway* (New York: Harcourt Brace Jovanovich, 1991), pp. 3, 288.

35. My account of this experiment is indebted to several sources: Peter Goodchild, *J. Robert Oppenheimer: Shatterer of Worlds* (1981; reprint ed., New York: Fromm International, 1985), pp. 132–33, 147; Rhodes, *Making of the Atomic Bomb*, pp. 610–12; and Eileen Welsome, *The Plutonium Files: America's Secret Medical Experiments in the Cold War* (New York: Dial Press, 1999), pp. 184–88.

Sprawling into Western Emptiness: The Metropolitan Frontier, Suburban Borderlands, Misbegotten Middle Landscapes

1. Roderick Nash, introductory note to the section The Dilemma of Urban Growth, *The Call of the Wild, 1900–1916*, ed. Roderick Nash (New York: Braziller, 1970), p. 26.

2. Carl Abbott, *The Metropolitan Frontier: Cities in the Modern American West* (Tucson: University of Arizona Press, 1993), pp. xix, xii, xi.

3. Charles Wilkinson, "Paradise Revised," in *Atlas of the New West: Portrait of a Changing Region*, ed. William E. Riebsame et al. (New York: Norton, 1997), pp. 29, 31.

4. William L. Fox, *The Void, the Grid, and the Sign: Traversing the Great Basin* (Salt Lake City: University of Utah Press, 2000), p. 213.

5. Frederick Turner, *Beyond Geography: The Western Spirit against the Wilderness* (1980; reprint ed., New Brunswick, NJ: Rutgers University Press, 1992), pp. 23, 32, 33.

6. Hayden White, "The Forms of Wildness: Archaeology of an Idea," in *The Wild Man Within: An Image in Western Thought from the Renaissance to Romanticism*, ed. Edward Dudley and Maximillian E. Novak (Pittsburgh, PA: University of Pittsburgh Press, 1972), p. 23.

7. John R. Stilgoe, *Common Landscape of America, 1580 to 1845* (New Haven, CT: Yale University Press, 1982), p. 3.

8. Gretel Ehrlich, "Letters to an Architect," in *Northern Lights: A Selection of New Writing from the American West*, ed. Deborah Clow and Donald Snow (New York: Vintage Books, 1994), pp. 28, 29.

9. See, for example, *Comstock Women: The Making of a Mining Community*, ed. Ronald M. James and C. Elizabeth Raymond (Reno: University of Nevada Press, 1997).

10. See Lawrence H. Larsen, *The Urban West at the End of the Frontier* (Lawrence: University Press of Kansas, 1978), pp. 111–22.

11. Abbott, *Metropolitan Frontier*, p. xiii. With regard, particularly, to how the economically attractive defense industry encouraged the outward, multicentered growth of Western cities, see Ric Dias, "The Great Cantonment: Cold War Cities in the American West," in *The Cold War American West, 1945–1989*, ed. Kevin J. Fernlund (Albuquerque: University of New Mexico Press, 1998), pp. 71–85.

12. Richard Slotkin, *The Fatal Environment: The Myth of the Frontier in the Age of Industrialization, 1800–1890* (New York: Atheneum, 1985), pp. 41, 114.

13. Roger W. Lotchin, "The Impending Urban Past: An Essay on the Twentieth-Century West," in *Researching Western History: Topics in the Twentieth Century*, ed. Gerald D. Nash and Richard W. Etulain (Albuquerque: University of New Mexico Press, 1997), p. 54.

14. Richard White, *"It's Your Misfortune and None of My Own": A New History of the American West* (Norman: University of Oklahoma Press, 1991), p. 435.

15. Slotkin, *Fatal Environment*, p. 35.

16. Garry Wills, *John Wayne's America: The Politics of Celebrity* (New York: Simon and Schuster, 1997), pp. 302, 303.

17. Daniel Kemmis, "The Art of the Possible in the Home of Hope," in *Northern Lights*, ed. Clow and Snow, p. 173.

18. White, *"It's Your Misfortune and None of My Own,"* p. 416.

19. Slotkin, *Fatal Environment*, pp. 5–6.

20. SueEllen Campbell, apropos of this irony, says, "I'm often afraid in cities and almost never in wild places. Freeways and sirens and the local newscasts make me uneasy, not weather or wild animals" ("Fear," in *Bringing the Mountain Home* [Tucson: University of Arizona Press, 1996], p. 64).

21. Andrew Light, "Urban Wilderness," in *Wild Ideas*, ed. David Rothenberg (Minneapolis: University of Minnesota Press, 1995), pp. 200, 201.

22. Roderick Nash, *Wilderness and the American Mind*, 3rd ed. (New Haven, CT: Yale University Press, 1982), pp. 143, xii.

23. Keith Thomas, *Man and the Natural World: Changing Attitudes in England, 1500–1800* (1983; reprint ed., New York: Oxford University Press, 1996), p. 253.

24. Rick Bass in Bill Stobb, "The Wild into the Word: An Interview with Rick Bass," *Interdisciplinary Studies in Literature and Environment* 5, no. 2 (Summer 1998): 102.

25. Zeese Papanikolas, *Trickster in the Land of Dreams* (Lincoln: University of Nebraska Press, 1995), p. 100.

26. White, *"It's Your Misfortune and None of My Own,"* pp. 531, 541.

27. An exemplary study of some of the oppositions at play in an area of expanding postwar urbanization is Arthur R. Gómez, *Quest for the Golden Circle: The Four Corners and the Metropolitan West, 1945–1970* (1994; reprint ed., Lawrence: University Press of Kansas, 2000).

28. William G. Robbins, *Colony and Empire: The Capitalist Transformation of the American West* (Lawrence: University Press of Kansas, 1994), pp. 166, 165, 182.

29. Abbott, *Metropolitan Frontier*, p. 190. Versions of this tension are much in evidence throughout *Open Spaces, City Places: Contemporary Writers on the Changing Southwest*, ed. Judy Nolte Temple (Tucson: University of Arizona Press, 1994), a collection of essays by city-dwellers about open country.

30. Gundars Rudzitis, *Wilderness and the Changing American West* (New York: Wiley, 1996), p. 166.

31. Lotchin, "Impending Urban Past," pp. 56, 60.

32. John R. Stilgoe, *Borderland: Origins of the American Suburb, 1820–1939* (New Haven, CT: Yale University Press, 1988), pp. 1, 2, 5.

33. Ibid., pp. 7, 8, 9.

34. White, *"It's Your Misfortune and None of My Own,"* pp. 546–47.

35. Pertinent to my invocation of landscape architect Frederick Law Olmsted is this remark from Robert Wilson (review of *A Clearing in the Distance: Frederick Law Olmsted and America in the Nineteenth Century*, by Witold Rybczynski, *American Scholar* 68, no. 3 [Summer 1999]: 144): "Olmsted's role was to bring nature back into the cities that had violated the earthly paradise the North American continent had once been. To do so, parks (and the ideal suburbs

Olmsted would also design) had to give the illusion of wilderness—but wilderness made better than itself, wildness tamed. These conflicting impulses are with us yet."

36. Yi-Fu Tuan, *Escapism* (Baltimore: Johns Hopkins University Press, 1998), p. 25. On farmland as a middle landscape, especially in relation to suburban consumerism, inner-city violence, and related phenomena, see Victor Davis Hanson, *The Land Was Everything: Letters from an American Farmer* (New York: Free Press, 2000).

37. Simon Schama, *Landscape and Memory* (New York: Vintage Books, 1995), p. 16.

38. Jennifer Price, *Flight Maps: Adventures with Nature in Modern America* (New York: Basic Books, 1999), p. 136.

39. Carolyn Merchant, "Reinventing Eden: Western Culture as a Recovery Narrative," in *Uncommon Ground: Rethinking the Human Place in Nature*, ed. William Cronon (New York: Norton, 1995), pp. 153–54.

40. Denis Cosgrove, "Habitable Earth: Wilderness, Empire, and Race in America," in *Wild Ideas*, ed. Rothenberg, p. 31.

41. Yi-Fu Tuan, *Topophilia: A Study of Environmental Perception, Attitudes, and Values* (1974; reprint ed., New York: Columbia University Press, 1990), pp. 196, 226, 238.

42. Alexander Wilson, *The Culture of Nature: North American Landscape from Disney to the Exxon Valdez* (Cambridge, MA: Blackwell, 1992), pp. 100, 108.

43. Abbott, *Metropolitan Frontier*, p. xxi.

Part Five: From the 1960s to the Present: The West as Postregion
Prelude and Overview

1. For the original, see Karl Marx, *Der achtzehnte Brumaire des Louis Bonaparte* (1852; reprint ed., Kempten, West Germany: Allgäuer Heimatverlag, 1965), p. 9.

2. Larry McMurtry, *Walter Benjamin at the Dairy Queen: Reflections at Sixty and Beyond* (New York: Simon and Schuster, 1999), p. 130.

3. Dennis McNally, "Prophets on the Burning Shore: Jack Kerouac, Gary Snyder, and San Francisco," in *A Literary History of the American West*, ed. J. Golden Taylor et al. (Fort Worth: Texas Christian University Press, 1987), pp. 483, 488.

4. Hal K. Rothman, *Devil's Bargains: Tourism in the Twentieth-Century American West* (Lawrence: University Press of Kansas, 1998), pp. 167, 228. Apropos of Rothman's construal of *On the Road*, Matt Herman argues that it's a book in which exaggerations present the West as a "democratic, free, sensual, and liberating" place where, in contrast to the world of the protagonist's suburban New Jersey home, "the illusion reigns that things are naturally as they naturally are" ("Literature, Growth, and Criticism in the New West," *Western American Literature* 38 [2003]: 52, 53).

5. See Lois Palken Rudnick, *Utopian Vistas: The Mabel Dodge Luhan House and the American Counterculture* (Albuquerque: University of New Mexico Press, 1996).

6. For an account of this revealing encounter between conservative control and radical wildness, see John M. Findlay, *Magic Lands: Western Cityscapes and American Culture after 1940* (Berkeley: University of California Press, 1992), pp. 112–13.

7. Jennifer Price, *Flight Maps: Adventures with Nature in Modern America* (New York: Basic Books, 1999), pp. 140, 139.

8. Roderick Nash, *Wilderness and the American Mind*, 3rd ed. (New Haven, CT: Yale University Press, 1982), p. 252.

9. Fred Erisman, "The Enduring Myth and the Modern West," in *Researching Western History: Topics in the Twentieth Century*, ed. Gerald D. Nash and Richard W. Etulain (Albuquerque: University of New Mexico Press, 1997), p. 179.

10. Richard W. Etulain, "Research Opportunities in Twentieth-Century Western Cultural History," in *Researching Western History*, ed. Nash and Etulain, p. 151.

11. Patricia Nelson Limerick, *The Legacy of Conquest: The Unbroken Past of the American West* (New York: Norton, 1987), p. 95.

12. Richard White, *"It's Your Misfortune and None of My Own": A New History of the American West* (Norman: University of Oklahoma Press, 1991), p. 606.

13. Leslie A. Fiedler, *The Return of the Vanishing American* (New York: Stein and Day, 1968), p. 25.

14. Robert F. Berkhofer Jr., *The White Man's Indian: Images of the American Indian from Columbus to the Present* (New York: Vintage Books, 1979), p. 98.

15. Philip J. Deloria, *Playing Indian* (New Haven, CT: Yale University Press, 1998), pp. 155, 157.

16. Fiedler, *Return of the Vanishing American*, p. 186.

17. Carl Abbott, *The Metropolitan Frontier: Cities in the Modern American West* (Tucson: University of Arizona Press, 1993), p. xvi. See also Steve Fox, "From the Beat Generation to the Sanctuary Movement: Cold War Resistance Cultures in the American West," in *The Cold War American West, 1945–1989*, ed. Kevin J. Fernlund (Albuquerque: University of New Mexico Press, 1998), pp. 139–66, a survey of such matters as how "countercultural values filtered through the West in different ways" and why their associated movement in the 1960s underwent "a winding down" (pp. 153, 152); and Eleanor Agnew, *Back from the Land: How Young Americans Went to Nature in the 1970's, and Why They Came Back* (Chicago: Dee, 2004).

18. Michael C. Steiner and David M. Wrobel, "Many Wests: Discovering a Dynamic Western Regionalism," in *Many Wests: Place, Culture, and Regional Identity*, ed. David M. Wrobel and Michael C. Steiner (Lawrence: University Press of Kansas, 1997), pp. 3, 7, 17.

19. Richard W. Etulain, *Re-imagining the Modern American West: A Century of Fiction, History, and Art* (Tucson: University of Arizona Press, 1996), p. 210.

20. Rothman, *Devil's Bargains*, p. 22.

21. Findlay, *Magic Lands*, p. 2. To get a sense of the role automotive traffic has played in Western urban sprawl, see *Atlas of the New West: Portrait of a Changing Region*, ed. William E. Riebsame et al. (New York: Norton, 1997), pp. 72–75. On technoburbs, see Jon C. Teaford, *Post-Suburbia: Government and Politics in the Edge Cities* (Baltimore: Johns Hopkins University Press, 1997). Concerning the metropolitan dominance of multicentered cities in California and Texas, see Abbott, *Metropolitan Frontier*, pp. 159–61. A sketch of the causes and effects of urban sprawl may be found in Rodger Doyle, "Sprawling into the Third Millennium," *Scientific American*, March 2001, p. 25. For a more comprehensive treatment of the subject, see Oliver Gillham, *The Limitless City: A Primer on the Urban Sprawl Debate* (Washington, DC: Island Press, 2002). In regard to the West specifically, see Raye C. Ringholz, *Paradise Paved: The Challenge of Growth in the New West* (Salt Lake City: University of Utah Press, 1996). Revealing interrelations between sprawl and the growth of the fast-food industry, with repeated reference to the West, may be found in Eric Schlosser, *Fast Food Nation: The Dark Side of the All-American Meal* (Boston: Houghton Mifflin, 2001).

22. Findlay, *Magic Lands*, pp. 2, 3, 5, 9. Regarding New Urbanism and its preoccupying issues, see Donald D. T. Chen, "The Science of Smart Growth," *Scientific American*, December 2000, pp. 84–91, and Peter Calthorpe and William Fulton, *The Regional City: Planning for the End of Sprawl* (Washington, DC: Island Press, 2001), both treatments that seem to find more reason for optimism through planning than does Findlay's book. Complementary or counter to such visions, depending on your point of view, are critiques of the idea that cities are separate from and exclude the nature they overrun—see *The Nature of Cities: Ecocriticism and Urban Environments*, ed. Michael Bennett and David W. Teague (Tucson: University of Arizona Press, 1999).

23. Abbott, *Metropolitan Frontiers*, p. 56.

24. Though a little out of date, a relevant history here is Carl Abbott, *Portland: Planning, Politics, and Growth in a Twentieth-Century City* (Lincoln: University of Nebraska Press, 1983). To catch up on more-recent plans for control of overdevelopment, see Robert D. Kaplan, *An Empire Wilderness: Travels into America's Future* (New York: Random House, 1998), pp. 330–36.

25. There's no dearth of histories of Los Angeles, but one of the best on growth issues is Greg Hise, *Magnetic Los Angeles: Planning the Twentieth-Century Metropolis* (Baltimore: Johns Hopkins University Press, 1997).

26. See Greg Hise and William Deverell, *Eden by Design: The 1930 Olmsted-Bartholomew Plan for the Los Angeles Region* (Berkeley: University of California Press, 2000).

27. Mike Davis, *City of Quartz: Excavating the Future in Los Angeles* (London: Verso, 1990), pp. 4, 6, 14. See also Davis's *Ecology of Fear: Los Angeles and the Imagination of Disaster* (New York: Metropolitan Books, 1998), an even more disturbing account of the city's counternatural pathology and its consequences.

28. William L. Fox, *The Void, the Grid, and the Sign: Traversing the Great Basin* (Salt Lake City: University of Utah Press, 2000), p. 210.

29. Kaplan, *Empire Wilderness*, p. 91.

30. Jean Baudrillard, *America*, trans. Chris Turner (London: Verso, 1988), pp. 125, 126.

31. Maxine Scates, "On the Poetry of Ann Stanford," *Writer's Chronicle*, October–November 2000, p. 29. Two observations about Californians (meaning, largely, Angelenos) are pertinent here: that, according to a statewide poll taken in the 1990s, "the California Dream—a dream of all the West, at that, a desire to live close to nature—was dying" (Timothy Egan, *Lasso the Wind: Away to the New West* [New York: Knopf, 1998], p. 244) and that most Californians "have forgotten nature" and experience primarily "discontinuity, fragmentation, even alienation" (Zeese Papanikolas, "The Perpetual Tourist," *Western American Literature* 34 [1999]: 193).

32. Baudrillard, *America*, p. 2.

33. Bruce Berger, "The Designer Deserts of Greater Phoenix," in *The Telling Distance: Conversations with the American Desert* (1991; reprint ed., Tucson: University of Arizona Press, 1997), pp. 100, 103, 104. For a history of Phoenix that takes full account of such twists, see Bradford Luckingham, *Phoenix: The History of a Southwestern Metropolis* (Tucson: University of Arizona Press, 1989). Because of the scale of its effects on the circumambient environment, the city has become the subject of an intensive, long-term ecological study—see Kim A. McDonald, "Ecology's Last Frontier: Studying Urban Areas to Monitor the Impact of Human Activity," *Chronicle of Higher Education*, 13 February 1998, pp. A18–19.

34. Kaplan, *Empire Wilderness*, pp. 151, 152.

35. María E. Montoya, "Landscapes of the Cold War West," in *The Cold War American West,* 1945–1989, ed. Fernlund, p. 20.

36. Elliott West, *The Contested Plains: Indians, Goldseekers, and the Rush to Colorado* (Lawrence: University Press of Kansas, 1998), p. 241.

37. Abbott, *Metropolitan Frontier,* p. 159.

38. Larry McMurtry, "A Handful of Roses," in *In a Narrow Grave: Essays on Texas* (1968; reprint ed., New York: Touchstone, 1989), pp. 119, 129, 120.

39. Kaplan, *Empire Wilderness,* pp. 65, 35, 33.

40. William Cronon, *Nature's Metropolis: Chicago and the Great West* (New York: Norton, 1991), pp. xviii, xvi, xvii.

41. Yi-Fu Tuan, *Topophilia: A Study of Environmental Perception, Attitudes, and Values* (1974; reprint ed., New York: Columbia University Press, 1990), p. 200.

A Sewer Runs through It

1. Timothy Egan, *Lasso the Wind: Away to the New West* (New York: Knopf, 1998), p. 47.

2. Philip Kimball, *Liar's Moon: A Long Story* (New York: Holt, 1999), p. 243.

3. See Patricia Nelson Limerick, "Haunted by Rhyolite: Learning from the Landscape of Failure," in *The Big Empty: Essays on Western Landscapes as Narrative,* ed. Leonard Engel (Albuquerque: University of New Mexico Press, 1994), pp. 27–47.

4. Gary Holthaus, Patricia Nelson Limerick, and Charles F. Wilkinson remark that, "with its appearance of having unused 'waste' spaces, the American West will always be the leading candidate for waste disposal" ("Speaking of the West," in *A Society to Match the Scenery: Personal Visions of the Future of the American West,* ed. Gary Holthaus, Patricia Nelson Limerick, Charles F. Wilkinson, and Eve Stryker Munson [Niwot: University Press of Colorado, 1991], p. 6.)

5. María E. Montoya, "Landscapes of the Cold War West," in *The Cold War American West,* 1945–1989, ed. Kevin J. Fernlund (Albuquerque: University of New Mexico Press, 1998), pp. 11, 24.

6. Mike Davis, "Dead West: Ecocide in Marlboro Country," in *Over the Edge: Remapping the American West,* ed. Valerie J. Matsumoto and Blake Allmendinger (Berkeley: University of California Press, 1999), p. 339. For an extended treatment of the history of and a host of issues associated with the Nevada Test Site, see Rebecca Solnit, *Savage Dreams: A Journey into the Landscape Wars of the American West* (New York: Vintage Books, 1995), pp. 3–212.

7. See Peter Goin's photographs of Hanford in his *Nuclear Landscapes* (Baltimore: Johns Hopkins University Press, 1991), pp. 66–99, and David Oates, "Real Losses: The Hanford Reach," in *Paradise Wild: Reimagining American Nature* (Corvallis: Oregon State University Press, 2003), pp. 182–95.

8. William Cronon, "Introduction: In Search of Nature," in *Uncommon Ground: Rethinking the Human Place in Nature,* ed. William Cronon (New York: Norton, 1995), p. 28.

9. Davis, "Dead West," pp. 341, 345, 346, 347. For numerous examples of photos from The Pit, see Anne Wilkes Tucker with Rebecca Solnit, *Crimes and Splendors: The Desert Cantos of Richard Misrach* (Boston: Bulfinch Press, 1996), pp. 98–103.

10. Valerie L. Kuletz, *The Tainted Desert: Environmental Ruin in the American West* (New York: Routledge, 1998), pp. xiii, 7, 12, 287. It's easy enough to make a *paysage moralisé* of Yucca Mountain and its environs for a number of reasons, not the least of which is its proximity to

mountains named Skull and Little Skull (a young volcano!), which recall the Aramaic etymology of *Golgotha* ("the place of a skull," in the Revised Standard Version translation of Matt. 27:33), the setting of the Crucifixion—see Goin's photo of Jackass Flats in his *Nuclear Landscapes*, p. 33.

11. Neil Campbell, *The Cultures of the American New West* (Edinburgh, UK: Edinburgh University Press, 2000), p. 36.

12. See Zeese Papanikolas, *Trickster in the Land of Dreams* (Lincoln: University of Nebraska Press, 1995), p. 128.

13. Montoya, "Landscapes of the Cold War West," p. 22.

14. On the troubled history of water rights in the West, see, in addition to works I cited in my earlier discussion of dams, the list of sources in Robert W. Cherny, "Research Opportunities in Twentieth-Century Western History: Politics," in *Researching Western History: Topics in the Twentieth Century*, ed. Gerald D. Nash and Richard W. Etulain (Albuquerque: University of New Mexico Press, 1997), p. 106n8.

15. Simon Schama, *Landscape and Memory* (New York: Vintage Books, 1995), pp. 258, 273. For alternative codifications, see Gretel Ehrlich, "On Water," in *The Solace of Open Spaces* (New York: Penguin Books, 1986), pp. 75–85, and Chris Bullock and George Newton, "A Wilderness of Rivers: River Writing in North America," in *Wilderness Tapestry: An Eclectic Approach to Preservation*, ed. Samuel I. Zeveloff, L. Mikel Vause, and William H. McVaugh (Reno: University of Nevada Press, 1992), pp. 67–79.

16. See Sharman Apt Russell, "Irrigation," in *Songs of the Fluteplayer: Seasons of Life in the Southwest* (Reading, MA: Addison-Wesley, 1991), p. 85.

17. Elliott West, *The Contested Plains: Indians, Goldseekers, and the Rush to Colorado* (Lawrence: University Press of Kansas, 1998), pp. 160, 161.

18. In an overview of fish species endangered in American rivers and lakes, especially those in the Southwest, Rodger Doyle declares, "Of all places on earth, rivers and lakes are the most dangerous for wildlife"—not only because "their natural ecology is segmented by dams and locks" and "their waters are diverted" but also because "they are the principal depositories of civilization's wastes" ("Freshwater Fish at Risk in the U.S.," *Scientific American*, December 1997, p. 32).

19. Concerning the history of this drastic domestication, see Robert Kelley Schneiders, *Big Sky Rivers: The Yellowstone and Upper Missouri* (Lawrence: University Press of Kansas, 2003).

20. Kenneth R. Olwig, "Reinventing Common Nature: Yosemite and Mount Rushmore—A Meandering Tale of a Double Nature," in *Uncommon Ground*, ed. Cronon, p. 404.

21. Richard White, *The Organic Machine* (New York: Hill and Wang, 1995), p. 108.

22. Donald Worster, *The Wealth of Nature: Environmental History and the Ecological Imagination* (New York: Oxford University Press, 1993), pp. 131, 134.

23. White, *Organic Machine*, p. 113.

24. See Blake Gumprecht, *The Los Angeles River: Its Life, Death, and Possible Rebirth* (Baltimore: Johns Hopkins University Press, 1999).

25. Larry McMurtry, *Duane's Depressed* (New York: Simon and Schuster, 1999), p. 142.

26. Denis Cosgrove, "Habitable Earth: Wilderness, Empire, and Race in America," in *Wild Ideas*, ed. David Rothenberg (Minneapolis: University of Minnesota Press, 1995), p. 29.

27. Sandra Alcosser, "Approaching August," in *Except by Nature* (Saint Paul, MN: Graywolf Press, 1998), p. 50.

1. Aldo Leopold, Foreword, *"A Sand Country Almanac" and "Sketches Here and There"* (1949; reprint ed., New York: Oxford University Press, 1989), p. 1.

2. Donald Worster, *The Wealth of Nature: Environmental History and the Ecological Imagination* (New York: Oxford University Press, 1993), p. 15.

3. Ronald Wallace, "Corn Snake," *Interdisciplinary Studies in Literature and Environment* 8, no. 2 (Summer 2001): 262.

4. There's a lot of literature on the consequences of Americans' mixed feelings about wildlife, but a starting point might be Lisa Mighetto's *Wild Animals and American Environmental Ethics* (Tucson: University of Arizona Press, 1991); likewise in respect of the West in particular, I'd suggest Dan Flores's *Horizontal Yellow: Nature and History in the Near Southwest* (Albuquerque: University of New Mexico Press, 2000). A companion piece to Flores's book might be Tom Wolf's "Beauty and the Beasts: Predators in the Sangre de Cristo Mountains," in *Wild Ideas*, ed. David Rothenberg (Minneapolis: University of Minnesota Press, 1995), pp. 163–81.

5. Larry McMurtry, *Walter Benjamin at the Dairy Queen: Reflections at Sixty and Beyond* (New York: Simon and Schuster, 1999), p. 186.

6. Jane Tompkins, *West of Everything: The Inner Life of Westerns* (New York: Oxford University Press, 1992), p. 101.

7. Frederick Turner, "Roping a Dream," in *Of Chiles, Cacti, and Fighting Cocks: Notes on the American West* (1990; reprint ed., New York: Owl Books, 1996), pp. 34, 39, 41.

8. Ibid., p. 45. A firsthand account of catching wild horses is Parley J. Paskett, *Wild Mustangs* (Logan: Utah State University Press, 1986). The classic natural-historical treatment of such horses is J. Frank Dobie's *The Mustangs* (Boston: Little, Brown, 1952). The iconography of the horse in the West is investigated in Luis Alberto Urrea's poem "Horses," in *The Fever of Being* (Albuquerque: West End Press, 1994), pp. 55–73, and Stephen Tatum's essay "The Solace of Animal Faces," *Arizona Quarterly* 50, no. 4 (Winter 1994): 133–56.

9. See Dan Flores, *The Natural West: Environmental History in the Great Plains and Rocky Mountains* (Norman: University of Oklahoma Press, 2001), p. 83. Jacob Fowler's account, which Flores quotes at length, may be found in *The Journal of Jacob Fowler*, ed. Elliott Coues (Lincoln: University of Nebraska Press, 1970), pp. 46–49.

10. J. E. Cirlot, *A Dictionary of Symbols*, trans. Jack Sage (New York: Philosophical Library, 1962), s.v. "bear."

11. Louis Owens, *Other Destinies: Understanding the American Indian Novel* (Norman: University of Oklahoma Press, 1992), p. 122.

12. Flores, *Natural West*, pp. 73, 74, 88. Flores's quotation from Paul Shepard is, as he acknowledges, from his *The Others: How Animals Made Us Human* (Washington, DC: Shearwater Books, 1996), p. 72. A fuller treatment of Ben Lilly's career may be found in David E. Brown, *The Grizzly in the Southwest: Documentary of an Extinction* (Norman: University of Oklahoma Press, 1985), pp. 177–88. The existence of grizzlies in present-day Colorado—specifically, in the San Juan Mountains—is a matter of much debate, with a lot of the searching for them having the feel of a snipe hunt, a lot of sightings (or all of them) mistaken or spurious. In *The Lost Grizzlies: A Search for Survivors in the Wilderness of Colorado* (Boston: Mariner Books, 1995), Rick Bass narrates his extensive seeking. In *Ghost Grizzlies* (New York: Holt, 1995), David Petersen writes of the "deep and lingering ambivalence" in attitudes toward the possibility of

grizzlies in Colorado (p. xiv). There's a considerable body of literature concerning the grizzly, to which a helpful introduction is Terrell Dixon, "Ways of Knowing Nature: Scientists, Poets, and Nature Writers View the Grizzly Bear," in *Wilderness Tapestry: An Eclectic Approach to Preservation*, ed. Samuel I. Zeveloff, L. Mikel Vause, and William H. McVaugh (Reno: University of Nevada Press, 1992), pp. 80–96. A classic account of the animal is Ernest Thompson Seton, *The Biography of a Grizzly* (1900; reprint ed., Lincoln: University of Nebraska Press, 1987).

13. SueEllen Campbell, "Fear," in *Bringing the Mountain Home* (Tucson: University of Arizona Press, 1996), p. 67.

14. Doug Peacock, *Grizzly Years: In Search of the American Wilderness* (New York: Owl Books, 1996), p. 67.

15. Patricia Nelson Limerick, *The Legacy of Conquest: The Unbroken Past of the American West* (New York: Norton, 1987), pp. 316, 317. On the controversies over the management of grizzlies in Yellowstone and related matters, see Paul Schullery, *The Bears of Yellowstone* (Boulder, CO: Rinehart, 1986), and John J. Craighead, Jay S. Sumner, and John A. Mitchell, *The Grizzly Bears of Yellowstone: Their Ecology in the Yellowstone Ecosystem, 1959–1992* (Washington, DC: Island Press, 1995).

16. Timothy Egan, *Lasso the Wind: Away to the New West* (New York: Knopf, 1998), pp. 170, 177. It should be noted that reintroduced wolves raised in captivity often have problems, partly because of inadequate hunting skills, in adapting to the wild. Concerning wolves' recent impact on the Yellowstone ecosystem, see Jim Robbins, "Lessons from the Wolf," *Scientific American*, June 2004, pp. 76–81.

17. William Trowbridge, "The Wolf's Advice to His Nephew," *Cottonwood*, no. 52 (Fall 1998), p. 92.

18. Rick Bass, *The Ninemile Wolves* (New York: Ballantine Books, 1993), p. 4.

19. Barry Lopez, *Of Wolves and Men* (New York: Scribners, 1978), p. 4.

20. Jim Brandenburg, *Brother Wolf: A Forgotten Promise* (Minocqua, WI: NorthWord Press, 1993), p. 82. His work, in verbal text and photographs alike, has to do with wolves in northern Minnesota, another place where their existence, more populous than in the West, is hotly contested along city–country and environmentalist–farmer/rancher divisions. An eloquent statement of the depth of human connection with wolves in the area is Linda Hogan's "Deify the Wolf," in *Dwellings: A Spiritual History of the Living World* (New York: Touchstone, 1996), pp. 63–76.

21. Irene Klaver, "Silent Wolves: The Howl of the Implicit," in *Wild Ideas*, ed. Rothenberg, pp. 118, 120.

22. Bill McKibben, *Hope, Human and Wild: True Stories of Living Lightly on the Earth* (Boston: Little, Brown, 1995), pp. 220, 222. As he acknowledges, his thinking here is indebted to Michael Pollan's *Second Nature: A Gardener's Education* (New York: Atlantic Monthly Press, 1991). A moving fictional treatment of the troubled borders (in several senses) between humans and wolves in a Western (and Mexican) setting is the first section of Cormac McCarthy's novel *The Crossing* (New York: Knopf, 1994), pp. 3–127.

23. Sharman Apt Russell, *Kill the Cowboy: A Battle of Mythology in the New West* (Reading, MA: Addison-Wesley, 1993), p. 98.

24. James Galvin, *The Meadow* (New York: Holt, 1992), p. 15.

25. A balanced and informative treatment of the mountain lion is Harley Shaw, *Soul among Lions: The Cougar as Peaceful Adversary* (1989; reprint ed., Tucson: University of Arizona Press,

2000). On the controversial situation of the lion in New Mexico, a state with high kill quotas, see Krista West, "Lion versus Lamb: In New Mexico, a Battle Brews between Two Rare Species," *Scientific American*, May 2002, pp. 20–21.

26. See David E. Brown and Carlos A. López González, *Borderland Jaguars: Tigres de la Frontera* (Salt Lake City: University of Utah Press, 2001).

27. Many of the issues of restoration I've mentioned are considered in case-study detail in *Large Mammal Restoration: Ecological and Sociological Challenges in the Twenty-first Century*, ed. David S. Maehr, Reed F. Noss, and Jeffery L. Larkin (Washington, DC: Island Press, 2001).

28. Alexander Wilson, *The Culture of Nature: North American Landscapes from Disney to the Exxon Valdez* (Cambridge, MA: Blackwell, 1992), p. 45.

29. Gary Snyder, "The Call of the Wild," in *Turtle Island* (New York: New Directions, 1974), p. 22. A number of studies of the ambiguous meanings of zoos (as sites of wildlife appreciation, control, commodification, and so on) recently have been published, among them these: Elizabeth Hanson, *Animal Attractions: Nature on Display in American Zoos* (Princeton, NJ: Princeton University Press, 2002); Randy Malamud, *Reading Zoos: Representations of Animals and Captivity* (New York: New York University Press, 1998); and Nigel Rothfels, *Savages and Beasts: The Birth of the Modern Zoo* (Baltimore: Johns Hopkins University Press, 2002).

30. Shepard, *The Others*, p. 151.

31. Dave Hickey, "Luis Jiménez and the Incarnation of the West," in Camille Flores-Turney, *Howl: The Artwork of Luis Jiménez* (Santa Fe: New Mexico Magazine, 1997), p. 9. The importance of nature's being at times dangerous shouldn't be forgotten, however; purging the West of most of the wildlife dangerous to people has contributed to numerous problems, including the illusion of triumph over the natural world—regarding which problems in both Western and global contexts, see David Quammen, *Monster of God: The Man-Eating Predator in the Jungles of History and the Mind* (New York: Norton, 2003).

32. John Rennie, "Cloning and Conservation," *Scientific American*, November 2000, p. 1. The article in the same issue to which he refers is Robert P. Lanza, Betsy L. Dresser, and Philip Damiani, "Cloning Noah's Ark," pp. 84–89.

33. William Kittredge, *Hole in the Sky: A Memoir* (New York: Knopf, 1992), pp. 234–35.

McWilderness: Disneyfying the Frontier

1. Richard Stayton, "Disneyland," in *Eyewitness to the American West: From the Aztec Empire to the Digital Frontier in the Words of Those Who Saw It Happen*, ed. David Colbert (New York: Viking, 1998), pp. 395, 396.

2. Umberto Eco, "Travels in Hyperreality," in *Travels in Hyperreality*, trans. William Weaver (New York: Harcourt Brace Jovanovich, 1986), pp. 8, 31.

3. Richard White, untitled lecture presented as part of a colloquium titled "Nature and Hollywood" held at the Hall Center for the Humanities at the University of Kansas, 21 February 1997.

4. Richard Schickel, *The Disney Version: The Life, Times, Art and Commerce of Walt Disney* (New York: Simon and Schuster, 1968), pp. 289, 290–91.

5. Alexander Wilson, *The Culture of Nature: North American Landscape from Disney to the Exxon Valdez* (Cambridge, MA: Blackwell, 1992), pp. 118, 124, 125, 134, 135.

6. On the interrelations of postmodernism, late capitalism, the commodification of heritage, and such, see David Harvey, *The Condition of Postmodernity: An Inquiry into the Origins of Cultural Change* (Cambridge, MA: Blackwell, 1990), pp. 62–63.

7. Louis Owens, "Where Things Can Happen: California and Writing," *Western American Literature* 34 (1999): 153.

8. Carl Abbott, *The Metropolitan Frontier: Cities in the Modern American West* (Tucson: University of Arizona Press, 1993), p. 184.

9. John M. Findlay, *Magic Lands: Western Cityscapes and American Culture after 1940* (Berkeley: University of California Press, 1992), pp. 57, 68, 69, 73, 85.

10. William Cronon, "Introduction: In Search of Nature," in *Uncommon Ground: Rethinking the Human Place in Nature*, ed. William Cronon (New York: Norton, 1995), p. 40.

11. Eco, "Travels in Hyperreality," pp. 43, 44, 48.

12. Michael Steiner, "Frontierland as Tomorrowland: Walt Disney and the Architectural Packaging of the Mythic West," *Montana: The Magazine of Western History* 48, no. 1 (Spring 1998): 6, 11.

13. Ibid., pp. 14, 15. Regarding the global commodification of the frontier not only in the Disney parks but also in Legoredo, the Old West section of Denmark's Legoland, see John D. Dorst, *Looking West* (Philadelphia: University of Pennsylvania Press, 1999), pp. 212–14. Also relevant *passim* are *Disney Discourse: Producing the Magic Kingdom*, ed. Eric Smoodin (New York: Routledge, 1994), and Carl Hiaasen, *Team Rodent: How Disney Devours the World* (New York: Ballantine, 1998).

14. Steiner, "Frontierland as Tomorrowland," p. 17. Sal Paradise's phrase is from Jack Kerouac, *On the Road* (New York: Viking, 1957), p. 309. Such muting strategies are applied also in touristic Western theme towns—see, for example, Bonnie Christensen's *Red Lodge and the Mythic West: Coal Miners to Cowboys* (Lawrence: University Press of Kansas, 2002).

15. Steiner, "Frontierland as Tomorrowland," p. 4.

16. Joy S. Kasson, *Buffalo Bill's Wild West: Celebrity, Memory, and Popular History* (New York: Hill and Wang, 2000), p. 8.

17. Yi-Fu Tuan, *Escapism* (Baltimore: Johns Hopkins University Press, 1998), pp. 6, 27.

18. Sven Birkerts, "American Nostalgias," in *Readings* (Saint Paul, MN: Graywolf Press, 1999), pp. 24–25, 24, 35, 36, 38.

19. Ibid., pp. 39–40, 41.

20. For further discussion of the pathology involved here, see Paul Shepard, "Virtually Hunting Reality in the Forests of Simulacra," in *Reinventing Nature? Responses to Postmodern Deconstruction*, ed. Michael E. Soulé and Gary Lease (Washington, DC: Island Press, 1995), pp. 17–29, and Scott Hess, "Postmodern Pastoral, Advertising, and the Masque of Technology," *Interdisciplinary Studies in Literature and Environment* 11, no. 1 (Winter 2004): 71–100.

21. Jim Brandenburg, *Brother Wolf: A Forgotten Promise* (Minocqua, WI: NorthWord Press, 1993), p. 35.

22. Jack Turner, "Wildness and the Defense of Nature," in *The Abstract Wild* (Tucson: University of Arizona Press, 1996), pp. 121, 109.

23. Jack Turner, "The Abstract Wild: A Rant," in *Abstract Wild*, pp. 23, 29.

24. Hayden White, "The Forms of Wildness: Archaeology of an Idea," in *The Wild Man Within: An Image in Western Thought from the Renaissance to Romanticism*, ed. Edward Dudley and Maximillian E. Novak (Pittsburgh, PA: University of Pittsburgh Press, 1972), p. 32.

25. Boria Sax, "The Mermaid and Her Sisters: From Archaic Goddess to Consumer Society," *Interdisciplinary Studies in Literature and Environment* 7, no. 2 (Summer 2000): 54.

26. Molly Wallace, "'A Bizarre Ecology': The Nature of Denatured Nature," *Interdisciplinary Studies in Literature and Environment* 7, no. 2 (Summer 2000): 137, 138. A fuller treatment

of the problematic postmodern intermingling of nature and culture, especially with respect to the former as an ideological construction of the latter, is Peter Goin's *Humanature* (Austin: University of Texas Press, 1996).

27. Donald Worster, *Under Western Skies: Nature and History in the American West* (New York: Oxford University Press, 1992), pp. 241, 254.

The Computer in the Cabin: Unsettling the Nouveau West

1. See Danny Lehman's photograph in Bart McDowell, "New Mexico: Between Frontier and Future," *National Geographic* 172 (1987): 602–3.

2. See Ted Wood's photograph in Jordan Bonfante, "Sky's the Limit," *Time*, 6 September 1993, pp. 20–21.

3. Tom Huth, "The Epicurean Cowboys," *Condé Nast Traveler*, September 1994, pp. 114, 121.

4. Lincoln Navigator, advertisement, *Scientific American*, June 1998, pp. 24–25.

5. Leo Marx, *The Machine in the Garden: Technology and the Pastoral Ideal in America* (London: Oxford University Press, 1964), pp. 6, 26, 27.

6. Bonfante, "Sky's the Limit," p. 23.

7. Patricia Nelson Limerick, "The Shadows of Heaven Itself," in *Atlas of the New West: Portrait of a Changing Region*, ed. William E. Riebsame et al. (New York: Norton, 1997), pp. 155, 157, 158.

8. Richard White, "Frederick Jackson Turner and Buffalo Bill," in *The Frontier in American Culture: An Exhibition at the Newberry Library, August 26, 1994–January 7, 1995: Essays by Richard White and Patricia Nelson Limerick*, ed. James R. Grossman (Berkeley: University of California Press, 1994), pp. 19–21.

9. Elliott West, "Selling the Myth: Western Images in Advertising," in *Wanted Dead or Alive: The American West in Popular Culture*, ed. Richard Aquila (Urbana: University of Illinois Press, 1996), pp. 272, 273.

10. *Atlas of the New West*, ed. Riebsame et al., p. 77.

11. David Brooks, *Bobos in Paradise: The New Upper Class and How They Got There* (New York: Simon and Schuster, 2000), p. 11.

12. West, "Selling the Myth," p. 273.

13. Carl Abbott, *The Metropolitan Frontier: Cities in the Modern American West* (Tucson: University of Arizona Press, 1993), p. 170.

14. Ibid., p. 171.

15. Neil Campbell, *The Cultures of the American New West* (Edinburgh, UK: Edinburgh University Press, 2000), pp. 143, 144, 149. Concerning Wallace Stegner's recommendation, see his "Variations on a Theme by Crèvecoeur," in *Where the Bluebird Sings to the Lemonade Springs: Living and Writing in the West* (1992; reprint ed., New York: Penguin Books, 1993), pp. 115–16, where he writes of towns, such as Missoula, Montana, and Corvallis, Oregon, that exemplify "the most quintessential West" (p. 115).

16. Chris Rojek, *Ways of Escape: Modern Transformations in Leisure and Travel* (Lanham, MD: Rowman and Littlefield, 1993), p. 177.

17. Hal K. Rothman, *Devil's Bargains: Tourism in the Twentieth-Century American West* (Lawrence: University Press of Kansas, 1998), p. 371.

18. Wally Gordon, "Letter from Silverton," *New Frontiers: The Magazine of New Mexico* 3, no. 4 (Winter 1996–97): 27.

19. Gary Holthaus, *Wide Skies: Finding a Home in the West* (Tucson: University of Arizona Press, 1997), p. xii. In this and related connections, see Jim Robbins, *Last Refuge: The Environmental Showdown in Yellowstone and the American West* (New York: Morrow, 1993), esp. pp. 206–67, and Raye C. Ringholz, *Little Town Blues: Voices from the Changing West* (Salt Lake City: Peregrine Smith Books, 1992).

20. William Kittredge, *Who Owns the West?* (San Francisco: Mercury House, 1996), p. 133.

21. Richard White, *"It's Your Misfortune and None of My Own": A New History of the American West* (Norman: University of Oklahoma Press, 1991), p. 633.

22. Paula Gunn Allen, "Cuentos de la Tierra Encantada: Magic and Realism in the Southwest Borderlands," in *Many Wests: Place, Culture, and Regional Identity*, ed. David M. Wrobel and Michael C. Steiner (Lawrence: University Press of Kansas, 1997), p. 355.

23. David Rothenberg, "Epilogue: Paradox Wild," in *Wild Ideas*, ed. David Rothenberg (Minneapolis: University of Minnesota Press, 1995), p. 217.

24. Mark Busby, "Sam Shepard and Frontier Gothic," in *Frontier Gothic: Terror and Wonder at the Frontier in American Literature*, ed. David Mogen, Scott P. Sanders, and Joanne B. Karpinski (Rutherford, NJ: Fairleigh Dickinson University Press, 1993), pp. 87–88.

25. Edwin H. Marston, "The American West: What Ideas Should Determine Its Future?" in *A Society to Match the Scenery: Personal Visions of the Future of the American West*, ed. Gary Holthaus, Patricia Nelson Limerick, Charles F. Wilkinson, and Eve Stryker Munson (Niwot: University Press of Colorado, 1991), p. 188.

26. Ibid., p. 189.

27. Adrian Herminio Bustamante, "The Human Element in the West: Contradictions, Contradictions, Contradictions," in *Society to Match the Scenery*, ed. Holthaus, Limerick, Wilkinson, and Munson, p. 76.

28. Gary Holthaus, Patricia Nelson Limerick, and Charles F. Wilkinson, "Speaking of the West," in *Society to Match the Scenery*, ed. Holthaus, Limerick, Wilkinson, and Munson, p. 9.

Wild(e) Style: Ralphlaurenizing the Range

1. For the details of Wilde's American tour, including *passim* those of the Western leg, see Richard Ellmann, *Oscar Wilde* (New York: Knopf, 1988), pp. 157–211. His Western itinerary is on p. 188.

2. Ray Allen Billington, *Land of Savagery, Land of Promise: The European Image of the American Frontier in the Nineteenth Century* (New York: Norton, 1981), p. 324. His examples of enthusiasm for the West are on pp. 324–30.

3. Richard White, *"It's Your Misfortune and None of My Own": A New History of the American West* (Norman: University of Oklahoma Press, 1991), pp. 631, 630.

4. Neil Campbell, *The Cultures of the American New West* (Edinburgh, UK: Edinburgh University Press, 2000), p. 144.

5. Richard Rodriguez, "True West," in *The Anchor Essay Annual: The Best of 1997*, ed. Phillip Lopate (New York: Doubleday, Anchor Books, 1997), pp. 321, 323.

6. Carole Cable, cartoon, *Chronicle of Higher Education*, 23 June 1995, p. B3.

7. David Thomson, *In Nevada: The Land, the People, God, and Chance* (New York: Knopf, 1999), p. 294.

8. René E. Riley, "Sensuous Skins," *Western Styles*, Fall 1993, p. 113.

9. Larry McMurtry, *Walter Benjamin at the Dairy Queen: Reflections at Sixty and Beyond* (New York: Simon and Schuster, 1999), p. 187.

10. Robert G. Athearn, *The Mythic West in Twentieth-Century America* (Lawrence: University Press of Kansas, 1986), p. 269.

11. Taos Country, advertisement, *Western Styles*, April 1995, p. 47.

12. Subaru Outback, advertisement, *Scientific American*, August 2002, pp. 10–11.

13. Elliott West, "Selling the Myth: Western Images in Advertising," in *Wanted Dead or Alive: The American West in Popular Culture*, ed. Richard Aquila (Urbana: University of Illinois Press, 1996), pp. 275, 276.

14. Ibid., p. 271.

15. Ibid., pp. 274, 275, 278.

16. Ibid., pp. 280, 281.

17. Ibid., pp. 282, 283, 286, 288. Insightful observations about the West as style may be found *passim* in Annie Gilbert Coleman, *Ski Style: Sport and Culture in the Rockies* (Lawrence: University Press of Kansas, 2004).

18. White, "*It's Your Misfortune and None of My Own*," p. 537.

19. In this connection, see Dagoberto Gilb's short story "Ballad," in *The Best of the West 4: New Stories from the Wide Side of the Missouri*, ed. James Thomas and Denise Thomas (New York: Norton, 1991), pp. 207–16.

20. Stephen Tatum, "Adventure in the Fashion System," *Western Humanities Review* 43, no. 1 (Spring 1989): 18.

21. Stephen Tatum, "'The Heart of the Wise Is in the House of Mourning,'" in *Eye on the Future: Popular Culture Scholarship into the Twenty-first Century*, ed. Marilyn F. Motz, John G. Nachbar, Michael T. Marsden, and Ronald J. Ambrosetti (Bowling Green, OH: Bowling Green State University Popular Press, 1994), pp. 61, 63.

Once in the Saddle I Used to Go Gay: Redoing Rodeo

1. May Swenson, "Bronco Busting, Event #1," in *May out West: Poems of May Swenson* (Logan: Utah State University Press, 1996), p. 44.

2. Wayne S. Wooden and Gavin Ehringer, *Rodeo in America: Wranglers, Roughstock, and Paydirt* (Lawrence: University Press of Kansas, 1996), p. 72.

3. See Kristine Fredriksson, *American Rodeo: From Buffalo Bill to Big Business* (College Station: Texas A&M University Press, 1985), pp. 183–200, for a brief postmodern history of what she calls "the cowboy plutocrat" in rodeo (p. 183).

4. Larry McMurtry, *Walter Benjamin at the Dairy Queen: Reflections at Sixty and Beyond* (New York: Simon and Schuster, 1999), p. 56.

5. Larry McMurtry, "Notes on Rodeo: Occasioned by the Arena Photography of Louise L. Serpa," in Louise L. Serpa, *Rodeo* (New York: Aperture Foundation, 1994), p. 83.

6. Larry McMurtry, *It's Always We Rambled: An Essay on Rodeo* (New York: Hallman, 1974), p. 20.

7. See Mary Lou LeCompte, *Cowgirls of the Rodeo: Pioneer Professional Athletes* (Urbana: University of Illinois Press, 1993); Wooden and Ehringer, *Rodeo in America*, pp. 186–200; and Michele Morris, *The Cowboy Life: A Saddlebag Guide for Dudes, Tenderfeet, and Cowpunchers Everywhere* (New York: Fireside, 1993), pp. 207–10.

8. Elizabeth Atwood Lawrence, *Rodeo: An Anthropologist Looks at the Wild and the Tame* (Knoxville: University of Tennessee Press, 1982), p. 130.

9. See Wooden and Ehringer, *Rodeo in America*, pp. 188–89.

10. Ibid., p. 196.

11. McMurtry, *Walter Benjamin at the Dairy Queen*, p. 139.

12. LeCompte, *Cowgirls of the Rodeo*, pp. 21, 187.

13. Stephen Tatum, "Literature Out-of-Doors," review of *Prose and Poetry of the American West*, ed. James C. Work, *American Literary History* 5 (1993): 312.

14. Blake Allmendinger, *Ten Most Wanted: The New Western Literature* (New York: Routledge, 1998), p. 67.

15. Blake Allmendinger, *The Cowboy: Representations of Labor in an American Work Culture* (New York: Oxford University Press, 1992), p. 13. Allmendinger is undoubtedly right about the lack of textual proof, but some texts surely come close to delivering it—see, for example, the cowboy song that Jim Wilke (who makes no bones about there being plenty of homosexuality in bunkhouses and on cattle trails) says "originated on the Texas Panhandle in the 1880s" in his "My Lover Is a Cowboy: Homosexuality on the Open Range," *Roundup: The Gay and Lesbian Western Magazine*, no. 9 (May 1996), p. 8.

16. Allmendinger, *Ten Most Wanted*, p. 157.

17. Lee Clark Mitchell, *Westerns: Making the Man in Fiction and Film* (Chicago: University of Chicago Press, 1996), pp. 159, 160, 159.

18. Wooden and Ehringer, *Rodeo in America*, p. 212.

19. Darrell Yates Rist, *Heartlands: A Gay Man's Odyssey across America* (New York: Dutton, 1992), p. 119.

20. McMurtry, *It's Always We Rambled*, p. 12. Worth remarking in this connection is the "strengthening gay identity in the West" (*Atlas of the New West: Portrait of a Changing Region*, ed. William E. Riebsame et al. [New York: Norton, 1997], p. 101). Nonetheless, outside urban areas the gay world still usually receives a cold welcome at best and therefore tends to be secretive—a predicament fictionalized by Annie Proulx in her short story "Brokeback Mountain," in *Close Range: Wyoming Stories* (New York: Scribner, 1999), pp. 253–83, which Ang Lee made into a movie with the same title in 2005.

21. Delmas Howe's series can be viewed small in his book *Rodeo Pantheon* (London: Éditions Aubrey Walter, 1993).

22. Annie Proulx, "The Mud Below," in *Close Range*, p. 62.

23. Jack Randolph Conrad, *The Horn and the Sword: The History of the Bull as a Symbol of Power and Fertility* (London: MacGibbon and Kee, 1959), p. 9. See also J. E. Cirlot, *A Dictionary of Symbols*, trans. Jack Sage (New York: Philosophical Library, 1962), s.v. "bull."

24. Bonney MacDonald, "Desire of the Middle Ground: Opposition, Dialectics, and Dialogic Context in Gretel Ehrlich's *The Solace of Open Spaces*," *Western American Literature* 33 (1998): 137. The quotations from Ehrlich, which are followed by parenthesized page numbers in Macdonald's original text, may be found in her "Rules of the Game: Rodeo," in *The Solace of Open Spaces* (New York: Penguin Books, 1986), pp. 93, 94. Apropos of this inversion of stereotypes, Ehrlich remarks in another essay in the same collection, "Other Lives," that in the West "the women I met—descendants of outlaws, homesteaders, ranchers, and Mormon pioneers—were as tough and capable as the men were softhearted" (p. 39).

25. Cheryll Glotfelty, "Old Folks in the New West: Surviving Change and Staying Fit in *The Misfits*," *Western American Literature* 37 (2002): 27, 32–33, 31, 43.

Las Vegas: Ambiguous Oasis

1. John McPhee, *Basin and Range* (New York: Noonday Press, 1990), p. 54.

2. Hunter S. Thompson, *Fear and Loathing in Las Vegas: A Savage Journey to the Heart of the American Dream* (1971; reprint ed., New York: Popular Library, 1971), pp. 6, 47.

3. Timothy Egan, *Lasso the Wind: Away to the New West* (New York: Knopf, 1998), pp. 95, 97, 95.

4. Richard White, *"It's Your Misfortune and None of My Own": A New History of the American West* (Norman: University of Oklahoma Press, 1991), p. 519.

5. Egan, *Lasso the Wind*, p. 105.

6. Hal K. Rothman, *Devil's Bargains: Tourism in the Twentieth-Century American West* (Lawrence: University Press of Kansas, 1998), pp. 288, 289, 293, 289, 294. For more history of Las Vegas since World War II, see the biography-based collection *The Players: The Men Who Made Las Vegas*, ed. Jack Sheehan (Reno: University of Nevada Press, 1997), and the multigenre anthology *Literary Las Vegas: The Best Writing about America's Most Fabulous City*, ed. Mike Tronnes (New York: Holt, 1995). The most thorough study of the city's history from the beginning to recent times is Hal Rothman's *Neon Metropolis: How Las Vegas Started the Twenty-first Century* (New York: Routledge, 2002).

7. See Katherine Jensen and Audie Blevins, *The Last Gamble: Betting on the Future in Four Rocky Mountain Mining Towns* (Tucson: University of Arizona Press, 1998).

8. Jean Baudrillard, *America*, trans. Chris Turner (London: Verso, 1988), p. 128.

9. Elizabeth Raymond, "When the Desert Won't Bloom: Environmental Limitation and the Great Basin," in *Many Wests: Place, Culture, and Regional Identity*, ed. David M. Wrobel and Michael C. Steiner (Lawrence: University Press of Kansas, 1997), p. 85.

10. Robert G. Athearn, *The Mythic West in Twentieth-Century America* (Lawrence: University Press of Kansas, 1986), p. 121.

11. Lee Clark Mitchell, *Westerns: Making the Man in Fiction and Film* (Chicago: University of Chicago Press, 1996), pp. 82–83. For a broader historical view of the cultural context of the explanations I offer in this paragraph, see John M. Findlay, *People of Chance: Gambling in American Society from Jamestown to Las Vegas* (New York: Oxford University Press, 1986).

12. Rothman, *Devil's Bargains*, p. 292.

13. David Spanier, *Welcome to the Pleasuredome: Inside Las Vegas* (Reno: University of Nevada Press, 1992), p. 1.

14. David Thomson, *In Nevada: The Land, the People, God, and Chance* (New York: Knopf, 1999), pp. 288, 289, 290.

15. Hal K. Rothman and Mike Davis, "Introduction: The Many Faces of Las Vegas," in *The Grit beneath the Glitter: Tales from the Real Las Vegas*, ed. Hal K. Rothman and Mike Davis (Berkeley: University of California Press, 2002), pp. 4, 9, 10.

16. Norman M. Klein, "Scripting Las Vegas: Noir Naïfs, Junking Up, and the New Strip," in *Grit beneath the Glitter*, ed. Rothman and Davis, p. 27.

17. Egan, *Lasso the Wind*, p. 98.

18. Klein, "Scripting Las Vegas," p. 25.

19. Zeese Papanikolas, *Trickster in the Land of Dreams* (Lincoln: University of Nebraska Press, 1995), pp. 137, 136.

20. Thomson, *In Nevada*, p. 280. Such etherealization is reflected even in the now-frequent use of the relatively vague word *gaming* in preference to the connotation-laden word *gambling*.

21. Neil Campbell, *The Cultures of the American New West* (Edinburgh, UK: Edinburgh University Press, 2000), pp. 152, 153, 154. "If the Mirage began the post-modernist phase in Las Vegas in November, 1989, then the MGM Grand, if it is built as planned, will complete it,"

Spanier wrote in 1992 (*Welcome to the Pleasuredome*, p. 250); but he's wrong on both counts: that phase began earlier (arguably in the 1960s) and isn't, years after the opening of the MGM Grand, over yet.

22. For an extended discussion of postmodernism, especially in relation to modernism, see David Harvey, *The Condition of Postmodernity: An Enquiry into the Origins of Cultural Change* (Cambridge, MA: Blackwell, 1990), pp. 3–65.

23. Egan, *Lasso the Wind*, pp. 102, 107.

24. Papanikolas, *Trickster in the Land of Dreams*, p. 144.

25. Thomson, *In Nevada*, p. 291.

Weird Weird West: Roswell and Other Landing Sites

1. James C. Work, *Ride South to Purgatory* (Unity, ME: Five Star, 1999), p. 68.

2. Paula Gunn Allen, "Cuentos de la Tierra Encantada: Magic and Realism in the Southwest Borderlands," in *Many Wests: Place, Culture, and Regional Identity*, ed. David M. Wrobel and Michael C. Steiner (Lawrence: University Press of Kansas, 1997), p. 359.

3. There's no shortage of versions of this story, but a concise one with the essential details may be found in Brendan Doherty, "Fact or Fiction: The Roswell Incident," *New Mexico Magazine*, February 1999, pp. 22–24.

4. Thomas E. Bullard, "UFOs: Lost in the Myths," in *UFOs and Abductions: Challenging the Borders of Knowledge*, ed. David M. Jacobs (Lawrence: University Press of Kansas, 2000), pp. 143, 153, 163, 164, 167, 179, 168. For background on the space-age mythology of UFOs, see *UFO Crash at Roswell: The Genesis of a Modern Myth*, ed. Benson Saler, Charles A. Ziegler, and Charles B. Moore (Washington, DC: Smithsonian Institution Press, 1997). In her study of memes, Susan Blackmore argues that tales of alien abduction are created and promulgated in order to make sense of sleep paralysis ("The Power of Memes," *Scientific American*, October 2000, p. 73). Her argument isn't refuted by anything said by members of the Los Angeles chapter of the UFO abductee support group visited by Mary Morris—as reported in her *Angels and Aliens: A Journey West* (New York: Picador USA, 1999), pp. 197–207—but at any rate my interest isn't so much in what the tales make sense of as in how they do so.

5. Phil Patton, *Travels inside the Secret World of Roswell and Area 51* (New York: Villard, 1998), pp. 3, 6, 10, 12–13. Despite claims to the contrary, experienced Area 51 watchers, like Patton, argue that the site is still functional. William L. Fox, for example, says there's no evidence to support "rumors that Area 51 has been abandoned by the military and its operations dispersed to other installations within the Great Basin" (*The Void, the Grid, and the Sign: Traversing the Great Basin* [Salt Lake City: University of Utah Press, 2000], p. 218).

6. David Perkins, "Heart of Weirdness," *Spirit: The Magazine of the Rocky Mountain Southwest*, Fall-Winter 1994–95, p. 20. For a probable (and nonextraterrestrial) explanation of the much-bruited cow mutilations, see Jack Hitt, "Operation Moo," *Gentleman's Quarterly*, February 1997, pp. 157–59.

7. Catherine L. Albanese, *Nature Religion in America: From the Algonkian Indians to the New Age* (Chicago: University of Chicago Press, 1990), pp. 154, 155.

8. Allen, "Cuentos de la Tierra Encantada," p. 343. For some background on the evolution of the Southwest as a fantasy space for white Americans, see Audrey Goodman, *Translating Southwestern Landscapes: The Making of an Anglo Literary Region* (Tucson: University of Arizona Press, 2002).

9. See Devon Jackson, "Shadow Play," *Santa Fean*, April 2002, pp. 37–45.

10. Stephen Fox, "Boomer Dharma: The Evolution of Alternative Spiritual Communities in Modern New Mexico," in *Religion in Modern New Mexico*, ed. Ferenc M. Szasz and Richard W. Etulain (Albuquerque: University of New Mexico Press, 1997), p. 148.

11. Patricia Nelson Limerick, "The Shadows of Heaven Itself," in *Atlas of the New West: Portrait of a Changing Region*, ed. William E. Riebsame et al. (New York: Norton, 1997), p. 167.

12. Robert Michael Pyle, *Where Bigfoot Walks: Crossing the Dark Divide* (Boston: Houghton Mifflin, 1995), pp. 1, 6, 8, 271.

13. Paul Shepard, *The Others: How Animals Made Us Human* (Washington, DC: Shearwater Books, 1996), pp. 185, 186.

14. Neil Campbell, *The Cultures of the American New West* (Edinburgh, UK: Edinburgh University Press, 2000), p. 37.

15. Boria Sax, "The Mermaid and Her Sisters: From Archaic Goddess to Consumer Society," *Interdisciplinary Studies in Literature and Environment* 7, no. 2 (Summer 2000): 50. For Lucian Boia's discussion of l'homme *différent*, see his *Entre l'ange et la bête: Le mythe de l'homme différent de l'antiquité à nos jours* (Paris: Plon, 1995).

16. Fox, *The Void, the Grid, and the Sign*, pp. 13, 206.

17. Donald Snow, "Ecocide," in *Northern Lights: A Selection of New Writing from the American West*, ed. Deborah Clow and Donald Snow (New York: Vintage Books, 1994), p. 237.

18. Philip J. Deloria, *Playing Indian* (New Haven, CT: Yale University Press, 1998), p. 3.

The Last Best Craze: Madness in Montana

1. *Daily Oklahoman*, 20 April 1995, p. 1.

2. Jonathan Raban, *Bad Land: An American Romance* (New York: Pantheon Books, 1996), pp. 298, 299.

3. Larry McMurtry, "On the Big Two-Hearted River," review of *The Cadence of Grass*, by Thomas McGuane, *New York Review of Books*, 27 June 2002, p. 22.

4. See William W. Bevis, *Ten Tough Trips: Montana Writers and the West* (Seattle: University of Washington Press, 1990), p. xv.

5. Timothy Egan, *Lasso the Wind: Away to the New West* (New York: Knopf, 1998), p. 163. The state doesn't say no even to bison hunting anymore. In late 2004 it approved, over protests, the issuance of licenses for such hunting north of Yellowstone, where some of the animals wander in search of winter forage.

6. K. Ross Toole, *Twentieth-Century Montana: A State of Extremes* (Norman: University of Oklahoma Press, 1972), pp. 5, xi.

7. John Taylor, "The Big Sky's the Limit," *Esquire*, March 1996, p. 115.

8. Raban, *Bad Land*, p. 303. For Ted Kaczynski's views, see "FC," *The Unabomber Manifesto: Industrial Society and Its Future* (Berkeley: Jolly Roger Press, 1995).

9. Roderick Nash, *Wilderness and the American Mind*, 3rd ed. (New Haven, CT: Yale University Press, 1982), p. 273.

10. Larry McMurtry, *Roads: Driving America's Great Highways* (New York: Simon and Schuster, 2000), p. 198.

11. Mary Murphy, "Searching for an Angle of Repose: Women, Work, and Creativity in Early Montana," in *Many Wests: Place, Culture, and Regional Identity*, ed. David M. Wrobel and Michael C. Steiner (Lawrence: University Press of Kansas, 1997), p. 172.

12. Robert D. Kaplan, *An Empire Wilderness: Travels into America's Future* (New York: Random House, 1998), p. 288.

13. David Brooks, *Bobos in Paradise: The New Upper Class and How They Got There* (New York: Simon and Schuster, 2000), pp. 220, 221, 224, 250.

14. Bevis, *Ten Tough Trips*, p. 149.

15. Raban, *Bad Land*, p. 7.

16. Sharman Apt Russell, "Biosphere II," in *Songs of the Fluteplayer: Seasons of Life in the Southwest* (Reading, MA: Addison-Wesley, 1991), p. 146.

17. Leslie Ryan, "The Clearing in the Clearing," in *Northern Lights: A Selection of New Writing from the American West*, ed. Deborah Clow and Donald Snow (New York: Vintage Books, 1994), pp. 351–52.

18. William Kittredge, "Yellowstone in Winter," in *Wilderness Tapestry: An Eclectic Approach to Preservation*, ed. Samuel I. Zeveloff, L. Mikel Vause, and William H. McVaugh (Reno: University of Nevada Press, 1992), pp. 113, 114, 116.

19. Bevis, *Ten Tough Trips*, pp. 198, 200, 205.

20. Ibid., p. 205.

Little Hassle on the Prairie: The Issue of Wise (Non)use

1. For illuminating perspectives on problems of this kind, see *American Forests: Nature, Culture, and Politics*, ed. Char Miller (Lawrence: University Press of Kansas, 1997), and *Contested Landscape: The Politics of Wilderness in Utah and the West*, ed. Doug Goodman and Daniel McCool (Salt Lake City: University of Utah Press, 1999).

2. Patricia Nelson Limerick, *The Legacy of Conquest: The Unbroken Past of the American West* (New York: Norton, 1987), pp. 46, 47.

3. For historical background on the environmental movement and the Sagebrush Rebellion, respectively, see Roderick Nash, *The Rights of Nature: A History of Environmental Ethics* (Madison: University of Wisconsin Press, 1989), and Donald J. Pisani, *Water, Land, and Law in the West: The Limits of Public Policy, 1850–1920* (Lawrence: University Press of Kansas, 1996). Two spiky treatments of public-lands controversies in the postregional West, particularly with respect to rangeland, are Edward Abbey, "Even the Bad Guys Wear White Hats: Cowboys, Ranchers, and the Ruin of the West," *Harper's*, January 1986, pp. 51–55, and Sharman Apt Russell, *Kill the Cowboy: A Battle of Mythology in the New West* (Reading, MA: Addison-Wesley, 1993), pp. 14–73. More detailed accounts of the Sagebrush Rebellion (and its antecedents) may be found in William L. Graf, *Wilderness Preservation and the Sagebrush Rebellions* (Savage, MD: Rowman and Littlefield, 1990), and R. McGreggor Cawley, *Federal Land, Western Anger: The Sagebrush Rebellion and Environmental Politics* (Lawrence: University Press of Kansas, 1993), esp. pp. 71–122.

4. J. Baird Callicott and Michael P. Nelson, Introduction, *The Great New Wilderness Debate*, ed. J. Baird Callicott and Michael P. Nelson (Athens: University of Georgia Press, 1998), p. 1.

5. Bruce Babbitt, "Public Use and the Future of the Federal Lands," in *A Society to Match the Scenery: Personal Visions of the Future of the American West*, ed. Gary Holthaus, Patricia Nelson Limerick, Charles F. Wilkinson, and Eve Stryker Munson (Niwot: University Press of Colorado, 1991), p. 163.

6. Ibid., p. 166.

7. Gundars Rudzitis, *Wilderness and the Changing American West* (New York: Wiley, 1996), pp. 173–74.

8. Jack Turner, "Economic Nature," in *The Abstract Wild* (Tucson: University of Arizona Press, 1996), p. 53.

9. William Kittredge, *Who Owns the West?* (San Francisco: Mercury House, 1996), pp. 133, 134.

10. Jim Robbins, *Last Refuge: The Environmental Showdown in Yellowstone and the West* (New York: Morrow, 1993), p. 12.

11. For further discussion and more examples of the ideas being advanced, see Nathan F. Sayre, *The New Ranch Handbook: A Guide to Restoring Western Rangelands* (Reno: University of Nevada Press, 2001); Sally K. Fairfax and Darla Guenzler, *Conservation Trusts* (Lawrence: University Press of Kansas, 2001); *The New Agrarianism: Land, Culture, and the Community of Life*, ed. Eric T. Freyfogle (Washington, DC: Shearwater Books, 2001); Nathan F. Sayre, *Ranching, Endangered Species, and Urbanization in the Southwest* (Tucson: University of Arizona Press, 2002); and *Ranching West of the 100th Meridian: Culture, Ecology, and Economics*, ed. Richard L. Knight, Wendell C. Gilbert, and Ed Marston (Washington, DC: Island Press, 2002).

12. Rudzitis, *Wilderness and the Changing American West*, pp. 181–82.

13. Peggy Simson Curry, "Abandoned Irrigation Ditch," in *Summer Range* (Story, WY: Dooryard Press, 1981), p. 14.

14. Paul S. Sutter, *Driven Wild: How the Fight against Automobiles Launched the Modern Wilderness Movement* (Seattle: University of Washington Press, 2002), p. 263.

15. Curt Meine, "The Utility of Preservation and the Preservation of Utility: Leopold's Fine Line," in *The Wilderness Condition: Essays on Environment and Civilization*, ed. Max Oelschlaeger (San Francisco: Sierra Club Books, 1992), p. 158.

16. T. S. Eliot, "Gerontion," in *Collected Poems, 1909–1962* (San Diego: Harcourt, Brace, Jovanovich, 1963), p. 30.

17. Some examples of that literature, besides sources I've cited elsewhere, are *The World of Wilderness: Essays on the Power and Purpose of Wild Country*, ed. T. H. Watkins and Patricia Byrnes (Niwot, CO: Rinehart, 1995), an encyclopedic collection on different approaches to land use; William Ashworth, *The Left Hand of Eden: Meditations on Nature and Human Nature* (Corvallis: Oregon State University Press, 1999), a book that makes a case against the preservation of wilderness as something separate from the human sphere; David M. Graber, "Resolute Biocentrism: The Dilemma of Wilderness in National Parks," in *Reinventing Nature? Responses to Postmodern Deconstruction*, ed. Michael E. Soulé and Gary Lease (Washington, DC: Island Press, 1995), pp. 123–35, a treatment of biocentrism that explores its problems and pushes for more research on ecosystem management; and Dick Carter, "Defending the Desert," in *Wilderness Issues in the Arid Lands of the Western United States*, ed. Samuel I. Zeveloff and Cyrus M. McKell (Albuquerque: University of New Mexico Press, 1992), pp. 105–16, an argument that emphasizes attending to Western wilderness through consensus.

18. *Atlas of the New West: Portrait of a Changing Region*, ed. William E. Riebsame et al. (New York: Norton, 1997), p. 149. For other possible features of such a vision, see *Return of the Wild: The Future of Our Natural Lands*, ed. Ted Kerasote (Washington, DC: Island Press, 2001); Tim Palmer, *The Heart of America: Our Landscape, Our Future* (Washington, DC: Island Press, 1999); R. Edward Grumbine, "Wise and Sustainable Uses: Revisioning Wilderness," in *Wild Ideas*, ed. David Rothenberg (Minneapolis: University of Minnesota Press, 1995), pp. 3–25; and William Kittredge, *Taking Care: Thoughts on Storytelling and Belief* (Minneapolis: Milkweed Editions, 1999).

Beyond John Wayne: Bewildering Westerns and Wild Wild Texts

1. John H. Lenihan, "Westbound: Feature Films and the American West," in *Wanted Dead or Alive: The American West in Popular Culture*, ed. Richard Aquila (Urbana: University of Illinois Press, 1996), p. 127.

2. Jon Tuska, *The American West in Film: Critical Approaches to the Western* (Westport, CT: Greenwood Press, 1985), p. 26.

3. Richard White, *"It's Your Misfortune and None of My Own": A New History of the American West* (Norman: University of Oklahoma Press, 1991), p. 626.

4. A. Carl Bredahl Jr., *New Ground: Western American Narrative and the Literary Canon* (Chapel Hill: University of North Carolina Press, 1989), pp. 162, 164.

5. Michael Kowalewski, "An Estranged Frontier: Landscape in Altman's *McCabe and Mrs. Miller*," in *The Big Empty: Essays on Western Landscapes as Narrative*, ed. Leonard Engel (Albuquerque: University of New Mexico Press, 1994), pp. 209, 223.

6. Neil Campbell, *The Cultures of the American New West* (Edinburgh, UK: Edinburgh University Press, 2000), p. 90.

7. Fred Erisman, "The Enduring Myth and the Modern West," in *Researching Western History: Topics in the Twentieth Century*, ed. Gerald D. Nash and Richard W. Etulain (Albuquerque: University of New Mexico Press, 1997), p. 173.

8. White, *"It's Your Misfortune and None of My Own,"* p. 626.

9. Christian Metz, *Language and Cinema*, trans. Donna Jean Umiker-Sebeok (The Hague: Mouton, 1974), p. 152.

10. Robert G. Athearn, *The Mythic West in Twentieth-Century America* (Lawrence: University Press of Kansas, 1986), p. 188.

11. Lee Clark Mitchell, *Westerns: Making the Man in Fiction and Film* (Chicago: University of Chicago Press, 1996), pp. 226, 229.

12. Thomas Schatz, "The Western," in *Handbook of American Film Genres*, ed. Wes D. Gehring (New York: Greenwood Press, 1988), p. 35.

13. Leslie A. Fiedler, *The Return of the Vanishing American* (New York: Stein and Day, 1968), p. 185.

14. Stephen Ives in Gregory Lalire, "The West according to Burns and Ives," interview with Ken Burns and Stephen Ives, *Wild West*, October 1996, p. 48.

15. Richard W. Etulain, *Re-imagining the Modern American West: A Century of Fiction, History, and Art* (Tucson: University of Arizona Press, 1996), pp. 193, 196, 205, 210.

16. William Kittredge, *Who Owns the West?* (San Francisco: Mercury House, 1996), p. 93.

17. Stephen Tatum, "From the Acting Editor," *Western American Literature* 35 (2000): 3.

18. Campbell, *Cultures of the American New West*, p. 21. For the sources of his terminology, see Edward W. Soja, *Thirdspace: Journeys to Los Angeles and Other Real-and-Imagined Places* (Cambridge, MA: Blackwell, 1996), esp. pp. 53–82, and Henri Lefebvre, *The Production of Space*, trans. Donald Nicholson-Smith (Cambridge, MA: Blackwell, 1991).

19. Russell Martin, Introduction, *Writers of the Purple Sage: An Anthology of Recent Western Writing*, ed. Russell Martin and Marc Barasch (New York: Viking, 1984), p. xix.

20. Timothy Egan, *Lasso the Wind: Away to the New West* (New York: Knopf, 1998), p. 10.

21. Patricia Nelson Limerick, *Something in the Soil: Legacies and Reckonings in the New West* (New York: Norton, 2000), p. 294.

22. Scott P. Sanders, "Southwestern Gothic: On the Frontier between Landscape and Locale," in *Frontier Gothic: Terror and Wonder at the Frontier in American Literature*, ed. David Mogen, Scott P. Sanders, and Joanne B. Karpinski (Rutherford, NJ: Fairleigh Dickinson University Press, 1993), p. 68.

23. Harold P. Simonson, *Beyond the Frontier: Writers, Western Regionalism and a Sense of Place* (Fort Worth: Texas Christian University Press, 1989), p. 4.

24. Etulain, *Re-imagining the Modern American West*, p. 159.

25. See, in this connection, Charles Kupfer, "The Cold War West as Symbol and Myth: Perspectives from Popular Culture," in *The Cold War American West, 1945–1989*, ed. Kevin J. Fernlund (Albuquerque: University of New Mexico Press, 1998), pp. 167–88.

26. Annie Proulx, "The Governors of Wyoming," in *Close Range: Wyoming Stories* (New York: Scribner, 1999), p. 211.

27. Craig Miller, "Nature and Cowboy Poetry," in *Cowboy Poets and Cowboy Poetry*, ed. David Stanley and Elaine Thatcher (Urbana: University of Illinois Press, 2000), pp. 236, 237.

28. See, for example, a number of essays by contemporary American ethnic writers in *The Colors of Nature: Culture, Identity, and the Natural World*, ed. Alison H. Deming and Lauret E. Savoy (Minneapolis: Milkweed Editions, 2002).

29. Andrew Smith, "Hearing Bats and Following Berdache: The Project of Survivance in Linda Hogan's *Mean Spirit*," *Western American Literature* 35 (2000): 177, 189.

30. Sheila Ruzycki O'Brien, "*Housekeeping*: New West Novel, Old West Film," in *Old West— New West: Centennial Essays*, ed. Barbara Howard Meldrum (Moscow: University of Idaho Press, 1993), pp. 173, 176.

31. Annette Van Dyke, "Marilynne Robinson's *Housekeeping*: A Landscape of Discontent," in *Big Empty*, ed. Engel, p. 160.

32. Kim Barnes and Mary Clearman Blew, Introduction, *Circle of Women: An Anthology of Contemporary Western Women Writers*, ed. Kim Barnes and Mary Clearman Blew (New York: Penguin Books, 1994), p. xi.

33. Mary Clearman Blew in "Western Autobiography and Memoir: A Panel of Writers," *Western American Literature* 37 (2002): 159, 160.

34. Etulain, *Re-imagining the Modern American West*, p. 153.

35. Bredahl, *New Ground*, p. 140.

36. Campbell, *Cultures of the American New West*, p. 76.

37. Brian W. Dippie, "American Wests: Historiographical Perspectives," in *Trails: Toward a New Western History*, ed. Patricia Nelson Limerick, Clyde A. Milner II, and Charles E. Rankin (Lawrence: University Press of Kansas, 1991), pp. 126, 135.

38. Richard W. Etulain, "Conclusion: Visions and Revisions: Recent Interpretations of the American West," in *Writing Western History: Essays on Major Western Historians*, ed. Richard W. Etulain (Albuquerque: University of New Mexico Press, 1991), p. 350.

39. Etulain, *Re-imagining the Modern American West*, pp. 145, 146.

40. Todd F. Tietchen, "Cowboy Tricksters and Devilish Wangols: Ishmael Reed's Hoo-Doo West," *Western American Literature* 36 (2002): 339.

41. Robert Murray Davis, *Playing Cowboys: Low Culture and High Art in the Western* (Norman: University of Oklahoma Press, 1991), p. 87.

42. Mark Busby, "Sam Shepard and Frontier Gothic," in *Frontier Gothic*, ed. Mogen, Sanders, and Karpinski, pp. 91–92.

43. Larry McMurtry alludes to the parallel between his novel and Miguel de Cervantes's *Don Quixote* in *Walter Benjamin at the Dairy Queen: Reflections at Sixty and Beyond* (New York: Simon and Schuster, 1999), p. 187.

44. For more extensive analyses of McCarthy's vision of the Western wild-tame dialectic, see Jonathan Pitts, "Writing On: *Blood Meridian* as Devisionary Western," *Western American Literature* 33 (1998): 7–25; James Bowers, *Reading Cormac McCarthy's "Blood Meridian"* (Boise, ID:

Boise State University, 1999); Mark Busby, "Into the Darkening Land, the World to Come: Cormac McCarthy's Border Crossings," in *Myth, Legend, Dust: Critical Responses to Cormac McCarthy*, ed. Rick Wallach (Manchester, UK: Manchester University Press, 2000), pp. 227–48; Barcley Owens, *Cormac McCarthy's Western Novels* (Tucson: University of Arizona Press, 2000); and Campell, *Cultures of the American New West*, pp. 23–29.

45. Campbell, *Cultures of the American New West*, p. 160.

46. Larry McMurtry, Introduction, *Still Wild: Short Fiction of the American West, 1950 to the Present*, ed. Larry McMurtry (New York: Simon and Schuster, 2000), p. 11.

47. Thomas J. Lyon, "The Literary West," in *The Oxford History of the American West*, ed. Clyde A. Milner II, Carol A. O'Connor, and Martha A. Sandweiss (New York: Oxford University Press, 1994), pp. 735, 736.

48. Louis Owens, "'Grinning Aboriginal Demons': Gerald Vizenor's *Bearheart* and the Indian's Escape from Gothic," in *Frontier Gothic*, ed. Mogen, Sanders, and Karpinski, p. 81. Vizenor's novel was later reprinted as *Bearheart: The Heirship Chronicles* (Minneapolis: University of Minnesota Press, 1990).

49. Campbell, *Cultures of the American New West*, p. 107.

50. Louis Owens, *Other Destinies: Understanding the American Indian Novel* (Norman: University of Oklahoma Press, 1992), p. 168.

51. Dan Flores, *The Natural West: Environmental History in the Great Plains and Rocky Mountains* (Norman: University of Oklahoma Press, 2001), pp. 6, 11.

52. Etulain, *Re-imagining the Modern American West*, p. 154.

53. Michael Kowalewski, Introduction, *Reading the West: New Essays on the Literature of the American West*, ed. Michael Kowalewski (Cambridge: Cambridge University Press, 1996), p. 12.

54. Lawrence Buell, *The Environmental Imagination: Thoreau, Nature Writing, and the Formation of American Culture* (Cambridge, MA: Belknap Press, 1995), p. 20.

55. Owens, *Other Destinies*, p. 126.

56. Alison Hawthorne Deming, "Preface: What the Land Has Inspired," in *Poetry of the American West: A Columbia Anthology*, ed. Alison Hawthorne Deming (New York: Columbia University Press, 1996), pp. xvi-xvii.

57. Lyon, "Literary West," p. 716.

58. Glen A. Love, "Revaluing Nature: Toward an Ecological Criticism," *Western American Literature* 25 (1990): 213.

59. Thomas J. Lyon, "Epilogue: What Is Happening in the West Today, and What It Might Mean," in *Updating the Literary West*, ed. Thomas J. Lyon et al. (Fort Worth: Texas Christian University Press, 1997), p. 963.

60. Louise Erdrich, Introduction, *Northern Lights: A Selection of New Writing from the American West*, ed. Deborah Clow and Donald Snow (New York: Vintage Books, 1994), p. xvi.

61. Interestingly, *hem*, an Anglo-Saxon word meaning "border," is cognate with *ham*, an Anglo-Saxon word meaning "home," as well as with the Middle High German *hemmen* ("to restrain"). Also pertinent here is William R. Handley's argument, concerning achieving a rapprochement between Western history and Western literature, that we need "not to choose between reality and representation (or past and present), but to learn how to inhabit the ground between them" (*Marriage, Violence, and the Nation in the American Literary West* [Cambridge: Cambridge University Press, 2002], p. 230).

Way Out Walden: Rewriting Western Nature

1. See William H. Goetzmann, *Exploration and Empire: The Explorer and the Scientist in the Winning of the American West* (1966; reprint ed., Austin: Texas State Historical Association, 1993), pp. 15–16, 187–88.

2. Donald A. Barclay, James H. Maguire, and Peter Wild, Epilogue, *Into the Wilderness Dream: Exploration Narratives of the American West, 1500–1805*, ed. Donald A. Barclay, James H. Maguire, and Peter Wild (Salt Lake City: University of Utah Press, 1994), p. 385.

3. Max Oelschlaeger, "Introduction: The Wilderness Condition Today," in *The Wilderness Condition: Essays on Environment and Civilization*, ed. Max Oelschlaeger (San Francisco: Sierra Club Books, 1992), pp. 2, 20.

4. Thomas J. Lyon, "Introduction: The Conquistador, the Lone Ranger, and Beyond," in *The Literary West: An Anthology of Western American Literature*, ed. Thomas J. Lyon (New York: Oxford University Press, 1999), pp. 15, 18.

5. Scott Slovic, "'Be Prepared for the Worst': Love, Anticipated Loss, and Environmental Valuation," *Western American Literature* 35 (2000): 258, 260. For additional discussions of Bass's approach to nature writing, see *The Literary Art and Activism of Rick Bass*, ed. O. Alan Weltzien (Salt Lake City: University of Utah Press, 2001).

6. Slovic, "'Be Prepared for the Worst,'" p. 260.

7. Frank Stewart, *A Natural History of Nature Writing* (Washington, DC: Shearwater Books, 1995), p. xv.

8. Paul Shepard, *The Others: How Animals Made Us Human* (Washington, DC: Shearwater Books, 1995), p. 11.

9. Rick Bass, *The Lost Grizzlies: A Search for Survivors in the Wilderness of Colorado* (Boston: Houghton Mifflin, Mariner Books, 1995), p. 67.

10. For some of the strategies of such advocacy, with lots of examples from Western nature writers, see Michael Frome, *Green Ink: An Introduction to Environmental Journalism* (Salt Lake City: University of Utah Press, 1999). For a broad view of some of the social issues that occupy Western nature writers as advocates, see *The Environmental Justice Reader: Politics, Poetics, and Pedagogy*, ed. Joni Adamson, Mei Mei Evans, and Rachel Stein (Tucson: University of Arizona Press, 2002).

11. Glen A. Love, "Et in Arcadia Ego: Pastoral Theory Meets Ecocriticism," *Western American Literature* 27 (1992): 203.

12. Peter Friederici, *The Suburban Wild* (Athens: University of Georgia Press, 1999), pp. 5, 6, 8, 7.

13. Emily Hiestand, Introduction, *Urban Nature: Poems about Wildlife in the City*, ed. Laure-Anne Bosselaar (Minneapolis: Milkweed Editions, 2000), pp. xv, xvii.

14. Jennifer Price, *Flight Maps: Adventures with Nature in Modern America* (New York: Basic Books, 1999), pp. xvi, xvii.

15. See *City Wilds: Essays and Stories about Urban Nature*, ed. Terrell Dixon (Athens: University of Georgia Press, 2002), which has a good selection of writers from the West. A more theoretical consideration of the topic, one much engaged with the problems of the nature–culture dichotomy, is Annabelle Sabloff, *Reordering the Natural World: Humans and Animals in the City* (Toronto: University of Toronto Press, 2001).

16. Pattiann Rogers, "Rolling Naked in the Morning Dew," in *Song of the World Becoming: New and Collected Poems, 1981–2001* (Minneapolis: Milkweed Editions, 2001), p. 312.

17. Krista Comer, "Feminism, Women Writers and the New Western Regionalism: Revising Critical Paradigms," in *Updating the West*, ed. Thomas J. Lyon et al. (Fort Worth: Texas Christian University Press, 1997), pp. 17, 31. For a fuller version of this argument, see Comer's *Landscapes of the New West: Gender and Geography in Contemporary Women's Writing* (Chapel Hill: University of North Carolina Press, 1999).

18. John P. O'Grady, *Pilgrims to the Wild: Everett Ruess, Henry David Thoreau, John Muir, Clarence King, Mary Austin* (Salt Lake City: University of Utah Press, 1993), p. xi. Regarding the tradition of women's nature writing, see Rochelle Johnson, "Susan Fenimore Cooper's *Rural Hours* and the 'Natural' Refinement of American Culture," *Interdisciplinary Studies in Literature and Environment* 7, no. 1 (Winter 2000): 47–77, and Vera L. Norwood, "Heroines of Nature: Four Women Respond to the American Landscape," in *The Ecocriticism Reader: Landmarks in Literary Ecology*, ed. Cheryll Glotfelty and Harold Fromm (Athens: University of Georgia Press, 1996), pp. 323–50. A representative—though far from comprehensive—chronological anthology of the tradition is *At Home on This Earth: Two Centuries of U.S. Women's Nature Writing*, ed. Lorraine Anderson and Thomas S. Edwards (Hanover, NH: University Press of New England, 2002). *Such News of the Land: U.S. Women Nature Writers*, ed. Thomas S. Edwards and Elizabeth A. De Wolfe (Hanover, NH: University Press of New England, 2001), offers a historically oriented collection of critical essays on the tradition that touch on many issues relevant to my discussion of Western women nature writers and the wild-tame dialectic.

19. With reference to the significance of Williams as an innovator in the portrayal of the wild as erotic space, see Boyd Petersen, "Landscapes of Seduction: Terry Tempest Williams's *Desert Quartet* and the Biblical Song of Songs," *Interdisciplinary Studies in Literature and Environment* 9, no. 1 (Winter 2002): 91–104.

20. Lorraine Anderson, Preface, *Sisters of the Earth: Women's Prose and Poetry about Nature*, ed. Lorraine Anderson (New York: Random House, Vintage Books, 1991), p. xvii.

21. For additional examples, see *American Nature Writing 2000: A Celebration of Women Writers*, ed. John Murray (Corvallis: Oregon State University Press, 2000), which includes work by Westerners such as Susan Zwinger, Kate Boyes, Emma Brown, Susan Marsh, and Ellen Meloy. For a fuller treatment of the nature-as-woman identification, see Stacy Alaimo, *Undomesticated Ground: Recasting Nature as Feminist Space* (Ithaca, NY: Cornell University Press, 2000).

22. In this connection, see Lawrence Buell, *Writing for an Endangered World: Literature, Culture, and Environment in the U.S. and Beyond* (Cambridge, MA: Belknap Press, 2001), as well as *Reading the Earth: New Directions in the Study of Literature and Environment*, ed. Michael P. Branch, Rochelle Johnson, Daniel Patterson, and Scott Slovic (Moscow: University of Idaho Press, 1998), and *Beyond Nature Writing: Expanding the Boundaries of Ecocriticism*, ed. Karla Armbruster and Kathleen R. Wallace (Charlottesville: University of Virginia Press, 2001). A historically informative collection of essays by predecessors to postmodern ecocriticism is *A Century of Early American Ecocriticism*, ed. David Mazel (Athens: University of Georgia Press, 2001). For a study of the intellectual foundations of ecocritical thinking, see Glen A. Love, *Practical Ecocriticism: Literature, Biology, and the Environment* (Charlottesville: University of Virginia Press, 2003).

23. Love, "Et in Arcadia Ego," 203, 202–3. That middle state, as he implies, covers a range of relatively tame or wild possibilities for resolving the wilderness–civilization tension—on which range, see Don Scheese, *Nature Writing: The Pastoral Impulse in America* (New York: Twayne, 1996), pp. 5–7.

24. With respect to the adaptations, mental and otherwise, for this getting-over, see Lawrence Hogue, *All the Wild and Lonely Places: Journeys in a Desert Landscape* (Washington, DC: Island Press, 2000).

25. Reg Saner, "Desert Wisdom," in *Reaching Keet Seel: Ruin's Echo and the Anasazi* (Salt Lake City: University of Utah Press, 1998), p. 5. That acknowledgment, he asserts, may be coming about: "Lately our minds have undergone complete reversal. Instead of seeing it as accursed, we lend the very emptiness of such regions a sacral aura" (p. 4).

26. Gary Snyder, "For the Children," in *Turtle Island* (New York: New Directions, 1974), p. 86. My sense that the global instructions in the italicized tercet have a special relevance for the West is justified in part, through logical conversion, by Snyder's general tendency to write of the West synecdochically, something he does most notably in his long 1996 poem *Mountains and Rivers without End*, which, as John P. O'Grady observes, "uses the western landscape as a metaphor for the whole planet" ("Living Landscape: An Interview with Gary Snyder," *Western American Literature* 33 [1998]: 289).

The Wild Woman in the Outback: Postregional Cowgirls

1. Richard W. Etulain, *Re-imagining the Modern American West: A Century of Fiction, History, and Art* (Tucson: University of Arizona Press, 1996), p. 141.

2. Glenda Riley, "Twentieth-Century Western Women: Research Issues and Possibilities," in *Researching Western History: Topics in the Twentieth Century*, ed. Gerald D. Nash and Richard W. Etulain (Albuquerque: University of New Mexico Press, 1997), p. 126.

3. Concerning that complicity as evidenced by the colonialist discourse of white women's diaries, novels, and such, see Brigitte Georgi-Findlay, *The Frontiers of Women's Writing: Women's Narratives and the Rhetoric of Westward Expansion* (Tucson: University of Arizona Press, 1996). On Native American women as warriors, see, for example, Jo Martín, "Women Warriors: Secret Weapon of the Apaches," *New Mexico Magazine*, August 1997, pp. 90–96.

4. Lawrence Buell, *The Environmental Imagination: Thoreau, Nature Writing, and the Formation of American Culture* (Cambridge, MA: Belknap Press, 1995), p. 34.

5. Patricia Nelson Limerick, *Something in the Soil: Legacies and Reckonings in the New West* (New York: Norton, 2000), pp. 71, 72. In reference to both Buell's point and Limerick's last one, see Blake Allmendinger, *Ten Most Wanted: The New Western Literature* (New York: Routledge, 1998), pp. 79–101, for a discussion of Opal Whiteley's 1920 children's book *The Story of Opal: The Journal of an Understanding Heart*, which "narrates two years in the imaginative life of a child, or alleged child, whose adventures in the forests of Oregon" make for a story that "confirms the process of replication as a frontier phenomenon" in telling how "Opal moves from the house of 'the mamma' to the forest, from civilization to wilderness, imaginatively transforming the forest into her version of a familiar society" (pp. 89, 91).

6. Patricia Nelson Limerick, "What Raymond Chandler Knew and Western Historians Forgot," in *Old West—New West: Centennial Essays*, ed. Barbara Howard Meldrum (Moscow: University of Idaho Press, 1993), p. 32.

7. See Carl W. Breihan, *Wild Women of the West* (New York: New American Library, Signet Books, 1982); Duncan Aikman, *Calamity Jane and the Lady Wildcats* (Lincoln: University of Nebraska Press, 1987); and *Wild Women of the Old West*, ed. Glenda Riley and Richard W. Etulain (Golden, CO: Fulcrum, 2003) for further examples.

8. Glenda Riley, *The Life and Legacy of Annie Oakley* (Norman: University of Oklahoma Press, 1994), p. xv.

9. Regarding dime-novel heroines, see Henry Nash Smith, *Virgin Land: The American West as Symbol and Myth* (1950; reprint ed., Cambridge, MA: Harvard University Press, 1970), pp. 112–20, as well as a discussion of their forerunners in the Crockett almanacs in Carroll Smith-Rosenberg, *Disorderly Conduct: Visions of Gender in Victorian America* (New York: Knopf, 1985), pp. 103–5. As a counter to later stereotypes, consider Victoria Lamont's assessment, in respect to women's prospects for their personal lives and also for a political voice in issues such as conservation a century ago, that "the alternative form of frontier individualism represented by Molly Stark was a very real possibility in American society at the turn of the last century" ("The Bovine Object of Ideology: History, Gender, and the Origins of the 'Classic' Western," *Western American Literature* 35 [2001]: 398).

10. Albert B. Tucker, "Reel Cowboys: Cowhands and Western Movies," in *The Cowboy Way: An Exploration of History and Culture*, ed. Paul H. Carlson (Lubbock: Texas Tech University Press, 2000), p. 181.

11. Teresa Jordan, *Cowgirls: Women of the American West* (Garden City, NY: Anchor Books, 1982), pp. xii, xx.

12. Richard White, *"It's Your Misfortune and None of My Own": A New History of the American West* (Norman: University of Oklahoma Press, 1991), pp. 627–28, 629.

13. Lee Clark Mitchell, *Westerns: Making the Man in Fiction and Film* (Chicago: University of Chicago Press, 1996), p. 82.

14. Robert G. Athearn, *The Mythic West in Twentieth-Century America* (Lawrence: University Press of Kansas, 1986), p. 171.

15. Larry McMurtry, "Eros in Archer County," in *In a Narrow Grave: Essays on Texas* (1968; reprint ed., New York: Touchstone, 1989), p. 55.

16. Larry McMurtry, *It's Always We Rambled: An Essay on Rodeo* (New York: Hallman, 1974), p. 21.

17. Tom Pilkington, Afterword, *Rockspring*, by R. G. Vliet (1974; reprint ed., Dallas, TX: Southern Methodist University Press, 1992), pp. 128, 129. Kate Horsley's novel *Crazy Woman* (Albuquerque, NM: La Alameda Press, 1992) bears comparison with Vliet's, as does CBS's 1997 made-for-television movie *Stolen Women: Captured Hearts*.

18. Stan Steiner, "Love in a Covered Wagon," in *The Waning of the West*, ed. Emily Skretny Drabanski (New York: St. Martin's Press, 1989), pp. 68, 70.

19. Irene Klaver, "Silent Wolves: The Howl of the Implicit," in *Wild Ideas*, ed. David Rothenberg (Minneapolis: University of Minnesota Press, 1995), p. 122.

20. See Sandra M. Gilbert and Susan Gubar, *The Madwoman in the Attic: The Woman Writer and the Nineteenth-Century Literary Imagination* (New Haven, CT: Yale University Press, 1979).

21. Hayden White, "The Forms of Wildness: Archaeology of an Idea," in *The Wild Man Within: An Image in Western Thought from the Renaissance to Romanticism*, ed. Edward Dudley and Maximillian E. Novak (Pittsburgh, PA: University of Pittsburgh Press, 1972), p. 21.

22. Sharon W. Tiffany and Kathleen J. Adams, *The Wild Woman: An Inquiry into the Anthropology of an Idea* (Cambridge, MA: Schenkman, 1985), p. 97.

23. Max Oelschlaeger, *The Idea of Wilderness: From Prehistory to the Age of Ecology* (New Haven, CT: Yale University Press, 1991), p. 310. I've altered slightly the mechanics of his list.

24. Sharman Apt Russell, *Kill the Cowboy: A Battle of Mythology in the New West* (Reading, MA: Addison-Wesley, 1993), pp. 193, 194, 196, 197.

25. Donald Worster, *An Unsettled Country: Changing Landscapes of the American West* (Albuquerque: University of New Mexico Press, 1994), p. 89.

26. Linda Hogan, Deena Metzger, and Brenda Peterson, Introduction, *Intimate Nature: The Bond between Women and Animals*, ed. Linda Hogan, Deena Metzger, and Brenda Peterson (New York: Fawcett Columbine, 1998), pp. xii, xiii.

27. See Alice Marriott, *Hell on Horses and Women* (Norman: University of Oklahoma Press, 1953), a book that offers a good deal of folksy insight into why "the world of the West was from the beginning a man's world" (p. 9) and maybe even a hint or two that that might not forever be the case.

28. See Tom Dorrance, *True Unity: Willing Communication between Horse and Human* (Sanger, CA: Word Dancer Press, 1994), and Bill Dorrance and Leslie Desmond, *True Horsemanship through Feel* (Guilford, CT: Lyons Press, 2001).

29. Peggy Simson Curry, "Growing Old," in *Summer Range* (Story, WY: Dooryard Press, 1981), p. 22. As regards the scope of paradoxical symbolic meanings of the horse, see Paul Shepard, *The Others: How Animals Made Us Human* (Washington, DC: Shearwater Books, 1996), pp. 250–66, where he discusses both "the historical alliance of horses with patriarchal cultures" (p. 255) and "the passionate association of horses with women" (pp. 251–52). On the horse as a symbol of creation, see J. E. Cirlot, *A Dictionary of Symbols*, trans. Jack Sage (New York: Philosophical Library, 1962), s.v. "horse."

30. Neila C. Seshachari, "Toward a Holistic Eco-vision: The Infusion of the Eco-feminine in Eco-philosophy," in *Wilderness Tapestry: An Eclectic Approach to Preservation*, ed. Samuel I. Zeveloff, L. Mikel Vause, and William H. McVaugh (Reno: University of Nevada Press, 1992), pp. 169, 170. For general background on this commitment, see *Ecofeminism: Women, Animals, Nature*, ed. Greta Gaard (Philadelphia: Temple University Press, 1993); Carolyn Merchant, *Earthcare: Women and the Environment* (New York: Routledge, 1996); and Vera Norwood, *Made from This Earth: American Women and Nature* (Chapel Hill: University of North Carolina Press, 1996).

31. Cynthia Taylor, "Claiming Female Space: Mary Austin's Western Landscape," in *The Big Empty: Essays on Western Landscapes as Narrative*, ed. Leonard Engel (Albuquerque: University of New Mexico Press, 1994), p. 130.

32. Clarissa Pinkola Estés, *Women Who Run with the Wolves: Myths and Stories of the Wild Woman Archetype* (New York: Ballantine Books, 1995), p. 6.

33. Leslie Ryan, "The Other Side of Fire," in *Northern Lights: A Selection of New Writing from the American West*, ed. Deborah Clow and Donald Snow (New York: Vintage Books, 1994), pp. 362, 369.

34. Susan Ewing, "Antelope, Annie Oakley and the Screaming Demons," in *Solo: On Her Own Adventure*, ed. Susan Fox Rogers (Seattle: Seal Press, 1996), pp. 70, 71, 75.

35. "Soul Mates," advertisement, *USA Weekend*, 17–19 December 1993, p. 13.

36. N. Scott Momaday, *The Ancient Child* (1989; reprint ed., New York: HarperPerennial, 1990), p. 247.

37. Ron Hansen, Introduction, *The Best of the West 4: New Stories from the Wide Side of the Missouri*, ed. James Thomas and Denise Thomas (New York: Norton, 1991), p. 14.

The Return of the Native: Reclaiming Identities

1. Vine Deloria Jr., *God Is Red: A Native View of Religion*, updated ed. (Golden, CO: Fulcrum, 1994), p. 9. For a full account, in the form of a memoir, of the occupation and events leading up to it, see Adam Fortunate Eagle with Tim Findley, *Heart of the Rock: The Indian Invasion of Alcatraz* (Norman: University of Oklahoma Press, 2002). For the deeper historical context of

such identity-claiming events, see Roger L. Nichols, *American Indians in U.S. History* (Norman: University of Oklahoma Press, 2003).

2. Deloria, *God Is Red*, pp. 20, 21, 24.

3. Ibid., pp. 1, 2, 3. For some background on this matter, see Richard White, "Indian Peoples and the Natural World: *Asking the Right Questions*," in *Rethinking American Indian History*, ed. Donald L. Fixico (Albuquerque: University of New Mexico Press, 1997), pp. 87–100.

4. Donald Worster, *Under Western Skies: Nature and History in the American West* (New York: Oxford University Press, 1992), pp. 109, 136, 150, 152.

5. Reginald Horsman, "Recent Trends and New Directions in Native American History," in *The American West: New Perspectives, New Dimensions*, ed. Jerome O. Steffen (Norman: University of Oklahoma Press, 1979), p. 142. Horsman surveys a good deal of revisionist Indian history, environmental and otherwise, but further and more recent overviews may be found in Richard W. Etulain, "Conclusion: Visions and Revisions: Recent Interpretations of the American West," in *Writing Western History: Essays on Major Western Historians*, ed. Richard W. Etulain (Albuquerque: University of New Mexico Press, 1991), pp. 341–42, 353, and, on ethnohistory especially, Margaret Connell Szasz, Introduction, *Between Indian and White Worlds: The Cultural Broker*, ed. Margaret Connell Szasz (Norman: University of Oklahoma Press, 1994), pp. 6–20. A treasury of Indian history by members of sundry tribes, mostly Western, is *Native American Testimony: An Anthology of Indian and White Relations: First Encounter to Dispossession*, ed. Peter Nabokov (New York: Harper and Row, 1978), which might be read alongside Nabokov's *A Forest of Time: American Indian Ways of History* (Cambridge: Cambridge University Press, 2002).

6. Of all the problems plaguing reservations, the most important in the long run may be those of water rights—see Daniel McCool, *Native Waters: Contemporary Indian Water Settlements and the Second Treaty Era* (Tucson: University of Arizona Press, 2002).

7. Patricia Nelson Limerick, *The Legacy of Conquest: The Unbroken Past of the American West* (New York: Norton, 1987), p. 330.

8. See Kathryn Gabriel, *Gambler Way: Indian Gaming in Mythology, History, and Archaeology in North America* (Boulder, CO: Johnson Books, 1996).

9. Fergus M. Bordewich, *Killing the White Man's Indian: Reinventing Native Americans at the End of the Twentieth Century* (New York: Doubleday, 1996), pp. 339–40.

10. With respect to both the pluses and the minuses of casino operations, see W. Dale Mason, *Indian Gaming: Tribal Sovereignty and American Politics* (Norman: University of Oklahoma Press, 2000).

11. Kristan Sarvé-Gorham, "Games of Chance: Gambling and Land Tenure in *Tracks, Love Medicine,* and *The Bingo Palace*," *Western American Literature* 34 (1999): 299.

12. Bordewich, *Killing the White Man's Indian*, pp. 336, 337.

13. Leslie Marmon Silko, *Almanac of the Dead* (New York: Simon and Schuster, 1991), p. 712.

14. Arnold Krupat, *The Turn to the Native: Studies in Criticism and Culture* (Lincoln: University of Nebraska Press, 1996), p. xii. On such concerns in urbanization, see Donald L. Fixico, *The Urban Indian Experience in America* (Albuquerque: University of New Mexico Press, 2000).

15. N. Scott Momaday, "The Morality of Indian Hating," in *The Man Made of Words: Essays, Stories, Passages* (New York: St. Martin's Press, 1997), pp. 71–72.

16. William H. Goetzmann and William N. Goetzmann, *The West of the Imagination* (New York: Norton, 1986), p. 398.

17. Kenneth Lincoln, *Sing with the Heart of a Bear: Fusions of Native and American Poetry, 1890–1999* (Berkeley: University of California Press, 2000), p. xvii.

18. Gerald Vizenor, *Fugitive Poses: Native American Indian Scenes of Absence and Presence* (Lincoln: University of Nebraska Press, 1998), p. 20. That consciousness is much at play in Owens's work, as Chris LaLonde demonstrates in his *Grave Concerns, Trickster Turns: The Novels of Louis Owens* (Norman: University of Oklahoma Press, 2002). On King's novel, see Bud Hirsch, "'Stay Calm, Be Brave, Wait for the Signs': Sign-offs and Send-ups in the Fiction of Thomas King," *Western American Literature* 39 (2004): 145–75.

19. William E. Bevis, "Region, Power, Place," in *Reading the West: New Essays on the Literature of the American West*, ed. Michael Kowalewski (Cambridge: Cambridge University Press, 1996), pp. 21, 22.

20. Philip Burnham, "The Return of the Native: The Politics of Identity in American Indian Fiction of the West," in *Reading the West*, ed. Kowalewski, p. 200.

21. Ibid., pp. 203, 206, 210.

22. Louis Owens, "'Grinning Aboriginal Demons': Gerald Vizenor's *Bearheart* and the Indians' Escape from Gothic," in *Frontier Gothic: Terror and Wonder at the Frontier in American Literature*, ed. David Mogen, Scott P. Sanders, and Joanne B. Karpinski (Rutherford, NJ: Fairleigh Dickinson University Press, 1993), pp. 72, 71, 71–72.

23. Ray Pierotti, quoted in Jane Hoskinson, "A Meeting of Cultures," *Report from the University of Kansas*, Summer 1994, p. 2.

24. Robert F. Berkhofer Jr., *The White Man's Indian: Images of the American Indian from Columbus to the Present* (New York: Vintage Books, 1979), p. 107.

25. Burnham, "Return of the Native," p. 206. See also Shari M. Huhndorf's *Going Native: Indians in the American Cultural Imagination* (Ithaca, NY: Cornell University Press, 2001), an analysis of the motives for several specific instances of appropriations of Indian identity during the twentieth century.

26. Louis Owens, *I Hear the Train: Reflections, Inventions, Refractions* (Norman: University of Oklahoma Press, 2001), pp. 217, 219.

27. Bordewich, *Killing the White Man's Indian*, p. 17.

28. In this connection, see Richard Rodriguez's essay "India," in *Days of Obligation: An Argument with My Mexican Father* (New York: Viking Penguin, 1992), pp. 1–25, where he writes of the Indian as "the mascot of an international ecology movement" (p. 6).

29. David H. Getches, "Land, Community, and Survival: Lessons for the West from American Indians," in *A Society to Match the Scenery: Personal Visions of the Future of the American West*, ed. Gary Holthaus, Patricia Nelson Limerick, Charles F. Wilkinson, and Eve Stryker Munson (Niwot: University Press of Colorado, 1991), pp. 65, 68.

30. Leslie A. Fiedler, *The Return of the Vanishing American* (New York: Stein and Day, 1968), pp. 14, 169, 175.

31. For discussion of an exemplary case in point, that of the mixed-blood Chippewa Sun Bear, see Catherine L. Albanese, *Nature Religion in America: From the Algonkian Indians to the New Age* (Chicago: University of Chicago Press, 1990), pp. 156–63.

32. S. Elizabeth Bird, "Savage Desires: The Gendered Construction of the American Indian in Popular Media," in *Selling the Indian: Commercializing and Appropriating American Indian Cultures*, ed. Carter Jones Meyer and Diana Royer (Tucson: University of Arizona Press, 2001), p. 76.

33. Philip J. Deloria, *Playing Indian* (New Haven, CT: Yale University Press, 1998), pp. 7, 185, 188. See also his *Indians in Unexpected Places* (Lawrence: University Press of Kansas, 2004),

which focuses on the modern history of discrepancies between anomalous Indian realities and the stereotypical images produced by that exercise.

34. Roy Harvey Pearce, *Savagism and Civilization: A Study of the Indian and the American Mind* (Baltimore: Johns Hopkins Press, 1967), p. 243.

35. Gundars Rudzitis, *Wilderness and the Changing American West* (New York: Wiley, 1996), p. 71.

36. Bordewich, *Killing the White Man's Indian*, pp. 343–44.

37. Ibid., p. 344.

Break on Through to the Other Side: The Postmodern Frontier Imperative

1. See Julia Prodis, "Tombstone, Ariz.: Armed and Dangerous," *Lawrence Journal-World*, 19 August 1996, p. 5A.

2. Zoë Ingalls, "In a New Mexico Forest, Art Students Learn to Push Their Limits," *Chronicle of Higher Education*, 26 July 1996, p. B4.

3. Richard Slotkin, *The Fatal Environment: The Myth of the Frontier in the Age of Industrialization, 1800–1890* (New York: Atheneum, 1985), p. 531.

4. Wallace Stevens, "The Poems of Our Climate," in *The Palm at the End of the Mind: Selected Poems and a Play by Wallace Stevens*, ed. Holly Stevens (New York: Vintage Books, 1972), p. 158.

5. Roderick Nash, Introduction, *The Call of the Wild, 1910–1916*, ed. Roderick Nash (New York: Braziller, 1970), pp. 11–12.

6. Timothy Egan, *Lasso the Wind: Away to the New West* (New York: Knopf, 1998), p. 247.

7. Michael S. Kimmel, "The Cult of Masculinity: American Social Character and the Legacy of the Cowboy," in *Beyond Patriarchy: Essays by Men on Pleasure, Power, and Change*, ed. Michael Kaufman (New York: Oxford University Press, 1987), p. 247. For a fuller discussion of frontier mythology as it metaphorically informed Reagan's presidency, see Richard Slotkin, *Gunfighter Nation: The Myth of the Frontier in Twentieth-Century America* (1992; reprint ed., New York: HarperPerennial, 1993), pp. 643–50.

8. Patricia Nelson Limerick, *Something in the Soil: Legacies and Reckonings in the New West* (New York: Norton, 2000), pp. 75, 86.

9. See David Schneider, "Buck Rogers, CEO," *Scientific American*, September 1997, pp. 34–36.

10. Louis L'Amour, *Education of a Wandering Man* (New York: Bantam Books, 1989), p. 137.

11. Slotkin, *Fatal Environment*, p. 24.

12. Lawrence Ferlinghetti, "I Am Waiting," in *A Coney Island of the Mind* (New York: New Directions, 1958), p. 49.

13. David Mogen, Scott P. Sanders, and Joanne B. Karpinski, Introduction, *Frontier Gothic: Terror and Wonder at the Frontier in American Literature*, ed. David Mogen, Scott P. Sanders, and Joanne B. Karpinski (Rutherford, NJ: Fairleigh Dickinson University Press, 1993), p. 22.

14. Larry McMurtry, "Southwestern Literature?" in *In a Narrow Grave: Essays on Texas* (1968; reprint ed., New York: Touchstone, 1989), p. 43.

15. Yi-Fu Tuan, *Topophilia: A Study of Environmental Perception, Attitudes, and Values* (1974; reprint ed., New York: Columbia University Press, 1990), p. 203.

16. Cheryl Lester, "Signifying at the Frontier," review of *Frontiers*, by Michel Butor, *Kansas English* 80, no. 2 (Spring 1995): 12.

17. Linda Kintz, "Conservative Cowboy Stories: Adventures of the Chosen Sons," in *Boys: Masculinities in Contemporary Culture*, ed. Paul Smith (Boulder, CO: Westview Press, 1996), pp. 236, 244, 236.

18. Stan Steiner in "Challenge and Gusto: A Life-long and Fertile Love Affair with the American West: Interview with Stan Steiner by László Borsányi," in Stan Steiner, *The Waning of the West*, ed. Emily Skretny Drabanski (New York: St. Martin's Press, 1989), p. 266.

19. Rebecca Solnit, *Savage Dreams: A Journey into the Landscape Wars of the American West* (New York: Vintage Books, 1995), p. 375.

20. Blake Allmendinger, *Ten Most Wanted: The New Western Literature* (New York: Routledge, 1998), p. 172.

21. David Mogen, "Wilderness, Metamorphosis, and Millennium: Gothic Apocalypse from the Puritans to the Cyberpunks," in *Frontier Gothic*, ed. Mogen, Sanders, and Karpinski, p. 102.

22. Leslie A. Fiedler, *The Return of the Vanishing American* (New York: Stein and Day, 1968), pp. 26–27.

23. Slotkin, *Gunfighter Nation*, p. 658.

24. Reg Saner, "The Road's Motion," in *Reaching Keet Seel: Ruin's Echo and the Anasazi* (Salt Lake City: University of Utah Press, 1998), p. 147.

25. Annette Kolodny, *The Lay of the Land: Metaphor as Experience and History in American Life and Letters* (Chapel Hill: University of North Carolina Press, 1975), p. 137.

26. Kim Addonizio and Dorianne Laux, *The Poet's Companion: A Guide to the Pleasures of Writing Poetry* (New York: Norton, 1997), p. 75. See also F. Marina Schauffler's discussion of the "spiral of growth" in her *Turning to Earth: Stories of Ecological Conversion* (Charlottesville: University of Virginia Press, 2003), p. 7.

Wildfire: A Taste of Authenticity

1. For some of the details in this account, I'm indebted to Steve Larese, "Los Alamos: From the Ashes Rises a Stronger Community," *New Mexico Magazine*, May 2001, pp. 32–39.

2. Edward Abbey, *Desert Solitaire: A Season in the Wilderness* (1968; reprint ed., New York: Ballantine Books, 1971), p. 13.

3. Richard Manning, *Grassland: The History, Biology, Politics, and Promise of the American Prairie* (New York: Viking, 1995), p. 272.

4. See Stephen J. Pyne, *Fire in America: A Cultural History of Wildland and Rural Fire* (Princeton, NJ: Princeton University Press, 1982), p. 15.

5. Concerning such matters in an especially fire-vulnerable section of the West, see *Forests under Fire: A Century of Ecosystem Mismanagement in the Southwest*, ed. Christopher J. Huggard and Arthur R. Gómez (Tucson: University of Arizona Press, 2001), as well as a related essay on fire in Mexico, Stephen J. Pyne's "Old Fire, New Fire," *Interdisciplinary Studies in Literature and Environment* 6, no. 2 (Summer 1999): 179–89. Concerning those matters in the wider West, see Douglas Gantenbein, "Burning Questions," *Scientific American*, November 2002, pp. 82–89, and David J. Strohmaier, *The Seasons of Fire: Reflections on Fire in the West* (Reno: University of Nevada Press, 2001). Concerning them in national, historical, and philosophical contexts, see *Wildfire: A Reader*, ed. Alianor True (Washington, DC: Island Press, 2001); Stephen J. Pyne, *Fire: A Brief History* (Seattle: University of Washington Press, 2001); Sheila Nickerson, "Earth on Fire," *Interdisciplinary Studies in Literature and Environment* 5, no. 1 (Winter 1998): 67–87; and Stephen J. Pyne, *Smokechasing* (Tucson: University of Arizona Press, 2003).

6. See Robert Glennon, *Water Follies: Groundwater Pumping and the Fate of America's Fresh Waters* (Washington, DC: Island Press, 2002).

7. Bruce Berger, "Fear in the Lower Sonoran," in *The Telling Distance: Conversations with the American Desert* (1991; reprint ed., Tucson: University of Arizona Press, 1997), p. 148.

8. Reg Saner, "Spirit Root," in *Reaching Keet Seel: Ruin's Echo and the Anasazi* (Salt Lake City: University of Utah Press, 1998), p. 179. The consequences of being unrealistic are documented in excruciating detail in Luis Alberto Urrea's *The Devil's Highway: A True Story* (New York: Little, Brown, 2004).

9. James K. Folsom, "Gothicism in the Western Novel," in *Frontier Gothic: Terror and Wonder at the Frontier in American Literature*, ed. David Mogen, Scott P. Sanders, and Joanne B. Karpinski (Rutherford, NJ: Fairleigh Dickinson University Press, 1993), p. 30.

10. Gary Short, "Driving Nevada/Reprise," in *Flying over Sonny Liston* (Reno: University of Nevada Press, 1996), p. 62.

11. Joseph Kanon, *Los Alamos* (New York: Broadway Books, 1997), p. 176.

12. Larry McMurtry, *Roads: Driving America's Great Highways* (New York: Simon and Schuster, 2000), p. 53.

13. Jane Hirshfield, *Nine Gates: Entering the Mind of Poetry* (New York: HarperCollins, 1997), p. 134.

14. Louis L'Amour, *Education of a Wandering Man* (New York: Bantam Books, 1989), p. 198.

15. Victor Davis Hanson, *Fields without Dreams: Defending the Agrarian Idea* (New York: Free Press, 1996), p. xiv.

16. Patricia Nelson Limerick, "The Real West," in *The Real West* (Denver, CO: Civic Center Cultural Complex, 1996), p. 13.

17. Larry McMurtry, "Cookie Pioneers," review of *Something in the Soil: Legacies and Reckonings in the New West*, by Patricia Nelson Limerick, and *Texas History Movies*, by John Rosenfield Jr. and Jack Patton, *New York Review of Books*, 25 May 2000, p. 30. See Patricia Nelson Limerick, "Making the Most of Words: Verbal Activity and Western America," in *Under an Open Sky: Rethinking America's Western Past*, ed. William Cronon, George Miles, and Jay Gitlin (New York: Norton, 1992), pp. 167–84, for a discussion that bears on that process.

18. Gary Lease, "Introduction: Nature under Fire," in *Reinventing Nature? Responses to Postmodern Deconstruction*, ed. Michael E. Soulé and Gary Lease (Washington, DC: Island Press, 1995), p. 9.

19. Virginia Scharff, "Honey, I Shrunk the West," *Pacific Historical Review* 67 (1998): 419. The "authentic West" in all its semantic precariousness is investigated from many points of view in *True West: Authenticity and the American West*, ed. William R. Handley and Nathaniel Lewis (Lincoln: University of Nebraska Press, 2004).

20. Yi-Fu Tuan, *Escapism* (Baltimore: Johns Hopkins University Press, 1998), p. 10.

21. William Cronon, "Introduction: In Search of Nature," in *Uncommon Ground: Rethinking the Human Place in Nature*, ed. William Cronon (New York: Norton, 1995), p. 25. Clements's idea of such organismic ecology was refuted early on by Henry Gleason, who saw continual and loosely structured change where Clements saw the uniform push toward and achievement of homeostasis, the former view one that Rod Romesburg finds refigured in Abbey's work as "a view of nature that values both order and disorder, evoking the paradoxical unity of deterministic chaos" ("Deterministic Chaos in Ed Abbey's *Desert Solitaire*," *Western American Literature* 39 [2004]: 209).

22. Richard Manning, "The Failure of Literature," in *Northern Lights: A Selection of New Writing from the American West*, ed. Deborah Clow and Donald Snow (New York: Vintage Books, 1994), pp. 72, 73. Cf. John N. Maclean's arguably more objective account of the 1994 South Canyon fire in western Colorado, *Fire on the Mountain: The True Story of the South Canyon Fire* (New York: Morrow, 1999).

23. Zeese Papanikolas, *Trickster in the Land of Dreams* (Lincoln: University of Nebraska Press, 1995), p. 107.

24. Zeese Papanikolas, "The Perpetual Tourist," *Western American Literature* 34 (1999): 193. On such follies, see also John McPhee, "Los Angeles against the Mountains," in *The Control of Nature* (New York: Farrar, Straus and Giroux, 1989), pp. 265–72.

25. Scott Hermanson, "Fear and Loathing in Los Angeles: Mike Davis as Nature Writer," *Western American Literature* 37 (2002): 293, 302.

26. Richard Hutson, "Ecce Cowboy: E. C. Abbott's *We Pointed Them North*," *Western American Literature* 37 (2002): 261.

27. Leslie A. Fiedler, *The Return of the Vanishing American* (New York: Stein and Day, 1968), pp. 140, 141.

28. John Sandlos, "The Coyote Came Back: The Return of an Ancient Song Dog in the Post-colonial Literature and Landscape of North America," *Interdisciplinary Studies in Literature and Environment* 6, no. 2 (Summer 1999): 105, 107. Jarold Ramsey, one of Sandlos's sources, comments that "to believe that the world as we have it is largely the work of a trickster is, in a mode of thought unfamiliar to our culture, to know and accept it *on its own terms*" ("Coyote and Friends: An Experiment in Interpretive Bricolage," in *Reading the Fire: Essays in the Traditional Indian Literatures of the Far West* [Lincoln: University of Nebraska Press, 1983], p. 41).

29. Patricia Nelson Limerick, *The Legacy of Conquest: The Unbroken Past of the American West* (New York: Norton, 1987), p. 321.

30. David Rothenberg, "Epilogue: Paradox Wild," in *Wild Ideas*, ed. David Rothenberg (Minneapolis: University of Minnesota Press, 1995), pp. 217–18.

Hunger for the Wild: Finding a True Western Heritage

1. John P. O'Grady, *Pilgrims to the Wild: Everett Ruess, Henry David Thoreau, John Muir, Clarence King, Mary Austin* (Salt Lake City: University of Utah Press, 1993), p. 1.

2. Bruce Berger, "Genius of the Canyons," in *The Telling Distance: Conversations with the American Desert* (1991; reprint ed., Tucson: University of Arizona Press, 1997), pp. 16, 24, 23.

3. O'Grady, *Pilgrims to the Wild*, pp. 4, 5, 10, 14. See also W. L. Rusho, *Everett Ruess: A Vagabond for Beauty* (Salt Lake City: Peregrine Smith Books, 1983). The somewhat similar but more postmodern story of Christopher Johnson McCandless, who walked into the Alaskan wilderness, is told by Jon Krakauer in his *Into the Wild* (New York: Villard, 1996), which includes a chapter on Ruess (pp. 87–97).

4. Bruce Berger, "Wild Interiors," in *Telling Distance*, pp. 25, 30. Remarking that "gourmet camping food is big business," SueEllen Campbell goes on to argue that "this kind of civilized eating now signals less an armor against, than a denial of, the wild in wilderness, a vision of the natural world as a garden for our delectation" ("Feasting in the Wilderness: The Language of Food in American Wilderness Narratives," *American Literary History* 6 [1994]: 14).

5. David Brooks, *Bobos in Paradise: The New Upper Class and How They Got There* (New York: Simon and Schuster, 2000), p. 209.

6. Yi-Fu Tuan, *Escapism* (Baltimore: Johns Hopkins University Press, 1998), pp. 22, 19. Apropos of Tuan's notion of impact is Douglas C. Daly's point that "our capacity still to be awestruck by nature is essential to our survival, because it prevents us from arrogance, from the obliviousness to the environment that leads us toward oblivion" ("A Whirlybird's-Eye View of the World," review of *Earth from Above*, by Yann Arthus-Bertrand, *Scientific American*, March 2000, p. 100). Relevant to the paradox Tuan notes, as well as to the observations from

Berger and Brooks, is Bill McKibben's comment—in a review of *The Complete Walker IV*, by Colin Fletcher and Chip Rawlins—in regard to hiking: "The biggest compromise is making yourself so laden and comfortable and safe and swaddled that you no longer feel exposed to the natural world—which is the only reason to go hiking in the first place" ("The Hiker's Gospel," *New York Review of Books*, 26 September 2002, p. 47).

7. Jim Harrison, "Meals of Peace and Restoration," in *The Raw and the Cooked: Adventures of a Roving Gourmand* (New York: Grove Press, 2001), p. 22.

8. Gretel Ehrlich, "The Solace of Open Spaces," in *The Solace of Open Spaces* (New York: Penguin Books, 1986), pp. 14, 15.

9. C. L. Rawlins, "The Meadow at the Corner of Your Eye," in *Northern Lights: A Selection of New Writing from the American West*, ed. Deborah Clow and Donald Snow (New York: Vintage Books, 1994), p. 393.

10. Diana Ossana, "White Line Fever," in *Still Wild: Short Fiction of the American West, 1950 to the Present*, ed. Larry McMurtry (New York: Simon and Schuster, 2000), p. 149.

11. Jack Turner, "The Abstract Wild: A Rant," in *The Abstract Wild* (Tucson: University of Arizona Press, 1996), p. 26.

12. Doug Peacock, *Grizzly Years: In Search of the American Wilderness* (1990; reprint ed., New York: Owl Books, 1996), p. 64.

13. Gary Snyder, "The Etiquette of Freedom," in *The Practice of the Wild* (New York: North Point Press, 1990), pp. 23, 24.

14. Reg Saner, "The Pleasures of Ruin," in *Reaching Keet Seel: Ruin's Echo and the Anasazi* (Salt Lake City: University of Utah Press, 1998), pp. 89, 90, 89.

Fear and Loathing in Santa Fe: Meatspace or Virtual Reality?

1. Concerning alife as well as other projects at the institute, see Roger Lewin, *Complexity: Life at the Edge of Chaos* (New York: Macmillan, 1992); George Johnson, *Strange Beauty: Murray Gell-Mann and the Revolution in Twentieth-Century Physics* (New York: Knopf, 1999); Stuart A. Kauffman, *Investigations* (New York: Oxford University Press, 2000); and Steven Johnson, *Emergence: The Connected Lives of Ants, Brains, Cities, and Software* (New York: Scribner, 2001).

2. Patricia Nelson Limerick, *Something in the Soil: Legacies and Reckonings in the New West* (New York: Norton, 2000), p. 278.

3. Devon Jackson, "Still the One," *Santa Fean*, September 2002, p. 35.

4. Hal K. Rothman, *Devil's Bargains: Tourism in the Twentieth-Century American West* (Lawrence: University Press of Kansas, 1998), p. 117. For a fuller history of how Santa Fe got scripted, see Chris Wilson, *The Myth of Santa Fe: Creating a Modern Regional Tradition* (Albuquerque: University of New Mexico Press, 1997).

5. Gary Paul Nabhan, "Cultural Parallax in Viewing North American Habitats," in *Reinventing Nature? Responses to Postmodern Deconstruction*, ed. Michael E. Soulé and Gary Lease (Washington, DC: Island Press, 1995), p. 98.

6. Sven Birkerts, "Fractured Being," *Hungry Mind Review*, Winter 1998–99, p. 11.

7. Daniel B. Botkin, *Discordant Harmonies: A New Ecology for the Twenty-first Century* (New York: Oxford University Press, 1990), p. 131.

8. Frieda Knobloch, *The Culture of Wilderness: Agriculture as Colonization in the American West* (Chapel Hill: University of North Carolina Press, 1996), p. 12.

9. Donald Worster, *The Wealth of Nature: Environmental History and the Ecological Imagination* (New York: Oxford University Press, 1993), pp. 162, 170.

10. Rick Bass, *The Lost Grizzlies: A Search for Survivors in the Wilderness of Colorado* (Boston: Houghton Mifflin, Mariner Books, 1995), pp. 237, 235, 236.

Conclusion: Some New Vision: Resolving the Western Paradox

1. Henry Nash Smith, *Virgin Land: The American West as Symbol and Myth* (1950; reprint ed., Cambridge, MA: Harvard University Press, 1970), p. 260.

2. Donald Worster, "A Tapestry of Change: Nature and Culture on the Prairie," in Terry Evans, *The Inhabited Prairie* (Lawrence: University Press of Kansas, 1998), p. xiv.

3. Donald Worster, *Under Western Skies: Nature and History in the American West* (New York: Oxford University Press, 1992), pp. 81, 90. Worster's notion of a new vision is not without its critics. Stephen Tatum, for instance, shares Worster's hope, but he argues that "any transcendence of the 'Western paradox' constitutes, paradoxically, a transcendence of history itself" ("The Problem of the 'Popular' in the New Western History," in *The New Western History: An Assessment*, ed. Forrest G. Robinson, a special issue of *Arizona Quarterly* 53, no. 2 [Summer 1997]: 185)—an alerting but, I think, refutable argument, for Worster uses "transcend" (p. 90) to mean something more like "break out of the limitations of" than absolutely "go beyond."

4. Hillel Schwartz, review of *The Cultivated Wilderness; or, What is Landscape?* by Paul Shepheard, *Journal of Unconventional History* 10, no. 2 (Winter 1999): 85.

5. William Kittredge, *Who Owns the West?* (San Francisco: Mercury House, 1996), pp. 98, 35.

6. In a discussion completely germane to the continuing development of the West, Martin Heidegger notes (in my translation) that "the old word *buan* not only tells us that *bauen* ["to build"] is really *wohnen* ["to dwell"] but as well gives us a hint as to how we ought to think about the dwelling it denominates," for *bauen* "means also *hegen* ["to preserve"] and *pflegen* ["to care for"] . . ." ("Bauen Wohnen Denken," in *Vorträge und Aufsätze*, 2d ed. [Pfullingen, West Germany: Neske, 1959], p. 147).

7. See Daniel B. Botkin, *Discordant Harmonies: A New Ecology for the Twenty-first Century* (New York: Oxford University Press, 1990), pp. 191–92. See also Botkin's *No Man's Garden: Thoreau and a New Vision for Civilization and Culture* (Washington, DC: Shearwater Books, 2001), as well as Terry Gifford's *Pastoral* (London: Routledge, 1999), which articulates a literary-theoretical but also ecologically practical notion of the "post-pastoral" as a mediator of nature and culture.

8. Bonney MacDonald, "Desire of the Middle Ground: Opposition, Dialectics, and Dialogic Context in Gretel Ehrlich's *The Solace of Open Spaces*," *Western American Literature* 33 (1998): 139, 140.

9. Patricia Nelson Limerick, *Something in the Soil: Legacies and Reckonings in the New West* (New York: Norton, 2000), p. 315. As John P. O'Grady argues, "the notion of sustainability is . . . very difficult to pin down"; but he nicely capsules the gist of what *sustainable development* means when he says that the concept "is akin to the lesson most people learn when quite young around the kitchen table: *Mind your manners and don't be greedy*" ("How Sustainable Is the Idea of Sustainability?" *Interdisciplinary Studies in Literature and Environment* 10, no. 1 [Winter 2003]: 3, 2). Apt reading here might be Kent Haruf's *Plainsong* (New York: Knopf, 1999), a novel that plays down or inverts traditional Western mythic values and emphasizes those of sustainable heroism and individuals interconnected in community.

10. Brenda Peterson in Mary Troychak, "Respect for the Other: An Interview with Nature Writer Brenda Peterson," *Bloomsbury Review* 16, no. 5 (September–October 1996): 15.

11. Donald Worster, *Rivers of Empire: Water, Aridity, and the Growth of the American West* (1985; reprint ed., New York: Oxford University Press, 1992), pp. 331, 332.

12. Lewis Hyde, *Trickster Makes This World: Mischief, Myth, and Art* (New York: Farrar, Straus and Giroux, 1998), p. 9.

13. Gretel Ehrlich, "Other Lives," in *The Solace of Open Spaces* (New York: Penguin Books, 1986), p. 42. Felicitous here, in a final note, is Edward Abbey's appeal for a love of wilderness that "is more than a hunger for what is always beyond reach" and thus "is also an expression of loyalty to the earth, the earth which bore us and sustains us, the only home we shall ever know, the only paradise we ever need—if only we had the eyes to see" (*Desert Solitaire: A Season in the Wilderness* [1968; reprint ed., New York: Ballantine Books, 1971], p. 190).

Index